Introduction to Logic

"This new edition is a significant improvement on an already excellent text. The virtues of the original remain including clear expositions, an intuitive proof procedure that generalizes naturally from propositional logic to more advanced logics and a wealth of problems drawn from philosophical sources. There are new chapters on the history of logic, deviant logics and the philosophy of logic and the accompanying LogiCola program has been improved. This is a student friendly approach to logic."

Michael Bradie, Bowling Green State University

Introduction to Logic combines likely the broadest scope of any logic textbook with clear, concise writing and interesting examples and arguments. Its key features, all retained in the **Second Edition**, include:

- Simpler ways to test arguments, including the star test for syllogisms
- A wide scope of materials, suiting it for introductory or intermediate courses
- Engaging examples, from everyday life and the great philosophers
- Useful for self-study and preparation for standardized tests, like the LSAT
- A reasonable price (a third the cost of some competitors)
- Exercises that correspond to the free LogiCola instructional program

This **Second Edition** also:

- Arranges chapters in a more natural way, going from easier to more difficult material
- Adds new chapters on history of logic, deviant logic, and philosophy of logic
- Refines many explanations and expands several sections (such as informal fallacies and relational translations)
- Includes a fuller index and a new appendix on suggested further readings
- Updates LogiCola, which is now more visually attractive and easier to download, update, and use (install from http://www.jcu.edu/philosophy/gensler/lc or http://www.routledge.com/textbooks/9780415996518)

Harry J. Gensler, S.J., is Professor of Philosophy at John Carroll University in Cleveland. Some of his other books include *Gödel's Theorem Simplified* (1984), *Formal Ethics* (1996), *Anthology of Catholic Philosophy* (2005), *Historical Dictionary of Logic* (2006), *Historical Dictionary of Ethics* (2008), and *Ethics: A Contemporary Introduction, Second Edition* (2011).

Introduction to Logic

Second Edition

Harry J. Gensler

Routledge
Taylor & Francis Group

NEW YORK AND LONDON

First published 2002
by Routledge

This edition published 2010
by Routledge
711 Third Avenue, New York, NY 10017

Simultaneously published in the UK
by Routledge
2 Park Square, Milton Park, Abingdon, Oxon OX14 4RN

Routledge is an imprint of the Taylor & Francis Group

Typeset in Aldus Roman by the author
Printed and bound in the United States of America
on acid-free paper by Edwards Brothers Inc

Library of Congress Cataloging-in-Publication Data
Gensler, Harry J., 1945—
Introduction to logic / Harry J. Gensler. – 2nd ed.
p. cm.
Includes index.
1. Logic. I. Title.
BC71.G37 2010
160–dc22
2009039539

British Library Cataloguing in Publication Data
A catalogue record for this book is available from the British Library.

ISBN: 978–0–415–99650–1, ISBN 10: 0–415–99650–3 (hback)
ISBN: 978–0–415–99651–8, ISBN 10: 0–415–99651–1 (pback)
ISBN: 978–0–203–85500–3, ISBN 10: 0–203–85500–0 (ebook)

Contents

PART ONE
SYLLOGISTIC, INFORMAL, AND INDUCTIVE LOGIC

PART TWO
CLASSICAL SYMBOLIC LOGIC

PART THREE
ADVANCED SYMBOLIC SYSTEMS

Chapter 10: Basic Modal Logic   228

Chapter 11: Further Modal Systems   248

Chapter 12: Deontic and Imperative Logic   267

Chapter 13: Belief Logic   290

Chapter 14: A Formalized Ethical Theory   313

PART FOUR
FURTHER VISTAS

Preface

This is a comprehensive *Introduction to Logic*. It covers:

- syllogisms;
- informal aspects of reasoning (like meaning and fallacies);
- inductive reasoning;
- propositional and quantificational logic;
- modal, deontic, and belief logic;
- the formalization of an ethical theory about the golden rule; and
- metalogic, history of logic, deviant logic, and philosophy of logic.

Because of its broad scope, this book can be used for basic logic courses (where teachers can choose from a variety of topics) or more advanced ones (including graduate courses). The teacher manual and the end of Chapter 1 both talk about which chapters are suitable for which type of course.

The first Routledge edition came out in 2002. Key features included: (a) clear, direct, concise writing; (b) interesting examples and arguments, often from everyday life or great philosophers; (c) simpler ways to test arguments, including the star test for syllogisms and an easier way to do proofs and refutations; (d) wide scope of materials (likely the widest of any logic text); (e) suitability for self-study and preparation for tests like the LSAT; (f) reasonable price (a third of the cost of some competitors); and (g) the companion LogiCola instructional program (which randomly generates problems, gives feedback on answers, provides help and explanations, and records progress). I'm happy with how the first edition has been received, often with lavish praise.

I have made many improvements to this second edition. I have arranged the chapters in a more logical way; so they now go, roughly, from easier to harder material. I added new chapters on history of logic, deviant logic, and philosophy of logic; so the book is even broader in scope than before. I beefed up informal fallacies, added inference to the best explanation, and corrected some typos. I overhauled three difficult sections: on relational translations, belief-logic proofs, and completeness. I did much tweaking of explanations (for example, see the sections on the star test, Venn diagrams, and proofs). I tweaked some exercises. I added an appendix on suggested further readings. I added a real index (previously there was only an index of names); so now it's easier to research a topic. And I added a convenient list of rules to the inside covers. I cut two parts that got little use: the appendix on how to download and use LogiCola (the program is now so easy to download and use that this appendix isn't needed) and the glossary (which just repeated definitions from the text). I tried to keep things brief; despite the additions, the book is only 23 pages longer than before. Finally, I did a massive rewrite of the Windows-based LogiCola instructional program (whose source has over 20,000 lines of code – which is longer than the book); the new LogiCola is easier to install and update, easier to use, more visually attractive, and improved in many other ways. LogiCola (with a score-processing program, teacher manual, class slides, flash cards, and sample quizzes) can be downloaded for free from either of these Web addresses:

http://www.jcu.edu/philosophy/gensler/lc
http://www.routledge.com/textbooks/9780415996518

All the supplementary materials are conveniently accessible from LogiCola's HELP menu; so I suggest that you just install LogiCola (teachers should check the option to install the score processor too).

I wish to thank all who have somehow contributed to this second edition. I thank the Routledge editorial staff and reviewers, who made good suggestions. I thank my logic students, especially the ones whose puzzled looks forced me to try to make things clearer. And I especially thank the many teachers, students, and self-learners who have e-mailed me about the book and software over the years, often saying things like "I love the book and software, but there's one thing that I'm having trouble with …." If this second edition is a genuine improvement – as I hope and trust that it is – then there are a lot of people to thank besides me.

Long live logic!

Harry J. Gensler
Philosophy Department
John Carroll University
Cleveland, OH 44118 USA

http://www.jcu.edu/philosophy/gensler

CHAPTER 1
Introduction

Logic is about reasoning – about going from premises to a conclusion. As we begin our study of logic, we need to be clearer on what logic is and why it's important. We also need to learn some concepts (like "valid" and "argument") that are central to the study of logic.

1.1 Logic

Logic[1] is *the analysis and appraisal of arguments*. When you do logic, you try to clarify reasoning and separate good from bad reasoning. As you work through this book, you'll examine reasoning on various topics, both philosophical (like free will and determinism, the existence of God, and the nature of morality) and non-philosophical (like backpacking, water pollution, football, Supreme Court decisions, and the Bible). You'll come to see logic not as an irrelevant game with funny symbols, but as a useful tool to clarify and evaluate our reasoning – whether on life's deeper questions or on everyday topics.

Why study logic? I can think of three main reasons. First, logic is important because reasoning is important. While you've been reasoning about things all your life, this may be the first time that you try to understand reasoning and become better at it. Reasoning and general analytical skills are important in law, politics, journalism, education, medicine, business, science, mathematics, computer science, and most other areas. This book is crammed with exercises; look at these as puzzles designed to help you think more clearly (so people can better understand what you're saying) and logically (so you better support your conclusions).

Second, logic can deepen your understanding of philosophy. **Philosophy** can be defined as *reasoning about the ultimate questions of life*. Philosophers ask questions like "Why accept or reject free will?" or "Can one prove or disprove God's existence?" or "How can one justify a moral belief?" If you don't know any logic, you'll have only a vague grasp of such issues; and you'll lack the tools needed to understand and evaluate philosophical reasoning. If you've studied philosophy, you'll likely recognize many of the pieces of philosophical

---

[1] Centrally important terms (like "**logic**") are introduced in bold type. Learn each such term and be able to give a definition.

reasoning in this book. If you haven't studied philosophy, you'll find this book a good introduction to the subject. In either case, you should get better at recognizing, understanding, and appraising philosophical reasoning.

Finally, logic can be fun. Doing logic is like playing a game or doing puzzles; logic will challenge your thinking processes in new ways. The rigor of logical systems will likely fascinate you. Most people find logic enjoyable.

1.2   Valid arguments

I begin my basic logic course with a multiple-choice test. The test has ten problems; each problem gives information and asks what conclusion necessarily follows. The problems are easy, but most students get about half wrong.[1]

Here are two of the problems – with the right answers boxed:

If you overslept, you'll be late. You aren't late.	If you overslept, you'll be late. You didn't oversleep.
Therefore:	Therefore:
(a) You did oversleep.	(a) You're late.
(b) You didn't oversleep.	(b) You aren't late.
(c) You're late.	(c) You did oversleep.
(d) None of these follows.	**(d) None of these follows.**

While almost everyone gets the first problem right, many students wrongly pick "(b)" for the second problem. Here "You aren't late" doesn't necessary follow, since you might be late for some other reason; maybe your car didn't start. Most students, once they grasp this point, will see that (b) is wrong.[2]

Untrained logical intuitions are often unreliable. But logical intuitions can be developed; yours will likely improve as you work through this book. You'll also learn special techniques for testing arguments.[3]

An **argument**, in the sense used in logic, is a set of statements consisting of premises and a conclusion. The **premises** are statements that give supporting evidence; the **conclusion** is what is allegedly supported by these statements. Arguments put into words a possible act of reasoning. Here's an example:

---

[1] The Web has my pretest at http://www.jcu.edu/philosophy/gensler/logic.htm in an interactive format. I suggest that you try it. I developed this test to help a psychologist friend put to an experimental test the idea that males are more logical than females; he found, of course, that males and females did equally well on the logic test.

[2] These two arguments were taken from Matthew Lipman's fifth-grade logic textbook: *Harry Stottlemeier's Discovery* (Caldwell, NJ: Universal Diversified Services, 1974).

[3] Many psychologists think we have two systems for drawing conclusions. Our *intuitive system* rests on feelings and works very quickly. Our *rational system* uses rules and works in a slower, step-by-step manner. Neither is always right. A logic course should develop both systems.

*Valid
argument* ➔ If you overslept, you'll be late.
You aren't late.
∴ You didn't oversleep.   ("∴" = *therefore*)

An argument is **valid** if it would be contradictory (impossible) to have the premises all true and conclusion false. In calling an argument *valid*, we aren't saying whether the premises are true. We're just saying that the conclusion *follows from* the premises – that if the premises were all true, then the conclusion also would have to be true. In saying this, we implicitly assume that there's no shift in the meaning or reference of the terms; hence we must use "overslept," "late," and "you" the same way throughout the argument.

Our argument is valid because of its *logical form* – its arrangement of logical notions (like "if-then" and "not") and content phrases (like "You overslept" and "You're late"). We can display an argument's form by using words or symbols for logical notions and letters for content phrases:

If you overslept, you'll be late.   If A then B   **Valid**
You aren't late.   Not-B
∴ You didn't oversleep.   ∴ Not-A

Our argument is valid because its *form* is correct. If we take another argument of the same form, but substitute other ideas for "A" and "B," then this second argument also will be valid. Here's an example:

If you're in France, you're in Europe.   If A then B   **Valid**
You aren't in Europe.   Not-B
∴ You aren't in France.   ∴ Not-A

Logic studies forms of reasoning. The content can deal with anything – backpacking, mathematics, cooking, physics, ethics, or whatever. When you learn logic, you're learning tools of reasoning that can be applied to any subject.

Consider our **invalid** example:

If you overslept, you'll be late.   If A then B   Invalid
You didn't oversleep.   Not-A
∴ You aren't late.   ∴ Not-B

Here the second premise denies the *first* part of the if-then; this makes it invalid. Intuitively, you might be late for some other reason – just as, in this similar argument, you might be in Europe because you're in Italy:

If you're in France, you're in Europe.   If A then B   Invalid
You aren't in France.   Not-A
∴ You aren't in Europe.   ∴ Not-B

1.3 Sound arguments

Logicians distinguish *valid* arguments from *sound* arguments:

> An argument is **valid** if it would be contradictory to have the premises all true and conclusion false.
>
> An argument is **sound** if it's valid and has every premise true.

Calling an argument "valid" says nothing about whether its premises are true. But calling it "sound" says that it's valid (the conclusion follows from the premises) *and* has true premises. Here's an example of a *sound* argument:

Valid	If you're reading this, you aren't illiterate.
and true ➔	You're reading this.
premises	∴ You aren't illiterate.

When we try to prove a conclusion, we try to give a *sound* argument. We must make sure that our premises are true and that our conclusion follows from our premises. If we have these two things, then our conclusion has to be true. The conclusion of a sound argument is always true.

An argument could be unsound in either of two ways: (1) it might have a false premise or (2) its conclusion might not follow from the premises:

First premise false:	*Conclusion doesn't follow:*
All logicians are millionaires.	All millionaires eat well.
Gensler is a logician.	Gensler eats well.
∴ Gensler is a millionaire.	∴ Gensler is a millionaire.

When we criticize an opponent's argument, we try to show that it's *unsound*. We try to show either that one of the premises is false or that the conclusion doesn't follow. If the argument has a false premise or is invalid, then our opponent hasn't proved the conclusion. But the conclusion still might be true – and our opponent might later discover a better argument for it. To show a view to be false, we must do more than just refute an argument for it; we must invent an argument of our own that shows the view to be false.

Besides asking whether premises are true, we could ask how certain they are, to ourselves or to others. We'd like our premises to be certain and obvious to everyone. We usually have to settle for less than this; our premises are often educated guesses or personal convictions. Our arguments are only as strong as their premises. This suggests a third strategy for criticizing an argument; we could try to show that one or more of the premises are very uncertain.

Here's another example of an argument. In fall 2008, before Barack Obama was elected US president, he was far ahead in the polls. But some thought he'd be defeated by the "Bradley effect," whereby many whites *say* they'll vote for a black candidate but in fact don't. Barack's wife Michelle, in a CNN interview with Larry King (October 8), argued that there wouldn't be a Bradley effect:[1]

> Barack Obama is the Democratic nominee.
> If there was going to be a Bradley effect, Barack wouldn't be the nominee
> [because the effect would have shown up in the primary elections].
> ∴ There isn't going to be a Bradley effect.

Once she gives this argument, we can't just say "Well, my opinion is that there *will* be a Bradley effect." Instead, we have to respond to her reasoning. It's clearly valid – the conclusion follows from the premises. Are the premises true? The first premise was undeniable. To dispute the second premise, we'd have to argue that the Bradley effect would appear in the final election but not in the primaries; but it's unclear how one might defend this. So an argument like this changes the nature of the discussion. (By the way, there was no Bradley effect when the general election took place a month later.)

Logic, while not itself resolving substantive issues, gives us intellectual tools to reason better about such issues. It can help us to be more aware of reasoning, to express reasoning clearly, to determine whether a conclusion follows from the premises, and to focus on key premises to defend or criticize.

I have two points on terminology. We'll call statements *true* or *false* (not *valid* or *invalid*). And we'll call arguments *valid* or *invalid* (not *true* or *false*). While this is conventional usage, it pains a logician's ears to hear "invalid statement" or "false argument."

So far we've seen **deductive** arguments, where the conclusion is claimed to follow with necessity. There also are **inductive** arguments, where the conclusion is claimed to follow only with probability; this claim is either implicit or else expressed by terms like "probably." Consider these examples:

Deductively valid	*Inductively strong*
All who live in France live in Europe.	Most who live in France speak French.
Pierre lives in France.	Pierre lives in France.
∴ Pierre lives in Europe.	This is all we know about the matter.
	∴ Pierre speaks French (probably).

The first argument has a tight connection between premises and conclusion; it would be impossible for the premises to all be true but the conclusion false. The second has a looser premise–conclusion connection. Relative to the premises, the conclusion is only a good guess; it's likely true but could be false (perhaps Pierre is the son of the Polish ambassador and speaks no French).

---

[1] These premises are Michelle Obama's own words. But often in this book, when I say that an argument is *from* a given thinker, I use my own phrasing.

1.4   The plan of this book

This book, being an introduction, starts simply and doesn't presume any previous study of logic. It covers a broad range of topics, from basic to rather advanced. The remaining chapters are divided into four groups:

- Part One. Chapters 2 to 5 cover syllogistic logic (an ancient branch of logic that focuses on "all," "no," and "some"), informal logic (which deals with meaning, definitions, informal fallacies, and other informal aspects of reasoning), and inductive reasoning.
- Part Two. Chapters 6 to 9 cover classical symbolic logic, which divides into propositional logic (about "if-then," "and," "or," and "not") and quantificational logic (which adds "all," "no," and "some").
- Part Three. Chapters 10 to 14 cover several advanced symbolic systems of philosophical interest: modal logic (about "necessary" and "possible"), deontic logic (about "ought" and "permissible"), belief logic (about consistent believing and willing), and a formalized ethical theory (which features a rigorous proof of the golden rule).
- Part Four. Chapters 15 to 18 introduce further vistas: metalogic (a study of logical systems), history of logic (from ancient times to the present), deviant logics (which question standard assumptions about logic), and philosophy of logic (which raises philosophical questions about logic).

Chapters 2–8 and 10 (and parts of 16 to 18) are suitable for a basic logic course, while the other chapters are more advanced. Since this book is so comprehensive, it has much more material than can be covered in a one-term course.[1]

Logic requires careful reading. While I've tried to explain things as clearly and concisely as possible, some points are difficult – especially for a beginner; you may sometimes have to read an explanation a few times before the ideas sink in. Since logic is so cumulative (with one idea building on another), it's especially important to keep up with the work; and "keeping up" involves being able to work out the problems yourself. You'll find the companion LogiCola software (see the Preface) a great help in this.

---

[1] Several chapters presume earlier chapters. Chapters 6 to 14 form a sequence, with each chapter building on previous chapters (except that Chapter 10 depends only on Chapters 6 and 7, and Chapter 11 isn't required for Chapters 12 to 14). Chapter 15 to 18 presume Chapter 6.

CHAPTER 2
Syllogistic Logic

Syllogistic logic studies arguments whose validity depends on "all," "no," "some," and similar notions. This branch of logic, which was the first to be developed, goes back to Aristotle (Section 16.1). It provides a fine preliminary to modern symbolic logic (Chapters 6–14).

2.1 Easier translations

We'll now create a little "syllogistic language," with precise rules for constructing arguments and testing validity. Our language will help us to test English arguments; here's how one such argument translates into our language:

All logicians are charming.		all L is C
Gensler is a logician.	➜	g is L
∴ Gensler is charming.		∴ g is C

Our language uses capital letters for general categories (like "logician") and small letters for specific individuals (like "Gensler"). It uses five words: "all," "no," "some," "is," and "not." Its grammatical sentences are called **wffs**, or **well-formed formulas**. Wffs are sequences having any of these eight forms (where other capital letters and other small letters may be used instead):[1]

all A is B	some A is B	x is A	x is y
no A is B	some A is not B	x is not A	x is not y

You must use one of these exact forms exactly (but perhaps using other capitals for "A" and "B," and other small letters for "x" and "y"). Here are examples of wffs (correct formulas) and non-wffs (misformed formulas):

wffs ➜	all L is C	no R is S	some C is D	g is C
non-wffs ➜	~~only L is C~~	~~all R is not S~~	~~some c is d~~	~~G is C~~

[1] Pronounce "wff" as "woof" (as in "wood"). We'll take upper and lower case forms (like A and a) to be different letters, and letters with primes (like A′ and A″) to be additional letters.

Be careful about whether you use upper or lower case; our rule for constructing wffs has implications about which to use:

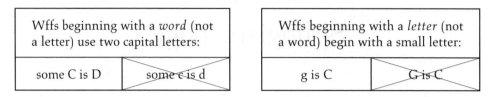

Wffs beginning with a *word* (not a letter) use two capital letters:	
some C is D	~~some c is d~~

Wffs beginning with a *letter* (not a word) begin with a small letter:	
g is C	~~G is C~~

If a wff begins with a small letter, however, then the second letter can be either capital or small; so "a is B" and "a is b" are both wffs. In this case, we have to look at the meaning of the term:

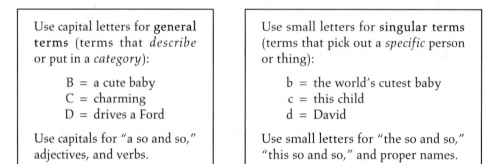

Use capital letters for **general terms** (terms that *describe* or put in a *category*):

    B = a cute baby
    C = charming
    D = drives a Ford

Use capitals for "a so and so," adjectives, and verbs.

Use small letters for **singular terms** (terms that pick out a *specific* person or thing):

    b = the world's cutest baby
    c = this child
    d = David

Use small letters for "the so and so," "this so and so," and proper names.

So these translations are correct:

$$\begin{array}{rcl} \text{Will Gensler is a cute baby} & = & \text{w is B} \\ \text{Will Gensler is the world's cutest baby} & = & \text{w is b} \end{array}$$

An argument's validity can depend on whether upper or lower case is used.

Be consistent when you translate English terms into logic; use the same letter for the same idea and different letters for different ideas. It matters little which letters you use; "a cute baby" could be "B" or "C" or any other capital. To keep ideas straight, use letters that remind you of the English terms.

Syllogistic wffs all have the verb "is." English sentences with a different verb should be rephrased to make "is" the main verb, and then translated. So "All dogs bark" is "all D is B" ("All dogs is [are] *barkers*"); and "Al drove the car" is "a is D" ("Al is *a person who drove the car*").

2.1a   Exercise – also LogiCola A (EM & ET)[1]

Translate these English sentences into wffs.

---

[1] Exercise sections have a boxed sample problem that is worked out for you. They also refer to corresponding LogiCola computer exercises (see the Preface). Selected problems 1, 3, 5, 10, 15, and so on are worked out at the back of the book (pp. 384–414).

> John left the room.

> j is L

1. This is a sentence.
2. This isn't the first sentence.
3. No logical positivist believes in God.
4. The book on your desk is green.
5. All dogs hate cats.
6. Kant is the greatest philosopher.
7. Ralph was born in Detroit.
8. Detroit is the birthplace of Ralph.
9. Alaska is a state.
10. Alaska is the biggest state.
11. Carol is my only sister.
12. Carol lives in Big Pine Key.
13. The idea of goodness is itself good.
14. All Michigan players are intelligent.
15. Michigan's team is awesome.
16. Donna is Ralph's wife.

2.2 The star test

A syllogism, roughly, is an argument using syllogistic wffs. Here's an English argument and its translation into a syllogism (the Cuyahoga is a river in Cleveland that used to be so polluted that it caught fire):

No pure water is burnable.	no P is B
Some Cuyahoga River water is burnable.	some C is B
∴ Some Cuyahoga River water isn't pure water.	∴ some C is not P

More precisely, a **syllogism** is a vertical sequence of one or more wffs in which each letter occurs twice and the letters "form a chain" (each wff has at least one letter in common with the wff just below it, if there is one, and the first wff has at least one letter in common with the last wff):

no P is B
some C is B
∴ some C is not P

(This is how the letters "form a chain.")

The last wff in a syllogism is the *conclusion*; any other wffs are *premises*. Here are three further syllogisms:

a is C
b is not C
∴ a is not b

some G is F
∴ some F is G

∴ all A is A

The last example is a premise-less syllogism. A premise-less syllogism is *valid* if and only if it's impossible for its conclusion to be false.

Before doing the star test, we need to learn the technical term "distributed":[1]

---

[1] Section 16.2 mentions the meaning of "distributed" in medieval logic. Here I suggest that you take a *distributed term* to be one that occurs just after "all" or anywhere after "no" or "not."

> An instance of a letter is **distributed** in a wff if it occurs just after "all" or anywhere after "no" or "not."

The <u>distributed</u> letters below are underlined:

all <u>A</u> is B	some A is B	x is A	x is y
no <u>A</u> is <u>B</u>	some A is not <u>B</u>	x is not <u>A</u>	x is not <u>y</u>

Note which letters are <u>distributed</u> (and underlined). By our definition:

- The first letter after "all" is distributed, but not the second.
- Both letters after "no" are distributed.
- The letter after "not" is distributed.

Once you know which terms are distributed, you're ready to learn the star test for validity. The star test is a gimmick, but a quick and effective one; for now it's best just to learn the test and not worry about why it works.

The **star test** for syllogisms goes as follows:

> Star premise letters that are distributed and conclusion letters that aren't distributed. Then the syllogism is **VALID** if and only if every capital letter is starred *exactly* once and there is *exactly* one star on the right-hand side.

The first few times you do the star test, I suggest that you use a three-part procedure: (1) underline distributed letters; (2) star; and (3) count the stars. Here's an example that comes out valid:

all <u>A</u> is B some C is A ∴ some C is B	(1) Underline distributed letters (only the first "A" is distributed).
all <u>A</u>* is B some C is A ∴ some C* is B*	(2) Star premise letters that are underlined and conclusion letters that aren't underlined.
all <u>A</u>* is B some C is A ∴ some C* is B*	(3) Count the stars. Every capital letter is starred exactly once and there is exactly one star on the right-hand side. So the argument is VALID.

Our second example comes out invalid:

no <u>A</u> is <u>B</u> no <u>C</u> is <u>A</u> ∴ no <u>C</u> is <u>B</u>	(1) Underline distributed letters (here all the letters are distributed – since they all occur after "no").
no <u>A</u>* is <u>B</u>* no <u>C</u>* is <u>A</u>* ∴ no <u>C</u> is <u>B</u>	(2) Star premise letters that are underlined and conclusion letters that aren't underlined.
no <u>A</u>* is <u>B</u>* no <u>C</u>* is <u>A</u>* ∴ no <u>C</u> is <u>B</u>	(3) Count the stars. Capital "A" is starred twice and there are two stars on the right-hand side. So the argument is INVALID.

A valid syllogism must satisfy two conditions: (a) each capital letter is starred in one and only one of its instances (small letters can be starred any number of times); and (b) one and only one right-hand letter (letter after "is" or "is not") is starred. Here's an example using only small letters:

a is not <u>b</u> ∴ b is not <u>a</u>	(1) Underline distributed letters (here just the letters after "not" are distributed).
a is not <u>b</u>* ∴ b* is not <u>a</u>	(2) Star premise letters that are underlined and conclusion letters that aren't underlined.
a is not <u>b</u>* ∴ b* is not <u>a</u>	(3) Count the stars. Since there are no capitals, each capital is starred exactly once (small letters can be starred any number of times). There's exactly one right-hand star. So the argument is VALID.

Here's an example without premises:

∴ all <u>A</u> is A	(1) Underline distributed letters.
∴ all <u>A</u> is A*	(2) Star conclusion letters that aren't underlined.
∴ all <u>A</u> is A*	(3) Count the stars. Each capital is starred exactly once and there's exactly one right-hand star. So the argument is VALID.

When you're used to how it works, skip the underlining and just star premise letters that are distributed and conclusion letters that aren't distributed. After a little practice, the star test takes about five seconds to do.[1]

---

[1] The star test is my invention; it came to me one day while I was watching a movie on television. For an explanation of why it works, see my "A simplified decision procedure for categorical syllogisms," *Notre Dame Journal of Formal Logic* 14 (1973): pages 457–66, or my explanation at http://www.jcu.edu/philosophy/gensler/star.htm.

Logic takes "some" to mean "one or more" – and so takes this to be valid:[1]

Gensler is a logician.	g is L	Valid
Gensler is mean.	g is M	
∴ Some logicians are mean.	∴ some L* is M*	

Similarly, logic takes this next argument to be invalid:

Some logicians are mean.	some L is M	Invalid
∴ Some logicians are not mean.	∴ some L* is not <u>M</u>	

If *one or more* logicians are mean, it needn't be that *one or more* aren't mean; maybe *all* logicians are mean.

2.2a   Exercise – No LogiCola exercise

Which of these are syllogisms?

no P is B
some C is B
∴ some C is not P

This is a syllogism. (Each formula is a wff, each letter occurs twice, and the letters form a chain.)

1. all C is D
    ∴ some C is not E

2. g is not l
    ∴ l is not g

3. no Y is E
    all G is Y
    ∴ no Y is E

4. ∴ all S is S

5. k is not L
    all M is L
    some N is M
    Z is N
    ∴ k is not Z

2.2b   Exercise – also LogiCola BH

Underline the distributed letters in the following wffs.

some R is not S

some R is not <u>S</u>

1. w is not s
2. some C is B
3. no R is S
4. a is C
5. all P is B
6. r is not D
7. s is w
8. some C is not P

2.2c   Exercise – also LogiCola B (H and S)

Valid or invalid? Use the star test.

---

[1] In English, "some" can have various meanings, including "one or more," "two or more," "several" (where it's vague how many this is), "one or more but not all," "two or more but not all," and "several but not all." Only the first meaning makes our argument valid.

no P is B	no <u>P</u>* is <u>B</u>* Valid
some C is B	some C is B
∴ some C is not P	∴ some C* is not <u>P</u>

1.   no P is B
     some C is not B
   ∴ some C is P

2.   x is W
     x is not Y
   ∴ some W is not Y

3.   no H is B
     no H is D
   ∴ some B is not D

4.   some J is not P
     all J is F
   ∴ some F is not P

5. ∴ g is g

6.   g is not s
   ∴ s is not g

7.   all L is M
     g is not L
   ∴ g is not M

8.   some N is T
     some C is not T
   ∴ some N is not C

9.   all C is K
     s is K
   ∴ s is C

10.   all D is A
   ∴ all A is D

11.   s is C
     s is H
   ∴ some C is H

12.   some C is H
   ∴ some C is not H

13.   a is b
     b is c
     c is d
   ∴ a is d

14.   no A is B
     some B is C
     some D is not C
     all D is E
   ∴ some E is A

2.3   English arguments

Most of the arguments in this book are in English. I suggest that you work them out in a dual manner. First use intuition. Read the argument and ask whether it seems valid; sometimes this will be clear, but sometimes not. Then symbolize the argument and do a validity test. If your intuition and the validity test agree, then you have a stronger basis for your answer. If they disagree, then something went wrong; so you have to reconsider your intuition, your translation, or how you did the validity test. This dual attack trains your logical intuitions and gives you a double-check on the results.

When you translate into logic, use the same letter for the same idea and different letters for different ideas. The "same idea" may be phrased in different ways[1]; often it's redundant or stilted to phrase an idea in the exact same way throughout an argument. If you can't remember which letter translates which phrase, underline the phrase in the argument and write the letter above it; or write out separately which letter goes with which phrase.

Translate singular terms into small letters, and general terms into capital letters (Section 2.1). Capitalization can make a difference to validity:

---

[1] "Express the same idea" can be tricky to apply. Consider "All Fuji apples are <u>nutritious</u>" and "All <u>nutritious apples</u> have vitamins." Use the same letter for both underlined phrases, since premise 1 would mean the same if rephrased as "All Fuji apples are <u>nutritious apples</u>."

Invalid	Al is *a man.*	Al is *the NY mayor.*	Valid
a is M	My best friend is *a man.*	My best friend is *the NY mayor.*	a is m
b is M			b is m
∴ a* is b*	∴ Al is my best friend.	∴ Al is my best friend.	∴ a* is b*

The invalid example uses a capital "M" (for "a man" – which could describe various people) while the valid one uses a small "m" (for "the NY mayor" – which refers to a specific person). We'd likely catch capitalization mistakes if we did the problems intuitively as well as mechanically.

2.3a   Exercise – also LogiCola BE

Valid or invalid? First appraise intuitively. Then translate into logic and use the star test to determine validity.

No pure water is burnable.	no P* is B* **Valid**
Some Cuyahoga River water is burnable.	some C is B
∴ Some Cuyahoga River water isn't pure water.	∴ some C* is not P

1. All segregation laws degrade human personality.
    All laws that degrade human personality are unjust.
    ∴ All segregation laws are unjust.   [From Dr Martin Luther King.]

2. All Communists favor the poor.
    All Democrats favor the poor.
    ∴ All Democrats are Communists.   [This reasoning could persuade if expressed emotionally in a political speech. It's less likely to persuade if put into a clear premise–conclusion form.]

3. All too-much-time penalties are called before play starts.
    No penalty called before play starts can be refused.
    ∴ No too-much-time penalty can be refused.

4. No one under 18 is permitted to vote.
    No faculty member is under 18.
    The philosophy chairperson is a faculty member.
    ∴ The philosophy chairperson is permitted to vote.   [Applying laws, like ones about voting, requires logical reasoning. Lawyers and judges need to be logical.]

5. All acts that maximize good consequences are right.
    Some punishing of the innocent maximizes good consequences.
    ∴ Some punishing of the innocent is right.   [This argument and the next give a mini-debate on utilitarianism, which holds that all acts that maximize the total of good consequences for everyone are right. Moral philosophy would try to evaluate the premises; logic just focuses on whether the conclusion follows.]

6. No punishing of the innocent is right.
    Some punishing of the innocent maximizes good consequences.
    ∴ Some acts that maximize good consequences aren't right.

7. All huevos revueltos are buenos para el desayuno.
    All café con leche is bueno para el desayuno.
    ∴ All café con leche is huevos revueltos.   [To test whether this argument is valid,
        you don't have to understand its meaning; you only have to grasp the form. In
        doing formal logic, you don't have to know what you're talking about; you only
        have to know the logical form of what you're talking about.]

8. The belief that there's a God is unnecessary to explain our experience.
    All beliefs unnecessary to explain our experience ought to be rejected.
    ∴ The belief that there's a God ought to be rejected.   [St Thomas Aquinas men-
        tioned this argument in order to dispute the first premise.]

9. The belief in God gives practical life benefits (courage, peace, zeal, love, …).
    All beliefs that give practical life benefits are pragmatically justifiable.
    ∴ The belief in God is pragmatically justifiable.   [From William James, an Ameri-
        can pragmatist philosopher.]

10. All sodium salt gives a yellow flame when put into the flame of a Bunsen burner.
    This material gives a yellow flame when put into the flame of a Bunsen burner.
    ∴ This material is sodium salt.

11. All abortions kill innocent human life.
    No killing of innocent human life is right.
    ∴ No abortions are right.

12. All acts that maximize good consequences are right.
    All socially useful abortions maximize good consequences.
    ∴ All socially useful abortions are right.

13. That drink is transparent.
    That drink is tasteless.
    All vodka is tasteless.
    ∴ Some vodka is transparent.

14. Judy isn't the world's best cook.
    The world's best cook lives in Detroit.
    ∴ Judy doesn't live in Detroit.

15. All men are mortal.
    My mother is a man.
    ∴ My mother is mortal.

16. All gender-neutral terms can be applied naturally to individual women.
    The term "man" can't be applied naturally to individual women. (We can't natu-
        rally say "My mother is a man"; see the previous argument.)
    ∴ The term "man" isn't a gender-neutral term.   [From the philosopher Janice
        Molton's discussion of sexist language.]

17. Some moral questions are controversial.
    No controversial question has a correct answer.
    ∴ Some moral questions don't have a correct answer.

18.   The idea of a perfect circle is a human concept.
      The idea of a perfect circle doesn't derive from sense experience.
      All ideas gained in our earthly existence derive from sense experience.
   ∴ Some human concepts aren't ideas gained in our earthly existence.   [This is from
      Plato. It led him to think that the soul gained ideas in a previous existence apart
      from the body, and so can exist apart from matter.]

19.   All beings with a right to life are capable of desiring continued existence.
      All beings capable of desiring continued existence have a concept of themselves as
      a continuing subject of experiences.
      No human fetus has a concept of itself as a continuing subject of experiences.
   ∴ No human fetus has a right to life.   [From Michael Tooley.]

20.   The bankrobber wears size-twelve hiking boots.
      You wear size-twelve hiking boots.
   ∴ You're the bankrobber.   [This is circumstantial evidence.]

21.   All moral beliefs are products of culture.
      No products of culture express objective truths.
   ∴ No moral beliefs express objective truths.

22.   Some books are products of culture.
      Some books express objective truths.
   ∴ Some products of culture express objective truths.   [How could we change this
      argument to make it valid?]

23.   Dr Martin Luther King believed in objective moral truths (about the wrongness
      of racism).
      Dr Martin Luther King disagreed with the moral beliefs of his culture.
      No people who disagree with the moral beliefs of their culture are absolutizing
      the moral beliefs of their own culture.
   ∴ Some who believed in objective moral truths aren't absolutizing the moral
      beliefs of their own culture.

24.   All claims that would still be true if no one believed them are objective truths.
      "Racism is wrong" would still be true if no one believed it.
      "Racism is wrong" is a moral claim.
   ∴ Some moral claims are objective truths.

25.   Some shivering people with uncovered heads have warm heads.
      All shivering people with uncovered heads lose much heat through their heads.
      All who lose much heat through their heads ought to put on a hat to stay warm.
   ∴ Some people who have warm heads ought to put on a hat to stay warm.   [From a
      ski magazine.]

2.3b   Mystery story exercise – No LogiCola exercise

Herman had a party at his house. Alice, Bob, Carol, David, George, and others were
there; one or more of these stole money from Herman's bedroom. You have the data in
the box, which may or may not give conclusive evidence about a given suspect:

> 1. Alice doesn't love money.
> 2. Bob loves money.
> 3. Carol knew where the money was.
> 4. David works for Herman.
> 5. David isn't the nastiest person at the party.
> 6. All who stole money love money.
> 7. All who stole money knew where the money was.
> 8. All who work for Herman hate Herman.
> 9. All who hate Herman stole money.
> 10. The nastiest person at the party stole money.

Did Alice steal money? If you can, prove your answer using a valid syllogism with premises from the box.

Alice *didn't* steal money:

a is not L* – #1
all S* is L – #6
∴ a* is not S

1. Did Bob steal money? If you can, prove your answer using a valid syllogism with premises from the box.
2. Did Carol steal money? If you can, prove your answer using a valid syllogism with premises from the box.
3. Did David steal money? If you can, prove your answer using a valid syllogism with premises from the box.
4. Based on our data, did more than one person steal money? Can you prove this using syllogistic logic?
5. Suppose that, from our data, we could deduce that a person stole money and also deduce that this same person didn't steal money. What would that show?

2.4   Harder translations

Suppose we want to test this argument:

Every human is mortal.	all H is M
Only humans are philosophers.	all P is H
∴ Every philosopher is mortal.	∴ all P is M

To symbolize such arguments, we need to translate idioms like "every" and "only" into our standard "all," "no," and "some." Here "every" is easy, since it just means "all." But "only" is more difficult; "Only humans are philosophers" really means "All philosophers are humans."

This box lists some common ways to express "all" in English:

Different ways to say "all A is B":

Every (each, any) A is B.	Only B's are A's.
Whoever is A is B.	None but B's are A's.
A's are B's.[1]	No one is A unless he or she is B.
Those who are A are B.	No one is A without being B.
If a person is A, then he or she is B.	A thing isn't A unless it's B.
If you're A, then you're B.	It's false that some A is not B.

The examples on the top right (with "only" and "none but") are tricky because they require switching the order of the letters:

	Only dogs are collies.		only D is C
=	All collies are dogs.	=	all C is D

So "only" translates as "all," but with the terms reversed; "none but" works the same way. The forms on the bottom right (starting with "no … unless") are tricky too, because here "no" with "unless" really means "all":

	Nothing is a collie unless it's a dog.		nothing is C unless it's D
=	All collies are dogs.	=	all C is D

Don't reverse the letters here; only reverse letters with "only" and "none but."
    This box lists some common ways to say "no A is B":

Different ways to say "no A is B":

A's aren't B's.	No one that's A is B.
Every (each, any) A is non-B.	There isn't a single A that's B.
Whoever is A isn't B.	Not any A is B.
If a person is A, then he or she isn't B.	It's false that there's an A that's B.
If you're A, then you aren't B.	It's false that some A is B.

Never use "all A is not B." Besides not being a wff, this form is ambiguous. "All cookies are not fattening" could mean "No cookies are fattening" or "Some cookies are not fattening."
    These last two boxes give some common ways to say "some":

---

[1] Logicians take "A's are B's" to mean "all A is B" – even though in ordinary English it also could mean "most A is B" or "some A is B."

some A is B   =
A's are sometimes B's.
One or more A's are B's.
There are A's that are B's.
It's false that no A is B.

some A is not B   =
One or more A's aren't B's.
There are A's that aren't B's.
Not all A's are B's.
It's false that all A is B.

Formulas "no A is B" and "some A is B" are contradictories: saying that one is false is equivalent to saying that the other is true:

It's false that no days are sunny	=	Some days are sunny.
It's false that some days are sunny	=	No days are sunny.

Similarly, "all A is B" and "some A is not B" are contradictories:

It's false that all cats are white	=	Some cats are not white.
It's false that some cats are not white	=	All cats are white.

Idiomatic sentences can be difficult to untangle, even though they're part of everyday speech. Our rules cover most cases. If you find an example that our rules don't cover, you have to puzzle out the meaning yourself; try substituting concrete terms, like "collie" and "dog," as we did above.

2.4a   Exercise – also LogiCola A (HM & HT)

Translate these English sentences into wffs.

Nothing is worthwhile unless it's difficult.

all W is D

1. Only free actions can justly be punished.
2. Not all actions are determined.
3. Socially useful actions are right.
4. None but Democrats favor the poor.
5. At least some of the shirts are on sale.
6. Not all of the shirts are on sale.
7. No one is happy unless they are rich.[1]
8. Only rich people are happy.
9. Every rich person is happy.
10. Not any selfish people are happy.
11. Whoever is happy is not selfish.
12. Altruistic people are happy.
13. All of the shirts (individually) cost $20.

[1] How would you argue against this statement (and the next two)? Would you go to the rich part of town and find a rich person who was miserable? Or would you go to the poor part of town and find a poor person who was happy?

14.   All of the shirts (together) cost $20.
15.   Blessed are the merciful.
16.   I mean whatever I say.
17.   I say whatever I mean.
18.   Whoever hikes the Appalachian Trail (AT) loves nature.
19.   No person hikes the AT unless he or she likes to walk.
20.   Not everyone who hikes the AT is in great shape.

2.5   Deriving conclusions

In the next exercise, you'll be given premises (like "All men are mortal" and "Socrates is a man") and have to derive a conclusion that follows validly. I suggest that you work out these problems in a dual manner: first use intuition and then use rules. With the intuitive approach, you'd read the premises reflectively, say "therefore" to yourself, hold your breath, and hope that the conclusion comes. If you get a conclusion, write it down; then symbolize the argument and test it for validity using the star test.

The rule approach uses four steps based on the star test:

(1) Translate the premises and star.	(2) Figure out the letters in the conclusion.	(3) Figure out the form of the conclusion.	(4) Add the conclusion and do the star test.

(1) Translate the premises into logic and star the distributed letters. Check to see if rules are broken. If you have two right-hand stars, or a capital letter that occurs twice without being starred exactly once, then no conclusion validly follows – and so you can write "no conclusion" and stop.

(2) Figure out which letters will occur in the conclusion. The conclusion letters are the two letters that occur just once in the premises.

(3) Figure out the form of the conclusion. There are eight possible forms:

If both conclusion letters are capitals: if *all* the premises are universal (have "all" or "no"), then use the "all A is B" or "no A is B" form in the conclusion; otherwise, use "some A is B" or "some A is not B."	*Use the negative form ("no" or "not") if there's a negative premise.*
If just one conclusion letter is small: use the "x is A" or "x is not A" form in the conclusion.	
If both conclusion letters are small: use the "x is y" or "x is not y" form in the conclusion.	

So if every premise has "all" (universal and positive), then the conclusion has "all"; but if the premises have a mix of "all" and "no" (universal but some negative), then the conclusion has "no."

(4) Add the conclusion and test for validity; if it comes out invalid, try switching the order of the letters to see if this makes it valid (the order matters with the "all A is B" and "some A is not B" forms). Finally, put the conclusion into English.

Suppose we want to derive a conclusion from the English premises on the left. We first translate the premise into logic and star:

<table>
<tr><td>Some cave dwellers use fire.</td><td>some C is F</td></tr>
<tr><td>All who use fire have intelligence.</td><td>all F* is I</td></tr>
</table>

No rules are broken. "C" and "I" will occur in the conclusion. The conclusion form will be "some … is …." We find that "some C is I" follows validly, and so we conclude "Some cave dwellers have intelligence." Equivalently, we could conclude "Some that have intelligence are cave dwellers."

Or suppose we want to derive a conclusion from these next premises. Again, we first translate the premises into logic and star:

<table>
<tr><td>No one held for murder is given bail.</td><td>no M* is B*</td></tr>
<tr><td>Smith isn't held for murder.</td><td>s is not M*</td></tr>
</table>

Here "M" is starred twice and there are two right-hand stars, and so rules are broken. So no conclusion follows. Do you intuitively want to conclude "Smith is given bail"? If so, consider that Smith might be held for something else, like kidnapping, for which bail is denied; or maybe Smith isn't held for anything.

Let's take yet another example:

<table>
<tr><td>Gensler is a logician.</td><td>g is L</td></tr>
<tr><td>Gensler is mean.</td><td>g is M</td></tr>
</table>

No rules are broken. "L" and "M" will occur in the conclusion. The conclusion form will be "some … is …." We find that "some L is M" follows validly, and so we conclude "Some logicians are mean." Equivalently, we could conclude "Some who are mean are logicians."

2.5a   Exercise – also LogiCola BD

Derive a conclusion in English (not in wffs) that follows validly from and uses all the premises. Leave blank or write "no conclusion" if no such conclusion validly follows.

No pure water is burnable. Some Cuyahoga River water is not burnable.	no P* is B* some C is not B*
	no conclusion

Do you want to conclude "Some Cuyahoga River water is pure water"? Consider that all of the river might be polluted by something that doesn't burn.

1. All human acts are determined (caused by prior events beyond our control).
   No determined acts are free.

2. Some human acts are free.
   No determined acts are free.

3. All acts where you do what you want are free.
   Some acts where you do what you want are determined.

4. All men are rational animals.
   No woman is a man.

5. All philosophers love wisdom.
   John loves wisdom.

6. Luke was a gospel writer.
   Luke was not an apostle.

7. All cheap waterproof raincoats block the escape of sweat.
   No raincoat that blocks the escape of sweat keeps you dry when hiking uphill.

8. All that is or could be experienced is thinkable.
   All that is thinkable is expressible in judgments.
   All that is expressible in judgments is expressible with subjects and predicates.
   All that is expressible with subjects and predicates is about objects and properties.

9. All moral judgments influence our actions and feelings.
   Nothing from reason influences our actions and feelings.

10. No feelings that diminish when we understand their origins are rational.
    All culturally taught racist feelings diminish when we understand their origin.

11.   I weigh 180 pounds.
      My mind does not weigh 180 pounds.
      _____

12.   No acts caused by hypnotic suggestion are free.
      Some acts where you do what you want are caused by hypnotic suggestion.
      _____

13.   All unproved beliefs ought to be rejected.
      "There is a God" is an unproved belief.
      _____

14.   All unproved beliefs ought to be rejected.
      "All unproved beliefs ought to be rejected" is an unproved belief.
      _____

15.   Jones likes raw steaks.
      Jones likes champagne.
      _____

16.   Some human beings seek self-destructive revenge.
      No one seeking self-destructive revenge is motivated only by self-interest.
      All purely selfish people are motivated only by self-interest.
      _____

17.   All virtues are praised.
      No emotions are praised.
      _____

18.   God is a perfect being.
      All perfect beings are self-sufficient.
      No self-sufficient being is influenced by anything outside of itself.
      _____

19.   God is a perfect being.
      All perfect beings know everything.
      All beings that know everything are influenced by everything.
      _____

20.   All basic moral norms hold for all possible rational beings as such.
      No principles based on human nature hold for all possible rational beings as such.
      _____

21.   All programs that discriminate simply because of race are wrong.
      All racial affirmative action programs discriminate simply because of race.
      _____

22.   Some racial affirmative action programs are attempts to make amends for past injustices toward a given group.
No attempts to make amends for past injustices toward a given group discriminate simply because of race. (They discriminate because of past injustices.)

23.   Some actions approved by reformers are right.
Some actions approved by society aren't approved by reformers.

24.   Some wrong actions are errors made in good faith.
No error made in good faith is blameworthy.

25.   All moral judgments are beliefs whose correctness cannot be decided by reason.
No objective truths are beliefs whose correctness cannot be decided by reason.

Here 1–3 defend the three classic views on free will: hard determinism, indeterminism, and soft determinism; 8 and 20 are from Immanuel Kant; 9 is from David Hume; 10 is from Richard Brandt; 17 and 18 are from Aristotle; and 19 is from Charles Hartshorne.

2.6   Venn diagrams

Now that we've mastered the star test, we'll learn a second test which is more intuitive (but also more difficult). **Venn diagrams** allow you to diagram the premises using three overlapping circles. We'll apply Venn diagrams only to *traditional syllogisms* (two-premise syllogisms with no small letters).
Here's how to do the Venn-diagram test:

> Draw three overlapping circles, labeling each with one of the syllogism's letters. Then draw the premises following the directions below. The syllogism is **VALID** if and only if drawing the premises *necessitates* drawing the conclusion.

First, we draw three overlapping circles:

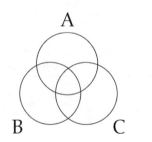

Visualize circle A containing all A things, circle B containing all B things, and circle C containing all C things.

Within the circles are seven distinct areas:

- The central area, where all three circles overlap, contains whatever has all three features (A and B and C).
- Three middle areas contain whatever has only two features (for example, A and B but not C).
- Three outer areas contain whatever has only one feature (for example, A but not B or C).

Each of the seven areas can be either empty or non-empty. We shade areas that we know to be empty. We put an "×" in areas that we know to contain at least one entity. An area without either shading or an "×" is unspecified; it could be either empty or non-empty.

Here is how we draw "no" and "some … is …":

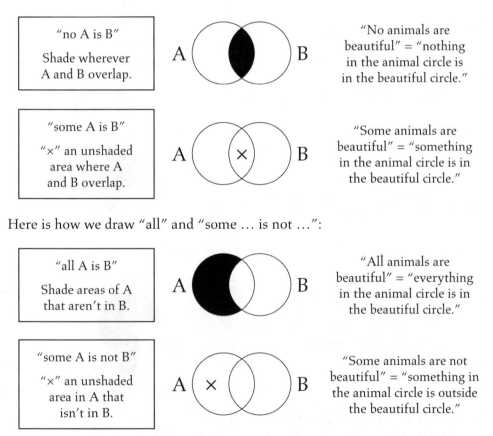

"no A is B"

Shade wherever A and B overlap.

"No animals are beautiful" = "nothing in the animal circle is in the beautiful circle."

"some A is B"

"×" an unshaded area where A and B overlap.

"Some animals are beautiful" = "something in the animal circle is in the beautiful circle."

Here is how we draw "all" and "some … is not …":

"all A is B"

Shade areas of A that aren't in B.

"All animals are beautiful" = "everything in the animal circle is in the beautiful circle."

"some A is not B"

"×" an unshaded area in A that isn't in B.

"Some animals are not beautiful" = "something in the animal circle is outside the beautiful circle."

Again, shading means that the area is empty, while an "×" means that there is something in the area.

Follow these four steps (for now you can ignore the complication on the right, since it doesn't come up in our first three examples):

1. Draw three overlapping circles.
2. First draw "all" and "no" premises by shading.
3. Then draw "some" premises by putting an "×" in some unshaded area.
4. If you *must* draw the conclusion, then the argument is valid; other-wise, it's invalid.

➡

3a. When you draw "some," you sometimes can put the "×" in either of two unshaded areas. Then the argument is invalid; to show this, put the "×" in an area that *doesn't* draw the conclusion. (I sug-gest you first put "×" in *both* areas and then erase the "×" that draws the conclusion.)

Let's try the test on the valid argument on the left:

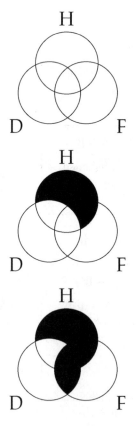

      all H is D Valid
      no F is D
    ∴ no H is F

We draw three overlapping circles.

We draw "all H is D" by shading areas of H that aren't in D.

We draw "no F is D" by shading where F and D overlap.

But then we've automatically drawn the conclusion "no H is F" – since we've shaded where H and F overlap. So the argument is valid.

    Here's an invalid argument:

no H is D   Invalid
no F is D
∴ no H is F

We draw "no H is D" by shading where
H and D overlap. We draw "no F is D"
by shading where F and D overlap.

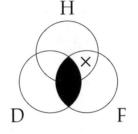

But then we haven't automatically drawn the conclusion "no H is F" (since we
haven't shaded all the areas where H and F overlap). So the argument is invalid.

Here's a valid argument using "some":

no D is F   Valid
some H is F
∴ some H is not D

We draw "no D is F" by shading where
D and F overlap. We draw "some H is F"
by putting "×" in some unshaded area
where H and F overlap.

But then we've automatically drawn the conclusion "some H is not D" – since
we've put an "×" in some area of H that's outside D. So the argument is valid.
(Recall that we draw "all" and "no" first, and then we draw "some.")

I earlier warned about a complication that sometimes occurs:

> 3a. When you draw "some," you sometimes can
> put the "×" in either of two unshaded areas. Then
> the argument is invalid; to show this, put the "×"
> in an area that *doesn't* draw the conclusion. (I
> suggest you first put "×" in *both* areas and then
> erase the "×" that draws the conclusion.)

Here's such an example:

no D is F   Invalid
some H is not D
∴ some H is F

We draw "no D is F" by shading where D
and F overlap. We draw "some H is not D"
by putting "×" in *both* unshaded areas in
H that are outside D (since either "×"
would draw the premise).

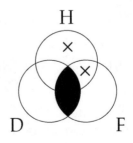

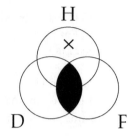

We then erase the "×" that draws the conclusion "some H is F." So then we've drawn the premises without drawing the conclusion.

Since it's possible to draw the premises without drawing the conclusion, the argument is invalid. Since this problem is tricky, you might reread the explanation a couple of times until it's clear in your mind.

2.6a   Exercise – also LogiCola BC

Test for validity using Venn diagrams.

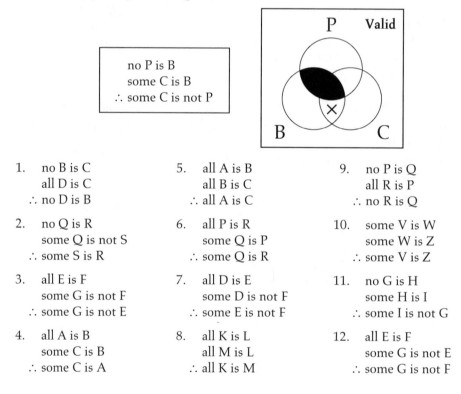

no P is B
some C is B
∴ some C is not P

1.   no B is C
       all D is C
   ∴ no D is B

2.   no Q is R
       some Q is not S
   ∴ some S is R

3.   all E is F
       some G is not F
   ∴ some G is not E

4.   all A is B
       some C is B
   ∴ some C is A

5.   all A is B
       all B is C
   ∴ all A is C

6.   all P is R
       some Q is P
   ∴ some Q is R

7.   all D is E
       some D is not F
   ∴ some E is not F

8.   all K is L
       all M is L
   ∴ all K is M

9.   no P is Q
       all R is P
   ∴ no R is Q

10.   some V is W
        some W is Z
    ∴ some V is Z

11.   no G is H
        some H is I
    ∴ some I is not G

12.   all E is F
        some G is not E
    ∴ some G is not F

2.7   Idiomatic arguments

Our arguments so far have been phrased in a clear premise–conclusion format. Unfortunately, real-life arguments are seldom so neat and clean. Instead we may find convoluted wording or extraneous material. Important parts of the argument may be omitted or only hinted at. And it may be hard to pick out the premises and conclusion. It often takes hard work to reconstruct a clearly stated argument from a passage.

Logicians like to put the conclusion last:

> "Socrates is human. All humans are mortal. *So Socrates is mortal.*"

> s is H
> all H is M
> ∴ s is M

But people sometimes put the conclusion first, or in the middle:

> "*Socrates must be mortal.*
> After all, he's human and
> all humans are mortal."

> "Socrates is human. *So he
> must be mortal* – since all
> humans are mortal."

In these examples, "must" and "so" indicate the conclusion (which always goes *last* when we translate the argument into logic). Here are some typical words that help us pick out the premises and conclusion:

These often indicate premises:		These often indicate conclusions:
Because, for, since, after all …	∴	Hence, thus, so, therefore …
I assume that, as we know …		It must be, it can't be …
For these reasons …		This proves (or shows) that …

When you don't have this help, ask yourself what is argued *from* (these are the premises) and what is argued *to* (this is the conclusion).

In reconstructing an argument, first pick out the conclusion. Then symbolize the premises and conclusion; this may involve untangling idioms like "Only A's are B's" (which translates as "all B is A"). If some letters occur only once, you may have to add unstated but implicit premises; using the "principle of charity," interpret unclear reasoning to give the best argument. Then test for validity.

Consider this twisted argument:

> "You aren't allowed in here! After all, only members are allowed."

First we pick out the premises and conclusion:

> Only members are allowed in here.
> ∴ You aren't allowed in here.

> all A is M
> ∴ u is not A

Since "M" and "u" occur only once, we need to add an implicit premise linking these to produce a syllogism. We add a plausible premise and test for validity:

You aren't a member. (implicit)	u is not M*	**Valid**
Only members are allowed in here.	all A* is M	
∴ You aren't allowed in here.	∴ u* is not A	

2.7a   Exercise – also LogiCola B (F & I)

First appraise intuitively. Then pick out the conclusion, translate into logic (using correct wffs and syllogisms), and determine validity using the star test. Supply implicit premises where needed; when two letters occur only once but stand for genuinely different ideas, we often need an implicit premise that connects the two.

Whatever is good in itself ought to be desired. But whatever ought to be desired is capable of being desired. So only pleasure is good in itself, since only pleasure is capable of being desired.	all G* is O **Valid** all O* is C all C* is P ∴ all G is P* The conclusion is *"Only pleasure is good in itself"*: *"all G is P."*

1. Racial segregation in schools generates severe feelings of inferiority among black students. Whatever generates such feelings treats students unfairly on the basis of race. Anything that treats students unfairly on the basis of race violates the 14th Amendment. Whatever violates the 14th Amendment is unconstitutional. Thus racial segregation in schools is unconstitutional.   [This is the reasoning behind the 1954 Brown vs. Topeka Board of Education Supreme Court decision.]
2. You couldn't have studied! The evidence for this is that you got an F- on the test.
3. God can't condemn agnostics for non-belief. For God is all-good, anyone who is all-good respects intellectual honesty, and no one who does this condemns agnostics for non-belief.
4. Only what is under a person's control is subject to praise or blame. Thus the consequences of an action aren't subject to praise or blame, since not all the consequences of an action are under a person's control.
5. No synthetic garment absorbs moisture. So no synthetic garment should be worn next to the skin while skiing.
6. Not all human concepts can be derived from sense experience. My reason for saying this is that the idea of "self-contradictory" is a human concept but isn't derived from sense experience.
7. Analyses of humans in purely physical-chemical terms are neutral about whether we have inner consciousness. So, contrary to Hobbes, we must conclude that no analysis of humans in purely physical-chemical terms fully explains our mental activities. Clearly, explanations that are neutral about whether we have inner consciousness don't fully explain our mental activities.
8. Only what is based on sense experience is knowledge about the world. It follows that no mathematical knowledge is knowledge about the world.
9. Not all the transistors in your radio can be silicon. After all, every transistor that works well at high temperatures is silicon and yet not all the transistors in your radio work well at high temperatures.

10. Moral principles aren't part of philosophy. This follows from these considerations: Only objective truths are part of philosophy. Nothing is an objective truth unless it's experimentally testable. Finally, of course, moral principles aren't experimentally testable. [From the logical positivist A. J. Ayer.]

11. At least some women are fathers. This follows from these facts: (1) Jones is a father, (2) Jones had a sex change to female, and (3) whoever had a sex change to female is (now) a woman.

12. Only language users employ generalizations. Not a single animal uses language. At least some animals reason. So not all reasoners employ generalizations. [From John Stuart Mill.]

13. Only pure studies in form have true artistic worth. This proves that a thing doesn't have true artistic worth unless it's abstract, for it's false that there's something that's abstract but that isn't a pure study in form.

14. Anything that relieves pressure on my blisters while I hike would allow me to finish my PCT (Pacific Crest Trail) hike from Mexico to Canada. Any insole with holes cut out for blisters would relieve pressure on my blisters while I hike. I conclude that any insole with holes cut out for blisters would allow me to finish my PCT hike from Mexico to Canada. [So I reasoned – and it worked.]

15. We know (from observing the earth's shadow on the moon during a lunar eclipse) that the earth casts a curved shadow. But spheres cast curved shadows. These two facts prove that the earth is a sphere.

16. Whatever is known is true, and whatever is true corresponds to the facts. We may conclude that no belief about the future is known.

17. No adequate ethical theory is based on sense experience, because any adequate ethical theory provides necessary and universal principles, and nothing based on sense experience provides such principles. [From Immanuel Kant.]

18. At least some active people are hypothermia victims. Active people don't shiver. It follows that not all hypothermia victims shiver. [From a ski magazine.]

19. Iron objects conduct electricity. We know this from what we learned last week – namely, that iron objects are metallic and that nothing conducts electricity unless it's metallic.

20. Only things true by linguistic convention are necessary truths. This shows that "God exists" can't be a necessary truth. After all, existence claims aren't true by linguistic convention.

21. No bundle of perceptions eats food. Hume eats food, and Hume is a human person. From this it follows (contrary to David Hume's theory) that no human person is a bundle of perceptions.

22. Any events we could experience as empirically real (as opposed to dreams or hallucinations) could fit coherently into our experience. So an uncaused event couldn't be experienced as empirically real. I assume that it's false that some uncaused event could fit coherently into our experience. [From Immanuel Kant.]

23. I think I'm seeing a chair. But some people who think they're seeing a chair are deceived by their senses. And surely people deceived by their senses don't really know that they're seeing an actual chair. So I don't really know that I'm seeing an actual chair.

24.   No material objects can exist unperceived. I say this for three reasons: (1) Material objects can be perceived. (2) Only sensations can be perceived. Finally, (3) no sensation can exist unperceived.   [Bertrand Russell criticized this argument for an idealist metaphysics.]

25.   Only those who can feel pleasure or pain deserve moral consideration. Not all plants can feel pleasure or pain. So not all plants deserve moral consideration.

26.   True principles don't have false consequences. There are plausible principles with false consequences. Hence not all true principles are plausible.

27.   Only what divides into parts can die. Everything that's material divides into parts. No human soul is material. This shows that no human soul can die.

2.8   The Aristotelian view

Historically, "Aristotelian" and "modern" logicians disagree about the validity of some syllogism forms. They disagree because of differing policies about allowing *empty terms* (general terms that don't refer to any existing beings).

Compare these two arguments:

All cats are animals.   All unicorns are animals.
∴ Some animals are cats.   ∴ Some animals are unicorns.

The first seems valid while the second seems invalid. Yet both have the same form – one that tests out as "invalid" using our star test:

all C* is A   Invalid
∴ some A* is C*

What's going on here?

When we read the first argument, we tend to presuppose that there's at least one cat. Given this as an assumed additional premise, it follows validly that some animals are cats. When we read the second argument, we don't assume that there's at least one unicorn.[1] Without this additional assumption, it doesn't follow that some animals are unicorns.

Logically, what we have is this:

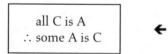

all C is A
∴ some A is C

← This is *valid* if we assume as a further premise that there are C's. It's *invalid* if we don't assume this.

The *Aristotelian view*, which assumes that each general term in a syllogism refers to at least one existing being, calls the argument "valid." The *modern view*, which allows empty terms like "unicorn" that don't refer to existing

---

[1] Unicorns are mythical creatures that are like horses but have a single horn on the forehead. Since there are no such beings, "unicorn" is an empty term and doesn't refer to existing beings.

beings, calls the argument "invalid."

I prefer the modern view, since we often reason without presupposing that our general terms refer to existing entities. Someone may write a paper disputing the existence of angels; it would be awkward if we couldn't reason using the term "angel" without presupposing that there are angels. Or a teacher may say, "All students with straight-100s may skip the final exam"; this rule doesn't presuppose that anyone in fact will get straight-100s. On the other hand, we sometimes *can* presuppose that our general terms all refer; then the Aristotelian test seems more sensible.

Suppose we have an argument with true premises that's valid on the Aristotelian view but invalid on the modern view. Should we draw the conclusion or not? We should draw the conclusion if we know that each general term in the premises refers to at least one existing being; otherwise, we shouldn't. Consider this pair of arguments with the same form (a form that's valid on the Aristotelian view but invalid on the modern view):

All cats are mammals.	All square circles are squares.
All cats are furry.	All square circles are circles.
∴ Some mammals are furry.	∴ Some squares are circles.

The first inference is sensible, because there are cats. The second inference isn't sensible, because there are no square circles.

Some logic books use the Aristotelian view, but most use the modern view. It makes a difference in very few cases; all the syllogisms in this chapter prior to this section test out the same on either view.

To adapt the star test to the Aristotelian view, word it so that each capital letter must be starred *at least once* (instead of "exactly once"). To adapt Venn diagrams to the Aristotelian view, add this rule: "If you have a circle with only one unshaded area, put an '×' in this area"; this is equivalent to assuming that the circle in question isn't entirely empty.

CHAPTER 3
Meaning and Definitions

Language is important when we appraise arguments. To decide whether an argument is sound, we need to appraise the truth of the premises; but this requires some understanding of what the premises mean. Meaning is often crucial. Imagine that someone proposes this argument:

> If there's a cosmic force, then there's a God.
> There's a cosmic force.
> ∴ There's a God.

While this is deductively valid, the premises are obscure. What is a "cosmic force"? Or, better yet, what (if anything) does the person proposing the argument mean by this phrase? We can't intelligently agree or disagree with these premises if we don't understand what they mean. *We need to understand before we criticize.*

In this chapter, after exploring some general uses of language, we'll examine definitions and other ways to make our meaning clear. Then we'll learn more about making distinctions and detecting unclarities. Finally, we'll consider the distinction between analytic and synthetic statements, and the related distinction between knowledge based on reason and knowledge based on experience. The goal of this investigation into language is to enhance our ability to analyze and appraise arguments.

3.1   Uses of language

Grammarians distinguish four sentence types, which broadly reflect four important uses of language:

Declarative:	"Michigan beat Ohio State."	*make assertions*
Interrogatory:	"Did Michigan win?"	*ask questions*
Imperative:	"Beat Ohio State."	*tell what to do*
Exclamatory:	"Hurrah for Michigan!"	*express feelings*

Sentences can do various jobs at the same time. While making assertions, we can also ask questions, tell what to do, or express feelings:

- "I wonder whether Michigan won." (This can ask a question.)
- "I want you to throw the ball." (This can tell what to do.)
- "Michigan won!" (This can express feelings of joy.)

Arguments too can exemplify different uses of language. Suppose someone argues this way about the Cleveland river that used to catch fire: "You can see that the Cuyahoga River is polluted from the fact that it can burn!" We could make this into an explicit argument:

> No pure water is burnable.
> Some Cuyahoga River water is burnable.
> ∴ Some Cuyahoga River water isn't pure water.

One who argues this way also can (perhaps implicitly) be raising a question, directing people to do something, or expressing feelings:

- What can we do to clean up this polluted river?
- Let's all resolve to take action on this problem.
- How disgusting is this polluted river!

Arguments have a wider human context and purpose. We should remember this when we study detached specimens of argumentation.

When we do logic, our focus narrows and we concentrate on assertions and reasoning. For this purpose, detached specimens are better. Expressing an argument in a clear, direct, emotionless way can make it easier to appraise the truth of the premises and the validity of the inference.

It's important to avoid emotional language when we reason. Of course, there's nothing wrong with feelings or emotional language. Reason and feeling are both important parts of life; we needn't choose between the two. But we often need to focus on one or the other for a given purpose. At times, expressing feelings is the important thing and argumentation only gets in the way. At other times, we need to reason things out in a cool-headed manner.

Emotional language can discourage clear reasoning. When reasoning about abortion, for example, it's wise to avoid slanted phrases like "the atrocious, murderous crime of abortion" or "Neanderthals who oppose the rights of women." Bertrand Russell gave this example of how we slant language:

> I am *firm*; you are *obstinate*; he is *pig-headed*.

Slanted phrases can mislead us into thinking we've defended our view by an argument (premises and conclusion) when in fact we've only expressed our feelings. Careful thinkers try to avoid highly emotional terms when constructing arguments.

In the rest of this chapter, we'll explore aspects of the "making assertions" side of language that relate closely to analyzing and appraising arguments.

3.1a   Exercise

For each word or phrase, say whether it has a positive, negative, or neutral emotional tone. Then find another word or phrase with more or less the same assertive meaning but a different emotional tone.

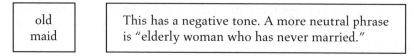

| old maid | This has a negative tone. A more neutral phrase is "elderly woman who has never married." |

(The term "old maid" suggests that a woman's goal in life is to get married and that an older woman who has never married is unfortunate. I can't think of a corresponding negative term for an older man who never married. A single word or phrase sometimes suggests a whole attitude toward life, and often an unexamined attitude.)

1. a cop
2. filthy rich
3. heroic
4. an extremist
5. an elderly gentleman
6. a bastard
7. baloney
8. a backward country
9. authoritarian
10. a do-gooder
11. a hair-splitter
12. an egghead
13. a bizarre idea
14. a kid
15. booze
16. a gay
17. abnormal
18. bureaucracy
19. abandoning me
20. babbling
21. brazen
22. an old broad
23. old moneybags
24. a busybody
25. a bribe
26. old–fashioned
27. brave
28. garbage
29. a cagey person
30. a whore

3.2   Lexical definitions

We noted earlier that the phrase "cosmic force" in this example is obscure:

> If there's a cosmic force, then there's a God.
> There's a cosmic force.
> ∴ There's a God.

Unless the speaker tells us what is meant by "cosmic force," we won't be able to understand what's said or tell whether it's true. But how can the speaker explain what he or she means by "cosmic force"? Or, more generally, how can we explain the meaning of a word or phrase?

Definitions are an important way to explain meaning, but not the only way. We'll consider definitions now and other ways to explain meaning later.

A **definition** is a rule of paraphrase intended to explain meaning. More precisely, a definition of a word or phrase is a rule saying how to eliminate this word or phrase in any sentence using it and produce a second sentence that means the same thing, the purpose of this being to explain or clarify the meaning of the word or phrase.

Suppose the person with the cosmic-force argument gives us this definition:

> "Cosmic force" means "force, in the sense used in
> physics, whose influence covers the entire universe."

This tells us that we can interchange "cosmic force" and a second phrase ("force, in the sense used in physics, whose influence covers the entire universe") in any sentence without changing the sentence's meaning. We can use this definition to paraphrase out the words "cosmic force" in the original argument. We'd get this equivalent argument:

> If there's a force, in the sense used in physics, whose influence
> covers the entire universe, then there's a God.
> There's a force, in the sense used in physics, whose influence
> covers the entire universe.
> ∴ There's a God.

This helps us to understand what the speaker is getting at and to see that the first premise is doubtful. Suppose there is a force, such as gravity, whose influence covers the entire universe. Why should we think that if there is such a force then there's a God? This is unclear.

So a definition is a rule of paraphrase intended to explain meaning. Definitions may be **lexical** (explaining current usage) or **stipulative** (specifying your own usage). Here's a correct lexical definition:

> "Bachelor" means "unmarried man."

This says we can interchange "bachelor" and "unmarried man" in any sentence; the resulting sentence will mean the same as the original, according to current usage. This leads to the interchange test for lexical definitions:

> **Interchange test:** To test a lexical definition claiming that A means B, try switching A and B in a variety of sentences. If some resulting pair of sentences doesn't mean the same thing, then the definition is incorrect.

According to our definition of "bachelor" as "unmarried man," for example, these two sentences would mean the same thing:

> "Al is a *bachelor*"   /   "Al is an *unmarried man*"

These two *do* seem to mean the same thing. To refute the definition, we'd have to find two sentences that are alike, except that "bachelor" and "unmarried man" are interchanged, and that don't mean the same thing.

Here's an incorrect lexical definition:

> "Bachelor" means "happy man."

This leads to incorrect paraphrases. If the definition were correct, then these two sentences would mean the same thing:

> "Al is a *bachelor*"   /   "Al is a *happy man*"

But they don't mean the same thing, since we could have one true but not the other. So the definition is wrong.

The interchange test is subject to at least two restrictions. First, definitions are often intended to cover just one sense of a word that has various meanings; we should then use the interchange test only on sentences using the intended sense. Thus it wouldn't be a good objection to our definition of "bachelor" as "unmarried man" to claim that these two sentences don't mean the same:

> "I have a *bachelor* of arts degree"   /   "I have an *unmarried man* of arts degree"

The first sentence uses "bachelor" in a sense the definition doesn't try to cover.

Second, we shouldn't use the test on sentences where the word appears in quotes. Consider this pair of sentences:

> "'*Bachelor*' has eight letters"   /   "'*Unmarried man*' has eight letters"

The two don't mean the same thing, since the first is true and the second false. But this doesn't show that our definition is wrong.

Lexical definitions are important in philosophy. Many philosophers, from Socrates to the present, have sought correct lexical definitions for some of the central concepts of human existence. They've tried to define concepts such as knowledge, truth, virtue, goodness, and justice. Such definitions are important for understanding and applying the concepts. Defining "good" as "what society approves of" would lead us to base our ethical beliefs on what is socially approved. We'd reject this method if we defined "good" as "what I like" or "what God desires," or if we regarded "good" as indefinable.

We can evaluate philosophical lexical definitions using the interchange test; Socrates was adept at this. Consider cultural relativism's definition of "good":

> "X is good" means "X is approved by my society."

To evaluate this, we'd try switching "good" and "approved by my society" in a sentence to get a second sentence. Here's such a pair of sentences:

> "Slavery is *good*"   /   "Slavery is *approved by my society*"

Then we'd see if the two sentences mean the same thing. Here they clearly don't, since it's consistent to affirm one but deny the other. Those who disagree with the norms of their society often say things like "Slavery is approved by my society, but it isn't good." Given this, we can argue against cultural relativism's definition of "good" as follows:

> If cultural relativism's definition is correct, then these
>   two sentences mean the same thing.
> They don't mean the same thing.
> ∴ Cultural relativism's definition isn't correct.

To counter this, the cultural relativist would have to claim that the sentences *do* mean the same thing. But this claim is implausible.

Here are five rules for good lexical definitions:

1. A good lexical definition is neither too broad nor too narrow.

Defining "bachelor" as "man" is too broad, since there are men who aren't bachelors. And defining "bachelor" as "unmarried male astronaut" is too narrow, since there are bachelors who aren't astronauts.

2. A good lexical definition avoids circularity and poorly understood terms.

Defining "true" as "known to be true" is circular, since it defines "true" using "true." And defining "good" as "having positive aretaic value" uses poorly understood terms, since "aretaic" is less clear than "good."

3. A good lexical definition matches in vagueness the term defined.

Defining "bachelor" as "unmarried male over 18 years old" is overly precise. The ordinary sense of "bachelor" is vague, since it's unclear on semantic grounds exactly at what age the term begins to apply. So "over 18" is too precise to define "bachelor." "Man" or "adult" are better choices, since these match "bachelor" fairly well in vagueness.

4. A good lexical definition matches, as far as possible, the emotional tone (positive, negative, or neutral) of the term defined.

It won't do to define "bachelor" as "*fortunate* man who never married" or "*unfortunate* man who never married." These have positive and negative emotional slants; the original term "bachelor" is fairly neutral.

5. A good lexical definition includes only properties essential to the term.

Suppose all bachelors live on the planet earth. Even so, living on planet earth isn't a property *essential* to the term "bachelor," since we could imagine a bachelor who lives on the moon. So it's wrong to include "living on planet earth" in the definition of "bachelor."

3.2a   Exercise – also LogiCola Q

Give objections to these proposed lexical definitions.

"Game" means "anything that involves competition between two parties, and winning and losing."	By this definition, solitaire isn't a game, but a military battle is. This goes against the normal usage of the word "game."

1. "Lie" means "false statement."
2. "Adolescent" means "person between 9 and 19 years old."
3. "God" means "object of ultimate concern."
4. "Metaphysics" means "any sleep-inducing subject."
5. "Good" means "of positive value."
6. "Human being" means "featherless biped."
7. "I know that P" means "I believe that P."
8. "I know that P" means "I believe that P, and P is true."
9. "Chair" means "what you sit on."
10. "True" means "believed."
11. "True" means "proved to be true."
12. "Valid argument" means "argument that persuades."
13. "Murder" means "killing."
14. "Morally wrong" means "against the law."
15. "Philosopher" means "someone who has a degree in philosophy" and "philosophy" means "study of the great philosophers."

3.2b   Exercise

Cultural relativism (CR) claims that "good" (in its ordinary usage) means "socially approved" or "approved by the majority (of the society in question)." What does this definition entail about the statements below? If this definition were correct, then would each of the following be true (1), false (0), or undecided by such considerations (?)?

If torturing for religious beliefs is *socially approved* in country X, then it's *good* in country X.	1 (for "true"). On cultural relativism, the statement would mean this (and thus be true): "If torturing for religious beliefs is *socially approved* in country X, then it's *socially approved* in country X."

1. Conclusions about what is good are deducible from sociological data (based, for example, on opinion surveys) describing one's society and what it approves.
2. If I say "Infanticide isn't good" but an ancient Roman says "Infanticide is good," then one or the other of us must be mistaken.

3. The norms set up by my society about what is good couldn't be mistaken.
4. Judgments about what is good aren't true or false.
5. It's good to respect the values of other societies.
6. If our society were to favor intolerance, then intolerance would be good.
7. Representational democracy will work anywhere.
8. From an analysis of how people use the word "good," it can be proved that whatever is socially approved must be good.
9. Different cultures accept different moral beliefs.
10. "The majority favors this" logically entails "This is good."
11. If the majority favors war (sexual stereotypes, conservative politics, abortion, and so on), then this has to be good.
12. "Do good" means "Do what the majority favors."
13. Doing something because it's good isn't the same as doing it because the majority favors it.
14. People who said "Racism is favored by the majority but it isn't good" were contradicting themselves.
15. Something that's bad might nevertheless be socially approved (because society may be misinformed or irrational in its evaluations).
16. The majority knows what it favors.
17. If Nazism became widespread and genocide came to be what most people favored, then genocide would have to be good.
18. It isn't necessarily good for me to do what society favors.
19. Suppose a survey showed that 90 percent of the population disapprove of people always following social approval. Then it follows that it's bad to always follow social approval – in other words, it's bad to always follow what is good.
20. Suppose your fellow Americans as a group and your fellow Anglicans as a group disapprove of racism, whereas your fellow workers and your social group (friends and relatives) approve of racism. Then racism is bad.

3.3   Stipulative definitions

A **stipulative definition** specifies how you're going to use a term. Since your usage may be a new one, it's unfair to criticize a stipulative definition for clashing with conventional usage. Stipulative definitions should be judged, not as correct or incorrect, but rather as useful or useless.

This book has many stipulative definitions. I continually define terms like "logic," "argument," "valid," "wff," and so forth. These definitions specify the meaning I'm going to use for the terms (which sometimes is close to their standard meaning). The definitions create a technical vocabulary.

A **clarifying definition** is one that stipulates a clearer meaning for a vague term. For example, a scientist might stipulate a technical sense of "pure water" in terms of bacteria level; this technical sense, while related to the normal one, is more scientifically precise. Likewise, courts might stipulate a more precise definition of "death" to resolve certain legal disputes; the definition might be chosen on moral and legal grounds to clarify the law.

Philosophers often use stipulative definitions. Here's an example:

> In this discussion, I use "rational" to mean "always adopting
> the means believed necessary to achieve one's goals."

This definition signals that the author will use "rational" to abbreviate a certain longer phrase; there's no claim that this exactly reflects the ordinary meaning of the term. Other philosophers may use "rational" in quite different senses, such as "logically consistent," "emotionless," or "always forming beliefs solely by the methods of science." These philosophers needn't be disagreeing; they may just be specifying their technical vocabulary differently. We could use subscripts for different senses; "rational$_1$" might mean "logically consistent," and "rational$_2$" might mean "emotionless." Don't be misled into thinking that, because being *rational* in one sense is desirable, therefore being *rational* in some other sense must also be desirable.

Stipulative definitions, while they needn't accord with current usage, should:

- use clear terms that the parties involved will understand,
- avoid circularity,
- allow us to paraphrase out the defined term,
- accord with how the person giving it is going to use the term, and
- aid our understanding and discussion of the subject matter.

Let me elaborate on the last norm. A stipulative definition is a device for abbreviating language. Chapter 1 of this book starts with a stipulative definition: "Logic is the analysis and appraisal of arguments." This definition lets us use the one word "logic" in place of the six words "the analysis and appraisal of arguments." Without the definition, our explanations would be wordier and harder to grasp; so the definition is useful.

Stipulative definitions should promote understanding. It's seldom useful to stipulate that a well–established term will be used in a radical new sense (for example, that "biology" will be used to mean "the study of earthquakes"); this would create confusion. And it's seldom useful to multiply stipulative definitions for terms that we'll seldom use. But at times we find ourselves repeating a cumbersome phrase over and over; then a stipulative definition can be helpful. Suppose your essay keeps repeating the phrase "action that satisfies criteria 1, 2, and 3 of the previous section"; your essay may be easier to follow if some short term were stipulated to mean the same as this longer phrase.

Some of our definitions seem to violate the "avoid circularity" norm. Section 6.1 defines "wffs" as sequences that are constructable using these rules:

> 1. Any capital letter is a wff.
> 2. The result of prefixing any wff with "~" is a wff.
> 3. The result of joining any two wffs by "•" or "∨" or "⊃" or "≡" and enclosing the result in parentheses is a wff.

Clauses 2 and 3 define "wff" in terms of "wff." And the definition doesn't seem to let us paraphrase out the term "wff"; we don't seem able to take a sentence using "wff" and say the same thing without "wff."

Actually, our definition is perfectly fine. We can rephrase it in the following way to avoid circularity and show how to paraphrase out the term "wff":

> "Wff" means "member of every set S of strings that satisfies these conditions: (1) Every capital letter is a member of set S; (2) the result of prefixing any member of set S with '~' is a member of set S; and (3) the result of joining any two members of set S by '•' or '∨' or '⊃' or '≡' and enclosing the result in parentheses is a member of set S."

Our definition of "wff" is a **recursive definition** – one that first specifies some things that the term applies to and then specifies that if the term applies to certain things, then it also applies to certain other things. Here's a recursive definition of "ancestor of mine":

> 1. My father and mother are ancestors of mine.
> 2. Any father or mother of an ancestor of mine is an ancestor of mine.

Here's an equivalent non-recursive definition:

> "Ancestor of mine" means "member of every set S that satisfies these conditions: (1) my father and mother are members of S; and (2) every father or mother of a member of S is a member of S."

3.4 Explaining meaning

If we avoid circular sets of definitions, we can't define all our terms; instead, we must leave some terms undefined. But how can we explain such *undefined* terms? One way is by examples.

To teach "red" to someone who understands no language that we speak, we could point to red objects and say "Red!" We'd want to point to different kinds of red object; if we pointed only to red shirts, the person might think that "red" meant "shirt." If the person understands "not," we also could point to non-red objects and say "Not red!" The person, unless color–blind, soon will catch our meaning and be able to point to red objects and say "Red!" This is a basic, primitive way to teach language. It explains a word, not by using other words, but by relating a word to concrete experiences.

We sometimes point to examples through words. We might explain "plaid" to a child by saying "It's a color pattern like that of your brother's shirt." We might explain "love" through examples: "Love is getting up to cook a sick person's breakfast instead of staying in bed, encouraging someone instead of complaining, and listening to other people instead of telling them how great you are." It's often helpful to combine a definition with examples, so the two reinforce each other; so Chapter 1 defined "argument" and then gave examples.

In abstract discussions, people sometimes use words so differently that they fail to communicate. People almost seem to speak different languages. Asking for definitions may then lead to the frustration of hearing one term you don't understand being defined using other terms you don't understand. In such cases, it may be more helpful to ask for examples instead of definitions. We might say, "Give me examples of an *analytic statement* (or of a *deconstruction*)." The request for examples can bring an bewilderingly abstract discussion back down to earth and mutual understanding.

Logical positivists and pragmatists suggested other ways to clarify statements. Positivists proposed that we explain the meaning of a statement by specifying which experiences would show the statement to be true, and which would show it to be false. Operational definitions such as these connect meaning to an experimental test:

- To say that rock A is "harder than" rock B means that A would scratch B but B wouldn't scratch A.
- To say that this string is "1 meter long" means that, if you stretch it over the standard meter stick, then the ends of both will coincide.
- To say that this person "has an IQ of 100" means that the person would get an average score on a standard IQ test.

Such definitions are important in science.

Logical positivists like A. J. Ayer appealed to the *verifiability criterion of meaning* as the cornerstone of their philosophy. We can formulate their principle (to be applied only to synthetic statements, see Section 3.6) as follows:

Logical Positivism (LP)

To help us find a statement's meaning, ask "How could the truth or falsity of the statement in principle be discovered by conceivable observable tests?"

If there's no way to test a statement, then it has no meaning (it makes no assertion that could be true or false). If tests are given, they specify the meaning.

There are problems with taking LP to be literally true. LP says *any untestable statement is without meaning*. But LP itself is untestable. Hence LP is without meaning on its own terms; it's self-refuting. For this reason and others, few hold this view anymore, even though it was popular decades ago.

Still, the LP way to clarify statements can sometimes be useful. Consider this claim of Thales, the ancient Greek alleged to be the first philosopher: "Water is the primal stuff of reality." The meaning here is unclear. We might ask Thales for a definition of "primal stuff"; this would clarify the claim. Or we might follow LP and ask, "How could we test whether your claim is correct?" Suppose Thales says the following, thus giving an operational definition:

> Try giving living things no water. If they die, then this
> proves my claim. If they live, then this refutes my claim.

We'd then understand Thales to be claiming that water is needed for life. Or suppose Thales replies this way:

> Let scientists work on the task of transforming each kind of matter
> (gold, rock, air, and so on) into water, and water back into each kind
> of matter. If they eventually succeed, then that proves my claim.

Again, this would help us understand the claim. But suppose Thales says this:

> No conceivable experimental test could show
> my claim to be true or show it to be false.

The positivists would immediately conclude that Thales's claim is meaningless – that it makes no factual assertion that could be true or false. Those of us who aren't positivists needn't draw this conclusion so quickly; but we may remain suspicious of Thales's claim and wonder what he's getting at.

LP demands that a statement *in principle* be able to be tested. The "in principle" qualification is important. Consider "There are mountains on the other side of the moon." When the positivists wrote, rocket technology was less advanced and we couldn't actually test this statement. But that didn't matter to its meaningfulness, since we could describe what a test would be like. That this claim was *testable in principle* was enough to make it meaningful.

LP hides an ambiguity when it speaks of "conceivable observable tests." Observable by whom? Is it enough that one person can make the observation? Or does it have to be publicly observable? Is a statement about my present feelings meaningful if I alone can observe whether it's true? Historically, most positivists demanded that a statement be *publicly verifiable*. But the weaker version of the theory that allows *verification by one person* seems better. After all, a statement about my present feelings makes sense, but only I can verify it.

William James suggested a related way to clarify statements. His "Pragmatism" essay suggests that we determine the meaning, or "cash value," of a statement by relating it to practical consequences. James's view is broader and more tolerant than that of the positivists. We can formulate his pragmatism principle as follows (again, it's to be applied only to synthetic statements):

> ### Pragmatism (PR)
>
> To help us find a statement's meaning, ask "What conceivable practical differences to someone could the truth or falsity of the statement make?" Here "practical differences to someone" covers what *experiences* one would have or what *choices* one ought to make.
>
> If the truth or falsity of a statement could make no practical difference to anyone, then it has no meaning (it makes no assertion that could be true or false). If practical differences are given, they specify the meaning.

I'm inclined to think that something close to PR is literally true. But here I'll just stress that PR can be useful in clarifying meaning.

In many cases, PR applies in much the same way as the weaker version of LP that allows verification by one person. LP focuses on what we could experience if the statement were true or false; and PR includes such experiences under practical differences.

PR also includes under "practical differences" what choices one ought to make. This makes PR broader than LP, since what makes a difference to choices needn't be testable by observation. Consider hedonism, which claims "Only pleasure is worth striving for." LP asks "How could the truth or falsity of hedonism in principle be discovered by conceivable observable tests?" Perhaps it can't; then LP would see hedonism as cognitively meaningless. PR asks "What conceivable practical differences to someone could the truth or falsity of hedonism make?" Here, "practical differences" include what *choices* one ought to make. The truth of hedonism could make many specifiable differences about choices; if hedonism is true, for example, then we should pursue knowledge not for its own sake but only insofar as it promotes pleasure. Ethical claims like hedonism are meaningless on LP but meaningful on the more tolerant PR.

In addition, PR isn't self-refuting. LP says "Any untestable statement is without meaning." But LP itself is untestable, and so is meaningless on its own terms. But PR says "Any statement whose truth or falsity could make no conceivable practical difference is without meaning." PR makes a practical difference to our choices about beliefs; presumably we shouldn't believe statements that fail the PR test. And so PR can be meaningful on its own terms.

So we can explain words by definitions, examples, verification conditions, and practical differences. Another way to convey the meaning of words is by contextual use: we use a word in such a way that its meaning can be gathered from surrounding "clues." Suppose a person getting in a car says "I'm getting in my C"; we can surmise that C means "car." We all learned most of our first language by picking up the meaning of words from their contextual use.

Some thinkers want us to pick up their technical terms in this same way. We are given no definitions of key terms, no examples to clarify their use, and no explanations in terms of verification conditions or practical differences. We are just told to dive in and catch the lingo by getting used to it. We should be suspicious of this. We may catch the lingo, but it may turn out to be empty and without meaning. That's why the positivists and pragmatists emphasized finding the "cash value" of ideas in terms of verification conditions or practical differences. We must be on guard against empty jargon.

3.4a Exercise

Would each claim be meaningful or meaningless on LP? (Take LP to require that a statement be publicly testable.) Would each be meaningful or meaningless on PR?

Unless we have strong reasons to the contrary, we *ought* to believe what sense experience seems to reveal.	This is meaningless on LP, since claims about what one ought to do aren't publicly testable. It's meaningful on PR, since its truth could make a difference about what choices we ought to make about beliefs.

1. It's cold outside.
2. That clock is fast.
3. There are five-foot-long blue ants in my bedroom.
4. Nothing is real.
5. Form is metaphysically prior to matter.
6. At noon all lengths, distances, and velocities in the universe will double.
7. I'm wearing an invisible hat that can't be felt or perceived in any way.
8. Regina has a pain in her little toe but shows no signs of this and will deny it if you ask her.
9. Other humans have no thoughts or feelings but only act as if they do.
10. Manuel will continue to have conscious experiences after his physical death.
11. Angels exist (that is, there are thinking creatures who have never had spatial dimensions or weights).
12. God exists (that is, there's a very intelligent, powerful, and good personal creator of the universe).
13. One ought to be logically consistent.
14. Any statement whose truth or falsity could make no conceivable practical difference is meaningless. (PR)
15. Any statement that isn't observationally testable is meaningless. (LP)

3.5 Making distinctions

Philosophers faced with difficult questions often begin by making distinctions:

> "If your question means ... [and then it's rephrased simply and clearly], then my answer is .... But if you're really asking ..., then my answer is ...."

The ability to formulate various possible meanings of a question is a valuable skill. Many of the questions that confront us are vague or confused; we often have to clarify a question before we can answer it intelligently. Getting clear on a question can be half the battle.

Consider this question (in which I underlined the tricky word "indubitable"):

"Are some beliefs <u>indubitable</u>?"

What does "indubitable" here mean? Does it mean not actually doubted? Or not able (psychologically) to be doubted? Or irrational to doubt? And what is it to doubt? Is it to refrain from believing? Or is it to have some suspicion toward the belief (although we might still believe it)? And indubitable by whom? By everyone (even crazy people)? By all rational persons? By at least some individuals? By me? Our little question hides a sea of ambiguities. Here are three of the many things that our little question could be asking:

- Are there some beliefs that no one at all has ever refused to believe? (To answer this, we'd need to know whether people in insane asylums sometimes refuse to believe that they exist or that "2 = 2.")
- Are there some beliefs that no rational person has suspicions about? (To answer this, we'd first have to decide what we mean by "rational.")
- Are there some beliefs that some specific individuals are psychologically unable to have any doubts about? (Perhaps many are unable to have any doubts about what their name is or where they live.)

It's unwise to try to answer such a question without first spelling out what we take it to mean.

Unnoticed ambiguities can block communication. Often people are unclear about what they're asking, or take another's question in an unintended sense. This is more likely if the discussion goes abstractly, without examples.

3.5a   Exercise

Each of the following questions is obscure or ambiguous as it stands. You are to distinguish at least three interesting senses of each question. Formulate each sense simply, clearly, and briefly – and without using the underlined words.

Can one <u>prove</u> that there are external objects?

- Can we deduce, from premises expressing immediate experience (like "I seem to see a blue shape"), that there are external objects?
- Can anyone give an argument that will convince (all or most) skeptics that there are external objects?

> • Can anyone give a good deductive or inductive argument, from premises expressing their immediate experience in addition to true principles of evidence, to conclude that it's reasonable to believe that there are external objects? (These "principles of evidence" might include things like "Unless we have strong reasons to the contrary, it's reasonable to believe what sense experience seems to reveal.")

1. Is ethics a <u>science</u>?
2. Is this monkey a <u>rational</u> animal?
3. Is this belief part of <u>common sense</u>?
4. Are material objects <u>objective</u>?
5. Are values <u>relative</u> (or <u>absolute</u>)?
6. Are scientific generalizations ever <u>certain</u>?
7. Was the action of that monkey a <u>free</u> act?
8. Is <u>truth</u> <u>changeless</u>?
9. How are moral beliefs <u>explainable</u>?
10. Is that judgment based on <u>reason</u>?
11. Is a fetus a <u>human being</u> (or <u>human person</u>)?
12. Are values <u>objective</u>?
13. What is the <u>nature</u> of <u>man</u>?
14. Can I ever <u>know</u> what someone else feels?
15. Do you have a <u>soul</u>?
16. Is the world <u>illogical</u>?

3.6 Analytic and synthetic

Immanuel Kant long ago introduced two related distinctions that have become very influential. He divided statements, on the basis of their meaning, into *analytic* and *synthetic* statements. He divided knowledge, on the basis of how it's known, into *a priori* and *a posteriori* knowledge. We'll consider these distinctions in this section and the next.[1]

First let's try to understand what an *analytic statement* is. One problem is that Kant gave two definitions:

1. An *analytic statement* is one whose subject contains its predicate.
2. An *analytic statement* is one that's self-contradictory to deny.

Consider these examples (and take "bachelor" to mean "unmarried man"):

(a) "All bachelors are unmarried."
(b) "If it's raining, then it's raining."

[1] I'll sketch a standard approach to these Kantian distinctions. Some thinkers, like W. V. O. Quine in his *Philosophy of Logic*, 2nd ed. (Cambridge, Mass.: Harvard University Press, 1986), criticize this standard approach.

Both examples are analytic by definition 2, since both are self-contradictory to deny. But only (a) is analytic by definition 1. In (a), the subject "bachelor" ("unmarried man") contains the predicate "unmarried"; but in (b), the subject "it" doesn't contain the predicate.

We'll adopt definition 2; so we define an **analytic statement** as one that's self-contradictory to deny. *Logically necessary truth* is another term for the same idea; such truths are based on logic, the meaning of concepts, or necessary connections between properties. Here are some further analytic statements:

"2 = 2"   "If everything is green, this is green."

"1 > 0"   "If there's rain, there's precipitation."

"All frogs are frogs."   "If this is green, this is colored."

By contrast, a **synthetic statement** is one that's neither analytic nor self-contradictory; *contingent* is another term for the same idea. Statements divide into analytic, synthetic, and self-contradictory; here's an example of each:[1]

Analytic: "All bachelors are unmarried."

Synthetic: "Daniel is a bachelor."

Self-contradictory: "Daniel is a married bachelor."

While there are three kinds of statement, there are only two kinds of truth: analytic and synthetic. Self-contradictory statements are necessarily false.

3.6a Exercise

Say whether each of these statements is analytic or synthetic. Take the various terms in their most natural senses. Some examples are controversial.

All triangles are triangles.	This is analytic. It would be self-contradictory to deny it and say "Some triangles aren't triangles."

1. All triangles have three angles.
2. 2+2 = 4.
3. Combining two drops of mercury with two other drops results in one big drop.
4. There are ants that have established a system of slavery.
5. Either some ants are parasitic or else none are.
6. No three-year-old is an adult.
7. No three-year-old understands symbolic logic.
8. Water boils at 90°C on that 10,000-foot mountain.
9. Water boils at 100°C at sea level.
10. No uncle who has never married is an only child.
11. All swans are white.

---

[1] Modal logic (Chapters 10 and 11) symbolizes "A is analytic (necessary)" as "$\Box$A," "A is synthetic (contingent)" as "$(\Diamond A \cdot \Diamond \sim A)$," and "A is self-contradictory" as "$\sim \Diamond A$."

12. Every material body is spatially located and has spatial dimensions.
13. Every material body has weight.
14. The sum of the angles of a Euclidian triangle equals 180°.
15. If all Parisians are French and all French are European, then all Parisians are European.
16. Every event has a cause.
17. Every effect has a cause.
18. We ought to treat a person not simply as a means but always as an end in itself.
19. One ought to be logically consistent.
20. God exists.
21. Given that we've observed that the sun rose every day in the past, it's reasonable for us to believe that the sun will rise tomorrow.
22. Unless we have strong reasons to the contrary, we ought to believe what sense experience seems to reveal.
23. Everything red is colored.
24. Nothing red is blue (at the same time and in the same part and respect).
25. Every synthetic statement that's known to be true is known on the basis of sense experience. (There's no synthetic *a priori* knowledge.)

3.7 *A priori* and *a posteriori*

Philosophers traditionally distinguish two kinds of knowledge. *A posteriori* **(empirical) knowledge** is knowledge based on sense experience. *A priori* **(rational) knowledge** is knowledge not based on sense experience. Here is an example of each kind of knowledge:

> *A posteriori*: "Some bachelors are happy."
> *A priori*: "All bachelors are unmarried."

While we know both to be true, *how* we know differs in the two cases. We know the first statement from our experience of bachelors; we've met many bachelors and recall that some of them have been happy. If we had to justify the truth of this statement to others, we'd appeal to experiential data about bachelors. In contrast, we know the second statement by grasping what it means and seeing that it must be true. If we had to justify the truth of this statements, we wouldn't have to gather experiential data about bachelors.

Most of our knowledge is *a posteriori* – based on sense experience. "Sense experience" here covers the five "outer senses" (sight, hearing, smell, taste, and touch). It also covers "inner sense" (the awareness of our own thoughts and feelings) and any other experiential access to the truth that we might have (perhaps mystical experience or extrasensory perception).

Logical and mathematical knowledge is generally *a priori*. To test the validity of an argument, we don't go out and do experiments. Instead, we just think and reason; sometimes we write things out to help our thinking. The validity tests in this book are rational (*a priori*) methods. "Reason" in a narrow sense (in which it contrasts with "experience") deals with what we can know *a priori*.

A priori knowledge requires some experience. We can't know that all bachelors are unmarried unless we've learned the concepts involved; this requires experience of language and of (married and unmarried) humans. And knowing that all bachelors are unmarried requires the experience of thinking. So *a priori* knowledge depends somewhat on experience (and thus isn't just something that we're born with). But it still makes sense to call such knowledge *a priori*. Suppose we've gained the concepts using experience. Then to justify the claim that all bachelors are unmarried, we don't have to appeal to any further experience, other than thinking. In particular, we don't have to investigate bachelors to see whether they're all unmarried.[1]

Here are some further examples of statements known *a priori*:

"2 = 2"	"If everything is green, this is green."
"1 > 0"	"If there's rain, there's precipitation."
"All frogs are frogs."	"If this is green, this is colored."

We also gave these as examples of analytic statements.

So far, we've used only analytic statements as examples of *a priori* knowledge and only synthetic statements as examples of *a posteriori* knowledge. Some philosophers think both distinctions coincide; they think there's only one distinction, although it's drawn in two ways. They suggest that:

a priori knowledge	=	analytic knowledge
a posteriori knowledge	=	synthetic knowledge

Is this view true? If it's true at all, it isn't true just because of how we defined the terms. By our definitions, the basis for the analytic / synthetic distinction differs from the basis for the *a priori* / *a posteriori* distinction. A statement is analytic or synthetic depending on whether its denial is self-contradictory. Knowledge is *a posteriori* or *a priori* depending on whether it rests on sense experience. Our definitions leave it open whether the two distinctions coincide.

These two combinations are very common:

analytic *a priori* knowledge   synthetic *a posteriori* knowledge

Most of our knowledge in math and logic is analytic and *a priori*. Most of our scientific knowledge and everyday knowledge about the world is synthetic and *a posteriori*. These next two combinations are more controversial:

---

[1] David Hume, who thought that all concepts come from experience, also defended *a priori* knowledge. By comparing two empirical concepts, we can sometimes recognize that the empirical conditions that would verify one ("bachelor") would also verify the other ("unmarried"); so by reflecting on our concepts, we can see that all bachelors must be unmarried.

analytic *a posteriori* knowledge   synthetic *a priori* knowledge

Can we know any analytic statements *a posteriori*? It seems that we can. "π is a little over 3" is presumably an analytic truth that can be known either by *a priori* calculations (the more precise way to compute π) – or by measuring circles empirically (as the ancient Egyptians did). And "It's raining or not raining" is an analytic truth that can be known either *a priori* (and justified by truth tables, see Section 6.6) – or by deducing it from the empirical statement "It's raining."

But perhaps any analytic statement that is known *a posteriori* also could be known *a priori*. This claim seems very plausible. Saul Kripke has questioned it, but his arguments are too complex to consider here.[1]

The biggest controversy has raged over this question: "Do we have any synthetic *a priori* knowledge?" This is asking whether there is any statement A such that:

- A is synthetic (neither self-contradictory to affirm nor self-contradictory to deny),
- we know A to be true, and
- our knowledge of A is based on reason (not on sense experience)?

In one sense of the term, an *empiricist* is one who rejects such knowledge – and who thus limits what we can know by pure reason to analytic statements. By contrast, a *rationalist* is one who accepts such knowledge – and who thus gives a greater scope to what we can know by pure reason.[2] Our view on this issue has an important impact on the rest of our philosophy.

Empiricists deny the possibility of synthetic *a priori* knowledge for two main reasons. First, it's difficult to understand how there could be such knowledge. Analytic *a priori* knowledge is fairly easy to grasp. Suppose a statement is true simply because of the meaning and logical relations of the concepts involved; then we can know it in an *a priori* fashion by reflecting on these concepts and logical relations. But suppose a statement could logically be either true or false. How could we then possibly know by pure thinking which it is?

Second, those who claim to know synthetic *a priori* truths don't agree much on what these truths are. They just seem to follow their prejudices and call them "deliverances of reason."

Rationalists affirm the existence of synthetic *a priori* knowledge for two main reasons. First, the opposite view (at least if it's claimed to be *known*) seems self-refuting. Consider empiricists who claim to know this to be true:

---

[1] Or perhaps he is claiming that there are non-analytic metaphysical necessities (such as that water is H_2O) that are *a posteriori*. See his *Naming and Necessity* (Cambridge, Mass.: Harvard University Press, 1980).

[2] More broadly, *empiricists* are those who emphasize *a posteriori* knowledge, while *rationalists* are those who emphasize *a priori* knowledge.

> "There's no synthetic *a priori* knowledge."

Any knowledge of this would have to be synthetic *a priori*. For the statement is synthetic (it isn't true by how we defined the terms "synthetic" and "*a priori,*" and it isn't self-contradictory to deny). And it would have to be known *a priori* (since we can't justify it by sense experience). So the empiricist's claim would have to be synthetic *a priori* knowledge, the very thing it rejects.

Second, we seem to have synthetic *a priori* knowledge of various truths, such as the following:

> If you believe that you see an object to be red and you have no
> special reason for doubting your perception [e.g., that the lighting
> is strange or that you're taking mind-altering drugs], then it's
> reasonable for you to believe that you see an actual red object.

This claim is synthetic; it isn't true because of how we've defined terms – and skeptics who think that all their perceptions may be delusive can deny it without self-contradiction. It's presumably known to be true; if we didn't know truths like this one, then we couldn't justify any empirical beliefs. And it's known *a priori*; it can't be based on sense experience – instead, knowledge from sense experience is based on truths like this one. So we have synthetic *a priori* knowledge of this claim. So there is synthetic *a priori* knowledge.

The dispute over synthetic *a priori* knowledge influences how we do philosophy. Consider this question: Can basic ethical principles be known *a priori*? Empiricists answer no; so they think knowledge of basic ethical principles is either empirical or non-existent. But rationalists can (and often do) think that we know basic ethical truths *a priori*, from reason alone (either through intuition or through some rational consistency test).

3.7a Exercise

Suppose we knew each of these statements to be true. Would our knowledge likely be *a priori* or *a posteriori*? Take the various terms in their most natural senses. Some examples are controversial.

All triangles are triangles.	This would be known *a priori*.

Use the examples from Section 3.6a.

CHAPTER 4
Fallacies and Argumentation

This chapter has five related topics. These deal with characteristics of a good argument, recognizing common fallacies, avoiding inconsistency, developing your own arguments, and analyzing arguments that you read.

4.1   Good arguments

A **good argument**, to be logically correct and to fulfill the purposes for which we use arguments, should:

1. be deductively valid (or inductively strong) and have all true premises;
2. have its validity and truth-of-premises be as evident as possible to the parties involved;
3. be clearly stated (using understandable language and making clear what the premises and conclusion are);
4. avoid circularity, ambiguity, and emotional language; and
5. be relevant to the issue at hand.

First, a good argument should be deductively valid (or inductively strong – see Chapter 5) and have all true premises. We often criticize an argument by trying to show that the conclusion doesn't follow from the premises or that one or more of the premises are false.

Second, a good argument should have its validity and truth-of-premises be as evident as possible to the parties involved. Arguments are less effective if they presume ideas that others see as false or controversial. Ideally, we'd like to use only premises that everyone will accept as immediately obvious; but in practice, this is too high an ideal. We often appeal to premises that will only be accepted by those of similar political, religious, or philosophical views. And sometimes we appeal to hunches, like "I can get to the gun before the thief does"; while not ideal, this may be the best we can do at a given moment.

Third, a good argument should be clearly stated; it should use understandable language and make clear what the premises and conclusion are. Obscure or overly complex language makes reasoning harder to grasp.

When we develop an argument, a good strategy is to put it on paper in a preliminary way and then reread it several times trying to make improvements.

Try to express the ideas more simply and clearly, and think how others may object or misunderstand. Often ideas emerge in a confused form; clarity comes later, after much hard work. While mushy thinking is often unavoidable in the early development of an idea, it isn't acceptable in the final product.

People often argue without making clear what their premises and conclusions are; sometimes we get stream-of-consciousness ramblings sprinkled with an occasional "therefore." While this is unacceptable, a good argument needn't spell everything out; it's often fine to omit premises that are obvious to the parties involved. If I'm hiking on the Appalachian Trail, I might say this to my hiking partner: "We can't still be on the right trail, since we don't see white blazes on the trees." This is fine if my partner knows that we'd see white blazes if we were on the right trail; then the full argument would be pedantic:

> We don't see white blazes on the trees.
> *If we were still on the right trail, then*
> *we'd see white blazes on the trees.*
> ∴ We aren't still on the right trail.

In philosophy, it's wise to spell out *all* our premises, since implicit ideas are often crucial but unexamined. Suppose someone argues: "We can't be free, since all our actions are determined." This assumes the italicized premise:

> All human actions are determined.
> *No determined action is free.*
> ∴ No human actions are free.

We should be aware that we're assuming this controversial premise.

So a good argument should be valid (or inductively strong) and have all true premises, this truth and validity should be evident, and the argument should be clearly stated. Our final conditions say that a good argument should (4) avoid circularity, ambiguity, and emotional language; and (5) be relevant to the issue at hand. Five common fallacies tie into these final conditions.

Our first fallacy is *circularity*:

An argument is **circular** if it presumes the truth of what is to be proved.	A series of arguments is **circular** if it uses a premise to prove a conclusion – and then uses that conclusion to prove the premise.

"The soul is immortal because it can't die" is circular; the premise here just repeats the conclusion in different words – so the argument takes for granted what it's supposed to prove. A circular *series* of arguments might say: "A is true because B is true, and B is true because A is true." A circular argument is also said to be *question begging*; this differs from the new (and somewhat confusing usage) in which "begging a question" means "raising a question."

Here's a second fallacy, and a crude argument that exemplifies the fallacy:

> An argument is **ambiguous** if it changes the meaning of a term or phrase within the argument.

> Love is an emotion.
> God is love.
> ∴ God is an emotion.

Premise 1 requires that we take "love" to mean "the feeling of love" – which makes premise 2 false or doubtful. Premise 2 requires that we take "love" to mean "a supremely loving person" or "the source of love" – which makes premise 1 false or doubtful. So we can have both premises clearly true only by shifting the meaning of "love." Ambiguity is also called *equivocation*.

Unclear sentence structures can bring ambiguities. For example, "pretty little girls' camp" can mean "camp for little girls who are pretty," "pretty camp for little girls," or "pretty camp that is little and for girls."

It's important to avoid emotionally slanted terms when we reason:

> To **appeal to emotion** is to stir up feelings instead of arguing in a logical manner.

Students, when asked to argue against a theory, often just describe the theory in derogatory language; so a student might dismiss Descartes by calling his views "superficial" or "overly dualistic." But such verbal abuse doesn't give any reason for thinking a view wrong. Often the best way to argue against a theory is to find some false implication and then reason as follows:

> If the theory is true, then this other thing also would be true.
> This other thing isn't true.
> ∴ The theory isn't true.

Recall that an argument consists of premises and a conclusion.

Our last condition says that a good argument must be relevant to the issue at hand. A clearly stated argument might prove something and yet still be defective, since it may be beside the point in the current context:

> An argument is **beside the point** if it argues for a conclusion irrelevant to the issue at hand.

Hitler, when facing a group opposed to the forceful imposition of dictatorships, sidetracked their attention by attacking pacifism; his arguments, even if sound, were beside the point. Such arguments are also called *red herrings*, after a practice used in training hunting dogs: a red herring fish would be dragged across the trail to distract the dog from tracking an animal. In arguing, we must keep the point at issue clearly in mind and not be misled by smelly fish.

Students sometimes use this "beside the point" label too broadly, to apply to almost any fallacy. Keep in mind that this fallacy isn't about the *premises being irrelevant* to the conclusion. Instead, it's about the *conclusion* (regardless of whether it's proved) *being irrelevant to the issue at hand*. To take another example, suppose a politician in a debate is asked "Where do you stand about the proposed tax cuts?" but evades answering, instead cleverly shifting to the issue of how we need a strong military. These statements are *beside the point*, since they don't answer the question.

One common form of this fallacy has its own name:

> A **straw man** argument misrepresents an opponent's views.

This is common in politics. Candidate A for mayor suggests cutting a few seldom-used stations on the rapid transit system. Then candidate B's campaign ad expresses shock that A wants to dismantle the whole transit system, which so many citizens depend on; the ad attacks, not what A actually holds, but only a "straw man" – a scarecrow of B's own invention. Campaign ads that distort an opponent's view have recently gotten so bad that "fact checkers" and "truth squads" have arisen to point out misleading language and downright falsehoods – regardless of which side engages in these.

Let's return to our discussion of good arguments. Briefly, a good argument is valid (or inductively strong) and has all true premises; has this validity and truth be as evident as possible to the parties involved; is clearly stated; avoids circularity, ambiguity, and emotional language; and is relevant to the issue.

A good argument normally convinces others, but it need not. Some people aren't open to rational argument on many issues. Some believe that the earth is flat, despite good arguments to the contrary. On the other hand, bad arguments sometimes convince people. Hitler's *beside the point* fallacy and the candidate's *straw man* fallacy can mislead and convince. Studying logic can help protect us from bad reasoning. The more people can distinguish good from bad reasoning, the less will politicians and others be able to promote causes by bad reasoning.

"Proof" is roughly like "good argument." But we can *prove* something even if our argument is unclear, contains emotional language, or is irrelevant to the issue at hand. And a proof must be *very* strong in its premises and in how it connects the premises to the conclusion; for the latter reason, it seems wrong to call inductive arguments "proofs." So we can define a **proof** as a non-circular, non-ambiguous, deductively valid argument with clearly true premises. A **refutation** of a statement is a proof of the statement's denial.

"Proof" can have other meanings. Chapters 7 to 14 use "proof" in the technical sense of "formal proof," to cover logical derivations that follow certain specified rules. And Exercise 3.5a explained that "prove" could have various meanings in the question, "Can we prove that there are external objects?" The word "proof" has a cluster of related meanings.

Students often misuse the words "prove" and "refute." These words properly apply only to successful arguments. If you *prove* something, it's true – and you've shown that it's true. If you *refute* something, it's false – and you've shown that it's false. Compare these two:

~~"Hume proved this, but Kant refuted him."~~	"Hume argued for this, but Kant criticized his reasoning."

The first is self-contradictory, since it implies that Hume's claim is both true and false – and that Hume showed it was true and Kant showed it was false.

4.2 Informal fallacies

A **fallacy** is a deceptive error of thinking; an **informal fallacy** is a fallacy that isn't covered by some system of deductive or inductive logic. In working out the conditions for a good argument, we introduced five informal fallacies: *circular, ambiguous, appeal to emotion, beside the point,* and *straw man.* We now add thirteen more, loosely divided into three groups. Bear in mind that there are many additional informal fallacies that aren't listed here. This section focuses on only some of the more common informal fallacies.

Our first group includes six fallacies that are neatly expressed in a premise–conclusion format. This one, with an example, appeals to our herd instincts:

Appeal to the crowd	Most people believe A. ∴ A is true.

Most people think Wheaties is very nutritious.
∴ Wheaties is very nutritious.

Despite popular opinion, perhaps influenced by health-oriented advertising, Wheaties cereal could have little nutritional value. Discovering its nutritional value requires checking its nutrient content; group opinion proves nothing. When we think about it, we all recognize the fallacy here; yet group opinion still may sway us. Reasoning that we know to be flawed may continue to influence us. We humans are only partially rational.

The *opposition fallacy* comes from dividing people into "our group" (which has the truth) and "our opponents" (who are totally wrong):

Opposition	Our opponents believe A. ∴ A is false.

Those blasted liberals say we should raise taxes.
∴ We shouldn't raise taxes.

The problem here is that our opponents are often right.

The *genetic fallacy* dismisses a belief on the basis of its origin:

Genetic	We can explain why you believe A. ∴ A is false.

Any psychologist would see that you believe A because of such and such. ∴ A is false.

One who has superficially studied a little psychology may dismiss the views of another in this way. An appropriate (but nasty) reply is, "And what is the psychological explanation for why you confuse psychological explanations with logical disproofs?" To show a belief to be false, we must argue against the *content* of the belief; it isn't enough to explain how the belief came to be.

This next one has two closely related forms:

Appeal to ignorance	No one has proved A. ∴ A is false. No one has disproved A. ∴ A is true.

No one has proved there's a God. ∴ There's no God.

No one has proved there's no God. ∴ There's a God.

Something that isn't proved might still be true, just as something that isn't disproved might still be false. An "appeal to ignorance" must have one of these forms; it isn't just any case where someone speaks out of ignorance.

This next one uses a Latin name for "after this therefore because of this":

Post hoc ergo propter hoc	A happened after B. ∴ A was caused by B.

Paul had a beer and then got 104% on his logic test. ∴ He got 104% because he had beer.

The premise was true (there were bonus points). Some students concluded: "So if I have a beer before the test, I'll get 104%" and "If I have a six-pack, I'll get 624%." Proving causal connections requires more than just the sequence of two factors; the factors might just *happen* to have occurred together. It isn't even enough that factors *always* occur together; day always follows night, and night always follows day, but neither causes the other. Proving causal connections is difficult (see Mill's methods in Section 5.7).

This next one is also called *division-composition*:

Part-whole	This is F. ∴ Every part of this is F. Every part of this is F. ∴ This is F.

My essay is good. ∴ Every sentence of my essay is good.

Every sentence of my essay is good. ∴ My essay is good.

The first argument is wrong because an essay might be good despite having some poor sentences. The second is wrong because each sentence of the essay might be good without the essay as a whole being good; the well-written individual sentences might not make sense together. So something might be true of a whole without being true of the parts; and something might be true of the parts without being true of a whole. A property that characterizes a whole but not any of its parts is sometimes called an *emergent property*; for example, being alive is an emergent property possessed by a cell but not by any of its component molecules – and water may be clear and wet without the individual H_2O molecules being clear or wet. More controversially, some say thinking is an emergent property possessed by the brain but not by any of its cells.

In rare cases, these fallacy forms might be abbreviated forms of good reasoning. Suppose you know that people in your society almost never have false beliefs; then this "appeal to the crowd" could be correct inductive reasoning:

> Almost always, what most people in my society believe is true.
> Most people in my society believe A.
> This is all we know about the matter.
> ∴ Probably A is true.

Or suppose you know that your opponent Jones is always wrong. Then this could be sound reasoning: "Everything Jones says is false, Jones says A, so A is false." But correct forms of these six fallacy forms are unusual in real life.

Our next group contains three types of reasoning that have common correct and fallacious forms. This first type of reasoning appeals to expert opinion:

Appeal to authority – correct form:	Incorrect forms omit premise 2 or 3, or conclude that A *must* be true.
X holds that A is true. X is an authority on the subject. The consensus of authorities agrees with X. ∴ There's a presumption that A is true.	

> Your doctor tells you A.
> She's an authority on the subject.   ← correct
> The other authorities agree with her.   ← form
> ∴ There's a presumption that A is true.

This conclusion means that we ought to believe A unless we have special evidence to the contrary. If our doctor is a great authority and the consensus of authorities is large, then the argument becomes stronger; but it's never totally conclusive. All the authorities in the world might agree on something that they later discover to be wrong; so we shouldn't think that something *must* be so because the authorities say it is. It's also wrong to appeal to a person who isn't an authority in the field (a sports hero endorsing coffee makers, for example).

And finally, it's weak to appeal to one authority (regarding the safety of an atomic power plant, for example) when the authorities disagree widely. The appeal to authority can go wrong in many ways. Yet many of our trusted beliefs (that Washington was the first US president, for example, or that there's such a country as Japan) rest quite properly on the say so of others.

An "authority" might be a calculator or computer instead of a human. My calculator has proved itself reliable, and it gives the same result as other reliable calculators. So I believe it when it tells me that $679 \cdot 177 = 120{,}183$.

This next one uses a Latin name for "against the person" (which is opposed to *ad rem*, "on the issue"):

Ad hominem – correct form:

X holds that A is true.
In holding this, X violates legitimate rational
   standards (for example, X is inconsistent,
   biased, or not correctly informed).
∴ X isn't fully reasonable in holding A.

Incorrect forms use factors irrelevant to rational competence (for example, X is a member of a hated group or beats his wife) or conclude that A is false.

Rick holds that people of this race ought to be treated poorly.
In holding this, Rick is inconsistent (because he doesn't think
   that he ought to be treated that way if he were in their exact
   place) and so violates legitimate rational standards.
∴ Rick isn't fully reasonable in his views.

← correct
← form

A "personal attack" argument can be either legitimate or fallacious. In our example, we legitimately conclude that Rick, because he violates rational standards, isn't fully reasonable in his beliefs. It would be fallacious to draw the stronger conclusion that his beliefs must be wrong; to show his beliefs to be wrong, we must argue against the beliefs, not against the person. A more extreme case of the *ad hominem* fallacy was exemplified by those Nazis who argued that Einstein's theories must be wrong since he was Jewish; being Jewish was irrelevant to Einstein's competence as a scientist.

This next form of reasoning lists and weighs reasons for and against:

Pro-con – correct form:

The reasons in favor of act A are ….
The reasons against act A are ….
The former reasons outweigh the latter.
∴ Act A ought to be done.

Incorrect form:

The reasons in favor of
act A are ….
∴ Act A ought to be done.

The reasons in favor of getting an internal-frame backpack are ....
The reasons against getting an internal-frame backpack are .... ← correct
The former reasons outweigh the latter. ← form
∴ I ought to get an internal-frame backpack.

People sometimes make decisions by folding a piece of paper in half and listing reasons in favor on one side and reasons against on the other; then they decide intuitively which side has stronger (not necessarily more) reasons. This method forces us to look at both sides of an issue. In the incorrect form, we just look at half of the picture; we say that you should do this (because of such and such advantages) or that you shouldn't do it (because of such and such disadvantages). This fallacy is also called "one-sided" or "stacking the deck."

We can expand our three correct forms into standard inductive and deductive arguments. A correct appeal to authority becomes a strong inductive argument if we add this inductively confirmed premise: "The consensus of authorities on a subject is usually right." Correct *ad hominem* arguments become deductively valid if we add: "Anyone who, in believing A, violates legitimate rational standards is thereby not fully reasonable in believing A." And correct pro-con arguments become deductively valid if we add: "If the reasons in favor of A outweigh the reasons against A, then A ought to be done."

Our final group has four miscellaneous fallacies. Here's the first fallacy (which is also called *false dilemma*):

> **Black-and-white** thinking oversimplifies by assuming that one or another of two extreme cases must be true.

One commits this fallacy in thinking that people must be *logical* or *emotional*, but can't be both. My thesaurus lists these terms as having opposite meanings; but if they really had opposite meanings, then no one could be both at once – which indeed is possible. In fact, all four combinations are common:

logical and emotional	illogical and emotional
logical and unemotional	illogical and unemotional

People who think in a black-and-white manner prefer simple dichotomies, like logical-emotional, capitalist-socialist, or intellectual-jock. Such people have a hard time seeing that the world is more complicated than that.

This next fallacy is also called *hasty generalization*:

> To use a **false stereotype** is to assume that the members of a certain group are more alike than they actually are.

People commit this fallacy in thinking that all Italians exist only on spaghetti, that all New Yorkers are uncaring, or that all who read Karl Marx want to overthrow the government. False stereotypes can be detrimental to the stereo-typed. A study compared scores on a math test of two otherwise identical groups of young girls; just the first group was told beforehand that girls are genetically inferior in math – and this group did much worse on the test.

This next fallacy substitutes violence for reasoning:

> To **appeal to force** is to use threats or intimidation to get a conclusion accepted.

A parent might say, "Just agree and shut up!" Parents and teachers hold inherently intimidating positions and are often tempted to appeal to force.

This last fallacy is also called *trick question*:

> A **complex question** is a question that assumes the truth of something false or doubtful.

The standard example is: "Are you still beating your wife?" A "yes" implies that you still beat your wife, while a "no" implies that you used to beat her. The question combines a statement with a question: "You have a wife and used to beat her; do you still beat her?" The proper response is: "Your question presumes something that's false, namely that I have a wife and used to beat her." Sometimes it's misleading to give a "yes" or "no" answer.

4.2a Exercise – also LogiCola R

Identify the fallacies in the following examples. Not all are clear-cut; some examples are controversial and some commit more than one fallacy. All the examples here are fallacious. Use these labels to identify the fallacies:

aa = appeal to authority	am = ambiguous	ge = genetic
ac = appeal to the crowd	bp = beside the point	op = opposition
ae = appeal to emotion	bw = black and white	pc = pro-con
af = appeal to force	ci = circular	ph = *post hoc*
ah = *ad hominem*	cq = complex question	pw = part-whole
ai = appeal to ignorance	fs = false stereotype	sm = straw man

> This sports hero advertises a popcorn popper on TV. He says it's the best popcorn popper, so this must be true.

> This is an incorrect appeal to authority. There's no reason to think the sports hero is an authority on popcorn poppers.

1. Are you still wasting time with all that book-learning at the university?

2. The Bible tells the truth because it's God's word. We know the Bible is God's word because the Bible says so and it tells the truth.

3. You should vote for this candidate because she's intelligent and has much experience in politics.

4. The Equal Rights Amendment was foolish because its feminist sponsors were nothing but bra-less bubbleheads.

5. No one accepts this theory anymore, so it must be wrong.

6. Either you favor a massive arms buildup, or you aren't a patriotic American.

7. The president's veto was the right move. In these troubled times we need decisive leadership, even in the face of opposition. We should all thank the president for his courageous move.

8. Each member of this team is unbeatable, so this team must be unbeatable.

9. My doctor told me to lose weight and give up smoking. But she's an overweight smoker herself, so I can safely ignore her advice.

10. Belief in God is explained in terms of one's need for a father figure; so it's false.

11. There are scientific laws. Where there are laws there must be a lawgiver. Hence someone must have set up the scientific laws to govern our universe, and this someone could only be God.

12. The lawyer for the defense claims that there's doubt that Smith committed the crime. But, I ask, are you going to let this horrible crime go unpunished because of this? Look at the crime; see how horrible it was! So you see clearly that the crime was horrible and that Smith should be convicted.

13. Free speech is for the common good, since unrestrained expression of opinion is in people's interest.

14. This is a shocking and stupid proposal. Its author must be either a dishonest bum or a complete idiot.

15. Aristotle said that heavy objects fall faster than light ones, so it must be true.

16. Each of these dozen cookies (or drinks) by itself isn't harmful; one little one won't hurt! Hence having these dozen cookies (or drinks) isn't harmful.

17. Before Barack Obama became the Democratic candidate for US president, he ran in a series of primary elections. He noted that he played basketball before the Iowa primary, and then won the vote, while he neglected to play before the New Hampshire primary, and then lost. He concluded (in jest) "At that point I was certain that we had to play on every primary."

18. Only men are rational animals. No woman is a man. Therefore no woman is a rational animal.

19. I'm right, because you flunk if you disagree with me!

20. The discriminating backpacker prefers South Glacier tents.

21. Those who opposed the war were obviously wrong; they were just a bunch of cowardly homosexual Communists.

22. We should legalize gambling in our state, because it would bring in new tax revenue, encourage tourists to come and spend money here, and cost nothing (just the passing of a new law).

23. Do you want to be a good little boy and go to bed?

24. This man is probably a Communist. After all, nothing in the files disproves his Communist connections.

25. People who read *Fortune* magazine make a lot of money. So if I subscribe to *Fortune*, then I too will make a lot of money.

26. Feminists deny all difference between male and female. But this is absurd, as anyone with eyes can see.

27. Each part of life (eyes, feet, and so on) has a purpose. Hence life itself must have a purpose.

28. So you're a business major? You must be one of those people who care only about the almighty dollar and aren't concerned about ideas.

29. My opponent hasn't proved that I obtained these campaign funds illegally. So we must conclude that I'm innocent.

30. Those dirty Communists said that we Americans should withdraw from the Panama Canal, so obviously we should have stayed there.

31. Karl Marx was a personal failure who couldn't even support his family, so his political theory must be wrong.

32. Religion originated from myth (which consists of superstitious errors). So religion must be false.

33. Suzy brushed with Ultra Brilliant and then attracted boys like a magnet! Wow – I'm going to get some Ultra Brilliant. Then I'll attract boys too!

34. Did you kill the butler because you hated him or because you were greedy?

35. My parents will be mad at me if I get a D, and I'll feel so stupid. Please? You know how I loved your course. I surely deserve at least a C.

36. Miracles are impossible because they simply can't happen.

37. I figure that a person must be a Communist if he doesn't think the American free-enterprise system is flawless and the greatest system in the world.

38. Everyone thinks this beer is simply the best. So it must be the best.

39. We ought to oppose this, since it's un-American.

40. Practically every heroin addict first tried marijuana. Therefore, marijuana causes heroin addiction.

41. Most college students are mainly concerned with sports, liquor, and sex. So this is normal. But Duane is mainly concerned with poetry. So he must be abnormal and thus unhealthy.

42. Each of the things in my backpack is light, so my loaded backpack must be light.

43. You're wrong in disagreeing with me, because what I said is true.

44. Everyone thinks the Democrat is the better candidate, so it must be true.

45. We should reject Mendel's genetic theories, since he was a monk and thus couldn't have known anything about science.

46. Every time I backpack it seems to rain. I'm going backpacking next week. So this will cause it to rain.

47. It hasn't been proved that cigarettes are dangerous, so it's only reasonable to conclude that they aren't dangerous.

48. In a commercial filled with superb scenery, sexy girls, and soft music: "Buy a Ford Mustang – it's a super car!"

49. Atheism is absurd. Atheists deny God because they can't see him. But who has seen electrons either?

50. President George W. Bush was in office for several years, and then the financial crisis occurred in 2008. Therefore the crisis occurred because Bush was in office.

51. Do you support freedom and the unrestricted right to buy weapons?

52. We don't know how the first forms of life could have emerged by natural causes from the primeval chemical soup that covered the earth. So we must assume that they didn't emerge by natural causes; so they had to have had a divine origin.
53. Since no atom in this rock is heavy or green, this rock cannot be heavy or green.
54. That car can't be any good, since it was made in Detroit.
55. All doctors are men with medical degrees. But no woman is a man with a medical degree. Therefore, no woman is a doctor.
56. If you don't keep quiet about our bank's dishonest practices, you're apt to lose your job.
57. A black cat crossed my path, and then later I flunked my logic test. So this proves that black cats are unlucky.
58. Either you respect and agree with your teacher, or you're insolent and don't deserve a good grade.
59. In spite of warnings from lifeguards, my girlfriend went swimming without a worry. She said that she didn't have to worry about man-eating sharks.
60. Will you contribute to our collection for famine relief, or are you insensitive to the suffering of other people?

4.2b   Another Fallacy Exercise – also LogiCola R

1. When are we going to guarantee all the people of this country the health care that they deserve?
2. When are we going to understand that the government cannot afford to pay for universal health care?
3. The professor's letter of recommendation said, "I cannot praise this student's study habits too highly."
4. No one has proven that humans are causing global warming; so we should assume that the heating of the earth has purely natural causes.
5. Christians are peaceful, Muslims are terrorists.
6. I never had problems with headaches before I studied logic. So studying logic must be the cause of my headaches.
7. This candidate's ideas are really scary; don't they make you afraid? I fear what would happen to our country if this candidate were elected.
8. Charles Darwin, who came up with the theory of evolution, presumably thought that his grandfather was a monkey.
9. You ask me why I deposited the company funds in my personal banking account. But why are you so doubtful about my integrity? Don't you believe that we all need to be more trusting?
10. American military experts testified in the first decade of the 21st century that Iraq was developing weapons of mass destruction; so this must be true.
11. If all persons in a group work to maximize their individual self-interest, then the group is working effectively to maximize its own self-interest.
12. The liberal elite media did it again! Those idiots are out to attack those of us who have solid, pro-American values.
13. My mother demands that I clean up after I make waffles. She is an incredible neatness freak! She wants me to devote my whole life to keeping her kitchen spotless!

14. Liberation theology got some of its concepts (like oppressive social structures) from atheistic Marxists, and so these concepts should be rejected.

15. This backpacking tent is very lightweight, and so this is the one you should get.

16. Everyone knows there ain't no gold in the Grand Canyon.

17. The Democrats want to raise tax rates on the rich and lower them on the middle class. This is part of their plan to move the country into socialism.

18. No one has given conclusive evidence showing that aliens from outside our planet didn't land near Roswell in 1947. So we should believe the witnesses who say that they encountered such aliens.

19. You should vote for me because I will lower your taxes.

20. Humans are "hardwired" so that, at least for the most part, they believe in God. So belief in God is rational.

21. Humans are "hardwired" so that, at least for the most part, they believe in God. So belief in God is irrational.

22. The second exam question asked me to describe Aristotle's approach to ethics. But since I didn't know anything about this, I instead described Plato's approach.

23. Those horrible city folk vote Democratic; so we country folk should vote Republican.

24. If you don't want to suffer an unfortunate accident, you'd better find my client innocent.

25. We should take either all of the Bible literally or else none of literally.

26. Men are logical, women are emotional.

27. Since there's no good evidence that there's intelligent life in other parts of the universe, it's only reasonable to conclude that there's no such life.

28. Since Martin Heidegger developed many of his ideas when he was a Nazi supporter in Germany, we should disregard his ideas.

29. Harry Gensler, who authored the Routledge *Introduction to Logic*, wears sandals with socks and claims that this is very fashionable; so this must be so.

30. We shouldn't listen when this Republican argues for tax relief for the rich; after all, her family was very rich.

31. If you don't buy some Girl Scout Cookies, I'll tell everyone how cheap you are.

32. My favorite Russian tennis star claims that Canon cameras are the best; so I plan to get one.

33. Where did you hide the dead body of your murder victim?

34. I read on the Internet that global warming is a hoax; so this must be true.

35. Cheating on exams can't be wrong; I mean, everyone does it.

36. The Republicans say that they are against "big government." But what they really want is to eliminate all social services for those in need, so that the rich can become even richer.

37. Last night I shot a burglar in my pajamas. I don't know how he got into my pajamas.

38. Are you going to admit that you're wrong?

39. Look at all the bad things that happened to our country while my opponent was in office! If you don't want to elect an official who'll bring about such bad things, then you should vote against my opponent.

40. Everything in the universe has a cause; so the universe also has a cause.

41. If you need another reference for my honesty, I can get Mariana Smith to vouch for me. Oh, you've never heard of Mariana Smith? Well, I can vouch for her.

42. I installed LogiCola on my computer, and then two weeks later my hard disk failed. LogiCola must be to blame!

43. So, you ask, which of my campaign promises will have to wait if we don't have enough funds to fulfill them all? Instead of responding, I'd like to address what's really troubling the people of this country, namely why the current administration is so dishonest.

44. Either you favor the Republicans or you aren't patriotic.

45. I had foolish and immature ideas like yours when I was your age.

46. Ancient Romans to Christians: "If you refuse to renounce your faith and worship the gods of Rome, we'll feed you to the lions."

47. All logicians are emotionless calculators.

48. When Harry Gensler baked his first batch of cookies, he used very good ingredients. Therefore the cookies that he baked were very good.

49. We shouldn't listen when this Democrat argues for tax relief for the poor; after all, her family was very poor.

50. God must have created the world, since surely *someone* must have created it.

51. Most Americans supported President George W. Bush's invasion of Iraq, so this invasion must have been a good thing.

52. You should take Gensler's logic course because he has a great sense of humor.

53. If you weren't so stupid, you'd agree with me.

54. To a junior Member of Congress: "If you don't vote for this Bill, you'll never be appointed to any important committees."

55. Why does my opponent want to lead our country into socialism?

56. Since each cell in the human organism is incapable of thought, thus the human organism itself is incapable of thought.

57. The Volkswagen was first developed by the Nazis, and so it must be an evil car.

58. Those crude country folk support this idea; so we city folk should be against it.

59. Dr Jones, you can't prove that I didn't come up independently with the same essay that occurs with word-by-word similarity on the Internet. So you must assume that I'm innocent of plagiarism.

60. Gensler's logic book is the best. My proof is that it says so inside, on page 69.

4.3   Inconsistency

Inconsistency is the most important fallacy – the most important deceptive error of thinking. Students writing on philosophical issues for the first time often express inconsistent views; this example is typical:

> Since morality is relative to culture, no duties bind universally. What's right in one culture is wrong in another. Universal duties are a myth. Relativism should make us tolerant toward others; we can't say that we're right and they're wrong. So everyone ought to respect the values of others.[1]

---

[1] See my *Ethics: A Contemporary Introduction*, 2nd ed. (New York: Routledge, 2011), Chapter 2.

Here the first statement is incompatible with the last:

1. No duties bind universally.
2. Everyone ought to respect the values of others.

If *everyone* ought to respect the values of others, then some duties bind universally. And if *no* duties bind universally, then neither does the duty to respect others. This inconsistency isn't trivial; it cuts deeply. The unexamined views that we use to guide our lives are often radically incoherent; putting these views into words often brings out their incoherence. The ancient Greek philosopher Socrates was adept at showing people how difficult it was to have consistent beliefs on the deeper questions of life.

Inconsistency is common in other areas too. Someone running for political office might talk to environmentalists one day and to industrialists the next. Each group might be told exactly what it wants to hear. The first group is told "I'll support stronger clean-air standards"; the second is told "I'll try to lower clean-air standards." We can be sure that the politician, if elected, will violate some of the promises. One can't fulfill incompatible promises.

We often aren't aware of our inconsistency. For example, one might believe all three of these:

1. God is good.
2. Predestination is true. (God immediately causes everything that happens.)
3. God damns sinners to eternal punishment.

These three beliefs aren't inconsistent in themselves. But the believer might have other beliefs that add to these three to make an inconsistent set:

4. If predestination is true, then God causes us to sin.
5. If God causes us to sin and yet damns sinners to eternal punishment, then God isn't good.

This set of five beliefs is inconsistent. Beliefs 2 and 4 entail "God causes us to sin." This, with 3 and 5, entails "God isn't good" – which contradicts 1. So the five beliefs can't all be true together. Someone who believes all five might not be aware of the inconsistency; the beliefs might not have come together in the person's consciousness at the same time.

Inconsistency is a sign that our belief system is flawed and that we need to change something. Logic can tell us that our belief system is inconsistent. But it can't tell us how to rearrange our beliefs to regain consistency; that's up to us.

Controversies often arise when a set of individually plausible statements can't consistently be combined. Consider this group of statements:

F = Some human actions are free.
D = All human actions are determined.
I = No determined actions are free.

Even though each claim by itself is plausible, the set is inconsistent. If we take any two of the statements as premises, we can infer the denial of the third. *Hard determinists* take D (determinism) and I (that determinism is incompatible with free will) as premises. They conclude not-F (that we have no free will):

All human actions are determined.   D
No determined actions are free.   I
∴ No human actions are free.   ∴ Not-F

Indeterminists take F (free will) and I (that determinism is incompatible with free will) as premises. They conclude not-D (the falsity of determinism):

Some human actions are free.   F
No determined actions are free.   I
∴ Some human actions aren't determined.   ∴ Not-D

Soft determinists take F (free will) and D (determinism) as premises. They conclude not-I (that determinism isn't incompatible with free will):

Some human actions are free.   F
All human actions are determined.   D
∴ Some determined actions are free.   ∴ Not-I

Each of the three arguments has plausible premises. All three arguments are valid, but at most only one of them can have true premises.

The three arguments relate to each other in an interesting way. Each argument is a "turnaround" of the other two. An argument is a *turnaround* of another argument if each results from the other by switching the denial of a premise with the denial of the conclusion. Here is an example:

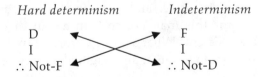

              Hard determinism   *Indeterminism*
                      D   F
                      I   I
                   ∴ Not-F   ∴ Not-D

As you'll see from the exercises, several classical philosophical disputes involve turnaround arguments. In each dispute, we have a set of individually plausible statements that can't consistently be combined.

A single statement may be inconsistent with itself. The most interesting case is that of a **self-refuting statement** – a statement that makes such a sweeping claim that it ends up denying itself. Suppose I tell you this:

> Everything that I tell you is false.

Could this be true? Not if I tell it to you; then it has to be false. The statement refutes itself. Here's another example:

> I know that there's no human knowledge.

This couldn't be true. If it were true, then there would be some human knowledge – thus refuting the claim. A self-refuting claim often starts as a seemingly big, bold insight. The bubble bursts when we see that it destroys itself.

Consistency relates ethical beliefs to actions in a special way. Suppose I believe that this man is bleeding. That belief doesn't commit me, under pain of inconsistency, to any specific act; how I live can't be inconsistent with this belief (taken by itself). But suppose I believe that I *ought* to call the doctor. This ethical belief does commit me, under pain of inconsistency, to action. If I don't act to call the doctor, then the way I live is inconsistent with my belief. Consistency requires a harmony between our ethical beliefs and how we live.

Many consistency arguments in ethics depend on the universalizability principle, which is one of the few principles on which almost all philosophers agree. Here's one formulation of the principle:

> Universalizability: Whatever is right (wrong, good, bad, etc.) in one case also would be right (wrong, good, bad, etc.) in any exactly or relevantly similar case, regardless of the individuals involved.

Here's an example adapted from the Good Samaritan parable (Luke 10:30–5). Suppose that, while I'm jogging, I see a man who's been beaten, robbed, and left to die. Should I help him, perhaps by making a phone call? I think of excuses why I shouldn't. I'm busy, don't want to get involved, and so on. I say to myself, "It would be all right for me not to help him." But then I consider an exactly reversed situation. I imagine myself in his place; I'm the one who's been beaten, robbed, and left to die. And I imagine him being in my place; he's jogging, sees me in my sad state, and has the same excuses. I ask myself, "Would it be all right for this man not to help me in this situation? Surely not!" But then I'm inconsistent. What's all right for me to do to another has to be all right for the other to do to me in an imagined exactly reversed situation.[1]

4.3a   Exercise

Construct a turnaround argument based on the three incompatible statements in the box. Include statement C as a premise of your argument.

---

[1] For more on consistency in ethics, see Chapters 13 and 14 of this present book – and Chapters 7 to 9 of my *Ethics: A Contemporary Introduction*, 2nd ed. (New York: Routledge, 2011).

A. There are no universal duties. B. Everyone ought to respect the dignity of others. C. If everyone ought to respect the dignity of others, then there are universal duties.

Everyone ought to respect the dignity of others. If everyone ought to respect the dignity of others, then there are universal duties. ∴ There are universal duties.

1. Construct a different turnaround argument based on the three statements in this first box. Again, include statement C as a premise of your argument.
2. Construct a turnaround argument based on the four incompatible statements in this second box. Include statement A as a premise of your argument.

A. If we have ethical knowledge, then either ethical truths are provable or there are self-evident ethical truths. B. We have ethical knowledge. C. Ethical truths aren't provable. D. There are no self-evident ethical truths.

3. Following the directions in 2, construct a second such turnaround argument.
4. Following the directions in 2, construct a third such turnaround argument.
5. Construct a turnaround argument based on the three incompatible statements in this third box.

A. All human concepts come from sense experience. B. The concept of logical validity is a human concept. C. The concept of logical validity doesn't come from sense experience.

6. Following the directions in 5, construct a second such turnaround argument.
7. Following the directions in 5, construct a third such turnaround argument.
8. If an argument is valid, then is its turnaround necessarily also valid? Argue for the correctness of your answer.

The next seven examples are self-refuting statements. Explain how each self-refutes.

9. No statement is true.
10. Every rule has an exception.
11. One ought not to accept statements that haven't been proved.
12. Any statement whose truth or falsity we can't decide through scientific experiments is meaningless.
13. There's no such thing as something being "true." There are only opinions, each being "true for" the person holding it, none being just "true."
14. We can know only what's been proved using experimental science. I know this.
15. It's impossible to express truth in human concepts.

4.4 Constructing arguments

This book presents many logical tools; these can help turn mushy thinking into clear reasoning. You should use these logical tools where appropriate in your own reading and writing.

Imagine that your teacher in business ethics gives you this assignment:

> Suppose you work for a small, struggling company called Mushy Software. You can get a lucrative contract for your company, but only by bribing an official of Enormity Incorporated. Would it be right for you to offer the bribe? Write a paper taking a position on this. Give a clear argument explaining the reasoning behind your answer.

Many of your fellow students probably don't even know what an argument is. But you've studied logic; you know that an argument is a set of statements divided into premises and a conclusion. The assignment tells you to construct a valid argument along these lines:

> [Insert plausible premise.]
> [Insert plausible premise.]
> ∴ Offering the bribe is/isn't right.

Phrase your argument as clearly and simply as possible, and make sure that it's valid in some acceptable logical system. After sketching various arguments, you might arrive at this (which is valid in syllogistic and quantificational logic):

> No dishonest act is right.
> Offering the bribe is a dishonest act.
> ∴ Offering the bribe isn't right.

When you propose an argument, it's wise to ask how an opponent could object to it. While the form here is clearly valid, there might be some difficulty with the premises. How could an opponent attack the premises?

One way to attack a universal claim is to find a counterexample:

Counterexample

To refute "all A is B," find something that's A but not B.
To refute "no A is B," find something that's A and also B.

Premise 1 says "No dishonest act is right." You could refute this by finding an action that's dishonest and also right. Can you think of any such action? Imagine a case in which the only way to provide food for your starving family is by stealing. Presumably, stealing here is dishonest but also right:

> This act of stealing is a dishonest act.
> This act of stealing is right.
> ∴ Some dishonest acts are right.

This is valid in syllogistic and quantificational logic. So if the premises here are true, then premise 1 of your original argument is false.

Modus tollens gives another simple way to attack a claim:

Modus tollens	
To refute claim A, find a clearly false claim B that A implies. Then argue as on the right:	If A then B. Not-B. ∴ Not-A.

Here you'd try to find some clearly false claim that one of the premises implies. This argument seems to work:

> If no dishonest act is right, then it wouldn't be right to
> steal food for your starving family when this is needed
> to keep them from starving.
> It would be right to steal food for your starving family
> when this is needed to keep them from starving.
> ∴ Some dishonest acts are right.

This is valid in propositional logic. If the premises are true, then premise 1 of your original argument is false. This *modus tollens* objection is similar in content to the counterexample objection, but phrased differently.

How can you respond to the objection? You have three options:

- *Counterattack*: Attack the arguments against your premise.
- *Reformulate*: Reword your original premises so they avoid the objection but still lead to your conclusion.
- *Change strategy*: Trash your argument and try another approach.

On the *counterattack* option, you'd maintain that the arguments against your premise either are invalid or else have false premises. Here you might claim that stealing is wrong in this hypothetical case. This would be *biting the bullet* – taking a stand that seems to go against common sense in order to defend your theory. Here you'd claim that it's wrong to steal to keep your family from starving; this is a difficult bullet to bite.

On the *reformulate* option, you'd rephrase premise 1 to avoid the objection but still lead to your conclusion. You might add the italicized qualification:

> No dishonest act *that isn't needed to avoid disaster* is right.

You'd have to explain what "avoid disaster" here means and you'd have to add another premise that says "Offering the bribe isn't needed to avoid disaster." Then you'd look for further objections to the revised argument.

On the *change strategy* option, you'd trash your original argument and try another approach. You might, for example, argue that offering the bribe is right (or wrong) because it's legal (or illegal), or accords with (or violates) the self-interest of the agent, or maximizes (or doesn't) the long-term interests of everyone affected by the action. Then, again, you'd have to ask whether there are objections to your new argument.

As you refine your reasoning, it's helpful to imagine a little debate going on. First present your argument to yourself. Then pretend to be your opponent and try to attack the argument. You might even enlist your friends to come up with objections; that's what professional philosophers do. Then imagine yourself trying to reply to your opponent. Then pretend to be your opponent and try to attack your reply. Repeat the process until you're content with the position you're defending and the argumentation behind it.

4.4a Exercise

Give a valid argument with plausible premises for or against these statements. For this exercise, you needn't believe these premises, but you have to regard them as plausible. Don't forget what you learned in Chapter 3 ("Meaning and Definitions") about the need to understand what a statement means before you defend or attack it.

Any act is right if and only if it's in the agent's self-interest. (This is called *ethical egoism*.)	If ethical egoism is true, then it would be right for Jones to torture and kill you if this were in Jones's self-interest. It wouldn't be right for Jones to torture and kill you if this were in Jones's self-interest. ∴ Ethical egoism isn't true.

1. Offering the bribe is in the agent's self-interest.
2. Every act is right if and only if it's legal.
3. All acts that maximize good consequences are right.
4. Offering the bribe maximizes the long-term interests of everyone concerned.
5. Offering the bribe is a dishonest act.
6. Some wrong actions are errors made in good faith.
7. No error made in good faith is blameworthy.
8. All socially useful acts are right.
9. No acts of punishing the innocent are right.
10. The belief that there is a God is unnecessary to explain our experience.
11. All beliefs unnecessary to explain our experience ought to be rejected.
12. All beliefs that give practical life benefits are pragmatically justifiable.
13. The idea of a perfect circle is a human concept.
14. The idea of a perfect circle doesn't derive from sense experience.

15.   All ideas gained in our earthly existence derive from sense experience.

[I took many examples from Section 2.3a. The exercises in this book with English arguments are a rich source of further problems for this exercise.]

4.5   Analyzing arguments

To get better at analyzing arguments, get into the habit of sketching out a formal version of arguments that you read or hear. Often the arguments will be as simple as a *modus tollens* ("If A then B, not-B, therefore not A"); but sometimes they'll get more complicated. It's important to listen and read carefully, with the aim of getting at the heart of the reasoning.

Here are four steps that you may find helpful in analyzing arguments in things you read. The steps are especially useful when you write an essay on an author's reasoning; but you also can use them to critique your own writing. The steps assume that the passage contains reasoning (and not just description).

1.   *Formulate the argument in English.* Identify and write out the premises and conclusion. Try to arrive at a valid argument expressed as clearly and directly as possible. Use the *principle of charity*: interpret unclear reasoning in the way that gives the best argument. Supply implicit premises where needed, avoid emotional terms, and phrase similar ideas in similar words. This step can be difficult if the author's argument is unclear.

2.   *Translate into some logical system and test for validity.* If the argument is invalid, you might return to step 1 and try a different formulation. If you can't get a valid argument, you can skip the next two steps.

3.   *Identify difficulties.* Star controversial premises. Underline obscure or ambiguous terms; explain what you think the author means by these.

4.   *Appraise the premises.* Try to decide if the premises are true. Look for informal fallacies, especially circularity and ambiguity. Give further arguments (your own or the author's) for or against the premises.

Let's try this on a famous passage from David Hume:

Since morals, therefore, have an influence on the actions and affections, it follows, that they cannot be deriv'd from reason; and that because reason alone, as we have already prov'd, can never have any such influence. Morals excite passions, and produce or prevent actions. Reason of itself is utterly impotent in this particular. The rules of morality, therefore, are not conclusions of our reason. No one, I believe, will deny the justness of this inference; nor is there any other means of evading it, than by denying that principle, on which it is founded. As long as it is allow'd, that reason has no influence on our passions and actions, 'tis in vain to pretend, that morality is discover'd only by a deduction of reason. An active principle can never be founded on an inactive ....[1]

First read the passage several times. Focus on the reasoning and try to put it into words; it usually takes several tries to get a clear argument. Here our argument might look like this:

> All moral judgments influence our actions and feelings.
> Nothing from reason influences our actions and feelings.
> ∴ No moral judgments are from reason.

Next translate into some logical system and test for validity. Here we could use either syllogistic or quantificational logic:

all M is I	$(x)(Mx \supset Ix)$
no R is I	$\sim(\exists x)(Rx \cdot Ix)$
∴ no M is R	∴ $\sim(\exists x)(Mx \cdot Rx)$

The argument tests out valid in either case.

Next identify difficulties. Star controversial premises and underline obscure or ambiguous terms:

> * All moral judgments <u>influence</u> our actions and feelings.
> * Nothing from <u>reason</u> <u>influences</u> our actions and feelings.
> ∴ No moral judgments are from <u>reason</u>.

Try to figure out what Hume meant by these underlined words. By "reason," Hume seems to mean "the discovery of truth or falsehood." Thus we can rephrase his argument as follows:

> * All moral judgments <u>influence</u> our actions and feelings.
> * No discovery of truth or falsehood <u>influences</u> our actions
>   and feelings.
> ∴ No moral judgments are a discovery of truth or falsehood.

"Influences" also is tricky. "X influences Y" could have either of two meanings:

"X *independently of* *our desires* influences Y."	"X *when combined with* *our desires* influences Y."

Finally, appraise the premises. Since "influences" has two senses, we have to appraise the premises using each sense. Taking "influences" in the first sense, premise 1 means:

---

[1] David Hume, *A Treatise of Human Nature* (Oxford: Clarendon Press, 1888), page 457 (Book III, Part I, Section I).

> All moral judgments, *independently of our
> desires*, influence our actions and feelings.

This seems false, since there are people who accept moral judgments but have no desire or motivation to follow them; the actions and feelings of such a person thus wouldn't be influenced by these moral judgments. Taking "influences" in the second sense, premise 2 means:

> No discovery of truth or falsehood, *when combined
> with our desires*, influences our actions and feelings.

This also seems false. The discovery of the truth that this flame would burn our finger, combined with our desire not to get burned, surely influences our actions and desires. Hume's argument is plausible because "influences" is ambiguous. Depending on how we take this term, one premise or the other becomes false or doubtful. So Hume's argument is flawed.

Here we've combined formal techniques with informal ones (common-sense judgments, definitions, and the fallacy of ambiguity). We've used these to formulate and criticize an argument on the foundations of ethics. Our criticisms, of course, might not be final. A Hume defender might attack our arguments against Hume's premises, suggest another reading of the argument, or rephrase the premises to avoid our criticisms. But our criticisms, if clearly and logically expressed, will help the discussion go forward. At its best, philosophical discussion involves reasoning together in a clear-headed, logical manner.

It's important to be fair when we criticize the reasoning of others. Such criticism can be part of a common search for truth; we shouldn't let it descend into a vain attempt to score points. In appraising the reasoning of others, we should follow the same standards of fairness that we want others to follow in their appraisal of *our* reasoning. Distortions and other fallacies are beneath the dignity of beings, such as ourselves, who are capable of reasoning.

CHAPTER 5
Inductive Reasoning

Much of our everyday reasoning deals with probabilities. We observe patterns and conclude that, based on these, such and such a belief is *probably* true. This is inductive reasoning.

5.1 The statistical syllogism

The Appalachian Trail (AT), a 2,160-mile footpath from Georgia to Maine in the eastern US, has a series of lean-to shelters. Suppose we backpack on the AT and plan to spend the night at Rocky Gap Shelter. We'd like to know beforehand whether there's water (a spring or stream) close by. If we knew that *all* AT shelters have water, or that *none* do, we could reason *deductively*:

All AT shelters have water.	No AT shelters have water.
Rocky Gap is an AT shelter.	Rocky Gap is an AT shelter.
∴ Rocky Gap has water.	∴ Rocky Gap doesn't have water.

Both are deductively valid. Both have a tight connection between premises and conclusion; if the premises are true, the conclusion *has* to be true. Deductive validity is an all-or-nothing affair. Deductive arguments can't be "half-valid," nor can one be "more valid" than another.

   In fact, most of the shelters have water, but a few don't. Of the shelters that I've visited, roughly 90 percent (depending on season and rainfall) have had water. If we knew that 90 percent had water, we could reason *inductively*:

> 90 percent of AT shelters have water.
> Rocky Gap is an AT shelter.
> This is all we know about the matter.
> ∴ Probably Rocky Gap has water.

This is a strong inductive argument. Relative to the premises, the conclusion is a good bet. But it's partially a guess; it could turn out false, even though the premises are all true.

   The "This is all we know about the matter" premise means "We have no further information that influences the probability of the conclusion." Suppose we just met a thirsty backpacker complaining that the water at Rocky Gap had dried up; that would change the probability of the conclusion. The premise claims that we have no such further information.

Two features set inductive arguments apart from deductive ones. (1) Inductive arguments vary in how strongly the premises support the conclusion. The premise "99 percent of AT shelters have water" supports the conclusion more strongly than does "60 percent of AT shelters have water." We have shades of gray here – not the black and white of deductive validity/invalidity. (2) Even a strong inductive argument has only a loose connection between premises and conclusion. The premises make the conclusion at most only highly probable; the premises might be true while the conclusion is false. Inductive reasoning is a form of guessing based on recognizing and extending known patterns and resemblances.

Let me sum up. A **deductive argument** claims that it's *logically necessary* that if the premises are all true, then so is the conclusion. An **inductive argument** claims that it's *likely* (but not logically necessary) that if the premises are all true, then so is the conclusion. While this book is mostly about deductive arguments, this chapter focuses on inductive ones.

If we refine our conclusion to specify a numerical probability, we get the classic **statistical syllogism** form:

Statistical Syllogism	90 percent of the AT shelters have water.
N percent of A's are B's.	Rocky Gap is an AT shelter.
X is an A.	This is all we know about the matter.
This is all we know about the matter.	∴ *It's 90 percent probable that* Rocky Gap has water.
∴ It's N percent probable that X is a B.	

Here's another example:

> 50 percent of coin tosses are heads.
> This is a coin toss.
> This is all we know about the matter.
> ∴ It's 50 percent probable that this is heads.

Suppose that all we know affecting the probability of the toss being heads is that 50 percent of coin tosses are heads and that this is a coin toss. Then it's 50 percent probable to us that the toss is heads. This holds if we hadn't yet tossed the coin, or if we tossed it but didn't yet know how it landed. The matter is different if we know how it landed. Then it's no longer just 50 percent probable to us that it's heads; rather, we *know* that it's heads or that it's tails.

Statistical syllogisms apply most cleanly if we know little about the subject. Suppose we know these two things about Michigan's football team:

1. It's first down – and Michigan runs 70 percent of the time on first down.
2. Michigan is behind – and passes 70 percent of the time when it's behind.

Relative to 1, Michigan probably will run. Relative to 2, Michigan probably will pass. But it's unclear what Michigan probably will do relative to 1 and 2. It gets worse if we add facts about the score, the time left, and the offensive formation. Each fact by itself may lead to a clear conclusion about what Michigan probably will do; but the combination muddies the issue. Too much information can confuse us when we apply statistical syllogisms.

Chapter 1 distinguished *valid* from *sound* deductive arguments. *Valid* asserts a correct relation between premises and conclusion, but says nothing about the truth of the premises; *sound* includes both "valid" and "has true premises." It's convenient to have similar terms for inductive arguments. Let's say that an argument is *strong* inductively if the conclusion is probable relative to the premises. And let's say that an argument is *reliable* inductively if it's strong and has true premises. Here's a chart:

	Deductively	Inductively
Correct premise/conclusion link ➔	*valid*	*strong*
This plus true premises ➔	*sound*	*reliable*

Here's a very strong inductive argument that isn't reliable:

> Michigan loses 99 percent of the time it plays.
> Michigan is playing today.
> This is all we know about the matter.
> ∴ Probably Michigan will lose today.

This is very strong, because in relation to the premises the conclusion is very probable. But the argument isn't reliable, since premise 1 is false.

We'll see that much of inductive logic is controversial and difficult to reduce to neat and tidy principles.

5.2   Probability calculations

Sometimes we can calculate probabilities rather precisely. Experience shows that coins tend to land *heads* half the time and *tails* the other half; so each coin has a 50 percent chance of landing heads and a 50 percent chance of landing tails. Suppose we toss two coins. There are four possible combinations of heads (**H**) and tails (**T**) for the two coins:

HH HT TH TT

Each case is equally probable. So our chance of getting two heads is 25 percent (.25 or ¼), since it happens in 1 out of 4 cases. Here's the rule (where "prob" is short for "the probability" and "favorable cases" are those in which A is true):

> This rule holds if every case is equally likely:
>
> $$\text{Prob of A} = \frac{\text{the number of favorable cases}}{\text{the total number of cases}}$$

Our chance of getting at least one head is 75 percent (.75 or ¾), since it happens in 3 of 4 cases.

With odds, the ratio concerns favorable and unfavorable cases ("unfavorable cases" are those in which A is false). The odds are in your favor if the number of favorable cases is greater (then your probability is greater than 50 percent):

> $$\text{The odds } \textit{in favor of } \text{A} = \frac{\text{the number of favorable cases}}{\text{the number of unfavorable cases}}$$

So the odds are 3 to 1 in favor of getting at least one head – since it happens in 3 cases and fails in only 1 case. The odds are against you if the number of unfavorable cases is greater (so your probability is less than 50 percent):

> $$\text{The odds } \textit{against } \text{A} = \frac{\text{the number of unfavorable cases}}{\text{the number of favorable cases}}$$

Odds are usually given in whole numbers, with the larger number first. We wouldn't say "The odds are 1 to 3 *in favor of* getting two heads"; rather, we'd put the larger number first and say "The odds are 3 to 1 *against* getting two heads." Here are examples of how to convert between odds and probability:

The odds are even (1 to 1) that we'll win	=	The probability of our winning is 50 percent.
The odds are 7 to 5 in favor of our winning	=	The probability of our winning is 7/12 (7 favorable cases out of 12 total cases, or 58.3 percent).
The odds are 7 to 5 against our winning	=	The probability of our winning is 5/12 (5 favorable cases out of 12 total cases, 41.7 percent).
The probability of our winning is 70 percent	=	The odds are 7 to 3 in favor of our winning (70 percent favorable to 30 percent unfavorable).
The probability of our winning is 30 percent	=	The odds are 7 to 3 against our winning (70 percent unfavorable to 30 percent favorable).

We'll now learn some rules for calculating probabilities. The first two rules are about necessary truths and self-contradictions:

If A is a necessary truth:
Prob of A = 100 percent.

If A is a self-contradiction:
Prob of A = 0 percent.

Our chance of a specific coin being *either heads or not heads* is 100 percent. And our chance of it being *both heads and not heads* (at one time) is 0 percent.

This next rule relates the probability of a given event happening to the probability of that event not happening:

Prob of not-A   =   100 percent - prob of A.

So if our chance of getting two heads is 25 percent, then our chance of *not* getting two heads is 75 percent (100 percent - 25 percent).

The next rule concerns events that are independent of each other, in that the occurrence of one doesn't make the occurrence of the other any more or any less likely (the first coin being heads, for example, doesn't make it any more or any less likely that the second coin will be heads):

If A and B are independent:
Prob of (A and B)   =   prob of A · prob of B.

Probabilities multiply with AND. So our chance of throwing two heads (25 percent) *and then* throwing two heads again (25 percent) is 6.25 percent (25 percent · 25 percent).

This next rule holds for events that are mutually exclusive, in that they can't both happen together:

If A and B are mutually exclusive:
Prob of (A or B)   =   prob of A + prob of B.

Probabilities add with OR. It can't happen that we throw two heads and also (on the same toss of two coins) throw two tails. The probability of either event is 25 percent. So the probability of one *or* the other happening (getting two heads *or* two tails) is 50 percent (25 percent + 25 percent). When the two events aren't mutually exclusive, we have to follow this more complex rule:

> This holds even if A and B aren't mutually exclusive:
>
> Prob of (A or B) = Prob of A + prob of B - prob of (A and B).

Suppose we calculate the probability of getting at least one head when we flip two coins. Coin 1 being heads and coin 2 being heads aren't mutually exclusive events, since they might both happen together; so we have to apply the more complex rule. The chance of coin 1 being heads *or* coin 2 being heads = the chance of coin 1 being heads (50 percent) + the chance of coin 2 being heads (50 percent) - the chance of coin 1 and coin 2 both being heads (25 percent). So our chance of getting at least one head is 75 percent (50 percent + 50 percent - 25 percent). If A and B are mutually exclusive, then the probability of (A and B) = 0; then the simpler rule gives the same result as the more complex rule.

Suppose we throw two dice. There are six equally probable possibilities for each die. Here are the possible combinations and resulting totals:

		1	2	3	4	5	6	← second die
	1	2	3	4	5	6	7	
	2	3	4	5	6	7	8	
first	3	4	5	6	7	8	9	
die	4	5	6	7	8	9	10	
	5	6	7	8	9	10	11	
	6	7	8	9	10	11	12	

There are 36 possible combinations; each has an equal 1/36 probability. The chance of getting a 12 is 1/36, since we get a 12 in only 1 of 36 cases. The chance of getting an 11 is 1/18 (2/36) – since we get an 11 in 2 of 36 cases. Similarly, we have a 1/6 (6/36) chance of getting a 10 or higher, and a 5/6 (30/36) chance of getting a 9 or lower.

Cards provide another example. What's our chance of getting 2 aces when dealt 2 cards from a standard 52-card deck? We might think that, since 1/13 of the cards are aces, our chance of getting two aces is 1/169 (1/13 · 1/13). But that's wrong. Our chance of getting an ace on the first draw is 1/13, since there are 4 aces in the 52 cards, and 4/52 = 1/13. But if we get an ace on the first draw, then there are only 3 aces left in the 51 cards. So our chance of getting a second ace is 1/17 (3/51). Thus, our chance of getting 2 aces when dealt 2 cards from a standard 52-card deck is 1/221 (1/13 · 1/17), or about 0.45 percent.

Here the events aren't independent. Getting an ace on the first card reduces the number of aces left and lowers our chance of drawing an ace for the second card. This is unlike coins, where getting heads on one toss doesn't affect our chance of getting heads on the next toss. If events A and B aren't independent, we need this rule for determining the probability of the conjunction (A and B):

> This holds even if A and B aren't independent:
>
> Prob of (A and B)   =   Prob of A · (prob of B after A occurs).

This reflects the reasoning we used to calculate our chance of getting 2 aces from a 52-card deck. What's our chance if we use a double 104-card deck? Our chance of getting a first ace is again 1/13 (since there are 8 aces among the 104 cards, and 8/104 = 1/13). After we get a first ace, there are 7 aces left in the 103 cards. Our chance of getting a second ace is 7/103. So the probability of getting a first ace and then a second ace = 1/13 (the probability of the first ace) · 7/103 (the probability of the second ace). This works out to 7/1339 (1/13 · 7/103), or about 0.52 percent. So our chance of getting 2 aces when dealt 2 cards from a double 104-card deck is about 0.52 percent. We have a better chance with the double deck (0.52 percent instead of 0.45 percent).

Mathematically fair betting odds are in reverse proportion to probability. Suppose we bet on whether, in drawing 2 cards from a standard 52-card deck, we'll draw 2 aces. There's a 1/221 chance of getting 2 aces, so the odds are 220 to 1 against us. If we bet $1, we should get $220 if we win. If we play for a long time under such betting odds, our gains and losses probably will roughly equalize. In practice, of course, the casino takes its cut; so we get less than mathematically fair earnings if we win. If we play for a long time under such odds, probably we'll lose and the casino will win. That's why Las Vegas casinos look like the palaces of emperors.

5.2a   Exercise – also LogiCola P (P, O, & C)

Work out the following problems. A calculator is useful for some of them.

> You're playing blackjack and your first card is an ace. What's your chance of getting a card worth 10 (a 10, jack, queen, or king) for your next card? You're using a standard 52-card deck.

> There are 16 such cards (one 10, J, Q, and K for each suit) from 51 remaining cards. So your chance is 16/51 (about 31.4 percent).

1. What would the answer to the sample problem be with a double 104-card deck?
2. Suppose the Cubs and Mets play baseball today. There's a 60 percent chance of rain, which would cancel the game. If the teams play, the Cubs have a 20 percent chance of winning. What chance do the Cubs have of winning today?
3. You're tossing coins. You tossed 5 heads in a row using a fair coin. What's the probability now that the next coin will be heads?
4. You're about to toss 6 coins. What's the probability that all 6 will be heads?
5. Suppose there's an 80 percent chance that the winner of the Michigan versus Ohio State game will go to the Rose Bowl, a 60 percent chance that Michigan will beat Ohio State, and a 30 percent chance that Michigan will win the Rose Bowl if it goes. Then what's the probability that Michigan will win the Rose Bowl?

6. Suppose you bet $10 that Michigan will win the Rose Bowl. Assuming the probabilities of the last example and mathematically fair betting odds, how much money should you win if Michigan wins the Rose Bowl?

7. You're playing blackjack and get an ace for the first card. You know that the cards used on the only previous hand were a 5, a 6, two 7s, and two 9s, and that all these are in the discard pile. What's your chance of getting a card worth 10 (a 10, jack, queen, or king) for the next card? You're using a standard 52-card deck.

8. What would the answer to the last problem be with a double 104-card deck?

9. You're throwing a pair of dice. Your sister bets you even money that you'll throw an even number (adding both together). Is she playing you for a sucker?

10. Your sister is throwing a pair of dice. She says, "I bet I'll throw a number divisible by three." What are the mathematically fair betting odds?

11. You're dealt five cards: two 3s, a 4, a 6, and a 7. If you get another card, what's the probability that it will be a 5? What's the probability that it will be a 3?

12. You're at a casino in Las Vegas and walk by a $1 slot machine that says "Win $2,000!" Assume that this is the only way you can win and that it gives mathematically fair odds or worse. What's your chance of winning if you deposit $1?

13. What's the antecedent probability that both your parents have their birthday on the same day of the year? (Ignore leap-year complications.)

14. Our football team, Michigan, is 2 points behind with a few seconds left. We have the ball, fourth and two, on the Ohio State 38. We could have the kicker try a long field goal, which would win the game. The probability of kicking this goal is 30 percent. Or we could try to make a first down and then kick from a shorter distance. There's a 70 percent probability of making a first down and a 50 percent probability of making the shorter field goal if we make the first down. Which alternative gives us a better chance to make the field goal?

15. Our team, Michigan, is 2 points ahead with a minute left. Ohio State is going for it on fourth down. It's 60 percent probable that they'll pass, and 40 percent probable that they'll run. We can defense the pass or defense the run. If we defense the pass, then we're 70 percent likely to stop a pass but only 40 percent likely to stop a run. If we defense the run, then we're 80 percent likely to stop a run but only 50 percent likely to stop a pass. What should we do?

5.3 Philosophical questions

We'll now consider four philosophical questions on probability. Philosophers disagree about how to answer these questions.

1. Are the ultimate scientific laws governing the universe *deterministic* or *probabilistic* in nature?

Some philosophers contend that all ultimate scientific laws are *deterministic*. We speak of probability only because we lack knowledge. Suppose we knew all the laws of nature and the complete state of the world at a given time, and could apply this knowledge. Then we could infallibly predict whether the coin will come up heads, whether it will rain three years from today, and who will win the World Cup in 30 years. This is the thesis of determinism.

Other philosophers say that some or all of the ultimate laws governing our world are *probabilistic*. Such laws say not that under given conditions a result must obtain, but rather that under these conditions a result *probably* obtains. The probabilistic laws of quantum physics show that the world is a dice game.

Since the empirical evidence is inconclusive, it's hard to be sure which side is correct. Physics today embraces probabilistic laws but could someday return to deterministic laws. The issue is complicated by the controversy over whether determinism is an empirical or an *a priori* issue (Section 3.7); some think reason (not experience) gives us certainty that the world is deterministic.

> 2.   What does "probable" mean? And can every statement be assigned a numerical probability relative to given evidence?

Philosophers distinguish various senses of "probable." "The *probability* of heads is 50 percent" could be taken in at least four ways:

- *Ratio of observed frequencies*: We've observed that coins land heads about half of the time.
- *Ratio of abstract possibilities*: Heads is one of the two equally likely abstract possibilities.
- *Measure of actual confidence*: We have the same confidence in the toss being heads as we have in it not being heads.
- *Measure of rational confidence*: It's rational to have the same confidence in the toss being heads as in it not being heads.

We used a *ratio of observed frequencies* to calculate the probability of finding water at Rocky Gap Shelter. And we used a *ratio of abstract possibilities* to calculate the probability of being dealt two aces. So sometimes these ratio approaches can give numerical probabilities. But sometimes they can't. Neither ratio approach gives a numerical probability to "Michigan will run" relative to information about ancient Greek philosophy – or relative to this combination:

1.   It's first down – and Michigan runs 70 percent of the time on first down.
2.   Michigan is behind – and passes 70 percent of the time when it's behind.

Only in special cases do the ratio approaches give numerical probabilities.

The *measure of actual confidence* sometimes yields numerical probabilities. Consider these statements:

> "There is life on other galaxies."
> "Michigan will beat Ohio State this year."
> "There is a God."

If you regard 1-to-1 betting odds on one of these as fair, then your actual confidence in the statement is 50 percent. But you may be unwilling to commit yourself to such odds. Maybe you can't say if your confidence in the statement is less or greater than your confidence that a coin toss will be heads. Then we can't assign numbers to your actual confidence. The *rational confidence view*, too, would have trouble assigning numerical probabilities in these cases.

Some doubt whether probability as rational confidence satisfies the standard probability rules of the last section. These rules say that necessary statements always have a probability of 100 percent. But consider a complex propositional logic formula that's a necessary truth, even though your evidence suggests that it isn't; perhaps your normally reliable logic teacher tells you that it isn't a necessary truth – or perhaps in error you get a truth-table line of false (see Section 6.6). Relative to your data, it seems rational not to put 100 percent confidence in the formula (even though it in fact is a necessary truth). So is probability theory wrong?

Probability theory is idealized rather than wrong. It describes the confidence an ideal reasoner would have, based on an ideal analysis of the data; an ideal reasoner would always recognize necessary truths and put 100 percent confidence in them. So we have to be careful applying probability theory to the beliefs of non-ideal human beings; we must be like physicists who give simple equations for frictionless bodies and then allow for the idealization when applying the equations to real cases.

Probability as *actual confidence* definitely can violate the probability rules. Many would calculate the probability of drawing 2 aces from a 52 or 104 card deck as 1/169 (1/13 · 1/13); so they'd regard 168-to-1 betting odds as fair. But the probability rules say this is wrong (Section 5.2).

3. How does probability relate to how ideally rational persons *believe*?

On one view, an ideally rational person would believe all and only those statements that are more than 50 percent probable relative to the person's data. But this view has strange implications. Suppose that Austria, Brazil, and China each has a 33⅓ percent chance of winning the World Cup. Then each of these three is 66⅔ percent probable:

> "Austria won't win the World Cup, but Brazil or China will."
> "Brazil won't win the World Cup, but Austria or China will."
> "China won't win the World Cup, but Austria or Brazil will."

On the view just described, an ideally rational person would believe all three statements. But this is silly; only a very confused person could do this.

The view has other problems. Why pick a 50 percent figure? Why wouldn't an ideally rational person believe all and only those statements that are at least 60 percent (or 75 percent or 90 percent) probable? There are further problems if sometimes (or usually) there's no way to work out numerical probabilities.

The view gives an ideal of selecting all beliefs in a way that's free of subjective factors (like feelings and practical interests). Some find this ideal attractive. Pragmatists find it repulsive. They believe in following subjective factors on issues that our intellects can't decide. They think numerical probability doesn't apply to life's deeper issues (like free will, God, or basic moral principles).

4.   How does probability relate to how ideally rational persons *act*?

On one view, an ideally rational person always acts to maximize **expected gain**. In working out what to do, such a person would list the possible alternative actions (A, B, C, ...) and then consider the possible outcomes (A1, A2, A3, ...) of each action. The gain or loss of each outcome would be multiplied by the probability of that outcome occurring; adding these together gives the action's expected gain. So an action's expected gain is the sum of probability-times-gain of its various possible outcomes. An ideally rational person, on this view, would always do whatever had the highest expected gain; this entails going for the lowest expected loss when every alternative loses.

What is "gain" here? Is it pleasure or desire-satisfaction – for oneself or for one's group or for all affected by the action? Or is it financial gain – for oneself or for one's company? To keep things concrete, let's focus on an economic version of the theory. Let's consider the view that ideally rational gamblers would always act to maximize their expected financial gain.

Imagine that you're such an "ideally rational gambler." You find a game of dice that pays $3,536 on a $100 bet if you throw a 12. You'd work out the expected gain of playing or not playing (alternatives P and N) in this way:

P.   PLAYING. There are two possible outcomes: P1 (I win) and P2 (I lose). P1 is 1/36 likely and gains $3,536; P1 is worth (1/36 · $3,536) or $98.22. P2 is 35/36 likely and loses $100; P2 is worth (35/36 · -$100), or -$97.22. The expected gain of alternative P is ($98.22 - 97.22), or $1.

N.   NOT PLAYING. On this alternative, I won't win or lose anything. The expected gain of alternative N is (100 percent · $0), or $0.

So then you'd play – unless you found another game with a greater expected gain. If you played this dice game only once, you'd be 97 percent likely to lose money. But the occasional payoff is great; you'd likely gain about a million dollars if you played a million times.

An "ideally rational gambler" would gamble if the odds were favorable, but not otherwise. Since Las Vegas casinos take their cut, their odds are against the individual gambler; so an ideally rational gambler wouldn't gamble at these places. But people have interests other than money; for many, gambling is great fun, and they're willing to pay for the fun.

Some whose only concern is money refuse to gamble even when the odds are in their favor. Their concern may be to have *enough* money. They may better satisfy this by being cautious; they don't want to risk losing what they have for the sake of gaining more. Few people would endanger their total savings for the 1-in-900 chance of gaining a fortune 1000 times as great.

Another problem with "maximize expected gain" is that it's often difficult or impossible to give objective numerical probabilities (except in cases involving things like dice or cards). How can we multiply probability by gain unless we can express both by numbers?

This imperative to "maximize expected gain" thus faces grave difficulties if taken as an overall guide to life. But it can sometimes be useful as a rough guide. At times it's helpful to work out the expected gain of the various alternatives, perhaps guessing at the probabilities and gains involved.

I once had two alternatives in choosing a flight for a hiking trip:

> Ticket A costs $250 and allows me to change my return date.

> Ticket B costs $200 and has a $125 charge if I change my return date.

Which ticket is a better deal for me? Intuitively, A is better if a change is very likely, while B is better if a change is very unlikely. But we can be more precise than that. Let x represent the probability of my changing the return. Then:

> Expected cost of A = $250.   Expected cost of B = $200 + ($125 · x).

Some algebra shows the expected costs to be identical if x is 40 percent. Thus A is better if a change is more than 40 percent likely, while B is better if a change is less likely than that. The actual probability of my having to change the return was clearly less than 40 percent; judging from my past, it was more like 10 percent. Thus, ticket B minimized my expected cost. So I bought ticket B.

In some cases, however, it might be more rational to pick A. Maybe I have $250 but I don't have the $325 that option B might cost me; so I'd be in great trouble if I had to change the return date. It might then be more rational to follow the "better safe than sorry" principle and pick A.

5.3a   Exercise – also LogiCola P (G, D, & V)

Suppose you decide to believe all and only statements that are more probable than not. You're tossing three coins; which of the next six statements would you believe?

> Either the first coin will be heads, or all three will be tails.

> You'd believe this, since it happens in 5 of 8 cases:
>
> **HHH** THH
> **HHT** THT
> **HTH** TTH
> **HTT** **TTT**

1. I'll get three heads.
2. I'll get at least one tail.
3. I'll get two heads and one tail.

4. I'll get either two heads and one tail, or else two tails and one head.
5. The first coin will be heads.

For problems 6 through 10, suppose you decide to do in all cases whatever would maximize your expected financial gain.

6. You're deciding whether to keep your life savings in a bank (which pays a dependable 10 percent) or invest in Mushy Software. If you invest in Mushy, you have a 99 percent chance of losing everything and a 1 percent chance of making 120 times your investment this year. What should you do?

7. You're deciding whether to get hospitalization insurance. There's a 1 percent chance per year that you'll have a $10,000 hospital visit (ignore other hospitalizations); the insurance would cover it all. What's the most you'd agree to pay per year for this insurance?

8. You're running a company that offers hospitalization insurance. There's a 1 percent chance per year that a customer will have a $10,000 hospital visit (ignore other hospitalizations); the insurance would cover it all. What's the least you could charge per year for this insurance to likely break even?

9. You're deciding whether to invest in Mushy Software or Enormity Incorporated. Mushy stock has a 30 percent probability of gaining 80 percent, and a 70 percent probability of losing 20 percent. Enormity stock has a 100 percent probability of gaining 11 percent. Which should you invest in?

10. You're deciding whether to buy a computer from Cut-Rate or Enormity. Both models perform identically. There's a 60 percent probability that either machine will need repair over the period you'll keep it. The Cut-Rate model is $600 but will be a total loss (requiring the purchase of another computer for $600) if it ever needs repair. The Enormity Incorporated model is $900 but offers free repairs. Which should you buy?

5.4 Reasoning from a sample

Recall our statistical syllogism about the Appalachian Trail:

> 90 percent of the AT shelters have water.
> Rocky Gap is an AT shelter.
> This is all we know about the matter.
> ∴ Probably Rocky Gap has water.

Premise 1 says 90 percent of the shelters have water. I might know this because I've checked all 300 shelters and found that 270 of them had water. But it's more likely that I base my claim on inductive reasoning. On my AT hikes, I've observed a large and varied group of shelters; about 90 percent of these have had water. I conclude that probably roughly 90 percent of *all* the shelters (including those not observed) have water:

> **Sample-Projection Syllogism**
>
> N percent of examined A's are B's.
> A large and varied group of A's has been examined.
> ∴ Probably roughly N percent of all A's are B's.

90 percent of examined AT shelters have water.
A large and varied group of AT shelters has been examined.
∴ Probably roughly 90 percent of all AT shelters have water.

Sample-projection reasoning presumes that a large and varied sample probably gives us a good idea of the whole. The strength of such reasoning depends on: (1) *size* of sample; (2) *variety* of sample; and (3) *cautiousness* of conclusion.

1. Other things being equal, a *larger sample* gives a stronger argument. A projection based on a small sample (ten shelters, for example) would be weak. My sample included about 150 shelters.

2. Other things being equal, a *more varied sample* gives a stronger argument. A sample is *varied* to the extent that it proportionally represents the diversity of the whole. AT shelters differ. Some are on high ridges, others are in valleys. Some are on the main trail, others are on blue-blazed side trails. Some are in wilderness areas, others are in rural areas. Our sample is varied to the extent that it reflects this diversity.

We'd have a weak argument if we examined only the dozen or so shelters in Georgia. This sample is small, has little variety, and covers only one part of the trail; but the poor sample might be all that we have to go on. Background information can help us to criticize a sample. Suppose we checked only AT shelters located on mountain tops or ridges. If we knew that water tends to be scarcer in such places, we'd judge this sample to be biased.

3. Other things being equal, we get a stronger argument if we have a *more cautious conclusion*. We have stronger reason for thinking the proportion of shelters with water is "between 80 and 95 percent" than for thinking that it's "between 89 and 91 percent." Our original argument says "roughly 90 percent." This is vague; whether it's too vague depends on our purposes.

Suppose our sample-projection argument is strong and has all true premises. Then it's likely that roughly 90 percent of the shelters have water. But the conclusion is only a rational guess; it could be far off. It's may even happen that every shelter we didn't check is bone dry. Inductive reasoning brings risk.

Here's another sample-projection argument:

> 52 percent of the voters we checked favor the Democrat.
> A large and varied group of voters has been checked.
> ∴ Probably roughly 52 percent of all voters favor the Democrat.

Again, our argument is stronger if we have a larger and more varied sample and a more cautious conclusion. A sample of 500 to 1000 people supposedly yields a margin of likely error of less than 5 percent; we should then construe our conclusion as "Probably between 57 percent and 47 percent of all voters favor the Democrat." To get a varied sample, we might select people using a random process that gives everyone an equal chance of being included. We also might try to have our sample proportionally represent groups (like farmers and the elderly) that tend to vote in a similar way. We should word our survey fairly and not intimidate people into giving a certain answer. And we should be clear whether we're checking registered voters or probable voters.

A sample-projection argument ends the way a statistical syllogism begins – with "N percent of all A's are B's." It's natural to connect the two:

> 90 percent of examined AT shelters have water.
> A large and varied group of AT shelters has been examined.
> ∴ Probably roughly 90 percent of all AT shelters have water.
> Rocky Gap is an AT shelter.
> This is all we know about the matter.
> ∴ It's roughly 90 percent probable that Rocky Gap has water.

Other variations are possible. We might use "all" instead of a percentage:

> All examined cats purr.
> A large and varied group of cats has been examined.
> ∴ Probably all cats purr.

This conclusion makes a strong claim, since a single non-purring cat would make it false; this makes the argument riskier and weaker. We could expand the argument further to draw a conclusion about a specific cat:

> All examined cats purr.
> A large and varied group of cats has been examined.
> ∴ Probably all cats purr.
> Socracat is a cat.
> ∴ Probably Socracat purrs.

Thus sample-projection syllogisms can have various forms.

5.4a   Exercise

Evaluate the following inductive arguments.

After contacting 2 million voters using telephone lists, we conclude that Landon will beat Roosevelt in 1936 by a landslide for the US presidency. (This was an actual prediction.)	The sample was biased. Those who could afford telephones during the Depression tended to be richer and more Republican. Roosevelt won easily.

1. I randomly examined 200 Loyola University of Chicago students at the law school and found that 15 percent were born in Chicago. So probably 15 percent of all Loyola students were born in Illinois.
2. I examined every Loyola student whose Social Security number ended in 3 and I found that exactly 78.4 percent of them were born in Chicago. So probably 78.4 percent of all Loyola students were born in Chicago.
3. Italians are generally fat and lazy. How do I know? Well, when I visited Rome for a weekend last year, all the hotel employees were fat and lazy – all six of them.
4. I meet many people in my daily activities; the great majority of them intend to vote for the Democrat. So the Democrat probably will win.
5. The sun has risen every day as long as humans can remember. So the sun will likely rise tomorrow. (How can we put this argument into standard form?)

Consider this inductive argument: "Lucy got an A on the first four logic quizzes, so probably she'll also get an A on the fifth logic quiz." Would each of the statements 6 through 10 strengthen or weaken this argument?

6. Lucy has been sick for the last few weeks and has missed most of her classes.
7. The first four quizzes were on formal logic, while the fifth is on informal logic.
8. Lucy has never received less than an A in her life.
9. A student in this course gets to drop the lowest of the five quizzes.
10. Lucy just took her Law School Admissions Test.

We'll see a deductive version of the classic argument from design for the existence of God in Section 7.1b (problem 4). The following inductive version of the argument has a sample-projection form and is very controversial. Evaluate the truth of the premises and the general inductive strength of the argument.

11. The universe is orderly (like a watch that follows complex laws).
    Most orderly things we've examined have intelligent designers.
    We've examined a large and varied group of orderly things.
    This is all we know about the matter.
    ∴ The universe probably has an intelligent designer.

5.5 Analogical reasoning

Suppose you're exploring your first Las Vegas casino. The casino is huge and filled with people. There are slot machines for nickels, dimes, quarters, and dollars. There are tables for blackjack and poker. There's a big roulette wheel. There's a bar and an inexpensive all-you-can-eat buffet.

You then go into your second Las Vegas casino and notice many of the same things: the size of the casino, the crowd, the slot machines, the blackjack and poker tables, the roulette wheel, and the bar. You're hungry. Recalling what you saw in your first casino, you conclude, "I bet this place has an inexpensive all-you-can-eat buffet, just like the first casino."

This is an argument by analogy. The first and second casinos are alike in many ways, so they're probably alike in some further way:

> Most things true of casino 1 also are true of casino 2.
> Casino 1 has an all-you-can-eat buffet.
> This is all we know about the matter.
> ∴ Probably casino 2 also has an all-you-can-eat buffet.

Here's a more wholesome example (about Appalachian Trail shelters):

> Most things true of the first AT shelter are true of this second one.
> The first AT shelter had a logbook for visitors.
> This is all we know about the matter.
> ∴ Probably this second shelter also has a logbook for visitors.

We argue that things similar in many ways are likely similar in a further way. Statistical and analogical arguments are closely related:

Statistical	*Analogical*
Most large casinos have buffets.	Most things true of casino 1 are true of casino 2.
Circus Circus is a large casino.	Casino 1 has a buffet.
That is all we know about it.	That is all we know about it.
∴ Probably Circus Circus has a buffet.	∴ Probably casino 2 has a buffet.

The first rests on our experience of *many casinos*, while the second rests on our experience of *many features* that two casinos have in common.

Here's the general form of the analogy syllogism:

> **Analogy Syllogism**
>
> Most things true of X also are true of Y.
> X is A.
> This is all we know about the matter.
> ∴ Probably Y is A.

Premise 1 is rough. In practice, we don't just count similarities; rather we look for how relevant the similarities are to the conclusion. While the two casinos were alike in many ways, they also differed in some ways:

- Casino 1 has a name whose first letter is "S," while casino 2 doesn't.
- Casino 1 has a name whose second letter is "A," while casino 2 doesn't.
- Casino 1 has quarter slot machines by the front entrance, while casino 2 has dollar slots there.

These factors aren't relevant and so don't weaken our argument that casino 2 has a buffet. But the following differences would weaken the argument:

- Casino 1 is huge, while casino 2 is small.
- Casino 1 has a bar, while casino 2 doesn't.
- Casino 1 has a big sign advertising a buffet, while casino 2 has no such sign.

These factors would make a buffet in casino 2 less likely.

So we don't just count similarities when we argue by analogy; many similarities are trivial and unimportant. Rather, we look to *relevant* similarities. But how do we decide which similarities are relevant? We somehow appeal to our background information about what things are likely to go together. It's difficult to give rules here – even vague ones.

Our "Analogy Syllogism" formulation is a rough sketch of a subtle form of reasoning. Analogical reasoning is elusive and difficult to put into strict rules.

5.5a Exercise – also LogiCola P (I)

Suppose you're familiar with this Gensler logic book but with no others. Your friend Sarah is taking logic and uses another book. You think to yourself, "My book discusses analogical reasoning, and so Sarah's book likely does too." Which of these bits of information would strengthen or weaken this argument – and why?

Sarah's course is a specialized graduate course on quantified modal logic.	This weakens the argument; such a course probably wouldn't discuss analogical reasoning. (This answer presumes background information.)

1. Sarah's book has a different color.
2. Sarah's book also has chapters on syllogisms, propositional logic, quantificational logic, and meaning and definitions.
3. Sarah's course is taught by a member of the mathematics department.
4. Sarah's chapter on syllogisms doesn't use the star test.
5. Sarah's book is abstract and has few real-life examples.
6. Sarah's book isn't published by Routledge Press.
7. Sarah's book is entirely on informal logic.
8. Sarah's book has cartoons.
9. Sarah's book has 100 pages on inductive reasoning.
10. Sarah's book has 10 pages on inductive reasoning.

Suppose your friend Tony at another school took an ethics course that discussed utilitarianism. You're taking an ethics course next semester. You think to yourself, "Tony's course discussed utilitarianism, and so my course likely will too." Which of these bits of information would strengthen or weaken this argument – and why?

11. Tony's teacher transferred to your school and will teach your course as well.
12. Tony's course was in medical ethics, while yours is in general ethical theory.

13.   Both courses use the same textbook.
14.   Tony's teacher has a good reputation, while yours doesn't.
15.   Your teacher is a Marxist, while Tony's isn't.

5.6   Analogy and other minds

We'll now study a classic philosophical example of analogical reasoning. This will help us to appreciate the elusive nature of such arguments.

Consider these two hypotheses:

> There are other con-
> scious beings besides me,
> other beings with inner
> thoughts and feelings.

> I'm the only conscious being. Other
> humans are like cleverly constructed
> robots; they have outer behavior but
> no inner thoughts and feelings.

We all accept the first hypothesis and reject the second. How can we justify this intellectually? Consider that I can directly feel my own pain, but not the pain of others. When I experience the *pain behavior* of others, how do I know that this behavior manifests an inner experience of pain?

One approach appeals to an argument from analogy:

> Most things true of me also are true of Jones. (We are both alike in
>   general behavior, nervous system, and so on.)
> I generally feel pain when showing outward pain behavior.
> This is all I know about the matter.
> ∴ Probably Jones also feels pain when showing outward pain behavior.

By this argument, Jones and I are alike in most respects. So probably we're alike in a further respect – that we both feel pain when we show pain behavior. But then there would be other conscious beings besides me.

Here are four ways to criticize this argument:

1.   Jones and I also *differ* in many ways. These differences, if relevant, would weaken the argument.

2.   Since I can't directly feel Jones's pain, I can't have direct access to the truth of the conclusion. This makes the argument peculiar and may weaken it.

3.   I have a sample-projection argument *against* the claim that there are other conscious beings besides me:

> All the conscious experiences that I've experienced are mine.
> I've examined a large and varied group of conscious experiences.
> ∴ Probably *all* conscious experiences are mine.

The conclusion is another way to say that I'm the only conscious being. Is this a strong argument? Can we disqualify my sample as "not varied" without already presuming that other conscious beings exist (which begs the question)? Any strength that this argument has detracts from the strength of the analogical argument for other minds.

4.   Since the analogical argument is weakened by such considerations, it at most makes it only *somewhat probable* that there are other conscious beings. But normally we take this belief to be *solidly based*.

Suppose we reject the analogical argument. Then *why* should we believe in other minds? Perhaps because it is a commonsense belief that hasn't been disproved and that's in our practical and emotional interests to accept. Or perhaps because of a special rule of evidence, not based on analogy, that experiencing another's behavior justifies beliefs about the other's mental states. Or perhaps because talk about mental states is really just talk about behavior (so "being in pain" means "showing pain behavior"). Or maybe there's no answer – and I don't really *know* if there are other conscious beings besides me.

The analogical argument for other minds highlights some problems with induction. Philosophers seldom dispute whether *deductive* arguments have a correct connection between premises and conclusion; instead, they dispute the truth of the premises. But *inductive* arguments are different. Here, it's often hotly disputed whether and to what extent the premises, if true, provide good reason for accepting the conclusion. Those who like things neat and tidy prefer deductive to inductive reasoning.

5.7   Mill's methods

John Stuart Mill, a 19th-century British philosopher, formulated five methods for arriving at and justifying beliefs about causes. We'll study three of his methods. His basic idea is that factors that regularly occur together are likely to be causally related.

Suppose Alice, Bob, Carol, and David were at a party. Alice and David got sick, and food poisoning is suspected. Hamburgers, pie, and ice cream were served. This chart shows who ate what and who got sick:

	Hamburger	Pie	Ice Cream	Sick
Alice	yes	yes	no	yes
Bob	no	no	yes	no
Carol	yes	no	no	no
David	no	yes	yes	yes

To find what caused the sickness, we'd search for a factor that correlates with the "yes" answers in the "sick" column. This suggests that the pie did it. Pie is the only thing eaten by all and only those who got sick. This reasoning reflects Mill's method of agreement:

Agreement	Sickness occurred more than once.
A occurred more than once. B is the only additional factor that occurred if and only if A occurred. ∴ Probably B caused A, or A caused B.	Eating pie is the only additional factor that occurred if and only if sickness occurred. ∴ Probably eating pie caused sickness, or sickness caused the eating of pie.

The second alternative, that sickness caused the eating of pie (perhaps by bringing about a special craving?), is interesting but implausible. So we'd conclude that the people probably got sick because of eating pie.

The "probably" is important. Eating the pie and getting sick might just happen to have occurred together; maybe there's no causal connection between the two. Some factor not on our chart might have caused the sickness; maybe Alice and David got sick from backpacking in the rain. Or maybe Alice's sickness and David's had different causes.

We took for granted a simplifying assumption. We assumed that the two cases of sickness had the same cause which was a single factor on our list and always caused sickness. Our investigation may force us to give up this assumption and consider more complex solutions. But it's good to try simple solutions first and avoid complex ones as long as we can.

We also can conclude that eating the hamburgers doesn't necessarily make a person sick, since Carol ate them but didn't get sick. Similarly, eating the ice cream doesn't necessarily make a person sick, since Bob ate it but didn't get sick. Let's call this sort of reasoning the "method of disagreement":

Disagreement	Eating the ice cream occurred in Bob's case.
A occurred in some case. B didn't occur in the same case. ∴ A doesn't necessarily cause B.	Sickness didn't occur in Bob's case. ∴ Eating the ice cream doesn't necessarily cause sickness.

Mill used this form of reasoning but didn't include it in his five methods.

Suppose *two* factors – eating pie and eating hamburgers – occurred in just those cases where someone got sick. Then the method of agreement wouldn't lead to any definite conclusion about which caused the sickness. To make sure it was the pie, we might do an experiment. We take two people, Eduardo and Frank, who are as alike as possible in health and diet. We give them all the same things to eat, except that we feed pie to Eduardo but not to Frank. (This is unethical, but it makes a good example.) Then we see what happens. Suppose Eduardo gets sick but Frank doesn't; then we can conclude that the pie probably caused the sickness. This follows Mill's method of difference:

Difference	
A occurred in the first case but not the second. The cases are otherwise identical, except that B also occurred in the first case but not in the second. ∴ Probably B is (or is part of) the cause of A, or A is (or is part of) the cause of B.	Sickness occurred in Eduardo's case but not Frank's. The cases are otherwise identical, except that eating pie occurred in Eduardo's case but not Frank's. ∴ Probably eating pie is (or is part of) the cause of the sickness, or the sickness is (or is part of) the cause of eating pie.

Since we caused Eduardo to eat the pie, we reject the second pair of alternatives. So probably eating pie is (or is part of) the cause of the sickness. The cause might simply be the eating of the pie (which contained a virus). Or the cause might be this combined with one's poor physical condition.

Another unethical experiment illustrates Mill's method of variation. This time we find four victims (George, Henry, Isabel, and Jodi) and feed them varying amounts of pie. They get sick in varying degrees:

	Pie	Sick
George	tiny slice	slightly
Henry	small slice	somewhat
Isabel	normal slice	very
Jodi	two slices	wants to die

We conclude that the pie probably caused the sickness. This follows Mill's method of variation:

Variation	
A changes in a certain way if and only if B also changes in a certain way. ∴ Probably B's changes caused A's, or A's caused B's, or some C caused both.	The person's sickness was greater if and only if the person ate more pie. ∴ Probably eating pie caused the sickness, or the sickness caused the eating of pie, or something else caused both the eating and the sickness.

The last two alternatives are implausible. So we conclude that eating pie probably caused the sickness.

Mill's methods often give us a conclusion with several alternatives. Sometimes we can eliminate an alternative because of temporal sequence; the cause can't happen after the effect. Suppose we conclude this:

> Either laziness during previous months caused the F on the final exam,
> or the F on the final exam caused laziness during the previous months.

Here we'd reject the second alternative.

In applying Mill's methods, we should know that "cause" can mean either "total cause" or "partial cause." Suppose Jones got shot and then died. Misapplying the method of disagreement, we might conclude that being shot didn't cause the death, since some who are shot don't die. But the proper conclusion is rather that being shot doesn't necessarily cause death. We also can conclude that being shot wasn't the *total* cause of Jones's death (even though it might be a partial cause). What caused Jones's death wasn't just that he was shot. What caused the death was that he was shot in a certain way (for example, through the head) in certain circumstances (for example, with no medical help available). This is the total cause; anyone shot in that exact way in those exact circumstances (including the same physical and mental condition) would have died. The method of disagreement deals with total causes, not partial causes.

The ambiguities of the word "cause" run deep. "Factor A causes factor B" could mean any combination of these:

> The presence of factor A will always (or probably) by itself (or in combination with some factor C) directly (or through a further causal chain) bring about the presence of factor B; or the absence of factor A will ... bring about the absence of factor B; or both.

The probabilistic sense is controversial. Suppose the incidence of lung cancer varies closely with heavy smoking, so heavy smokers are much more likely to get lung cancer. Could this probabilistic connection be enough for us to say that heavy smoking is a (partial) cause of lung cancer? Or is it wrong to use "cause" unless we come up with some factor C such that heavy smoking when combined with factor C *always* results in lung cancer? At least part of the debate over whether a "causal connection" exists between heavy smoking and lung cancer is semantic. Does it make sense to use "cause" with probabilistic connections? If we can speak of Russian roulette *causing* death, then we can speak of heavy smoking *causing* lung cancer.

5.7a   Exercise – also LogiCola P (M & B)

Draw whatever conclusions you can using Mill's methods; supplement Mill's methods by common sense when appropriate. Say which method you're using, what alternatives you conclude from the method itself, and how you narrow the conclusion down to a single alternative. Also say when Mill's methods lead to no definite conclusion.

> Kristen's computer gave error messages when she booted up. We changed things one at a time to see what would stop the messages. What worked was updating the video driver.

> By the difference method, probably updating the driver caused (or partially caused) the error messages to stop, or stopping the messages caused (or partially caused) us to update the driver. The latter can't be, since the cause can't happen after the effect. So probably updating the driver caused (or partially caused) the error messages to stop.

1. Experiments show that a person's reaction time is much longer after a few drinks but is relatively uninfluenced by a series of other factors.

2. A study showed that people with no bacteria in their mouth get no cavities – and that people with no food particles in their mouth get no cavities. However, people with both bacteria and food particles in their mouth get cavities.

3. Whenever Michelle drinks scotch and *soda*, she has a hangover the next day. Whenever she drinks gin and *soda*, she gets a hangover. Likewise, whenever she drinks rum and *soda*, she gets a hangover.

4. The morning disc jockey on a Cleveland radio station remarked in early December that the coldest temperature of the day seemed to occur later and later in the morning. The weather person pointed out that the sunrise had been getting later and later. In a few weeks both processes would reverse themselves, with the sunrise and the coldest temperature of the day both occurring earlier every day.

5. Our research team at the medical center just discovered a new blood factor called "factor K." Factor K occurs in everyone who has cancer but in no one else.

6. When I sat eating on the rock slab in Grand Gulch, armies of little ants invaded the slab. Later I sat on the slab the same way except that I didn't eat anything. In the second case the ants didn't invade the slab.

7. We just did an interesting study comparing the vacation periods of employees and the disappearance of food items. We found that when Megan is working, the items disappear, and when she's away, they don't disappear.

8. People in several parts of the country have lower rates of tooth decay. Investigations show that the only thing different about these places is that their water supply contains fluoride.

9. We did an experiment where we selected two more or less identical groups and put fluoride in the first group's water but not in the second group's. The first group had a lower rate of tooth decay.

10. Many backpackers think eating raw garlic gives you an odor that causes mosquitoes not to bite you. When hiking a mosquito-infested part of the Bruce Trail, I ate much raw garlic. The mosquitoes bit me in their usual bloodthirsty manner.

11. Little Will throws food on the floor and receives signs of disapproval from Mommy and Daddy. Such things happen regularly. When he eats his food without throwing it on the floor, he doesn't get any disapproval.

12. Everyone in our study who became a heroin addict had first tried marijuana.

13. If you rub two surfaces together, the surfaces get warm. They'll get warmer and warmer as you rub the surfaces together harder and faster.

14. When we plot how many hours Alex studies against the grades he gets for his various exams, we see a close correlation.

15. Matches that aren't either heated or struck don't light. Matches that are wet don't light. Matches that aren't in the presence of oxygen don't light. Matches that are heated or struck, dry, and in the presence of oxygen do light.

16. Little Will made a discovery. He keeps moving the lever on the radio up and down. He notices that the music gets louder and softer when he does this.

17. We made a careful study of the heart rate of athletes and how it correlates with various factors. The only significant correlation we found is that those who do aerobic exercise (and those alone) have lower heart rates.

18. We investigated many objects with a crystalline structure. The only thing they have in common is that all solidified from a liquid state. (Mill used this example.)

19. After long investigation, we found a close correlation between night and day. If you have night, then there invariably, in a few hours, follows day. If you have day, then invariably, in a few hours, there follows night.

20. Young Will has been experimenting with his electrical meter. He found that if he increases the electrical voltage, then he also increases the current.

21. Whenever Kurt wears his headband, he makes all his field goals. Whenever he doesn't wear it, he misses them all. This has been going on for many years.

22. The fish in my father's tank all died. We suspected either the fish food or the water temperature. We bought more fish and did everything the same except for changing the fish food. All the fish died. We then bought more fish and did everything the same except for changing the water temperature. The fish lived.

23. Bacteria introduced by visitors from the planet Krypton are causing an epidemic. We've found that everyone exposed to the bacteria gets sick and dies – except those who have a higher-than-normal heart rate.

24. When we chart the inflation rate next to the growth in the national debt over several years, we find a close correlation.

25. On my first backpack trip, I hiked long distances but wore only a single pair of socks. I got bad blisters on my feet. On my second trip, I did everything the same except that I wore two pairs of socks. I got only minor blisters.

5.8 Scientific laws

Ohm's Law is an important principle with many electrical applications. "Law" here suggests great scientific dignity and backing. Ohm's Law is more than a mere *hypothesis* (preliminary conjecture) or even a *theory* (with more backing than a hypothesis but less than a law).

Ohm's Law is a formula relating electric current, voltage, and resistance:

Ohm's Law	where:	I = current (in amps)
I = E/R		E = voltage (in volts)
		R = resistance (in ohms)

An electric current of 1 amp (ampere) is a flow of 6,250,000,000,000,000,000 electrons per second; a 100-watt bulb draws almost an amp, and the fuse blows if you draw over 15 amps. To push the electrons, you need a voltage; your outlet may have 117 volts and your flashlight battery 1.5 volts. The voltage encounters an electrical resistance, which influences how many electrons flow per second. A short thick wire has low resistance (less than an ohm) while an inch of air has high resistance (billions of ohms). Small carbon resistors go from less than an ohm to millions of ohms. Ohm's Law says that the current increases if you raise the voltage or lower the resistance.

Electric current is like the flow of water through a garden hose. Voltage is like water pressure. Electrical resistance is like the resistance to the water flow provided by your hose; a long, thin hose has greater resistance than a short, thick one. The current or flow of water is measured in gallons per minute; it increases if you raise the water pressure or use a hose with less resistance.

Ohm's Law is a mathematical formula that lets us calculate various results. Suppose we put a 10-ohm resistor across your 117-volt electrical outlet; we'd get a current of 11.7 amps (not quite enough to blow your fuse):

$$I = E/R = 117 \text{ volts}/10 \text{ ohms} = 11.7 \text{ amps}.$$

Ohm's Law deals with unobservable properties (current, voltage, resistance) and entities (electrons). Science allows unobservables if they have testable consequences or can somehow be measured. The term "unobservable" is vague. Actually we can feel certain voltages. The 1.5 volts from your flashlight battery can't normally be felt, slightly higher voltages give a slight tingle, and the 117 volts from your outlet can give a dangerous jolt. Philosophers dispute the status of unobservable entities. Are the ultimate elements of reality unobservables like atoms and electrons, or commonsense objects like chairs, or both? Or are atoms and chairs both just fictions to help us talk about our sensations?

We can ask how scientific laws are *discovered*, or we can ask how they're *verified*. History can tell us how Georg Simon Ohm discovered his law in 1827; philosophy is more concerned with how such laws are verified (or shown to be true), regardless of their origins. Basically, scientific laws are verified by a combination of observation and argument; but the details get complicated.

Suppose we want to verify Ohm's Law. We are given batteries and resistors. We also are given a meter for measuring current, voltage, and resistance. The meter simplifies our task; we don't have to worry about defining the fundamental units (ampere, volt, and ohm) and inventing ways to measure them. Wouldn't the meter make our task too easy? Couldn't we just do a few experiments and then base Ohm's Law on the results, using standard deductive and inductive reasoning? Unfortunately, it isn't that simple.

Suppose we hook up batteries of different voltages to a resistor:

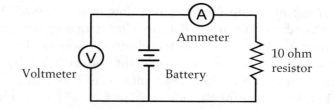

The voltmeter measures the voltage, and the ammeter measures the current. We start with a 10-ohm resistor. We try voltages of 1 volt and 2 volts and get currents of .1 amp and .2 amp. Here's a chart with the results:

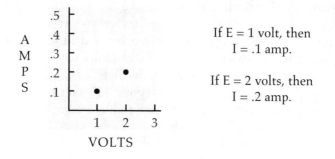

If E = 1 volt, then
I = .1 amp.

If E = 2 volts, then
I = .2 amp.

This accords with Ohm, since:

If E = 1 volt, then I = .1 amp.
(I = E/R = 1/10 = .1)

If E = 2 volts, then I = .2 amp.
(I = E/R = 2/10 = .2)

On this basis, we argue inductively as follows:

All examined voltage-resistance-current cases follow Ohm.
A large and varied group of such cases has been examined.
∴ Probably all such cases follow Ohm.

Premise 2 is weak, since we tried only two cases. But we can easily perform more experiments; after we do so, Ohm would seem to be securely based.

The problem is that we can give an equally strong inductive argument for a second and incompatible hypothesis: "I = (E^2 - 2E + 2)/R." Let's call this *Mho's Law* (although it isn't a "law"). Surprisingly, our test results also accord with Mho:

If E = 1 volt, then I = .1 amp.

I = (E^2 - 2E + 2)/R
= (1^2 - 2·1 + 2)/10
= (1 - 2 + 2)/10 = 1/10 = .1

If E = 2 volts, then I = .2 amp.

I = (E^2 - 2E + 2)/R
= (2^2 - 2·2 + 2)/10
= (4 - 4 + 2)/10 = 2/10 = .2

So each examined case follows Mho. We can argue inductively as follows:

All examined voltage-resistance-current cases follow Mho.
A large and varied group of such cases has been examined.
∴ Probably all such cases follow Mho.

This inductive argument for Mho seems as strong as the one we gave for Ohm. Judging just from these arguments and test results, there seems to be no reason for preferring Ohm over Mho, or Mho over Ohm.

The two laws, while agreeing on both test cases so far, give conflicting predictions for further cases. Ohm says we'll get 0 amps with 0 volts, and .3 amp with 3 volts; Mho says we'll get .2 amp with 0 volts, and .5 amp with 3 volts:

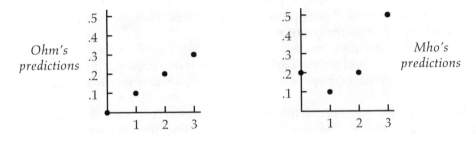

The two laws are genuinely different, even though both give the same results for a voltage of 1 or 2 volts.

We have to try a crucial experiment to decide between the theories. What happens with 3 volts? Ohm says we'll get .3 amp, but Mho says we'll get .5 amp. If we do the experiment and get .3 amp, this would falsify Mho:

	Valid
If Mho is correct and we apply 3 volts to this 10-ohm resistor, then we get .5 amp current.	If M and A, then G
We apply 3 volts to this 10-ohm resistor.	A
We don't get .5 amp current.	Not-G
∴ Mho isn't correct.	∴ Not-M

Premise 1 links a scientific hypothesis (Mho) to antecedent conditions (that 3 volts have been applied to the 10-ohm resistor) to give a testable prediction (that we'll get .5 amp current). Premise 2 says the antecedent conditions have been fulfilled. But premise 3 says the results conflict with what was predicted. Since this argument has true premises and is deductively valid, our experiment shows Mho to be wrong.

Does our experiment similarly show that Ohm is correct? Unfortunately not. Consider this argument:

	Invalid
If Ohm is correct and we apply 3 volts to this 10-ohm resistor, then we get .3 amp current.	If O and A, then G
We apply 3 volts to this 10-ohm resistor.	A
We get .3 amp current.	G
∴ Ohm is correct.	∴ O

This is invalid, as we could check using propositional logic (Chapter 6). So the premises don't prove that Ohm is correct; and Ohm might fail for further cases. But the experiment strengthens our inductive argument for Ohm, since it gives a larger and more varied sample. So we can have greater trust that the pattern observed to hold so far will continue to hold.

Here are three aspects of scientific method:

- *Scientists often set up crucial experiments to decide between conflicting theories.* Scientists like to dream up alternative theories and look for ways to decide between them.
- *We can sometimes deductively refute a theory through a crucial experiment.* Experimental results, when combined with other suitable premises, can logically entail the falsity of a theory.
- *We can't deductively prove a theory using experiments.* Experiments can inductively support a theory and deductively refute opposing theories. But they can't eliminate the possibility of the theory's failing for further cases.

Recall how the Mho problem arose. We had two test cases that agreed with Ohm. These test cases also agreed with another formula, one we called "Mho"; and the inductive argument for Mho seemed as strong as the one for Ohm. But Ohm and Mho gave conflicting predictions for further test cases. So we did a crucial experiment to decide between the two. Ohm won.

But there's always another Mho behind the bush – so our problems aren't over. However many experiments we do, there are always alternative theories that agree with all test cases so far but disagree on some further predictions. In fact, there's always an *infinity* of theories that do this. No matter how many dots we put on the chart (representing test results), we could draw an unlimited number of lines that go through all these dots but otherwise diverge.

Suppose we conduct 1000 experiments in which Ohm works. There are alternative theories Pho, Qho, Rho, and so on that agree on these 1000 test cases but give conflicting predictions about further cases. And each theory seems to be equally supported by the same kind of inductive argument:

> All examined voltage-resistance-current cases follow this theory.
> A large and varied group of such cases has been examined.
> ∴ Probably all such cases follow this theory.

Even after 1000 experiments, Ohm is just one of infinitely many formulas that seem equally probable on the basis of the test results and inductive logic.

In practice, we prefer Ohm on the basis of *simplicity*. Ohm is the simplest formula that agrees with all our test results. So we prefer Ohm to the alternatives and see Ohm as firmly based.

What is simplicity and how can we decide which of two scientific theories is simpler? We don't have neat and tidy answers to these questions. In practice, though, we can tell that Ohm is simpler than Mho; we judge that Ohm's formula and straight line are simpler than Mho's formula and curved line. We don't have a clear and satisfying definition of "simplicity"; yet we can apply this notion in a rough way in many cases.

We can express the simplicity criterion this way (this is a form of *Ockham's Razor* – see Section 16.2):

> **Simplicity criterion:** Other things being equal, we ought to prefer a simpler theory to a more complex one.

The "other things being equal" qualification is important. Experiments may force us to accept very complex theories; but we shouldn't take such theories seriously unless we're forced to.

It's unclear how to justify the simplicity criterion. Since inductive reasoning stumbles unless we presuppose the criterion, an inductive justification would be circular. Perhaps the criterion is a self-evident truth not in need of justification. Or perhaps the criterion is pragmatically justified:

If the simplicity criterion isn't correct, then no scientific laws are justified.
Some scientific laws are justified.
∴ The simplicity criterion is correct.

Does premise 2 beg the question against the skeptic? Can this premise be defended without appealing to the criterion? The simplicity criterion is vague and raises complex problems, but we can't do without it.

Coherence is another factor that's important for choosing between theories:

> **Coherence criterion:** Other things being equal, we ought to prefer a theory that harmonizes with existing well-established beliefs.

Mho has trouble here, since it predicts that 0 volts across a 10-ohm resistor produces a .2 amp current. But then it follows, using an existing well-grounded belief that current through a resistor produces heat, that a 10-ohm resistor with no voltage applied produces heat. While nice for portable handwarmers, this would be difficult to harmonize with the conservation of energy. So the coherence criterion leads us to doubt Mho.

Do further tests continue to confirm Ohm? The answer is complicated. Some resistors give, not a straight-line chart, but a curve; this happens if we use an incandescent light bulb for the resistor. Instead of rejecting Ohm, scientists say that heating the resistor changes the resistance. This seems satisfactory, since the curve becomes straighter if the resistor is kept cooler. And we can measure changes in resistance when the resistor is heated externally.

Another problem is that resistors will burn up or explode if enough voltage is applied. This brings an irregularity into the straight-line chart. But again, scientists regard this as changing the resistance, and not as falsifying Ohm.

A more serious problem is that some devices don't even roughly approximate the pattern predicted by Ohm. A Zener diode, for example, draws almost no current until a critical voltage is reached; then it draws a high current:

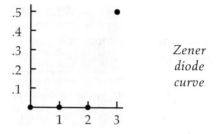

Do such devices refute Ohm? Not necessarily. Scientists implicitly qualify Ohm so it applies just to "pure resistances" and not to things like Zener diodes. This seems circular. Suppose that a "pure resistor" is any device that satisfies Ohm. Then isn't it circular to say that Ohm holds for "pure resistors"? Doesn't this just mean that Ohm works for any device for which it works?

In practice, people working in electronics quickly learn which devices satisfy Ohm and which don't. The little tubular "resistors" follow Ohm closely (neglecting slight changes caused by heating and major changes when we burn up the resistor). Zener diodes, transistors, and other semiconductors generally don't follow Ohm. So Ohm can be a useful principle, even though it's difficult to specify in any precise and non-circular manner the cases where it applies.

5.8a   Exercise

Sketch in a rough way how we might verify or falsify these hypotheses. Point out any special difficulties likely to arise.

| Women have less innate logical ability than men. | We'd give a logic test to large and varied groups of either sex, and see how results differ. If women tested lower [they don't – judging from a test I designed for a friend in psychology], this wouldn't itself prove lower innate ability, since the lower scores might come from different social expectations or upbringing. It would be difficult to avoid this problem completely; but we might try testing groups in cultures with less difference in social expectations and upbringing. |

1. Neglecting air resistance, objects of any weight fall at the same speed.
2. Germs cause colds.
3. A huge Ice-Age glacier covered most of Wisconsin about 10,000 years ago.
4. Regular moderate use of marijuana is no more harmful than regular moderate use of alcohol.

5. When couples have several children, the child born first tends to have greater innate intelligence than the one born last.
6. Career-oriented women tend to have marriages that are more successful than those of home-oriented women.
7. Factor K causes cancer.
8. Water is made up of molecules consisting of two atoms of hydrogen and one atom of oxygen.
9. Organisms of a given biological species randomly develop slightly different traits; organisms with survival-promoting traits tend to survive and pass these traits to their offspring. New biological species result when this process continues over millions of years. This is how complex species developed from simple organisms, and how humans developed from lower species.
10. Earth was created 5,000 years ago, complete with all current biological species.

5.9   Best-explanation reasoning

Suppose you made fudge in the morning for an afternoon party. When you later open the refrigerator, you find that most of the fudge is gone. You also find that your five-year-old son, who has a history of stealing deserts, has fudge on his face. The child denies that he ate the fudge. He contends that Martians appeared, ate the fudge, and spread some on his face. But you aren't fooled. The better and more likely explanation is the child ate the fudge. And so this is what you believe.

This is an example of an **inference to the best explanation**. The principle behind such reasoning is that we should accept the best explanation for the data. Consider what we said about Ohm's Law in the previous section. Ohm's Law explains a wide range of phenomena about electrical voltage, current, and resistance. Besides having testable implications that accord well with our experience, the law also has other virtues, including clarity, simplicity, and coherence with existing well-established beliefs. Unless someone comes up with a better explanation of the data, we should accept Ohm's Law.

Our best argument for the theory of evolution has a similar form:

> We ought to accept the best explanation for the wide range of empirical facts about biological organisms (including comparative structure, embryology, geographical distribution, and fossil records).
> The best explanation for the wide range of empirical facts about biological organisms is evolution.
> ∴ We ought to accept evolution.

A fuller formulation would elaborate on what these empirical facts are, alternative ways to explain them, and why evolution provides a better explanation than its rivals. Some say that our core beliefs about most things, including the existence of material objects, other minds, and perhaps even God, are to be justified as inferences to the best explanation.

Particularly interesting is the related "fine-tuning" inference for the existence of God. Here the empirical data to be explained is that the basic physical constants that govern the universe (like the gravitational constant "g," the charge and mass of the proton, the density of water, and the total mass of the universe) are within the exceedingly narrow range that makes it possible for life to evolve. Steven Hawking gives this example: "If the rate of expansion one second after the big bang had been smaller by even one part in a hundred thousand million million, the universe would have recollapsed before it ever reached its present size"[1] – which would have blocked the evolution of life. So life requires the expansion rate to be correct to the 17th decimal place; and other constants are similar. How is this empirical data to be explained? Could this precise combination of physical constants have come about by chance? Some atheists propose that there are an infinity of parallel universes, each governed by a different physics, and that it was highly likely that *some* of these parallel universes could produce life. Many theists claim that the simplest and best explanation involves God: that the universe was caused by a great mind who "fine tuned" its physical laws to make possible the emergence of life.

The general form of the inference to the best explanation raises some issues. On what grounds should we evaluate one explanation as "better" than another? Should we accept the *best possible* explanation (even though no one may yet have thought of it) or the *best currently available* explanation (even though none of the current explanations may be very good)? And why is the best explanation most likely to be the true one?

5.10   Problems with induction

We've seen in previous sections that inductive logic isn't as neat and tidy as deductive logic. Now we'll consider two further perplexing problems: how to *formulate* principles of inductive logic and how to *justify* these principles.

We've formulated inductive principles in rough ways that if taken literally can lead to absurdities. For example, our statistical-syllogism formulation can lead to this absurd inference:

> 60 percent of all Cleveland voters are Democrats.
> This non-Democrat is a Cleveland voter.
> This is all we know about the matter.
> ∴ It's 60 percent probable that this non-Democrat is a Democrat.

---

[1] *A Brief History of Time*, tenth anniversary edition (New York: Bantam Books, 1998), page 126; he also gives other examples and discusses their theological implications. See also Anthony Flew's *There Is a God* (New York: HarperCollins, 2007), pages 113–21, and Francis S. Collins's *The Language of God* (New York: Free Press, 2006), pages 63–84. For a computer-game version of the argument, see http://www.jcu.edu/philosophy/gensler/genesis.exe (Windows only).

Actually, "This non-Democrat is a Democrat" is 0 percent probable, since it's a self-contradiction. So our statistical syllogism principle isn't entirely correct.

We noted that the analogy syllogism is oversimplified in its formulation. We need to rely on *relevant similarities* instead of just counting resemblances. But "relevant similarities" is hard to pin down.

Sample-projection syllogisms suffer from a problem raised by Nelson Goodman. Consider this argument:

> All examined diamonds are hard.
> A large and varied group of diamonds has been examined.
> ∴ Probably all diamonds are hard.

Suppose the premises are true; then the argument would seem to be a good one. But consider this second argument, which has the same form except that we substitute a more complex phrase for "hard":

> All examined diamonds are such that they are hard-if-
> and-only-if-they-were-examined-before-2222.
> A large and varied group of diamonds has been examined.
> ∴ Probably all diamonds are such that they are hard-if-and-
> only-if-they-were-examined-before-2222.

Premise 1 is tricky to understand. It isn't yet 2222. So if all examined diamonds are hard, then they are such that they are hard-if-and-only-if-they-were-examined-before-2222. So premise 1 is true. Premise 2 also is true. Then this second argument also would seem to be a good one.

Consider a diamond X that will first be examined after 2222. By our first argument, diamond X probably *is* hard; by the second, it probably *isn't* hard. So our sample projection argument leads to conflicting conclusions.

Philosophers have discussed this problem for decades. Some suggest that we qualify the sample-projection syllogism form to outlaw the second argument; but it's not clear how to eliminate the bad apples without also eliminating the good ones. As yet, there's no agreement on how to solve the problem.

Goodman's problem is somewhat like one we saw in the last section. Here we had similar inductive arguments for two incompatible laws: Ohm and Mho:

All examined electrical cases follow Ohm's Law.	All examined electrical cases follow Mho's Law.
A large and varied group of cases has been examined.	A large and varied group of cases has been examined.
∴ Probably all electrical cases follow Ohm's Law.	∴ Probably all electrical cases follow Mho's Law.

Even after 1000 experiments, there still are an *infinity* of theories that give the same test results in these 1000 cases but conflicting results in further cases.

And we could "prove," using an inductive argument, that each of these incompatible theories is probably true. But this is absurd. We can't have each of an infinity of conflicting theories be probably true. Our sample-projection syllogism thus leads to absurdities.

We got around this problem in the scientific-theory case by appealing to simplicity: "Other things being equal, we ought to prefer a *simpler* theory to a more complex one." While "simpler" here is vague and difficult to explain, we seem to need some such simplicity criterion to justify any scientific theory.

Simplicity is important in our diamond case, since 1 is simpler than 2:

> 1.   All diamonds are hard.
> 2.   All diamonds are such that they are hard-if-and-only-if-they-were-examined-before-2222.

By our simplicity criterion, we ought to prefer 1 to 2, even if both have equally strong inductive backing. So the sample-projection syllogism seems to need a simplicity qualification too; but it's not clear how to formulate it.

So it's difficult to formulate clear inductive-logic principles that don't lead to absurdities. Inductive logic is less neat and tidy than deductive logic.

Our second problem is how to justify inductive principles. For now, let's ignore the problem we just talked about. Let's pretend that we have clear inductive principles that roughly accord with our practice and don't lead to absurdities. Why follow these principles?

Consider this inductive argument (which says roughly that the sun will probably come up tomorrow, since it has come up every day in the past):

> All examined days are days in which the sun comes up.
> A large and varied group of days has been examined.
> Tomorrow is a day.
> ∴ Probably tomorrow is a day in which the sun comes up.

But even though the sun has come up every day in the past, it still might not come up tomorrow. Why think that the premise gives good reason for accepting the conclusion? Why accept this or any inductive argument?

David Hume several centuries ago raised this problem about the justification of induction. We'll discuss five responses.

1. Some suggest that, to justify induction, we need to presume that nature is uniform. If nature works in regular patterns, then the cases we haven't examined will likely follow the same patterns as the ones we have examined.

There are two problems with this suggestion. First, what does it mean to say "Nature is uniform"? Let's be concrete. What would this principle imply about the regularity (or lack thereof) of Cleveland weather patterns? "Nature is uniform" seems either obviously false or hopelessly vague.

Second, what's the backing for the principle? Justifying "Nature is uniform" by experience would require inductive reasoning. But then we're arguing in a circle – using the uniformity idea to justify induction, and then using induction to justify the uniformity idea. This presumes what's being doubted: that it's reasonable to follow inductive reasoning in the first place. Or is the uniformity idea perhaps a self-evident truth not in need of justification? But it's implausible to claim self-evidence for a claim about what the world is like.

2. Some suggest that we justify induction by its success. Inductive methods work. Using inductive reasoning, we know what to do for a toothache and how to fix cars. We use such reasoning continuously and successfully in our lives. What better justification for inductive reasoning could we have than this?

This seems like a powerful justification. But there's a problem. Let's assume that inductive reasoning has worked in the past; how can we then conclude that it probably will work in the future? The argument is inductive, much like our sunrise argument:

Induction has worked in the past. ∴ Induction probably will work in the future.	The sun has come up every day in the past. ∴ The sun probably will come up tomorrow.

So justifying inductive reasoning by its past success is circular; it uses inductive reasoning and thus presupposes that such reasoning is legitimate.

3. Some suggest that it's part of the meaning of "reasonable" that beliefs based on inductive reasoning are *reasonable*. "Reasonable belief" just means "belief based on experience and inductive reasoning." So it's true by definition that beliefs based on experience and inductive reasoning are reasonable.

There are two problems with this. First, the definition is wrong. It really isn't true by definition that all and only things based on experience and inductive reasoning are reasonable. There's no contradiction in disagreeing with this standard of reasonableness – as there would be if this definition were correct. Mystics see their higher methods as reasonable, and skeptics see the ordinary methods as unreasonable. Both groups might be wrong, but they aren't simply contradicting themselves.

Second, even the correctness of the definition wouldn't solve the problem. Suppose that standards of inductive reasoning are built into the conventional meaning of our word "reasonable." Suppose that "reasonable belief" simply means "belief based on experience and inductive reasoning." Then why follow what's "reasonable" in this sense? Why not instead follow the skeptic's advice and avoid believing such things? So this approach doesn't answer the main question: Why follow inductive reasoning at all?

4. Karl Popper suggests that we avoid inductive reasoning. But we seem to need such reasoning in our lives; without inductive reasoning, we have no basis for believing that bread nourishes and arsenic kills. And suggested substitutes for inductive reasoning don't seem adequate.

5. Some suggest that we approach justification in inductive logic the same

way we approach it in deductive logic. How can we justify the validity of a deductive principle like *modus ponens* ("If A then B, A ∴ B")? Can we prove such a principle? Perhaps we can prove *modus ponens* by doing a truth table (Section 6.6) and then arguing this way:

> If the truth table for *modus ponens* never gives true premises and a false conclusion, then *modus ponens* is valid.
> The truth table for *modus ponens* never gives true premises and a false conclusion.
> ∴ *Modus ponens* is valid.

Premise 1 is a necessary truth and premise 2 is easy to check. The conclusion follows. Therefore, *modus ponens* is valid. But the problem is that the argument itself uses *modus ponens*. So this attempted justification is circular, since it presumes from the start that *modus ponens* is valid.

Aristotle long ago showed that every proof must eventually rest on something unproved; otherwise, we'd need an infinite chain of proofs or else circular arguments – and neither is acceptable. So why not just accept the validity of *modus ponens* as a self-evident truth – a truth that's evident but can't be based on anything more evident? If we have to accept some things as evident without proof, why not accept *modus ponens* as evident without proof?

I have some sympathy with this approach. But, if we accept it, we shouldn't think that picking logical principles is purely a matter of following "logical intuitions." Logical intuitions vary enormously among people. The pretest that I give my class shows that most beginning logic students have poor intuition about the validity of simple arguments. Even though untrained logical intuitions differ, still we can reach agreement on basic principles of logic. Early on, we introduce the notion of logical form. And we distinguish between valid and invalid forms – such as these two:

Modus ponens:		*Affirming the consequent:*	
If A then B	Valid	If A then B	Invalid
A		B	
∴ B		∴ A	

Students at first are poor at distinguishing valid from invalid forms. They need concrete examples like these:

If you're a dog, then you're an animal.	Valid	If you're a dog, then you're an animal.	Invalid
You're a dog.		You're an animal.	
∴ You're an animal.		∴ You're a dog.	

After enough well-chosen examples, the validity of *modus ponens* and the invalidity of affirming the consequent become clear.

So, despite the initial clash of intuitions, we eventually reach clear logical principles of universal rational appeal. We do this by searching for clear formulas that lead to intuitively correct results in concrete cases without leading to any clear absurdities. We might think that this procedure proves *modus ponens*:

> If *modus ponens* leads to intuitively correct results in concrete cases
> without leading to any clear absurdities, then *modus ponens* is valid.
> *Modus ponens* leads to intuitively correct results in concrete cases
> without leading to any clear absurdities.
> ∴ *Modus ponens* is valid.

But this reasoning itself uses *modus ponens*; the justification is circular, since it presumes from the start that *modus ponens* is valid. So this procedure of testing *modus ponens* by checking its implications doesn't prove *modus ponens*. But I think it gives a "justification" for it, in some sense of "justification." This is vague, but I don't know how to make it more precise.

I suggested that we justify inductive principles the same way we justify deductive ones. Realizing that we can't prove everything, we wouldn't demand a proof. Rather, we'd search for clear formal inductive principles that lead to intuitively correct results in concrete cases without leading to any clear absurdities. Once we reached such inductive principles, we'd rest content with them and not look for any further justification.

This is the approach that I'd use in justifying inductive principles. But the key problem is the one discussed earlier. As yet we seem unable to find clear formal inductive principles that lead to intuitively correct results in concrete cases without leading to any clear absurdities. We just don't know how to formulate inductive principles very rigorously. This is what makes the current state of inductive logic intellectually unsatisfying.

Inductive reasoning has been very useful. Inductively, we assume that it will continue to be useful. In our lives, we can't do without it. But the intellectual basis for inductive reasoning is shaky.

CHAPTER 6
Basic Propositional Logic

Propositional logic studies arguments whose validity depends on "if-then," "and," "or," "not," and similar notions. This chapter covers the basics and the next covers proofs. Our later systems build on what we learn here.

6.1   Easier translations

We'll now create a "propositional language," with precise rules for constructing arguments and testing validity. Our language uses capital letters for true-or-false statements, parentheses for grouping, and five special *logical connectives*:

~P	=	Not-P	"~" (squiggle)
(P · Q)	=	Both P and Q	"·" (dot)
(P ∨ Q)	=	Either P or Q	"∨" (vee)
(P ⊃ Q)	=	If P then Q	"⊃" (horseshoe)
(P ≡ Q)	=	P if and only if Q	"≡" (threebar)

A grammatically correct formula of our language is called a **wff**, or **well-formed formula**. Wffs are sequences that we can construct using these rules:[1]

> 1.   Any capital letter is a wff.
> 2.   The result of prefixing any wff with "~" is a wff.
> 3.   The result of joining any two wffs by "·" or "∨" or "⊃" or "≡" and enclosing the result in parentheses is a wff.

These rules let us build wffs like the following:

P	=	I live in Paris.
~Q	=	I don't live in Quebec.
(P · ~Q)	=	I live in Paris and I don't live in Quebec.
(N ⊃ (P · ~Q))	=	If I'm Napoleon, then I live in Paris and not Quebec.

---

[1] Pronounce "wff" as "woof" (as in "wood"). We'll take letters with primes (like A´ and A´´) to be additional letters.

"~P" doesn't need or use parentheses. A wff requires a pair of parentheses for each "•," "∨," "⊃," or "≡." So "~P • Q" is malformed and not a wff; this ambiguous formula could be given parentheses in two ways:

$$(\sim P \cdot Q) \quad = \quad \text{Both not-P and Q}$$
$$\sim(P \cdot Q) \quad = \quad \text{Not both P and Q}$$

The first is definite and says that P is false and Q is true. The second just says that not both are true (at least one is false). Don't read both the same way, as "not P and Q." Read "both" for the left-hand parenthesis, or use pauses:

$$(\sim P \cdot Q) \quad = \quad \text{Not-P (pause) and (pause) Q}$$
$$\sim(P \cdot Q) \quad = \quad \text{Not (pause) P and Q}$$

Logic is easier if you read the formulas correctly. These two also differ:

$$(P \cdot (Q \supset R)) \quad = \quad \text{P, and if Q then R}$$
$$((P \cdot Q) \supset R) \quad = \quad \text{If P-and-Q, then R}$$

The first says P is definitely true, but the second leaves us in doubt about this.

Here's a useful rule for translating from English into logic, with examples:

Put "(" wherever you see "both," "either," or "if."		
Either not A or B	=	$(\sim A \vee B)$
Not either A or B	=	$\sim(A \vee B)$
If both A and B, then C	=	$((A \cdot B) \supset C)$
Not both not A and B	=	$\sim(\sim A \cdot B)$

Our translation rules have exceptions and need to be applied with common sense. So don't translate "I saw them both" as "S(" – which isn't a wff.

Here's another rule:

Group together parts on either side of a comma.		
If A, then B and C	=	$(A \supset (B \cdot C))$
If A then B, and C	=	$((A \supset B) \cdot C)$

If you're confused on where to divide a sentence without a comma, ask yourself where a comma would naturally go and then translate accordingly:

| If it snows then I'll go outside and I'll ski | = | If it snows, then I'll go outside and I'll ski | = | $(S \supset (G \cdot K))$ |

Be sure that your capital letters stand for whole statements. "Gensler is happy" is just "G"; don't use "(G • H)" ("Gensler *and* happy"?). Similarly, "Bob and Lauren got married to each other" is just "M"; "(B • L)" would be wrong, since the English sentence doesn't mean "Bob got married and Lauren got married" (which omits "to each other"). However, it would be correct to translate "Bob and Lauren were sick" as "(B · L)"; here "and" connects whole statements since the English means "Bob was sick and Lauren was sick."

It doesn't matter what letters you use, as long as you're consistent. Use the same letter for the same idea and different letters for different ideas. If you use "P" for "I went to Paris," then use "~P" for "I didn't go to Paris."

Some common equivalences can help us to understand the formulas better. First, order and grouping don't matter in wffs using "·," "∨," or "≡" as the only connective; so we have the *commutation* and *association* equivalences:[1]

$$\begin{array}{lll} \textit{Commutation:} & (A · B) & = & (B · A) \\ \textit{Association:} & ((A · B) · C) & = & (A · (B · C)) \end{array}$$

But the order matters with "⊃"; these two make different claims:

$$\begin{array}{lll} \text{If it's a dog, then it's an animal} & = & (D ⊃ A) \\ \text{If it's an animal, then it's a dog} & = & (A ⊃ D) \end{array}$$

We can switch the parts of an if-then if we negate them; so "If it's a dog, then it's an animal" is equivalent to the *contrapositive* "If it's not an animal, then it's not a dog":

$$\textit{Contrapositive:} \quad (D ⊃ A) \quad = \quad (\sim A ⊃ \sim D)$$

Finally, *De Morgan* (Section 16.3) lets us convert between "and" and "or":

De Morgan:	~(A · B)	=	(~A ∨ ~B)
	Not both A and B		Either not-A or not-B
De Morgan:	~(A ∨ B)	=	(~A · ~B)
	Not either A or B		Both not-A and not-B

6.1a   Exercise – also LogiCola C (EM & ET)[2]

Translate these English sentences into wffs.

Both not A and B.	(~A · B)

1.   Not both A and B.
2.   Both A and either B or C.
3.   Either both A and B or C.

---

[1] Commutation fails in English when "and" means "and then"; "Suzy got married and had a baby" differs from "Suzy had a baby and got married." Our "·" is simpler and more abstract, and ignores temporal sequence. Sections 7.5 and 15.2 have additional equivalences.
[2] Exercise sections have a boxed sample problem that is worked out for you. They also refer to corresponding LogiCola computer exercises (see the Preface). Problems 1, 3, 5, 10, 15, and so on are worked out at the back of the book.

4.   If A, then B or C.
5.   If A then B, or C.
6.   If not A, then not either B or C.
7.   If not A, then either not B or C.
8.   Either A or B, and C.
9.   Either A, or B and C.
10. If A then not both not B and not C.
11. If you get an error message, then the disk is bad or it's a Macintosh disk.
12. If I bring my digital camera, then if my batteries don't die then I'll take pictures of my backpack trip and put the pictures on my Web site.
13. If you both don't exercise and eat too much, then you'll gain weight.
14. The statue isn't by either Cellini or Michelangelo.
15. If I don't have either $2 in exact change or a bus pass, I won't ride the bus.
16. If Michigan and Ohio State play each other, then Michigan will win.
17. Either you went through both Dayton and Cinci, or you went through Louisville.
18. If she had hamburgers then she ate junk food, and she ate French fries.
19. I'm going to Rome or Florence and you're going to London.
20. Everyone is male or female.

6.2   Simple truth tables

Let "P" stand for "I went to Paris" and "Q" for "I went to Quebec." Each could be *true* or *false* (the two **truth values**) – represented by "1" and "0" (or sometimes "T" and "F"). There are four possible combinations:

P Q	
0 0	Both are false
0 1	Just Q is true
1 0	Just P is true
1 1	Both are true

In the first case, I went to neither Paris nor Quebec. In the second, I went to Quebec but not Paris. And so on.

A **truth table** gives a logical diagram for a wff. It lists all possible truth-value combinations for the letters and says whether the wff is true or false in each case. The truth table for "·" ("and") is very simple:

P Q	(P · Q)	
0 0	0	"I went to Paris and
0 1	0	I went to Quebec."
1 0	0	"(P · Q)" is a **conjunction**;
1 1	1	P and Q are its **conjuncts**.

"(P · Q)" claims that *both* parts are true. So "I went to Paris *and* I went to

Quebec" is false in the first three cases (where one or both parts are false) – and true only in the last case. These truth equivalences give the same information:

$$(0 \cdot 0) = 0 \qquad (\text{false} \cdot \text{false}) = \text{false}$$
$$(0 \cdot 1) = 0 \qquad (\text{false} \cdot \text{true}) = \text{false}$$
$$(1 \cdot 0) = 0 \qquad (\text{true} \cdot \text{false}) = \text{false}$$
$$(1 \cdot 1) = 1 \qquad (\text{true} \cdot \text{true}) = \text{true}$$

Here "$(0 \cdot 0) = 0$" says that an AND statement is false if both parts are false. The next two say that an AND is false if one part is false and the other part is true. And "$(1 \cdot 1) = 1$" says that an AND is true if both parts are true.

Here are the truth table and equivalences for "$\vee$" ("or"):

P Q	(P $\vee$ Q)
0 0	0
0 1	1
1 0	1
1 1	1

$(0 \vee 0) = 0$
$(0 \vee 1) = 1$
$(1 \vee 0) = 1$
$(1 \vee 1) = 1$

"I went to Paris or I went to Quebec."

"(P $\vee$ Q)" is a **disjunction**; P and Q are its **disjuncts**.

"(P $\vee$ Q)" claims that *at least one* part is true. So "I went to Paris *or* I went to Quebec" is true just if I went to one or both places. Our "$\vee$" symbolizes the *inclusive* sense of "or"; English also can use "or" in an *exclusive* sense, which claims that at least one part is true *but not both*. Both senses of "or" can translate into our symbolism:

- *Inclusive "or"*: A or B or both   =   (A $\vee$ B)
- *Exclusive "or"*: A or B but not both   =   ((A $\vee$ B) $\cdot$ ~(A $\cdot$ B))

The exclusive sense requires a longer symbolization.[1]

Here are the truth table and equivalences for "$\supset$" ("if-then"):

P Q	(P $\supset$ Q)
0 0	1
0 1	1
1 0	0
1 1	1

$(0 \supset 0) = 1$
$(0 \supset 1) = 1$
$(1 \supset 0) = 0$
$(1 \supset 1) = 1$

"If I went to Paris, then I went to Quebec."

"(P $\supset$ Q)" is a **conditional**; P is the **antecedent** and Q the **consequent**.

"(P $\supset$ Q)" claims that what we *don't* have is the first part true and the second false. Suppose you say this:

"*If* I went to Paris, *then* I went to Quebec."

By our table, you speak truly if you went to neither place, or to both places, or

---

[1] People sometimes use "*Either* A or B" for the exclusive "or." We won't do this; instead, we'll use "either" to indicate grouping and we'll translate it as a left-hand parenthesis.

to Quebec but not Paris. You speak falsely if you went to Paris but not Quebec. Does that seem right to you? Most people think so, but some have doubts.

Our truth table can produce strange results. Take this example:

If I had eggs for breakfast, then $(E \supset W)$
the world will end at noon.

Suppose I didn't have eggs, and so E is false. By our table, the conditional is then *true* – since if E is false then "$(E \supset W)$" is true. This is strange. We'd normally tend to take the conditional to be *false* – since we'd take it to claim that my having eggs would *cause* the world to end. So translating "if-then" as "$\supset$" doesn't seem satisfactory. Something fishy is going on here.

Our "$\supset$" symbolizes a simplified "if-then" that ignores causal connections and temporal sequence. "$(P \supset Q)$" has a very simple meaning; it just *denies* that we have P-true-and-Q-false:

$(P \supset Q)$ If P is true, then Q is true.	=	$\sim(P \cdot \sim Q)$ We don't have P true and Q false.

Translating "if-then" this way is a useful simplification, since it captures the part of "if-then" that normally determines validity. The simplification usually works; in the few cases where it doesn't, we can use a more complex translation (as we'll sometimes do in the chapters on modal logic).

The truth conditions for "$\supset$" are hard to remember. These slogans may help:

Falsity implies anything.	$(0 \supset \ ) = 1$
Anything implies truth.	$(\ \supset 1) = 1$
Truth doesn't imply falsity.	$(1 \supset 0) = 0$

The "Falsity implies anything" slogan, for example, means that the whole if-then is true if the first part is false; so "If I'm a billionaire, then ..." is true, regardless of what replaces "...," since I'm *not* a billionaire.

Here are the table and equivalences for "$\equiv$" ("if-and-only-if"):

P Q	$(P \equiv Q)$		
0 0	1	$(0 \equiv 0) = 1$	"I went to Paris if and only
0 1	0	$(0 \equiv 1) = 0$	if I went to Quebec."
1 0	0	$(1 \equiv 0) = 0$	"$(P \equiv Q)$" is a **biconditional**.
1 1	1	$(1 \equiv 1) = 1$	

"$(P \equiv Q)$" claims that both parts have the *same* truth value: both are true or both are false. So "$\equiv$" is much like "equals."

Here are the table and equivalences for "~" ("not"):

P	~P
0	1
1	0

$\sim 0 = 1$
$\sim 1 = 0$

"I didn't go to Paris."
"~P" is a **negation**.

"~P" has the *opposite* value of "P." If "P" is true then "~P" is false, and if "P" is false then "~P" is true.

Much of the rest of this book presupposes these truth equivalences; try to master them right away. Let me sum up how they work:

$(P \cdot Q)$ AND says *both* parts are true.
$(P \vee Q)$ OR says *at least one* part is true.
$(P \supset Q)$ IF-THEN says we don't have *first part true & second part false.*
$(P \equiv Q)$ IF-AND-ONLY-IF says both parts have the *same* truth value.
$\sim P$ NOT *reverses* the truth value.

6.2a   Exercise – also LogiCola D (TE & FE)

Calculate each truth value.

$(0 \cdot 1)$	$(0 \cdot 1) = 0$

1. $(0 \vee 1)$
2. $(0 \cdot 0)$
3. $(0 \supset 0)$
4. ~ 0
5. $(0 \equiv 1)$

6. $(1 \cdot 0)$
7. $(1 \supset 1)$
8. $(1 \equiv 1)$
9. $(0 \vee 0)$
10. $(0 \supset 1)$

11. $(0 \equiv 0)$
12. $(1 \vee 1)$
13. $(1 \cdot 1)$
14. $(1 \supset 0)$
15. ~ 1

16. $(1 \vee 0)$
17. $(1 \equiv 0)$

6.3   Truth evaluations

We can calculate the truth value of a wff if we know the truth value of its letters. Consider this problem:

Suppose that P=1, Q=0, and R=0.
What is the truth value of "$((P \supset Q) \equiv \sim R)$"?

To figure this out, we write "1" for "P," "0" for "Q," and "0" for "R"; then we simplify from the inside out, using our equivalences, until we get "1" or "0":

$((P \supset Q) \equiv \sim R)$ ←   original formula
$((1 \supset 0) \equiv \sim 0)$ ←   substitute "1" and "0" for the letters
$(0 \equiv 1)$ ←   put "0" for "$(1 \supset 0)$," and "1" for "~ 0"
0 ←   put "0" for "$(0 \equiv 1)$"

Here the formula is false.

Simplify parts inside parentheses first. With a wff of the form "~(...)," first work out the part inside parentheses to get 1 or 0; then apply "~" to the result:

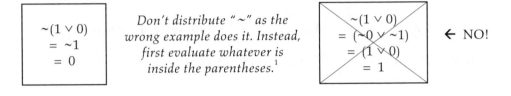

$\sim(1 \vee 0)$
$= \sim 1$
$= 0$

Don't distribute "~" as the wrong example does it. Instead, first evaluate whatever is inside the parentheses.[1]

$\sim(1 \vee 0)$
$= (\sim 0 \vee \sim 1)$ ← NO!
$= (1 \vee 0)$
$= 1$

6.3a   Exercise – also LogiCola D (TM & TH)

Assume that A=1 and B=1 (A and B are both true) while X=0 and Y=0 (X and Y are both false). Calculate the truth value of each wff below.

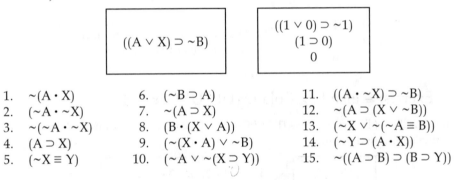

$((A \vee X) \supset \sim B)$

$((1 \vee 0) \supset \sim 1)$
$(1 \supset 0)$
0

1. $\sim(A \cdot X)$
2. $(\sim A \cdot \sim X)$
3. $\sim(\sim A \cdot \sim X)$
4. $(A \supset X)$
5. $(\sim X \equiv Y)$

6. $(\sim B \supset A)$
7. $\sim(A \supset X)$
8. $(B \cdot (X \vee A))$
9. $(\sim(X \cdot A) \vee \sim B)$
10. $(\sim A \vee \sim(X \supset Y))$

11. $((A \cdot \sim X) \supset \sim B)$
12. $\sim(A \supset (X \vee \sim B))$
13. $(\sim X \vee \sim(\sim A \equiv B))$
14. $(\sim Y \supset (A \cdot X))$
15. $\sim((A \supset B) \supset (B \supset Y))$

6.4   Unknown evaluations

We can sometimes figure out a formula's truth value even if we don't know the truth value of some letters. Take this example:

Suppose that P=1 and Q=? (unknown). What is the truth value of "$(P \vee Q)$"?

We first substitute "1" for "P" and "?" for "Q":

$$(1 \vee \text{?})$$

---

[1] Some want to distribute the "~" because they think it works that way in math. But don't worry about math; NOT might not work the same as MINUS. And we can't distribute in math either: "$-(2 \cdot 2)$" (which equals -4) differs from "$(-2 \cdot -2)$" (which equals +4).

We might just see that this is true, since an OR is true if at least one part is true. Or we might try it both ways; we write "1" above the "?" and "0" below it – and we evaluate the formula for each case:

$$1 = 1$$
$$(1 \lor ?)$$
$$0 = 1$$

The formula is true, since it's true either way.

Here's another example:

Suppose that P=1 and Q=? What is the truth value of "(P · Q)"?

We first substitute "1" for "P" and "?" for "Q":

$$(1 \cdot ?)$$

We might see that this is unknown, since the truth value of the whole depends on the unknown letter. Or we might try it both ways; we write "1" above the "?" and "0" below it – and we evaluate the formula for each case:

$$1 = 1$$
$$(1 \cdot ?)$$
$$0 = 0$$

The formula is unknown, since it could be either true or false.

6.4a   Exercise – also LogiCola D (UE, UM, & UH)

Assume that T=1 (T is true), F=0 (F is false), and U=? (U is unknown). Calculate the truth value of each wff below.

$(\sim T \cdot U)$	$(\sim 1 \cdot ?) = (0 \cdot ?) = 0$

1.	$(U \cdot F)$	4.	$(\sim F \cdot U)$	7.	$(U \supset \sim T)$	10.	$(U \supset \sim F)$
2.	$(U \supset \sim T)$	5.	$(F \supset U)$	8.	$(\sim F \lor U)$	11.	$(U \cdot \sim T)$
3.	$(U \lor \sim F)$	6.	$(\sim T \lor U)$	9.	$(T \cdot U)$	12.	$(U \lor F)$

6.5   Complex truth tables

A truth table for a wff is a diagram listing all possible truth-value combinations for the wff's letters and saying whether the wff would be true or false in each case. We've done simple tables already; now we'll do complex ones.

With n distinct letters we have 2^n possible truth-value combinations:

A	A B	A B C
0	0 0	0 0 0
1	0 1	0 0 1
	1 0	0 1 0
	1 1	0 1 1
		1 0 0
		1 0 1
		1 1 0
		1 1 1

One letter gives 2 (2^1) combinations.
Two letters give 4 (2^2) combinations.
Three letters give 8 (2^3) combinations.

n letters give 2^n combinations.

To get every combination, alternate 0's and 1's for the last letter the required number of times. Then alternate 0's and 1's for each earlier letter at half the previous rate: by twos, fours, and so on. This numbers the rows in base 2.

We begin a truth table for "~(A ∨ ~B)" like this:

A B	~(A ∨ ~B)
0 0	
0 1	
1 0	
1 1	

The right side has the wff. The left side has each letter used in the wff; we write each letter just once, regardless of how often it occurs. Below the letters, we write all possible truth-value combinations.

Then we figure out the wff's truth value for each line. The first line has A and B both false – which makes the whole wff false:

~(A ∨ ~B)   ← original formula
~(0 ∨ ~0)   ← substitute "0" for each letter
~(0 ∨ 1)   ← put "1" for "~0"
~1   ← put "1" for "(0 ∨ 1)"
0   ← put "0" for "~1"

The wff comes out "1," "0," and "0" for the next three lines; so we get:

A B	~(A ∨ ~B)
0 0	0
0 1	1
1 0	0
1 1	0

"~(A ∨ ~B)" is true if and only if A is false and B is true. The simpler wff "(~A · B)" is equivalent, in that it's true in the same cases. Both wffs are true in some cases and false in others – making them *contingent statements*.

"(P ∨ ~P)" is a *tautology*, since it comes out true in all cases:

P	(P ∨ ~P)
0	1
1	1

"I went to Paris or
I didn't go to Paris."

This formula, called the **law of the excluded middle**, says that every statement is true or false. This law holds in propositional logic, since we stipulated that capital letters stand for true-or-false statements. The law doesn't always hold in English, since English allows statements that are too vague to be true or false. Is "It's raining" true if there's a slight drizzle? Is "My shirt is white" true if it's a light cream color? Such claims can be too vague to be true or false. So the law is an idealization when applied to English.

"(P • ~P)" is a **self-contradiction**, since it comes out false in all cases:

P	(P • ~P)
0	0
1	0

"I went to Paris and
I didn't go to Paris."

"P and not-P" is always false in propositional logic, which presupposes that "P" stands for the same statement throughout. English is looser and lets us shift the meaning of a phrase in the middle of a sentence. "I went to Paris and I didn't go to Paris" may express a truth if it means this:

> "I went to Paris (in that I landed once at the Paris airport) – but I
> didn't really go there (in that I saw almost nothing of the city)."

Because of the shift in meaning, this would better translate as "(P • ~Q)."

6.5a Exercise – also LogiCola D (FM & FH)

Do a truth table for each formula.

P Q R	((P ∨ Q) ⊃ R)
0 0 0	1
0 0 1	1
0 1 0	0
0 1 1	1
1 0 0	0
1 0 1	1
1 1 0	0
1 1 1	1

((P ∨ Q) ⊃ R)

1. (P ≡ ~Q)
2. (~P • Q)
3. (P ∨ (Q • ~R))
4. ((P • ~Q) ⊃ R)
5. ((P ≡ Q) ⊃ Q)
6. ((P ∨ ~Q) ⊃ R)
7. (~Q ⊃ ~P)
8. (P ≡ (P • P))
9. ~(P • (Q ∨ ~R))

6.6   The truth-table test

Recall how VALID and INVALID are defined for arguments:

VALID = No possible case has premises all true and conclusion false.	1 1 ∴ 0	1 1 ∴ 0	INVALID = Some possible case has premises all true and conclusion false.

To use the truth-table test on a propositional argument:

> Construct a truth table showing the truth value of the premises and conclusion for all possible cases. The argument is **VALID** if and only if no possible case has premises all true and conclusion false.

Suppose we want to test this invalid argument:

If you're a dog, then you're an animal.	(D ⊃ A)
You're not a dog.	~D
∴ You're not an animal.	∴ ~A

First we do a truth table for the premises and conclusion. We start as follows:

D A	(D ⊃ A), ~D ∴ ~A
0 0	
0 1	
1 0	
1 1	

Then we evaluate the three wffs on each truth combination. The first combination has D=0 and A=0, which makes all three wffs true:

$$
\begin{array}{ccc}
\text{(D} \supset \text{A)} & \text{~D} & \text{~A} \\
\text{(0} \supset \text{0)} & \text{~0} & \text{~0} \\
1 & 1 & 1
\end{array}
$$

So the first line of our truth table looks like this:

D A	(D ⊃ A), ~D ∴ ~A
0 0	1 1 1

We work out the other three lines:

D A	(D ⊃ A),	~D	∴	~A	
0 0	1	1		1	
0 1	1	1		0	← Invalid
1 0	0	0		1	
1 1	1	0		0	

The argument is invalid, since some possible case has premises all true and conclusion false. Perhaps you aren't a dog but you are an animal (maybe a cat).
   Consider this valid argument:

If you're a dog, then you're an animal.	(D ⊃ A)
You're a dog.	D
∴ You're an animal.	∴ A

Again we do a truth table for the premises and conclusion:

D A	(D ⊃ A),	D	∴	A	Valid
0 0	1	0		0	
0 1	1	0		1	
1 0	0	1		0	
1 1	1	1		1	

This is valid, since no possible case has premises all true and conclusion false.
   The test has a short-cut version. Recall that we're looking for 110 (premises all true and conclusion false). The argument is invalid if 110 sometimes occurs; otherwise, it's valid. To save time, we can first evaluate an easy wff and cross out lines that can't be 110. In our last example, we might work out "D" first:

D A	(D ⊃ A),	D	∴	A
0 0	– – – – – – – – 0 – – – – –			
0 1	– – – – – – – – 0 – – – – –			
1 0	1			
1 1	1			

The first two lines can't be 110 (since the second digit is 0). So we cross them out and ignore them.

Next we might evaluate "A":

D A	(D ⊃ A),	D	∴	A
0 0	– – – – – – – – 0 – – – – –			
0 1	– – – – – – – – 0 – – – – –			
1 0	1			0
1 1	– – – – – – – – 1 – – – 1 –			

The bottom line can't be 110 (since the last digit is 1). So we cross it out.

Then we have to evaluate "(D ⊃ A)" for only one case – for which it comes out false. Since we never get 110, the argument is valid:

D A	(D ⊃ A), D ∴ A	Valid
0 0	– – – – – – – 0 – – – – –	
0 1	– – – – – – – 0 – – – – –	
1 0	– – – 0 – – – 1 – – – 0 –	
1 1	– – – – – – – 1 – – – 1 –	

Since we never get 110
(true premises and false
conclusion), the argument
is valid.

The short-cut method can save much time if otherwise we'd have to evaluate a long formula for eight or more cases.

With a two-premise argument, we look for 110. With three premises, we look for 1110. In general, we look for a case having premises all true and conclusion false. The argument is valid if and only if this never occurs.

The truth-table test can get tedious for long arguments. Arguments with 6 letters need 64 lines – and ones with 10 letters need 1024 lines. So we'll use the truth-table test only on fairly simple arguments.[1]

6.6a   Exercise – also LogiCola D (AE, AM, & AH)

First appraise intuitively. Then translate into logic (using the letters given) and use the truth-table test to determine validity.

It's in my left hand or
my right hand.
It's not in my left hand.
∴ It's in my right hand.

L R	(L ∨ R),	~L	∴	R	Valid
0 0	0	1		0	
0 1	1	1		1	we never
1 0	1	0		0	get 110
1 1	1	0		1	

1.   If you're a collie, then you're a dog.
     You're a dog.
  ∴ You're a collie.   [Use C and D.]

2.   If you're a collie, then you're a dog.
     You're not a dog.
  ∴ You're not a collie.   [Use C and D.]

3.   If television is always right, then Anacin is better than Bayer.
     If television is always right, then Anacin isn't better than Bayer.
  ∴ Television isn't always right.   [Use T and B.]

4.   If it rains and your tent leaks, then your down sleeping bag will get wet.
     Your tent won't leak.
  ∴ Your down sleeping bag won't get wet.   [R, L, W]

---

[1] An argument that tests out "invalid" may be valid on grounds that go beyond the system in question. For example, "This is green, therefore something is green" translates into propositional logic as "T ∴ S" and tests out invalid; but it's valid as "Gt ∴ (∃x)Gx" in quantificational logic.

5. If I get Grand Canyon reservations and get a group together, then I'll explore canyons during spring break.
   I've got a group together.
   I can't get Grand Canyon reservations.
   ∴ I won't explore canyons during spring break.   [R, T, E]

6. There's an objective moral law.
   If there's an objective moral law, then there's a source of the moral law.
   If there's a source of the moral law, then there's a God. (Other possible sources, like society or the individual, are claimed not to work.)
   ∴ There's a God.   [Use M, S, and G; this is from C. S. Lewis.]

7. If ethics depends on God's will, then something is good because God desires it.
   Something isn't good *because* God desires it. (Instead, God desires something because it's already good.)
   ∴ Ethics doesn't depend on God's will.   [Use D and B; this is from Plato's *Euthyphro*.]

8. It's an empirical fact that the basic physical constants are precisely in the narrow range of what is required for life to be possible. (This "anthropic principle" has considerable evidence behind it.)
   The best explanation for this fact is that the basic physical constants were caused by a great mind intending to produce life. (The main alternatives are the "chance coincidence" and "parallel universe" explanations.)
   If these two things are true, then it's reasonable to believe that the basic structure of the world was set up by a great mind (God) intending to produce life.
   ∴ It's reasonable to believe that the basic structure of the world was set up by a great mind (God) intending to produce life.   [Use E, B, and R; see Section 5.9.]

9. I'll go to Paris during spring break if and only if I'll win the lottery.
   I won't win the lottery.
   ∴ I won't go to Paris during spring break.   [P, W]

10. If we have a simple concept proper to God, then we've directly experienced God and we can't rationally doubt God's existence.
    We haven't directly experienced God.
    ∴ We can rationally doubt God's existence.   [S, E, R]

11. If there is a God, then God created the universe.
    If God created the universe, then matter didn't always exist.
    Matter always existed.
    ∴ There is no God.   [G, C, M]

12. If this creek is flowing, then either the spring upstream has water or this creek has some other water source.
    This creek has no other water source.
    This creek isn't flowing.
    ∴ The spring upstream has no water.   [F, S, O]

6.7 The truth-assignment test

Recall again how VALID and INVALID are defined for arguments:

VALID = No possible case has premises all true and conclusion false.	1 1 ∴ 0		1 1 ∴ 0	INVALID = Some possible case has premises all true and conclusion false.

To use the truth-assignment test on a propositional argument:

> Set each premise to 1 and the conclusion to 0. Figure out the truth value of as many letters as possible. The argument is VALID if and only if no possible way to assign 1 and 0 to the letters will keep the premises all 1 and conclusion 0.

Suppose we want to test this valid argument:

It's in my left hand or my right hand.	$(L \vee R)$
It's not in my left hand.	$\sim L$
∴ It's in my right hand.	∴ R

Here's how we work it out:

$(L \vee R) = 1$ $\sim L = 1$ ∴ $R = 0$	First we set each premise to 1 and the conclusion to 0.
$(L^0 \vee R) = 1$ $\sim L^0 = 1$ ∴ $R = 0$	Since premise 2 has $\sim L{=}1$, making L=0, we write 0 above each L.
$(L^0 \vee R^0) = 1$ $\sim L^0 = 1$ ∴ $R^0 = 0$	Since the conclusion has R=0, we write 0 above each R.
$(L^0 \vee R^0) \neq 1$ $\sim L^0 = 1$ ∴ $R^0 = 0$	But then premise 1 can't be true. So we can't have true premises and a false conclusion.

Valid

In doing the test, we first assign 1 to the premises and 0 to the conclusion (just to see if this could work). Then we figure out the truth values for the letters and then for the longer formulas. If we have to cross something out, then the initial assignment isn't possible, and so the argument is valid.

This shows how we work out an invalid argument:

It's in my left hand or my right hand.	$(L \lor R)$
It's not in my left hand.	$\sim L$
$\therefore$ It's not in my right hand.	$\therefore \sim R$

$(L \lor R) = 1$ $\sim L = 1$ $\therefore \sim R = 0$	First we set each premise to 1 and the conclusion to 0.
$(L^0 \lor R) = 1$ $\sim L^0 = 1$ $\therefore \sim R = 0$	Since premise 2 has $\sim L=1$, making $L=0$, we write 0 above each L.
$(L^0 \lor R^1) = 1$ $\sim L^0 = 1$ $\therefore \sim R^1 = 0$	Since the conclusion has $\sim R=0$, making $R=1$, we write 1 above each R.
$(L^0 \lor R^1) = 1$ $\sim L^0 = 1$ $\therefore \sim R^1 = 0$ Invalid	So we can have true premises and a false conclusion.

Since we can make the premises all true and conclusion false, the argument is invalid. A truth-table gives the same result when L=0 and R=1:

L R	$(L \lor R)$,	$\sim L$	$\therefore$	$\sim R$	
0 1	1	1		0	$\leftarrow$ Invalid

The truth-assignment test gives this result more quickly.[1]

Here's another invalid argument:

It's in my left hand or my right hand.	$(L \lor R)$
$\therefore$ It's in my right hand.	$\therefore R$

If we work this out, we get R false, but we get no value for L:

$(L \lor R) = 1$ $\therefore R = 0$	First we set the premise to 1 and the conclusion to 0.
$(L \lor R^0) = 1$ $\therefore R^0 = 0$	Since the conclusion has $R=0$, we write 0 above each R.

---

[1] Some find lines like "$\sim L^0 = 1$" confusing. Here the larger complex "$\sim L$" is true but the letter "L" is false. When I write an 0-superscript above the letter, I mean that the letter is false.

$$(L^1 \vee R^0) = 1$$
$$\therefore R^0 = 0$$

We can make the premise true if we make L true.

$$(L^1 \vee R^0) = 1$$
$$\therefore R^0 = 0$$

Invalid

So we can have true premises and a false conclusion.

If you don't get a value for a letter, try it both ways (as 1 and as 0); if either gives you true premises and a false conclusion, then the argument is invalid.

In working out the truth values for the letters, try to make premises all true and conclusion false. The argument is invalid if there's some way to do this.

6.7a   Exercise – also LogiCola ES

Test for validity using the truth-assignment test.

$$(K \supset (I \vee S))$$
$$\sim I$$
$$K$$
$$\therefore S$$

$$(K^1 \supset (I^0 \vee S^0)) \neq 1 \quad \textbf{Valid}$$
$$\sim I^0 = 1$$
$$K^1 = 1 \qquad \text{(we can't}$$
$$\therefore S^0 = 0 \qquad \text{have 1110)}$$

1. $\sim(N \equiv H)$
    N
    $\therefore \sim H$

2. $((J \cdot \sim D) \supset Z)$
    $\sim Z$
    D
    $\therefore \sim J$

3. $((T \vee M) \supset Q)$
    M
    $\therefore Q$

4. P
    $\therefore (P \cdot Q)$

5. $((L \cdot F) \supset S)$
    S
    F
    $\therefore L$

6. $((A \cdot U) \supset \sim B)$
    B
    A
    $\therefore \sim U$

7. $((W \cdot C) \supset Z)$
    $\sim Z$
    $\therefore \sim C$

8. Q
    $\therefore (P \supset Q)$

9. $(E \vee (Y \cdot X))$
    $\sim E$
    $\therefore X$

10. $(\sim T \supset (P \supset J))$
    P
    $\sim J$
    $\therefore T$

11. $\sim P$
    $\therefore \sim(Q \supset P)$

12. $((\sim M \cdot G) \supset R)$
    $\sim R$
    G
    $\therefore M$

13. $\sim(Q \equiv I)$
    $\sim Q$
    $\therefore I$

14. $((Q \cdot R) \equiv S)$
    Q
    $\therefore S$

15. A
    $\sim A$
    $\therefore B$

6.7b   Exercise – also LogiCola EE

First appraise intuitively. Then translate into logic and use the truth-assignment test to determine validity.

> If our country will be weak, then there will be war.
> Our country will not be weak.
> ∴ There will not be war.

$$(K^0 \supset R^1) = 1 \quad \textbf{Invalid}$$
$$\sim K^0 = 1 \quad \text{(we can}$$
$$\therefore \sim R^1 = 0 \quad \text{have 110)}$$

1. Some things are caused (brought into existence).
   Anything caused is caused by another.
   If some things are caused and anything caused is caused by another, then either there's a first cause or there's an infinite series of past causes.
   There's no infinite series of past causes.
   ∴ There's a first cause.   [A "first cause" (often identified with God) is a cause that isn't itself caused by another. This is from St Thomas Aquinas.]

2. If you pass and it's intercepted, then the other side gets the ball.
   You pass.
   It isn't intercepted.
   ∴ The other side doesn't get the ball.

3. If God exists in the understanding and not in reality, then there can be conceived a being greater than God (namely, a similar being that also exists in reality).
   "There can be conceived a being greater than God" is false (since "God" is defined as "a being than which no greater can be conceived").
   God exists in the understanding.
   ∴ God exists in reality.   [This is St Anselm's famous ontological argument.]

4. If existence is a perfection and God by definition has all perfections, then God by definition must exist.
   Existence is a perfection.
   God by definition has all perfections.
   ∴ God by definition must exist.   [From René Descartes.]

5. If we have sensations of alleged material objects and yet no material objects exist, then God is a deceiver.
   God isn't a deceiver.
   We have sensations of alleged material objects.
   ∴ Material objects exist.   [From René Descartes, who thus based our knowledge of the external material world on our knowledge of God.]

6. If "good" is definable in experimental terms, then ethical judgments are scientifically provable and ethics has a rational basis.
   Ethical judgments aren't scientifically provable.
   ∴ Ethics doesn't have a rational basis.

7. If it's right for me to lie and not right for you, then there's a relevant difference between our cases.
   There's no relevant difference between our cases.
   It's not right for you to lie.
   ∴ It's not right for me to lie.

8.   If Newton's gravitational theory is correct and there's no undiscovered planet near Uranus, then the orbit of Uranus would be such-and-such.
     Newton's gravitational theory is correct.
     The orbit of Uranus isn't such-and-such.
     ∴ There's an undiscovered planet near Uranus.   [This reasoning led to the discovery of the planet Neptune.]

9.   If attempts to prove "God exists" fail in the same way as our best arguments for "There are other conscious beings besides myself," then belief in God is reasonable if and only if belief in other conscious beings is reasonable.
     Attempts to prove "God exists" fail in the same way as our best arguments for "There are other conscious beings besides myself."
     Belief in other conscious beings is reasonable.
     ∴ Belief in God is reasonable.   [From Alvin Plantinga.]

10. If you pack intelligently, then either this teddy bear will be useful on the hiking trip or you won't pack it.
     This teddy bear won't be useful on the hiking trip.
     You won't pack it.
     ∴ You pack intelligently.

11. If knowledge is sensation, then pigs have knowledge.
     Pigs don't have knowledge.
     ∴ Knowledge isn't sensation.   [From Plato.]

12. If capital punishment is justified and justice doesn't demand a vindication for past wrongs, then capital punishment either reforms the offender or effectively deters crime.
     Capital punishment doesn't reform the offender.
     Capital punishment doesn't effectively deter crime.
     ∴ Capital punishment isn't justified.

13. If belief in God were a purely intellectual matter, then either all smart people would be believers or all smart people would be non-believers.
     Not all smart people are believers.
     Not all smart people are non-believers.
     ∴ Belief in God isn't a purely intellectual matter.

14. If you're lost, then you should call for help or head downstream.
     You're lost.
     ∴ You should call for help.

15. If maximizing human enjoyment is always good and the sadist's dog-torturing maximizes human enjoyment, then the sadist's act is good.
     The sadist's dog-torturing maximizes human enjoyment.
     The sadist's act isn't good.
     ∴ Maximizing human enjoyment isn't always good.

16. If there's knowledge, then either some things are known without proof or we can prove every premise by previous arguments infinitely.
   We can't prove every premise by previous arguments infinitely.
   There's knowledge.
   ∴ Some things are known without proof.   [From Aristotle.]

17. If you modified your computer or didn't send in the registration card, then the warranty is void.
   You didn't modify your computer.
   You sent in the registration card.
   ∴ The warranty isn't void.

18. If "X is good" means "Hurrah for X!" and it makes sense to say "If X is good," then it makes sense to say "If hurrah for X!"
   It makes sense to say "If X is good."
   It doesn't make sense to say "If hurrah for X!"
   ∴ "X is good" doesn't mean "Hurrah for X!"   [From Hector-Neri Castañeda.]

19. If we have an idea of substance, then "substance" refers either to a simple sensation or to a complex constructed out of simple sensations.
   "Substance" doesn't refer to a simple sensation.
   ∴ We don't have an idea of substance.   [From David Hume.]

20. If we have an idea of "substance" and we don't derive the idea of "substance" from sensations, then "substance" is a thought category of pure reason.
   We don't derive the idea of "substance" from sensations.
   We have an idea of "substance."
   ∴ "Substance" is a thought category of pure reason.   [From Immanuel Kant.]

21. If "good" means "socially approved," then what is socially approved is necessarily good.
   What is socially approved isn't necessarily good.
   ∴ "Good" doesn't mean "socially approved."

22. [Generalizing the last argument, G. E. Moore argued that we can't define "good" in terms of any empirical term "F" – like "desired" or "socially approved."]
   If "good" means "F," then what is F is necessarily good.
   What is F isn't necessarily good. (We can consistently say "Some F things may not be good" without thereby violating the meaning of "good.")
   ∴ "Good" doesn't mean "F."

23. If moral realism (the belief in objective moral truths) were true, then it could explain the moral diversity in the world.
   Moral realism can't explain the moral diversity in the world.
   ∴ Moral realism isn't true.

6.8   Harder translations

Now we'll learn how to symbolize idiomatic English. We'll still use our rules to group together parts on either side of a comma and to write "(" for "both," "either," or "if." Here are three additional rules, with examples:

Translate "but" ("yet," "however," "although," and so on) as "and."

Michigan played *but* it lost   = $(P \cdot L)$

The translation loses the contrast (or surprise), but this doesn't affect validity.

Translate "unless" as "or."

You'll die *unless* you breathe   = $(D \vee B)$ = $(B \vee D)$
Unless you breathe you'll die   = $(D \vee B)$ = $(B \vee D)$

"Unless" is also equivalent to "if not"; so we also could use "$(\sim B \supset D)$" ("If you don't breathe, then you'll die").

Translate "just if" and "iff" (a logician word) as "if and only if."

I'll agree *just if* you pay me \$1,000   = $(A \equiv P)$
I'll agree *iff* you pay me \$1,000   = $(A \equiv P)$

The order of the letters doesn't matter with "$\cdot$" or "$\vee$" or "$\equiv$."
  Our next two rules are tricky. The first governs most conditional words:

The part after "if" ("provided that," "assuming that," and so on) is the if-part (the antecedent, the part before the horseshoe).

If A, then B   = $(A \supset B)$
Provided that A, B   = $(A \supset B)$
A, if B   = $(B \supset A)$
A, provided that B   = $(B \supset A)$

You're an animal, *if* you're a dog   = $(D \supset A)$
Provided that you're a dog, you're an animal   = $(D \supset A)$

"Only if" is different and follows its own rule:

The part after "only if" is the then-part (the consequent, the part after the horseshoe). (Or just write "$\supset$" for "only if.")

A only if B   = $(A \supset B)$
Only if A, B   = $(B \supset A)$

You're alive *only if* you have oxygen   = $(A \supset O)$
Only if you have oxygen, are you alive   = $(A \supset O)$

The *contrapositive* translation "$(\sim O \supset \sim A)$" ("If you don't have oxygen, then you aren't alive") is equivalent and often sounds more intuitive.

Here's the rule for "sufficient" and "necessary":

> "A is *sufficient* for B" means "If A then B."
> "A is *necessary* for B" means "If not A then not B."
> "A is *necessary and sufficient* for B" means "A if and only if B."

$$\text{Oxygen is } \textit{sufficient for } \text{life} \quad = \quad (O \supset L)$$
$$\text{Oxygen is } \textit{necessary for } \text{life} \quad = \quad (\sim O \supset \sim L)$$
$$\text{Oxygen is } \textit{necessary and sufficient for } \text{life} \quad = \quad (O \equiv L)$$

The order of the letters matters with "$\supset$," but not with "$\equiv$."

These translation rules are rough and don't always work. Sometimes you have to puzzle out the meaning on your own.

6.8a Exercise – also LogiCola C (HM & HT)

Translate these English sentences into wffs.

> A, assuming that B. $(B \supset A)$

1. If she goes, then you'll be alone but I'll be here.
2. Your car will start only if you have fuel.
3. I will quit unless you give me a raise.
4. Taking the final is a sufficient condition for passing.
5. Taking the final is necessary for you to pass.
6. You're a man just if you're a rational animal.
7. Unless you have faith, you'll die.
8. She neither asserted it nor hinted at it.
9. Getting at least 96 is a necessary and sufficient condition for getting an A.
10. Only if you exercise are you fully alive.
11. I'll go, assuming that you go.
12. Assuming that your belief is false, you don't know.
13. Having a true belief is a necessary condition for having knowledge.
14. You get mashed potatoes or French fries, but not both.
15. You're wrong if you say that.

6.9 Idiomatic arguments

Our arguments so far have been phrased in a clear premise–conclusion format. Unfortunately, real-life arguments are seldom so neat and clean. Instead we often find convoluted wording or extraneous material. Important parts of the argument may be omitted or only hinted at. And it may be hard to pick out the premises and conclusion. It often takes hard work to reconstruct a clearly stated argument from a passage.

Logicians like to put the conclusion last:

Socrates is human. If he's	H
human, then he's mortal.	(H ⊃ M)
So Socrates is mortal.	∴ M

But people sometimes put the conclusion first, or in the middle:

Socrates must be mortal.	Socrates is human. *So he*
After all, he's human. And	*must be mortal* – since if
if he's human, he's mortal.	he's human, he's mortal.

In these examples, "must" and "so" indicate the conclusion (which always goes *last* when we translate the argument into logic). Here are some typical words that help us pick out the premises and conclusion:

These often indicate premises:	∴	*These often indicate conclusions:*
Because, for, since, after all …		Hence, thus, so, therefore …
I assume that, as we know …		It must be, it can't be …
For these reasons …		This proves (or shows) that …

When you don't have this help, ask yourself what is argued *from* (these are the premises) and what is argued *to* (this is the conclusion).

In reconstructing an argument, first pick out the conclusion. Then symbolize the premises and conclusion; this may involve untangling idioms like "A unless B" (which translates as "A or B"). If you don't get a valid argument, try adding unstated but implicit premises (you may need to add a premise that uses letters that only occur once); using the "principle of charity," interpret unclear reasoning in the way that gives the best argument.

Here's an easy example:

The gun must have been shot recently! It's still hot.

First we pick out the premises and conclusion:

The gun is still hot.	H
∴ The gun was shot recently.	∴ S

Since this seems to presume an implicit premise, we add the most plausible one that we can think of and that makes the argument valid. Then we translate into logic and test for validity:

If the gun is still hot, then it
was shot recently. (implicit)
The gun is still hot.
∴ The gun was shot recently.

$$(H \supset S) \quad \textbf{Valid}$$
$$H$$
$$\therefore S$$

6.9a   Exercise – also LogiCola E (F & I)

First appraise intuitively. Then pick out the conclusion, translate into logic, and determine validity using the truth-assignment test. Supply implicit premises if needed.

Knowledge is good in itself only if it's desired for its own sake. So knowledge is good in itself, since it's desired for its own sake.

$$(G^0 \supset D^1) = 1 \quad \textbf{Invalid}$$
$$D^1 = 1$$
$$\therefore G^0 = 0$$

(The conclusion is *"So knowledge is good in itself"* – *"G."*)

1. Knowledge can't be sensation. If it were, then we couldn't know something that we aren't presently sensing.   [From Plato.]
2. Presuming that we followed the map, then unless the map is wrong there's a pair of lakes just over the pass. We followed the map. There's no pair of lakes just over the pass. Hence the map is wrong.
3. If they blitz but don't get to our quarterback, then our wide receiver will be open. So our wide receiver won't be open, as shown by the fact that they won't blitz.
4. My true love will marry me only if I buy her a Rolls Royce. It follows that she'll marry me, since I'll buy her a Rolls Royce.
5. The basic principles of ethics can't be self-evident truths, since if they were then they'd largely be agreed upon by intelligent people who have studied ethics.
6. That your views are logically consistent is a necessary condition for your views to be sensible. Your views are logically consistent. So your views are sensible.
7. If Ohio State wins but Nebraska doesn't, then the Ohio Buckeyes will be national champions. So it looks like the Ohio Buckeyes won't be national champs, since Nebraska clearly is going to win.
8. The filter capacitor can't be blown. This is indicated by the following facts. You'd hear a hum, presuming that the silicon diodes work but the filter capacitor is blown. But you don't hear a hum. And the silicon diodes work.
9. There's oxygen present. And so there will be a fire! My reason for saying this is that only if there's oxygen present will there be a fire.
10. We have no moral knowledge. This is proved by the fact that if we did have moral knowledge then basic moral principles would be either provable or self-evident. But they aren't provable. And they aren't self-evident either.
11. It must be a touchdown! We know that it's a touchdown if the ball broke the plane of the end zone.
12. Assuming that it wasn't an inside job, then the lock was forced unless the thief stole the key. The thief didn't steal the key. We may infer that the robbery was an inside job, inasmuch as the lock wasn't forced.

13. It must be the case that we don't have any tea bags. After all, we'd have tea bags if your sister Carol drinks tea. Of course, Carol doesn't drink tea.

14. We can't still be on the right trail. We'd see the white Appalachian Trail blazes on the trees if we were still on the right trail.

15. If God is omnipotent, then he could make hatred inherently good – unless there's a contradiction in hatred being inherently good. But there's no contradiction in this. And God is omnipotent. I conclude that God could make hatred inherently good. [From William of Ockham, who saw morality as depending on God's will.]

16. Taking the exam is a sufficient condition for getting an A. You didn't take the exam. This means you don't get an A.

17. If Texas or Arkansas wins, then I win my $10 bet. I guess I win $10. Texas just beat Oklahoma 17-14!

18. Unless you give me a raise, I'll quit. Therefore I'm quitting!

19. Empirical knowledge must be impossible. My reason for saying this is that there's no independent way to prove that our senses are reliable. Empirical knowledge would be possible, of course, only if there were an independent way to prove that our senses are reliable.

20. It's virtuous to try to do what's good. On the other hand, it isn't virtuous to try to do what's socially approved. I conclude that, contrary to cultural relativism, "good" doesn't mean "socially approved." I assume, of course, that if "good" meant "socially approved" and it was virtuous to try to do what's good, then it would be virtuous to try to do what's socially approved.

21. Moral conclusions can be deduced from non-moral premises only if "good" is definable using non-moral predicates. But "good" isn't so definable. So moral conclusions can't be deduced from non-moral premises.

22. The world can't need a cause. If the world needed a cause, then so would God.

6.10   S-rules

We'll now learn some **inference rules**, which state that certain formulas can be derived from certain other formulas. Most of these rules reflect common forms of reasoning. These rules also provide the building blocks for formal proofs, which we start in the next chapter; formal proofs reduce a complex argument to a series of small steps, each based on an inference rule.

The **S-rules** of this section are used to *simplify* statements. Our first S-rule is called "AND"; here it is in English and in symbols:

AND	This and that. ∴ This. ∴ That.	$\dfrac{(P \cdot Q)}{P, Q}$	AND statement, so both parts are true.

From an AND statement, we can infer each part: "It's cold and windy; therefore it's cold, therefore it's windy." Negative parts work the same way:

It isn't cold and it isn't windy.
∴ It isn't cold.
∴ It isn't windy.

$$\frac{(\sim C \cdot \sim W)}{\sim C, \sim W}$$

But from a *negative* AND statement (where "~" is outside the parentheses), we can infer nothing about the truth or falsity of each part:

You're *not both* in Paris and in Quebec.
∴ No conclusion.

$$\frac{\sim(P \cdot Q)}{nil}$$

You can't be in both cities at the same time. But you might be in Paris (and not Quebec), or in Quebec (and not Paris), or in some third place (perhaps Miami). From "~(P · Q)" we can't tell the truth value for P or for Q; we only know that *not both* are true (at least one is false).

Our second S-rule is called "NOR" or "NOT-EITHER":

NOR	Not either this or that. ∴ Not this. ∴ Not that.	$\dfrac{\sim(P \vee Q)}{\sim P, \sim Q}$	NOT-EITHER is true, so both are false.

From a NOT-EITHER statement, we can infer the opposite of each part: "It isn't either cold or windy, therefore it isn't cold, therefore it isn't windy." Negative parts work the same way: we infer the opposite of each part (the opposite of "~A" being "A"):

Not either not-A or not-B.
∴ A
∴ B

$$\frac{\sim(\sim A \vee \sim B)}{A, B}$$

But from a *positive* OR statement we can infer nothing about the truth or falsity of each part:

You're in either Paris or Quebec.
∴ No conclusion.

$$\frac{(P \vee Q)}{nil}$$

You might be in Paris (and not Quebec), or in Quebec (and not Paris). From "(P ∨ Q)" we can't tell the truth value for P or for Q; we only know that *at least one* is true.

Our third S-rule is called "NIF" or "FALSE IF-THEN":

NIF	FALSE IF-THEN. ∴ First part true. ∴ Second part false.	$\dfrac{\sim(P \supset Q)}{P, \sim Q}$

Recall that "(P ⊃ Q)" means "We *don't* have P-true-and-Q-false"; so then "~(P ⊃ Q)" means "We *do* have P-true-and-Q-false." This FALSE IF-THEN rule isn't very intuitive; I suggest memorizing it instead of appealing to logical intuitions or concrete examples. You'll use this rule so much in doing proofs that it'll soon become second nature.

If a FALSE IF-THEN has negative parts, we again infer part 1 and the opposite of part 2:

$$\frac{\sim(\sim A \supset B)}{\sim A, \sim B} \qquad \frac{\sim(A \supset \sim B)}{A, B} \qquad \frac{\sim(\sim A \supset \sim B)}{\sim A, B}$$

This diagram might help you follow what is going on here:

$$\frac{\sim (\text{p a r t } 1 \supset \text{p a r t } 2)}{\text{write part 1} \qquad \text{write opposite of part 2}}$$

If the IF-THEN is itself *positive* (there's no "~" outside the parentheses), then we can infer nothing about the truth or falsity of each part. So from "(A ⊃ B)" alone we can infer nothing about A or about B.

To sum up: we can simplify the forms on the left, but not those on the right:

AND	(P · Q) → P, Q
NOR	~(P ∨ Q) → ~P, ~Q
NIF	~(P ⊃ Q) → P, ~Q

~(P · Q)
(P ∨ Q)
(P ⊃ Q)

To understand why these rules work as they do, recall our basic truth tables:

- For an AND to be true, both parts have to be true.
- For an OR to be false, both parts have to be false.
- For an IF-THEN to be false, we need part 1 true and part 2 false.

You need to learn these S-rules so well that they become automatic.

6.10a Exercise – also LogiCola F (SE & SH)

Draw any simple conclusions (a letter or its negation) that follow from these premises. If nothing follows, leave blank.

$$\frac{(C \cdot \sim R)}{} \qquad \frac{(C \cdot \sim R)}{C, \sim R}$$

1. $\underline{(P \cdot U)}$ 2. $\underline{(L \vee C)}$ 3. $\underline{(\sim N \supset S)}$ 4. $\underline{\sim(F \supset M)}$

5.   ~(R ∨ S)   9.   (~Q · B)   13.   ~(~N ∨ ~E)   17.   ~(~Y ⊃ G)

6.   ~(J · ~N)   10.   ~(H ⊃ ~I)   14.   ~(Q · T)   18.   ~(~A · ~J)

7.   ~(I ∨ ~V)   11.   (~O ∨ ~X)   15.   (M ∨ ~W)   19.   ~(~U ⊃ ~L)

8.   (F ⊃ ~G)   12.   (~T ⊃ ~H)   16.   (~D · ~Z)   20.   (~K ∨ B)

6.11   I-rules

The I-rules are used to *infer* a conclusion from two premises. Our first two I-rules are called "CS" or "conjunctive syllogism":

CS	Not both are true.	~(P · Q)	~(P · Q)	*Deny* AND.
	This one is true.	P	Q	*Affirm* one part.
	∴ The other isn't.	~Q	~P	∴ *Deny* other part.

With a NOT-BOTH, we must affirm one part. Here are examples:

You're *not both* in Paris   You're *not both* in Paris
  and also in Quebec.   and also in Quebec.
You're in Paris.   You're in Quebec.
∴ You're not in Quebec.   ∴ You're not in Paris.

Negative parts work the same way; if we affirm one, we can deny the other:

~(~A · ~B)	~(A · ~B)	~(A · ~B)
~A	A	~B
B	B	~A

In each case, the second premise affirms (says the same as) one part. And the conclusion denies (says the opposite of) the other part.

   If we deny one part, we can't draw a conclusion about the other part:

Not both are true.	~(P · Q)
The first is false.	~P
No conclusion.	nil

You may want to conclude Q; but maybe Q is false too (maybe both parts are false). Here's an example:

You're *not both* in Paris and also in Quebec.
You're not in Paris.
∴ No conclusion.

You needn't be in Quebec; maybe you're in Chicago. To get a conclusion from a NOT-BOTH, we must *affirm* one part.

Our second two I-rules are called "DS" or "disjunctive syllogism":

DS				
	At least one is true.	(P ∨ Q)	(P ∨ Q)	*Affirm OR.*
	This one isn't.	~P	~Q	*Deny one part.*
	∴ The other is.	Q	P	∴ *Affirm other part.*

With an OR, we must deny one part. Here are examples:

At least one hand (left
or right) has candy.
The left hand doesn't.
∴ The right hand does.

At least one hand (left
or right) has candy.
The right hand doesn't.
∴ The left hand does.

Negative parts work the same; if we deny one part, we can affirm the other:

$$\frac{(\sim A \lor \sim B) \quad A}{\sim B} \qquad \frac{(A \lor \sim B) \quad \sim A}{\sim B} \qquad \frac{(A \lor \sim B) \quad B}{A}$$

In each case, the second premise denies (says the opposite of) one part. And the conclusion affirms (says the same as) the other part.

If we affirm one part, we can't draw a conclusion about the other part:

At least one is true.
The first is true.
————————————
No conclusion.

(L ∨ R)
L
———
nil

You may want to conclude ~R; but maybe R is true too (maybe both parts are true). Here's an example:

At least one hand (left or right) has candy.
The left hand has candy.
∴ No conclusion.

We can't conclude "The right hand doesn't have candy," since maybe both hands have it. To get a conclusion from an OR, we must *deny* one part.

Here's a helpful trick. To infer with NOT-AND or OR, the premises must *alternate* between affirming and denying:

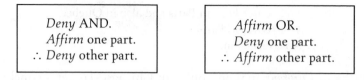

Nothing follows if the premises don't alternate. So nothing follows if we deny AND and then deny one part – or if we affirm OR and then affirm one part.

Our final I-rules are *modus ponens* (Latin for "affirming mode") and *modus tollens* (Latin for "denying mode"). Both deal with "if-then":

MP

IF-THEN.	$(P \supset Q)$
Affirm first.	P
∴ Affirm second.	Q

MT

IF-THEN.	$(P \supset Q)$
Deny second.	~Q
∴ Deny first.	~P

With an if-then, we must affirm the first part or deny the second part:

If you're a dog, then
  you're an animal.
You're a dog.
∴ You're an animal.

$(D \supset A)$
D
———
A

If you're a dog, then
  you're an animal.
You're not an animal.
∴ You're not a dog.

$(D \supset A)$
~A
———
~D

Negative parts work the same. If we affirm the first, we can affirm the second:

$(\sim A \supset \sim B)$ $(A \supset \sim B)$ $(\sim A \supset B)$
~A   A   ~A
———   ———   ———
~B   ~B   B

And if we deny the second, we can deny the first:

$(\sim A \supset \sim B)$ $(A \supset \sim B)$ $(\sim A \supset B)$
B   B   ~B
———   ———   ———
A   ~A   A

If we deny the first part or affirm the second, we can't conclude anything about the other part:

If you're a dog, then
  you're an animal.
You're not a dog.
∴ No conclusion.

$(D \supset A)$
~D
———
nil

If you're a dog, then
  you're an animal.
You're an animal.
∴ No conclusion.

$(D \supset A)$
A
———
nil

In the first case, you may want to conclude "You're not an animal"; but you might be a cat. In the second, you may want to conclude "You're a dog"; but again, you might be a cat. *To infer with an if-then, we need the first part true or the second part false*: "(+ ⊃ -)."

Since formal proofs depend so much on the S- and I-rules, it's important to master these rules before starting the next chapter.

6.11a   Exercise – also LogiCola F (IE & IH)

Draw any simple conclusions (a letter or its negation) that follow from these premises. If nothing follows, leave blank.

(~Q ∨ ~M)	(~Q ∨ ~M)
Q	Q
——	——
	~M

1. ~(W • T)
    W
    ——————

2. (S ∨ L)
    S
    ——————

3. (H ⊃ ~B)
    H
    ——————

4. (X ⊃ E)
    E
    ——————

5. ~(B • S)
    ~S
    ——————

6. (~Y ⊃ K)
    Y
    ——————

7. (K ∨ ~R)
    R
    ——————

8. ~(~S • W)
    ~W
    ——————

9. (U ⊃ G)
    U
    ——————

10. (~I ∨ K)
    K
    ——————

11. (C ⊃ ~V)
    ~C
    ——————

12. (~N ∨ ~A)
    A
    ——————

13. ~(V • H)
    ~V
    ——————

14. (~A ⊃ ~E)
    ~E
    ——————

15. ~(~F • ~O)
    ~O
    ——————

16. (Y ∨ ~C)
    ~C
    ——————

17. (~L ⊃ M)
    ~M
    ——————

18. (~M ∨ ~B)
    ~M
    ——————

19. ~(~F • ~Q)
    F
    ——————

20. ~(A • ~Y)
    A
    ——————

6.12   Mixing S- and I-rules

Our next exercise mixes S- and I-rule inferences. This should cause you little trouble, so long as you remember to use S-rules to simplify *one* premise and I-rules to infer from *two* premises. Here's a quick review:

	S-rules (Simplifying)	I-rules (Inferring)	

<table>
<tr><td>AND</td><td>$(P \cdot Q) \rightarrow P, Q$</td></tr>
<tr><td>NOR</td><td>$\sim(P \vee Q) \rightarrow \sim P, \sim Q$</td></tr>
<tr><td>NIF</td><td>$\sim(P \supset Q) \rightarrow P, \sim Q$</td></tr>
</table>

$\sim(P \cdot Q), P \rightarrow \sim Q$		CS
$\sim(P \cdot Q), Q \rightarrow \sim P$		
$(P \vee Q), \sim P \rightarrow Q$		DS
$(P \vee Q), \sim Q \rightarrow P$		
$(P \supset Q), P \rightarrow Q$		MP
$(P \supset Q), \sim Q \rightarrow \sim P$		MT

6.12a   Exercise – also LogiCola F (CE & CH)

Draw any simple conclusions (a letter or its negation) that follow from these premises. If nothing follows, leave blank.

$$\frac{\begin{array}{c}(A \supset \sim B)\\ \sim A\end{array}}{}$$

(no conclusion)

1. $\sim(U \cdot T)$
    $\dfrac{T}{}$

2. $\sim(\sim B \vee C)$
    $\overline{}$

3. $(X \supset F)$
    $\dfrac{\sim X}{}$

4. $(\sim S \vee T)$
    $\overline{}$

5. $(P \cdot \sim Q)$
    $\overline{}$

6. $(\sim I \supset \sim N)$
    $\dfrac{N}{}$

7. $(D \vee \sim J)$
    $\dfrac{D}{}$

8. $\sim(L \cdot M)$

9. $\sim(\sim C \supset D)$
    $\overline{}$

10. $\sim(\sim R \cdot A)$
    $\dfrac{\sim R}{}$

11. $\sim(M \vee \sim I)$
    $\overline{}$

12. $\sim(R \cdot \sim G)$
    $\dfrac{\sim G}{}$

13. $(\sim L \cdot S)$
    $\overline{}$

14. $(\sim L \vee \sim T)$
    $\dfrac{L}{}$

15. $(A \supset \sim B)$
    $\overline{}$

16. $\sim(W \cdot \sim X)$
    $\dfrac{\sim W}{}$

6.13   Extended inferences

From an AND statement, we can conclude that both parts are true; so from "$(P \cdot Q)$," we can get "P" and also "Q." The rule also works on larger formulas:

$$\frac{((C \equiv D) \cdot (E \supset F))}{(C \equiv D), (E \supset F)}$$ AND statement, so both parts are true.

Visualize the premise as a big AND with two parts – blurring out the details: "$(\$\$\$\$\$ \cdot \#\#\#\#\#)$." We can infer each part, even if these parts are complex.

Here's another inference using an S-rule:

$$\frac{\sim((C \cdot D) \supset (E \supset F))}{(C \cdot D), \sim(E \supset F)}$$

FALSE IF-THEN, so first
part true, second part false.

Again, blur the details; read the long formula as just "FALSE IF-THEN." From such a formula, we can conclude that the first part is true and the second false; so we write the first part and the opposite of the second.

Consider this formula (which I suggest you read to yourself as "IF-THEN"):

$$((C \cdot D) \supset (E \supset F))$$

Since this is an if-then, we can't break it down using an S-rule. But we can conclude something from it if we have the first part true or second part false:

$$\frac{\begin{array}{c}((C \cdot D) \supset (E \supset F)) \\ (C \cdot D)\end{array}}{(E \supset F)}$$
IF-THEN.
Affirm first.

Affirm second.

$$\frac{\begin{array}{c}((C \cdot D) \supset (E \supset F)) \\ \sim(E \supset F)\end{array}}{\sim(C \cdot D)}$$
IF-THEN.
Deny second.

Deny first.

These are the only legitimate I-rule inferences. We get no conclusion if we deny the first part or affirm the second – or if we affirm or deny a smaller part:

$$\frac{\begin{array}{c}((C \cdot D) \supset (E \supset F)) \\ \sim(C \cdot D)\end{array}}{\text{nil}}$$

$$\frac{\begin{array}{c}((C \cdot D) \supset (E \supset F)) \\ (E \supset F)\end{array}}{\text{nil}}$$

$$\frac{\begin{array}{c}((C \cdot D) \supset (E \supset F)) \\ E\end{array}}{\text{nil}}$$

In the last example, we don't know that "(E ⊃ F)" is true – but just that it *would* be true if "(C · D)" were true.

6.13a   Exercise – No LogiCola exercise

Draw any conclusions that follow from these premises by a single application of the S- or I-rules. If nothing follows in this way, then leave blank.

$$\boxed{\frac{\sim(\sim A \lor (B \cdot C))}{}}$$

$$\boxed{\frac{\sim(\sim A \lor (B \cdot C))}{A, \sim(B \cdot C)}}$$

1. $\dfrac{\sim((A \cdot B) \supset \sim C)}{}$

2. $\dfrac{\begin{array}{c}((A \cdot B) \supset \sim C) \\ \sim(A \cdot B)\end{array}}{}$

3. $\dfrac{\sim((G \lor H) \cdot (I \lor J))}{}$

4. $\dfrac{\begin{array}{c}\sim((G \lor H) \cdot (I \lor J)) \\ (G \lor H)\end{array}}{}$

5. $\dfrac{((A \cdot B) \lor (C \supset D))}{}$

6. $\dfrac{\begin{array}{c}((A \cdot B) \lor (C \supset D)) \\ C\end{array}}{}$

7.   ~((A ⊃ B) ∨ C)   8.   ((A ⊃ B) ⊃ C)   9.   ((G ≡ H) ⊃ ~(I · J))
                                   (A ⊃ B)   ~(I · J)

6.14   Logic and computers

Before leaving this chapter, let us note that digital computers were developed using ideas from propositional logic. The key insight is that electrical devices can simulate logic formulas.

Computers represent "1" and "0" by different physical states; "1" might be a positive voltage and "0" a zero voltage. An *and-gate* would then be a physical device with two inputs and one output, where the output has a positive voltage if and only if *both* inputs have positive voltages:

A →
          | AND-GATE | →   (A · B)
B →

An *or-gate* would be similar, except that the output has a positive voltage if and only if *at least one* input has a positive voltage. For any formula, we can construct an input-output device (a *logic gate*) that mimics that formula.

A computer basically converts input information into 1's and 0's, manipulates these by logic gates and memory devices, and converts the resulting 1's and 0's back into a useful output. So propositional logic is central to the operation of computers. One of my logic teachers at the University of Michigan, Art Burks, was part of the team in the 1940s that produced the ENIAC, the first large-scale electronic computer. So logic had an important role in moving us into the computer age.

CHAPTER 7

Propositional Proofs

Formal proofs are a convenient way to test arguments of various systems and, in addition, help to develop reasoning skills. From now on, formal proofs will be our main method of testing arguments.

7.1 Easier proofs

A formal proof breaks a complicated argument into a series of small steps. Since most steps are based on our S- and I-rules (Sections 6.10–13), it's good to review these now and then as you learn to do proofs.

We'll be using an indirect proof strategy, where we first assume the opposite of what we want to prove. You may remember such proofs from geometry; to prove that two angles are equal, you'd assume that they *aren't* equal – and then show that this is impossible, because it leads to a contradiction. Similarly, to prove that the butler committed the murder, we'll assume that he *didn't* do it – and then show that this is impossible, because it leads to a contradiction.

Suppose that we know premises 1 to 4 to be true and we want to prove that the butler committed the murder. Here's an English version of a formal proof:

1	The only people in the mansion were the butler and the maid.
2	If the only people in the mansion were the butler and the maid, then the butler or the maid did it.
3	If the maid did it, then she had a motive.
4	The maid didn't have a motive. ⇐
	[∴ The butler did it.
5	⌐ Assume: The butler didn't do it.
6	∴ The butler or the maid did it. {from 1 and 2}
7	∴ The maid did it. {from 5 and 6}
8	∟ ∴ The maid had a motive. {from 3 and 7} ⇐
9	∴ The butler did it. {from 5; 4 contradicts 8}

We first assume that the butler *didn't* do it (line 5). Then we derive a contradiction (between lines 4 and 8). So, given our premises, the assumption that he didn't do it is impossible. So the butler is guilty – throw him in jail!

Mirroring how we reasoned in English, we now construct a formal proof using a three-step strategy (START, S&I, RAA):

1	T	
2	(T ⊃ (B ∨ M))	
3	(M ⊃ H)	
4	~H	
	[∴ B	
5	asm: ~B	

(1) START: Block off the conclusion and add "asm:" (for "assume") followed by the conclusion's simpler contradictory.

Blocking off a line reminds us not to use it in deriving further lines.

	1	T	
*	2	(T ⊃ (B ∨ M))	
*	3	(M ⊃ H)	
	4	~H ⇐	
		[∴ B	
	5	asm: ~B	
*	6	∴ (B ∨ M) {from 1 and 2}	
	7	∴ M {from 5 and 6}	
	8	∴ H {from 3 and 7} ⇐	

(2) S&I: Go through the complex wffs that aren't starred or blocked off and use these to derive new wffs using the S- and I-rules. Star any wff you simplify using an S-rule, or the longer wff used in an I-rule inference.

We go from "T" & "(T ⊃ (B ∨ M))" to "(B ∨ M)" – from "(B ∨ M)" & "~B" to "M" – and from "(M ⊃ H)" & "M" to "H."

Lines 4 and 8 contradict.

	1	T	Valid
*	2	(T ⊃ (B ∨ M))	
*	3	(M ⊃ H)	
	4	~H	
		[∴ B	
	5	⌈ asm: ~B	
*	6	│ ∴ (B ∨ M) {from 1 and 2}	
	7	│ ∴ M {from 5 and 6}	
	8	⌊ ∴ H {from 3 and 7}	
	9	∴ B {from 5; 4 contradicts 8}	

(3) RAA: When some pair of not-blocked-off lines contradicts, apply RAA and derive the original conclusion.

Our proof is done!

(1) START: We start a proof by blocking off the original conclusion (blocking off tells us to ignore a line for the rest of the proof) and assuming its simpler *contradictory*. Two wffs are **contradictories** if they are exactly alike except that one starts with an additional "~." So if our conclusion is "A," then we assume "~A"; but if our conclusion is "~A," then we assume "A." And if our conclusion is "(A ⊃ B)," then we assume "~(A ⊃ B)." Our first assumption always adds or subtracts an initial squiggle to the original conclusion.

(2) S&I: Then we derive further lines using the S- and I-rules until we get a contradiction. We focus on what we can derive using *complex wffs that aren't starred or blocked off.* A **simple wff** is a letter or its negation; any other wff is **complex.** So our first inference in our sample proof has to involve lines 2 or 3, which are the only complex wffs. From lines 1 and 2 we derive line 6. We then derive lines 7 and 8, and notice that lines 4 and 8 ("~H" and "H") contradict.

There often are alternative ways to do a proof; so instead of deriving "H" in line 8, we could have used 3 and 4 to get "~M," which would contradict 7.

We starred lines 2, 3, and 6. Here are the starring rules – with examples:

<table>
<tr><td>Star any wff that you
simplify using an S-rule.</td><td>Star the longer wff used
in an I-rule inference.</td></tr>
<tr><td>* (A · B)
———
∴ A
∴ B</td><td>* (A ⊃ B)
A
———
∴ B</td></tr>
</table>

Starred lines are redundant, since shorter lines have the same information. When we do a proof, we can focus on *complex wffs that aren't starred or blocked off* and what can be derived from them. While starring is optional, it simplifies our work because it leads us to ignore lines that won't help us to derive further formulas.

(3) RAA: Our goal in the S&I part is to derive a contradiction – a pair of wffs (like "H" and "~H") that is identical except that one starts with an additional squiggle. These contradictory wffs may occur anywhere in the proof (as premises or assumptions or derived lines), so long as neither is blocked off. Once we derive a contradiction, we apply **RAA**, our new *reductio ad absurdum* (reduction to absurdity) rule, which says that an assumption that leads to a contradiction must be false. As we apply RAA, we block off lines 5 through 8 to show that we can't use them in deriving further lines. Thus we prove the argument valid.

In doing the S&I part, we'll use these inference rules, which hold regardless of what pairs of contradictory wffs replace "P" / "~P" and "Q" / "~Q" (here "→" means we can infer whole lines from left to right):

S-rules *(Simplifying)*	I-rules *(Inferring)*
(P · Q) → P, Q ~(P ∨ Q) → ~P, ~Q ~(P ⊃ Q) → P, ~Q ~~P → P (P ≡ Q) → (P ⊃ Q), (Q ⊃ P) ~(P ≡ Q) → (P ∨ Q), ~(P · Q)	~(P · Q), P → ~Q ~(P · Q), Q → ~P (P ∨ Q), ~P → Q (P ∨ Q), ~Q → P (P ⊃ Q), P → Q (P ⊃ Q), ~Q → ~P

Read "(P · Q) → P, Q" as "from '(P · Q)' one may derive 'P' and also 'Q.'"

Three S-rules are new. The fourth S-rule ("double negation" or "DN") eliminates "~~" from the beginning of a wff. The fifth S-rule ("IFF") breaks a biconditional into two conditionals. The last S-rule ("NIFF") breaks up the denial of a biconditional; since "(P ≡ Q)" says that P and Q have the same truth value, "~(P ≡ Q)" says that P and Q have different truth values – so one or the other is true, but not both. These three rules aren't used much.[1]

Here are some key definitions:

- A **premise** is a line consisting of a wff by itself (with no "asm:" or "∴").
- An **assumption** is a line consisting of "asm:" and then a wff.
- A **derived line** is a line consisting of "∴" and then a wff.
- A **formal proof** is a vertical sequence of zero or more premises followed by one or more assumptions or derived lines, where each derived line follows from previously not-blocked-off lines by RAA or one of the S- and I-rules listed above, and each assumption is blocked off using RAA.[2]

Rule RAA says an assumption is false if it leads to contradictory wffs; these wffs may occur anywhere in the proof (as premises or assumptions or derived lines), so long as neither is blocked off. Here's a more precise formulation:

> RAA: Suppose some pair of not-blocked-off lines has contradictory wffs. Then block off all the lines from the last not-blocked-off assumption on down and infer a line consisting in "∴" followed by a contradictory of that assumption.

Here's a proof of a premiseless argument (which is valid because the conclusion is a logically necessary truth):

[∴ ((A · B) ⊃ A) **Valid**	(1) START: We block off the conclusion and assume its contradictory (line 1).
* 1 ⌐ asm: ~((A · B) ⊃ A)	
2 │ ∴ (A · B) {from 1}	(2) S&I: We use S-rules to get lines 2 to 4 and a contradiction.
3 │ ∴ ~A {from 1} ⇐	
4 └ ∴ A {from 2} ⇐	(3) RAA: We use RAA to finish the proof (line 5).
5 ∴ ((A · B) ⊃ A) {from 1; 3 contradicts 4}	

A formal proof, as we've defined it, must use the specified S- and I-rules or RAA to derive further lines. We can't just use any intuitive inferences that we think will work (although advanced users sometimes take such shortcuts). Some logicians like to mention the inference rule (like "MP" or "DS" or "AND") in the justifications. Our proof strategy will get more complex later, as we bring in invalid arguments and multiple assumptions.

---

[1] The S-rules also work in the other direction (for example, "(A · B)" follows from "A" and "B"); but our proofs and software use the S-rules only to simplify. The LogiCola software does, however, let you use two additional rules for the biconditional: (1) Given "(A ≡ B)": if you have one side true, you can get the other side true – and if you have one side false, you can get the other side false. (2) Given "~(A ≡ B)": if you have one side true, you can get the other side false – and if you have one side false, you can get the other side true.

[2] By this definition, the stars, line numbers, blocked off original conclusion, and justifications aren't strictly part of the proof; instead, they are unofficial helps.

While a proof, as we've defined it, must derive only lines that are licensed by the inference rules, there still can be legitimate variations in how to do proofs. For example, one person might always simplify "(A • B)" automatically into the two parts, "A" first and then "B." Another person might derive "B" first and then "A." Yet another person might derive just the part needed to get a contradiction. All three approaches are fine.

7.1a   Exercise – also LogiCola F (TE & TH) and GEV

Prove each of these arguments to be valid (all are valid).

```
        *    1      (A ∨ B)   Valid
                  [ ∴ (~A ⊃ B)
        *    2    ┌ asm: ~(~A ⊃ B)
             3    │  ∴ ~A   {from 2}
             4    │  ∴ ~B   {from 2}
             5    └  ∴ B    {from 1 and 3}
             6     ∴ (~A ⊃ B)   {from 2; 4 contradicts 5}
```

```
   (A ∨ B)
∴ (~A ⊃ B)
```

1.   (A ⊃ B)
  ∴ (~B ⊃ ~A)

2.   A
  ∴ (A ∨ B)

3.   (A ⊃ B)
     (~A ⊃ B)
  ∴ B

4.   ((A ∨ B) ⊃ C)
  ∴ (~C ⊃ ~B)

5.   (A ∨ B)
     (A ⊃ C)
     (B ⊃ D)
  ∴ (C ∨ D)

6.   (A ⊃ B)
     (B ⊃ C)
  ∴ (A ⊃ C)

7.   (A ≡ B)
  ∴ (A ⊃ (A • B))

8.   ~(A ∨ B)
     (C ∨ B)
     ~(D • C)
  ∴ ~D

9.   (A ⊃ B)
     ~B
  ∴ (A ≡ B)

10. (A ⊃ (B ⊃ C))
  ∴ ((A • B) ⊃ C)

7.1b   Exercise – also LogiCola F (TE & TH) and GEV

First appraise intuitively. Then translate into logic (using the letters given) and prove to be valid (all are valid).

1.   If Heather saw the butler putting the tablet into the drink and the tablet was poison, then the butler killed the deceased.
     Heather saw the butler putting the tablet into the drink.
   ∴ If the tablet was poison, then the butler killed the deceased.   [Use H, T, and B.]

2.   If we had an absolute proof of God's existence, then our will would be irresistibly attracted to do right.
     If our will were irresistibly attracted to do right, then we'd have no free will.
   ∴ If we have free will, then we have no absolute proof of God's existence.   [Use P, I, and F. This is from Immanuel Kant and John Hick, who used it to explain why God doesn't make his existence more evident.]

3. If racism is clearly wrong, then either it's factually clear that all races have equal abilities or it's morally clear that similar interests of all beings ought to be given equal consideration.

   It's not factually clear that all races have equal abilities.

   If it's morally clear that similar interests of all beings ought to be given equal consideration, then similar interests of animals and humans ought to be given equal consideration.

   ∴ If racism is clearly wrong, then similar interests of animals and humans ought to be given equal consideration. [Use W, F, M, and A. This argument is from Peter Singer, who fathered the animal liberation movement.]

4. The universe is orderly (like a watch that follows complex laws).

   Most orderly things we've examined have intelligent designers.

   We've examined a large and varied group of orderly things.

   If most orderly things we've examined have intelligent designers and we've examined a large and varied group of orderly things, then probably most orderly things have intelligent designers.

   If the universe is orderly and probably most orderly things have intelligent designers, then the universe probably has an intelligent designer.

   ∴ The universe probably has an intelligent designer. [Use U, M, W, P, and D. This is a form of the argument from design for the existence of God.]

5. If God doesn't want to prevent evil, then he isn't all good.

   If God isn't able to prevent evil, then he isn't all powerful.

   Either God doesn't want to prevent evil, or he isn't able.

   ∴ Either God isn't all powerful, or he isn't all good. [Use W, G, A, and P. This form of the problem-of-evil argument is from the ancient Greek Empiricus.]

6. If Genesis gives the literal facts, then birds were created before humans. (Genesis 1:20–26)

   If Genesis gives the literal facts, then birds were not created before humans. (Genesis 2:5–20)

   ∴ Genesis doesn't give the literal facts. [Use L and B. Origen, an early Christian thinker, gave similar textual arguments against taking Genesis literally.]

7. The world had a beginning in time.

   If the world had a beginning in time, there was a cause for the world's beginning.

   If there was a cause for the world's beginning, a personal being caused the world.

   ∴ A personal being caused the world. [Use B, C, and P. This "Kalam argument" for the existence of God is from William Craig and James Moreland; they defend premise 1 by various considerations, including the big-bang theory, the law of entropy, and the impossibility of an actual infinite.]

8. If the world had a beginning in time and it didn't just pop into existence without any cause, then the world was caused by God.

   If the world was caused by God, then there is a God.

   There is no God.

   ∴ Either the world had no beginning in time, or it just popped into existence without any cause. [Use B, P, C, and G. This is from J. L. Mackie, who based his "There is no God" premise on the problem-of-evil argument.]

9. Closed systems tend toward greater entropy (a more randomly uniform distribution of energy). (This is the second law of thermodynamics.)
    If closed systems tend toward greater entropy and the world has existed through endless time, then the world would have achieved almost complete entropy (for example, everything would be about the same temperature).
    The world has not achieved almost complete entropy.
    If the world hasn't existed through endless time, then the world had a beginning in time.
    ∴ The world had a beginning in time.   [Use G, E, C, and B. This is from William Craig and James Moreland.]

10. If time stretches back infinitely, then today wouldn't have been reached.
    If today wouldn't have been reached, then today wouldn't exist.
    Today exists.
    If time doesn't stretch back infinitely, then there was a first moment of time.
    ∴ There was a first moment of time.   [I, R, T, F]

11. If there are already laws preventing discrimination against women, then if the Equal Rights Amendment (ERA) would rob women of many current privileges then it is the case both that passage of the ERA would be against women's interests and that women ought to work for its defeat.
    The ERA would rob women of many current privileges (like draft exemption).
    ∴ If there are already laws preventing discrimination against women, then women ought to work for the defeat of the ERA.   [L, R, A, W]

12. If women ought never to be discriminated against, then we should work for current laws against discrimination and prevent future generations from imposing discriminatory laws against women.
    The only way to prevent future generations from imposing discriminatory laws against women is to pass an Equal Rights Amendment (ERA).
    If we should prevent future generations from imposing discriminatory laws against women and the only way to do this is to pass an ERA, then we ought to pass an ERA.
    ∴ If women ought never to be discriminated against, then we ought to pass an ERA. [N, C, F, O, E]

13. If the claim that knowledge-is-impossible is true, then we understand the word "know" but there are no cases of knowledge.
    If we understand the word "know," then the meaning of "know" comes either from a verbal definition or from experienced examples of knowledge.
    If the meaning of "know" comes from a verbal definition, then there's an agreed-upon definition of "know."
    There's no agreed-upon definition of "know."
    If the meaning of "know" comes from experienced examples of knowledge, then there are cases of knowledge.
    ∴ The claim that knowledge-is-impossible is false.   [Use I, U, C, D, E, and A. This is a form of the paradigm-case argument.]

14. If *p* is the greatest prime, then *n* (we may stipulate) is one plus the product of all the primes less than *p*.

If *n* is one plus the product of all the primes less than *p*, then either *n* is prime or else *n* isn't prime but has prime factors greater than *p*.

If *n* is prime, then *p* isn't the greatest prime.

If *n* has prime factors greater than *p*, then *p* isn't the greatest prime.

∴ *p* isn't the greatest prime. [Use G, N, P, and F. This proof that there's no greatest prime number is from the ancient Greek mathematician Euclid.]

7.2 Easier refutations

The beginning of this chapter featured an argument that the butler committed the murder. But now let's suppose that doubts arise about the key premise that *the maid didn't have a motive*; and so we drop this premise. The reasoning then doesn't work – it's invalid:

> The only people in the mansion were the butler and the maid.
> If the only people in the mansion were the butler and the maid, then the butler or the maid did it.
> If the maid did it, then she had a motive.
> ∴ The butler did it.

$$T$$
$$(T \supset (B \vee M))$$
$$(M \supset H)$$
$$\therefore B$$

If we gave this weakened argument, the butler's lawyers could object: "Yes, we know that the only people in the mansion were the butler and the maid, and so one of them did the killing. But maybe the maid did the killing – not the butler – and the maid had a motive. Since the known facts are consistent with this possibility, these known facts don't show that the butler did it." We have here a **refutation** – a set of truth conditions making the premises all true and conclusion false. A refutation shows that the argument is invalid.

If we attempt to prove this invalid argument, we'll begin by assuming that the butler *didn't* do the killing. But this won't lead to a contradiction. Instead we'll reach a refutation that shows that the argument is invalid:

	1	T	
*	2	$(T \supset (B \vee M))$	
*	3	$(M \supset H)$	
		[∴ B	
	4	asm: ~B	
*	5	∴ $(B \vee M)$	{from 1 and 2}
	6	∴ M	{from 4 and 5}
	7	∴ H	{from 3 and 6}

As usual, we assume the opposite of the conclusion. Then we use S- and I-rules to derive whatever we can.

But now we get no contradiction.

```
      1     T
*     2     (T ⊃ (B ∨ M))
*     3     (M ⊃ H)
       [ ∴ B
      4     asm: ~B
*     5     ∴ (B ∨ M)   {from 1 and 2}
      6     ∴ M   {from 4 and 5}
      7     ∴ H   {from 3 and 6}
```

$$\boxed{\text{T, M, H, } \sim\text{B}}$$

We construct a refutation box – which contains the simple wffs (letters or their negation) from not-blocked-off lines (1, 4, 6, and 7).

```
      1     T¹ = 1                    Invalid
*     2     (T¹ ⊃ (B⁰ ∨ M¹)) = 1
*     3     (M¹ ⊃ H¹) = 1
       [ ∴ B⁰ = 0
      4     asm: ~B
*     5     ∴ (B ∨ M)   {from 1 and 2}
      6     ∴ M   {from 4 and 5}
      7     ∴ H   {from 3 and 6}
```

$$\boxed{\text{T, M, H, } \sim\text{B}}$$

To check the refutation, we plug the values into the argument to see if they make the premises all true and conclusion false. They do!

With invalid arguments, we don't get a contradiction; instead, we get a refutation. To construct the refutation box, we take the simple wffs (letters or their negation) from not-blocked-off lines and put them in a box (their order doesn't matter). Our box also could be written in either of these two ways:

$$\boxed{\text{T=1, M=1, H=1, B=0}} \qquad \boxed{\text{T}^1\text{, M}^1\text{, H}^1\text{, B}^0}$$

Then we plug the truth values into the original argument. If the refutation box has a letter by itself (like "T" or "M"), then we mark that letter *true* ("1") in the argument; if it has the negation of a letter (like "~B"), then we mark that letter *false* ("0"); any letters that don't occur in the box are *unknown* ("?" – we can sometimes refute an argument even though not all the letters have values). Then we figure out if these values make the premises all true and conclusion false; if they do, then that shows that the argument is invalid.

What if we don't get the premises all true and conclusion false? Then we did something wrong. The faulty line (a 0 or ? premise, or a 1 or ? conclusion) is the source of the problem; maybe we derived something incorrectly from this line, or didn't derive something we should have derived. So our strategy can tell us when something went wrong and where to look to fix the problem.

Here's another invalid argument and its refutation:

```
        1     (A⁰ ⊃ B¹) = 1   Invalid
    *   2     (C⁰ ∨ B¹) = 1
              [∴ (C⁰ ∨ A⁰) = 0
    *   3     asm: ~(C ∨ A)
        4     ∴ ~C   {from 3}
        5     ∴ ~A   {from 3}
        6     ∴ B   {from 2 and 4}
```

$$\boxed{B, \sim A, \sim C}$$

Since we don't get a contradiction, we construct a refutation box. We plug the values into the argument and find that we get the premises all true and conclusion false.

We may be tempted to use line 1 with 5 or 6 to derive a further conclusion – and a contradiction. But we can't derive anything validly here:

$$\frac{(A \supset B)}{\sim A} \qquad \frac{(A \supset B)}{B}$$
$$\text{nil} \qquad\qquad \text{nil}$$

If we misapply the I-rules, we can wrongly "prove" the argument to be valid.

Let me summarize. Suppose we want to show that, given certain premises, the butler must be guilty. We assume that he's innocent and try to show that this leads to a contradiction. If we get a contradiction, then his innocence is impossible – and so he must be guilty. But if we get no contradiction, then we may be able to show how the premises could be true while yet he is innocent – thus showing that the argument against him is invalid.

I suggest this strategy for proving or refuting a propositional argument:

1. START: Block off the conclusion and add "asm:" followed by the conclusion's simpler contradictory.

2. S&I: Go through the complex wffs that aren't starred or blocked off and use these to derive new wffs using S- and I-rules. Star any wff you simplify using an S-rule, or the longer wff used in an I-rule inference.

   - If you get a contradiction, then go to RAA (step 3).
   - If you can't derive anything further and yet have no contradiction, then go to REFUTE (step 4).

3. RAA: Apply the RAA rule. You've proved the argument valid.

4. REFUTE: Construct a refutation box containing any simple wffs (letters or their negation) that aren't blocked off. In the original argument, mark each letter "1" or "0" or "?" depending on whether the box has the letter or its negation or neither. If these truth conditions make the premises all true and conclusion false, then this shows the argument to be invalid.

This strategy can prove or refute most propositional arguments. We'll see later that some arguments need a more complex strategy and multiple assumptions.

7.2a   Exercise – also LogiCola GEI

Prove each of these arguments to be invalid (all are invalid).

$$\begin{array}{l} (A \supset B) \\ \therefore (B \supset A) \end{array}$$

1	$(A^0 \supset B^1) = 1$	Invalid
	$[\therefore (B^1 \supset A^0) = 0$	
* 2	asm: $\sim(B \supset A)$	$B, \sim A$
3	$\therefore B$ {from 2}	
4	$\therefore \sim A$ {from 2}	

1. $(A \lor B)$
  $\therefore A$

2. $(A \supset B)$
  $(C \supset B)$
  $\therefore (A \supset C)$

3. $\sim(A \cdot \sim B)$
  $\therefore \sim(B \cdot \sim A)$

4. $(A \supset (B \cdot C))$
  $(\sim C \supset D)$
  $\therefore ((B \cdot \sim D) \supset A)$

5. $((A \supset B) \supset (C \supset D))$
  $(B \supset D)$
  $(A \supset C)$
  $\therefore (A \supset D)$

6. $(A \equiv B)$
  $(C \supset B)$
  $\sim(C \cdot D)$
  D
  $\therefore \sim A$

7. $((A \cdot B) \supset C)$
  $\therefore (B \supset C)$

8. $((A \cdot B) \supset C)$
  $((C \lor D) \supset \sim E)$
  $\therefore \sim(A \cdot E)$

9. $\sim(A \cdot B)$
  $(\sim A \lor C)$
  $\therefore \sim(C \cdot B)$

10. $\sim(\sim A \cdot \sim B)$
  $\sim C$
  $(D \lor \sim A)$
  $((C \cdot \sim E) \supset \sim B)$
  $\sim D$
  $\therefore \sim E$

7.2b   Exercise – also LogiCola GEC

First appraise intuitively. Then translate into logic (using the letters given) and say whether valid (and give a proof) or invalid (and give a refutation).

1.   If the butler shot Jones, then he knew how to use a gun.
  If the butler was a former marine, then he knew how to use a gun.
  The butler was a former marine.
 $\therefore$ The butler shot Jones.   [Use S, K, and M.]

2.   If virtue can be taught, then either there are professional virtue-teachers or there are amateur virtue-teachers.
  If there are professional virtue-teachers, then the Sophists can teach their students to be virtuous.
  If there are amateur virtue-teachers, then the noblest Athenians can teach their children to be virtuous.
  The Sophists can't teach their students to be virtuous and the noblest Athenians (such as the great leader Pericles) can't teach their children to be virtuous.
 $\therefore$ Virtue can't be taught.   [Use V, P, A, S, and N. This is from Plato's *Meno*.]

3. It would be equally wrong for a sadist (through a drug injection that would blind you but not hurt your mother) to have blinded you permanently before or after your birth.

    If it would be equally wrong for a sadist (through such a drug injection) to have blinded you permanently before or after your birth, then it's false that one's moral right to equal consideration begins at birth.

    If infanticide is wrong and abortion isn't wrong, then one's moral right to equal consideration begins at birth.

    Infanticide is wrong.

    ∴ Abortion is wrong.   [Use E, R, I, and A.]

4. If you hold a moral belief and don't act on it, then you're inconsistent.

    If you're inconsistent, then you're doing wrong.

    ∴ If you hold a moral belief and act on it, then you aren't doing wrong.   [Use M, A, I, and W. Is the conclusion plausible? What more plausible conclusion follows from these premises?]

5. If Socrates escapes from jail, then he's willing to obey the state only when it pleases him.

    If he's willing to obey the state only when it pleases him, then he doesn't really believe what he says and he's inconsistent.

    ∴ If Socrates really believes what he says, then he won't escape from jail.   [Use E, W, R, and I. This is from Plato's *Crito*. Socrates had been jailed and sentenced to death for teaching philosophy. He discussed with his friends whether he ought to escape from jail instead of suffering the death penalty.]

6. Either Socrates's death will be perpetual sleep, or if the gods are good then his death will be an entry into a better life.

    If Socrates's death will be perpetual sleep, then he shouldn't fear death.

    If Socrates's death will be an entry into a better life, then he shouldn't fear death.

    ∴ Socrates shouldn't fear death.   [Use P, G, B, and F. This is from Plato's *Crito* – except for which dropped premise?]

7. If predestination is true, then God causes us to sin.

    If God causes us to sin and yet damns sinners to eternal punishment, then God isn't good.

    ∴ If God is good, then either predestination isn't true or else God doesn't damn sinners to eternal punishment.   [Use P, C, D, and G. This attacks the views of the American colonial thinker Jonathan Edwards.]

8. If determinism is true, then we have no free will.

    If Heisenberg's interpretation of quantum physics is correct, some events aren't causally necessitated by prior events.

    If some events aren't causally necessitated by prior events, determinism is false.

    ∴ If Heisenberg's interpretation of quantum physics is correct, then we have free will.   [D, F, H, E]

9. Government's function is to protect life, liberty, and the pursuit of happiness.
    The British colonial government doesn't protect these.
    The only way to change it is by revolution.
    If government's function is to protect life, liberty, and the pursuit of happiness
      and the British colonial government doesn't protect these, then the British co-
      lonial government ought to be changed.
    If the British colonial government ought to be changed and the only way to
      change it is by revolution, then we ought to have a revolution.
    ∴ We ought to have a revolution.   [Use G, B, O, C, and R. This summarizes the
      reasoning behind the American Declaration of Independence. Premise 1 was
      claimed to be self-evident, premises 2 and 3 were backed by historical data, and
      premises 4 and 5 were implicit conceptual bridge premises.]

10. The apostles' teaching either comes from God or is of human origin.
    If it comes from God and we kill the apostles, then we will be fighting God.
    If it's of human origin, then it'll collapse of its own accord.
    If it'll collapse of its own accord and we kill the apostles, then our killings will be
      unnecessary.
    ∴ If we kill the apostles, then either our killings will be unnecessary or we will be
      fighting God.   [Use G, H, K, F, C, and U. This argument, from Rabbi Gamaliel
      in Acts 5:34–9, is perhaps the most complex reasoning in the Bible.]

11. If materialism (the view that only matter exists) is true, then idealism is false.
    If idealism (the view that only minds exist) is true, then materialism is false.
    If mental events exist, then materialism is false.
    If materialists *think* their theory is true, then mental events exist.
    ∴ If materialists *think* their theory is true, then idealism is true.   [M, I, E, T]

12. If determinism is true and cruelty is wrong, then the universe contains unavoid-
      able wrong actions.
    If the universe contains unavoidable wrong actions, then we ought to regret the
      universe as a whole.
    If determinism is true and regretting cruelty is wrong, then the universe contains
      unavoidable wrong actions.
    ∴ If determinism is true, then either we ought to regret the universe as a whole (the
      pessimism option) or else cruelty isn't wrong and regretting cruelty isn't wrong
      (the "nothing matters" option).   [Use D, C, U, O, and R. This sketches the rea-
      soning in William James's "The Dilemma of Determinism." James thought
      that when we couldn't prove one side or the other to be correct (as on the issue
      of determinism), it was more rational to pick our beliefs in accord with practical
      considerations. He argued that these weighed against determinism.]

13. If a belief is proved, then it's worthy of acceptance.
    If a belief isn't disproved but is of practical value to our lives, then it's worthy of
      acceptance.
    If a belief is proved, then it isn't disproved.
    ∴ If a belief is proved or is of practical value to our lives, then it's worthy of accept-
      ance.   [P, W, D, V]

14. If you're consistent and think that stealing is normally permissible, then you'll consent to the idea of others stealing from you in normal circumstances.

   You don't consent to the idea of others stealing from you in normal circumstances.

   ∴ If you're consistent, then you won't think that stealing is normally permissible. [C, N, Y]

15. If the meaning of a term is always the object it refers to, then the meaning of "Fido" is Fido.

   If the meaning of "Fido" is Fido, then if Fido is dead then the meaning of "Fido" is dead.

   If the meaning of "Fido" is dead, then "Fido is dead" has no meaning.

   "Fido is dead" has meaning.

   ∴ The meaning of a term isn't always the object it refers to.   [Use A, B, F, M, and H. This is from Ludwig Wittgenstein, except for which dropped premise?]

16. God is all powerful.

   If God is all powerful, then he could have created the world in any logically possible way and the world has no necessity.

   If the world has no necessity, then we can't know the way the world is by abstract speculation apart from experience.

   ∴ We can't know the way the world is by abstract speculation apart from experience.   [Use A, C, N, and K. This is from the medieval William of Ockham.]

17. If God changes, then he changes for the worse or for the better.

   If he's perfect, then he doesn't change for the worse.

   If he changes for the better, then he isn't perfect.

   ∴ If God is perfect, then he doesn't change.   [C, W, B, P]

18. If belief in God has scientific backing, then it's rational.

   No conceivable scientific experiment could decide whether there is a God.

   If belief in God has scientific backing, then some conceivable scientific experiment could decide whether there is a God.

   ∴ Belief in God isn't rational.   [B, R, D]

19. Every event with finite probability eventually takes place.

   If the nations of the world don't get rid of their nuclear weapons, then there's a finite probability that humanity will eventually destroy the world.

   If every event with finite probability eventually takes place and there's a finite probability that humanity will eventually destroy the world, then humanity will eventually destroy the world.

   ∴ Either nations of the world will get rid of their nuclear weapons, or humanity will eventually destroy the world.   [E, R, F, H]

20. If the world isn't ultimately absurd, then conscious life will go on forever and the world process will culminate in an eternal personal goal.

   If there is no God, then conscious life won't go on forever.

   ∴ If the world isn't ultimately absurd, then there is a God.   [Use A, F, C, and G. This is from the Jesuit scientist, Pierre Teilhard de Chardin.]

21.   If it rained here on this date 500 years ago and there's no way to know whether it rained here on this date 500 years ago, then there are objective truths that we cannot know.
      If it didn't rain here on this date 500 years ago and there's no way to know whether it rained here on this date 500 years ago, then there are objective truths that we cannot know.
      There's no way to know whether it rained here on this date 500 years ago.
   ∴ There are objective truths that we cannot know.   [R, K, O]

22.   If you know that you don't exist, then you don't exist.
      If you know that you don't exist, then you know some things.
      If you know some things, then you exist.
   ∴ You exist.   [K, E, S]

23.   We have an idea of a perfect being.
      If we have an idea of a perfect being, then this idea is either from the world or from a perfect being.
      If this idea is from a perfect being, then there is a God.
   ∴ There is a God.   [Use I, W, P, and G. This is from René Descartes, except for which dropped premise?]

24.   The distance from A to B can be divided into an infinity of spatial points.
      One can cross only one spatial point at a time.
      If one can cross only one spatial point at a time, then one can't cross an infinity of spatial points in a finite time.
      If the distance from A to B can be divided into an infinity of spatial points and one can't cross an infinity of spatial points in a finite time, then one can't move from A to B in a finite time.
      If motion is real, then one can move from A to B in a finite time.
   ∴ Motion isn't real.   [Use D, O, C, M, and R. This is from the ancient Greek Zeno of Elea, who denied the reality of motion.]

25.   If the square root of 2 equals some fraction of positive whole numbers, then (we stipulate) the square root of 2 equals x/y and x/y is simplified as far as it can be.
      If the square root of 2 equals x/y, then $2 = x^2/y^2$.
      If $2 = x^2/y^2$, then $2y^2 = x^2$.
      If $2y^2 = x^2$, then x is even.
      If x is even and $2y^2 = x^2$, then y is even.
      If x is even and y is even, then x/y isn't simplified as far as it can be.
   ∴ The square root of 2 doesn't equal some fraction of positive whole numbers.
      [F, E, S, T, T′, X, Y]

7.3   Harder proofs

Our present proof strategy doesn't work with the following argument:

> If the butler was at the party, then he fixed
> the drinks and poisoned the deceased.
> If the butler wasn't at the party, then the
> detective would have seen him leave the
> mansion and would have reported this.
> The detective didn't report this.
> ∴ The butler poisoned the deceased.

```
(A ⊃ (F · P))
(~A ⊃ (S · R))
~R
∴  P
```

If we assume "~P," then we get stuck. We can't apply the S- or I-rules or RAA; and we don't have enough simple wffs for a refutation. What can we do? On our expanded strategy, when we get stuck we'll make another assumption.

Here's a proof that uses our expanded strategy:

1	(A ⊃ (F · P))	We're stuck. We can't derive any-thing, and so we can't get a proof or refutation.
2	(~A ⊃ (S · R))	
3	~R	
	[∴ P	So we make another assumption.
4	asm: ~P	

1	(A ⊃ (F · P))	We pick a complex wff we haven't used yet (1 or 2), pick left or right side, and assume it or its negation.
2	(~A ⊃ (S · R))	
3	~R	
	[∴ P	
4	asm: ~P	Here we decide to assume the negation of the left side of line 1.
5	asm: ~A {break 1}	

	1	(A ⊃ (F · P))	
**	2	(~A ⊃ (S · R))	We use S- and I-rules to derive further lines. But now we use two stars (one for each assumption).
	3	~R ⇐	
		[∴ P	
	4	asm: ~P	
	5	asm: ~A {break 1}	Lines 3 and 8 contradict.
**	6	∴ (S · R) {from 2 and 5}	
	7	∴ S {from 6}	
	8	∴ R {from 6} ⇐	

1	(A ⊃ (F · P))	Since we have a contradiction, we:
2	(~A ⊃ (S · R))	
3	~R ⇐	• block off the lines from the last assumption on down,
	[∴ P	
4	asm: ~P	• derive the opposite of this last assumption, and
5	⌐ asm: ~A {break 1}	
6	∴ (S · R) {from 2 and 5}	• erase star strings with more stars than the number of remaining assumptions.
7	∴ S {from 6}	
8	⌊ ∴ R {from 6} ⇐	
9	∴ A {from 5; 3 contradicts 8}	

```
  *   1    (A ⊃ (F • P))
      2    (~A ⊃ (S • R))
      3    ~R
         [ ∴ P
      4      asm: ~P   ⇦
      5    ┌ asm: ~A   {break 1}
      6    │  ∴ (S • R)   {from 2 and 5}
      7    │  ∴ S   {from 6}
      8    └  ∴ R   {from 6}
      9      ∴ A   {from 5; 3 contradicts 8}
  *  10      ∴ (F • P)   {from 1 and 9}
     11      ∴ F   {from 10}
     12      ∴ P   {from 10}   ⇦
```

We use S- and I-rules to derive further lines, and we get a second contradiction (lines 4 and 12).

We ignore blocked-off lines (the original conclusion and lines 5 to 8) as we derive further lines and look for a contradiction.

```
  *   1    (A ⊃ (F • P))          Valid
      2    (~A ⊃ (S • R))
      3    ~R
         [ ∴ P
      4    ┌ asm: ~P
      5    │ ┌ asm: ~A   {break 1}
      6    │ │  ∴ (S • R)   {from 2 and 5}
      7    │ │  ∴ S   {from 6}
      8    │ └  ∴ R   {from 6}
      9    │   ∴ A   {from 5; 3 contradicts 8}
  *  10    │   ∴ (F • P)   {from 1 and 9}
     11    │   ∴ F   {from 10}
     12    └   ∴ P   {from 10}
     13      ∴ P   {from 4; 4 contradicts 12}
```

Finally, we apply RAA again, this time on our original assumption.

To prove the argument valid, we need a contradiction for each assumption.

Our proof is done!

The most difficult part of multiple-assumption proofs is knowing *when* to make another assumption and *what* to assume.

(1) *Make another assumption when you're stuck.* This means that you can't apply S- or I-rules further – and yet you can't prove the argument VALID (since you don't have a contradiction) or INVALID (since you don't have enough simple wffs for a refutation). Don't make additional assumptions too soon; it's "too soon" if you can still apply S- or I-rules or RAA. Always use S- and I-rules and RAA to their limit before resorting to further assumptions.

(2) *When you're stuck, make an assumption that breaks a complex wff.* Look for a complex wff that isn't starred, blocked off, or *broken* (a wff is broken if we already have one side or its negation but not what we need to conclude anything new). This wff will have one of these forms:

$$~(A • B) \qquad (A ∨ B) \qquad (A ⊃ B)$$

Assume either side or its negation. Here we could use any of these:

asm: A   asm: ~A   asm: B   asm: ~B

While any of the four will work, our proof will go differently depending on which we use. Suppose we want to break "(A ⊃ B)"; compare what happens if we assume "A" or assume "~A":

(immediate gratification)	(A ⊃ B) asm: A ∴ B	(A ⊃ B) asm: ~A ...	*(delayed gratification)*

In the first case, we assume "A" and get immediate gratification; we can use an I-rule on "(A ⊃ B)" right away to get "B." In the second case, we assume "~A" and get delayed gratification; we'll be able to use an I-rule on "(A ⊃ B)" only later, after the "~A" assumption dies (if it does) and we derive "A." The "delayed gratification" approach tends to produce shorter proofs; it saves an average of one line, with all the gain coming on invalid arguments. So sometimes a proof is simpler if you assume one thing rather than another.

Follow the same strategy on wffs that are more complicated. To break "((A · B) ⊃ (C · D))," we could make any of these four assumptions:

asm: (A · B)   asm: ~(A · B)   asm: (C · D)   asm: ~(C · D)

Assume one side or its negation. Never assume the denial of a whole line.

Also, never make an assumption to break a wff that's already *broken*. A wff is *broken* if we already have one side or its negation but not what we need to conclude anything new. So a "(A ⊃ B)" line, for example, is broken if we already have a not-blocked-off line with "~A" or "B." In such a case, it won't help us to make an assumption to break "(A ⊃ B)."

After making our second assumption, we star the same things as before – except that we now use more stars:

Star any wff that you simplify using an S-rule. ** (A · B) ───── ∴ A ∴ B	*Use one star for each live assumption.*	Star the *longer* wff used in an I-rule inference. ** (A ⊃ B) A ───── ∴ B

A *live assumption* is one that isn't blocked off. So if we have two live assumptions, then we use two stars. And if we have three live assumptions, then we use three stars. As before, starred lines are redundant; when we do a proof, we can focus on *complex wffs that aren't starred or blocked off* and what can be derived from them. Multiple stars mean "You can ignore this line for now, but you may have to use it later."

When we have multiple live assumptions and find a contradiction:

- we block off the lines from the last live assumption on down (this indicates that these lines are no longer to be used in the proof – since they depend on an assumption that we've concluded to be false);
- we derive the opposite of this last assumption; and
- we erase star strings with more stars than the number of remaining live assumptions (we do this because the lines that make these starred lines re-dundant are now blocked off).

Note the part about erasing star strings with more stars than the number of remaining live assumptions. So if our second assumption dies, leaving us with just one live assumption, then we erase double-stars ("**").

When our last live assumption leads to a contradiction, we've proved the argument to be valid. Valid arguments seldom require more than two assumptions. But if we get stuck again after making a second assumption, then we'll need to make a third assumption.

Our final proof strategy can prove or refute any propositional argument (as we'll show in Section 15.4):

1. START: Block off the conclusion and add "asm:" followed by the conclusion's simpler contradictory.

2. S&I: Go through the complex wffs that aren't starred or blocked off and use these to derive new wffs using S- and I-rules. Star (with one star for each live assumption) any wff you simplify using an S-rule, or the longer wff used in an I-rule inference.
   - If you get a contradiction, then go to RAA (step 3).
   - If you can't derive anything further but there is a complex wff that isn't starred or blocked off or broken, then go to ASSUME (step 4).
   - If you can't derive anything further and every complex wff is starred or blocked off or broken, then go to REFUTE (step 5).

3. RAA: Apply the RAA rule. If all assumptions are now blocked off, you've proved the argument valid. Otherwise, erase star strings having more stars than the number of live assumptions and return to step 2.

4. ASSUME: Pick a complex wff that isn't starred or blocked off or broken. This wff will have one of these forms: "~(A • B)," "(A ∨ B)," or "(A ⊃ B)." Assume one side or its negation and return to step 2.

5. REFUTE: Construct a refutation box containing any simple wffs (letters or their negation) that aren't blocked off. In the original argument, mark each letter "1" or "0" or "?" depending on whether the box has the letter or its negation or neither. These truth conditions should make the premises all true and conclusion false – thus showing the argument to be invalid.

Here's another example of a multiple-assumption valid argument (we'll get to invalid ones later):

	1	(A ⊃ (B · C))
	2	(B ⊃ (A · C))
		[∴ ((A ∨ B) ⊃ C)
*	3	asm: ~((A ∨ B) ⊃ C)
	4	∴ (A ∨ B) {from 3}
	5	∴ ~C {from 3}

After deriving a few lines, we get stuck and can't go further. So we need to make another assumption. We could assume the left or right sides (or their denials) of lines 1, 2, or 4.

**	1	(A ⊃ (B · C))
	2	(B ⊃ (A · C))
		[∴ ((A ∨ B) ⊃ C)
*	3	asm: ~((A ∨ B) ⊃ C)
	4	∴ (A ∨ B) {from 3}
	5	∴ ~C {from 3} ⇐
	6	asm: A {break 1}
**	7	∴ (B · C) {from 1 and 6}
	8	∴ B {from 7}
	9	∴ C {from 7} ⇐

We decide to assume the left side of line 1. Then we derive further lines until we get a contradiction (lines 5 and 9).

We do double stars, since we have two live assumptions.

	1	(A ⊃ (B · C))
	2	(B ⊃ (A · C))
		[∴ ((A ∨ B) ⊃ C)
*	3	asm: ~((A ∨ B) ⊃ C)
	4	∴ (A ∨ B) {from 3}
	5	∴ ~C {from 3} ⇐
	6	⌐ asm: A {break 1}
	7	│ ∴ (B · C) {from 1 and 6}
	8	│ ∴ B {from 7}
	9	∟ ∴ C {from 7} ⇐
	10	∴ ~A {from 6; 5 contradicts 9}

We block off from assumption 6 down, conclude its opposite in line 10, and then (since we now have only one live assumption) erase double stars.

We ignore blocked-off lines (the original conclusion and lines 6 to 9) as we continue the proof.

	1	(A ⊃ (B · C))	**Valid**
*	2	(B ⊃ (A · C))	
		[∴ ((A ∨ B) ⊃ C)	
*	3	⌐ asm: ~((A ∨ B) ⊃ C)	
*	4	│ ∴ (A ∨ B) {from 3}	
	5	│ ∴ ~C {from 3}	
	6	│ ⌐ asm: A {break 1}	
	7	│ │ ∴ (B · C) {from 1 and 6}	
	8	│ │ ∴ B {from 7}	
	9	│ ∟ ∴ C {from 7}	
	10	│ ∴ ~A {from 6; 5 contradicts 9} ⇐	
	11	│ ∴ B {from 4 and 10}	
	12	│ ∴ (A · C) {from 2 and 11}	
	13	∟ ∴ A {from 12} ⇐	
	14	∴ ((A ∨ B) ⊃ C) {from 3; 10 contradicts 13}	

We derive further lines and get our second contradiction (lines 10 and 13). We apply RAA again, this time on our original assumption.

To prove the argument valid, we need a contradiction for each assumption.

Our proof is done!

7.3a   Exercise – also LogiCola GHV

Prove each of these arguments to be valid (all are valid).

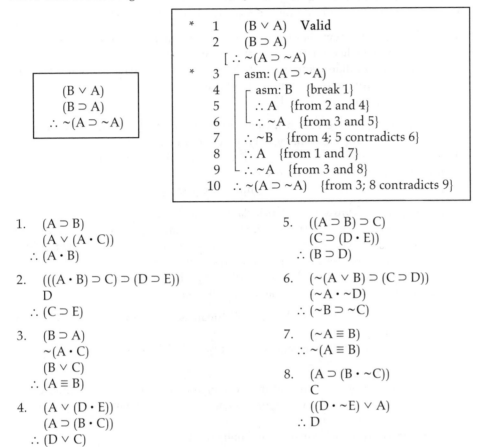

```
    *    1     (B ∨ A)   Valid
         2     (B ⊃ A)
              [ ∴ ~(A ⊃ ~A)
    *    3     ┌ asm: (A ⊃ ~A)
         4     │  ┌ asm: B   {break 1}
         5     │  │ ∴ A   {from 2 and 4}
         6     │  └ ∴ ~A   {from 3 and 5}
         7     │  ∴ ~B   {from 4; 5 contradicts 6}
         8     │  ∴ A   {from 1 and 7}
         9     └ ∴ ~A   {from 3 and 8}
        10     ∴ ~(A ⊃ ~A)   {from 3; 8 contradicts 9}
```

1.   (A ⊃ B)
     (A ∨ (A · C))
     ∴ (A · B)

2.   (((A · B) ⊃ C) ⊃ (D ⊃ E))
     D
     ∴ (C ⊃ E)

3.   (B ⊃ A)
     ~(A · C)
     (B ∨ C)
     ∴ (A ≡ B)

4.   (A ∨ (D · E))
     (A ⊃ (B · C))
     ∴ (D ∨ C)

5.   ((A ⊃ B) ⊃ C)
     (C ⊃ (D · E))
     ∴ (B ⊃ D)

6.   (~(A ∨ B) ⊃ (C ⊃ D))
     (~A · ~D)
     ∴ (~B ⊃ ~C)

7.   (~A ≡ B)
     ∴ ~(A ≡ B)

8.   (A ⊃ (B · ~C))
     C
     ((D · ~E) ∨ A)
     ∴ D

7.3b   Exercise – also LogiCola GHV

First appraise intuitively. Then translate into logic (using the letters given) and prove to be valid (all are valid).

1.   Either the butler fixed the drink and poisoned the deceased, or the butler added poison later and poisoned the deceased.
     If the butler poisoned the deceased, then the butler is guilty.
     ∴ The butler poisoned the deceased and is guilty.   [Use F, P, A, and G.]

2.   If I'm coming down with a cold and I exercise, then I'll get worse and feel awful.
     If I don't exercise, then I'll suffer exercise deprivation and I'll feel awful.
     ∴ If I'm coming down with a cold, then I'll feel awful.   [Use C, E, W, A, and D. This one is easier if you break premise 1 (not 2) to make your assumption.]

3. You'll get an A if and only if you either get a hundred on the final exam or else bribe the teacher.
    You won't get a hundred on the final exam.
    ∴ You'll get an A if and only if you bribe the teacher.   [Use A, H, and B.]

4. If President Nixon knew about the massive Watergate cover-up, then he lied to the American people on national television and he should resign.
    If President Nixon didn't know about the massive Watergate cover-up, then he was incompetently ignorant and he should resign.
    ∴ Nixon should resign.   [K, L, R, I]

5. If you don't compromise your principles, then you won't get campaign money.
    If you won't get campaign money, then you won't be elected.
    If you compromise your principles, then you'll appeal to more voters.
    If you appeal to more voters, then you'll be elected.
    ∴ You'll be elected if and only if you compromise your principles.   [C, M, E, A]

6. Moral judgments express either truth claims or feelings.
    If moral judgments express truth claims, then "ought" expresses either a concept from sense experience or an objective concept that isn't from sense experience.
    "Ought" doesn't express a concept from sense experience.
    "Ought" doesn't express an objective concept that isn't from sense experience.
    ∴ Moral judgments express feelings and not truth claims.   [T, F, S, O]

7. If Michigan either won or tied, then Michigan is going to the Rose Bowl and Gensler is happy.
    ∴ If Gensler isn't happy, then Michigan didn't tie.   [W, T, R, H]

8. There are moral obligations.
    If there are moral obligations and moral obligations are explainable, then either there's an explanation besides God's existence or else God's existence would explain moral obligations.
    God's existence wouldn't explain moral obligation.
    ∴ Either moral obligations aren't explainable, or else there's an explanation besides God's existence.   [M, E, B, G]

9. If determinism is true and Dr Freudlov correctly predicts (using deterministic laws) what I'll do, then if she tells me her prediction I'll do something else.
    If Dr Freudlov tells me her prediction and yet I'll do something else, then Dr Freudlov doesn't correctly predict (using deterministic laws) what I'll do.
    ∴ If determinism is true, then Dr Freudlov doesn't correctly predict (using deterministic laws) what I'll do or else she won't tell me her prediction.   [D, P, T, E]

10. If you make this demand on your son [that he leave Suzy or else not have his graduate schooling financed] and he leaves Suzy, then he'll regret being forced to leave her and he'll always resent you.
    If you make this demand on your son and he doesn't leave Suzy, then he'll regret not going to graduate school and he'll always resent you.
    ∴ If you make this demand on your son, then he'll always resent you.   [Use D, L, F, A, and G; this one is difficult.]

7.4   Harder refutations

Multiple-assumption invalid arguments work like other invalid arguments – except that we need to make further assumptions before we reach our refutation. Here's an example:

If the butler was at the party, he fixed the drinks and poisoned the deceased.

If the butler wasn't at the party, he was at a neighbor's house.

∴ The butler poisoned the deceased.

	1	$(A^0 \supset (F^? \cdot P^0)) = 1$	Invalid
**	2	$(\sim A^0 \supset N^1) = 1$	
		$[\therefore P^0 = 0$	
	3	asm: ~P	
	4	asm: ~A {break 1}	
	5	∴ N {from 2 and 4}	

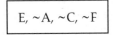

N, ~A, ~P

We derive all we can and make additional assumptions when needed. But now we reach no contradiction; instead, we reach a refutation in which the butler was at a neighbor's house, wasn't at the party, and didn't poison the deceased. This refutation makes the premises all true and conclusion false.

As we work out our proof, we can follow the five-step proof strategy of the previous section until we get a proof or a refutation. If every assumption leads to a contradiction, then we get a proof of validity. But when do we know that the argument is invalid? When do we stop making further assumptions and instead construct our refutation box? *We stop and refute when we can't derive anything further (using S- or I-rules or RAA) and every complex wff is starred or blocked off or broken.* (Recall that a complex wff is "broken" if we have one side or its negation but not what we need to conclude anything new.)

Here's an example of an invalid argument that requires three assumptions:

	1	$(A^0 \supset B^?) = 1$ Invalid
	2	$(C^0 \supset D^?) = 1$
	3	$(F^0 \supset (C^0 \cdot D^?)) = 1$
		$[\therefore (E^1 \supset C^0) = 0$
*	4	asm: ~(E ⊃ C)
	5	∴ E {from 4}
	6	∴ ~C {from 4}
	7	asm: ~A {break 1}
	8	asm: ~F {break 3}

E, ~A, ~C, ~F

We continue until we can derive nothing further and all complex wffs are either starred (line 4) or blocked off (original conclusion) or broken (lines 1–3). Our refutation has no values for "B" or "D"; but it still makes the premises all true and conclusion false.

Our proof strategy, if applied correctly, will always give a proof or refutation. How these go may depend on which lines we do first and what we decide to assume; proofs and refutations may differ but still be correct.

7.4a   Exercise – also LogiCola GHI

Prove each of these arguments to be invalid (all are invalid).

$$
\begin{array}{ll}
(A \lor \sim(B \supset C)) \\
(D \supset (A \supset B)) \\
\therefore (C \supset \sim(D \lor A))
\end{array}
$$

	1	$(A^1 \lor \sim(B^? \supset C^1)) = 1$	Invalid
	2	$(D^0 \supset (A^1 \supset B^?)) = 1$	$A,\ C,\ \sim D$
		$[\therefore (C^1 \supset \sim(D^0 \lor A^1)) = 0$	
*	3	asm: $\sim(C \supset \sim(D \lor A))$	
	4	$\therefore C$ {from 3}	
	5	$\therefore (D \lor A)$ {from 3}	
	6	asm: A {break 1}	
	7	asm: $\sim D$ {break 2}	

1. $\sim(A \cdot B)$
    $\therefore (\sim A \cdot \sim B)$

2. $(A \supset \sim B)$
    $\therefore \sim(A \supset B)$

3. $(A \supset B)$
    $(C \supset (\sim D \cdot E))$
    $\therefore (D \lor F)$

4. $\sim(A \cdot B)$
    $\therefore \sim(A \equiv B)$

5. $(A \supset (B \cdot C))$
    $((D \supset E) \supset A)$
    $\therefore (E \lor C)$

6. $(\sim A \lor \sim B)$
    $\therefore \sim(A \lor B)$

7. $((A \cdot B) \supset \sim(C \cdot D))$
    C
    $(E \supset B)$
    $\therefore \sim E$

8. $(A \supset (B \supset C))$
    $(B \lor \sim(C \supset D))$
    $\therefore (D \supset \sim(A \lor B))$

7.4b   Exercise – also LogiCola G (HC & MC)

First appraise intuitively. Then translate into logic (using the letters given) and say whether valid (and give a proof) or invalid (and give a refutation).

1.   If the maid prepared the drink, then the butler didn't prepare it.
     The maid didn't prepare the drink.
     If the butler prepared the drink, then he poisoned the drink and is guilty.
     ∴ The butler is guilty.   [Use M, B, P, and G.]

2.   If you tell your teacher that you like logic, then your teacher will think that you're insincere and you'll be in trouble.
     If you don't tell your teacher that you like logic, then your teacher will think that you dislike logic and you'll be in trouble.
     ∴ You'll be in trouble.   [Use L, I, T, and D.]

3.   If we don't get reinforcements, then the enemy will overwhelm us and we won't survive.
     ∴ If we do get reinforcements, then we'll conquer the enemy and we'll survive.
     [Use R, O, S, and C.]

4.   If Socrates didn't approve of the laws of Athens, then he would have left Athens or would have tried to change the laws.
     If Socrates didn't leave Athens and didn't try to change the laws, then he agreed to obey the laws.
     Socrates didn't leave Athens.
     ∴ If Socrates didn't try to change the laws, then he approved of the laws and agreed to obey them.   [Use A, L, C, and O. This is from Plato's *Crito*, which argued that Socrates shouldn't disobey the law by escaping from jail.]

5.   If I hike the Appalachian Trail and go during late spring, then I'll get maximum daylight and maximum mosquitoes.
     If I'll get maximum mosquitoes, then I won't be comfortable.
     If I go right after school, then I'll go during late spring.
∴ If I hike the Appalachian Trail and don't go right after school, then I'll be comfortable.   [A, L, D, M, C, S]

6.   [Logical positivism says "*Every genuine truth claim is either experimentally testable or true by definition.*" This view, while once popular, is self-refuting and hence not very popular today.]
     If LP (logical positivism) is true and is a genuine truth claim, then it's either experimentally testable or true by definition.
     LP isn't experimentally testable.
     LP isn't true by definition.
     If LP isn't a genuine truth claim, then it isn't true.
∴ LP isn't true.   [T, G, E, D]

7.   If you give a test, then students either do well or do poorly.
     If students do well, then you think you made the test too easy and you're frustrated.
     If students do poorly, then you think they didn't learn any logic and you're frustrated.
∴ If you give a test, then you're frustrated.   [Use T, W, P, E, F, and L. This is from a class who tried to talk me out of giving a test.]

8.   If the world contains moral goodness, then the world contains free creatures and the free creatures sometimes do wrong.
     If the free creatures sometimes do wrong, then the world is imperfect and the creator is imperfect.
∴ If the world doesn't contain moral goodness, then the creator is imperfect.   [M, F, S, W, C]

9.   We'll find your action's cause, if and only if your action has a cause and we look hard enough.
     If all events have causes, then your action has a cause.
     All events have causes.
∴ We'll find your action's cause, if and only if we look hard enough.   [F, H, L, A]

10. Herman sees that the piece of chalk is white.
     The piece of chalk is the smallest thing on the desk.
     Herman doesn't see that the smallest thing on the desk is white. (He can't see the whole desk and so can't tell that the piece of chalk is the smallest thing on it.)
     If Herman sees a material thing, then if he sees that the piece of chalk is white and the piece of chalk is the smallest thing on the desk, then he sees that the smallest thing on the desk is white.
     If Herman doesn't see a material thing, then he sees a sense datum.
∴ Herman doesn't see a material thing, but he does see a sense datum.   [Use H, P, H´, M, and S. This argument attacks direct realism – the view that we directly perceive material things and not just sensations or sense data.]

11. If the final capacitor in the transmitter is arcing, then the SWR (standing wave ratio) is too high and the efficiency is lowered.
    If you hear a cracking sound, then the final capacitor in the transmitter is arcing.
    ∴ If you don't hear a cracking sound, then the SWR isn't too high.   [A, H, L, C]

12. If we can know that God exists, then we can know God by experience or we can know God by logical inference from experience.
    If we can't know God empirically, then we can't know God by experience and we can't know God by logical inference from experience.
    If we can know God empirically, then "God exists" is a scientific hypothesis and is empirically falsifiable.
    "God exists" isn't empirically falsifiable.
    ∴ We can't know that God exists.   [K, E, L, M, S, F]

13. If I perceive, then my perception is either delusive or veridical.
    If my perception is delusive, then I don't directly perceive a material object.
    If my perception is veridical and I directly perceive a material object, then my experience in veridical perception would always differ qualitatively from my experience in delusive perception.
    My experience in veridical perception doesn't always differ qualitatively from my experience in delusive perception.
    If I perceive and I don't directly perceive a material object, then I directly perceive a sensation.
    ∴ If I perceive, then I directly perceive a sensation and I don't directly perceive a material object.   [Use P, D, V, M, Q, and S. This argument from illusion attacks direct realism – the view that we directly perceive material objects and not just sensations or sense data.]

14. If you're romantic and you're Italian, then Juliet will fall in love with you and will want to marry you.
    If you're Italian, then you're romantic.
    ∴ If you're Italian, then Juliet will want to marry you.   [R, I, F, M]

15. If emotions can rest on factual errors and factual errors can be criticized, then we can criticize emotions.
    If we can criticize emotions and moral judgments are based on emotions, then beliefs about morality can be criticized and morality isn't entirely non-rational.
    ∴ If morality is entirely non-rational, then emotions can't rest on factual errors.
    [E, F, W, M, B, N]

7.5   Other proof methods

The proof method in this book tries to combine the best features of two other methods: traditional proofs and truth trees. These three approaches (plus an axiomatic approach that we'll mention in Section 15.5), while differing in how they do proofs, can prove all the same arguments.

Traditional proofs use a standard set of inference rules and equivalence rules. The nine inference rules are like our S- and I-rules, in that they let us infer whole lines from previous whole lines:

$$
\begin{array}{ll}
(P \cdot Q) \rightarrow P & (P \supset Q), P \rightarrow Q \\
P, Q \rightarrow (P \cdot Q) & (P \supset Q), {\sim}Q \rightarrow {\sim}P \\
(P \vee Q), {\sim}P \rightarrow Q & (P \supset Q), (Q \supset R) \rightarrow (P \supset R) \\
P \rightarrow (P \vee Q) & (P \supset Q) \rightarrow (P \supset (P \cdot Q)) \\
\end{array}
$$

$$((P \supset Q) \cdot (R \supset S)), (P \vee R) \rightarrow (Q \vee S)$$

The 16 equivalence rules let us replace parts of formulas with equivalent parts (I've dropped outer parentheses here to promote readability):

$$
\begin{array}{ll}
P \equiv {\sim}{\sim}P & (P \supset Q) \equiv ({\sim}P \vee Q) \\
P \equiv (P \cdot P) & (P \cdot (Q \cdot R)) \equiv ((P \cdot Q) \cdot R) \\
P \equiv (P \vee P) & (P \vee (Q \vee R)) \equiv ((P \vee Q) \vee R) \\
(P \cdot Q) \equiv (Q \cdot P) & (P \cdot (Q \vee R)) \equiv ((P \cdot Q) \vee (P \cdot R)) \\
(P \vee Q) \equiv (Q \vee P) & (P \vee (Q \cdot R)) \equiv ((P \vee Q) \cdot (P \vee R)) \\
{\sim}(P \cdot Q) \equiv ({\sim}P \vee {\sim}Q) & (P \equiv Q) \equiv ((P \supset Q) \cdot (Q \supset P)) \\
{\sim}(P \vee Q) \equiv ({\sim}P \cdot {\sim}Q) & (P \equiv Q) \equiv ((P \cdot Q) \vee ({\sim}P \cdot {\sim}Q)) \\
(P \supset Q) \equiv ({\sim}Q \supset {\sim}P) & ((P \cdot Q) \supset R) \equiv (P \supset (Q \supset R)) \\
\end{array}
$$

Our approach uses a simpler and more understandable set of rules.

Traditional proofs can be *indirect proofs* (where we assume the opposite of the conclusion and then derive a contradiction); but they more often are *direct proofs* (where we just derive things from the premises and eventually derive the desired conclusion) or *conditional proofs* (where we prove "(P ⊃ Q)" by assuming "P" and then deriving "Q"). Here's an argument proved two ways:

	Traditional proof			*Our proof*

Traditional proof

1 ((A ⊃ B) • (C ⊃ D))
  [∴ ((A • C) ⊃ (B ∨ D))
2 ∴ (A ⊃ B) {from 1}
3 ∴ (~A ∨ B) {from 2}
4 ∴ ((~A ∨ B) ∨ D) {from 3}
5 ∴ (~A ∨ (B ∨ D)) {from 4}
6 ∴ ((~A ∨ (B ∨ D)) ∨ ~C) {from 5}
7 ∴ (~C ∨ (~A ∨ (B ∨ D))) {from 6}
8 ∴ ((~C ∨ ~A) ∨ (B ∨ D)) {from 7}
9 ∴ ((~A ∨ ~C) ∨ (B ∨ D)) {from 8}
10 ∴ (~(A • C) ∨ (B ∨ D)) {from 9}
11 ∴ ((A • C) ⊃ (B ∨ D)) {from 10,
    giving the original conclusion}

Our proof

* 1 ((A ⊃ B) • (C ⊃ D))
  [∴ ((A • C) ⊃ (B ∨ D))
* 2 ⌐ asm: ~((A • C) ⊃ (B ∨ D))
* 3 │ ∴ (A ⊃ B) {from 1}
4 │ ∴ (C ⊃ D) {from 1}
* 5 │ ∴ (A • C) {from 2}
6 │ ∴ ~(B ∨ D) {from 2}
7 │ ∴ A {from 5}
8 │ ∴ C {from 5}
9 │ ∴ B {from 3 and 7}
10 ∟ ∴ ~B {from 6}
11 ∴ ((A • C) ⊃ (B ∨ D)) {from
    2; 9 contradicts 10}

Both proofs have the same number of lines; but this can vary, depending on how we do each proof.[1] Our lines typically have shorter formulas. Our proofs tend to simplify larger formulas into smaller ones, while traditional proofs tend to manipulate longer formulas (often by substituting equivalents) to get the desired result. Our proofs are easier to do, since they use an automatic strategy that students learn quickly; traditional proofs require guesswork and intuition. Also, our system refutes invalid arguments; it can separate valid from invalid arguments, prove valid ones to be valid, and refute invalid ones. In contrast, the traditional system is only a proof method; if we try to prove an invalid argument, we'll fail but won't necessarily learn that the argument is invalid.

Another common approach is *truth trees*, which decompose formulas into the cases that make them true. Truth trees use simplifying rules and branching rules. The simplifying rules are like our S-rules, in that they let us simplify a formula into smaller parts and then ignore the original formula. These four simplifying rules (which apply to whole lines) are used:

$$
\begin{array}{l}
\sim\sim P \;\rightarrow\; P \\
(P \cdot Q) \;\rightarrow\; P, Q \\
\sim(P \vee Q) \;\rightarrow\; \sim P, \sim Q \\
\sim(P \supset Q) \;\rightarrow\; P, \sim Q
\end{array}
$$

Each form that can't be simplified is branched into the two sub-cases that would make it true; for example, since "$\sim(P \cdot Q)$" is true just if "$\sim P$" is true or "$\sim Q$" is true, it branches into these two formulas. There are five branching rules:

$\sim(P \cdot Q)$	$(P \vee Q)$	$(P \supset Q)$	$(P \equiv Q)$	$\sim(P \equiv Q)$
$\sim P$ $\sim Q$	P Q	$\sim P$ Q	P $\sim P$ Q $\sim Q$	P Q $\sim Q$ $\sim P$

To test an argument, we write the premises, block off the original conclusion (showing that it is to be ignored in constructing the tree), and add the denial of the conclusion. Then we apply the simplifying and branching rules to each formula, and to each further formula that we get, until every branch either dies (contains a pair of contradictory wffs) or contains only simple wffs (letters or their negation). The argument is valid if and only if every branch dies. Here's an argument proved two ways:

---

[1] Our proof still works if we skip lines 4 and 8 (which are prescribed by our proof strategy). If we skip these, then our proof becomes two lines shorter.

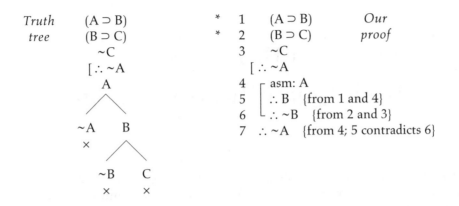

In the truth tree, we write the premises, block off the original "∴ A" conclusion (and henceforth ignore it), and add its contradictory "A." Then we branch "(A ⊃ B)" into its two sub-cases: "~A" and "B." The left branch dies, since it contains "A" and "~A"; we indicate this by putting "×" at its bottom. Then we branch "(B ⊃ C)" into its two sub-cases: "~B" and "C." Each branch dies; the left branch has "B" and "~B," while the right has "C" and "~C." Since every branch of the tree dies, no possible truth conditions would make the premises all true and conclusion false, and so the argument is valid.

An argument is invalid if some branch of the tree doesn't die. Then the simple wffs on each branch that doesn't die give a refutation of the argument – truth conditions making the premises all true and conclusion false.

Truth trees have two main advantages over traditional proofs: truth trees are easier to do (since they rely on an easily learnable strategy) and can refute invalid arguments (so they provide an efficient way to test whether an argument is valid or invalid). But truth trees don't mirror ordinary reasoning very well; they give a mechanical way to test validity instead of a way to help develop reasoning skills. And branching can get messy. Our method avoids these disadvantages but keeps the main advantages of truth trees.

Our method is a marriage between truth trees and traditional proofs. In its stress on simplifying formulas down to their basic parts, our method resembles truth trees; but branching is replaced by I-rules and multiple assumptions. In its stress on giving a linear derivation of formulas, our method resembles traditional proofs. Our goal is to combine the best features of both systems in a practical and easily learnable method for constructing proofs and refutations.

CHAPTER 8
Basic Quantificational Logic

Quantificational logic builds on propositional logic and studies arguments whose validity depends on "all," "no," "some," and similar notions.[1] This chapter covers the basics and the next adds relations and identity.

8.1   Easier translations

To help us evaluate quantificational arguments, we'll construct a little quantificational language. Our language builds on propositional logic and includes all of its vocabulary, wffs, inference rules, and proofs. We add two new vocabulary items: small letters and "∃." Here are sample formulas:

Ir	=	Romeo is Italian.
Ix	=	x is Italian.
(x)Ix	=	For all x, x is Italian (all are Italian).
(∃x)Ix	=	For some x, x is Italian (some are Italian).

"Romeo is Italian" is "Ir"; write the capital letter first. Here "I" is for the general category "Italian" and "r" is for the specific individual "Romeo":

Use capital letters for **general terms** (terms that *describe* or put in a *category*):

Use capital letters for **general terms** (terms that *describe* or put in a *category*):

    I = an Italian
    C = charming
    F = drives a Ford

Use capitals for "a so and so," adjectives, and verbs.

Use small letters for **singular terms** (terms that pick out a *specific* person or thing):

    i = the richest Italian
    c = this child
    r = Romeo

Use small letters for "the so and so," "this so and so," and proper names.

---

[1] While overlapping with syllogistic logic (Chapter 2), quantificational logic is more powerful because it builds on propositional logic. For example, it can express statements like "If everything that is A or B is then C if and only if it's D, then either something is E or nothing is F."

Capital and small letters have various uses. Capitals can represent statements, general terms, or relations (which we take in the next chapter):

A capital letter alone (not followed by small letters) represents a *statement*.	S	*It is snowing.*
A capital letter followed by a single small letter represents a *general term*.	Ir	Romeo is *Italian*.
A capital letter followed by two or more small letters represents a *relation*.	Lrj	Romeo *loves* Juliet.

Similarly, small letters can be constants or variables:

A small letter from "a" to "w" is a **constant** – and stands for a specific person or thing.	Ir	*Romeo* is Italian.
A small letter from "x" to "z" is a **variable** – and doesn't stand for a specific person or thing.	Ix	*x* is Italian.

"Ix" ("x is Italian"), which uses the variable "x," is incomplete, and thus not true or false, since we haven't said whom we are talking about; but we can add a quantifier to complete the claim.

A **quantifier** is a sequence of the form "(x)" or "(∃x)" – where any variable may replace "x":

"(x)" is a **universal quantifier**. It claims that the formula that follows is true for *all* values of x.	"(∃x)" is an **existential quantifier**. It claims that the formula that follows is true for *at least one* value of x.

(x)Ix   =   For all x, x is Italian.
       =   All are Italian.
	(∃x)Ix = For some x, x is Italian.
	        = Some are Italian.

Quantifiers express "all" and "some" by saying in how many cases the following formula is true.

As before, a grammatically correct formula is called a *wff*, or *well-formed formula*. For now, wffs are strings that we can construct using the propositional rules plus these two rules:

> 1. The result of writing a capital letter and then a small letter is a wff.
> 2. The result of writing a quantifier and then a wff is a wff.

These rules let us build wffs that we've already mentioned: "Ir," "Ix," "(x)Ix," and "(∃x)Ix." Don't use additional parentheses with these:

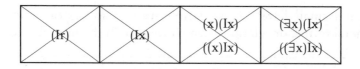

Use a pair of parentheses for each quantifier and for each instance of "·," "∨," "⊃," and "≡"; use no other parentheses. Here are some further wffs:

~(x)Ix	=	Not all are Italian.
	=	It is not the case that, for all x, x is Italian.
~(∃x)Ix	=	No one is Italian.
	=	It is not the case that, for some x, x is Italian.
(Ix ⊃ Lx)	=	If x is Italian then x is a lover.
(Ix · Lx)	=	x is Italian and x is a lover.

Translating from English sentences to wffs can be difficult. We'll begin with sentences that translate into wffs starting with a quantifier, or with "~" and then a quantifier. This rule tells where to put what quantifier:

If the English begins with	then begin the wff with
all (every)	(x)
not all (not every)	~(x)
some	(∃x)
no	~(∃x)

Here are basic examples:

All are Italian	=	(x)Ix		Some are Italian	=	(∃x)Ix
Not all are Italian	=	~(x)Ix		No one is Italian	=	~(∃x)Ix

Here are harder examples:

All are rich or Italian	=	(x)(Rx ∨ Ix)
Not everyone is non-Italian	=	~(x)~Ix
Some aren't rich	=	(∃x)~Rx
No one is rich and non-Italian	=	~(∃x)(Rx · ~Ix)

When the English begins with "all," "some," "not all," or "no," the quantifier must go *outside* all parentheses:

All are rich or Italian	=	(x)(Rx ∨ Ix)	≠	((x)Rx ∨ Ix)

The *wrong* formula means "Either everyone is rich, or x is Italian" – which isn't what we want to say.

If the English sentence specifies a logical connective (like "or," "and," or "if-then"), then use the corresponding logical symbol. When the English doesn't specify the connective, use these rules:

| With "all … is …," use "⊃" for the *middle* connective. | *Otherwise* use "·" for the connective. |

"All (every) A is B" uses "⊃," while "Some A is B" and "No A is B" use "·"; here are examples:

All Italians are lovers = (x)(Ix ⊃ Lx)
  = For all x, *if* x is Italian *then* x is a lover.

Some Italians are lovers = (∃x)(Ix · Lx)
  = For some x, x is Italian *and* x is a lover.

No Italians are lovers = ~(∃x)(Ix · Lx)
  = It is not the case that, for some x, x is Italian *and* x is a lover.

When you see "All Italians," think "For all x, *if* x is Italian *then* …" – and when you see "Some Italians," think "For some x, x is Italian *and* …." This next example illustrates both boxed rules:

All rich Italians are lovers = (x)((Rx · Ix) ⊃ Lx)
  = For all x, *if* x is rich *and* Italian, *then* x is a lover.

We use "⊃" as the *middle* connective ("*If* rich Italian, *then* lover") and "·" in the *other* place ("If rich *and* Italian, then lover"). Note carefully the connectives in the next two examples:

Not all Italians are lovers = ~(x)(Ix ⊃ Lx)
  = It is not the case that, for all x, *if* x is Italian *then* x is a lover.

All are rich Italians = (x)(Rx · Ix)
  = For all x, x is rich *and* Italian.

In case of doubt, phrase out the symbolic formula to yourself and see if it means the same as the English sentence.

Sentences with a main verb other than "is" should be rephrased to make "is" the main verb – and then translated. Here's an example:

	=	All dogs are cat-haters.
All dogs hate cats	=	For all x, if x is a dog then x is a cat-hater.
	=	(x)(Dx ⊃ Hx)

The **universe of discourse** is the set of entities that words like "all," "some," and "no" range over in a given context. In translating arguments about some one kind of entity (such as persons or statements), we can simplify our formulas by restricting the universe of discourse to that one kind of entity. We did this implicitly when we translated "All are Italian" as "(x)Ix" – instead of as "(x)(Px ⊃ Ix)" ("All persons are Italians"); here our "(x)" really means "For all persons x." We'll often restrict the universe of discourse to persons.

English has many idiomatic expressions; so our translation rules are rough and don't always work. After you symbolize an English sentence, it's wise to read your formula carefully, to make sure it reflects what the English means.

8.1a   Exercise – also LogiCola H (EM & ET)

Translate these English sentences into wffs.

Not all logicians run.	~(x)(Lx ⊃ Rx)

1.   x isn't a cat.
2.   Something is a cat.
3.   Something isn't a cat.
4.   It isn't the case that there is something that isn't a cat.
5.   Everything is a cat.
6.   If x is a dog, then x is an animal.
7.   All dogs are animals.
8.   No one is evil.
9.   Some logicians are evil.
10.   No logician is evil.
11.   All black cats are unlucky.
12.   Some dogs are large and hungry.
13.   Not all hungry dogs bark.
14.   Some animals aren't barking dogs.
15.   Some animals are dogs who don't bark.
16.   All dogs who bark are frightening.
17.   Not all non-dogs are cats.
18.   Some cats who aren't black are unlucky.
19.   Some cats don't purr.
20.   Not every cat purrs.
21.   Not all animals are dogs or cats.
22.   All who are either dogs or cats are animals.
23.   All who are both dogs and cats are animals.
24.   All dogs and cats are animals.
25.   Everyone is a crazy logician.

8.2   Easier proofs

Quantificational proofs work much like propositional ones but use four new inference rules for quantifiers.

These two reverse-squiggle (RS) rules hold regardless of what variable replaces "x" and what pair of contradictory wffs replaces "Fx" / "~Fx"; here "→" means we can infer whole lines from left to right:

<table>
<tr><td rowspan="2">Reverse
squiggle</td><td>~(x)Fx → (∃x)~Fx</td></tr>
<tr><td>~(∃x)Fx → (x)~Fx</td></tr>
</table>

So "Not everyone is funny" entails "Someone isn't funny." Similarly, "It is not the case that someone is funny" ("No one is funny") entails "Everyone is non-funny." We can reverse squiggles on longer formulas, so long as the whole formula begins with "~" and then a quantifier (so the third box is wrong):

~(∃x)~Gx	~(x)(Lx · ~Mx)	~~(Ir ⊃ ~(x)Gx)~~
∴ (x)~~Gx	∴ (∃x)~(Lx · ~Mx)	~~∴ (Ir ⊃ (∃x)~Gx)~~

In the first box, it would be simpler to conclude "(x)Gx" (eliminating the double negation). Reverse squiggles whenever you have a wff that begins with "~" and then a quantifier; reversing a squiggle moves the quantifier to the beginning of the formula, so we can later drop it.

We drop quantifiers using the next two rules (which hold regardless of what variable replaces "x" and what wffs replace "Fx" / "Fa" – provided that the two wffs are identical except that wherever the variable occurs freely[1] in the former the same constant occurs in the latter). Here's the drop-existential (DE) rule:

<table>
<tr><td>Drop
existential</td><td>(∃x)Fx → Fa,
use a new constant</td></tr>
</table>

Suppose *someone* robbed the bank; we can give this person a name – like "Al" – but it must be an *arbitrary name* that we make up. Likewise, when we drop an existential, we'll label this "someone" with a *new constant* – one that hasn't yet occurred in earlier lines of the proof. In proofs, we'll use the next unused letter in alphabetical order – starting with "a," then "b," and so on:

---

[1] *Technical footnote:* An instance of a variable occurs "freely" if it doesn't occur as part of a wff that begins with a quantifier using that variable; just the first instance of "x" in "(Fx · (x)Gx)" occurs freely. So we'd go from "(∃x)(Fx · (x)Gx)" to "(Fa · (x)Gx)."

$(\exists x)Mx$ Someone is male, someone is female;
$(\exists x)Fx$ let's call the male "a" and the female "b."
———
$\therefore$ Ma   ←   "a" is OK since it occurs in no earlier line.
$\therefore$ Fb   ←   Since "a" has now occurred, we use "b."

We can drop existentials from complicated formulas if the quantifier begins the wff and we replace the variable with the same new constant throughout:

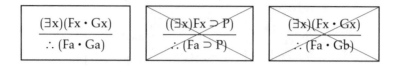

The second formula doesn't *begin* with a quantifier; instead, it begins with a left-hand parenthesis. *Drop only initial quantifiers.*[1]

Here's the drop-universal (DU) rule:

Drop universal
$$(x)Fx \;\;\rightarrow\;\; Fa,$$
use any constant

If *everyone* is funny, then Al is funny, Bob is funny, and so on. From "$(x)Fx$" we can derive "Fa," "Fb," and so on – using any constant. However, it's bad strategy to use a new constant unless we really have to; normally we should use old constants. As before, the quantifier must begin the wff and we must replace the variable with the same constant throughout:

$(x)(Fx \supset Gx)$	$((x)Fx \supset (x)Gx)$	$(x)(Fx \supset Gx)$
$\therefore (Fa \supset Ga)$	$\therefore (Fa \supset Ga)$	$\therefore (Fa \supset Gb)$

The second inference is wrong because the quantifier doesn't *begin* the formula (a left-hand parenthesis begins it). "$((x)Fx \supset (x)Gx)$" is an if-then and follows the if-then rules: if we have the first part "$(x)Fx$" true, we can get the second true; if we have the second part "$(x)Gx$" false, we can get the first false; and if we get stuck, we need to make another assumption.

Here's an English version of a quantificational proof:

---

[1] *Technical footnote:* This paragraph needs three qualifications. (1) If *someone* robbed the bank, then maybe *more than one* person did; then our name (or constant) will refer to a random *one* of the robbers. (2) Using a new name is consistent with the robber being someone mentioned in the argument so far; different names (like "Jim" and "Smith") might refer to the same individual. (3) Rule DE should be used only when there is at least one not-blocked-off assumption; otherwise, the symbolic version of "Someone is a thief, so Gensler is a thief" would be a two-line proof.

1   All logicians are funny.
2   Someone is a logician.
 [∴ Someone is funny.
3   ┌ Assume: It is not the case that someone is funny.
4   │ ∴ Everyone is non-funny.   {from 3, reverse squiggles}
5   │ ∴ a is a logician.   {from 2, drop existential, call the logician "a"}
6   │ ∴ If a is a logician then a is funny.   {from 1, drop universal}
7   │ ∴ a is funny.   {from 5 and 6}   ⇐
8   └ ∴ a is non-funny.   {from 4, drop universal}   ⇐
9   ∴ Someone is funny.   {from 3; 7 contradicts 8}

Our symbolic version adds three quantificational steps (reverse squiggles, drop existentials, drop universals) to our propositional-proof strategy:

	1	(x)(Lx ⊃ Fx) **Valid**
*	2	(∃x)Lx
		[∴ (∃x)Fx
*	3	┌ asm: ~(∃x)Fx
	4	│ ∴ (x)~Fx {from 3}
	5	│ ∴ La {from 2}
*	6	│ ∴ (La ⊃ Fa) {from 1}
	7	│ ∴ Fa {from 5 and 6} ⇐
	8	└ ∴ ~Fa {from 4} ⇐
	9	∴ (∃x)Fx {from 3; 7 contradicts 8}

(1) Reverse squiggles: go from "~(∃x)Fx" to "(x)~Fx" (line 4).

(2) Drop initial existentials, using a new letter each time: go from "(∃x)Lx" to "La" (line 5).

(3) Lastly, drop each initial universal once for each old letter: go from "(x)(Lx ⊃ Fx)" to "(La ⊃ Fa)" – and from "(x)~Fx" to "~Fa."

We starred lines 2, 3, and 6. As before, starred lines largely can be ignored in deriving further lines. Here are the new starring rules – with examples:

Star any wff on which you reverse squiggles.	Star any wff from which you drop an existential.
* ~(x)Fx	* (∃x)Fx
―――――――	―――――――
∴ (∃x)~Fx	∴ Fa

When we reverse squiggles or drop existentials, the new line has the same information. Don't star when dropping a universal; we can never exhaust an "all" statement by deriving instances – and we may have to derive further things from it later in the proof.

Here's another quantificational proof:

```
        1      (x)(Fx · Gx)   Valid
           [ ∴ (x)Fx
  *     2  ┌ asm: ~(x)Fx
  *     3  │ ∴ (∃x)~Fx   {from 2}
        4  │ ∴ ~Fa   {from 3}
        5  │ ∴ (Fa · Ga)   {from 1}
        6  └ ∴ Fa   {from 5}
        7  ∴ (x)Fx   {from 2; 4 contradicts 6}
```

(1) Reverse squiggles: go from "~(x)Fx" to "(∃x)~Fx" (line 3).

(2) Drop initial existentials, using a new letter each time: go from "(∃x)~Fx" to "~Fa" (line 4).

(3) Lastly, drop each initial universal once for each old letter: go from "(x)(Fx · Gx)" to "(Fa · Ga)."

It would be wrong to switch lines 4 and 5. If we drop the universal first using "a," then we can't drop the existential next using "a" (since "a" would be old).

Our proof strategy works much like before. We first assume the opposite of the conclusion; then we use our four new quantificational rules plus the S- and I-rules to derive whatever we can. If we find a contradiction, we apply RAA. If we get stuck and need to break a wff of the form "~(A · B)" or "(A ∨ B)" or "(A ⊃ B)," then we make another assumption. If we get no contradiction and yet can't do anything further, then we try to refute the argument.

Here's a fuller statement of the three quantificational steps of our strategy:

1. FIRST REVERSE SQUIGGLES: For each unstarred, not-blocked-off line that begins with "~" and then a quantifier, derive a line using the reverse-squiggle rules. Star the original line.

2. AND DROP EXISTENTIALS: For each unstarred, not-blocked-off line that begins with an existential quantifier, derive an instance using the next available *new* constant (unless some such instance already occurs in previous not-blocked-off lines). Star the original line.

    Note: Don't drop an existential if you already have a not-blocked-off instance in previous lines – there's no point in deriving a second instance. So don't drop "(∃x)Fx" if you already have "Fc."

3. LASTLY DROP UNIVERSALS: For each not-blocked-off line that begins with a universal quantifier, derive instances using each *old* constant. Don't star the original line; you might have to use it again.

    Note: Drop a universal using a *new* letter only if you've done everything else possible (making further assumptions if needed) and still have no old letters. This is unusual, but happens if we try to prove "(x)~Fx ∴ ~(x)Fx."

Drop existentials before universals. Introduce a new letter each time you drop an existential, and use the same old letters when you drop a universal. And drop only initial quantifiers.

8.2a   Exercise – also LogiCola IEV

Prove each of these arguments to be valid (all are valid).

```
  *   1      ~(∃x)Fx          Valid
           [ ∴ (x)~(Fx • Gx)
  *   2    ┌ asm: ~(x)~(Fx • Gx)
  *   3    │ ∴ (∃x)(Fx • Gx)   {from 2}
      4    │ ∴ (x)~Fx   {from 1}
      5    │ ∴ (Fa • Ga)   {from 3}
      6    │ ∴ ~Fa   {from 4}
      7    └ ∴ Fa   {from 5}
      8    ∴ (x)~(Fx • Gx)   {from 2; 6 contradicts 7}
```

```
~(∃x)Fx
∴ (x)~(Fx • Gx)
```

1. (x)Fx
    ∴ (x)(Gx ∨ Fx)

2. ~(∃x)(Fx • ~Gx)
    ∴ (x)(Fx ⊃ Gx)

3. ~(∃x)(Fx • Gx)
    (∃x)Fx
    ∴ (∃x)~Gx

4. (x)((Fx ∨ Gx) ⊃ Hx)
    ∴ (x)(~Hx ⊃ ~Fx)

5. (x)(Fx ⊃ Gx)
    (∃x)Fx
    ∴ (∃x)(Fx • Gx)

6. (x)(Fx ∨ Gx)
    ~(x)Fx
    ∴ (∃x)Gx

7. (x)~(Fx ∨ Gx)
    ∴ (x)~Fx

8. (x)(Fx ⊃ Gx)
    (x)(Fx ⊃ ~Gx)
    ∴ (x)~Fx

9. (x)(Fx ⊃ Gx)
    (x)(~Fx ⊃ Hx)
    ∴ (x)(Gx ∨ Hx)

10. (x)(Fx ≡ Gx)
    (∃x)~Gx
    ∴ (∃x)~Fx

8.2b Exercise – also LogiCola IEV

First appraise intuitively. Then translate into logic (using the letters given) and prove to be valid (all are valid).

1. All who deliberate about alternatives believe in free will (at least implicitly).
    All deliberate about alternatives.
    ∴ All believe in free will.   [Use Dx and Bx. This is from William James.]

2. Everyone makes mistakes.
    ∴ Every logic teacher makes mistakes.   [Use Mx and Lx.]

3. No feeling of pain is publicly observable.
    All chemical processes are publicly observable.
    ∴ No feeling of pain is a chemical process.   [Use Fx, Ox, and Cx. This attacks a form of materialism that identifies mental events with material events. We also could test this argument using syllogistic logic (Chapter 2).]

4. All (in the electoral college) who do their jobs are useless.
    All (in the electoral college) who don't do their jobs are dangerous.
    ∴ All (in the electoral college) are useless or dangerous.   [Use Jx for "x does their job," Ux for "x is useless," and Dx for "x is dangerous." Use the universe of discourse of electoral college members: take "(x)" to mean "for every electoral college member x" and don't translate "in the electoral college."]

5. All that's known is experienced through the senses.
   Nothing that's experienced through the senses is known.
   ∴ Nothing is known.   [Use Kx and Ex. Empiricism (premise 1) plus skepticism
   about the senses (premise 2) yields general skepticism.]

6. No pure water is burnable.
   Some Cuyahoga River water is burnable.
   ∴ Some Cuyahoga River water isn't pure water.   [Use Px, Bx, and Cx. The Cuya-
   hoga is a river in Cleveland that used to catch fire.]

7. Everyone who isn't with me is against me.
   ∴ Everyone who isn't against me is with me.   [Use Wx and Ax. These claims from
   the Gospels are sometimes thought to be incompatible.]

8. All basic laws depend on God's will.
   ∴ All basic laws about morality depend on God's will.   [Bx, Dx, Mx]

9. Some lies in unusual circumstances aren't wrong.
   ∴ Not all lies are wrong.   [Lx, Ux, Wx]

10. Nothing based on sense experience is certain.
    Some logical inferences are certain.
    All certain things are truths of reason.
    ∴ Some truths of reason are certain and aren't based on sense experience.   [Bx, Cx,
    Lx, Rx]

11. No truth by itself motivates us to action.
    Every categorical imperative would by itself motivate us to action.
    Every categorical imperative would be a truth.
    ∴ There are no categorical imperatives.   [Use Tx, Mx, and Cx. Immanuel Kant
    claimed that commonsense morality accepts categorical imperatives (objectively
    true moral judgments that command us to act and that we must follow if we are
    to be rational); but some thinkers argue against the idea.]

12. Every genuine truth claim is either experimentally testable or true by definition.
    No moral judgments are experimentally testable.
    No moral judgments are true by definition.
    ∴ No moral judgments are genuine truth claims.   [Use Gx, Ex, Dx, and Mx. This is
    logical positivism's argument against moral truths.]

13. Everyone who can think clearly would do well in logic.
    Everyone who would do well in logic ought to study logic.
    Everyone who can't think clearly ought to study logic.
    ∴ Everyone ought to study logic.   [Tx, Wx, Ox]

8.3   Easier refutations

Applying our proof strategy to an invalid argument leads to a refutation:

	1	(x)(Lx ⊃ Fx)	Invalid
*	2	(∃x)Lx	a, b
		[∴ (x)Fx	

*	3	asm: ~(x)Fx
*	4	∴ (∃x)~Fx {from 3}
	5	∴ La {from 2}
	6	∴ ~Fb {from 4}
*	7	∴ (La ⊃ Fa) {from 1}
*	8	∴ (Lb ⊃ Fb) {from 1}
	9	∴ Fa {from 5 and 7}
	10	∴ ~Lb {from 6 and 8}

All logicians are funny.
Someone is a logician.
∴ Everyone is funny.

La, Fa
~Lb, ~Fb

After making the assumption (line 3), we reverse a squiggle to move a quantifier to the outside (line 4). Then we drop the two existential quantifiers, using a new and different constant each time (lines 5 and 6). We drop the universal quantifier twice, first using "a" and then using "b" (lines 7 and 8). Since we get no contradiction, we gather the simple pieces to give a refutation. Our refutation is a little possible world with two people, a and b:

a is a logician.	a is funny.
b isn't a logician.	b isn't funny.

Here the premises are true, since all logicians are funny, and someone is a logician. The conclusion is false, since someone isn't funny. Since the premises are all true and the conclusion false, our argument is invalid.

If we try to prove an invalid argument, we'll instead be led to a refutation – a little possible world with various individuals (like a and b) and simple truths about these individuals (like La and ~Lb) that would make the premises all true and conclusion false. In evaluating the premises and conclusion, evaluate each wff that starts with a quantifier according to these rules:

An *existential* wff is true if and only if *at least one case* is true.	A *universal* wff is true if and only if *all cases* are true.

In our world, universal premise "(x)(Lx ⊃ Fx)" is true, since all cases are true:

$$(La \supset Fa) = (1 \supset 1) = 1$$
$$(Lb \supset Fb) = (0 \supset 0) = 1$$

Existential premise "(∃x)Lx" is true, since at least one case is true (we have "La" – "a is a logician"). But universal conclusion "(x)Fx" is false, since at least one case is false (we have "~Fb" – "b isn't funny"). So our possible world makes the premises all true and the conclusion false.

Be sure to check that your refutation works. If you don't get premises all 1 and conclusion 0, then you did something wrong – and the source of the problem is likely what you did with the formula that came out wrong.

Here's another example:

*	1	~(∃x)(Fx · Gx)	Invalid	
*	2	(∃x)Fx		
		[∴ ~(∃x)Gx	a, b	
*	3	asm: (∃x)Gx		
	4	∴ (x)~(Fx · Gx) {from 1}	Fa, ~Ga	
	5	∴ Fa {from 2}	Gb, ~Fb	
	6	∴ Gb {from 3}		
*	7	∴ ~(Fa · Ga) {from 4}		
*	8	∴ ~(Fb · Gb) {from 4}		
	9	∴ ~Ga {from 5 and 7}		
	10	∴ ~Fb {from 6 and 8}		

In this world, some things are F and some things are G, but nothing is both at once. In evaluating premise "~(∃x)(Fx · Gx)," first evaluate the subformula that starts with the quantifier. "(∃x)(Fx · Gx)" is false since no case is true:

$$(Fa \cdot Ga) \;=\; (1 \cdot 0) \;=\; 0$$
$$(Fb \cdot Gb) \;=\; (0 \cdot 1) \;=\; 0$$

So the denial "~(∃x)(Fx · Gx)" is true. Premise "(∃x)Fx" is true since at least one case is true (namely, Fa). In evaluating conclusion "~(∃x)Gx," again first evaluate the subformula that starts with the quantifier. "(∃x)Gx" is true since at least one case is true (namely, Gb); so the denial "~(∃x)Gx" is false. So we get the premises all true and the conclusion false.

These two rules are crucial for working out proofs and refutations:

(1) For each initial *existential quantifier*, introduce a *new constant*.
(2) For each initial *universal quantifier*, derive an instance for each *old constant*.

In our last example, we'd violate (1) if we derived "Ga" in line 6 – since "a" at this point is old; then we'd "prove" the argument to be valid. We'd violate (2) if we didn't derive "~(Fb · Gb)" in line 8. Then our refutation would have no truth value for "Fb"; so "Fb" and premise 1 would both be "?" (unknown truth value) – showing that we had to do something further with premise 1.

Possible worlds for refutations must contain at least one entity. Seldom do we need more than two entities.

8.3a   Exercise – also LogiCola IEI

Prove each of these arguments to be invalid (all are invalid).

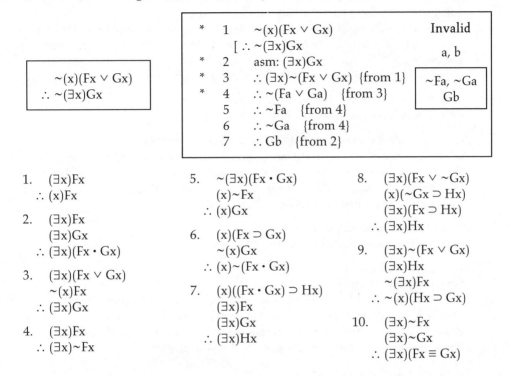

1.   (∃x)Fx
     ∴ (x)Fx

2.   (∃x)Fx
     (∃x)Gx
     ∴ (∃x)(Fx · Gx)

3.   (∃x)(Fx ∨ Gx)
     ~(x)Fx
     ∴ (∃x)Gx

4.   (∃x)Fx
     ∴ (∃x)~Fx

5.   ~(∃x)(Fx · Gx)
     (x)~Fx
     ∴ (x)Gx

6.   (x)(Fx ⊃ Gx)
     ~(x)Gx
     ∴ (x)~(Fx · Gx)

7.   (x)((Fx · Gx) ⊃ Hx)
     (∃x)Fx
     (∃x)Gx
     ∴ (∃x)Hx

8.   (∃x)(Fx ∨ ~Gx)
     (x)(~Gx ⊃ Hx)
     (∃x)(Fx ⊃ Hx)
     ∴ (∃x)Hx

9.   (∃x)~(Fx ∨ Gx)
     (∃x)Hx
     ~(∃x)Fx
     ∴ ~(x)(Hx ⊃ Gx)

10. (∃x)~Fx
     (∃x)~Gx
     ∴ (∃x)(Fx ≡ Gx)

8.3b   Exercise – also LogiCola IEC

First appraise intuitively. Then translate into logic (using the letters given) and say whether valid (and give a proof) or invalid (and give a refutation).

1.   Some butlers are guilty.
     ∴ All butlers are guilty.   [Use Bx and Gx.]

2.   No material thing is infinite.
     Not everything is material.
     ∴ Something is infinite.   [Use Mx and Ix.]

3.   Some smoke.
     Not all have clean lungs.
     ∴ Some who smoke don't have clean lungs.   [Use Sx and Cx.]

4.   Some Marxists plot violent revolution.
     Some faculty members are Marxists.
     ∴ Some faculty members plot violent revolution.   [Mx, Px, Fx]

5. All valid arguments that have "ought" in the conclusion also have "ought" in the premises.
   All arguments that seek to deduce an "ought" from an "is" have "ought" in the conclusion but don't have "ought" in the premises.
   ∴ No argument that seeks to deduce an "ought" from an "is" is valid.   [Use Vx for "x is valid," Cx for "x has 'ought' in the conclusion," Px for "x has 'ought' in the premises," Dx for "x seeks to deduce an 'ought' from an 'is,'" and the universe of discourse of arguments. This one is difficult to translate.]

6. Every kick returner who is successful is fast.
   ∴ Every kick returner who is fast is successful.   [Kx, Sx, Fx]

7. All exceptionless duties are based on the categorical imperative.
   All non-exceptionless duties are based on the categorical imperative.
   ∴ All duties are based on the categorical imperative.   [Use Ex, Bx, and the universe of discourse of duties. This is from Kant, who based all duties on his supreme moral principle, called "the categorical imperative."]

8. All who aren't crazy agree with me.
   ∴ No one who is crazy agrees with me.   [Cx, Ax]

9. Everything can be conceived.
   Everything that can be conceived is mental.
   ∴ Everything is mental.   [Use Cx and Mx. This is from George Berkeley, who attacked materialism by arguing that everything is mental and that matter doesn't exist apart from mental sensations; so a chair is just a collection of experiences. Bertrand Russell thought premise 2 was confused.]

10. All sound arguments are valid.
    ∴ All invalid arguments are unsound.   [Use Sx and Vx and the universe of discourse of arguments.]

11. All trespassers are eaten.
    ∴ Some trespassers are eaten.   [Use Tx and Ex. The premise is from a sign on the Appalachian Trail in northern Virginia. Traditional logic (Section 2.8) takes "all A is B" to entail "some A is B"; modern logic takes "all A is B" to mean "whatever is A also is B" – which can be true even if there are no A's.]

12. Some necessary being exists.
    All necessary beings are perfect beings.
    ∴ Some perfect being exists.   [Use Nx and Px. Kant claimed that the cosmological argument for God's existence at most proves premise 1; it doesn't prove the existence of God (a perfect being) unless we add premise 2. But premise 2, by the next argument, presupposes the central claim of the ontological argument – that some perfect being is a necessary being. So, Kant claimed, the cosmological argument presupposes the ontological argument.]

13. All necessary beings are perfect beings.
    ∴ Some perfect being is a necessary being.   [Use Nx and Px. Kant followed traditional logic (see problem 11) in taking "all A is B" to entail "some A is B."]

14.   No one who isn't a logical positivist holds the verifiability criterion of meaning.
∴ All who hold the verifiability criterion of meaning are logical positivists.   [Use
Lx and Hx. The verifiability criterion of meaning says that every genuine truth
claim is either experimentally testable or true by definition.]

15.   No pure water is burnable.
Some Cuyahoga River water isn't burnable.
∴ Some Cuyahoga River water is pure water.   [Use Px, Bx, and Cx.]

8.4   Harder translations

We'll now start using statement letters (like "S" for "It is snowing") and
individual constants (like "r" for "Romeo") in our translations and proofs:

If it's snowing, then Romeo is cold   =   (S ⊃ Cr)

Here "S," since it's a capital letter not followed by a small letter, represents a
whole statement. And "r," since it's a small letter between "a" and "w," is a
constant that stands for a specific person or thing.

We'll also start using multiple and non-initial quantifiers. From now on, use
this expanded rule about what quantifier to use and where to put it:

Wherever the English has	put this in the wff
all (every)	(x)
not all (not every)	~(x)
some	(∃x)
no	~(∃x)

Here's an example:

If all are Italian, then Romeo is Italian   =   ((x)Ix ⊃ Ir)

Since "if" translates as "(," likewise "if all" translates as "((x)." As you translate, mimic the English word order:

all not	=	(x)~	all either	=	(x)(	if all either	=	((x)(
not all	=	~(x)	either all	=	((x)	if either all	=	(((x)

Use a separate quantifier for each "all," "some," and "no":

If all are Italian,
then all are lovers   =   ((x)Ix ⊃ (x)Lx)

If not everyone is Italian, then some aren't lovers.	=	$(\sim(x)Ix \supset (\exists x)\sim Lx)$
If no Italians are lovers, then some Italians are not lovers	=	$(\sim(\exists x)(Ix \cdot Lx) \supset (\exists x)(Ix \cdot \sim Lx))$

"Any" differs in subtle ways from "all" (which translates into a "(x)" that mirrors where "all" occurs in the English sentence). "Any" is governed by two different but equivalent rules; here's the easier rule, with examples:

(1) To translate "any," first rephrase the sentence so it means the same thing but doesn't use "any"; then translate the second sentence.	"Not any …" = "No …." "If any …" = "If some …." "Any …" = "All …."

Not anyone is rich	=	No one is rich.
	=	$\sim(\exists x)Rx$
Not any Italian is a lover	=	No Italian is a lover.
	=	$\sim(\exists x)(Ix \cdot Lx)$
If anyone is just, there will be peace	=	If someone is just, there will be peace.
	=	$((\exists x)Jx \supset P)$

Our second rule usually gives a different formula, but an equivalent one:

(2) To translate "any," put a "(x)" at the *beginning* of the wff, regardless of where the "any" occurs in the sentence.

Not anyone is rich	=	$(x)\sim Rx$
	=	For all x, x isn't rich.
Not any Italian is a lover	=	$(x)\sim(Ix \cdot Lx)$ ← Note the "·" here!
	=	For all x, x isn't both Italian and a lover.
If anyone is just, there will be peace	=	$(x)(Jx \supset P)$
	=	For all x, if x is just there will be peace.

"Any" at the beginning of a sentence usually just means "all." So "Any Italian is a lover" just means "All Italians are lovers."

8.4a   Exercise – also LogiCola H (HM & HT)

Translate these English sentences into wffs. Recall that our translation rules are rough guides and sometimes don't work; so read your formula carefully to make sure it reflects what the English means.

| If everyone is evil, then Gensler is evil. | ((x)Ex ⊃ Eg) |

1. Gensler is either crazy or evil.
2. If Gensler is a logician, then some logicians are evil.
3. If everyone is a logician, then everyone is evil.
4. If all logicians are evil, then some logicians are evil.
5. If someone is evil, it will rain.
6. If everyone is evil, it will rain.
7. If anyone is evil, it will rain.
8. If Gensler is a logician, then someone is a logician.
9. If no one is evil, then no one is an evil logician.
10. If all are evil, then all logicians are evil.
11. If some are logicians, then some are evil.
12. All crazy logicians are evil.
13. Everyone who isn't a logician is evil.
14. Not everyone is evil.
15. Not anyone is evil.
16. If Gensler is a logician, then he's evil.
17. If anyone is a logician, then Gensler is a logician.
18. If someone is a logician, then he or she is evil.
19. Everyone is an evil logician.
20. Not any logician is evil.

8.5 Harder proofs

Now we come to proofs using formulas with multiple or non-initial quantifiers. Such proofs, while they require no new inference rules, often are tricky and require multiple assumptions. As before, drop only initial quantifiers:

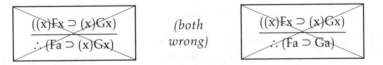

The formula "((x)Fx ⊃ (x)Gx)" is an if-then; to infer with it, we need the first part true or the second part false – as in these examples:

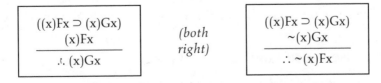

If we get stuck, we may need to assume one side or its negation.

Here's a proof using a formula with multiple quantifiers:

If *some* are enslaved, then all have their freedom threatened.
∴ If this person is enslaved, then I have my freedom threatened.

```
*    1    ((∃x)Sx ⊃ (x)Tx)   Valid
          [ ∴ (St ⊃ Ti)
*    2   ┌ asm: ~(St ⊃ Ti)
     3   │ ∴ St   {from 2}
     4   │ ∴ ~Ti  {from 2}
     5   │ ┌ asm: ~(∃x)Sx   {break 1}
     6   │ │ ∴ (x)~Sx   {from 5}
     7   │ └ ∴ ~St   {from 6}
     8   │ ∴ (∃x)Sx   {from 5; 3 contradicts 7}
     9   │ ∴ (x)Tx   {from 1 and 8}
    10   └ ∴ Ti   {from 9}
    11   ∴ (St ⊃ Ti)   {from 2; 4 contradicts 10}
```

After making the assumption, we apply an S-rule to get lines 3 and 4. Then we're stuck, since we can't drop the non-initial quantifiers in 1. So we make a second assumption in line 5, get a contradiction, and derive 8. We soon get a second contradiction to complete the proof.

Here's a similar invalid argument:

If *all* are enslaved, then all have their freedom threatened.
∴ If this person is enslaved, then I have my freedom threatened.

```
     1    ((x)Sx ⊃ (x)Tx)          Invalid
          [ ∴ (St ⊃ Ti)
                                    t, i, a
*    2    asm: ~(St ⊃ Ti)
     3    ∴ St   {from 2}           ┌──────────────┐
     4    ∴ ~Ti  {from 2}           │ St, ~Ti, ~Sa │
**   5    asm: ~(x)Sx  {break 1}    └──────────────┘
**   6    ∴ (∃x)~Sx   {from 5}
     7    ∴ ~Sa   {from 6}
```

In evaluating the premise here, first evaluate subformulas that start with quantifiers:

((x)Sx ⊃ (x)Tx)   ← Our premise. We first evaluate "(x)Sx" and "(x)Tx":
                      "(x)Sx" is false because "Sa" is false.
                      "(x)Tx" is false because "Ti" is false.
(0 ⊃ 0)   ← So we substitute "0" for "(x)Sx" and "0" for "(x)Tx."
1   ← So "((x)Sx ⊃ (x)Tx)" is true.

So the premise is true. Since the conclusion is false, the argument is invalid.

8.5a Exercise – also LogiCola I (HC & MC)

Say whether each is valid (and give a proof) or invalid (and give a refutation).

```
        1     (x)(Mx ∨ Fx)                    Invalid
      [ ∴ ((x)Mx ∨ (x)Fx)
 *     2     asm: ~((x)Mx ∨ (x)Fx)             a, b
 *     3     ∴ ~(x)Mx   {from 2}
 *     4     ∴ ~(x)Fx   {from 2}            Fa, ~Ma
 *     5     ∴ (∃x)~Mx  {from 3}            Mb, ~Fb
 *     6     ∴ (∃x)~Fx  {from 4}
       7     ∴ ~Ma   {from 5}
       8     ∴ ~Fb   {from 6}
 *     9     ∴ (Ma ∨ Fa)  {from 1}
 *    10     ∴ (Mb ∨ Fb)  {from 1}
      11     ∴ Fa   {from 7 and 9}
      12     ∴ Mb   {from 8 and 10}
```

(x)(Mx ∨ Fx)
∴ ((x)Mx ∨ (x)Fx)

(This is like arguing that, since everyone is male or female, thus either everyone is male or everyone is female.)

1. (x)(Fx ∨ Gx)
    ~Fa
    ∴ (∃x)Gx

2. (x)(Ex ⊃ R)
    ∴ ((∃x)Ex ⊃ R)

3. ((x)Ex ⊃ R)
    ∴ (x)(Ex ⊃ R)

4. ((∃x)Fx ∨ (∃x)Gx)
    ∴ (∃x)(Fx ∨ Gx)

5. ((∃x)Fx ⊃ (∃x)Gx)
    ∴ (x)(Fx ⊃ Gx)

6. (x)((Fx ∨ Gx) ⊃ Hx)
    Fm
    ∴ Hm

7. Fj
    (∃x)Gx
    (x)((Fx · Gx) ⊃ Hx)
    ∴ (∃x)Hx

8. ((∃x)Fx ⊃ (x)Gx)
    ~Gp
    ∴ ~Fp

9. (∃x)(Fx ∨ Gx)
    ∴ ((x)~Gx ⊃ (∃x)Fx)

10. ~(∃x)(Fx · Gx)
     ~Fd
     ∴ Gd

11. (x)(Ex ⊃ R)
     ∴ ((x)Ex ⊃ R)

12. (x)(Fx · Gx)
     ∴ ((x)Fx · (x)Gx)

13. (R ⊃ (x)Ex)
     ∴ (x)(R ⊃ Ex)

14. ((x)Fx ∨ (x)Gx)
     ∴ (x)(Fx ∨ Gx)

15. ((∃x)Ex ⊃ R)
     ∴ (x)(Ex ⊃ R)

8.5b   Exercise – also LogiCola I (HC & MC)

First appraise intuitively. Then translate into logic (using the letters given) and say whether valid (and give a proof) or invalid (and give a refutation).

1. Everything has a cause.
    If the world has a cause, then there is a God.
    ∴ There is a God. [Use Cx for "x has a cause," w for "the world," and G for "There is a God" (which we needn't here break down into "(∃x)Gx" – "For some x, x is a God"). A student of mine suggested this argument; but the next example shows that premise 1 can as easily lead to the opposite conclusion.]

2. Everything has a cause.
    If there is a God, then something doesn't have a cause (namely, God).
    ∴ There is no God. [Use Cx and G. The next example qualifies "Everything has a cause" to avoid the problem; some prefer an argument based on "Every *contingent being or set of such beings* has a cause."]

3. Everything that began to exist has a cause.
The world began to exist.
If the world has a cause, then there is a God.
∴ There is a God. [Use Bx, Cx, w, and G. This "Kalam argument" is from William Craig and James Moreland; they defend premise 2 by appealing to the big-bang theory, the law of entropy, and the impossibility of an actual infinite.]

4. If everyone litters, then the world will be dirty.
∴ If you litter, then the world will be dirty. [Lx, D, u]

5. Anything enjoyable is either immoral or fattening.
∴ If nothing is immoral, then everything that isn't fattening isn't enjoyable. [Ex, Ix, Fx]

6. Anything that can be explained either can be explained as caused by scientific laws or can be explained as resulting from a free choice of a rational being.
The totality of basic scientific laws can't be explained as caused by scientific laws (since this would be circular).
∴ Either the totality of basic scientific laws can't be explained or else it can be explained as resulting from a free choice of a rational being (God). [Use Ex for "x can be explained," Sx for "x can be explained as caused by scientific laws," Fx for "x can be explained as resulting from a free choice of a rational being," and t for "the totality of scientific laws." This one is from R. G. Swinburne.]

7. If someone knows the future, then no one has free will.
∴ No one who knows the future has free will. [Kx, Fx]

8. If everyone teaches philosophy, then everyone will starve.
∴ Everyone who teaches philosophy will starve. [Tx, Sx]

9. No proposition based on sense experience is logically necessary.
∴ Either no mathematical proposition is based on sense experience, or no mathematical proposition is logically necessary. [Use Sx, Nx, and Mx, and the universe of propositions. This is from the logical positivist A. J. Ayer.]

10. Any basic social rule that people would agree to if they were free and rational but ignorant of their place in society (whether rich or poor, white or black, male or female) is a principle of justice.
The equal-liberty principle and the difference principle are basic social rules that people would agree to if they were free and rational but ignorant of their place in society.
∴ The equal-liberty principle and the difference principle are principles of justice. [Use Ax, Px, e, and d. This is from John Rawls. The equal-liberty principle says that each person is entitled to the greatest liberty compatible with an equal liberty for all others. The difference principle says that wealth is to be distributed equally, except for inequalities that serve as incentives that ultimately benefit everyone and are equally open to all.]

11. If there are no necessary beings, then there are no contingent beings.
∴ All contingent beings are necessary beings. [Use Nx and Cx. Aquinas accepted the premise but not the conclusion.]

12.   Anything not disproved that is of practical value to one's life to believe ought to be believed.
      Free will isn't disproved.
   ∴ If free will is of practical value to one's life to believe, then it ought to be believed.   [Use Dx, Vx, Ox, f (for "free will"), and the universe of discourse of beliefs. This is from William James.]

13.   If the world had no temporal beginning, then some series of moments before the present moment is a completed infinite series.
      There's no completed infinite series.
   ∴ The world had a temporal beginning.   [Use Tx for "x had a temporal beginning," w for "the world," Mx for "x is a series of moments before the present moment," and Ix for "x is a completed infinite series." This one and the next are from Immanuel Kant, who thought our intuitive metaphysical principles lead to conflicting conclusions and thus can't be trusted.]

14.   Everything that had a temporal beginning was caused to exist by something previously in existence.
      If the world was caused to exist by something previously in existence, then there was time before the world began.
      If the world had a temporal beginning, then there was no time before the world began.
   ∴ The world didn't have a temporal beginning.   [Use Tx for "x had a temporal beginning," Cx for "x was caused to exist by something previously in existence," w for "the world," and B for "There was time before the world began."]

15.   If emotivism is true, then "X is good" means "Hurrah for X!" and all moral judgments are exclamations.
      All exclamations are inherently emotional.
      "This dishonest income tax exemption is wrong" is a moral judgment.
      "This dishonest income tax exemption is wrong" isn't inherently emotional.
   ∴ Emotivism isn't true.   [T, H, Mx, Ex, Ix, t]

16.   If everything is material, then all prime numbers are composed of physical particles.
      Seven is a prime number.
      Seven isn't composed of physical particles.
   ∴ Not everything is material.   [Mx, Px, Cx, s]

17.   If everyone lies, the results will be disastrous.
   ∴ If anyone lies, the results will be disastrous.   [Lx, D]

18.   Everyone makes moral judgments.
      Moral judgments logically presuppose beliefs about God.
      If moral judgments logically presuppose beliefs about God, then everyone who makes moral judgments believes (at least implicitly) that there is a God.
   ∴ Everyone believes (at least implicitly) that there is a God.   [Use Mx for "x makes moral judgments," L for "Moral judgments logically presuppose beliefs about God," and Bx for "x believes (at least implicitly) that there is a God." This is from the Jesuit theologian Karl Rahner.]

19.   "x=x" is a basic law.
      "x=x" is true in itself, and not true because someone made it true.
      If "x=x" depends on God's will, then "x=x" is true because someone made it true.
   ∴ Some basic laws don't depend on God's will.   [Use e (for "x=x"), Bx, Tx, Mx, and Dx.]

20.   Nothing that isn't caused can be integrated into the unity of our experience.
      Everything that we could experientially know can be integrated into the unity of our experience.
   ∴ Everything that we could experientially know is caused.   [Use Cx, Ix, and Ex. This is from Immanuel Kant. The conclusion is limited to objects of possible experience – since it says "Everything *that we could experientially know* is caused"; Kant thought that the unqualified "Everything is caused" leads to contradictions (see problems 1 and 2).]

21.   If everyone deliberates about alternatives, then everyone believes (at least implicitly) in free will.
   ∴ Everyone who deliberates about alternatives believes (at least implicitly) in free will.   [Dx, Bx]

22.   All who are consistent and think that abortion is normally permissible will consent to the idea of their having been aborted in normal circumstances.
      You don't consent to the idea of your having been aborted in normal circumstances.
   ∴ If you're consistent, then you won't think that abortion is normally permissible. [Use Cx, Px, Ix, and u. See my article in January 1986 *Philosophical Studies* or the synthesis chapter of my *Ethics: A Contemporary Introduction*, 2nd ed. (New York: Routledge, 2011).]

CHAPTER 9
Relations and Identity

This chapter brings quantificational logic up to full power by adding **identity** statements (like "a=b") and **relational statements** (like "Lrj" for "Romeo loves Juliet").

9.1 Identity translations

Our third rule for forming quantificational wffs introduces "=" ("equals"):

> 3. The result of writing a small letter and then "=" and then a small letter is a wff.

This rule lets us construct wffs like these:

x=y	=	x equals y.
r=l	=	Romeo is the lover of Juliet.
~p=l	=	Paris isn't the lover of Juliet.

We negate an identity wff by writing "~" in front. Neither "r=l" nor "~p=l" use parentheses, since these aren't needed to avoid ambiguity.

The simplest use of "=" is to translate an "is" that goes between singular terms. Recall the difference between general and singular terms:

Use capital letters for **general terms** (terms that *describe* or put in a *category*):

L = a lover
C = charming
F = drives a Ford

Use capitals for "a so and so," adjectives, and verbs.

Use small letters for **singular terms** (terms that pick out a *specific* person or thing):

l = the lover of Juliet
c = this child
r = Romeo

Use small letters for "the so and so," "this so and so," and proper names.

Compare these two forms:

Predication	Identity
Lr	r=l
Romeo is a lover.	Romeo is the lover of Juliet.

Use "=" for "is" if both sides are singular terms (and thus represented by small letters). The "is" of identity can be replaced with "is identical to" or "is the same entity as," and can be reversed (so if x=y then y=x).

We can translate "other than," "besides," and "alone" using identity:

Someone *other than* Romeo is rich = Someone who isn't Romeo is rich.
= Someone *besides* Romeo is rich = For some x, x ≠ Romeo and x is rich.
= $(\exists x)(\sim x=r \cdot Rx)$

Romeo *alone* is rich = Romeo is rich and no one besides Romeo is rich.
= $(Rr \cdot \sim(\exists x)(\sim x=r \cdot Rx))$

We also can translate some numerical notions, for example:

At least two are rich = For some x and some y: x≠y, x is rich, and y is rich.
= $(\exists x)(\exists y)(\sim x=y \cdot (Rx \cdot Ry))$

The pair of quantifiers "$(\exists x)(\exists y)$" ("for some x and some y") doesn't say whether x and y are identical; so we need "$\sim x=y$" to say that they aren't.

Henceforth we'll often need more variable letters than just "x" to keep references straight. It doesn't matter what letters we use; these two are equivalent:

$(\exists x)Rx$ = For some x, x is rich = At least one being is rich.
$(\exists y)Ry$ = For some y, y is rich = At least one being is rich.

Here's how we translate "exactly one" and "exactly two":

Exactly one being is rich = For some x: x is rich and there's no y such that y≠x and y is rich.
= $(\exists x)(Rx \cdot \sim(\exists y)(\sim y=x \cdot Ry))$

Exactly two beings are rich = For some x and some y: x is rich and y is rich and x≠y and there's no z such that z≠x and z≠y and z is rich.
= $(\exists x)(\exists y)(((Rx \cdot Ry) \cdot \sim x=y) \cdot \sim(\exists z)((\sim z=x \cdot \sim z=y) \cdot Rz))$

Our notation thus can express "There are exactly n F's" for any specific whole number n.

We also can express addition. Here's an English paraphrase of "1+1 = 2" and the corresponding formula:

If exactly one being is F	$((((\exists x)(Fx \cdot \sim(\exists y)(\sim y=x \cdot Fy))$
and exactly one being is G	$\cdot (\exists x)(Gx \cdot \sim(\exists y)(\sim y=x \cdot Gy)))$
and nothing is F-and-G,	$\cdot \sim(\exists x)(Fx \cdot Gx)) \supset$
then exactly two beings	$(\exists x)(\exists y)(((Fx \vee Gx) \cdot (Fy \vee Gy)) \cdot (\sim x=y$
are F-or-G.	$\cdot \sim(\exists z)((\sim z=x \cdot \sim z=y) \cdot (Fz \vee Gz)))))$

We could prove our "1+1 = 2" formula by assuming its denial and deriving a contradiction. While this would be tedious to do, it's interesting that it could be done. In principle, we could prove "2+2 = 4" and "5+7 = 12" – and the additions on your income tax form. Some mean logic teachers assign such things for homework.

9.1a Exercise – also LogiCola H (IM & IT)

Translate these English sentences into wffs.

Jim is the goalie and is a student.	$(j=g \cdot Sj)$

1. Aristotle is a logician.
2. Aristotle is the greatest logician.
3. Aristotle isn't Plato.
4. Someone besides Aristotle is a logician.
5. There are at least two logicians.
6. Aristotle alone is a logician.
7. All logicians other than Aristotle are evil.
8. No one besides Aristotle is evil.
9. The philosopher is Aristotle.
10. There's exactly one logician.
11. There's exactly one evil logician.
12. Everyone besides Aristotle and Plato is evil.
13. If the thief is intelligent, then you aren't the thief.
14. Carol is my only sister.
15. Alice runs but isn't the fastest runner.
16. There's at most one king.
17. The king is bald.
18. There's exactly one king and he is bald.

9.2 Identity proofs

We need two new rules for identity. This self-identity (SI) rule holds regardless of what constant replaces "a":

Self-identity | a=a |

This is an **axiom** – a basic assertion that isn't proved but can be used to prove other things. Rule SI says that we may assert a self-identity as a "derived line" anywhere in a proof, no matter what the earlier lines are. Adding "a=a" can be useful if we already have "~a=a" (since then we get a contradiction) or if we already have a line like "(a=a ⊃ Gb)" (since then we can apply an I-rule).

The substitute-equals (SE) rule is based on the idea that identicals are interchangeable: if a=b, then whatever is true of a also is true of b, and vice versa. This rule holds regardless of what constants replace "a" and "b" and what wffs replace "Fa" and "Fb" – provided that the two wffs are alike except that the constants are interchanged in one or more occurrences:

Substitute
equals | a=b, Fa → Fb |

Here's a simple identity proof:

	1	Wi	Valid

I weigh 180 pounds.
My mind doesn't weigh 180 pounds.
∴ I'm not identical to my mind.

1   Wi   Valid
2   ~Wm
[∴ ~i=m
3   ⌈ asm: i=m
4   ⌊ ∴ Wm   {from 1 and 3}
5   ∴ ~i=m   {from 3; 2 contradicts 4}

Line 4 follows by substituting equals; if i and m are identical, then whatever is true of one is true of the other.

Here's a simple invalid argument and its refutation:

The bankrobber wears size-twelve shoes.
You wear size-twelve shoes.
∴ You're the bankrobber.

1   Wb   Invalid   b, u
2   Wu
[∴ u=b | Wb, Wu, ~u=b |
3   asm: ~u=b

Since we can't infer anything here (we can't do much with "~u=b"), we set up a possible world to refute the argument. This world contains two distinct persons, the bankrobber and you, each wearing size-twelve shoes. Since the premises are all true and conclusion false in this world, our argument is invalid.

Our next example involves *pluralism* and *monism*:

Pluralism	*Monism*
There's more than one being.	There's exactly one being.
(∃x)(∃y)~x=y	(∃x)(y)y=x
For some x and some y: x≠y.	For some x, every y is identical to x.

Here's a proof that pluralism entails the falsity of monism:

*	1	(∃x)(∃y)~x=y	Valid
		[∴ ~(∃x)(y)y=x	
*	2	┌ asm: (∃x)(y)y=x	
*	3	│ ∴ (∃y)~a=y {from 1}	
	4	│ ∴ ~a=b {from 3}	
	5	│ ∴ (y)y=c {from 2}	
	6	│ ∴ a=c {from 5}	
	7	│ ∴ b=c {from 5}	
	8	└ ∴ a=b {from 6 and 7}	
	9	∴ ~(∃x)(y)y=x {from 2; 4 contradicts 8}	

There's more than one being.
∴ It's false that there's exactly one being.

Lines 1 and 2 have back-to-back quantifiers. We can drop only quantifiers that are initial and hence outermost; so we have to drop the quantifiers one at a time, starting from the outside. After dropping quantifiers, we substitute equals to get line 8: our "b=c" premise lets us take "a=c" and substitute "b" for the "c," thus getting "a=b."

We didn't bother to derive "c=c" from "(y)y=c" in line 5. From now on, it'll often be too tedious to drop universal quantifiers using *every* old constant. So we'll just derive instances likely to be useful for our proof or refutation.

Our substitute-equals rule seems to hold universally in arguments about matter or mathematics. But the rule can fail with mental phenomena. Consider this argument (where "Bx" stands for "Jones believes that x is on the penny"):

Jones believes that Lincoln is on the penny.	Bl
Lincoln is the first Republican US president.	l=r
∴ Jones believes that the first Republican US president is on the penny.	∴ Br

If Jones is unaware that Lincoln was the first Republican president, the premises could be true while the conclusion is false. So the argument is invalid. But yet we can derive the conclusion from the premises using our substitute-equals rule. So something is wrong here.

To avoid the problem, we'll disallow translating into quantificational logic any predicates or relations that violate the substitute-equals rule. So we won't let "Bx" stand for "Jones believes that x is on the penny." Statements about beliefs and other mental phenomena often violate this rule; so we have to be careful translating such statements into quantificational logic.[1]

So the mental seems to follow different logical patterns from the physical. Does this refute the materialist project of reducing the mental to the physical? Philosophers dispute this question.

---

[1] Chapter 13 will develop special ways to symbolize belief formulas and will explicitly restrict the use of the substitute-equals rule with such formulas (Section 13.2).

9.2a   Exercise – also LogiCola IDC

Say whether each is valid (and give a proof) or invalid (and give a refutation).

a=b
∴ b=a

```
1      a=b   Valid
   [ ∴ b=a
2    ┌ asm: ~b=a
3    │ ∴ ~b=b   {from 1 and 2}
4    └ ∴ b=b   {self-identity, to contradict 3}
5    ∴ b=a   {from 2; 3 contradicts 4}
```

1.   Fa
∴ ~(∃x)(Fx • ~x=a)

2.   (a=b ⊃ ~(∃x)Fx)
∴ (Fa ⊃ ~Fb)

3.   a=b
b=c
∴ a=c

4.   ~a=b
c=b
∴ ~a=c

5.   ~a=b
~c=b
∴ a=c

6.   a=b
∴ (Fa ≡ Fb)

7.   a=b
(x)(Fx ⊃ Gx)
~Ga
∴ ~Fb

8.   Fa
∴ (x)(x=a ⊃ Fx)

9.   ∴ (∃x)(y)y=x

10.   ∴ (∃x)(∃y)~y=x

9.2b   Exercise – also LogiCola IDC

First appraise intuitively. Then translate into logic and say whether valid (and give a proof) or invalid (and give a refutation). You'll have to figure out what letters to use; be careful about deciding between small and capital letters.

1.   Keith is my only nephew.
My only nephew knows more about BASIC than I do.
Keith is a ten-year-old.
∴ Some ten-year-olds know more about BASIC than I do.   [I wrote this argument many years ago; now Keith is older and I have two nephews.]

2.   Some are logicians.
Some aren't logicians.
∴ There's more than one being.

3.   This chemical process is publicly observable.
This pain isn't publicly observable.
∴ This pain isn't identical to this chemical process.   [This attacks the identity theory of the mind, which identifies mental events with chemical processes.]

4.   The person who left a lighter is the murderer.
The person who left a lighter is a smoker.
No smokers are backpackers.
∴ The murderer isn't a backpacker.

5. The murderer isn't a backpacker.
    You aren't a backpacker.
    ∴ You're the murderer.

6. If Speedy Jones looks back to the quarterback just before the hike, then Speedy
    Jones is the primary receiver.
    The primary receiver is the receiver you should try to cover.
    ∴ If Speedy Jones looks back to the quarterback just before the hike, then Speedy
    Jones is the receiver you should try to cover.

7. Judy isn't the world's best cook.
    The world's best cook lives in Detroit.
    ∴ Judy doesn't live in Detroit.

8. Patricia lives in North Dakota.
    Blondie lives in North Dakota.
    ∴ At least two people live in North Dakota.·

9. Your grade is the average of your tests.
    The average of your tests is B.
    ∴ Your grade is B.

10. Either you knew where the money was, or the thief knew where it was.
    You didn't know where the money was.
    ∴ You aren't the thief.

11. The man of Suzy's dreams is either rich or handsome.
    You aren't rich.
    ∴ If you're handsome, then you're the man of Suzy's dreams.

12. If someone confesses, then someone goes to jail.
    I confess.
    I don't go to jail.
    ∴ Someone besides me goes to jail.

13. David stole money.
    The nastiest person at the party stole money.
    David isn't the nastiest person at the party.
    ∴ At least two people stole money.   [See problem 4 of Section 2.3b.]

14. No one besides Carol and the detective had a key.
    Someone who had a key stole money.
    ∴ Either Carol or the detective stole money.

15. Exactly one person lives in North Dakota.
    Paul lives in North Dakota.
    Paul is a farmer.
    ∴ Everyone who lives in North Dakota is a farmer.

16. The wildcard team with the best record goes to the playoffs.
    Cleveland isn't the wildcard team with the best record.
    ∴ Cleveland doesn't go to the playoffs.

17. If the thief is intelligent, then you aren't the thief.
    ∴ You aren't intelligent.

18. You aren't intelligent.
    ∴ If the thief is intelligent, then you aren't the thief.

9.3 Easier relations

Our last rule for forming quantificational wffs introduces relations:

> 4. The result of writing a capital letter and then two or more small letters is a wff.

$$\begin{array}{rcl} \text{Lrj} & = & \text{Romeo loves Juliet.} \\ \text{Gxyz} & = & \text{x gave y to z.} \end{array}$$

Translating relational sentences into logic can be difficult, since there are few rules to help us. We mostly have to study examples and catch the patterns. This section covers translations that require at most one quantifier; the next section covers translations that require two or more quantifiers.

Here are further examples without quantifiers:

$$\begin{array}{rcl} \text{Juliet loves Romeo} & = & \text{Ljr} \\ \text{Juliet loves herself} & = & \text{Ljj} \\ \text{Juliet loves Romeo but not Paris} & = & \text{(Ljr} \cdot \text{~Ljp)} \end{array}$$

And here are some easy examples with quantifiers:

$$\begin{array}{rcl} \text{Everyone loves him/herself} & = & \text{(x)Lxx} \\ \text{Someone loves him/herself} & = & \text{(∃x)Lxx} \\ \text{No one loves him/herself} & = & \text{~(∃x)Lxx} \end{array}$$

Normally put quantifiers *before* relations:

> Someone (everyone, no one) loves Romeo
>
> =
>
> For some (all, no) x,
> x loves Romeo.

> Romeo loves someone (everyone, no one)
>
> =
>
> For some (all, no) x,
> Romeo loves x.

In the box on the right, English puts the quantifier last – but logic puts it first. Here are fuller translations:

Someone loves Romeo = (∃x)Lxr
For some x, x loves Romeo

Everyone loves Romeo = (x)Lxr
For all x, x loves Romeo

No one loves Romeo = ~(∃x)Lxr
It's not the case that, for
some x, x loves Romeo

Romeo loves someone = (∃x)Lrx
For some x, Romeo loves x

Romeo loves everyone = (x)Lrx
For all x, Romeo loves x

Romeo loves no one = ~(∃x)Lrx
It's not the case that, for
some x, Romeo loves x

These examples are more complicated:

Some Montague loves Juliet = (∃x)(Mx · Lxj)

| For some x, | x is a Montague and | x loves Juliet |

All Montagues love Juliet = (x)(Mx ⊃ Lxj)

| For all x, | if x is a Montague then | x loves Juliet |

Romeo loves some Capulet = (∃x)(Cx · Lrx)

| For some x, | x is a Capulet and | Romeo loves x |

Romeo loves all Capulets = (x)(Cx ⊃ Lrx)

| For all x, | if x is a Capulet then | Romeo loves x |

And here are some further examples:

Some Montague besides Romeo loves Juliet = (∃x)((Mx · ~x=r) · Lxj)

| For some x, | x is a Montague and x isn't Romeo and | x loves Juliet |

Romeo loves all Capulets besides Juliet = (x)((Cx · ~x=j) ⊃ Lrx)

| For all x, | if x is a Capulet and x isn't Juliet then | Romeo loves x |

Romeo loves all Capulets who love themselves = (x)((Cx · Lxx) ⊃ Lrx)

| For all x, | if x is a Capulet and x loves x then | Romeo loves x |

Finally, here are examples with two different relations:

All who know Juliet love Juliet = (x)(Kxj ⊃ Lxj)

| For all x, | if x knows Juliet then | x loves Juliet |

| All who know themselves love themselves | = | (x)(Kxx ⊃ Lxx) |

| For all x, | if x knows x then | x loves x |

It's helpful to rephrase the English into the quantificational idiom before translating into logic, as in the examples given here.

9.3a   Exercise – also LogiCola H (RM & RT)

Using these equivalences, translate these English sentences into wffs.

Lxy	=	x loves y	Ix	=	x is Italian	t	=	Tony
Cxy	=	x caused y	Rx	=	x is Russian	o	=	Olga
Gxy	=	x is greater than y	Ex	=	x is evil	g	=	God

| God caused nothing that is evil. | ~(∃x)(Ex • Cgx) |

1.   Tony loves Olga and Olga loves Tony.
2.   Not every Russian loves Olga.
3.   Tony loves everyone who is Russian.
4.   Olga loves someone who isn't Italian.
5.   Everyone loves Olga but not everyone is loved by Olga.
6.   All Italians love themselves.
7.   Olga loves every Italian besides Tony.
8.   Tony loves everyone who loves Olga.
9.   No Russian besides Olga loves Tony.
10.   Olga loves all who love themselves.
11.   Tony loves no Russians who love themselves.
12.   Olga is loved.
13.   God caused everything besides himself.
14.   Nothing caused God.
15.   Everything that God caused is loved by God.
16.   Nothing caused itself.
17.   God loves himself.
18.   If God did not cause himself, then there is something that God did not cause.
19.   Nothing is greater than God.
20.   God is greater than anything that he caused.

9.4   Harder relations

This relational sentence requires two quantifiers:

| Someone loves someone | = | (∃x)(∃y)Lxy |

| For some x and for some y, | x loves y |

This could be true because some love themselves ("(∃x)Lxx") or because some love another ("(∃x)(∃y)(~x=y • Lxy)"). These also require two quantifiers:

Some Montague hates some Capulet	=	(∃x)(∃y)((Mx • Cy) • Hxy)	
For some x and for some y,	x is a Montague and y is a Capulet and	x hates y	

Everyone loves everyone	=	(x)(y)Lxy
For all x and for all y,	x loves y	

Every Montague hates every Capulet	=	(x)(y)((Mx • Cy) ⊃ Hxy)	
For all x and for all y,	if x is a Montague and y is a Capulet then	x hates y	

Study carefully this next pair – which differs only in the quantifier order:

Everyone loves someone. For all x there's some y, such that x loves y. (x)(∃y)Lxy	There's someone who everyone loves. There's some y such that, for all x, x loves y. (∃y)(x)Lxy

In the first case, we might love *different* people. In the second, we love the *same* person; perhaps we all love God. These pairs emphasize the difference:

Everyone loves someone	≠	There's someone who everyone loves.
Everyone lives in some house	≠	There's some house where everyone lives.
Everyone makes some error	≠	There's some error that everyone makes.

The sentences on the right make the stronger claim.

With back-to-back quantifiers, the order doesn't matter if both quantifiers are of the same type; but the order matters if the quantifiers are mixed:

$$(x)(y) = (y)(x) \qquad (∃x)(∃y) = (∃y)(∃x) \qquad (x)(∃y) ≠ (∃y)(x)$$

Also, it doesn't matter which variable letters we use, so long as the reference pattern is the same. These three are equivalent:

Each has a universal, then an existential, then "L," then the variable used in the existential, and finally the variable used in the universal.

Here are some mixed-quantifier examples of greater complexity:

Every Capulet loves some Montague = (x)(Cx ⊃ (∃y)(My · Lxy))

| For all x, | if x is a Capulet then | x loves some Montague |
| | | for some y, y is a Montague and x loves y |

Every Capulet loves someone = (x)(Cx ⊃ (∃y)Lxy)

| For all x, | if x is a Capulet then | x loves someone |
| | | for some y, x loves y |

Everyone loves some Montague = (x)(∃y)(My · Lxy)

| For all x, | x loves some Montague |
| | for some y, y is a Montague and x loves y |

When you see "Every Capulet," think "For all x, if x is a Capulet then ..." – and when you see "Some Montague," think "For some x, x is a Montague and ..."; you'll sometimes have to use a variable other than "x" to keep the references straight. Here are cases where we have "some" and then "every":

Some Capulet loves every Montague = (∃x)(Cx · (y)(My ⊃ Lxy))

| For some x, | x is a Capulet and | x loves every Montague |
| | | for all y, if y is a Montague then x loves y |

Some Capulet loves everyone = (∃x)(Cx · (y)Lxy)

| For some x, | x is a Capulet and | x loves everyone |
| | | for all y, x loves y |

Someone loves every Montague = (∃x)(y)(My ⊃ Lxy)

| For some x, | x loves every Montague |
| | for all y, if y is a Montague then x loves y |

Here are some miscellaneous examples:

There is an unloved lover = (∃x)(~(∃y)Lyx · (∃y)Lxy)

| For some x, | x is unloved | and | x is a lover |
| | it is false that for some y, y loves x | | for some y, x loves y |

Everyone loves a lover = (x)((∃y)Lxy ⊃ (y)Lyx)

| For all x, | if x is a lover | then | everyone loves x |
| | if, for some y, x loves y | | for all y, y loves x |

Romeo loves all and only those who don't love themselves			$=$ $(x)(Lrx \equiv {\sim}Lxx)$
For all x,	Romeo loves x	if and only if	x doesn't love x

All who know any person love that person		$=$ $(x)(y)(Kxy \supset Lxy)$
For all x and for all y,	if x knows y then	x loves y

While there are few mechanical rules for translating relational sentences, it often helps to keep paraphrasing the sentence according to the quantificational idiom into parts that are progressively more finely grained.

Many relations have special properties, such as reflexivity, symmetry, or transitivity. Here are examples:

"Is identical to" is *reflexive*.
= Everything is identical to itself.
= $(x)x=x$ [Identity is a relation with a special symbol.]

"Taller than" is *irreflexive*.
= Nothing is taller than itself.
= ${\sim}(\exists x)Txx$

"Being a relative of" is *symmetrical*.
= In all cases, if x is a relative of y, then y is a relative of x.
= $(x)(y)(Rxy \supset Ryx)$

"Being a parent of" is *asymmetrical*.
= In all cases, if x is a parent of y then y isn't a parent of x.
= $(x)(y)(Pxy \supset {\sim}Pyx)$

"Being taller than" is *transitive*.
= In all cases, if x is taller than y and y is taller than z, then
    x is taller than z.
= $(x)(y)(z)((Txy \cdot Tyz) \supset Txz)$

"Being a foot taller than" is *intransitive*.
= In all cases, if x is a foot taller than y and y is a foot taller
    than z, then x isn't a foot taller than z.
= $(x)(y)(z)((Txy \cdot Tyz) \supset {\sim}Txz)$

Love fits none of these six categories. Love is neither reflexive nor irreflexive: sometimes people love themselves and sometimes they don't. Love is neither symmetrical nor asymmetrical: if x loves y, then sometimes y loves x in return and sometimes not. Love is neither transitive nor intransitive: if x loves y and y loves z, then sometimes x loves z and sometimes not.

9.4a   Exercise – also LogiCola H (RM & RT)

Using these equivalences, translate these English sentences into wffs.

Lxy	=	x loves y	Ix	=	x is Italian	t	=	Tony
Cxy	=	x caused y	Rx	=	x is Russian	o	=	Olga
Gxy	=	x is greater than y	Ex	=	x is evil			

Every Russian loves everyone.

$(x)(Rx \supset (y)Lxy)$
or $(x)(y)(Rx \supset Lxy)$

1.   Everyone loves every Russian.
2.   Some Russians love someone.
3.   Someone loves some Russians.
4.   Some Russians love every Italian.
5.   Every Russian loves some Italian.
6.   There is some Italian that every Russian loves.
7.   Everyone loves everyone else.
8.   Every Italian loves every other Italian.
9.   Some Italians love no one.
10. No Italians love everyone.
11. No one loves all Italians.
12. Someone loves no Italians.
13. No Russians love all Italians.
14. If everyone loves Olga, then there is some Russian that everyone loves.
15. If Tony loves everyone, then there is some Italian who loves everyone.
16. It is not always true that if a first thing caused a second, then the first is greater than the second.
17. In all cases, if a first thing is greater than a second, then the second isn't greater than the first.
18. Everything is greater than something.
19. There's something than which nothing is greater.
20. Everything is caused by something.
21. There's something that caused everything.
22. Something evil caused all evil things.
23. In all cases, if a first thing caused a second and the second caused a third, then the first caused the third.
24. There's a first cause (there's some x that caused something but nothing caused x).
25. Anyone who caused anything loves that thing.

9.5   Relational proofs

In relational proofs, as before, we'll reverse squiggles, drop existentials (using new constants), and lastly drop universals. But now back-to-back quantifiers will be common (as in line 3 of this next proof); we'll drop such quantifiers one at a time, starting at the outside, since we can drop only an *initial* quantifier:

Paris loves Juliet.
Juliet doesn't love Paris.
∴ It's not always true that if a first person loves a second then the second loves the first.

```
       1     Lpj   Valid
       2     ~Ljp
       [ ∴ ~(x)(y)(Lxy ⊃ Lyx)
       3   ┌ asm: (x)(y)(Lxy ⊃ Lyx)
       4   │ ∴ (y)(Lpy ⊃ Lyp)  {from 3}
*      5   │ ∴ (Lpj ⊃ Ljp)  {from 4}
       6   └ ∴ Ljp  {from 1 and 5}
       7   ∴ ~(x)(y)(Lxy ⊃ Lyx)  {from
                        3; 2 contradicts 6}
```

Our older proof strategy would have us drop each initial universal quantifier twice, once using "p" and once using "j." But now this would be tedious; so henceforth we'll derive only what will be useful for our proof or refutation.

Here's another relational proof:

There's someone that everyone loves.
∴ Everyone loves someone.

```
*      1     (∃y)(x)Lxy   Valid
       [ ∴ (x)(∃y)Lxy
*      2   ┌ asm: ~(x)(∃y)Lxy
*      3   │ ∴ (∃x)~(∃y)Lxy  {from 2}
*      4   │ ∴ ~(∃y)Lay  {from 3}
       5   │ ∴ (y)~Lay  {from 4}
       6   │ ∴ (x)Lxb  {from 1}
       7   │ ∴ Lab  {from 6}
       8   └ ∴ ~Lab  {from 5}
       9   ∴ (x)(∃y)Lxy  {from 2; 7 contradicts 8}
```

This should be valid intuitively – since if there's one specific person (God, for example) that everyone loves, then everyone loves at least one person.

Relational proofs raise interesting problems. With quantificational arguments that lack relations and identity:

1. there are mechanical strategies (like that sketched in Section 8.2) that always will give a proof or refutation in a finite number of lines; and
2. a refutation at most needs 2^n entities (where n is the number of distinct predicates in the argument) and never needs an infinite number of entities.

Neither feature holds for relational arguments. Against 1, there's no possible mechanical strategy that always will give us a proof or refutation of a relational argument. This result is called *Church's theorem*, after Alonzo Church. As a result, working out relational arguments sometimes requires ingenuity and not just mechanical methods; the defect with our proof strategy, we'll see, is that it can lead into endless loops.[1] Against 2, refuting invalid relational arguments

---

[1] The computer program LogiCola, which goes with this book, follows mechanical rules (algorithms) for constructing proofs. If left to itself, LogiCola would go into an endless loop for some invalid relational arguments. But LogiCola is told beforehand which arguments would go into an endless loop and which refutations to then give, so it can stop the loop at a reasonable point.

sometimes requires a possible world with an infinite number of entities.

Instructions lead into an **endless loop** if they command the same sequence of actions over and over, endlessly. I've written computer programs with endless loops by mistake. I put an endless loop into the Index for fun:

Endless loop. See loop, endless.	Loop, endless. See endless loop.

Our quantificational proof strategy can lead into such a loop. If you see this coming, quit the strategy and improvise your own refutation.

Trying to prove "~(x)(∃y)x=y" ("Not everything is identical to something") leads into an endless loop:

[∴ Not everything is identical to something.	[∴ ~(x)(∃y)x=y **Invalid**
Assume: Everything is identical to something.	1 asm: (x)(∃y)x=y
∴ a is identical to something.	2 ∴ (∃y)a=y {from 1}
∴ a is identical to b.	3 ∴ a=b {from 2}
∴ b is identical to something.	4 ∴ (∃y)b=y {from 1}
∴ b is identical to c.	5 ∴ b=c {from 4}
∴ c is identical to something....	6 ∴ (∃y)c=y {from 1} ...

We drop the universal quantifier in 1, using a new constant "a" (since there are no old constants) to get 2; a line later, we get new constant "b." We drop the universal in 1 using "b" to get 4; a line later, we get new constant "c." And so on endlessly. To refute the argument, we can use a world with a single entity, a, that is identical to itself:

In this world, everything is identical to something – and hence the conclusion is false. We have to think up this world for ourselves. The strategy doesn't provide it automatically; instead, it leads into an endless loop.

Wffs that begin with a universal/existential quantifier combination, like "(x)(∃y)," often lead into an endless loop. Here's another example:[1]

Everyone loves someone.	(x)(∃y)Lxy **Invalid**
∴ There's someone that everyone loves.	∴ (∃y)(x)Lxy

Here the premise by itself leads into an endless loop:

[1] This example is like arguing "Everyone lives in some house, so there must be some (one) house that everyone lives in." Some great minds have committed this quantifier-shift fallacy. Aristotle argued, "Every agent acts for an end, so there must be some (one) end for which every agent acts." St Thomas Aquinas argued, "If everything at some time fails to exist, then there must be some (one) time at which everything fails to exist." And John Locke argued, "Everything is caused by something, so there must be some (one) thing that caused everything."

Everyone loves someone.	(x)(∃y)Lxy
∴ a loves someone.	∴ (∃y)Lay
∴ a loves b.	∴ Lab
∴ b loves someone.	∴ (∃y)Lby
∴ b loves c.	∴ Lbc
∴ c loves someone….	∴ (∃y)Lcy …

Again we must improvise, since our strategy doesn't automatically give us a proof or refutation. With some ingenuity, we can construct this possible world, with beings a and b, that makes the premise true and conclusion false:

$$\text{a, b} \quad \boxed{\begin{array}{l} \text{Laa, ~Lab} \\ \text{Lbb, ~Lba} \end{array}} \quad \begin{array}{l} \text{(egoistic} \\ \text{world)} \end{array}$$

Here all love themselves, and only themselves. This makes "Everyone loves someone" true but "There's someone that everyone loves" false. Here's another refutation:

$$\text{a, b} \quad \boxed{\begin{array}{l} \text{Lab, ~Laa} \\ \text{Lba, ~Lbb} \end{array}} \quad \begin{array}{l} \text{(altruistic} \\ \text{world)} \end{array}$$

Here all love the other but not themselves; this again makes the premise true and conclusion false.

We don't automatically get a refutation with invalid arguments that lead into an endless loop. Instead, we have to think out the refutation by ourselves. While there's no strategy that always works, I'd suggest that you:

1. try breaking out of the loop before introducing your third constant (often it suffices to use two beings, a and b; don't multiply entities unnecessarily),
2. begin your refutation with values you already have (maybe, for example, you already have "Lab" and "Laa"), and
3. experiment with adding other wffs to make the premises true and conclusion false (if you already have "Lab" and "Laa," then try adding "Lba" or "~Lba" – and "Lbb" or "~Lbb" – until you get a refutation).

We have to fiddle with the values until we find a refutation that works.

Refuting a relational argument sometimes requires a universe with an infinite number of entities. Here's an example:

In all cases, if x is greater than y and y is
   greater than z then x is greater than z.
In all cases, if x is greater than y then y
   isn't greater than x.
b is greater than a.
∴ There's something than which nothing
   is greater.

$(x)(y)(z)((Gxy \cdot Gyz) \supset Gxz)$
$(x)(y)(Gxy \supset {\sim}Gyx)$
Gba
∴ $(\exists x){\sim}(\exists y)Gyx$

Given these premises, every world with a finite number of beings must have
some being unsurpassed in greatness (making the conclusion true). But we can
imagine a world with an infinity of beings – in which each being is surpassed in
greatness by another. So the argument is invalid.

We can refute the argument by giving another of the same form with true
premises and a false conclusion. Let's take the natural numbers (0, 1, 2, ...) as
the universe of discourse. Let "a" refer to 0 and "b" refer to 1 and "Gxy" mean
"x > y." On this interpretation, the premises are all true. But the conclusion,
which says "There's a number than which no number is greater," is false. This
shows that the form is invalid.

So relational arguments raise problems about infinity (endless loops and
infinite worlds) that other kinds of argument we've studied don't raise.

9.5a   Exercise – also LogiCola I (RC & BC)

Say whether each is valid (and give a proof) or invalid (and give a refutation).

```
*    1      (∃x)(∃y)Lxy    Valid
       [ ∴ (∃y)(∃x)Lxy
*    2   ┌ asm: ~(∃y)(∃x)Lxy
     3   │ ∴ (y)~(∃x)Lxy    {from 2}
*    4   │ ∴ (∃y)Lay    {from 1}
     5   │ ∴ Lab    {from 4}
*    6   │ ∴ ~(∃x)Lxb    {from 3}
     7   │ ∴ (x)~Lxb    {from 6}
     8   └ ∴ ~Lab    {from 7}
     9   ∴ (∃y)(∃x)Lxy    {from 2; 5 contradicts 8}
```

$(\exists x)(\exists y)Lxy$
∴ $(\exists y)(\exists x)Lxy$

1. $(x)Lxa$
    ∴ $(x)Lax$

2. $(\exists x)(y)Lxy$
    ∴ $(\exists x)Lxa$

3. $(x)(y)(Lxy \supset x=y)$
    ∴ $(x)Lxx$

4. $(x)(\exists y)Lxy$
    ∴ Laa

5. $(x)(y)Lxy$
    ∴ $(x)(y)((Fx \cdot Gy) \supset Lxy)$

6. $(x)(y)(Uxy \supset Lxy)$
    $(x)(\exists y)Uxy$
    ∴ $(x)(\exists y)Lxy$

7. $(x)Lxx$
    ∴ $(\exists x)(y)Lxy$

8. (x)Gaxb
    ∴ (∃x)(∃y)Gxcy

9. (x)(y)Lxy
    ∴ (∃x)Lax

10. Lab
    Lbc
    ∴ (∃x)(Lax • Lxc)

11. (x)Lxx
    ∴ (x)(y)(Lxy ⊃ x=y)

12. (∃x)Lxa
    ~Laa
    ∴ (∃x)(~a=x • Lxa)

13. (x)(y)(z)((Lxy • Lyz) ⊃ Lxz)
    (x)(y)(Kxy ⊃ Lyx)
    ∴ (x)Lxx

14. (x)Lxa
    (x)(Lax ⊃ x=b)
    ∴ (x)Lxb

15. (x)(y)(Lxy ⊃ (Fx • ~Fy))
    ∴ (x)(y)(Lxy ⊃ ~Lyx)

9.5b   Exercise – also LogiCola I (RC & BC)

First appraise intuitively. Then translate into logic and say whether valid (and give a proof) or invalid (and give a refutation).

1. Juliet loves everyone.
    ∴ Someone loves you.   [Use Lxy, j, and u.]

2. Nothing caused itself.
    ∴ There's nothing that caused everything.   [Use Cxy.]

3. Alice is older than Betty.
    ∴ Betty isn't older than Alice.   [Use Oxy, a, and b. What implicit premise would make this valid?]

4. There's something that everything depends on.
    ∴ Everything depends on something.   [Dxy]

5. Everything depends on something.
    ∴ There's something that everything depends on.   [Dxy]

6. Paris loves all females.
    No females love Paris.
    Juliet is female.
    ∴ Paris loves someone who doesn't love him.   [Lxy, p, Fx, j]

7. In all cases, if a first thing caused a second, then the first exists before the second.
    Nothing exists before it exists.
    ∴ Nothing caused itself.   [Use Cxy and Bxy (for "x exists before y exists").]

8. Everyone hates my enemy.
    My enemy hates no one besides me.
    ∴ My enemy is me.   [Hxy, e, m]

9. Not everyone loves everyone.
    ∴ Not everyone loves you.   [Lxy, u]

10.   There's someone that everyone loves.
∴ Some love themselves.

11.   Andy shaves all and only those who don't shave themselves.
∴ It is raining.   [Sxy, a, R]

12.   No one hates themselves.
I hate all logicians.
∴ I am not a logician.   [Hxy, i, Lx]

13.   Juliet loves everyone besides herself.
Juliet is Italian.
Romeo is my logic teacher.
My logic teacher isn't Italian.
∴ Juliet loves Romeo.   [j, Lxy, Ix, r, m]

14.   Romeo loves either Lisa or Colleen.
Romeo doesn't love anyone who isn't Italian.
Colleen isn't Italian.
∴ Romeo loves Lisa.   [Lxy, r, l, c]

15.   Everyone loves all lovers.
Romeo loves Juliet.
∴ I love you.   [Use Lxy, r, j, i, and u. This one is difficult.]

16.   Everyone loves someone.
∴ Some love themselves.

17.   Nothing caused itself.
This chemical brain process caused this pain.
∴ This chemical brain process isn't identical to this pain.   [Cxy, b, p]

18.   For every positive contingent truth, something explains why it's true.
The existence of the world is a positive contingent truth.
If something explains the existence of the world, then some necessary being explains the existence of the world.
∴ Some necessary being explains the existence of the world.   [Use Cx, Exy, e, and Nx. This argument for the existence of God is from Richard Taylor.]

19.   That girl is Miss Novak.
∴ If you don't like Miss Novak, then you don't like that girl.   [Use t, m, u, and Lxy. This is from the movie, *The Little Shop around the Corner*: "If you don't like Miss Novak, I can tell you right now that you won't like that girl. Why? Because it is Miss Novak."]

20.   Everyone who is wholly good prevents every evil that he can prevent.
Everyone who is omnipotent can prevent every evil.
If someone prevents every evil, then there's no evil.
There's evil.
∴ Either God isn't omnipotent, or God isn't wholly good.   [Use Gx, Ex, Cxy (for "x can prevent y"), Pxy (for "x prevents y"), Ox, and g. This is from J. L. Mackie.]

21.   Your friend is wholly good.
      Your knee pain is evil.
      Your friend can prevent your knee pain.
      Your friend doesn't prevent your knee pain (since he could prevent it only by amputating your leg – which would bring about a worse situation).
∴   "Everyone who is wholly good prevents every evil that he can prevent" is false. [Use f, Gx, k, Ex, Cxy, and Pxy. Alvin Plantinga thus attacked premise 1 of the previous argument; he proposed instead roughly this: "Everyone who is wholly good prevents every evil that he knows about if he can do so without thereby eliminating a greater good or bringing about a greater evil."]

22.   For everything contingent, there's some time at which it fails to exist.
∴   If everything is contingent, then there's some time at which everything fails to exist.   [Use Cx for "x is contingent"; Ext for "x exists at time t"; t for a time variable; and t′, t″, t‴, … for time constants. This is a critical step in St Thomas Aquinas's third argument for the existence of God.]

23.   If everything is contingent, then there's some time at which everything fails to exist.
      If there's some time at which everything fails to exist, then there's nothing in existence now.
      There's something in existence now.
      Everything that isn't contingent is necessary.
∴   There's a necessary being.   [Besides the letters for the previous argument, use Nx for "x is necessary" and n for "now." This continues Aquinas's argument; here premise 1 is from the previous argument.]

24.   [The great logician Gottlob Frege tried to systematize mathematics. One of his axioms said that *every sentence with a free variable[1] determines a set*. So then "x is blue" determines a set: there's a set y containing all and only blue things. While this seems sensible, Bertrand Russell showed that Frege's axiom entails that "x doesn't contain x" determines a set – so there's a set y containing all and only those things that don't contain themselves – and this leads to the self-contradiction "y contains y if and only if y doesn't contain y." The foundations of mathematics haven't been the same since "Russell's paradox."]
      If every sentence with a free variable determines a set, then there's a set y such that, for all x, y contains x if and only if x doesn't contain x.
∴   Not every sentence with a free variable determines a set.   [Use D for "Every sentence with a free variable determines a set," Sx for "x is a set," and Cyx for "y contains x." See Section 16.4.]

25.   All dogs are animals.
∴   All heads of dogs are heads of animals.   [Use Dx, Ax, and Hxy (for "x is a head of y"). Translate "x is a head of a dog" as "for some y, y is a dog and x is a head of y." Augustus De Morgan in the 19th century claimed that this was a valid argument that traditional logic couldn't validate.]

---

[1] An instance of a variable is "free" in a wff if it doesn't occur as part of a wff that begins with a quantifier using that variable; each instance of "x" is free in "Fx" but not in "(x)Fx."

9.6 Definite descriptions

Phrases of the form "the so and so" are called **definite descriptions**, since they're meant to pick out a definite (single) person or thing. This final section sketches Bertrand Russell's influential ideas on definite descriptions. While philosophical discussions about these and about proper names can get complex and controversial, I'll try to keep things fairly simple.

Consider these two sentences and how we've been symbolizing them:

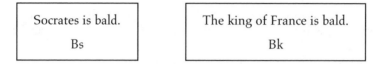

The first sentence has a proper name ("Socrates") while the second has a definite description ("the king of France"); both seem to ascribe a *property* (baldness) to a particular *object* or entity. Russell argued that this object-property analysis is misleading in the second case;[1] sentences with definite descriptions (like "the king of France") were in reality more complicated and should be analyzed in terms of a complex of predicates and quantifiers:

> The king of France is bald.
> = There's exactly one king of France, and he is bald.
> = For some x: x is king of France, there's no y such
>   that y≠x and y is king of France, and x is bald.
> = $(\exists x)((Kx \cdot \sim(\exists y)(\sim y=x \cdot Ky)) \cdot Bx)$

Russell saw his analysis as having several advantages; I'll mention two.

First, "The king of France is bald" might be false for any of three reasons:

1. There's no king of France;
2. there's more than one king of France; or
3. there's exactly one king of France, and he has hair on his head.

In fact, "The king of France is bald" is false for reason 1: France is a republic and has no king. This accords well with Russell's analysis. By contrast, the object-property analysis suggests that if "The king of France is bald" is false, then "The king of France isn't bald" would have to be true[2] – and so the king of France would have to have hair! So Russell's analysis seems to express better the logical complexity of definite descriptions.

Second, the object-property analysis of definite descriptions can easily lead us into metaphysical errors, like positing existing things that aren't real. The

---

[1] He also thought the analysis misleading in the first case; but I don't want to discuss this now.
[2] On Russell's analysis, "The king of France isn't bald" is false too – since it means "There's exactly one king of France, and he isn't bald."

philosopher Alexius Meinong argued roughly as follows:

> "The round square does not exist" is a true
>   statement about the round square.
> If there's a true statement about something,
>   then that something has to exist.
> ∴ The round square exists.
>   But the round square isn't a real thing.
> ∴ Some things that exist aren't real things.

Russell once accepted this argument. Later he came to see the belief in non-real existing things as foolish; he rejected Meinong's first premise and appealed to the theory of descriptions to clear up the confusion.

According to Russell, Meinong's error comes from his naïve object-property understanding of the following statement:

> The round square does not exist.

This, Russell contended, isn't a true statement ascribing non-existence to some object called "the round square." If it were a true statement about the round square, then the round square would have to exist – which the statement denies. Instead, the statement just denies that there's exactly one round square. So Russell's analysis keeps us from having to accept that there are existing things that aren't real.

CHAPTER 10
Basic Modal Logic

Modal logic studies arguments whose validity depends on "necessary," "possible," and similar notions. This chapter covers the basics and the next gets into further modal systems.

10.1 Translations

To help us evaluate modal arguments, we'll construct a little modal language. For now, our language builds on propositional logic, and thus include all the vocabulary, wffs, inference rules, and proofs of the latter. Our language adds two new vocabulary items: "◇" and "□" (diamond and box):

◇A	=	It's possible that A	=	A is true in some possible world.
A	=	It's true that A	=	A is true in the actual world.
□A	=	It's necessary that A	=	A is true in all possible worlds.

Calling something *possible* is a weak claim – weaker than calling it *true*. Calling something *necessary* is a strong claim; it says, not just that the thing is true, but that it *has* to be true – it *couldn't* be false.

"Possible" here means *logically possible* (*not self-contradictory*). "I run a mile in two minutes" may be physically impossible; but because there's no self-contradiction in the idea, it's logically possible. Likewise, "necessary" means *logically necessary* (*self-contradictory to deny*). "2+2 = 4" and "All bachelors are unmarried" are examples of **necessary truths**; such truths are based on logic, the meaning of concepts, or necessary connections between properties.

We can rephrase "possible" as *true in some possible world* – and "necessary" as *true in all possible worlds*. A **possible world** is a consistent and complete[1] description of how things might have been or might in fact be. Picture a possible world as a *consistent story* (or novel). The story is *consistent*, in that its statements don't entail self-contradictions; it describes a set of possible situations that are all possible together. The story may or may not be true. The **actual world** is the story that's true – the description of how things in fact are.

---

[1] Since we are finite beings, we will in practice only give partial (not "complete") descriptions.

As before, a grammatically correct formula is called a *wff*, or *well-formed formula*. For now, wffs are strings that we can construct using the propositional rules plus this additional rule:

> The result of writing "◇" or "□," and then a wff, is a wff.

Don't use parentheses with "◇A" and "□A":

Parentheses here would serve no purpose.

Now we'll focus on how to translate English sentences into modal logic. Here are some simpler examples:

$$
\begin{array}{rcl}
\text{A is possible (consistent, could be true)} & = & \diamondsuit A \\
\text{A is necessary (must be true, has to be true)} & = & \Box A
\end{array}
$$

$$
\begin{array}{rclcl}
\text{A is impossible (self-contradictory)} & = & \sim\diamondsuit A & = & \text{A couldn't be true.} \\
 & = & \Box\sim A & = & \text{A has to be false.}
\end{array}
$$

An impossible statement (like "2 ≠ 2") is one that's false in every possible world.
These examples are more complicated:

$$
\begin{array}{rcl}
\text{A is consistent (compatible) with B} & = & \text{It's possible that A and B are both true.} \\
 & = & \diamondsuit(A \cdot B)
\end{array}
$$

$$
\begin{array}{rcl}
\text{A entails B} & = & \text{It's necessary that if A then B.} \\
 & = & \Box(A \supset B)
\end{array}
$$

"Entails" makes a stronger claim than plain "if-then." Compare these two:

$$
\begin{array}{rcl}
\text{"There's rain" entails "There's precipitation"} & = & \Box(R \supset P) \\
\text{If it's Saturday, then I don't teach class} & = & (S \supset \sim T)
\end{array}
$$

The first if-then is logically necessary; every conceivable situation with rain also has precipitation. The second if-then just happens to be true; we can consistently imagine me teaching on Saturday – even though in fact I never do.
These common forms negate the whole wff:

$$
\begin{array}{rcl}
\text{A is inconsistent with B} & = & \text{It's not possible that A and B are both true.} \\
 & = & \sim\diamondsuit(A \cdot B)
\end{array}
$$

$$
\begin{array}{rcl}
\text{A doesn't entail B} & = & \text{It's not necessary that if A then B.} \\
 & = & \sim\Box(A \supset B)
\end{array}
$$

Here is how we translate "contingent":

A is a contingent statement	=	A is possible and not-A is possible.
	=	$(\Diamond A \cdot \Diamond \sim A)$
A is a contingent truth	=	A is true but could have been false.
	=	$(A \cdot \Diamond \sim A)$

Statements are necessary, impossible, or contingent. But truths are only necessary or contingent (since impossible statements are false).

When translating, it's usually good to mimic the English word order:

necessary not	=	$\Box \sim$	necessary if	=	$\Box($
not necessary	=	$\sim \Box$	if necessary	=	$(\Box$

Use a separate box or diamond for each "necessary" or "possible":

If A is necessary and B is possible, then C is possible = $((\Box A \cdot \Diamond B) \supset \Diamond C)$

Sometimes an English sentence is ambiguous between two kinds of necessity; translate such a sentence into two modal wffs and say that it could mean one or the other. So this next sentence could have either of two meanings:

"If you're a bachelor, then you must be unmarried."

Simple Necessity $(B \supset \Box U)$	Conditional Necessity $\Box(B \supset U)$
If you're a bachelor, then you're *inherently unmarriable* (in no possible world would anyone ever marry you).	It's necessary that *if* you're a bachelor *then* you're unmarried.
If B, then U (by itself) is necessary.	It's necessary that if-B-then-U.

The **box-inside** "$(B \supset \Box U)$" posits a *simple (inherent) necessity*: given your bachelorhood, "You're unmarried" is inherently necessary. This version is insulting and presumably false. By contrast, the **box-outside** "$\Box(B \supset U)$" posits a *conditional necessity*: what is necessary is, not "You're a bachelor" or "You're unmarried" by itself, but the connection between the two. This second version is trivially true because "bachelor" means *unmarried man*. Our English sentence ("*If you're a bachelor, then you must be unmarried*") is ambiguous; its wording suggests simple necessity (which denies your freedom to marry) but it's more likely meant as conditional necessity.

The medievals called the box-inside form the "necessity of the *consequent*" (the second part being necessary); they called the box-outside form the "necessity of the *consequence*" (the whole if-then being necessary). The ambiguity is important philosophically; several intriguing but fallacious philosophical arguments depend on the ambiguity for their plausibility.

It's not ambiguous if you say that the second part is "by itself" or "intrinsically" necessary or impossible – or if you use "entails" or start with "necessary." These forms aren't ambiguous:

If A, then B (by itself) is necessary	=	$(A \supset \Box B)$
If A, then B is intrinsically necessary	=	$(A \supset \Box B)$
A entails B	=	$\Box(A \supset B)$
Necessarily, if A then B	=	$\Box(A \supset B)$
It's necessary that if A then B	=	$\Box(A \supset B)$
"If A then B" is a necessary truth	=	$\Box(A \supset B)$

The ambiguous forms have if-then with a strong modal term (like "necessary," "must," "impossible," or "can't") in the then-part:[1]

"*If A is true, then it's necessary (must be) that B*" could mean "$(A \supset \Box B)$" or "$\Box(A \supset B)$."	"*If A is true, then it's impossible (couldn't be) that B*" could mean "$(A \supset \Box{\sim}B)$" or "$\Box(A \supset {\sim}B)$."

When you translate an ambiguous English sentence, say that it's ambiguous and give both translations. When you do an argument with an ambiguous premise, give both translations and work out both versions of the argument.

10.1a   Exercise – also LogiCola J (BM & BT)

Translate these into wffs. Be sure to translate ambiguous forms both ways.

"God exists and evil doesn't exist" entails "There's no matter."	$\Box((G \cdot {\sim}E) \supset {\sim}M)$

1. It's necessary that God exists.
2. "There's a God" is self-contradictory.
3. It isn't necessary that there's matter.
4. It's necessary that there's no matter.
5. "There's rain" entails "There's precipitation."
6. "There's precipitation" doesn't entail "There's rain."
7. "There's no precipitation" entails "There's no rain."
8. If rain is possible, then precipitation is possible.
9. God exists.

---

[1] There's an exception to these boxed rules: if the if-part is a claim about necessity or possibility, then just use the box-inside form. So "If A is necessary then B is necessary" is just "$(\Box A \supset \Box B)$" – and "If A is possible then B is impossible" is just "$(\Diamond A \supset {\sim}\Diamond B)$."

10. If there's rain, then there must be rain.
11. It isn't possible that there's evil.
12. It's possible that there's no evil.
13. If you get more points than your opponent, then it's impossible for you to lose.
14. It's necessary that if you see that B is true then B is true.
15. If B has an all-1 truth table, then B is inherently necessary.
16. Necessarily, if there's a God then there's no evil.
17. If there's a God, then there can't be evil.
18. If there must be matter, then there's evil.
19. Necessarily, if there's a God then "There's evil" (by itself) is self-contradictory.
20. It's necessary that it's heads or tails.
21. Either it's necessary that it's heads or it's necessary that it's tails.
22. "There's rain" is a contingent statement.
23. "There's rain" is a contingent truth.
24. "If there's rain, then there's evil" is a necessary truth.
25. If there's rain, then "There's evil" (by itself) is logically necessary.
26. If there's rain, then it's necessary that there's evil.
27. It's necessary that it's possible that there's matter.
28. "There's a God" isn't a contingent truth.
29. If there's a God, then it must be that there's a God.
30. It's necessary that if there's a God then "There's a God" (by itself) is necessary.

10.2 Proofs

Modal proofs work much like propositional proofs; but we need to add possible worlds and four new inference rules.

A **world prefix** is a string of zero or more instances of "W." So " " (zero instances), "W," "WW," and so on are world prefixes; these represent possible worlds, with the blank world prefix (" ") representing the actual world. A *derived line* is now a line consisting of a world prefix and then "∴" and then a wff. And an *assumption* is now a line consisting of a world prefix and then "asm:" and then a wff. Here are examples of derived lines and assumptions:

∴ A	(So A is true in the actual world.)	asm: A	(Assume A is true in the actual world.)
W ∴ A	(So A is true in world W.)	W asm: A	(Assume A is true in world W.)
WW ∴ A	(So A is true in world WW.)	WW asm: A	(Assume A is true in world WW.)

Seldom do we need to assume something in another world.

We'll still use S- and I-rules and RAA in modal proofs. Unless otherwise specified, we can use an inference rule only within a given world; so if we have "(A ⊃ B)" and "A" in the same world, then we can infer "B" in this same world. RAA needs additional wording (*italicized below*) for world prefixes:

> RAA: Suppose some pair of not-blocked-off lines *using the same world prefix* has contradictory wffs. Then block off all the lines from the last not-blocked-off assumption on down and infer a line consisting in *this assumption's world prefix followed by ".·."* followed by a contradictory of the assumption.

To apply RAA, lines with the same world prefix must have contradictory wffs. Having "W ∴ A" and "WW ∴ ~A" isn't enough; "A" may well be true in one world but false in another. But "WW ∴ A" and "WW ∴ ~A" provide a genuine contradiction. The line derived using RAA must have the same world prefix as the assumption; if "W asm: A" leads to a contradiction in any world, then RAA lets us derive "W ∴ ~A."

Modal proofs use four new inference rules. These two reverse-squiggle (RS) rules hold regardless of what pair of contradictory wffs replaces "A" / "~A" (here "→" means we can infer whole lines from left to right):

Reverse squiggle	$\sim\Box A \quad \rightarrow \quad \Diamond\sim A$ $\sim\Diamond A \quad \rightarrow \quad \Box\sim A$

These let us go from "not necessary" to "possibly false" – and from "not possible" to "necessarily false." Use these rules only within the same world. We can reverse squiggles on complicated formulas, so long as the whole formula begins with "~□" or "~◇" (so the third box is wrong):

$\sim\Diamond\sim B$ $\therefore \Box\sim\sim B$	$\sim\Box(C \cdot \sim D)$ $\therefore \Diamond\sim(C \cdot \sim D)$	~~$(P \supset \sim\Box Q)$~~ ~~$\therefore (P \supset \Diamond\sim Q)$~~

In the first box, it would be simpler to conclude "□B" (eliminating the double negation). Reverse squiggles whenever you have a wff that begins with "~" and then a modal operator; reversing a squiggle moves the modal operator to the beginning of the formula, so we can later drop it.

We drop modal operators using the next two rules (which hold regardless of what wff replaces "A"). Here's the drop-diamond (DD) rule:

Drop diamond	$\Diamond A \quad \rightarrow \quad W \therefore A,$ use a *new* string of W's

Here the line with "◇A" can use any world prefix – and the line with "∴ A" must use a *new* string (one not occurring in earlier lines) of one or more W's. If

"A" is possible, then "A" is thereby true in *some* possible world; we can give this world a name – but a *new* name, since "A" needn't be true in any of the worlds used in the proof so far. In proofs, we'll use "W" for the first diamond we drop, "WW" for the second, and so forth. So if we drop two diamonds, then we must introduce two worlds:

◇H	Heads is possible, tails is possible; call an imagined
◇T	world with heads "W," and one with tails "WW."
W ∴ H ←	"W" is OK because it occurs in no earlier line.
WW ∴ T ←	Since "W" has now occurred, we use "WW."

We can drop diamonds from complicated formulas, so long as the diamond *begins* the wff:

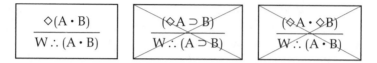

The last two formulas don't *begin* with a diamond; instead, they begin with "(." Drop only *initial* operators (diamonds or boxes) – and introduce a new and different world prefix whenever you drop a diamond.

Here's the drop-box (DB) rule:

Drop	□A → W ∴ A,
box	use any world prefix

The line with "□A" can use any world prefix – and the line with "∴ A" can use any world prefix too (including the blank one). If "A" is necessary, then "A" is true in *all* possible worlds, and so we can put "A" in any world we like. However, it's bad strategy to drop a box into a new world; instead, stay in old worlds. As before, we can drop boxes from complicated formulas, so long as the box *begins* the wff:

The last two formulas begin, not with a box, but with a left-hand parenthesis. "(□A ⊃ B)" and "(□A ⊃ □B)" are if-then forms and follow the if-then rules: if we have the first part true, we can get the second true; if we have the second part false, we can get the first false; and if we get stuck, we need to make another assumption.

Here's an example of a valid modal argument:

Necessarily, if there's rain then there's
precipitation.
It's possible that there's rain.
∴ It's possible that there's precipitation.

$$\boxed{\begin{array}{l} \Box(R \supset P) \\ \Diamond R \\ \therefore \Diamond P \end{array}}$$

Our proof adds three modal steps (reverse squiggles, drop diamonds, drop boxes) to our propositional-proof strategy:

	1	□(R ⊃ P) **Valid**
*	2	◇R
		[∴ ◇P
*	3	┌ asm: ~◇P
	4	│ ∴ □~P {from 3}
	5	│ W ∴ R {from 2}
*	6	│ W ∴ (R ⊃ P) {from 1}
	7	│ W ∴ P {from 5 and 6}
	8	└ W ∴ ~P {from 4}
	9	∴ ◇P {from 3; 7 contradicts 8}

(1) Reverse squiggles: go from "~◇P" to "□~P" (line 4).

(2) Drop initial diamonds, using a new world each time: go from "◇R" to "W ∴ R" (line 5).

(3) Lastly, drop each initial box once for each old world: go from "□(R ⊃ P)" to "W ∴ (R ⊃ P)" – and from "□~P" to "W ∴ ~P."

We starred lines 2, 3, and 6. As before, starred lines largely can be ignored in deriving further lines. Here are the new starring rules – with examples:

Star any wff on which
you reverse squiggles.

$$\frac{*\ \sim\Box A}{\therefore \Diamond\sim A}$$

Star any wff from which
you drop a diamond.

$$\frac{*\ \Diamond A}{W \therefore A}$$

When we reverse squiggles or drop diamonds, the new line has the same information. Don't star when dropping a box; we can never exhaust a "necessary" statement – and we may have to use it again later in the proof.

Here's another modal proof:

	1	□(A · B) **Valid**
		[∴ □A
*	2	┌ asm: ~□A
*	3	│ ∴ ◇~A {from 2}
	4	│ W ∴ ~A {from 3}
	5	│ W ∴ (A · B) {from 1}
	6	└ W ∴ A {from 5}
	7	∴ □A {from 2; 4 contradicts 6}

(1) Reverse squiggles: go from "~□A" to "◇~A" (line 3).

(2) Drop initial diamonds, using a new world each time: go from "◇~A" to "W ∴ ~A" (line 4).

(3) Lastly, drop each initial box once for each old world: go from "□(A · B)" to "W ∴ (A · B)."

It would be wrong to switch lines 4 and 5; if we drop the box first using world W, then we can't drop the diamond next using W (since W would be old).

In this proof, it would be useless and bad strategy to drop the box into the actual world – to go from "□(A • B)" in line 1 to "∴ (A • B)" with no initial W's. Drop a box into the actual world in only two cases:

> Drop a box into the actual world just if:
>
> - you have an unmodalized instance of a letter in your original premises or conclusion, or
> - you've done everything else possible (including further assumptions if needed) and still have no other worlds.

These two proofs illustrate the two cases (the first case is more common):

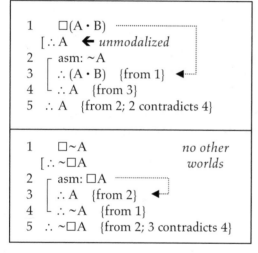

The instance of "A" in the conclusion is *unmodalized* (it doesn't occur as part of a larger wff beginning with a box or diamond). Whenever our original premises or conclusion have an unmodalized instance of a letter, our standard strategy is to drop all boxes into the actual world.[1]

Here we drop a box into the actual world because there are no other old worlds to use (since there was no "◇" to drop) and we've done everything else that we can do.

Our "standard strategy" about dropping boxes into the actual world will always give us a proof, but sometimes it gives us lines that we don't need. If we see that we can complete the proof without these lines, then it's OK to skip them.

Our proof strategy works much like before. We first assume the opposite of the conclusion; then we use our four new rules plus the S- and I-rules to derive whatever we can. If we find a contradiction, we apply RAA. If we get stuck and need to break a wff of the form "~(A • B)" or "(A ∨ B)" or "(A ⊃ B)," then we make another assumption. If we get no contradiction and yet can't do anything further, then we try to refute the argument.

Here's a fuller statement of the three modal steps of our strategy:

1. FIRST REVERSE SQUIGGLES: For each unstarred, not-blocked-off line that begins with "~" and then a box or diamond, derive a line using the reverse-squiggle rules. Star the original line.

[1] In "(A • ◇B)," the first letter is unmodalized; if this formula was a premise or conclusion, then our standard strategy would be to drop all boxes into the actual world.

2. AND DROP DIAMONDS: For each unstarred, not-blocked-off line that begins with a diamond, derive an instance using the next available *new* world prefix (unless some such instance already occurs in previous not-blocked-off lines). Star the original line.

Note: Don't drop a diamond if you already have a not-blocked-off instance in previous lines – there's no point in deriving a second instance. For example, don't drop "◇A" if you already have "W ∴ A."

3. LASTLY DROP BOXES: For each not-blocked-off line that begins with a box, derive instances using each *old* world. [Drop boxes into the actual world under the two conditions given on the previous page.] Don't star the original line; you might have to use it again.

Drop diamonds before boxes. Introduce a new world each time you drop a diamond, and use the same old worlds when you drop a box. And drop only initial diamonds and boxes.

10.2a Exercise – also LogiCola KV

Prove each of these arguments to be valid (all are valid).

$$\begin{array}{c} \Box(A \supset B) \\ \Diamond {\sim} B \\ \therefore \Diamond {\sim} A \end{array}$$

```
      1     □(A ⊃ B)    Valid
  *   2     ◇~B
            [ ∴ ◇~A
  *   3   ┌ asm: ~◇~A
      4   │ ∴ □A    {from 3}
      5   │ W ∴ ~B    {from 2}
  *   6   │ W ∴ (A ⊃ B)   {from 1}
      7   │ W ∴ A    {from 4}
      8   └ W ∴ B    {from 6 and 7}
      9     ∴ ◇~A    {from 3; 5 contradicts 8}
```

1. ◇(A · B)
   ∴ ◇A

2. A
   ∴ ◇A

3. ~◇(A · ~B)
   ∴ □(A ⊃ B)

4. □(A ∨ ~B)
   ~□A
   ∴ ◇~B

5. (◇A ∨ ◇B)
   ∴ ◇(A ∨ B)

6. (A ⊃ □B)
   ◇~B
   ∴ ◇~A

7. ~◇(A · B)
   ◇A
   ∴ ~□B

8. □A
   ∴ ◇A

9. □A
   ~□B
   ∴ ~□(A ⊃ B)

10. □(A ⊃ B)
    ∴ (□A ⊃ □B)

10.2b Exercises – also LogiCola KV

First appraise intuitively. Then translate into logic (using the letters given) and prove to be valid (all are valid).

1. "You knowingly testify falsely because of threats to your life" entails "You lie."
    It's possible that you knowingly testify falsely because of threats to your life but don't intend to deceive. (Maybe you hope no one will believe you.)
    ∴ "You lie" is consistent with "You don't intend to deceive." [Use T, L, and I. This is from Tom Carson, who writes on the morality of lying.]

2. Necessarily, if you don't decide then you decide not to decide.
    Necessarily, if you decide not to decide then you decide.
    ∴ Necessarily, if you don't decide then you decide. [Use D for "You decide" and N for "You decide not to decide." This is adapted from Jean-Paul Sartre.]

3. If truth is a correspondence with the mind, then "There are truths" entails "There are minds."
    "There are minds" isn't logically necessary.
    Necessarily, if there are no truths then it is not true that there are no truths.
    ∴ Truth isn't a correspondence with the mind. [Use C, T, and M.]

4. There's a perfect God.
    There's evil in the world.
    ∴ "There's a perfect God" is logically compatible with "There's evil in the world." [Use G and E. Most who doubt the conclusion would also doubt premise 1.]

5. "There's a perfect God" is logically compatible with T.
    T logically entails "There's evil in the world."
    ∴ "There's a perfect God" is logically compatible with "There's evil in the world." [Use G, T, and E. Here T (for "theodicy") is a possible explanation of why God permits evil that's consistent with God's perfection and entails the existence of evil. T might say: "The world has evil because God, who is perfect, wants us to make significant free choices to struggle to bring a half-completed world toward its fulfillment; moral evil comes from the abuse of human freedom and physical evil from the half-completed state of the world." This basic argument (but not the specific T) is from Alvin Plantinga.]

6. "There's a perfect God and there's evil in the world and God has some reason for permitting the evil" is logically consistent.
    ∴ "There's a perfect God and there's evil in the world" is logically consistent. [Use G, E, and R. This is Ravi Zacharias's version of Plantinga's argument.]

7.   God is omnipotent.
     "You freely always do the right thing" is logically possible.
     If "You freely always do the right thing" is logically possible and God is omnipo-
     tent, then it's possible for God to bring it about that you freely always do the
     right thing.
     ∴ It's possible for God to bring it about that you freely always do the right thing.
     [Use O, F, and B. This is from J. L. Mackie. He thought God had a third option
     besides making robots who always act rightly and free beings who sometimes
     act wrongly: he could make free beings who always act rightly.]

8.   "God brings it about that you do A" is inconsistent with "You freely do A."
     "God brings it about that you freely do A" entails "God brings it about that you
     do A."
     "God brings it about that you freely do A" entails "You freely do A."
     ∴ It's impossible for God to bring it about that you freely do A.   [Use B, F, and G.
     This attacks the conclusion of the previous argument.]

9.   "This is a square" entails "This is composed of straight lines."
     "This is a circle" entails "This isn't composed of straight lines."
     ∴ "This is a square and also a circle" is self-contradictory.   [S, L, C]

10. "This is red and there's a blue light that makes red things look violet to normal
     observers" entails "Normal observers won't sense redness."
     "This is red and there's a blue light that makes red things look violet to normal
     observers" is logically consistent.
     ∴ "This is red" doesn't entail "Normal observers will sense redness."   [Use R, B,
     and N. This is from Roderick Chisholm.]

11. "All brown dogs are brown" is a necessary truth.
     "Some dog is brown" isn't a necessary truth.
     "Some brown dog is brown" entails "Some dog is brown."
     ∴ "All brown dogs are brown" doesn't entail "Some brown dog is brown."   [Use A
     for "All brown dogs are brown," X for "Some dog is brown," and S for "Some
     brown dog is brown." This attacks a doctrine of traditional logic (Section 2.8),
     that "all A is B" entails "some A is B."]

12. It's necessary that, if God exists as a possibility but does not exist in reality, then
     there could be a being greater than God (namely, a similar being that also exists
     in reality).
     "There could be a being greater than God" is self-contradictory (since "God" is
     defined as "a being than which no greater could be").
     It's necessary that God exists as a possibility.
     ∴ It's necessary that God exists in reality.   [Use P for "God exists as a possibility,"
     R for "God exists in reality," and G for "There's a being greater than God."
     This is a modal version of St Anselm's ontological argument.]

13. If "X is good" and "I like X" are interchangeable, then "I like hurting people" logically entails "Hurting people is good."
"I like hurting people but hurting people isn't good" is consistent.
∴ "X is good" and "I like X" aren't interchangeable. [Use I, L, and G. This argument attacks subjectivism.]

14. "You sin" entails "You know what you ought to do and you're able to do it and you don't do it."
It's necessary that if you know what you ought to do then you want to do it.
It's necessary that if you want to do it and you're able to do it then you do it.
∴ It's impossible for you to sin. [S, K, A, D, W]

15. Necessarily, if it's true that there are no truths then there are truths.
∴ It's necessary that there are truths. [Use T for "There are truths."]

10.3 Refutations

Applying our proof strategy to an invalid argument leads to a refutation:

* 1 ◇~H   Invalid

2 □(H ∨ T)

[∴ □T   W | H, ~T |

* 3 asm: ~□T

* 4 ∴ ◇~T {from 3}   WW | T, ~H |

5 W ∴ ~T {from 4}

6 WW ∴ ~H {from 1}

* 7 W ∴ (H ∨ T) {from 2}

* 8 WW ∴ (H ∨ T) {from 2}

9 W ∴ H {from 5 and 7}

10 WW ∴ T {from 6 and 8}

It's possible that it's not heads.
It's necessary that it's heads or tails.
∴ It's necessary that it's tails.

After making the assumption (line 3), we reverse a squiggle to move the modal operator to the outside (line 4). Then we drop the two diamonds, using a new and different world each time (lines 5 and 6). We drop the box twice, using first world W and then world WW (lines 7 and 8). Since we reach no contradiction, we gather the simple pieces to give a refutation. Here our refutation has two possible worlds: one with heads-and-not-tails and another with tails-and-not-heads. Presumably, our refutation will make premises true and conclusion false, and thus show the argument to be invalid. But how are we to calculate the truth value of the premises and conclusion?

In evaluating the premises and conclusion, evaluate each wff that starts with a diamond or box according to these rules:

| | "◇A" is true if and only if *at least one world* has "A" true. | | "□A" is true if and only if *all worlds* have "A" true. |

Recall the galaxy of possible worlds that we reached for our last argument:

W	H, ~T
WW	T, ~H

This galaxy makes our premises true and conclusion false. Here's how we'd evaluate each wff:

◇~H   ←   First premise: by our rule, this is true if and only if *at least one world* has "~H" true.
           But world WW has "~H" true.
1   ←   So "◇~H" is true.

□(H ∨ T)   ←   Second premise: by our rule, this is true if and only if *all worlds* have "(H ∨ T)" true.
           In world W: (H ∨ T) = (1 ∨ 0) = 1.
           In world WW: (H ∨ T) = (0 ∨ 1) = 1.
1   ←   So "□(H ∨ T)" is true.

□T   ←   Conclusion: by our rule, this is true if and only if *all worlds* have T true.
           But world W has T false.
0   ←   So "□T" is false.

So this galaxy of possible worlds shows our argument to be invalid.

As before, it's important to check that our refutation works. If we don't get the premises all true and conclusion false, then we did something wrong – and we should check what we did with the formula that didn't come out right. Often the problem is that we didn't drop a box into all the old worlds.

So far we've evaluated formulas that begin with a diamond or box, like "◇~H" or "□(H ∨ T)." But some formulas, like "(◇H ⊃ □T)," have the diamond or box further inside. In these cases, we'd first evaluate subformulas that begin with a diamond or box, and then substitute "1" or "0" for these. With "(◇H ⊃ □T)," we'd first evaluate "◇H" and "□T" to see whether these are "1" or "0"; then we'd substitute "1" or "0" for these parts and determine the truth value of the whole formula.

I'll give examples to show how this works. Let's assume the same galaxy:

W	H, ~T
WW	T, ~H

Now let's evaluate three sample wffs:

~□H   ←   Here we'd first evaluate "□H." This is true if and
          only if *all worlds* have H true.
          Since world WW has H false, "□H" is false.
~0   ←   So we substitute "0" for "□H."
1   ←   So "~□H" is true.

(◇H ⊃ □T)   ←   Here we'd first evaluate "◇H" and "□T."
                "◇H" is true if and only if *at least one world* has H
                true. Since world W has H true, "◇H" is true.
                "□T" is true if and only if *all worlds* have T true.
                Since world W has T false, "□T" is false.
(1 ⊃ 0)   ←   So we substitute "1" for "◇H" and "0" for "□T."
0   ←   So "(◇H ⊃ □T)" is false.

~□(H ⊃ ~T)   ←   Here we'd first evaluate "□(H ⊃ ~T)." This is true
                 if and only if *all worlds* have "(H ⊃ ~T)" true.
                 In world W: (H ⊃ ~T) = (1 ⊃ ~0) = (1 ⊃ 1) = 1.
                 In world WW: (H ⊃ ~T) = (0 ⊃ ~1) = (0 ⊃ 0) = 1.
~1   ←   So "□(H ⊃ ~T)" is true; so we substitute "1" for it.
0   ←   So "~□(H ⊃ ~T)" is false.

The key thing is to evaluate each subformula that starts with a diamond or box, and then substitute "1" or "0" for it.

In working out English modal arguments, we'll sometimes find an ambiguous premise – as in the following argument:

If you're a bachelor, then you must be unmarried.
You're a bachelor.
∴ It's logically necessary that you're unmarried.

Premise 1 here could have either of these two meanings:

(B ⊃ □U)	□(B ⊃ U)
If you're a bachelor, then you're *inherently unmarriable* – in no possible world would anyone ever marry you. (We hope this is false.)	It's necessary that *if* you're a bachelor *then* you're unmarried. (This is trivially true because "bachelor" means *unmarried man*.)

In such cases, say that the argument is ambiguous and work out both versions:

Box-inside version: *Box-outside version:*

```
* 1     (B ⊃ □U)   Valid          1     □(B ⊃ U)              Invalid
  2     B                         2     B
    [ ∴ □U                          [ ∴ □U                    ┌──────────┐
  3   ┌ asm: ~□U              * 3     asm: ~□U         W    │  B, U    │
  4   └ ∴ □U {from 1 and 2}   * 4     ∴ ◇~U  {from 3}      ├──────────┤
  5   ∴ □U {from 3; 3 contradicts 4}  5     W ∴ ~U  {from 4}      │ ~B, ~U  │
                                * 6     W ∴ (B ⊃ U)  {from 1}  └──────────┘
    (While this is valid,       * 7     ∴ (B ⊃ U)  {from 1}
    premise 1 is false.)          8     W ∴ ~B  {from 5 and 6}
                                  9     ∴ U  {from 2 and 7}
```

Both versions are flawed; the first has a false premise, while the second is invalid. So the proof that you're inherently unmarriable ("□U" – "It's logically necessary that you're unmarried") fails.

In the second version, the refutation uses an actual world and a possible world W. An unmodalized instance of a letter, like B in premise 2, should be evaluated according to the actual world; so here B is true. Premise 1 "□(B ⊃ U)" also comes out true, since "(B ⊃ U)" is true in both worlds:

$$\text{In the actual world:} \quad (B ⊃ U) = (1 ⊃ 1) = 1$$
$$\text{In world W:} \quad (B ⊃ U) = (0 ⊃ 0) = 1$$

And conclusion "□U" is false, since "U" is false in world W. So the galaxy makes the premises all true and the conclusion false, establishing invalidity.

Arguments with a modal ambiguity often have one interpretation with a false premise and another that's invalid. Such arguments often seem sound until we focus on the ambiguity.

10.3a Exercise – also LogiCola KI

Prove each of these arguments to be invalid (all are invalid).

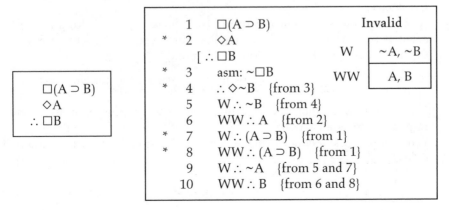

```
□(A ⊃ B)
◇A
∴ □B
```

```
    1     □(A ⊃ B)                    Invalid
  * 2     ◇A
    [ ∴ □B                    W    ┌──────────┐
  * 3     asm: ~□B                  │ ~A, ~B  │
  * 4     ∴ ◇~B  {from 3}    WW   ├──────────┤
    5     W ∴ ~B  {from 4}          │  A, B   │
    6     WW ∴ A  {from 2}         └──────────┘
  * 7     W ∴ (A ⊃ B)  {from 1}
  * 8     WW ∴ (A ⊃ B)  {from 1}
    9     W ∴ ~A  {from 5 and 7}
   10     WW ∴ B  {from 6 and 8}
```

1. ◇A
    ∴ □A

2. A
    ∴ □A

3. ◇A
    ◇B
    ∴ ◇(A · B)

4. □(A ⊃ ~B)
    B
    ∴ □~A

5. (□A ⊃ □B)
    ∴ □(A ⊃ B)

6. ◇A
    ~□B
    ∴ ~□(A ⊃ B)

7. □(C ⊃ (A ∨ B))
    (~A · ◇~B)
    ∴ ◇~C

8. □(A ∨ ~B)
    ∴ (~◇B ∨ □A)

9. □((A · B) ⊃ C)
    ◇A
    ◇B
    ∴ ◇C

10. ~□A
    □(B ≡ A)
    ∴ ~◇B

10.3b   Exercise – also LogiCola KC

First appraise intuitively. Then translate into logic (using the letters given) and say whether valid (and give a proof) or invalid (and give a refutation). Translate ambiguous English arguments both ways; prove or disprove each symbolization separately.

1. If the pragmatist view of truth is right, then "A is true" entails "A is useful to believe."
    "A is true but not useful to believe" is consistent.
    ∴ The pragmatist view of truth isn't right.   [Use P, T, and B.]

2. You know.
    "You're mistaken" is logically possible.
    ∴ "You know and are mistaken" is logically possible.   [Use K and M.]

3. Necessarily, if this will be then this will be.
    ∴ If this will be, then it's necessary (in itself) that this will be.   [Use B. This illustrates two senses of "Que será será" – "Whatever will be will be." The first sense is a truth of logic while the second is a form of fatalism.]

4. I'm still.
    If I'm still, then it's necessary that I'm not moving.
    If it's necessary that I'm not moving, then whether I move is not a matter of my free choice.
    ∴ Whether I move is not a matter of my free choice.   [Use S, M, and F. This is adapted from the medieval thinker Boethius, who used a similar example to explain the box-inside/box-outside distinction.]

5. It's necessarily true that if you're morally responsible for your actions then you're free.
    It's necessarily true that if your actions are uncaused then you aren't morally responsible for your actions.
    ∴ "You're free" doesn't entail "Your actions are uncaused."   [Use R, F, and U. This is from A. J. Ayer.]

6. If "One's conscious life won't continue forever" entails "Life is meaningless," then a finite span of life is meaningless.
    If a finite span of life is meaningless, then an infinite span of life is meaningless.
    If an infinite span of life is meaningless, then "One's conscious life will continue forever" entails "Life is meaningless."
    ∴ If it's possible that life is not meaningless, then "One's conscious life won't continue forever" doesn't entail "Life is meaningless."   [C, L, F, I]

7. If you have money, then you couldn't be broke.
    You could be broke.
    ∴ You don't have money.   [Use M and B. Is this argument just a valid instance of *modus tollens*: "(P ⊃ Q), ~Q ∴ ~P"?]

8. If you know, then you couldn't be mistaken.
    You could be mistaken.
    ∴ You don't know.   [Use K and M. Since we could repeat this reasoning for any alleged item of knowledge, the argument seems to show that genuine knowledge is impossible.]

9. It's necessary that if there's a necessary being then "There's a necessary being" (by itself) is necessary.
    "There's a necessary being" is logically possible.
    ∴ "There's a necessary being" is logically necessary.   [Use N for "There's a necessary being" or "There's a being that exists of logical necessity"; this being is often identified with God. This is from Charles Hartshorne and St Anselm; it's sometimes called "Anselm's second ontological argument." The proof raises logical issues that we'll deal with in the next chapter.]

10. It's necessary that either I'll do it or I won't do it.
    If it's necessary that I'll do it, then I'm not free.
    If it's necessary that I won't do it, then I'm not free.
    ∴ I'm not free.   [Use D for "I'll do it." Aristotle and the Stoic Chrysippus discussed this argument. The flaw in this argument relates to a point made by Chrysippus, that "□(D ∨ ~D) ∴ (□D ∨ □~D)" is invalid and is like arguing "Everything is either A or non-A; therefore either everything is A or everything is non-A."]

11. "This agent's actions were all determined" is consistent with "I describe this agent's character in an approving way."
    "I describe this agent's character in an approving way" is consistent with "I praise this agent."
    ∴ "This agent's actions were all determined" is consistent with "I praise this agent."
    [D, A, P]

12. If thinking is just a chemical brain process, then "I think" entails "There's a chemical process in my brain."
    "There's a chemical process in my brain" entails "I have a body."
    "I think but I don't have a body" is logically consistent.
    ∴ Thinking isn't just a chemical brain process.   [Use J, T, C, and B. This argument attacks a form of materialism.]

13.   If "I did that on purpose" entails "I made a prior purposeful decision to do that," then there's an infinite chain of previous decisions to decide.
It's impossible for there to be an infinite chain of previous decisions to decide.
∴ "I did that on purpose" is consistent with "I didn't make a prior purposeful decision to do that."   [Use D, P, and I. This is from Gilbert Ryle.]

14.   God knew that you'd do it.
If God knew that you'd do it, then it was necessary that you'd do it.
If it was necessary that you'd do it, then you weren't free.
∴ You weren't free.   [Use K, D, and F. This argument is the focus of an ancient controversy. Would divine foreknowledge preclude human freedom? If it would, then should we reject human freedom (as did Luther) or divine foreknowledge (as did Charles Hartshorne)? Or perhaps (as the medieval thinkers Boethius, Aquinas, and Ockham claimed) is there a flaw in the argument that divine fore-knowledge precludes human freedom?]

15.   If "good" means "socially approved," then "Racism is socially approved" logically entails "Racism is good."
"Racism is socially approved but not good" is consistent.
∴ "Good" doesn't mean "socially approved." [Use M, S, and G. This argument attacks cultural relativism.]

16.   Necessarily, if God brings it about that A is true, then A is true.
A is a self-contradiction.
∴ It's impossible for God to bring it about that A is true.   [Use B and A, where B is for "God brings it about that A is true."]

17.   If this is experienced, then this must be thought about.
"This is thought about" entails "This is put into the categories of judgments."
∴ If it's possible for this to be experienced, then it's possible for this to be put into the categories of judgments.   [Use E, T, and C. This is from Immanuel Kant, who argued that our mental categories apply, not necessarily to everything that exists, but rather to everything that we could experience.]

18.   Necessarily, if formula B has an all-1 truth table then B is true.
∴ If formula B has an all-1 truth table, then B (taken by itself) is necessary.   [Use A and B. This illustrates the box-outside versus box-inside distinction.]

19.   Necessarily, if you mistakenly think that you exist then you don't exist.
Necessarily, if you mistakenly think that you exist then you exist.
∴ "You mistakenly think that you exist" is impossible.   [Use M and E. This relates to Descartes's "I think, therefore I am" ("Cogito ergo sum").]

20.   If "good" means "desired by God," then "This is good" entails "There's a God."
"There's no God, but this is good" is consistent.
∴ "Good" doesn't mean "desired by God." [Use M, A, and B. This attacks one form of the divine command theory of ethics. Some (see problems 9 and 26 of this section and problem 12 of Section 10.2b) would dispute premise 2 and say that "There's no God" is logically impossible.]

21.   If Plato is right, then it's necessary that ideas are superior to material things.
      It's possible that ideas aren't superior to material things.
   ∴ Plato isn't right.   [P, S]

22.   "I seem to see a chair" doesn't entail "There's an actual chair that I seem to see."
      If we directly perceive material objects, then "I seem to see a chair and there's an
         actual chair that I seem to see" is consistent.
   ∴ We don't directly perceive material objects.   [S, A, D]

23.   "There's a God" is logically incompatible with "There's evil in the world."
      There's evil in the world.
   ∴ "There's a God" is self-contradictory.   [G, E]

24.   If you do all your homework right, then it's impossible that you get this problem
         wrong.
      It's possible that you get this problem wrong.
   ∴ You don't do all your homework right.   [R, W]

25.   "You do what you want" is compatible with "Your act is determined."
      "You do what you want" entails "Your act is free."
   ∴ "Your act is free" is compatible with "Your act is determined."   [W, D, F]

26.   It's necessarily true that if God doesn't exist in reality then there's a being greater
         than God (since then any existing being would be greater than God).
      It's not possible that there's a being greater than God (since "God" is defined as
         "a being than which no being could be greater").
   ∴ It's necessary that God exists in reality.   [Use R and B. This is a simplified modal
      form of St Anselm's ontological argument.]

27.   It was always true that you'd do it.
      If it was always true that you'd do it, then it was necessary that you'd do it.
      If it was necessary that you'd do it, then you weren't free.
   ∴ You weren't free.   [Use A (for "It was always true that you'd do it" – don't use a
      box here), D, and F. This argument is much like problem 14. Are statements
      about future contingencies (for example, "I'll brush my teeth tomorrow") true
      or false before they happen? Should we do truth tables for such statements in
      the normal way, assigning them "1" or "0"? Does this preclude human free-
      dom? If so, should we then reject human freedom? Or should we adopt a many-
      valued logic that says that statements about future contingencies aren't "1" or
      "0" but must instead have some third truth value (maybe "½")? Or is the
      argument fallacious?]

CHAPTER 11
Further Modal Systems

Modal logic studies arguments whose validity depends on "necessary," "possible," and similar notions. The previous chapter presented a basic system that builds on propositional logic. This present chapter considers alternative systems of propositional and quantified modal logic.

11.1 Galactic travel

While logicians usually agree on which arguments are valid, there are some disagreements about modal arguments. Many of the disputes involve arguments in which one modal operator occurs within the scope of another – like "◇◇A ∴ ◇A" and "□(A ⊃ □B), ◇A ∴ B."

These disputes reflect differences in how to formulate the box-dropping rule. So far, we've assumed a system called "S5," which lets us go from any world to any world when we drop a box (Section 10.2):

Drop box	□A → W ∴ A, use any world prefix	Here the line with "□A" can use any world prefix – and so can the line with "∴ A."

This assumes that whatever is necessary in *any* world is thereby true in *all* worlds without restriction. A further implication is that whatever is necessary in one world is thereby necessary in all worlds.

Some weaker views reject these ideas. On these views, what is necessary only has to be true in all "suitably related" worlds; so these views restrict the drop-box rule. All the views in question let us go from "□A" in a world to "A" in the *same* world. But we can't always go from "□A" in one world to "A" in *another* world; traveling between worlds requires a suitable "travel ticket."

We get travel tickets when we drop diamonds. Let "W1" and "W2" stand for world prefixes. Suppose we go from "◇A" in world W1 to "A" in new world W2. Then we get a travel ticket from W1 to W2, and we'll write "W1 ⇒ W2":

W1 ⇒ W2	We have a ticket to move from world W1 to world W2.

Here's an example. Suppose we're doing a proof with wffs "◇◇A" and "◇B." We'd get these travel tickets when we drop diamonds (here "#" stands for the actual world):

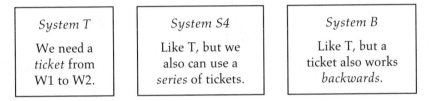

		Travel tickets:
1	◇◇A	
2	◇B	
11	W ∴ ◇A {from 1}	# ⇒ W
12	WW ∴ A {from 11}	W ⇒ WW
13	WWW ∴ B {from 2}	# ⇒ WWW

Dropping a diamond gives us a travel ticket from the world in the "from" line to the world in the "to" line. So in line 11 we get ticket "# ⇒ W" – because we moved from "◇◇A" in the actual world ("#") to "◇A" in world W.

Tickets are reusable; we can use "W1 ⇒ W2" any number of times. The rules for using tickets vary. System T lets us use only one ticket at a time, and only in the direction of the arrow; system S4 lets us combine a series of tickets, while system B lets us use them in a backwards direction. Suppose we have "□A" in world W1 and want to put "A" in world W2:

System T	*System S4*	*System B*
We need a *ticket* from W1 to W2.	Like T, but we also can use a *series* of tickets.	Like T, but a ticket also works *backwards*.

Suppose we have three travel tickets:

$$\# \Rightarrow W \qquad W \Rightarrow WW \qquad \# \Rightarrow WWW$$

System T would let us, when we drop boxes, go from # to W, from W to WW, and from # to WWW. The other systems allow these and more. System S4 lets us use a *series* of tickets in the direction of the arrow; this lets us go from # to WW. System B lets us use single tickets *backwards*; this lets us go from W to #, from WW to W, and from WWW to #. In contrast, system S5 lets us go from any world to any world; this is equivalent to letting us use any ticket or series of tickets in either direction.

S5 is the most liberal system and accepts the most valid arguments; so S5 is the strongest system. T is the weakest system, allowing the fewest proofs. S4 and B are intermediate, each allowing some proofs that the other doesn't. The four systems give the same result for most arguments. But some arguments are valid in one system but invalid in another; these arguments use wffs that apply a modal operator to a wff already containing a modal operator.

This argument is valid in S4 or S5 but invalid in T or B:

```
        1    □A          Valid
            [∴ □□A
  *     2  ┌ asm: ~□□A
  *     3  │  ∴ ◇~□A  {from 2}
  *     4  │  W ∴ ~□A  {from 3}            # ⇒ W
  *     5  │  W ∴ ◇~A  {from 4}
        6  │  WW ∴ ~A  {from 5}           W ⇒ WW
        7  └  WW ∴ A  {from 1}         Need S4 or S5
        8   ∴ □□A  {from 2; 6 contradicts 7}
```

Line 7 requires that we combine a series of tickets in the direction of the arrow. Tickets "# ⇒ W" and "W ⇒ WW" then let us go from actual world # (line 1) to world WW (line 7). This requires systems S4 or S5.

This next one is valid in B or S5 but invalid in T or S4:

```
        1    A           Valid
            [∴ □◇A
  *     2  ┌ asm: ~□◇A
  *     3  │  ∴ ◇~◇A  {from 2}
  *     4  │  W ∴ ~◇A  {from 3}            # ⇒ W
        5  │  W ∴ □~A  {from 4}
        6  └  ∴ ~A  {from 5}            Need B or S5
        7   ∴ □◇A  {from 2; 1 contradicts 6}
```

Line 6 requires using ticket "# ⇒ W" backwards, to go from world W (line 5) to the actual world # (line 6). This requires systems B or S5.

This last one is valid in S5 but invalid in T or B or S4:

```
  *     1    ◇A          Valid
            [∴ □◇A
  *     2  ┌ asm: ~□◇A
  *     3  │  ∴ ◇~◇A  {from 2}
  *     4  │  W ∴ ~◇A  {from 3}            # ⇒ W
        5  │  W ∴ □~A  {from 4}
        6  │  WW ∴ A  {from 1}            # ⇒ WW
        7  └  WW ∴ ~A  {from 5}           Need S5
        8   ∴ □◇A  {from 2; 6 contradicts 7}
```

Line 7 requires combining a series of tickets and using some backwards. Tickets "# ⇒ W" and "# ⇒ WW" then let us go from W (line 5) to WW (line 7). This requires system S5.

S5 is the simplest system in several ways:

• We can formulate S5 more simply. The box-dropping rule doesn't have to mention travel tickets; we need only say that, if we have "□A" in any world, then we can put "A" in any world (the same or a different one).

- S5 captures simple intuitions about necessity and possibility: what is *necessary* is what is true in *all* worlds, what is *possible* is what is true in *some* worlds, and what is necessary or possible doesn't vary between worlds.

- On S5, any string of boxes and diamonds simplifies to the last element of the string. So "□□" and "◇□" simplify to "□" – and "◇◇" and "□◇" simplify to "◇."

Which is the best system? This depends on what we take the box and diamond to mean. If we take them to be about the logical necessity and possibility of *ideas*, then S5 is the best system. If an idea (for example, the claim that 2=2) is logically necessary, then it couldn't have been other than logically necessary. So if A is logically necessary, then it's logically necessary that A is logically necessary ["(□A ⊃ □□A)"]. Similarly, if an idea is logically possible, then it's logically necessary that it's logically possible ["(◇A ⊃ □◇A)"]. Of the four systems, only S5 accepts both these formulas. All this presupposes that we use the box to talk about the logical necessity of *ideas*.

Alternatively, we could take the box to be about the logical necessity of *sentences*. Now the *sentence* "2=2" just happens to express a necessary truth; it wouldn't have expressed one if English had used "=" to mean "≠." So the *sentence* is necessary, but it isn't necessary that it's necessary; this makes "(□A ⊃ □□A)" false. But the *idea* that "2=2" now expresses is both necessary and necessarily necessary – and a change in how we use language wouldn't make this *idea* false. So whether S5 is the best system can depend on whether we take the box to be about the necessity of *ideas* or of *sentences*.

There are still other ways to take "necessary." Sometimes calling something "necessary" might mean that it's "physically necessary," "proven," "known," or "obligatory." Some logicians like the weak system T because it holds for various senses of "necessary"; such logicians might still use S5 for arguments about the logical necessity of *ideas*. While I have sympathy with this view, most of the modal arguments I'm interested in are about the logical necessity of ideas. So I use S5 as the standard system of modal logic but feel free to switch to weaker systems for arguments about other kinds of necessity.

Here we've considered the four main modal systems. We could invent other systems – for example, ones in which we can combine travel tickets only in groups of three. Logicians develop such systems, not to help us in analyzing real arguments, but rather to explore interesting formal structures.[1]

11.1a   Exercise – also LogiCola KG

Using system S5, prove each of these arguments to be valid (all are valid in S5). Also say in which systems the argument is valid: T, B, S4, or S5.

---

[1] For more on alternative modal systems, consult G. E. Hughes and M. J. Cresswell, *A New Introduction to Modal Logic* (London: Routledge, 1996).

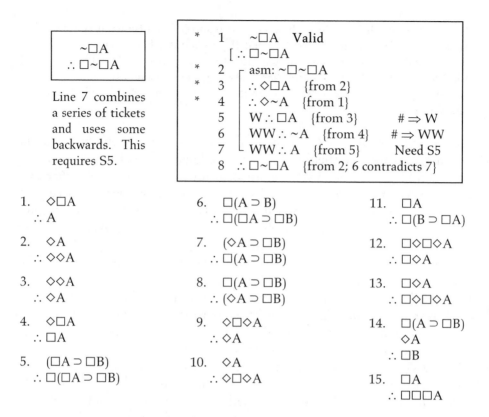

~□A
∴ □~□A

Line 7 combines a series of tickets and uses some backwards. This requires S5.

```
*  1      ~□A   Valid
      [ ∴ □~□A
*  2    ┌ asm: ~□~□A
*  3    │ ∴ ◇□A    {from 2}
*  4    │ ∴ ◇~A    {from 1}
   5    │ W ∴ □A    {from 3}        # ⇒ W
   6    │ WW ∴ ~A   {from 4}        # ⇒ WW
   7    └ WW ∴ A    {from 5}        Need S5
   8   ∴ □~□A    {from 2; 6 contradicts 7}
```

1. ◇□A
    ∴ A

2. ◇A
    ∴ ◇◇A

3. ◇◇A
    ∴ ◇A

4. ◇□A
    ∴ □A

5. (□A ⊃ □B)
    ∴ □(□A ⊃ □B)

6. □(A ⊃ B)
    ∴ □(□A ⊃ □B)

7. (◇A ⊃ □B)
    ∴ □(A ⊃ □B)

8. □(A ⊃ □B)
    ∴ (◇A ⊃ □B)

9. ◇□◇A
    ∴ ◇A

10. ◇A
    ∴ ◇□◇A

11. □A
    ∴ □(B ⊃ □A)

12. □◇□◇A
    ∴ □◇A

13. □◇A
    ∴ □◇□◇A

14. □(A ⊃ □B)
    ◇A
    ∴ □B

15. □A
    ∴ □□□A

11.1b   Exercise – also LogiCola KG

First appraise intuitively. Then translate into logic (using the letters given) and prove to be valid in system S5 (all are valid in S5). Also say in which systems the argument is valid: T, B, S4, or S5.

1. It's necessary that if there's a necessary being then "There's a necessary being" (by itself) is necessary.
    "There's a necessary being" is logically possible.
    ∴ "There's a necessary being" is logically necessary. [Use N for "There's a necessary being" or "There's a being that exists of logical necessity"; this being is often identified with God. This argument (which we saw before in Section 10.3b) is from Charles Hartshorne and St Anselm. Its validity depends on which system of modal logic is correct. Some philosophers defend the argument, often after defending a modal system needed to make it valid. Others argue that the argument is invalid, and so any modal system that would make it valid must be wrong. Still others deny the theological import of the conclusion; they say that a necessary being could be a prime number or the world and needn't be God.]

2. "There's a necessary being" isn't a contingent statement.
    "There's a necessary being" is logically possible.
    ∴ There's a necessary being. [Use N. This version of the Anselm–Hartshorne argument is more clearly valid.]

3. Prove that the first premise of argument 1 is logically equivalent to the first premise of argument 2. (You can prove that two statements are logically equivalent by first deducing the second from the first, and then deducing the first from the second.) In which systems does this equivalence hold?

4. It's necessary that if there's a necessary being then "There's a necessary being" (by itself) is necessary.
    "There's no necessary being" is logically possible.
    ∴ There's no necessary being.   [Use N. Some object that the first premise of the Anselm–Hartshorne argument just as easily leads to an opposite conclusion.]

5. It's necessary that 2+2 = 4.
    It's possible that no language ever existed.
    If all necessary truths hold because of language conventions, then "It's necessary that 2+2 = 4" entails "Some language has sometime existed."
    ∴ Not all necessary truths hold because of language conventions.   [Use T, L, and N. This attacks the linguistic theory of logical necessity.]

11.2   Quantified translations

We'll now develop a system of quantified modal logic that combines our quantificational and modal systems. We'll call this our "naïve" system, since it ignores certain problems; later we'll add refinements.[1]

Many quantified modal translations follow familiar patterns. For example, "everyone" translate into a universal quantifier that follows the English word order – while "anyone," regardless of where it occurs, translates into a universal quantifier at the beginning of the wff:

	=	Everyone could be above average. (FALSE)
◇(x)Ax	=	It's possible for everyone to be above average.
	=	It's possible that, for all x, x is above average.
	=	Anyone could be above average. (TRUE)
(x)◇Ax	=	It's possible for anyone to be above average.
	=	For all x, it's possible that x is above average.

Quantified modal logic can express the difference between necessary and contingent properties. Numbers seem to have both kinds of property. The number 8, for example, has the necessary properties of being even and of being one greater than seven; 8 couldn't have lacked these properties. But 8 also has contingent properties, ones it could have lacked, such as being my favorite number and being less than the number of chapters in this book. We can

---

[1] My understanding of quantified modal logic follows Alvin Plantinga's *The Nature of Necessity* (London: Oxford University Press, 1974). For related discussions, see Saul Kripke's *Naming and Necessity* (Cambridge, Mass.: Harvard University Press, 1980) and Kenneth Konyndyk's *Introductory Modal Logic* (Notre Dame, Ind.: Notre Dame Press, 1986).

symbolize "necessary property" and "contingent property" as follows:

$\Box Fx$
- = F is a necessary (essential) property of x.
- = x has the necessary property of being F.
- = x is necessarily F.
- = In all possible worlds, x would be F.

$(Fx \cdot \Diamond {\sim} Fx)$
- = F is a contingent (accidental) property of x.
- = x is F but could have lacked F.
- = x is contingently F.
- = In the actual world x is F; but in some possible world x isn't F.

Humans have mostly contingent properties. Socrates had contingent properties, like having a beard and being a philosopher; these are contingent, because he could (without self-contradiction) have been a clean-shaven non-philosopher. But Socrates also had necessary properties, like being self-identical and not being a square circle; every being has these properties of necessity.

Aristotelian essentialism is the controversial view that there are properties that some beings have of necessity but some other beings totally lack. Plantinga, supporting this view, suggests that Socrates had of necessity these properties (that some other beings totally lack): not being a prime number, being snubnosed in W (a specific possible world), being a person (capable of conscious rational activity), and being identical with Socrates. The last property differs from that of being named "Socrates."

Plantinga explains "necessary property" as follows. Suppose "a" names a being and "F" names a property. Then the entity named by "a" has the property named by "F" necessarily, if and only if the proposition expressed by "a is non-F" is logically impossible. Then to say that Socrates necessarily has the property of not being a prime number is to say that the proposition "Socrates is a prime number" (with the name "Socrates" referring to the person Socrates) is logically impossible. We must use names (like "Socrates") here and not definite descriptions (like "the entity I'm thinking about").

We talked before about the **box-inside/box-outside** ambiguity. This quantified modal sentence similarly could have either of two meanings:

"All bachelors are necessarily unmarried."

Simple Necessity	Conditional Necessity
$(x)(Bx \supset \Box Ux)$	$\Box(x)(Bx \supset Ux)$
All bachelors are *inherently unmarriable* – in no possible world would anyone ever marry them. (We hope this is false.)	It's necessarily true that all bachelors are unmarried. (This is trivially true because "bachelor" means *unmarried man*.)

When you translate a statement of the form "All A's are necessarily B's," say that it's ambiguous and give both possible translations. When you do an argument with an ambiguous premise, give both translations and give a proof or refutation for each translation. As before, various philosophical fallacies result from confusing the forms.

Discussions about Aristotelian essentialism frequently involve such modal ambiguities. This following sentence could have either of two meanings:

"All persons are necessarily persons."

Simple Necessity $(x)(Px \supset \Box Px)$	Conditional Necessity $\Box(x)(Px \supset Px)$
Everyone who in fact is a person has the necessary property of being a person.	It's necessary that all persons are persons.

The first form is more controversial and attributes to each person the necessary property of being a person; the medievals called this *de re* ("of the thing") necessity. If this first form is true, then you couldn't have been a non-person – the idea of your existing as a non-person is self-contradictory; this would exclude, for example, the possibility of your being reincarnated as an unconscious doorknob. In contrast, the second form is trivially true and attributes necessity to the proposition (or saying) "All persons are persons"; the medievals called this *de dicto* ("of the saying") necessity.

11.2a Exercise – also LogiCola J (QM & QT)

Translate these English sentences into wffs; translate ambiguous forms both ways.

It's necessary that all mathematicians have the necessary property of being rational.	$\Box(x)(Mx \supset \Box Rx)$

Here the first box symbolizes *de dicto* necessity ("It's necessary that ..."), while the second symbolizes *de re* necessity ("have the necessary property of being rational").

1. It's possible for anyone to be unsurpassed in greatness. [Use Ux.]
2. It's possible for everyone to be unsurpassed in greatness.
3. John has the necessary property of being unmarried. [Use Ux and j.]
4. All experts are necessarily smart. [Ex, Sx]
5. Being named "Socrates" is a contingent property of Socrates. [Nx, s]
6. It's necessary that everything is self-identical. [Use "=."]
7. Every entity has the necessary property of being self-identical.
8. John is necessarily sitting. [Sx, j]
9. Everyone that is observed to be sitting is necessarily sitting. [Ox, Sx]
10. All numbers have the necessary property of being abstract entities. [Nx, Ax]

11. It's necessary that all living beings in this room are persons.   [Lx, Px]
12. All living beings in this room have the necessary property of being persons.
13. All living beings in this room have the contingent property of being persons.
14. Any contingent claim could be true.   [Cx, Tx]
15. "All contingent claims are true" is possible.
16. All mathematicians are necessarily rational.   [Mx, Rx]
17. All mathematicians are contingently two-legged.   [Mx, Tx]
18. All mathematical statements that are true are necessarily true.   [Mx, Tx]
19. It's possible that God has the necessary property of being unsurpassed in greatness.   [Ux, g]
20. Some being has the necessary property of being unsurpassed in greatness.   [Ux]

11.3 Quantified proofs

Proofs use the same quantificational and modal inference rules as before. Here's an example of a quantified modal proof:

It's necessary that everything is self-identical.
∴ Every entity has the necessary property of being self-identical.

```
        1     □(x)x=x   Valid
            [∴ (x)□x=x
 *      2   ┌ asm: ~(x)□x=x
 *      3   │ ∴ (∃x)~□x=x   {from 2}
 *      4   │ ∴ ~□a=a   {from 3}
 *      5   │ ∴ ◇~a=a   {from 4}
        6   │ W∴ ~a=a   {from 5}
        7   │ W∴ (x)x=x   {from 1}
        8   └ W∴ a=a   {from 7}
        9   ∴ (x)□x=x   {from 2; 6 contradicts 8}
```

In working out English modal arguments, we'll sometimes find an ambiguous premise – as in the following argument:

> All bachelors are necessarily unmarried.
> You're a bachelor.
> ∴ "You're unmarried" is logically necessary.

Premise 1 could be taken to assert either the simple necessity "$(x)(Bx \supset \Box Ux)$" ("All bachelors are *inherently unmarriable*") or the conditional necessity "$\Box(x)(Bx \supset Ux)$" ("It's necessarily true that all bachelors are unmarried"). In such cases, we need to say that the argument is ambiguous and give a proof or refutation for each translation:

Box-inside version:

```
1   (x)(Bx ⊃ □Ux)   Valid
2   Bu
    [ ∴ □Uu
3   ┌ asm: ~□Uu
*  4 │ ∴ (Bu ⊃ □Uu) {from 1}
5   └ ∴ □Uu {from 4 and 2}
6   ∴ □Uu {from 3; 3 contra-
        dicts 5}
```

(While this is valid,
premise 1 is false.)

Box-outside version:

```
1    □(x)(Bx ⊃ Ux)        Invalid
2    Bu
     [ ∴ □Uu
*  3  asm: ~□Uu
*  4  ∴ ◇~Uu {from 3}
5    W ∴ ~Uu {from 4}
6    W ∴ (x)(Bx ⊃ Ux) {from 1}
7    ∴ (x)(Bx ⊃ Ux) {from 1}
*  8  W ∴ (Bu ⊃ Uu) {from 6}
*  9  ∴ (Bu ⊃ Uu) {from 7}
10   W ∴ ~Bu {from 5 and 8}
11   ∴ Uu {from 2 and 9}
```

```
          ┌─────────────┐
        W │   Bu, Uu    │
          ├─────────────┤
          │  ~Bu, ~Uu   │
          └─────────────┘
```

Both versions are flawed; the first has a false premise while the second is invalid. So the proof that you're inherently unmarriable fails.

Our refutation has two possible worlds, each with only one entity – you. In the actual world, you're a bachelor and unmarried; in world W, you're not a bachelor and not unmarried. In this galaxy, the premises are true (since in both worlds all bachelors are unmarried – and in the actual world you're a bachelor) but the conclusion is false (since in world W you're not unmarried).

Arguments with a modal ambiguity often have one interpretation with a false premise and another that's invalid. Such arguments often seem sound until we focus on the ambiguity.

As with relational arguments, applying our proof strategy mechanically will sometimes lead into an endless loop. In the following case, we keep getting new letters and new worlds, endlessly:

It's possible for anyone to be
above average.
∴ It's possible for everyone to be
above average.

```
                      1    (x)◇Ax
                           [ ∴ ◇(x)Ax
                  *   2    asm: ~◇(x)Ax
                      3    ∴ □~(x)Ax {from 2}
New letter ➔      *   4    ∴ ◇Aa {from 1}
New world  ➔          5    W ∴ Aa {from 4}
                  *   6    W ∴ ~(x)Ax {from 3}
                  *   7    W ∴ (∃x)~Ax {from 6}
New letter ➔          8    W ∴ ~Ab {from 7}
                  *   9    ∴ ◇Ab {from 1}
New world  ➔          10   WW ∴ Ab {from 9}
                  *   11   WW ∴ ~(x)Ax {from 3}
                  *   12   WW ∴ (∃x)~Ax {from 11}
New letter ➔          13   WW ∴ ~Ac {from 12}
                  …   14   ∴ ◇Ac {from 1} …
```

Using ingenuity, we can devise a refutation with two entities and two worlds:

	a, b
W	Aa, ~Ab
WW	Ab, ~Aa

Here each person is above average in some world or other – but in no world is every person above average. For now, we'll assume in our refutations that every world contains the same entities (and at least one such entity).

11.3a   Exercise – also LogiCola KQ

Say whether valid (and give a proof) or invalid (and give a refutation).

```
          1   (x)□Fx   Valid
         [ ∴ □(x)Fx
 *   2   ┌ asm: ~□(x)Fx
 *   3   │ ∴ ◇~(x)Fx   {from 2}
 *   4   │ W ∴ ~(x)Fx   {from 3}
 *   5   │ W ∴ (∃x)~Fx   {from 4}
     6   │ W ∴ ~Fa   {from 5}
     7   │ ∴ □Fa   {from 1}
     8   └ W ∴ Fa   {from 7}
     9   ∴ □(x)Fx   {from 2; 6 contradicts 8}
```

(x)□Fx
∴ □(x)Fx

This is called a "Barcan inference," after Ruth Barcan Marcus. It's doubtful that our naïve quantified modal logic gives the right results for this argument and for several others. We'll discuss this argument again in Section 11.4.

1.   (∃x)□Fx
     ∴ □(∃x)Fx

2.   a=b
     ∴ (□Fa ⊃ □Fb)

3. ∴ □(∃x)x=a

4. ∴ (∃x)□x=a

5.   ◇(x)Fx
     ∴ (x)◇Fx

6. ∴ (x)□x=x

7. ∴ □(x)x=x

8.   □(x)(Fx ⊃ Gx)
     ∴ (x)(Fx ⊃ □Gx)

9.   ◇(∃x)Fx
     ∴ (∃x)◇Fx

10.   (∃x)◇Fx
     ∴ ◇(∃x)Fx

11.   (◇(x)Fx ⊃ (x)◇Fx)
     ∴ ((∃x)~Fx ⊃ □(∃x)~Fx)

12. ∴ (x)(y)(x=y ⊃ □x=y)

13.   □(x)(Fx ⊃ Gx)
     □Fa
     ∴ □Ga

14.   ~a=b
     ∴ □~a=b

11.3b   Exercise – also LogiCola KQ

First appraise intuitively. Then translate into logic (using the letters given) and say whether valid (and give a proof) or invalid (and give a refutation). Translate ambiguous English arguments both ways; prove or disprove each symbolization separately.

1.   I have a beard.
     ∴ "Whoever doesn't have a beard isn't me" is a necessary truth.   [Use Bx and i.
        G. E. Moore criticized such reasoning, which he saw as essential to the idealistic
        metaphysics of his day and its claim that every property of a thing is necessary.
        The conclusion entails that "I have a beard" is logically necessary. Moore would
        say that, given that premise 1 is true, "Whoever doesn't have a beard isn't me"
        is only a contingent truth.]

2.   "Whoever doesn't have a beard isn't me" is a necessary truth.
     ∴ "I have a beard" is logically necessary.   [Use Bx and i.]

3.   Aristotle isn't identical to Plato.
     If some being has the property of being necessarily identical to Plato but not all
        beings have the property of being necessarily identical to Plato, then some
        beings have necessary properties that other beings lack.
     ∴ Some beings have necessary properties that other beings lack.   [Use a, p, and S
        (for "Some beings have necessary properties that other beings lack"). This
        defense of Aristotelian essentialism is essentially from Alvin Plantinga.]

4.   All mathematicians are necessarily rational.
     Paul is a mathematician.
     ∴ Paul is necessarily rational.   [Mx, Rx, p]

5.   Necessarily there exists something unsurpassed in greatness.
     ∴ There exists something that necessarily is unsurpassed in greatness.   [Ux]

6.   The number that I'm thinking of isn't necessarily even.
     8 = the number that I'm thinking of.
     ∴ 8 isn't necessarily even.   [Use n, E, and e. Does our naïve quantified modal logic
        correctly decide whether this argument is valid?]

7.   "I'm a thinking being, and there are no material objects" is logically possible.
     Every material object has the necessary property of being a material object.
     ∴ I'm not a material object.   [Use Tx, Mx, and i. This is from Alvin Plantinga.]

8.   All humans are necessarily rational.
     All living beings in this room are human.
     ∴ All living beings in this room are necessarily rational.   [Use Hx, Rx, and Lx. This
        is from Aristotle, who was the first logician and the first to combine quantifica-
        tion with modality.]

9.   It isn't necessary that all cyclists are rational.
     Paul is a cyclist.
     Paul is rational.
     ∴ Paul is contingently rational.   [Cx, Rx, p]

10. "Socrates has a pain in his toe but doesn't show pain behavior" is consistent.
     It's necessary that everyone who has a pain in his toe is in pain.
     ∴ "All who are in pain show pain behavior" isn't a necessary truth.   [Use s, Tx for
        "x has a pain in his toe," Bx for "x shows pain behavior," and Px for "x is in
        pain." This attacks a behaviorist analysis of the concept of "pain."]

11. If Q (the question "Why is there something and not nothing?") is a meaningful question, then it's possible that there's an answer to Q.
Necessarily, every answer to Q refers to an existent that explains the existence of other things.
Necessarily, nothing that refers to an existent that explains the existence of other things is an answer to Q.
∴ Q isn't a meaningful question.   [M, Ax, Rx]

12. The number of apostles is 12.
12 is necessarily greater than 8.
∴ The number of apostles is necessarily greater than 8.   [Use n, t, e, and Gxy. Does our naïve system correctly decide whether this argument is valid?]

13. All (well-formed) cyclists are necessarily two–legged.
Paul is a (well-formed) cyclist.
∴ Paul is necessarily two–legged.   [Cx, Tx, p]

14. Something exists in the understanding than which nothing could be greater. (In other words, there's some x such that x exists in the understanding and it isn't possible that there be something greater that x.)
Anything that exists in reality is greater than anything that doesn't exist in reality.
Socrates exists in reality.
∴ Something exists in reality than which nothing could be greater. (In other words, there's some x such that x exists in reality and it isn't possible that there be something greater than x.)   [Use Ux for "x exists in the understanding," Rx for "x exists in reality," Gxy for "x is greater than y," and s for "Socrates." Use a universe of discourse of *possible beings* – including fictional beings like Santa Claus in addition to actual beings. (Is this legitimate?) This is a form of St Anselm's first ontological argument for the existence of God.]

15. "Someone is unsurpassably great" is logically possible.
"Everyone who is unsurpassably great is, in every possible world, omnipotent, omniscient, and morally perfect" is necessarily true.
∴ Someone is omnipotent, omniscient, and morally perfect.   [Use Ux and Ox. This is a simplified form of Alvin Plantinga's ontological argument for the existence of God. Plantinga regards the second premise as true by definition; he sees the first premise as controversial but reasonable.]

16. Anything could cease to exist.
∴ Everything could cease to exist.   [Use Cx for "x ceases to exist." Some see Aquinas's third argument for the existence of God as requiring this inference.]

11.4   A sophisticated system

Our naïve quantified modal logic has two problems. First, it mishandles definite descriptions (terms of the form "the so and so"). So far, we've translated these using small letters; but this can cause problems in modal contexts. To solve the problems, we'll use Russell's analysis of definite descriptions (Section 9.6).

Consider how we've been translating this English sentence:

The number I'm thinking of is necessarily odd   =   □On

This sentence is ambiguous; it could mean either of two things (where "Tx" means "I'm thinking of number x"):

Box Inside	Box Outside
$(\exists x)((Tx \cdot \sim(\exists y)(\sim x=y \cdot Ty)) \cdot \Box Ox)$	$\Box(\exists x)((Tx \cdot \sim(\exists y)(\sim x=y \cdot Ty)) \cdot Ox)$
I'm thinking of just one number, and it has the necessary property of being odd.	This is necessary: "I'm thinking of just one number and it's odd."

The first form might be true – if, for example, the number 7 has the necessary property of being odd and I'm thinking of just the number 7. But the second form is definitely false, since it's possible that I'm thinking of no number, or more than one number, or an even number.

So our naïve way to translate "the so and so" is ambiguous. To fix this problem, our sophisticated system will require that we symbolize "the so and so" using Russell's "there is just one ..." analysis – as we do in the above boxes. This analysis also blocks the proof of invalid arguments like this one:

8 is the number I'm thinking of.	e=n
It's necessary that 8 is 8.	□e=e
∴ It's necessary that 8 is the number I'm thinking of.	∴ □e=n

This is invalid – since it may be only contingently true that 8 is the number I'm thinking of. The argument is provable in naïve quantified modal logic, since the conclusion follows from the premises by the substitute-equals rule (Section 9.2). Our sophisticated system avoids the problem by requiring the longer analysis of "the number I'm thinking of." So "8 is the number I'm thinking of" gets changed into "I'm thinking of just one number and it is 8" – and the above argument becomes this:

I'm thinking of just one number and it is 8.	$(\exists x)((Tx \cdot \sim(\exists y)(\sim x=y \cdot Ty)) \cdot x=e)$
It's necessary that 8 is 8.	□e=e
∴ This is necessary: "I'm thinking of just one number and it is 8."	∴ $\Box(\exists x)((Tx \cdot \sim(\exists y)(\sim x=y \cdot Ty)) \cdot x=e)$
	Invalid

So translated, the argument becomes invalid and not provable.

The second problem is that our naïve system assumes that the same entities exist in all possible worlds. This leads to implausible results; for example, it makes Gensler (and everyone else) into a logically necessary being:

$$[\; \therefore \; \Box(\exists x)x=g \qquad \text{Valid ???}$$

*	1	┌ asm: ~□(∃x)x=g	
*	2	│ ∴ ◇~(∃x)x=g	{from 1}
*	3	│ W ∴ ~(∃x)x=g	{from 2}
	4	│ W ∴ (x)~x=g	{from 3}
	5	│ W ∴ ~g=g	{from 4} ← ???
	6	└ W ∴ g=g	{self-identity}
	7	∴ □(∃x)x=g	{from 1; 5 contradicts 6}

∴ In every possible world, there exists a being who is Gensler.

But Gensler isn't a logically necessary being – since there are impoverished possible worlds without me. So something is wrong here.

There are two ways out of the problem. One way is to change how we take "(∃x)." The provable "□(∃x)x=g" is false if we take "(∃x)" to mean "for some *existing being* x." But we might take "(∃x)" to mean "for some *possible being* x"; then "□(∃x)x=g" would mean the more plausible: "In every possible world, there's a *possible being* who is Gensler." Perhaps there's a possible being Gensler in every world; in some of these worlds Gensler exists, and in others he doesn't. This view would need an existence predicate "Ex" to distinguish between possible beings that exist and those that don't; we could then use the formula "(∃x)~Ex" to say that there are possible beings that don't exist.

This view is paradoxical, since it posits non-existent beings. Alvin Plantinga defends the opposite view, which he calls "actualism." *Actualism* holds that to be a being and to exist is the same thing; there neither are nor could have been non-existent beings. Of course there could have been beings other than those that now exist. But this doesn't mean that there *now* are beings that don't exist. Actualism denies the latter claim.

Since I favor actualism, I'll avoid non-existent beings and continue to take "(∃x)" to mean "for some existing being." On this reading, "□(∃x)x=g" means "It's necessary that there's an existing being who is Gensler." This is false, since I might not have existed. So we must reject some line of the above proof.

The faulty line seems to be the derivation of 5 from 4:

In W, every existing being is distinct from Gensler.   4 W ∴ (x)~x=g
∴ In W, Gensler is distinct from Gensler.   5 W ∴ ~g=g   {from 4}

This inference shouldn't be valid – unless we presuppose the additional premise "W ∴ (∃x)x=g" – that Gensler is an existing being in world W.

Rejecting this line requires moving to a *free logic* – one that is free of the assumption that individual constants like "g" always refer to existing beings. Recall our drop-universal rule DU of Section 8.2:

DU	(x)Fx → Fa, use any constant	Every existing being is F. ∴ a is F.

Suppose that every existing being is F; "a" might not denote an existing being, and so "a is F" might not be true. So we need to modify the rule to require the premise that "a" denotes an existing being:

DU*

(x)Fx, (∃x)x=a → Fa, use any constant

Every existing being is F.
a is an existing being.
∴ a is F.

Here we symbolize "a is an existing being" by "(∃x)x=a" ("For some existing being x, x is identical to a"). With this change, "□(∃x)x=g" ("Gensler is a necessary being") is no longer provable.

If we weaken DU, we should strengthen our drop-existential rule DE:

DE*

(∃x)Fx → Fa, (∃x)x=a, use a *new* constant

Some existing being is F.
∴ a is F.
∴ a is an existing being.

When we drop an existential using DE*, we get an existence claim (like "(∃x)x=a") that we can use in dropping universals with DU*. The resulting system can prove almost everything we could prove before – except that the proofs are now a few lines longer. The main effect is to block a few proofs; we can no longer prove that Gensler exists in all possible worlds.

Our free-logic system also blocks the proof of this Barcan inference:

Every existing being has the necessary property of being F.
∴ In every possible world, every existing being is F.

	1	(x)□Fx	Invalid
		[∴ □(x)Fx	
*	2	asm: ~□(x)Fx	
*	3	∴ ◇~(x)Fx {from 2}	
*	4	W ∴ ~(x)Fx {from 3}	
*	5	W ∴ (∃x)~Fx {from 4}	
	6	W ∴ ~Fa {from 5}	
	7	W ∴ (∃x)x=a {from 5}	

b exists
a doesn't
Fb, ~Fa

a & b exist
Fb, ~Fa

W

Our new rule for dropping "(∃x)" tells us that "a" denotes an existing being in world W (line 7). But we don't know if "a" denotes an existing being in the actual world; so we can't conclude "□Fa" from "(x)□Fx" in line 1. With our naïve system, we could conclude "□Fa" – and then put "Fa" in world W to contradict line 6; but now the line is blocked, and the proof fails.

While we don't automatically get a refutation, we can invent one on our own. Our refutation lists which entities exist in which worlds; it uses "a exists" for "(∃x)x=a." Here "Every existing being has the necessary property of being F" is true – since entity-b is the only existing being and in every world it is F. But "In every possible world, every existing being is F" is false – since in world W there is an existing being, a, that isn't F.

Here's another objection to the argument. Suppose only abstract objects (numbers, sets, etc.) existed and all these had the necessary property of being abstract. Then "Every existing being has the necessary property of being abstract" would be true. But "In every possible world, every existing being is abstract" could still be false – if other possible worlds had concrete entities.[1]

Our new approach allows different worlds to have different existing entities. Gensler might exist in one world but not another. We shouldn't picture existing in different worlds as anything spooky; it's just a way of talking about different possibilities. I might not have existed. We can tell consistent stories where my parents didn't meet and where I never came into existence. If the stories had been true, then I wouldn't have existed. So I don't exist in these stories (although I might exist in other stories). Existing in a possible world is much like existing in a story; a "possible world" is just a technical analogue of a "consistent story." "I exist in world W" just means "If world W had been actual, then I would have existed."

We also could allow possible worlds with no entities. In such worlds, all wffs starting with existential quantifiers are false and all those starting with universal quantifiers are true.

Should we allow this as a possible world when we do our refutations?

$$\text{W} \quad \boxed{\text{a doesn't exist, Fa}}$$

It seems incoherent to claim that "a has property F" is true while a doesn't exist. It seems that only existing beings have positive properties; in a consistent story where Gensler doesn't exist, Gensler couldn't be a logician or a backpacker. So if "a exists" isn't true in a possible world, then "a has property F" isn't true in that world either. We can put this idea into an inference rule PE* (for "property existence"):

$$\text{PE*} \quad \boxed{\text{Fa} \quad \rightarrow \quad (\exists x)x{=}a} \qquad \begin{array}{l} \text{a has property F.} \\ \therefore \text{ a is an existing being.} \end{array}$$

Rule PE* holds regardless of what constant replaces "a," what variable replaces "x," and what wff containing only a capital letter and "a" and perhaps other small letters (but nothing else) replaces "Fa." By PE*, "Descartes thinks" entails "Descartes exists." Conversely, the falsity of "Descartes exists" entails the falsity of "Descartes thinks." Rule PE* expresses that it's a necessary truth that only existing objects have properties. Plantinga calls this view "serious actualism"; actualists who reject PE* are deemed frivolous.

The first example below isn't a correct instance of PE* (since the wff substituted for "Fa" in PE* can't contain "~"), but the second is:

---

[1] Or suppose God created nothing and all uncreated beings had the necessary property of being uncreated. Then "Every existing being has the necessary property of being uncreated" would be true. But "In every possible world, every existing being is uncreated" could still be false – since there could have been possible worlds with created beings.

This point is confusing because "a isn't F" in English can have two different senses. "Descartes doesn't think" could mean either of these:

Descartes is an existing being who doesn't think   = $(\exists x)(x{=}d \cdot {\sim}Td)$

It's false that Descartes is an existing being who thinks   = ${\sim}(\exists x)(x{=}d \cdot Td)$

The first form is *de re* (about the thing); it affirms the property of being a non-thinker of the entity Descartes. Taken this first way, "Descartes doesn't think" entails "Descartes exists." The second form is *de dicto* (about the saying); it denies the statement "Descartes thinks" (which may be false either because Descartes is a non-thinking entity or because Descartes doesn't exist). Taken this second way, "Descartes doesn't think" doesn't entail "Descartes exists."

One might object to PE* on the grounds that Santa Claus has properties (such as being fat) but doesn't exist. But various stories predicate conflicting properties to Santa; they differ, for example, on which day he delivers presents. Does Santa have contradictory properties? Or is one Santa story uniquely "true"? What would that mean? When we say "Santa is fat," we mean that in such and such a story (or possible world) there's a being called Santa who is fat. We shouldn't think of Santa as a non-existing being in our actual world who has properties such as being fat. Rather, what exists in our actual world is stories about there being someone with certain properties – and children who may believe these stories. So Santa needn't make us give up PE*.

We need to modify our current definition of "necessary property":

$$\text{F is a necessary property of a} \quad \begin{aligned} &= \quad \Box Fa \\ &= \quad \text{In all possible worlds, a is F.} \end{aligned}$$

Let's grant that Socrates has properties only in worlds where he exists – and that there are worlds where he doesn't exist. Then there are worlds where Socrates has no properties – and so there aren't any properties that Socrates has in all worlds. By our definition, Socrates would have no necessary properties.

Socrates still might have some necessary *combinations* of properties. Perhaps it's true in all worlds that if Socrates exists then Socrates is a person. This suggests a looser definition of "necessary property":

$$\text{F is a necessary property of a} \quad \begin{aligned} &= \quad \Box((\exists x)x{=}a \supset Fa) \\ &= \quad \text{In all possible worlds where} \\ &\qquad \text{a exists, a is F.} \end{aligned}$$

This looser definition reflects more clearly what philosophers mean when they speak of "necessary properties." It also lets us claim that Socrates has the necessary property of being a person. This would mean that Socrates is a person in every possible world where he exists; equivalently, in no possible world does Socrates exist as anything other than a person. Here's an analogous definition of "contingent property":

$$
\begin{aligned}
\text{F is a contingent property of a} \quad &= \quad (\text{Fa} \cdot \Diamond((\exists x)x=a \cdot \sim\!\text{Fa})) \\
&= \quad \text{a is F; but in some possible world} \\
&\qquad \text{where a exists, a isn't F.}
\end{aligned}
$$

These refinements would overcome problems but make our system much harder to use. We seldom need the refinements. So we'll keep the naïve system of earlier sections as our "official system" and build on it in the following chapters. But we'll be conscious that this system is oversimplified in various ways. If and when the naïve system gives questionable results, we can appeal to the sophisticated system to clear things up.

CHAPTER 12
Deontic and Imperative Logic

Imperative logic studies arguments with imperatives, like "Don't do this." Deontic logic, by contrast, studies arguments whose validity depends on "ought," "permissible," and similar notions. We'll take imperative logic first and then build deontic logic on it.[1]

12.1 Imperative translations

Imperative logic builds on previous systems and adds two ways to form wffs:

> 1. Any underlined capital letter is a wff.
> 2. The result of writing a capital letter and then one or more small letters, one small letter of which is underlined, is a wff.

Underlining turns indicatives into imperatives:

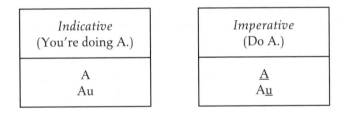

Indicative (You're doing A.)	*Imperative* (Do A.)
A Au	<u>A</u> A<u>u</u>

Here are some further translations:

$$
\begin{array}{rcl}
\text{Don't do A} & = & \sim\underline{A} \\
\text{Do A and B} & = & (\underline{A} \cdot \underline{B}) \\
\text{Do A or B} & = & (\underline{A} \vee \underline{B}) \\
\text{Don't do either A or B} & = & \sim(\underline{A} \vee \underline{B})
\end{array}
$$

---

[1] We'll mostly follow Hector-Neri Castañeda's approach. See his "Imperative reasonings," *Philosophy and Phenomenological Research* 21 (1960): pages 21–49; "Outline of a theory on the general logical structure of the language of action," *Theoria* 26 (1960): pages 151–82; "Actions, imperatives, and obligations," *Proceedings of the Aristotelian Society* 68 (1967–68): pages 25–48; and "On the semantics of the ought-to-do," *Synthese* 21 (1970): pages 448–68.

$$
\begin{array}{rcl}
\text{Don't both do A and do B} & = & \\
\text{Don't combine doing A with doing B} & = & \sim(\underline{A} \cdot \underline{B})
\end{array}
$$

$$
\begin{array}{rcl}
\text{Don't combine doing A with not doing B} & = & \\
\text{Don't do A without doing B} & = & \sim(\underline{A} \cdot \sim\underline{B})
\end{array}
$$

Underline imperative parts but not factual ones:

$$
\begin{array}{rcl}
\text{You're doing A and you're doing B} & = & (A \cdot B) \\
\text{You're doing A, but do B} & = & (A \cdot \underline{B}) \\
\text{Do A and B} & = & (\underline{A} \cdot \underline{B})
\end{array}
$$

$$
\begin{array}{rcl}
\text{If you're doing A, then you're doing B} & = & (A \supset B) \\
\text{If you (in fact) are doing A, then do B} & = & (A \supset \underline{B}) \\
\text{Do A, only if you (in fact) are doing B} & = & (\underline{A} \supset B)
\end{array}
$$

Since English doesn't put an imperative after "if," we can't read "$(\underline{A} \supset B)$" as "If do A, then you're doing B." But we can read it as the equivalent "Do A, only if you're doing B." This means the same as "$(\sim B \supset \sim\underline{A})$: "If you aren't doing B, then don't do A."

There's a subtle difference between these two:

$$
\begin{array}{rcl}
\text{If you (in fact) are doing A, then don't do B} & = & (A \supset \sim\underline{B}) \\
\text{Don't combine doing A with doing B} & = & \sim(\underline{A} \cdot \underline{B})
\end{array}
$$

"A" is underlined in the second but not the first; otherwise, the two wffs would be equivalent. The if-then "$(A \supset \sim\underline{B})$" says that if A is done then you aren't to do B. But the don't-combine "$\sim(\underline{A} \cdot \underline{B})$" just forbids a combination: doing A and B together. If you're doing A, it doesn't follow that you aren't to do B; it may be better to do B and stop doing A. We'll see more on this distinction later.

These examples underline the letter for the agent:

$$
\begin{array}{rcl}
\text{X, do (or be) A} & = & A\underline{x} \\
\text{X, do A to Y} & = & A\underline{x}y
\end{array}
$$

These use quantifiers:

$$
\begin{array}{rcl}
\text{Everyone does A} & = & (x)Ax \\
\text{Let everyone do A} & = & (x)A\underline{x}
\end{array}
$$

$$
\begin{array}{rcl}
\text{Let everyone who (in fact) is doing A do B} & = & (x)(Ax \supset B\underline{x})
\end{array}
$$

$$
\begin{array}{rcl}
\text{Let someone who (in fact) is doing A do B} & = & (\exists x)(Ax \cdot B\underline{x}) \\
\text{Let someone both do A and do B} & = & (\exists x)(A\underline{x} \cdot B\underline{x})
\end{array}
$$

Notice which letters are underlined.

12.1a Exercise – also LogiCola L (IM & IT)

Translate these English sentences into wffs; take each "you" as a singular "you."

If the cocoa is about to boil,
remove it from the heat

$(B \supset \underline{R})$

Our sentence also could translate as "$(B \supset R\underline{u})$" or "$(Bc \supset R\underline{u}c)$."

1.   Leave or shut up.   [Use L and S.]
2.   If you don't leave, then shut up.
3.   Do A, only if you want to do A.   [Use A and W.]
4.   Do A, only if you want to do A.   [This time use Au and Wu.]
5.   Don't combine accelerating with braking.
6.   If you accelerate, then don't brake.
7.   If you brake, then don't accelerate.
8.   If you believe that you ought to do A, then do A.   [Use A for "You do A" and B for "You believe that you ought to do A."]
9.   Don't combine believing that you ought to do A with not doing A.
10.   If everyone does A, then do A yourself.
11.   If you have a headache, then take aspirin.   [Hx, Ax, u]
12.   Let everyone who has a headache take aspirin.
13.   Gensler, rob Jones.   [Rxy, g, j]
14.   If Jones hits you, then hit Jones.   [Hxy, j, u]
15.   If you believe that A is wrong, then don't do A.   [Use A for "You do A" and B for "You believe that A is wrong."]
16.   If you do A, then don't believe that A is wrong.
17.   Don't combine believing that A is wrong with doing A.
18.   Would that someone be sick and also be well.   [Sx, Wx]
19.   Would that someone who is sick be well.
20.   Would that someone be sick who is well.

12.2   Imperative proofs

Imperative proofs work much like indicative ones and require no new inference rules. But we must treat "A" and "$\underline{A}$" as different wffs. "A" and "$\sim\underline{A}$" aren't contradictories; it's consistent to say "You're now doing A, but don't."

Here's an imperative argument that follows an I-rule inference:

If you're accelerating, then don't brake.	$(A \supset \sim\underline{B})$	Valid
You're accelerating.	A	
∴ Don't brake.	∴ $\sim\underline{B}$	

While this seems intuitively valid, there's a problem with calling it "valid," since we defined "valid" using "true" and "false" (Section 1.2):

> An argument is *valid* if it would be contradictory to
> have the premises all *true* and conclusion *false*.

"Don't brake" and other imperatives aren't true or false. So how can the valid/invalid distinction apply to imperative arguments?

We need a broader definition of "valid" that applies equally to indicative and imperative arguments. This one (which avoids "true" and "false") does the job:

> An argument is *valid* if the conjunction of its premises
> with the contradictory of its conclusion is inconsistent.

To say that our argument is *valid* means that this combination is inconsistent:

"If you're accelerating, then don't brake; you're accelerating; brake."

The combination *is* inconsistent. So our argument is *valid* in this new sense.[1]

This next argument is just like the first except that it uses a *don't-combine* premise, which makes it invalid:

Don't combine accelerating with braking.	$\sim(\underline{A} \cdot \underline{B})$ **Invalid**
You're accelerating.	A
∴ Don't brake.	∴ $\sim\underline{B}$

The first premise forbids us to accelerate and brake together. Suppose we're accelerating. It doesn't follow that we shouldn't brake; maybe, to avoid hitting a car, we should brake and stop accelerating. So the argument is invalid. It's consistent to conjoin the premises with the contradictory of the conclusion:

Don't combine accelerating with braking – never do both together;
you in fact are accelerating right now; but you'll hit a car unless you
slow down; so stop accelerating right away – and brake immediately.

Here it makes good consistent sense to endorse the premises while also adding the denial of the conclusion ("Brake").

We'd work out the symbolic argument this way (being careful to treat "A" and "$\underline{A}$" as different wffs, almost as if they were different letters):

---

[1] We could equivalently define a *valid argument* as one in which every set of imperatives and indicatives that is consistent with the premises also is consistent with the conclusion.

```
 *  1     ~(A° · B¹) = 1    Invalid
    2     A¹ = 1
        [∴ ~B¹ = 0          ┌──────────┐
                            │ A, ~A, B │
                            └──────────┘
    3     asm: B
    4     ∴ ~A   {from 1 and 3}
```

On our refutation:

$$A = 1$$
$$\underline{A} = 0$$
$$\underline{B} = 1$$

We quickly get a refutation – a set of assignments of 1 and 0 to the letters that make the premises 1 but conclusion 0. Our refutation says this:

> You're accelerating; don't accelerate; instead, brake.

But there's a problem here. Our refutation assigns *false* to the imperative "Accelerate" – even though imperatives aren't true or false. So what does "$\underline{A} = 0$" mean?

We can generically read "1" as "correct" and "0" as "incorrect." Applied to indicatives, these mean "true" or "false." Applied to imperatives, these mean that the prescribed action is "correct" or "incorrect" relative to some standard that divides actions prescribed by the imperative letters into *correct* and *incorrect* actions. The standard could be of different sorts, based on things like morality, law, or traffic safety goals; generally we won't specify the standard.

Suppose we have a propositional-logic argument with imperative letters added. The argument is *valid* if and only if, relative to every assignment of "1" or "0" to the indicative and imperative letters, if the premises are "1," then so is the conclusion. Equivalently, the argument is *valid* if and only if, relative to any possible facts and any possible standards for correct actions, if all the premises are correct then so is the conclusion.

So our refutation amounts to this – where we imagine certain facts being true/false and certain actions being correct/incorrect:

$$A = 1 \qquad \text{"You're accelerating" is true.}$$
$$\underline{A} = 0 \qquad \text{Accelerating is incorrect.}$$
$$\underline{B} = 1 \qquad \text{Braking is correct.}$$

Our argument could have all the premises correct but not the conclusion.

Compare the two imperative arguments that we've considered:

If you're accelerating, then don't brake.	$(A \supset \sim\underline{B})$ Valid
You're accelerating.	A
∴ Don't brake.	∴ ~$\underline{B}$
Don't combine accelerating with braking.	$\sim(\underline{A} \cdot \underline{B})$ Invalid
You're accelerating.	A
∴ Don't brake.	∴ ~$\underline{B}$

Both arguments are the same, except that the first uses an if-then "$(A \supset \sim\underline{B})$," while the second uses a don't-combine "$\sim(\underline{A} \cdot \underline{B})$." Since one argument is valid and the other isn't, the two wffs aren't equivalent.

Consider these three forms:

$$(A \supset \sim\underline{B}) \quad = \quad \text{If you're accelerating, then don't brake.}$$
$$(B \supset \sim\underline{A}) \quad = \quad \text{If you're braking, then don't accelerate.}$$
$$\sim(\underline{A} \cdot \underline{B}) \quad = \quad \text{Don't combine accelerating with braking.}$$

The first two mix indicatives and imperatives; they tell you exactly what to do under specified conditions. The last is a pure imperative of the don't-combine form; it just tells you to avoid a certain combination of actions: it tells you not to do certain things together.

Imagine that you find yourself accelerating and braking (making "A" and "B" both true) – thus wearing down your brakes and wasting energy. Then you violate all three imperatives. But the three differ on what to do next. The first tells you not to brake. The second tells you not to accelerate. But the third leaves it open whether you're to stop accelerating or stop braking. Maybe you need to brake (and stop accelerating) to avoid hitting another car; or maybe you need to accelerate (and stop braking) to pass another car. The don't-combine form doesn't tell a person in this forbidden combination exactly what to do.

This if-then/don't-combine distinction is crucial for consistency imperatives. Consider these three forms (using A for "You do A" and B for "You believe that A is wrong"):

$$(A \supset \sim\underline{B}) \quad = \quad \text{If you do A, then don't believe that A is wrong.}$$
$$(B \supset \sim\underline{A}) \quad = \quad \text{If you believe that A is wrong, then don't do A.}$$
$$\sim(\underline{B} \cdot \underline{A}) \quad = \quad \text{Don't combine believing that A is wrong with doing A.}$$

Imagine that you believe that A is wrong and yet you do A. Then you violate all three imperatives; but the three differ on what to do next. The first tells you to stop believing that A is wrong; the second tells you to stop doing A. Which of these is better advice depends on the situation. Maybe your belief in the wrongness of A is correct and well-founded, and you need to stop doing A; then the first form is faulty, since it tells you to change your belief. Or maybe your action is fine but your belief is faulty (maybe you treat dark-skinned people fairly but think this is wrong); then the second form is faulty, since it tells you to change your action. So the two if-then forms can give bad advice.

The third form is a don't-combine imperative forbidding this combination:

 +

This combination always has a faulty element. If your believing is correct, then your doing is faulty; if your doing is correct, then your believing is faulty. If you believe that A is wrong and yet do A, then your belief clashes with your action. How should you regain consistency? We saw that this depends on the situation; sometimes it's better to change your belief and sometimes it's better to change your action. The don't-combine form forbids an inconsistency, but it doesn't tell a person in this forbidden combination exactly what to do.

Here's an analogous pair:

$$(B \supset \underline{A}) \quad = \quad \text{If you believe that you ought to do A, then do A.}$$
$$\sim(\underline{B} \cdot \sim\underline{A}) \quad = \quad \text{Don't combine believing that you ought to do A}$$
$$\text{with not doing A.}$$

"Follow your conscience" is often seen as equivalent to the first form; but this form can tell you to do evil things when you have faulty beliefs (see example 5 of Section 12.2b). The don't-combine form is better; it just forbids an inconsistent belief-action combination. If your beliefs conflict with your actions, you have to change one or the other; either may be defective.

Before leaving this section, let me point out problems in two alternative ways to understand imperative logic. Consider this argument:

If you get 100 percent, then celebrate.	$(G \supset \underline{C})$	Invalid
Get 100 percent.	$\underline{G}$	
∴ Celebrate.	∴ $\underline{C}$	$\underline{G}, \sim G, \sim \underline{C}$

This is intuitively invalid. Don't celebrate yet – maybe you'll flunk. To derive the conclusion, we need, not an imperative second premise, but rather a factual one saying that you *did* get 100 percent.

Two proposed ways of understanding imperative logic would wrongly judge this argument to be valid. The *obedience view* says that an imperative argument is valid just if doing what the premises prescribe necessarily involves doing what the conclusion prescribes. This is fulfilled in the present case; if you do what both premises say, you'll get 100 percent and celebrate. So the obedience view says our argument is valid. So the obedience view is wrong.

The *threat view* analyzes the imperative "Do A" as "Either you will do A or else S will happen" – where sanction "S" is some unspecified bad thing. So "$\underline{A}$" is taken to mean "(A ∨ S)." But if we replace "$\underline{C}$" with "(C ∨ S)" and "$\underline{G}$" with "(G ∨ S)," and then our argument becomes valid. So the threat view says our argument is valid. So the threat view is wrong.

12.2a   Exercise – also LogiCola MI

Say whether valid (and give a proof) or invalid (and give a refutation).

$(A \supset \sim\underline{B})$
$(\sim A \supset \sim\underline{C})$
$\therefore \sim(\underline{B} \cdot \underline{C})$

```
*  1    (A ⊃ ~B)    Valid
*  2    (~A ⊃ ~C)
        [ ∴ ~(B · C)
*  3  ┌ asm: (B · C)
   4  │ ∴ B    {from 3}
   5  │ ∴ C    {from 3}
   6  │ ∴ ~A   {from 1 and 4}
   7  └ ∴ A    {from 2 and 5}
   8  ∴ ~(B · C)   {from 3; 6 contradicts 7}
```

1. $\sim\underline{A}$
    $\therefore \sim(\underline{A} \cdot \underline{B})$

2. $\sim(\underline{A} \cdot \sim\underline{B})$
    $\therefore (A \supset \underline{B})$

3. $(A \supset \underline{B})$
    $\therefore (\sim B \supset \sim\underline{A})$

4. $(A \supset \underline{B})$
    $\therefore \sim(\underline{A} \cdot \sim\underline{B})$

5. $\sim\Diamond(A \cdot \underline{B})$
    $\sim(\underline{C} \cdot \sim\underline{A})$
    $\therefore \sim(\underline{C} \cdot \underline{B})$

6. $(x)(Fx \supset G\underline{x})$
    $F\underline{a}$
    $\therefore G\underline{a}$

7. $(x)\sim(F\underline{x} \cdot G\underline{x})$
    $(x)(Hx \supset F\underline{x})$
    $\therefore (x)(G\underline{x} \supset \sim Hx)$

8. $(x)(Fx \supset G\underline{x})$
    $(x)(Gx \supset H\underline{x})$
    $\therefore (x)(Fx \supset H\underline{x})$

9. $(\sim\underline{A} \vee \sim\underline{B})$
    $\therefore \sim(\underline{A} \cdot \underline{B})$

10. $\sim(\underline{A} \cdot \sim\underline{B})$
    $\therefore (\sim\underline{A} \vee \underline{B})$

12.2b   Exercise – also LogiCola MI

First appraise intuitively. Then translate into logic (using the letters given) and say whether valid (and give a proof) or invalid (and give a refutation).

1.   Make chicken for dinner or make eggplant for dinner.
     Peter is a vegetarian.
     If Peter is a vegetarian, then don't make chicken for dinner.
     ∴ Make eggplant for dinner.   [Use C, E, and V. This one is from Peter Singer.]

2.   Don't eat cake.
     If you don't eat cake, then give yourself a gold star.
     ∴ Give yourself a gold star.   [Use E and G.]

3.   If this is greasy food, then don't eat this.
     This is greasy food.
     ∴ Don't eat this.   [Use G and E. This is from Aristotle, except that he saw the
        conclusion of an imperative argument as an action: since you accept the premis-
        es, you don't eat the thing. I'd prefer to say that if you accept these premises
        and are consistent, then you won't eat the thing.]

4.   Don't both drive and watch the scenery.
     Drive.
     ∴ Don't watch the scenery.   [D, W]

5. If you believe that you ought to commit mass murder, then commit mass murder.
   You believe that you ought to commit mass murder.
   ∴ Commit mass murder. [Use B and C. Suppose we take "Follow your conscience" to mean "If you believe that you ought to do A, then do A." Then this principle can tell us to do evil things. Would the corresponding don't-combine form also tell us to do evil things? See the next example.]

6. Don't combine believing that you ought to commit mass murder with not committing mass murder.
   You believe that you ought to commit mass murder.
   ∴ Commit mass murder. [B, C]

7. Don't combine having this end with not taking this means.
   Don't take this means.
   ∴ Don't have this end. [E, M]

8. Lie to your friend only if you want people to lie to you under such circumstances.
   You don't want people to lie to you under such circumstances.
   ∴ Don't lie to your friend. [Use L and W. Premise 1 is based on a simplified version of Immanuel Kant's formula of universal law; we'll see a more sophisticated version in Chapter 14.]

9. Studying is needed to become a teacher.
   "Become a teacher" entails "Do what is needed to become a teacher."
   "Do what is needed to become a teacher" entails "If studying is needed to become a teacher, then study."
   ∴ Either study or don't become a teacher. [Use N for "Studying is needed to become a teacher," B for "You become a teacher," D for "You do what is needed to become a teacher," and S for "You study." This example shows that we can deduce complex ends–means imperatives from purely descriptive premises.]

10. Winn Dixie is the largest grocer in Big Pine Key.
    ∴ Either go to Winn Dixie or don't go to the largest grocer in Big Pine Key. [w, l, Gxy, u]

11. Drink something that is available.
    The only things available are juice and soda.
    ∴ Drink some juice or soda. [Dxy, u, Ax, Jx, Sx]

12. If the cocoa is about to boil, remove it from the heat.
    If the cocoa is steaming, it's about to boil.
    ∴ If the cocoa is steaming, remove it from the heat. [B, R, S]

13. Don't shift.
    ∴ Don't combine shifting with not pedaling. [S, P]

14. If he's in the street, wear your gun.
    Don't wear your gun.
    ∴ He isn't in the street. [Use S and G. This imperative argument, from Hector-Neri Castañeda, has a factual conclusion; calling it "valid" means that it's inconsistent to conjoin the premises with the denial of the conclusion.]

15.   If you take logic, then you'll make logic mistakes.
      Take logic.
   ∴ Make logic mistakes.   [T, M]

16.   Get a soda.
      If you get a soda, then pay a dollar.
   ∴ Pay a dollar.   [G, P]

17. ∴ Either do A or don't do A.   [This (vacuous) imperative tautology is analogous to
      the logical truth "You're doing A or you aren't doing A."]

18.   Don't combine believing that A is wrong with doing A.
   ∴ Either don't believe that A is wrong, or don't do A.   [B, A]

19.   Mail this letter.
   ∴ Mail this letter or burn it.   [Use M and B. This one was used to try to discredit
      imperative logic. The argument is valid, since this is inconsistent: "Mail this
      letter; don't either mail this letter or burn it." Note that "Mail this letter or
      burn it" doesn't entail "You may burn it"; it's consistent to follow "Mail this
      letter or burn it" with "Don't burn it."]

20.   Let every incumbent who will be honest be endorsed.
   ∴ Let every incumbent who won't be endorsed not be honest.   [Use Hx, Ex, and
      the universe of discourse of incumbents.]

12.3   Deontic translations

Deontic logic adds two operators: "O" (for "ought") and "R" (for "all right" or
"permissible"); these attach to imperatives to form deontic wffs:

O$\underline{A}$	=	It's obligatory that A.	R$\underline{A}$	=	It's permissible that A.
OA$\underline{x}$	=	X ought to do A.	RA$\underline{x}$	=	It's all right for X to do A.
OA$\underline{xy}$	=	X ought to do A to Y.	RA$\underline{xy}$	=	It's all right for X to do A to Y.

"O"/"□" (moral/logical necessity) are somewhat analogous, as are "R"/"◇"
(moral/logical possibility).

   "Ought" here is intended in the all-things-considered, normative sense that
we often use in discussing moral issues. This sense of "ought" differs from at
least two other senses that may follow different logical patterns:

   • *Prima facie* senses of "ought" (which give a moral consideration that may
     be overridden in a given context): "Insofar as I promised to go with you to
     the movies, I ought to do this [*prima facie* duty]; but insofar as my wife
     needs me to drive her to the hospital, I ought to do this instead [*prima facie*
     duty]. Since my duty to my wife is more urgent, in the last analysis I ought
     to drive my wife to the hospital [all-things-considered duty]."

- Descriptive senses of "ought" (which state what is required by conventional social rules but needn't express one's own positive or negative evaluation): "You ought [by company regulations] to wear a tie to the office."

I'll be concerned with logical connections between ought judgments, where "ought" is taken in this all-things-considered, normative sense.[1] I'll mostly avoid metaethical issues, like how to further analyze "ought," whether moral judgments are objectively true or false, and how to justify ethical principles.[2] While my explanations sometimes assume that ought judgments are true or false, what I say could be rephrased to avoid this assumption.

Here are some further translations:

$$\text{Act A is obligatory (required, a duty)} \quad = \quad O\underline{A}$$
$$\text{Act A is all right (right, permissible, OK)} \quad = \quad R\underline{A}$$

$$\text{Act A is wrong} \quad \begin{matrix} = & {\sim}R\underline{A} & = & \text{Act A isn't all right.} \\ = & O{\sim}\underline{A} & = & \text{Act A ought not to be done.} \end{matrix}$$

$$\text{It ought to be that A and B} \quad = \quad O(\underline{A} \cdot \underline{B})$$
$$\text{It's all right that A or B} \quad = \quad R(\underline{A} \vee \underline{B})$$

$$\text{If you do A, then you ought not to do B} \quad = \quad (A \supset O{\sim}\underline{B})$$
$$\text{You ought not to combine doing A with doing B} \quad = \quad O{\sim}(\underline{A} \cdot \underline{B})$$

The last two are deontic if-then and don't-combine forms.

Here are translations using quantifiers:

$$\text{It's obligatory that everyone do A} \quad = \quad O(x)A\underline{x}$$
$$\text{It isn't obligatory that everyone do A} \quad = \quad {\sim}O(x)A\underline{x}$$
$$\text{It's obligatory that not everyone do A} \quad = \quad O{\sim}(x)A\underline{x}$$
$$\text{It's obligatory that everyone refrain from doing A} \quad = \quad O(x){\sim}A\underline{x}$$

These two are importantly different:

$$\text{It's obligatory that someone answer the phone} \quad = \quad O(\exists x)A\underline{x}$$
$$\text{There's someone who has the obligation to answer the phone} \quad = \quad (\exists x)OA\underline{x}$$

The first might be true while the second is false; it might be obligatory (on the group) that someone or other in the office answer the phone – while yet no specific person has the obligation to answer it. To prevent the "Let the other person do it" mentality in such cases, we sometimes need to assign duties.

Compare these three:

---

[1] I'm also taking imperatives in an all-things-considered (not *prima facie*) sense. So I don't take "Do A" to mean "Other-things-being-equal, do A."

[2] For a discussion of these issues, see my *Ethics: A Contemporary Introduction*, 2nd ed. (New York: Routledge, 2011).

It's obligatory that some who kill repent $\quad = \quad O(\exists x)(Kx \cdot \underline{Rx})$

It's obligatory that some kill who repent $\quad = \quad O(\exists x)(\underline{Kx} \cdot Rx)$

It's obligatory that some both kill and repent $\quad = \quad O(\exists x)(\underline{Kx} \cdot \underline{Rx})$

These three are importantly different; underlining in the wffs shows which parts are obligatory: repenting, killing, or killing-and-repenting. If we just attached "O" to indicatives, our formulas couldn't distinguish the forms; all three would translate as "$O(\exists x)(Kx \cdot Rx)$." Because of such examples, we need to attach "O" to imperative wffs, not to indicative ones.[1]

Wffs in deontic logic divide broadly into *descriptive, imperative,* and *deontic* wffs. Here are examples of each:

Descriptive	*Imperative*	*Deontic (normative)*	
You're doing A.	Do A.	You ought to do A.	It's all right for you to do A.
A	$\underline{A}$	O$\underline{A}$	R$\underline{A}$
Au	A$\underline{u}$	OA$\underline{u}$	RA$\underline{u}$

The type of wff can matter; for example, "O" and "R" must attach to *imperative* wffs. So we'll now give rules for distinguishing the three types of wff:

1. Any not-underlined capital letter not immediately followed by a small letter is a *descriptive* wff. Any underlined capital letter not immediately followed by a small letter is an *imperative* wff.

2. The result of writing a not-underlined capital letter and then one or more small letters, none of which are underlined, is a *descriptive* wff. The result of writing a not-underlined capital letter and then one or more small letters, one small letter of which is underlined, is an *imperative* wff.

3. The result of prefixing any wff with "~" is a wff and is *descriptive, imperative,* or *deontic,* depending on what the original wff was.

4. The result of joining any two wffs by "•" or "∨" or "⊃" or "≡" and enclosing the result in parentheses is a wff. The resulting wff is *descriptive* if both original wffs were descriptive; it's *imperative* if at least one was imperative; it's *deontic* if both were deontic or if one was deontic and the other descriptive.

5. The result of writing a quantifier and then a wff is a wff – and is *descriptive, imperative,* or *deontic,* depending on what the original wff was.

6. The result of writing a small letter and then "=" and then a small letter is a *descriptive* wff.

---

[1] We can't distinguish the three as "$(\exists x)(Kx \cdot ORx)$," "$(\exists x)(OKx \cdot Rx)$," and "$(\exists x)O(Kx \cdot Rx)$" – since putting "$(\exists x)$" outside the "O" changes the meaning. See the previous paragraph.

7. The result of writing "◇" or "□," and then a wff, is a *descriptive* wff.

8. The result of writing "O" or "R," and then an imperative wff, is a *deontic* wff.

12.3a Exercise – also LogiCola L (DM & DT)

Translate these English sentences into wffs; take each "you" as a singular "you."

"You ought to do A" entails "It's possible that you do A."	□(O<u>A</u> ⊃ ◇A)

Here "◇A" doesn't use underlining; "◇A" means "It's possible that you do A" – while "◇<u>A</u>" means "The imperative 'Do A' is logically consistent." Our sample sentence also could translate as "□(OA<u>u</u> ⊃ ◇Au)."

1. If you're accelerating, then you ought not to brake. [Use A and B.]
2. You ought not to combine accelerating with braking.
3. If A is wrong, then don't do A.
4. Do A, only if A is permissible.
5. "Do A" entails "A is permissible."
6. Act A is morally indifferent (morally optional).
7. If A is permissible and B is permissible, then A-and-B is permissible.
8. It isn't your duty to do A, but it's your duty not to do A.
9. If you believe that you ought to do A, then you ought to do A. [Use B for "You believe that you ought to do A" and A for "You do A."]
10. You ought not to combine believing that you ought to do A with not doing A.
11. "Everyone does A" doesn't entail "It would be all right for you to do A." [Ax, u]
12. If it's all right for X to do A to Y, then it's all right for Y to do A to X. [Axy]
13. It's your duty to do A, only if it's possible for you to do A.
14. It's obligatory that the state send only guilty persons to prison. [Gx, Sxy, s]
15. If it isn't possible for everyone to do A, then you ought not to do A. [Ax, u]
16. If it's all right for someone to do A, then it's all right for everyone to do A.
17. If it's all right for you to do A, then it's all right for anyone to do A.
18. It isn't all right for anyone to do A.
19. It's permissible that everyone who isn't sinful be thankful. [Sx, Tx]
20. It's permissible that everyone who isn't thankful be sinful.

12.4 Deontic proofs

We'll now add six inference rules. The first four, following the modal and quantificational pattern, are for reversing squiggles and dropping "R" and "O."

These reverse-squiggle (RS) rules hold regardless of what pair of contradictory imperative wffs replaces "<u>A</u>"/"~<u>A</u>":

<table>
<tr><td>Reverse
squiggle</td><td>~O<u>A</u> → R~<u>A</u>
~R<u>A</u> → O~<u>A</u></td></tr>
</table>

These let us go from "not obligatory to do" to "permissible not to do" – and from "not permissible to do" to "obligatory not to do." Use these rules only within the same world and only when the formula begins with "~O" or "~R."

We need to expand our worlds. From now on, a **possible world** is a consistent and complete set of indicatives and imperatives. And a **deontic world** is a possible world (in this expanded sense) in which (a) the indicative statements are all true and (b) the imperatives prescribe some jointly permissible combination of actions. So then these equivalences hold:

O<u>A</u>	=	Act A is obligatory.
	=	"Do A" is in *all* deontic worlds.

R<u>A</u>	=	Act A is permissible.
	=	"Do A" is in *some* deontic worlds.

Suppose I have an 8 am class (C), I ought to get up before 7 am (O<u>G</u>), it would be permissible for me to get up at 6:45 am (R<u>A</u>), and it would be permissible for me to get up at 6:30 am (R<u>B</u>). Then every deontic world would have "C" and "G"; but some deontic worlds would have "<u>A</u>" while others would have "<u>B</u>."

A **world prefix** is a string of zero or more instances of "W" or "D." As before, world prefixes represent possible worlds. "D," "DD," and so on represent deontic worlds; we can use these in derived lines and assumptions, such as:

D ∴ A   (So A is true in deontic world D.)

DD asm: A   (Assume A is true in deontic world DD.)

We can drop deontic operators using the next two rules (which hold regardless of what imperative wff replaces "<u>A</u>"). Here's the drop-"R" (DR) rule:

Drop "R"	R<u>A</u> → D ∴ <u>A</u>, use a *new* string of D's

Here the line with "R<u>A</u>" can use any world prefix – and the line with "∴ <u>A</u>" must use a world prefix that is the same except that it ends with a *new* string (a string not occurring in earlier lines) of one or more D's. If act A is permissible, then "Do A" is in some deontic world; we may give this world an arbitrary and hence *new* name – corresponding to a new string of D's. We'll use "D" for the first "R" we drop, "DD" for the second, and so forth. So if we drop two R's, then we must introduce two deontic worlds:

R<u>A</u>	Act A is permissible, act B is permissible; so some
R<u>B</u>	deontic world has "Do A" and another has "Do B."
D ∴ <u>A</u>	← "D" is OK because it occurs in no earlier line.
DD ∴ <u>B</u>	← Since "D" has now occurred, we use "DD."

Permissible options need not be combinable; if it's permissible to marry Ann and permissible to marry Beth, it needn't be permissible to marry both Ann and Beth (bigamy). We can drop an "R" from formulas that are more complicated, so long as "R" *begins* the wff:

R(<u>A</u> · <u>B</u>)	~~(R<u>A</u> ⊃ <u>B</u>)~~	~~(R<u>A</u> · R<u>B</u>)~~
D ∴ (<u>A</u> · <u>B</u>)	~~D ∴ (<u>A</u> ⊃ <u>B</u>)~~	~~D ∴ (<u>A</u> · <u>B</u>)~~

The last two formulas don't *begin* with "R"; instead, they begin with a left-hand parenthesis. Drop only an *initial* "R" – and introduce a new and different deontic world whenever you drop an "R."

Here's the drop-"O" (DO) rule:

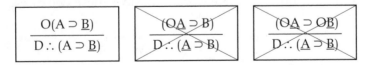

Drop "O"	O<u>A</u> → D ∴ <u>A</u>, use a blank or any string of D's

Here the line with "O<u>A</u>" can use any world prefix, and the line with "∴ <u>A</u>" must use a world prefix which is either the same or else the same except that it adds one or more D's at the end. If act A is obligatory, then "Do A" is in all deontic worlds. So if we have "O<u>A</u>" in the actual world, then we can derive "∴ <u>A</u>," "D ∴ <u>A</u>," "DD ∴ <u>A</u>," and so on; but it's good strategy to stay in *old* deontic worlds when dropping "O" (and use the actual world if there are no world with D's). As before, we can drop an "O" from formulas that are more complicated, so long as "O" *begins* the wff:

O(A ⊃ <u>B</u>)	~~(O<u>A</u> ⊃ B)~~	~~(O<u>A</u> ⊃ O<u>B</u>)~~
D ∴ (A ⊃ <u>B</u>)	~~D ∴ (<u>A</u> ⊃ B)~~	~~D ∴ (<u>A</u> ⊃ B)~~

The last two formulas begin not with "O," but with "(." "(O<u>A</u> ⊃ B)" and "(O<u>A</u> ⊃ O<u>B</u>)" are if-then forms and follow the if-then rules: if we have the first part true, we can get the second true; if we have the second part false, we can get the first false; and if we get stuck, we need to make another assumption.

Rule DO lets us go from "O<u>A</u>" in a world to "<u>A</u>" in the same world. This accords with "Hare's Law" (named after R. M. Hare):

Hare's Law □(O<u>A</u> ⊃ <u>A</u>)	An ought judgment entails the corresponding imperative: "You ought to do A" entails "Do A."

Hare's Law (also called "prescriptivity") equivalently claims that "You ought to do it, but don't" is inconsistent. This law fails for some weaker *prima facie* or descriptive senses of "ought"; there's no inconsistency in this: "You ought (according to company policy) to do it, but don't do it." But the law seems to hold for the all-things-considered, normative sense of "ought"; this seems inconsistent: "All things considered, you ought to do it; but don't do it." However, some philosophers reject Hare's Law; those who reject it would want to specify that in applying rule DO the world prefix of the derived line has to end in a "D" (and so we can't use a blank world prefix in the derived line).

Here's a deontic proof using these rules:

```
    1      O~(A · B)   Valid
    2      OA
         [ ∴ O~B
*   3    ┌ asm: ~O~B
*   4    │ ∴ RB    {from 3}
    5    │ D ∴ B    {from 4}
*   6    │ D ∴ ~(A · B)   {from 1}
    7    │ D ∴ A    {from 2}
    8    └ D ∴ ~B    {from 6 and 7}
    9    ∴ O~B    {from 3; 5 contradicts 8}
```

(1) Reverse squiggles: go from "~O~B" to "RB" (line 4).

(2) Drop each initial "R," using a new deontic world each time: go from "RB" to "D ∴ B" (line 5).

(3) Lastly, drop each initial "O" once for each old deontic world: go from "O~(A · B)" to "D ∴ ~(A · B)" – and from "OA" to "D ∴ A."

This is like a modal proof, except for underlining and having "O," "R," and "D" in place of "□," "◇," and "W." As with modal logic, we can star (and then ignore) a line when we use a reverse-squiggle or "R"-dropping rule on it.

Things get more complicated if we use the rules for dropping "R" and "O" on a formula in some other possible world. Consider these two cases:

```
    R A              W ∴ R A
    O B              W ∴ O B
  ───────          ─────────
   D ∴ A            WD ∴ A
   D ∴ B            WD ∴ B
```

In the case on the left, formulas "RA" and "OB" are in the actual world (using the blank world prefix); and so we put the corresponding imperatives in a deontic world "D." In the case on the right, formulas "RA" and "OB" are in world W; so here we keep the "W" and just add "D." The rules for dropping "R" and "O" allow these moves. Here world WD is a deontic world that *depends on* possible world W; this means that (a) the indicative statements in

WD are those of world W, and (b) the imperatives of WD prescribe some set of actions that are jointly permissible according to the deontic judgments of world W. The following proof uses world prefix "WD" in lines 7 to 9:

		[∴ □(O(A · B) ⊃ OA) Valid
*	1	⌐ asm: ~□(O(A · B) ⊃ OA)
*	2	∴ ◇~(O(A · B) ⊃ OA) {from 1}
*	3	W ∴ ~(O(A · B) ⊃ OA) {from 2}
	4	W ∴ O(A · B) {from 3}
*	5	W ∴ ~OA {from 3}
*	6	W ∴ R~A {from 5}
	7	WD ∴ ~A {from 6}
	8	WD ∴ (A · B) {from 4}
	9	⌐ WD ∴ A {from 8}
	10	∴ □(O(A · B) ⊃ OA) {from 1; 7 contradicts 9}

When we drop the "R" in line 6 ("W ∴ R ~A"), we add a new deontic world D to world W, so we get "WD ∴ ~A."

The next two chapters will often use complex world prefixes like "WD."

We have two additional inference rules. The indicative-transfer rule IT lets us transfer indicatives freely between a deontic world and whatever world it depends on; we can do this because these two worlds have the same indicative (descriptive or deontic) wffs. IT holds regardless of what descriptive or deontic wff replaces "A":

Indicative transfer
$$D \therefore A \;\; \rightarrow \;\; A$$

The world prefixes of the derived and deriving lines must be identical except that one ends in one or more additional D's. IT is to be used only with indicatives (including deontic judgments) – so the last box is wrong:

A		D ∴ A		OA		A̷
D ∴ A		∴ A		D ∴ OA		D̷ ∴ A̷

It can be useful to move an indicative between world D and the actual world (or vice versa) when we need to do so to get a contradiction or apply an I-rule.

Our final inference rule KL is named for Immanuel Kant:

Kant's Law
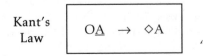
$$OA \;\; \rightarrow \;\; ◇A$$

"Ought" implies "can": "You ought to do A" entails "It's possible for you to do A."

This holds regardless of what imperative wff replaces "A" and what indicative wff replaces "A," provided that the former is like the latter except for underlin-ing, and every wff out of which the former is constructed is an imperative.[1] Kant's Law is often useful with arguments having both deontic ("O" or "R") and modal operators ("□" or "◇"); note that you infer "◇A" ("It's possible for you to do A") and not "◇A" ("The imperative 'Do A' is consistent").

Kant's Law equivalently claims that "You ought to do it, but it's impossible" is inconsistent. This law fails for some weaker *prima facie* or descriptive senses of "ought"; since company policy may require impossible things, there's no inconsistency in this: "You ought (according to company policy) to do it, but it's impossible." But the law seems to hold for the all-things-considered, normative sense of "ought"; this seems inconsistent: "All things considered, you ought to do it; but it's impossible to do it." We can't have an all-things-considered moral obligation to do the impossible.

KL is a weak form of Kant's Law. Kant thought that what we ought to do is not just *logically possible*, but also what we are *capable of doing* (physically and psychologically). Our rule KL expresses only the "logically possible" part; but, even so, it's still useful for many arguments. And it won't hurt if some-times we informally interpret "◇" in terms of what we're *capable of doing*.

We've already mentioned the first two of these four "laws":[2]

> Hare's Law: An "ought" entails the corresponding imperative.
> Kant's Law: "Ought" implies "can."
> Hume's Law: We can't deduce an "ought" from an "is."
> Poincaré's Law: We can't deduce an imperative from an "is."

Now we'll briefly consider the last two.

Hume's Law (named for David Hume) claims that we can't validly deduce what we *ought* to do from premises that don't contain "ought" or similar notions.[3] Hume's Law fails for some weak senses of "ought." Given descrip-tions of company policy and the situation, we can sometimes validly deduce what ought (according to company policy) to be done. But Hume's Law seems to hold for the all-things-considered, normative sense of "ought."

Here's a careful wording of Hume's Law:

---

[1] The proviso outlaws "O(∃x)(Lx • ~Lx) ∴ ◇(∃x)(Lx • ~Lx)" ("It's obligatory that someone who is lying not lie ∴ It's possible that someone both lie and not lie"). Since "Lx" in the premise isn't an imperative wff, this (incorrect) derivation doesn't satisfy KL.

[2] The word "law," although traditional here, is really too strong, since all four are controversial and subject to qualifications.

[3] Some philosophers disagree and claim we can deduce moral conclusions using only premises about social conventions, personal feelings, God's will, or something similar. For views on both sides, see my *Ethics: A Contemporary Introduction*, 2nd ed. (New York: Routledge, 2011).

Hume's Law ~□(B ⊃ O<u>A</u>)	We can't deduce an "ought" from an "is": If B is a consistent non-evaluative statement and A is a simple contingent action, then B doesn't entail "Act A ought to be done."

The complex wording here sidesteps some trivial cases (Section 12.4a) where we clearly *can* deduce an "ought" from an "is."

Poincaré's Law (named for the mathematician Jules Henri Poincaré) similarly claims that we can't validly deduce an imperative from indicative premises that don't contain "ought" or similar notions. Here's a careful wording:

Poincaré's Law ~□(B ⊃ <u>A</u>)	We can't deduce an imperative from an "is": If B is a consistent non-evaluative statement and A is a simple contingent action, then B doesn't entail the imperative "Do act A."

Again, the qualifications block objections (like problems 9 and 10 of Section 12.2b). We won't build Hume's or Poincaré's Law into our system.

Our deontic proof strategy is much like the modal strategy. First we reverse squiggles to put "O" and "R" at the beginning of a formula. Then we drop each initial "R," putting each permissible thing into a *new* deontic world. Lastly we drop each initial "O," putting each obligatory thing into each *old* deontic world. Drop obligatory things into the actual world just if:

- the premises or conclusion have an instance of an underlined letter that isn't part of some wff beginning with "O" or "R"; or
- you've done everything else possible (including further assumptions if needed) and still have no old deontic worlds.

Use the indicative transfer rule if you need to move an indicative between the actual world and a deontic world (or vice versa). Consider using Kant's Law if you see a letter that occurs underlined in a deontic wff and not-underlined in a modal wff; some of the proofs that use Kant's Law get tricky.

From now on, we won't do refutations for invalid arguments, since refutations get too messy when we mix various kinds of world.

12.4a Exercise – also LogiCola M (D & M)

Say whether valid (and give a proof) or invalid (no refutation necessary).

$$\therefore \sim\!\Diamond(O\underline{A} \cdot O\!\sim\!\underline{A})$$

		$[\; \therefore \sim\!\Diamond(O\underline{A} \cdot O\!\sim\!\underline{A})$ **Valid**
*	1	asm: $\Diamond(O\underline{A} \cdot O\!\sim\!\underline{A})$
*	2	W $\therefore (O\underline{A} \cdot O\!\sim\!\underline{A})$ {from 1}
	3	W $\therefore O\underline{A}$ {from 2}
	4	W $\therefore O\!\sim\!\underline{A}$ {from 2}
	5	W $\therefore \underline{A}$ {from 3}
	6	W $\therefore \sim\!\underline{A}$ {from 4}
	7	$\therefore \sim\!\Diamond(O\underline{A} \cdot R\!\sim\!\underline{A})$ {from 1; 5 contradicts 6}

This wff says "It isn't logically possible that you ought to do A and also ought not to do A"; this formula is correct if we take "ought" in the all-things-considered, normative sense. Morality can't make impossible demands on us; if we think otherwise, our lives will likely be filled with irrational guilt for not fulfilling impossible demands. But "$\sim\!\Diamond(O\underline{A} \cdot O\!\sim\!\underline{A})$" would be incorrect if we took "O" in it to mean something like "ought according to company policy" or *prima facie* ought." Inconsistent company policies may require that we do A and also require that we not do A; and we can have a *prima facie* duty to do A and another to omit doing A.

1. $O\!\sim\!\underline{A}$
    $\therefore O\!\sim\!(\underline{A} \cdot \underline{B})$

2. $(\exists x)OA\underline{x}$
    $\therefore O(\exists x)A\underline{x}$

3. $b=c$
    $\therefore (OF\underline{a}b \supset OF\underline{a}c)$

4. $\therefore O(O\underline{A} \supset \underline{A})$

5. $\therefore O(\underline{A} \supset O\underline{A})$

6. $\therefore O(\underline{A} \supset R\underline{A})$

7. $O\underline{A}$
    $O\underline{B}$
    $\therefore O(\underline{A} \cdot \underline{B})$

8. $(x)OF\underline{x}$
    $\therefore O(x)F\underline{x}$

9. $O(\underline{A} \vee \underline{B})$
    $\therefore (\sim\!\Diamond A \supset R\underline{B})$

10. $(A \supset O\underline{B})$
    $\therefore O(A \supset \underline{B})$

11. $\Box(\underline{A} \supset \underline{B})$
    $O\underline{A}$
    $\therefore O\underline{B}$

12. $O\underline{A}$
    $R\underline{B}$
    $\therefore R(\underline{A} \cdot \underline{B})$

13. A
    $\therefore O(\underline{B} \vee \sim\!\underline{B})$

14. $(x)RA\underline{x}$
    $\therefore R(x)A\underline{x}$

15. $O\underline{A}$
    $O\underline{B}$
    $\therefore \Diamond(A \cdot B)$

16. $\therefore (R\underline{A} \vee R\!\sim\!\underline{A})$

17. $(O\underline{A} \supset \underline{B})$
    $\therefore R(\underline{A} \cdot \underline{B})$

18. $\sim\!\Diamond A$
    $\therefore R\!\sim\!\underline{A}$

19. A
    $\sim\!A$
    $\therefore O\underline{B}$

20. $O(x)(Fx \supset G\underline{x})$
    $OF\underline{a}$
    $\therefore OG\underline{a}$

21. $O(A \supset \underline{B})$
    $\therefore (A \supset O\underline{B})$

22. $O(x)A\underline{x}$
    $\therefore (x)OA\underline{x}$

23. $\therefore O(\sim\!R\underline{A} \supset \sim\!\underline{A})$

24. A
    $\therefore (A \vee O\underline{B})$

25. $(A \vee O\underline{B})$
    $\sim\!A$
    $\therefore O\underline{B}$

Problems 3, 13, and 19 show how to deduce an "ought" from an "is." If "$(A \vee O\underline{B})$" is an "ought," then 24 gives another example; if it's an "is," then 25 gives another example. Problem 20 of Section 12.4b gives yet another example. We formulated Hume's Law so that these examples don't refute it.

12.4b   Exercise – also LogiCola M (D & M)

First appraise intuitively. Then translate into logic (using the letters given) and say whether valid (and give a proof) or invalid (no refutation necessary).

1.   It isn't all right for you to combine boozing with driving.
     You ought to drive.
     ∴ Don't booze.   [Use B and D.]

2. ∴ Either it's your duty to do A or it's your duty not to do A.   [The conclusion, if taken to apply to every action A, is *rigorism*, the view that there are no morally neutral acts (acts permissible to do and also permissible not to do).]

3.   I did A.
     I ought not to have done A.
     If I did A and it was possible for me not to have done A, then I have free will.
     ∴ I have free will.   [Use A and F. Immanuel Kant thus argued that ethics requires free will.]

4. ∴ If you ought to do A, then do A.

5. ∴ If you ought to do A, then you'll in fact do A.

6.   It isn't possible for you to be perfect.
     ∴ It isn't your duty to be perfect.   [Use "P" for "You are perfect."]

7.   You ought not to combine boozing with driving.
     You don't have a duty to drive.
     ∴ It's all right for you to booze.   [B, D]

8. ∴ Do A, only if it would be all right for you to do A.

9.   If it's all right for you to insult Jones, then it's all right for Jones to insult you.
     ∴ If Jones ought not to insult you, then don't you insult Jones.   [Use Ixy, u, and j. The premise follows from the universalizability principle ("What is right for one person is right for anyone else in similar circumstances") plus the claim that the cases are similar. The conclusion is a distant relative of the golden rule.]

10.   It's all right for someone to do A.
      ∴ It's all right for anyone to do A.   [Can you think of an example where the premise would be true and conclusion false?]

11.   If fatalism (the view that whatever happens couldn't have been otherwise) is true and I do A, then my doing A (taken by itself) is necessary.
      ∴ If fatalism is true and I do A, then it's all right for me to do A.   [F, A]

12.   If it's all right for you to complain, then you ought to take action.
      ∴ You ought to either take action or else not complain.   [Use C and T. This is the "Put up or shut up" argument.]

13.   I ought to stay with my brother while he's sick in bed.
      It's impossible for me to combine these two things: staying with my brother while he's sick in bed and driving you to the airport.
      ∴ It's all right for me not to drive you to the airport.   [S, D]

14. Jones ought to be happy in proportion to his moral virtue.
Necessarily, if Jones is happy in proportion to his moral virtue, then Jones will be rewarded either in the present life or in an afterlife.
It isn't possible for Jones to be rewarded in the present life.
If it's possible for Jones to be rewarded in an afterlife, then there is a God.
∴ There is a God. [Use H for "Jones is happy in proportion to his moral virtue," P for "Jones will be rewarded in the present life," A for "Jones will be rewarded in an afterlife," and G for "There is a God." This is Kant's moral argument for the existence of God. To make premise 3 plausible, we must take "possible" as "factually possible" (instead of "logically possible"). But does "ought to be" (premise 1 uses this – and not "ought to do") entail "is factually possible"?]

15. If killing the innocent is wrong, then one ought not to intend to kill the innocent.
If it's permissible to have a nuclear retaliation policy, then intending to kill the innocent is permissible.
∴ If killing the innocent is wrong, then it's wrong to have a nuclear retaliation policy. [K, I, N]

16. If it's all right for you to do A, then you ought to do A.
If you ought to do A, then it's obligatory that everyone do A.
∴ If it's impossible that everyone do A, then you ought not to do A. [Use Ax and u. The premises and conclusion are doubtful; the conclusion entails "If it's impossible that everyone become the first woman president, then you ought not to become the first woman president." The conclusion is a relative of Kant's formula of universal law; it's also a faulty "formal ethical principle" – an ethical principle that we can formulate using abstract logical notions but leaving unspecified the meaning of the individual, property, relational, and statement letters.]

17. It's obligatory that Smith help someone or other whom Jones is beating up.
∴ It's obligatory that Jones beat up someone. [Use Hxy, Bxy, s, and j. This "good Samaritan paradox" is provable in most deontic systems that attach "O" to indicatives. There are similar examples where the evil deed happens after the good one. It may be obligatory that Smith warn someone or other whom Jones will try to beat up; this doesn't entail that Jones ought to try to beat up someone.]

18. If it isn't right to do A, then it isn't right to promise to do A.
∴ Promise to do A, only if it's all right to do A. [A, P]

19. It's obligatory that someone answer the phone.
∴ There's someone who has the obligation to answer the phone. [Ax]

20. Studying is needed to become a teacher.
"Become a teacher" entails "Do what is needed to become a teacher."
"Do what is needed to become a teacher" entails "If studying is needed to become a teacher, then study."
∴ You ought to either study or not become a teacher. [Use N for "Studying is needed to become a teacher," B for "You become a teacher," D for "You do what is needed to become a teacher," and S for "You study." This is an ought-version of problem 9 of Section 12.2b. It shows that we can deduce a complex ought judgment from purely descriptive premises.]

21. If it's right for you to litter, then it's wrong for you to preach concern for the environment.
    ∴ It isn't right for you to combine preaching concern for the environment with littering. [L, P]

22. If you ought to be better than everyone else, then it's obligatory that everyone be better than everyone else.
    "Everyone is better than everyone else" is self-contradictory.
    ∴ It's all right for you not to be better than everyone else. [Use Bx (for "x is better than everyone else") and u.]

23. You ought not to combine braking with accelerating.
    You ought to brake.
    ∴ You ought to brake and not accelerate. [B, A]

24. "Everyone breaks promises" is impossible.
    ∴ It's all right for there to be someone who doesn't break promises. [Use Bx. Kant thought universal promise-breaking would be impossible, since no one would make promises if everyone broke them. But he wanted to draw the stronger conclusion that it's always wrong to break promises. See problem 16.]

25. It's all right for you to punish Judy for the accident, only if Judy ought to have stopped her car more quickly.
    Judy couldn't have stopped her car more quickly.
    ∴ You ought not to punish Judy for the accident. [P, S]

26. You ought to pay by check or pay by MasterCard.
    If your MasterCard is expired, then you ought not to pay by MasterCard.
    ∴ If your MasterCard is expired, then pay by check. [C, M, E]

27. You ought to help your neighbor.
    It ought to be that, if you (in fact) help your neighbor, then you say you'll help him.
    You don't help your neighbor.
    If you don't help your neighbor, then you ought not to say you'll help him.
    ∴ You ought to say you'll help him, and you ought not to say you'll help him. [Use H and S. Roderick Chisholm pointed out that this clearly invalid argument was provable in many systems of deontic logic. Is it provable in our system?]

28. If you take logic, then you'll make mistakes.
    You ought not to make mistakes.
    ∴ You ought not to take logic. [T, M]

29. If I ought to name you acting mayor because you served on the city council, then I ought to name Jennifer acting mayor because she served on the city council.
    I can't name both you and Jennifer acting mayor.
    ∴ It's not the case that I ought to name you acting mayor because you served on the city council. [U, J]

CHAPTER 13
Belief Logic

Belief logic is "logic" in an extended sense. Instead of studying what follows from what, our belief logic studies patterns of consistent believing and willing; it generates consistency norms that prescribe that we be consistent in various ways. We'll start with a simplified system and then add refinements.

13.1 Belief translations

We'll use ":" to construct descriptive and imperative belief formulas:

> 1. The result of writing a small letter and then ":"
>   and then a wff is a *descriptive* wff.
> 2. The result of writing an underlined small letter
>   and then ":" and then a wff is an *imperative* wff.

Statements about beliefs translate into *descriptive* belief formulas:

$$\text{You believe that A is true} \quad = \quad \text{u:A}$$

$$\text{You don't believe that A is true} \quad = \quad \sim\text{u:A}$$
$$\text{You believe that A is false} \quad = \quad \text{u:}\sim\text{A}$$
$$\text{You don't believe A and you don't believe not-A} \quad = \quad (\sim\text{u:A} \cdot \sim\text{u:}\sim\text{A})$$

If you refrain from believing A, you might believe that A is false or you might take no position on A. Here are some further translations:

$$\text{You believe that you ought to do A} \quad = \quad \text{u:OA}\underline{\text{u}}$$
$$\text{Everyone believes that they ought to do A} \quad = \quad (\text{x})\text{x:OA}\underline{\text{x}}$$

$$\text{You believe that if A then not-B} \quad = \quad \text{u:(A} \supset \sim\text{B)}$$
$$\text{If you believe A, then you don't believe B} \quad = \quad (\text{u:A} \supset \sim\text{u:B})$$

Since our belief logic generates norms *prescribing* consistency, it focuses on *imperative* belief formulas – which we express by underlining the small letter:

Believe that A is true	=	u:A
Don't believe that A is true	=	~u:A
Believe that A is false	=	u:~A
Don't believe A and don't believe not-A	=	(~u:A · ~u:~A)
Believe that you ought to do A	=	u:OAu
Let everyone believe that they ought to do A	=	(x)x:OAx

As before, we distinguish between if-then and don't-combine forms:

If you in fact believe A, then don't believe B	=	(u:A ⊃ ~u:B)
Don't combine believing A with believing B	=	~(u:A · u:B)

13.1a   Exercise – also LogiCola N (BM & BT)

Translate these sentences into wffs (use "u" for "you" and "G" for "There's a God").

You believe that there's a God. (You're a theist.)	u:G

1. You believe that there's no God. (You're an atheist.)
2. You take no position on whether there's a God. (You're an agnostic.)
3. You don't believe that there's a God. (You're a non-theist.)
4. You believe that "There's a God" is self-contradictory.
5. Necessarily, if you're a theist then you aren't an atheist. (Is this statement true?)
6. Believe that there's a God.
7. If "There's a God" is self-contradictory, then don't believe that there's a God.
8. If you believe A, then you don't believe not-A.
9. If you believe A, then don't believe not-A.
10. Don't combine believing A with believing not-A.

13.2   Belief proofs

There are three approaches that we might take to belief logic. The first approach would study what belief formulas validly follow from what other belief formulas. We might try to prove arguments such as this one:

You believe A.	u:A
∴ You don't believe not-A.	∴ ~u:~A

But this is invalid, since people can be confused and illogical. Students and politicians can assert A and assert not-A almost in the same breath; given that someone believes A, we can deduce little or nothing about what else the person believes. So this first approach is doomed from the start.

A second approach would study how people would believe if they were *completely consistent believers* (an idealized notion):

> Person X is a **completely consistent believer** if and only if:
>
> - X believes some things,
> - the set S of things that X believes is logically consistent, and
> - X believes anything that follows logically from set S.

Our previous argument would be valid if we added, as an additional premise, that you're a completely consistent believer:

> (You're a completely consistent believer.)
> You believe A.
> ∴ You don't believe not-A.

Such a belief logic would take "You're a completely consistent believer" as an implicit premise of its arguments. This premise would be assumed, even though it's false, to help us explore what belief patterns a consistent believer would follow. While this approach to belief logic works,[1] I prefer a third approach, in view of what I want to do in the next chapter.

My approach generates belief consistency imperatives, like these:

$$\sim(\underline{u}{:}A \cdot \underline{u}{:}{\sim}A) \qquad\qquad \sim(\underline{u}{:}(A \cdot B) \cdot {\sim}\underline{u}{:}A)$$

<table>
<tr><td>Don't combine believing
A with believing not-A.</td><td>Don't combine believing
A-and-B with not believing A.</td></tr>
</table>

This approach assumes the premise that *we ought to be consistent*[2] – that we ought not to combine inconsistent beliefs and that we ought not to believe something without also believing what follows from it.

Our belief logic adds **belief worlds** and two inference rules. We represent a belief world by a string of one or more instances of a small letter. Since most of our belief norms involve a generic "you," our belief worlds will typically be "u," "uu," "uuu," and so on. A **world prefix** is now a string of zero or more instances of letters from the set <W, D, a, b, c, …>, where <a, b, c, …> is the set of small letters. Our two inference rules use belief worlds; while it's fairly easy to use these inference rules in a mechanical way, it's devilishly hard to get an intuitive grasp of how it all works. Let me try to explain this.

First, let a *belief policy* be a set of imperatives about what someone (typically a generic "you") is or is not to believe. Here's an example:

---

[1] Jaakko Hintikka used roughly this second approach in his classic *Knowledge and Belief* (Ithaca, New York: Cornell University Press, 1962).

[2] We'll see later (Section 13.7) that this premise requires some qualifications.

| Believe that Michigan will play. Be neutral about whether Michigan will win. | <u>u</u>:P (~<u>u</u>:W • ~<u>u</u>:~W) |

This policy prescribes a way to believe that's consistent (but boring). In general, a belief policy prescribes a *consistent way to believe* if and only if (1) the set S of things that the person is told to believe is logically consistent, and (2) the person isn't forbidden to believe something that follows logically from set S. Our task is to put this idea into inference rules that use the powerful mechanism of possible worlds that we've developed in previous chapters.

Our belief logic is interested in rejecting belief policies, such as the following one, that prescribe an *inconsistent way to believe*:

| Believe A. Believe not-A. | <u>u</u>:A <u>u</u>:~A |

This belief policy violates our first condition given above, since the set S of things that the person is told to believe *isn't* logically consistent. But how do we express this in terms of possible worlds?

A **belief world** (relative to a belief policy) is a possible world that contains everything the person is told to believe. So if you're told to believe A, then all your belief worlds have A. Individual belief worlds may contain further statements. For example, if you're told to be neutral about B (not to believe B and not to believe not-B), then some of your belief worlds will have B and some will have not-B. What is common to all of your belief worlds is what you're told to believe. Being possible worlds, belief worlds must be consistent.

Our first inference rule, B+, requires that there be belief worlds and they all contain everything the person is told to believe. Here's a rough formulation:

B+ If you're told to believe A, then put A in all of your belief worlds.

This leads to a proof of "Don't combine believing A with believing not-A." We start by assuming its opposite ("Believe A, and believe not-A") and then try to construct belief worlds containing everything you're told to believe:

```
      [ ∴ ~(u:A • u:~A)   Valid
 *  1  ┌ asm: (u:A • u:~A)
    2  │ ∴ u:A   {from 1}
    3  │ ∴ u:~A   {from 1}
    4  │ u ∴ A   {from 2}    ⇐
    5  └ u ∴ ~A   {from 3}   ⇐
    6  ∴ ~(u:A • u:~A)   {from
          1; 4 contradicts 5}
```

Using B+, we try to construct a non-empty set of belief worlds containing everything you're told to believe.

Since lines 4 and 5 contradict, our assumption prescribes an inconsistent combination of belief attitudes. So we reject it and derive the original conclusion.

The belief-world mechanism shows that the belief policy in the assumption prescribes an inconsistency. So by RAA we derive its opposite: "Don't combine believing A with believing not-A." Our proof doesn't show that this conclusion is logically necessary; instead, it shows that it follows from an implicit "One ought to be consistent" premise.

We expressed rule B+ above in a rough and intuitive way: "If you're told to believe A, then put A in all of your belief worlds." Now we need to give a more precise formulation. Rule B+ operates on *positive imperative belief formulas*; here any wff can replace "A" and any small letter can replace "u":

$$\text{B+} \qquad \boxed{\begin{array}{l} \underline{u}{:}A \quad \to \quad u \therefore A, \\ \text{use any string of } u\text{'s} \end{array}}$$

The line with "$\underline{u}{:}A$" can use any world prefix not containing small letters or "W"[1] – and the line with "$\therefore A$" must use a world prefix that is the same except that it adds at the end a string of one or more instances of "u" (or of the small letter that replaces "u"). If we have "u $\therefore$ A" in a proof, "u" refers to a belief world based on what you're told to believe in the assumption and premises. If instead we have "Du $\therefore$ A," then we have a belief world based on what you're told to believe in deontic world D.

Here's another belief policy that tells you to be inconsistent:

Believe A-and-B.	$\underline{u}{:}(A \cdot B)$
Don't believe A.	$\sim\underline{u}{:}A$

You're told to believe something and also forbidden to believe what logically follows from it. To reject such cases, we need a second inference rule, which we can express roughly as follows:

> B- If you're told to *refrain* from believing A, then
> put not-A in a *new* belief world of yours.

With B-, we can now prove "Don't combine believing A-and-B with not believing A." We start by assuming its opposite ("Believe A-and-B, and don't believe A") and then use B- and then B+ to construct our belief worlds:

---

[1] This proviso (about small letters and "W") blocks proofs of perhaps questionable wffs that place one imperative belief operator within another, like "$\underline{b}{:}\sim(\underline{c}{:}A \cdot \underline{c}{:}\sim A)$," or claim logical necessity for consistency imperatives, like "$\Box\sim(\underline{x}{:}A \cdot \underline{x}{:}\sim A)$."

```
        [ ∴ ~(u:(A • B) • ~u:A)   Valid
*   1   ┌ asm: (u:(A • B) • ~u:A)
    2   │  ∴ u:(A • B)   {from 1}
*   3   │  ∴ ~u:A   {from 1}
    4   │  u ∴ ~A   {from 3}   ⇦
    5   │  u ∴ (A • B)   {from 2}
    6   └  u ∴ A   {from 5}   ⇦
    7    ∴ ~(u:(A • B) • ~u:A)   {from
             1; 4 contradicts 6}
```

We first use B- on "~u:A" in line 3. We put "~A" in a new belief world to get line 4.

Then we use B+ on "u:(A • B)" in line 2. We put "(A • B)" in this same belief world to get line 5.

Since lines 4 and 6 contradict, our assumption prescribes inconsistent belief attitudes.

The assumption's belief policy prescribes an inconsistency. So by RAA we derive its opposite: "Don't combine believing A-and-B with not believing A."

We expressed rule B- above in a rough and intuitive way: "If you're told to *refrain* from believing A, then put not-A in a *new* belief world of yours." Now we need a more precise formulation. Rule B- operates on *negative imperative belief formulas*; here any pair of contradictory wffs can replace "A"/"~A" and any small letter can replace "u":

B-
$$\boxed{\begin{array}{c} \text{~u:A} \;\;\rightarrow\;\; \text{u ∴ ~A,} \\ \text{use a } \textit{new} \text{ string of u's} \end{array}}$$

The line with "~u:A" can use any world prefix not containing small letters or "W" – and the line with "∴ ~A" must use a world prefix that is the same except that it ends with a *new* string (one not occurring in earlier lines) of one or more instances of "u" (or of the small letter that replaces "u").

Our B- rule is peculiar in that it doesn't follow the usual pattern. Our last three systems had strong operators (ALL, NECESSARY, OUGHT), and weak operators (SOME, POSSIBLE, PERMISSIBLE). They had reverse-squiggle rules, a rule for dropping the weak operator using a new constant-or-world, and a rule for dropping the strong operator using (preferably) an old constant-or-world. Why doesn't belief logic follow the same pattern? The answer is that English has no weak operator to correspond to the strong operator BELIEVES. Suppose we did modal logic with just the strong operator NECESSARY; then we'd use two rules much like the two belief rules:

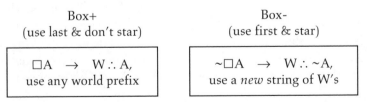

Box+	Box-
(use last & don't star)	(use first & star)

$$\boxed{\begin{array}{c} \Box A \;\;\rightarrow\;\; \text{W ∴ A,} \\ \text{use any world prefix} \end{array}} \qquad \boxed{\begin{array}{c} \sim\Box A \;\;\rightarrow\;\; \text{W ∴ ~A,} \\ \text{use a } \textit{new} \text{ string of W's} \end{array}}$$

Our Box- rule would let us go from "~□A" to "W ∴ ~A" in a new world W, without the intermediate step of deriving "◇~A"; the Box- rule would replace the reverse-squiggle and diamond-dropping rules. If we had developed modal logic that way, then our belief rules would look very familiar:

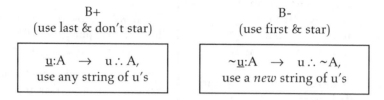

B+ (use last & don't star)	B- (use first & star)
u:A → u ∴ A, use any string of u's	~u:A → u ∴ ~A, use a *new* string of u's

But fear not, you'll soon get used to our belief rules.

Our proof strategy goes as follows:

- First use rule B- on *negative imperative belief formulas* (formulas that say to *refrain* from believing something). Use a new belief world each time. You can star (and then ignore) a line when you use B- on it.

- Then use B+ on *positive imperative belief formulas* (formulas that say to believe something). Use *each* old belief world of the person in question each time. (Use a single new belief world if you have no old ones.) Don't star a line when you use B+ on it.

Both rules operate only on *imperative* belief formulas (like "~u:A" or "u:A") – not on *descriptive* ones (like "~u:A" or "u:A"). Our belief worlds are about what a belief policy *tells* you to believe, not about what you *actually* believe.

Our consistency norms have a don't-combine form, forbidding inconsistent belief policies. They tell you to make your beliefs coherent with each other; but they don't say what beliefs to add or subtract to bring this about. Suppose that P (*premise*) logically entails C (*conclusion*); compare these three forms:

(u:P ⊃ u:C)	If you believe *premise*, then believe *conclusion*.
(~u:C ⊃ ~u:P)	If you don't believe *conclusion*, then don't believe *premise*.
~(u:P • ~u:C)	Don't combine believing *premise* with not believing *conclusion*.

Suppose you believe *premise* but don't believe *conclusion*; then you violate all three imperatives. What should you do? The first form tells you to believe *conclusion*; but maybe *conclusion* is irrational and you should reject both *premise* and *conclusion*. The second tells you to drop *premise*; but maybe *premise* is solid and you should accept both *premise* and *conclusion*. So the first two forms can tell you to do the wrong thing. The third is better; it simply forbids the inconsistent combination of believing *premise* but not believing *conclusion* – but it doesn't say what to do if we get into this forbidden combination.

Here's another example. Assume that A is logically inconsistent with B; compare these three forms:

(u:A ⊃ ~<u>u</u>:B)	If you believe A, then don't believe B.
(u:B ⊃ ~<u>u</u>:A)	If you believe B, then don't believe A.
~(<u>u</u>:A · <u>u</u>:B)	Don't combine believing A with believing B.

Suppose you believe A and also believe B, even though the two are inconsistent. The first form tells you to drop B, while the second tells you to drop A; but which you should drop depends on the situation. The last form is better; it simply tells us to avoid the inconsistent combination.

Doing proofs with different kinds of operator can be confusing. This chart tells what order to use in dropping operators:

First drop these weak operators:	Then drop these strong operators:
◇ ~<u>x</u>: R (∃x)	□ <u>x</u>: O (x)
Use new worlds/constants; star the old line.	Use old worlds/constants if you have them; don't star the old line.

Within each group, the dropping order doesn't matter – except that it's wise to drop "<u>x</u>:" and "O" before dropping the very strong "□."

Section 9.2 noted that our "substitute equals" rule can fail in arguments about beliefs. Consider this argument:

Jones believes that Lincoln is on the penny.	j:Pl
Lincoln is the first Republican US president.	l=r
∴ Jones believes that the first Republican US president is on the penny.	∴ j:Pr

If Jones is unaware that Lincoln was the first Republican president, the premises could be true while the conclusion is false. So the argument is invalid. But yet we can derive the conclusion from the premises using our substitute-equals rule. So we need to qualify this rule so it doesn't apply in belief contexts. So from now on, the substitute-equals rule holds only if no interchanged instance of the constants occurs within a wff immediately preceded by ":" and then a small letter (underlined or not).

13.2a   Exercise – also LogiCola OB

Say whether valid (and give a proof) or invalid (no refutation necessary).

```
        1      □(A ⊃ B)   Invalid
             [ ∴ (u:A ⊃ u:B)
  *     2      asm: ~(u:A ⊃ u:B)
        3      ∴ u:A   {from 2}
  *     4      ∴ ~u:B   {from 2}
        5      u ∴ ~B   {from 4}
  *     6      u ∴ (A ⊃ B)   {from 1}
        7      u ∴ ~A   {from 5 and 6}
```

```
□(A ⊃ B)
∴ (u:A ⊃ u:B)
```

Since rules B+ and B- work only on *imperative* belief formulas, we can't go from "u:A" in line 3 to "u ∴ A." The conclusion here has the faulty if-then form. Suppose that A entails B and you believe A; it doesn't follow that you should believe B – maybe you should reject A and also reject B.

1. ~◇(A · B)
    ∴ ~(u:A · u:B)

2. ~◇(A · B)
    ∴ (u:A ⊃ ~u:B)

3. ~◇(A · B)
    ∴ (u:A ⊃ ~u:B)

4. ~◇(A · B)
    ∴ (~u:A ∨ ~u:B)

5. ~◇(A · B)
    ∴ (u:~A ∨ u:~B)

6. □(A ⊃ B)
    u:A
    ∴ u:B

7. □(A ⊃ B)
    u:A
    ∴ u:B

8. □(A ⊃ B)
    ~u:~A
    ∴ ~u:~B

9. □(A ⊃ B)
    ~u:B
    ∴ u:~A

10. ~◇(A · B)
    ∴ ~(u:A · ~u:~B)

13.2b   Exercise – also LogiCola OB

First appraise intuitively. Then translate into logic and say whether valid (and give a proof) or invalid (no refutation necessary).

1. A logically entails B.
    Don't believe B.
    ∴ Don't believe A.

2. You believe A.
    ∴ You don't believe not-A.

3. You believe A.
    ∴ Don't believe not-A.

4. ∴ If A is self-contradictory, then don't believe A.

5. ∴ Either believe A or believe not-A.

6. Believe A.
    ∴ Don't believe not-A.

7. ∴ Don't combine believe that A is true with not believing that A is possible.

8. (A and B) entails C.
    ∴ Don't combine believing A and believing B and not believing C.

9.   A logically entails (B and C).
      Don't believe that B is true.
   ∴. Believe that A is false.

10. ∴. If A is true, then believe A.

13.3   Believing and willing

Now we'll expand belief logic to cover willing as well as believing. We'll do this by treating "willing" as *accepting an imperative* – just as we previously treated "believing" as *accepting an indicative*:

$$u{:}A \quad \begin{matrix} = \\ = \end{matrix} \quad \begin{matrix} \text{You accept (endorse, assent to, say in your heart) "A is true."} \\ \text{You believe that A.} \end{matrix}$$

$$u{:}\underline{A} \quad \begin{matrix} = \\ = \end{matrix} \quad \begin{matrix} \text{You accept (endorse, assent to, say in your heart) "Let act A be done."} \\ \text{You will that act A be done.} \end{matrix}$$

In translating "u:$\underline{A}$," we'll often use terms more specific than "will" – terms like "act," "resolve to act," or "desire."[1] Which of these fits depends on whether the imperative is present or future, and whether it applies to oneself or to another. Here are three examples:

If A is present:	u:A$\underline{u}$	=	You accept the imperative for you to do A now.
		=	You act (in order) to do A.
If A is future:	u:A$\underline{u}$	=	You accept the imperative for you to do A in the future.
		=	You're resolved to do A.
If u≠x:	u:A$\underline{x}$	=	You accept the imperative for X to do A.
		=	You desire (or want) that X do A.

And to accept "Would that I had done that" is to wish that you had done it. There's a subtle difference between "u:A$\underline{u}$" and "Au":

u:A$\underline{u}$	=	You act (in order) to do A.
	=	You say in your heart, "Do A" (addressed to yourself).

Au	=	You do A.

The left box is about what you try or intend to do, while the right box is about what you actually do (perhaps accidentally).

[1] "Desire" and similar terms can have a *prima facie* sense ("I have some desire to do A") or an all-things-considered sense ("All things considered, I desire to do A"). Here I intend the all-things-considered sense.

Section 12.3 noted that we'd lose important distinctions if we prefixed "O" only to indicatives. Something similar applies here. Consider these three wffs:

u:(∃x)(Kx • R<u>x</u>)	=	You desire that some who kill *repent*.
	=	You say in your heart "Would that some who kill *repent*."
u:(∃x)(K<u>x</u> • Rx)	=	You desire that some *kill* who repent.
	=	You say in your heart "Would that some *kill* who repent."
u:(∃x)(K<u>x</u> • R<u>x</u>)	=	You desire that some both *kill* and *repent*.
	=	You say in your heart "Would that some *kill* and *repent*."

The three are very different. The underlining shows which parts are desired: repenting, or killing, or killing-and-repenting. If we attached "desire" only to indicative formulas, all three would translate the same way, as "You desire that (∃x)(Kx • Rx)" ("You desire that there's someone who both kills and repents"). So "desire" is better symbolized in terms of accepting an imperative.

This imperative formula *tells* you to will something:

<u>u</u>:A	=	Accept (endorse, assent to, say in your heart) "Let act A be done."
	=	Will that act A be done.

Again, our translation can use terms more specific than "will":

If A is present:	<u>u</u>:A<u>u</u>	=	Accept the imperative for you to do A now.
		=	Act (in order) to do A.
If A is future:	<u>u</u>:A<u>u</u>	=	Accept the imperative for you to do A in the future.
		=	Be resolved to do A.
If u≠x:	<u>u</u>:A<u>x</u>	=	Accept the imperative for X to do A.
		=	Desire (or want) that X do A.

Be careful about underlining. Underlining before ":" makes the formula an imperative (instead of an indicative). Underlining after ":" makes the formula about willing (instead of believing). Here are the basic cases:

Indicatives		
u:A	=	You believe A.
u:<u>A</u>	=	You will A.

Imperatives		
<u>u</u>:A	=	Believe A.
<u>u</u>:<u>A</u>	=	Will A.

And here are some baseball examples that may be helpful:

Hub	=	You hit the ball.
H_ub_	=	Hit the ball.
OHub	=	You ought to hit the ball.
RH_ub_	=	It's all right for you to hit the ball.

u:Hub	=	You believe that you'll hit the ball.
u:H_ub_	=	You act (with the intention) to hit the ball.
_u_:Hub	=	Believe that you'll hit the ball.
_u_:H_ub_	=	Act (with the intention) to hit the ball.

13.3a   Exercise – also LogiCola N (WM & WT)

Translate these English sentences into wffs (use "u" for "you").

Don't act to do A without believing that A would be all right.	~(_u_:A_u_ • ~_u_:RA_u_)

1. You want Al to sit down.   [Use a for "Al" and Sx for "x sits down."]
2. Believe that Al is sitting down.
3. You believe that Al ought to sit down.
4. Believe that Al intends to sit down.
5. Desire that Al sit down.
6. Eat nothing.   [Use Exy for "x eats y."]
7. Resolve to eat nothing.
8. You fall down, but you don't act (in order) to fall down.   [Fx]
9. You act to kick the goal, but you don't in fact kick the goal.   [Kx]
10. If you believe that you ought to do A, then do A.
11. Don't combine believing that you ought to do A with not acting to do A.
12. Do A, only if you want everyone to do A. (Act only as you'd want everyone to act.)   [This is a crude form of Kant's formula of universal law.]
13. If X does A to you, then do A to X. (Treat others as they treat you.)   [Use Axy. This principle entails "If X knocks out your eye, then knock out X's eye."]
14. If you do A to X, then X will do A to you. (People will treat you as you treat them.)   [This is often confused with the golden rule.]
15. If you want X to do A to you, then do A to X. (Treat others as you want to be treated.)   [This is the "literal golden rule."]
16. Don't combine acting in order to do A to X with wanting X not to do A to you.

13.4   Willing proofs

Besides inconsistency in beliefs, there's also inconsistency in will. For example, I might have inconsistent desires, violate ends–means consistency, or have my moral beliefs conflict with how I live. Belief logic also generates norms about consistent willing.

Except for having more underlining, proofs with willing formulas work like before. Here's an example:

$$[\therefore \sim(\underline{u}{:}O{\sim}A\underline{u} \cdot \underline{u}{:}A\underline{u}) \quad \text{Valid}$$

∴ Don't combine *believing* that
it's wrong for you to do A
with *acting* to do A.

```
*  1  ┌ asm: (u:O~Au · u:Au)
   2  │ ∴ u:O~Au   {from 1}
   3  │ ∴ u:Au     {from 1}
   4  │ u ∴ O~Au   {from 2}
   5  │ u ∴ Au     {from 3}
   6  └ u ∴ ~Au    {from 4}
   7  ∴ ~(u:O~Au · u:Au)   {from 1;
            5 contradicts 6}
```

This formula forbids combining these two:

believing that it's wrong to do A	acting (in order) to do A

The second part is expressed as "$\underline{u}{:}A\underline{u}$" (which is about what you try or intend to do) and not "$A\underline{u}$" (which is about what you actually do, perhaps accidentally). The faulty translation "$\sim(\underline{u}{:}O{\sim}A\underline{u} \cdot A\underline{u})$" forbids unintentionally doing what one thinks is wrong; there's no inconsistency in this, except maybe externally. The correct version forbids this inconsistent combination: thinking that A is wrong and at the same time acting with the intention of doing A.

13.4a   Exercise – also LogiCola OW

Say whether valid (and give a proof) or invalid (no refutation necessary).

∴ (u:O~Au ⊃ ~u:Au)

```
          [ ∴ (u:O~Au ⊃ ~u:Au)   Invalid
*  1  asm: ~(u:O~Au ⊃ ~u:Au)
   2  ∴ u:O~Au   {from 1}
   3  ∴ u:Au     {from 1}
   4  u ∴ Au     {from 3}
```

This formula says: "If you believe that it's wrong for you to do A, then don't act to do A"; this leads to absurdities because it doesn't have the correct don't-combine form and because your belief may be mistaken. Maybe you believe that it's wrong to treat people fairly; then this formula tells you not to act to treat them fairly.

1. ∴ ~(u:A · u:~A)

2. ∴ u:(Ba ⊃ RBa)

3. ∴ (u:Ba ∨ u:~Ba)

4. ∴ ~((u:(A ⊃ B) · u:A) · ~u:B)

5. u:(x)OAx
    ∴ u:Au

6. ~u:Au
    ∴ ~u:OAu

7. ∴ u:(OAu ⊃ Au)

8. ∴ (u:Au ∨ ~u:OAu)

9. u:Au
    ∴ ~u:O~Au

10. □(A ⊃ B)
    ∴ ~(u:OA · ~u:B)

13.4b   Exercise – also LogiCola OW

First appraise intuitively. Then translate into logic and say whether valid (and give a proof) or invalid (no refutation necessary).

1. ∴ Don't combine believing that everyone ought to do A with not acting/resolving to do A yourself.   [This is belief logic's version of "Practice what you preach."]

2. ∴ Don't combine resolving to eat nothing with acting to eat this.   [Use Exy and t.]

3. "Attain this end" entails "If taking this means is needed to attain this end, then take this means."
   ∴ Don't combine (1) *wanting* to attain this end and (2) *believing* that taking this means is needed to attain this end and (3) *not acting* to take this means.   [Use E for "You attain this end," N for "Taking this means is needed to attain this end," M for "You take this means," and u. The conclusion is an ends–means consistency imperative; you violate it if you want to become a doctor and believe that studying is needed for you to do this and yet you don't act to study.]

4. "Attain this end" entails "If taking this means is needed to attain this end, then take this means."
   ∴ If you want to attain this end and believe that taking this means is needed to attain this end, then act to take this means.   [Use E, N, M, and u. This formulation could tell people with evil ends to do evil things.]

5. ∴ Don't accept "For all x, it's wrong for x to kill," without being resolved that if killing were needed to save your family, then you wouldn't kill.   [Kx, N]

6. ∴ Don't accept "For all x, it's wrong for x to kill," without it being the case that if killing were needed to save your family then you wouldn't kill.   [Use Kx and N. A draft board challenged a pacifist friend of mine, "If killing were needed to save your family, then would you kill?" My friend answered, "I don't know – I might lose control and kill (it's hard to predict what you'll do in a panic situation); but I now firmly hope and resolve that I wouldn't kill." Maybe my friend didn't satisfy this present formula; but he satisfied the previous one.]

7. ∴ Don't combine accepting "It's wrong for Bob to do A" with wanting Bob to do A.

8. ∴ Don't combine believing that the state ought to execute all murderers with not desiring that if your friend is a murderer then the state execute your friend. [Use s for "the state," Exy for "x executes y," Mx for "x is a murderer," f for "your friend," and u for "you."]

9. ∴ Don't combine acting to do A with not accepting that A is all right.

10. ∴ If you act to do A, then accept that act A is all right.

11. ∴ Don't combine acting to do A with not accepting that A is obligatory.

12. Believe that you ought to do A.
    ∴ Act to do A.

13. "It's all right for you to do A" entails "It's obligatory that everyone do A."
∴ Don't combine acting to do A with not willing that everyone do A. [The conclusion is a crude version of Kant's formula of universal law. To see that the premise and conclusion are questionable, substitute "become a doctor" for "do A" in both. We'll see a better version of the formula in the next chapter.]

13.5 Rationality translations

Beliefs can be "evident" or "reasonable" for a given person. As I shade my eyes from the bright sun, my belief that it's sunny is *evident*; it's very solidly grounded. As I hear the prediction of rain, my belief that it will rain is *reasonable*; my belief accords with reason but isn't solid enough to be evident. "Evident" expresses a higher certitude than does "reasonable." We'll symbolize these two notions as follows:

$$
\begin{aligned}
&= \quad \text{A is evident to you.} \\
\text{O\underline{u}:A} \quad &= \quad \text{It's obligatory (rationally required) that you believe A.} \\
&= \quad \text{Insofar as intellectual considerations are concerned (including} \\
&\qquad\quad \text{your experiences), you ought to believe A.}
\end{aligned}
$$

$$
\begin{aligned}
&= \quad \text{A is reasonable for you to believe.} \\
\text{R\underline{u}:A} \quad &= \quad \text{It's all right (rationally permissible) that you believe A.} \\
&= \quad \text{Insofar as intellectual considerations are concerned (including} \\
&\qquad\quad \text{your experiences), it would be all right for you to believe A.}
\end{aligned}
$$

Neither entails that you believe A; to say that a proposition A that you believe is evident or reasonable, we'll use "(u:A • O\underline{u}:A)" or "(u:A • R\underline{u}:A)." "Evident" and "reasonable" are relational; "It's raining" might be evident to someone outside but not to someone inside in a windowless room.

Here are further translations:

It would be unreasonable for you to believe A	=	∼R\underline{u}:A
It's obligatory that you not believe A	=	O∼\underline{u}:A
It would be reasonable for you to take no position on A	=	R(∼\underline{u}:A • ∼\underline{u}:∼A)
It's evident to you that if A then B	=	O\underline{u}:(A ⊃ B)
If it's evident to you that A, then it's evident to you that B	=	(O\underline{u}:A ⊃ O\underline{u}:B)
You ought not to combine believing A with believing not-A	=	O∼(\underline{u}:A • \underline{u}:∼A)

Since "O" and "R" attach only to imperatives, "Ou:A" and "Ru:A" aren't wffs.

We can almost define "knowledge" in this simple way:

$$knowledge \quad = \quad evident\ true\ belief$$

You know that A $\quad = \quad$ A is evident to you, A is true, and you believe A.

$$uKA \quad = \quad (O\underline{u}{:}A \cdot (A \cdot u{:}A))$$

Knowing requires more than just true belief; if you guess right, you have not knowledge, but only true belief. Knowledge must be well-grounded; it must be more than just *reasonable* (permitted by the evidence), it must be *evident* (required by the evidence). The claim that *knowledge* is *evident true belief* is plausible. But there are cases (like example 10 of Section 13.6b) where we can have one but not the other. So this simple definition of "knowledge" is flawed; but it's still a useful approximation.

13.5a   Exercise – also LogiCola N (RM & RT)

Translate these English sentences into wffs. When an example says a belief is evident or reasonable, but doesn't say *to whom*, assume it means evident or reasonable *to you*.

You ought to want Al to sit down.	O\underline{u}{:}S\underline{a}

We can paraphrase the sentence as "It's obligatory that you say in your heart 'Would that Al sit down.'"

1.   You ought to believe that Al is sitting down.
2.   It's evident to you that Al is sitting down.
3.   It's reasonable for you to believe that Al ought to sit down.
4.   Belief in God is reasonable (for you).   [G]
5.   Belief in God is unreasonable for everyone.
6.   It isn't reasonable for you to believe that belief in God is unreasonable for everyone.
7.   Belief in God is reasonable only if "There is a God" is logically consistent.
8.   You ought not to combine believing that there is a God with not believing that "There is a God" is logically consistent.
9.   You ought not to combine believing that you ought to do A with not acting to do A.
10.   You know that x=x.   [Use the flawed definition of knowledge given previously.]
11.   If agnosticism is reasonable, then theism isn't evident.   [Agnosticism = not believing G and not believing not-G; theism = believing G.]
12.   You have a true belief that A.   [You believe that A, and it's true that A.]
13.   You mistakenly believe A.
14.   It would be impossible for you mistakenly to believe A.
15.   A is evident to you, if and only if it would be impossible for you mistakenly to believe A.   [This idea is attractive but quickly leads to skepticism.]
16.   It's logically possible that you have a belief A that is evident to you and yet false.
17.   It's evident to all that if they doubt then they exist.   [Dx, Ex]
18.   If A entails B, and B is unreasonable, then A is unreasonable.
19.   It's permissible for you to do A, only if you want everyone to do A.

20. If you want X to do A to you, then you ought to do A to X.   [Use Axy. This one and the next are versions of the golden rule.]
21. You ought not to combine acting to do A to X with wanting X not to do A to you.
22. It's necessary that, if you're in pain, then it's evident to you that you're in pain. [Use Px. This claims that "I'm in pain" is a self-justifying belief. Many think that there are two kinds of self-justifying belief: those of experience (as in this example) and those of reason (as in the next example).]
23. It's necessary that, if you believe that x=x, then it's evident to you that x=x. [Perhaps believing "x=x" entails understanding it, and this makes it evident.]
24. If you have no reason to doubt your perceptions and it's evident to you that you believe that you see a red object, then it's evident to you that there is an actual red object.   [Use Dx for "x has reason to doubt his or her perceptions," Sx for "x sees a red object," and R for "There is an actual red object." Roderick Chisholm claimed that we need evidential principles like this (but more complex) to show how beliefs about external objects are based on beliefs about perceptions.]
25. If you have no reason to doubt Jenny's sincerity and it's evident to you that she shows pain behavior, then it's evident to you that Jenny feels pain.   [Use Bx, Dx, Fx, and j. This exemplifies an evidential principle about knowing other minds.]

13.6   Rationality proofs

Deontic belief proofs, while not requiring further inference rules, often use complex world prefixes like "Du" or "Duu." Here's a proof of a conscientiousness principle, "You ought not to combine *believing* that it's wrong for you to do A with *acting* to do A":

```
        [ ∴ O~(u:O~Au • u:Au)      Valid
  *  1  ┌ asm: ~O~(u:O~Au • u:Au)
  *  2  │ ∴ R(u:O~Au • u:Au)   {from 1}
  *  3  │ D ∴ (u:O~Au • u:Au)   {from 2}
     4  │ D ∴ u:O~Au   {from 3}
     5  │ D ∴ u:Au   {from 3}
     6  │ Du ∴ O~Au   {from 4}
     7  │ Du ∴ Au   {from 5}
     8  └ Du ∴ ~Au   {from 6}
     9  ∴ O~(u:O~Au • u:Au)   {from 1;
            7 contradicts 8}
```

We get to line 5 using propositional and deontic rules.

Lines 6 and 7 follow using rule B+. Here we write belief world prefix "u" after the deontic world prefix "D" used in lines 4 and 5; world Du is a belief world of u that depends on what deontic world D tells u to accept.

We soon get a contradiction.

"O~(u:O~Au • u:Au)" is a **formal ethical principle** – an ethical principle that can be formulated using the abstract notions of our logical systems plus variables (like "u" and "A") that stand for any person and action. The next chapter will focus on another formal ethical principle – the golden rule.

13.6a Exercise – also LogiCola O (R & M)

Say whether valid (and give a proof) or invalid (no refutation necessary).

```
        Ru:O(A · B)
        ∴ Ru:OA
```

(If you can follow
this example, you
needn't fear proofs
involving complex
world prefixes.)

```
      1    Ru:O(A · B)   Valid
      [ ∴ Ru:OA
*     2  ┌ asm: ~Ru:OA
      3  │ ∴ O~u:OA      {from 2}
      4  │ D ∴ u:O(A · B)  {from 1}
*     5  │ D ∴ ~u:OA     {from 3}
*     6  │ Du ∴ ~OA      {from 5}
      7  │ Du ∴ O(A · B)  {from 4}
*     8  │ Du ∴ R~A      {from 6}
      9  │ DuDD ∴ ~A     {from 8}
     10  │ DuDD ∴ (A · B)  {from 7}
     11  └ DuDD ∴ A      {from 10}
     12   ∴ Ru:OA        {from 2; 9 contradicts 11}
```

1. □(A ⊃ B)
    ~Ru:B
    ∴ ~Ru:A

2. O~u:A
    ∴ Ou:~A

3. R(~u:A · ~u:~A)
    ∴ ~Ou:A

4. Ru:~A
    ∴ R~u:A

5. Oa:(C · D)
    ∴ Ob:C

6. ∴ O~(u:A · ~u:◇A)

7. ∴ (Ru:A ⊃ ◇A)

8. □(A ⊃ B)
    ∴ (R~u:B ⊃ Ru:~A)

9. Ru:OAu
    ∴ Ru:◇Au

10. Ou:(A ⊃ OBu)
     ∴ ~(u:A · ~u:Bu)

13.6b Exercise – also LogiCola O (R & M)

First appraise intuitively. Then translate into logic and say whether valid (and give a
proof) or invalid (no refutation necessary). Use G for "There is a God" and u for "you."
When an example says a belief is evident or reasonable, but don't say *to whom,* assume
it means evident or reasonable *to you.*

1. Theism is evident.
    ∴ Atheism is unreasonable.   [Theism = believing G; atheism = believing not-G.]

2. Theism isn't evident.
    ∴ Atheism is reasonable.

3. ∴ You ought not to combine *believing* you ought to do A with *not acting* to do A.

4. ∴ If you believe you ought to do A, then you ought to do A.

5. "All men are endowed by their creator with certain unalienable rights" is evident.
    "All men are endowed by their creator with certain unalienable rights" entails
    "There is a creator."
    ∴ "There is a creator" is evident.   [Use E and C. The opening lines of the US Dec-
    laration of Independence claim E to be self-evident.]

6.   It would be reasonable for you to believe that A is true.
      It would be reasonable for you to believe that B is true.
      ∴ It would be reasonable for you to believe that A and B are both true.

7.   "If I'm hallucinating, then physical objects aren't as they appear to me" is evident
         to me.
      It isn't evident to me that I'm not hallucinating.
      ∴ It isn't evident to me that physical objects are as they appear to me.   [Use H, P,
         and i. This argument for skepticism is essentially from Descartes.]

8.   "If I'm hallucinating, then physical objects aren't as they appear to me" is evident
         to me.
      If I have no special reason to doubt my perceptions, then it's evident to me that
         physical objects are as they appear to me.
      I have no special reason to doubt my perceptions.
      ∴ It's evident to me that I'm not hallucinating.   [Use H, P, D, and i. This is John
         Pollock's answer to the previous argument.]

9.   It's evident to you that taking this means is needed to attain this end.
      "Attain this end" entails "If taking this means is needed to attain this end, then
         take this means."
      ∴ You ought not to combine wanting to attain this end with not acting to take this
         means.   [Use N for "Taking this means is needed to attain this end," E for
         "You attain this end," M for "You take this means," and u.]

10.   Al believes that Smith owns a Ford.
       It's evident to Al that Smith owns a Ford.
       Smith doesn't own a Ford.
       Smith owns a Chevy.
       Al believes that Smith owns a Ford or a Chevy.
       Al doesn't know that Smith owns a Ford or a Chevy.
      ∴ Al has an evident true belief that Smith owns a Ford or a Chevy; but Al doesn't
         know that Smith owns a Ford or a Chevy.   [Use a for "Al," F for "Smith owns
         a Ford," C for "Smith owns a Chevy," and K for "Al knows that Smith owns a
         Ford or a Chevy." This argument from Edmund Gettier attacks the definition of
         knowledge as *evident true belief*.]

11.   It's evident to you that if it's all right for you to hit Al then it's all right for Al to
         hit you.
      ∴ Don't combine acting to hit Al with believing that it would be wrong for Al to hit
         you.   [Use Hxy, u, and a. The premise is normally true; but it could be false if
         you and Al are in different situations (maybe Al needs to be hit to dislodge food
         he's choking on). The conclusion resembles the golden rule.]

12. ∴ It's reasonable to want A to be done, only if it's reasonable to believe that A
       would be all right.

13.   It's evident that A is true.
      ∴ A is true.

14. It's reasonable to combine believing that there is a perfect God with believing T.
T entails that there's evil in the world.

∴ It's reasonable to combine believing that there is a perfect God with believing that there's evil in the world. [Use G, T, and E. Here T (for "theodicy") is a reasonable explanation of why God permits evil. T might say: "The world has evil because God, who is perfect, wants us to make significant free choices to struggle to bring a half-completed world toward its fulfillment; moral evil comes from the abuse of human freedom and physical evil from the half-completed state of the world."]

15. It's evident to you that if there are moral obligations then there's free will.

∴ Don't combine accepting that there are moral obligations with not accepting that there's free will. [M, F]

16. Theism is reasonable.

∴ Atheism is unreasonable.

17. Theism is evident.

∴ Agnosticism is unreasonable. [Agnosticism = not believing G and not believing not-G.]

18. ∴ It's reasonable for you to believe that God exists, only if "God exists" is consistent. [Belief logic regards a belief as "reasonable" only if *in fact* it's consistent. In a more subjective sense, someone could "reasonably" believe a proposition that's reasonably but incorrectly taken to be consistent.]

19. ∴ If A is unreasonable, then don't believe A.

20. You ought not to combine accepting A with not accepting B.

∴ If you accept A, then accept B.

21. ∴ You ought not to combine wanting A not to be done with believing that A would be all right.

22. It's reasonable not to believe that there is an external world.

∴ It's reasonable to believe that there's no external world. [E]

23. It's reasonable to believe that A ought to be done.

∴ It's reasonable to want A to be done.

24. ∴ Either theism is reasonable or atheism is reasonable.

25. It's evident to you that if the phone is ringing then you ought to answer it.
It's evident to you that the phone is ringing.

∴ Act on the imperative "Answer the phone." [P, Ax]

26. A entails B.
Believing A would be reasonable.

∴ Believing B would be reasonable.

27. Atheism isn't evident.

∴ Theism is reasonable.

28.   Atheism is unreasonable.
      Agnosticism is unreasonable.
      ∴ Theism is evident.

29.   A entails B.
      You accept A.
      It's unreasonable for you to accept B.
      ∴ Don't accept A, and don't accept B.

30.   It would be reasonable for anyone to believe A.
      ∴ It would be reasonable for everyone to believe A.   [Imagine a controversial issue
         where everyone has the same evidence. Could it be more reasonable for the
         community to disagree? If so, the premises of this argument might be true but
         the conclusion false.]

13.7   A sophisticated system

The system of belief logic that we've developed is oversimplified in three ways.
We'll now sketch a more sophisticated system.

First, our "One ought to be consistent" principle requires qualification. For
the most part, we do have a duty to be consistent. But, since "ought" implies
"can," this duty is nullified when we're unable to be consistent; such inability
can come from emotional turmoil or our incapacity to grasp complex inferences. And the obligation to be consistent can be overridden by other factors; if
Dr Evil would destroy the world unless we were inconsistent in some respect,
then surely our duty to be consistent would be overridden. And the duty to be
consistent applies, when it does, only to persons; yet our principles so far would
entail that rocks and trees also have a duty to be consistent.

For these reasons, it would be better to qualify our "One ought to be consistent" principle, as in the following formulation:[1]

> If X is a person who is able to be consistent in certain ways, who
> does (or should) grasp the logical relationships involved, and
> whose being consistent in these ways wouldn't have disastrous
> consequences, then X ought to be consistent in these ways.

Let's abbreviate the qualification in the box ("X is ...") as "Px." Then we can
reformulate our inference rules by adding a required "Px" premise:

B+ | $\underline{x}$:A, Px → x ∴ A, | B- | ~$\underline{x}$:A, Px → x ∴ ~A, |
     | use any string of x's | | use a *new* string of x's |

---

[1] Section 2.3 of my *Formal Ethics* (London: Routledge, 1996) has additional qualifications.

So now we'd need a "Px" premise to apply either rule. If we made these changes, we'd have to qualify most of our arguments with a premise like "Pu" – or else our arguments would be invalid.

A second problem is that our system can prove a questionable *conjunctivity principle*:

You ought not to combine believing A and believing B and not believing (A · B). $\quad O\sim((\underline{u}{:}A \cdot \underline{u}{:}B) \cdot \sim\underline{u}{:}(A \cdot B))$

This leads to questionable results in "the lottery paradox." Suppose six people have an equal chance to win a lottery. You know that one of the six will win; but the probability is against any given person winning. Presumably it could be reasonable for you to accept statements 1 to 6 without also accepting statement 7 (which means "None of the six will win"):

1. Person 1 won't win.
2. Person 2 won't win.
3. Person 3 won't win.
4. Person 4 won't win.
5. Person 5 won't win.
6. Person 6 won't win.
7. Person 1 won't win, person 2 won't win, person 3 won't win, person 4 won't win, person 5 won't win, and person 6 won't win.

But multiple uses of our conjunctivity principle would entail that one ought not to accept statements 1 to 6 without also accepting their conjunction 7. So the conjunctivity principle, which is provable using our rules B+ and B-, sometimes leads to questionable results.

I'm not completely convinced that it is reasonable to accept statements 1 to 6 but not accept 7. If it *is* reasonable, then we have to reject the conjunctivity principle; this would force us to modify our ideas on what sort of consistency is desirable. Let's call the ideal of "completely consistent believer" defined in Section 13.2 *broad consistency*. Perhaps we should strive, not for broad consistency, but for *narrow consistency*. To explain this, let S be the non-empty set of indicatives and imperatives that X accepts; then:

X is *broadly consistent* just if:	X is *narrowly consistent* just if:
• set S is logically consistent, and • X accepts anything that follows from set S.	• every pair of items of set S is logically consistent, and • X accepts anything that follows from any single item of set S.

Believing the six lottery statements but not their conjunction is narrowly consistent but not broadly consistent.

To have our rules mirror the ideal of narrow consistency, we'd need an additional proviso on rule B+: "The world prefix in the derived line cannot have occurred more than once in earlier lines." With this modification, only a few examples in this chapter would cease being provable. And many of these could still be salvaged by adding an additional conjunctivity premise like the following (which would be true in many cases):

You ought not to combine believing A and believing B and not believing (A · B).

$$O{\sim}((\underline{u}{:}A \cdot \underline{u}{:}B) \cdot {\sim}\underline{u}{:}(A \cdot B))$$

Conjunctivity presumably fails only in rare lottery-type cases.

The third problem is that we've been translating these two statements the same way, as "O$\underline{u}$:A," even though they don't mean the same thing:

"You ought to believe A."   "A is evident to you."

Suppose you have an obligation to trust your wife and give her the benefit of every reasonable doubt. It could be that you *ought to believe* what she says, even though the evidence isn't so strong as to make this belief *evident*. So there's a difference between "ought to believe" and "evident." So it may be better to use a different symbol (perhaps "O*") for "evident":

O$\underline{u}$:A	=	You ought to believe A.
	=	All things considered, you ought to believe A.
O*$\underline{u}$:A	=	A is evident to you.
	=	Insofar as intellectual considerations are concerned (including your experiences), you ought to believe A.

"O" is an all-things-considered "ought," while "O*" is a *prima facie* "ought" that considers only the intellectual basis for the belief. If we added "O*" to our system, we'd need corresponding deontic inference rules for it. Since "O*$\underline{A}$" is a *prima facie* "ought," it wouldn't entail the corresponding imperative or commit one to action; so we'd have to weaken the rule for dropping "O*" so we couldn't derive "$\underline{u}$:A" from "O*$\underline{u}$:A."

These refinements would overcome problems but make our system much harder to use. We seldom need the refinements. So we'll keep the naïve belief logic of earlier sections as our "official system" and build on it in the next chapter. But we'll be conscious that this system is oversimplified in various ways. If and when the naïve system gives questionable results, we can appeal to the sophisticated system to clear things up.

CHAPTER 14
A Formalized Ethical Theory

This chapter gives a precise logical formulation of an ethical theory, one that builds on ideas from Immanuel Kant and R. M. Hare.[1] This gives an example of how to use logical systems to formalize larger philosophical views. As in the chapter on belief logic, we'll systematize *consistency norms*. But now our norms will be stronger and will feature a version of the golden rule (roughly, "Treat others as you want to be treated").

We'll first consider practical rationality in general terms, highlighting the role of consistency. Then we'll focus on one consistency principle: the golden rule. After seeing problems with the usual wording, we'll formulate a better rule and give an intuitive argument for it. We'll then add logical machinery (symbols and inference rules) to formalize these ideas. We'll end by giving a formal proof of the golden rule in logical symbols.

14.1 Practical rationality

While non-rational forces (like emotional and cultural influences) play a big role in our moral thinking, rational forces also can be important. Here I'll distinguish three central dimensions of practical rationality: factual understanding, imagination, and consistency.

Factual understanding requires that we know the facts of the case: circumstances, alternatives, consequences, and so on. To the extent that we're misinformed or ignorant, our moral thinking is flawed. Of course, we can never know *all* the facts; and often we have no time to research a problem and must act quickly. But we can act out of greater or lesser knowledge. Other things being equal, a more informed judgment is a more rational one.

We also need to understand ourselves, and how our feelings and moral beliefs originated; this is important because we can to some extent neutralize our biases if we understand their origin. For example, some people are hostile toward a group because they were taught this when they were young. Their

---

[1] For a fuller account of my approach, see my technical *Formal Ethics* (London: Routledge, 1996) or my simpler *Ethics: A Contemporary Introduction*, 2nd ed. (New York: Routledge, 2011). See also Immanuel Kant's *Groundwork of the Metaphysics of Morals* (New York: Harper & Row, 1964) and R. M. Hare's *Freedom and Reason* (New York: Oxford University Press, 1963).

attitudes might change if they understood the source of their hostility and broadened their experience; if so, then their attitudes are less rational, since they exist because of a lack of self-knowledge and experience.

Imagination (role reversal) is a vivid and accurate awareness of what it would be like to be in the place of those affected by our actions. This differs from just knowing facts. So in dealing with poor people, besides knowing facts about them, we also need to appreciate and envision what these facts mean to their lives; movies, literature, and personal experience can help us to visualize another's life. We also need to appreciate future consequences of our actions on ourselves; knowing that drugs would have harmful effects on us differs from being able to imagine these effects in a vivid and accurate way.

Consistency demands a coherence among our beliefs, between our ends and means, and between our moral judgments and how we live; it also, I'll argue, includes golden-rule consistency – that we not act toward another in a way that we're unwilling to be treated in the same situation. The rest of this chapter will focus on consistency; as a logician, I have more to say about this dimension. Appeals to consistency in ethics are frequently dubious; my goal is to clarify and defend consistency norms. But keep in mind that we need all the dimensions of moral rationality working together for our practical thinking to be fully reasonable; consistency is important but isn't everything.

Holistic rationality includes all these aspects of rationality, and others that I haven't mentioned. A more traditional term is "practical wisdom." We are "rational" (or "wise") in our ethical beliefs to the extent that we satisfy a variety of considerations. Only God (knowing everything, imagining vividly the inner life of each person, being consistent in every way, and so on) could fulfill them completely. We humans find practical rationality difficult, and we satisfy its requirements only to a lesser or greater degree.

To dramatize the problem of practical rationality, let's imagine that you were brought up in a racist society that practiced Nazism, slavery, or apartheid. Suppose that racist norms were drilled into your moral intuitions; so, because of your training, it seemed "intuitively obvious" to you that it was right for whites to enslave blacks, but not vice versa. Is there any way that you could use your intelligence to criticize these racist norms? If so, how?

Let's consider parallel cases in other areas. Suppose your society taught you that there was a highest prime number or that the earth was flat. You could in principle use your intelligence to criticize these beliefs. There's a good argument going back to Euclid that there's no highest prime (see problem 14 in Section 7.1b); and there are indirect signs that the earth is round, or you could build a spaceship and go out and look at the earth. In practice, few people will have the independence, energy, and intelligence to pursue such ideas; but eventually someone will, and the word will spread. The morality case is similar.

To rationally criticize inherited racist norms requires the things we mentioned before: *factual accuracy* (understanding facts about race and how the victims suffer), *imagination* (role reversal: visualizing what it would be like for ourselves and our families to be treated in like manner), and *consistency* (especially the golden rule, which tells us to treat others only as we are willing to be treated ourselves in the same situation). Historically, people who criticized racist norms often appealed to the golden rule and to these other factors.

14.2   Consistency

Consistency itself has many dimensions. These include consistency among beliefs, between ends and means, and between our moral judgments and how we live. Our chapter on belief logic touched on these three consistency norms:[1]

> **Logicality**: Avoid inconsistency in beliefs.
>
> **Ends–means consistency**: Keep your means in harmony with your ends.
>
> **Conscientiousness**: Keep your actions, resolutions, and desires in harmony with your moral beliefs.

Our belief logic contains *logicality* norms forbidding inconsistent beliefs:

$(\sim\!\diamond(A \cdot B) \supset \sim\!(\underline{u}{:}A \cdot \underline{u}{:}B))$	=	Don't combine inconsistent beliefs.
	=	If A is inconsistent with B, then don't combine *believing A* with *believing B*.
$(\square(A \supset B) \supset \sim\!(\underline{u}{:}A \cdot \sim\!\underline{u}{:}B))$	=	Don't believe something without believing what follows from it.
	=	If A logically entails B, then don't combine *believing A* with *not believing B*.

We often appeal to such things when we argue about ethics. You say that such and such is wrong, and I ask why. You respond with an argument consisting in a factual premise, a moral premise, and a moral conclusion. The factual premise is challengeable on grounds of factual accuracy. The moral premise is challengeable on grounds of consistency; we look for cases where you'd reject the implications of your own principle (perhaps cases where the principle applies to how we should treat you).

Here's a concrete example. When I was ten years old, I heard a racist argue something like this: "Blacks ought to be treated poorly, because they're inferior." How can we respond? Should we dispute the racist's factual premise and say "All races are genetically equal"? Or should we counter with our own

---

[1] We noted at the end of the last chapter that consistency duties require qualifiers like "insofar as you are able to be consistent in these ways and no disaster would result from so doing …." This also applies to the golden rule. We'll regard such a qualifier as implicit throughout.

moral principle and say "People of all races ought to be treated equally"? Either strategy will likely lead to a stalemate, where the racist has his views and we have ours, and neither side can convince the other.

I suggest instead that we formulate the racist's argument clearly and then watch it explode in his face. First we need to clarify what the racist means by "inferior." Is "being inferior" a matter of IQ, education, wealth, physical strength, or what? Suppose he defines "inferior" as "having an IQ of less than 80." Since the racist's conclusion is about how *all* blacks ought to be treated, his premises also have to use "all." So his argument goes:

> All blacks have an IQ of less than 80.
> All who have an IQ of less than 80 ought to be treated poorly.
> ∴ All blacks ought to be treated poorly.

While this is valid, we can easily appeal to factual accuracy against premise 1 and to consistency against premise 2. Regarding consistency, we could ask the racist whether he accepts what his premise 2 logically entails about whites:

> All who have an IQ of less than 80 ought to be treated poorly.
> ∴ All *whites* who have an IQ of less than 80 ought to be treated poorly.

The racist won't accept this conclusion. But then he inconsistently believes a premise but refuses to believe what follows from it. To restore consistency, he must either give up his principle or else accept its implications about whites. It would be very difficult for the racist to reformulate his argument to avoid such objections; he needs some criterion that crisply divides the races (as IQ doesn't) and that he applies consistently (including to people of his own race).

Appealing to consistency in beliefs is often useful in moral disputes. The appeal is powerful, since it doesn't presume material moral premises (which the other party may reject) but just points out problems in one's belief system. But at times, of course, consistency won't do the job by itself and we need other ways to carry the argument further.

Our belief logic can prove this *ends–means consistency* argument (problem 3 of Section 13.4b):

$$\Box(\underline{E} \supset (N \supset \underline{M}))$$
$$\therefore \sim((\underline{u}{:}\underline{E} \cdot \underline{u}{:}N) \cdot \sim\underline{u}{:}M)$$

"Attain this end" entails "If taking this means is needed to attain this end, then take this means."
∴ Don't combine (1) *wanting* to attain this end and (2) *believing* that taking this means is needed to attain this end and (3) *not acting* to take this means.

It's easy to violate the conclusion. Many want to lose weight and believe that eating less is needed to do this; yet they don't take steps to eat less. Insofar as we violate ends–means consistency, we're flawed in our rationality. People of all cultures implicitly recognize this, or else they wouldn't survive.

We could incorporate ends–means consistency more fully into our system if we added the symbol "⊡" for "It's causally necessary that."[1] Then we could translate "Taking this means is needed to attain this end" as "⊡(~M ⊃ ~E)" ("It's causally necessary that if you don't take this means then you won't attain this end"); our premise above would then be "□(E ⊃ (⊡(~M ⊃ ~E) ⊃ M))." If we added rules of inference to prove this premise, then this form of the conclusion would be provable by itself:

$$\sim((\underline{u}{:}\underline{E} \cdot \underline{u}{:}\boxdot(\sim M \supset \sim E)) \cdot \sim \underline{u}{:}\underline{M})$$

> Don't combine (1) *wanting* to attain this end and (2) *believing* that taking this means is needed to attain this end and (3) *not acting* to take this means.

While all this would be easy to do, we won't do it here.

Our belief logic also can prove *conscientiousness* principles that prescribe a harmony between our moral beliefs and how we live. Here's one example:

$$\sim(\underline{u}{:}O{\sim}A\underline{u} \cdot \underline{u}{:}A\underline{u}))$$

> Don't combine *believing* that it's wrong for you to do A with *acting* to do A.

This is a **formal ethical principle** – an ethical principle that can be formulated using the abstract notions of our logical systems plus variables (like "u" and "A") that stand for any person and action. All our consistency requirements are *formal* in this sense.

Here are three further formal consistency requirements:

> **Impartiality**: Make similar evaluations about similar actions, regardless of the individuals involved.
>
> **Golden rule**: Treat others only as you consent to being treated in the same situation.
>
> **Formula of universal law**: Act only as you're willing for anyone to act in the same situation – regardless of imagined variations of time or person.

We'll add logical machinery for all three, but mostly focus on the golden rule.

14.3   The golden rule

The golden rule (GR) says "Treat others as you want to be treated." All the major religions and many non-religious thinkers teach this rule. For example,

---

[1] For more about "⊡" and the logic of causal necessity, see pages 337–478 of Arthur Burks's *Chance, Cause, Reason* (Chicago: University of Chicago Press, 1977).

Jesus gave the rule as the summary of the Law and the Prophets (Mt 7:12), the Rabbi Hillel used it to summarize the Jewish Law, and Confucius used it to sum up his teachings. And GR is important in our own culture.

The golden rule seems clear and simple; but this clarity and simplicity disappear when we try to explain what the rule means. We can't take the usual wording of the rule literally. GR seems to say this:

> **Literal golden rule (LR)**
>
> If you want X to do A to you, then do A to X.
>
> (u:A$\underline{x}$u $\supset$ A$\underline{u}$x)

LR often works well. Suppose you want Suzy to be kind to you; then LR tells you to be kind to her. Or suppose you want Tom not to hurt you (or rob you, or be selfish to you); then you are not to do these things to him. These applications seem sensible. But LR can lead to absurdities in two types of case. First, you may be in *different circumstances* from X:

- To a patient: If you want the doctor to remove your appendix, then remove the doctor's appendix.
- To a violent little boy who loves to fight: If you want your sister to fight with you, then fight with her.
- To a parent: If you want your child not to punish you, then don't punish him.

Second, you may have *defective desires* about how you are to be treated:

- To one who desires hatred: If you want others to hate you, then hate them.

LR leads to absurdities because its wording is defective.[1]

I suggest that the following wording will avoid the objections:

> **Golden rule**
>
> Treat others only as you consent to being treated in the same situation.

> GR forbids this combination:
>
> - I do something to another.
> - I'm unwilling that this be done to me in the same situation.

Our formulation has a don't-combine form (forbidding a combination) and has you imagine an exactly reversed situation where you are on the receiving end

---

[1] Some suggest that we apply GR only to "general" actions (such as treating someone with kindness) and not to "specific" ones (such as removing someone's appendix). But our last example used a general action; so this restriction wouldn't solve the problem.

of the action. These features avoid the objections to the "literal golden rule."

GR's same-situation clause avoids the first kind of objection. Consider this case. I speak loudly to my father (who is hard of hearing); but I don't want him to speak loudly to me (since my hearing is normal). While this is sensible, it violates the literal golden rule (LR). LR says that if I want my father to speak normally (not loudly) to me, then this is how I am to speak to him. LR ignores differences in circumstances. LR says: "If you want others to treat you in a given way in your present situation, then this is how you are to treat them – even if their situation is very different."

With GR, I'd ask how I desire that I'd be treated if I were in the *same situation* as my father (and thus hard of hearing). I desire that if I were in his same situation then people would speak loudly to me. So I'd speak loudly to him.

We can take "same" situation here as "exactly similar" or "relevantly similar." In the first approach, I'd imagine myself in my father's *exact place* (with all his properties). In the second, I'd imagine myself having those of his properties (such as being hard of hearing) that I think are or might be *relevant* to deciding how loudly one should speak to him. Either approach works fine.

The same-situation clause is important also for the appendix case. Recall that LR told the patient to remove the doctor's appendix. The same-situation clause would block this, since the patient clearly doesn't desire that if he were in the place of his doctor (with a healthy appendix), then his appendix be removed by a sick patient ignorant of medicine. In applying GR, we need to ask, "Am I willing that the same thing be done to me *in the same situation*?"

In the fighting case, LR told the violent little boy to fight with his sister. The same-situation clause would block this. The little boy should imagine himself in the place of his sister (who is terrorized by fighting) and ask "Am I willing that I be fought with in this way if I were in her place?" Since the answer is "no," he wouldn't fight with his sister.

We need to be careful about something else. GR is about *our present reaction to a hypothetical case*. It isn't about how we would react if we were in the hypothetical case. We have to ask the first question, not the second:

Am I now willing that if I were in X's place in the reversed situation then A be done to me?	~~If I were in X's place in the reversed situation, would I then be willing that A be done to me?~~

The difference here is important, but subtle. Let me try to clarify it.

Suppose I have a two-year-old son, little Will, who keeps putting his fingers into electrical outlets. I try to discourage him from doing this, but nothing works. Finally, I decide that I need to spank him when he does it. I want to see if I can spank him without violating GR. In determining this, I should ask the first question, not the second:

Am I now willing that if I were in Will's place in the reversed situation then I be spanked?	~~If I were in Will's place in the reversed situation, would I then be willing to be spanked?~~

This has "willing that if."
It's about my present adult desire
toward a hypothetical case.

This has "if" before "willing."
It's about the desires I'd have
as a small child.

With the first question, I imagine the case in the following box:

> I'm a two-year-old child. I put my fingers into electrical outlets, and the only thing that will stop me is a spanking. As a two-year old, I don't understand electricity and so I desire not to be spanked.

As an adult, I say "I *now* desire that if I were in this situation then I be spanked." I might add, "I'm thankful that my parents spanked me in such cases, even though I wasn't pleased then." Thus I can spank my child without breaking GR, since I'm willing that I would have been treated the same way in the same situation.

On the other hand, if I were in Will's place, and thus judged things from a two-year-old mentality, then I'd desire not to be spanked. That's what the crossed-out question is about. If we formulated GR using this, then I'd break GR if I spanked Will. But this is absurd. We need to formulate GR correctly, in terms of my present reaction to a hypothetical case. I can satisfy GR because I'm now (as an adult) willing that I would have been spanked in this situation.

This point is subtle, but of central importance. If you don't get the idea, I suggest you reread the last few paragraphs a few times until it comes through.

This distinction is crucial when we deal with someone who isn't very rational – such as a person who is in a coma, or who is senile or confused. We need to ask the correct question:

Am I now willing that if I were in a coma then this be done to me?	~~If I were in a coma, would I then willing that this be done to me?~~

GR is about our *present* attitude toward a hypothetical case. To use GR correctly, say "I AM WILLING THAT IF"; don't say "I WOULD BE WILLING."

Let me sum up where we are. Recall that the literal golden rule LR can lead to absurdities in two types of case. First, you might be in *different circumstances* from the other person. We can get around these by including a same-situation clause and being careful to ask the correct question. Second, you may have *defective desires* about how you are to be treated. LR can tell a person with defective desires to do evil things. For example, it can tell someone who desires hatred to hate others. Here we'll consider a simpler case that shows why we need to take GR not as a direct guide to action, but rather as prescribing consistency between our actions (toward another) and our desires (about a reversed-situation action).

Imagine this case. We own a profitable coal mine but act wrongly in paying our workers a miserly $1 a day. People ask if we're willing to be paid $1 a day in their place. We answer "yes" and thus are consistent. But we answer "yes" only because we think (incorrectly) that our workers can live tolerably on this much. If we knew the truth, we wouldn't answer "yes." So we're consistent and follow GR, but only because we're ignorant. We need to correct our view of the facts; only then can GR show us our error in how we pay our workers.

In the coal-mine case, we satisfy GR-consistency but act wrongly (because we're misinformed).[1] This shows that we shouldn't take GR by itself as an infallible guide on right and wrong. Properly understood, GR doesn't tell us what specific action to take; instead, it forbids inconsistent combinations. Formally, GR is a don't-combine consistency principle – not an if-then:

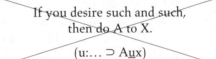

The golden rule forbids this combination: • I do something to another. • I'm unwilling that this be done to me in the same situation.	~~This formulation is defective, since your desires can be defective:~~ ~~"If you desire that you be treated in a given way in similar circumstances, then treat others this way."~~
Don't combine acting to do A to X with desiring such and such. $\sim(\underline{u}{:}A\underline{u}x \cdot \sim \underline{u}{:}...)$	~~If you desire such and such, then do A to X.~~ ~~$(u{:}... \supset A\underline{u}x)$~~

We've seen that other consistency principles require this *don't-combine* form, and that the *if-then* form can lead to absurdities when we have defective beliefs or desires. So our GR formulation has three key features:

- a same-situation clause,
- a present attitude toward a hypothetical situation, and
- a don't-combine form.

We need these features to avoid absurd implications.

Suppose that I'm about to do something to another, and I want to see if I can treat the other this way without violating GR. I'd imagine myself in the other person's place on the receiving end of the action; and I'd ask "Am I willing that if I were in this person's exact place then this be done to me?" If I do something

---

[1] Another example is ignorant Electra, who gives others severe electrical shocks because she thinks this causes them pleasure; she says "I'm willing that I be shocked this way in their place."

to another, and yet am unwilling that this be done to me in the same situation, then I'm inconsistent and I violate GR.

As I stressed before, consistency principles like the golden rule aren't sufficient in themselves. To apply GR most rationally, we need to know how our actions would influence the lives of others, and we need to develop and exercise the ability to imagine ourselves in the place of another. When combined with these and other elements, GR can be a powerful tool of ethical thinking.

But we shouldn't make excessive claims for the golden rule. It doesn't give all the answers to ethical problems. It doesn't separate concrete actions into "right actions" and "wrong actions." It only prescribes consistency: that we not have our actions (toward another) be out of harmony with our desires (about a reversed-situation action). Despite its limitations, GR is very useful. The golden rule expresses a formal rational condition that we often violate.

14.4 Starting the GR proof

What sort of *inconsistency* do we have when we violate the golden rule? Clearly we don't have an inconsistency between beliefs; what clashes here isn't beliefs but rather actions and desires. But why is it inconsistent to violate GR?

Consistency in a broad sense is more than just logical consistency in beliefs. It also includes things like consistency between ends and means. More important here are the consistency (which I call *conscientiousness*) between our moral beliefs and how we live (our actions, intentions, and desires) – and the consistency (which I call *impartiality*) between our evaluations of similar cases. GR is a consequence of these two kinds of consistency. Suppose that you're *conscientious* and *impartial* in these senses, and yet you want to steal Detra's bicycle. Being conscientious, you won't steal her bicycle unless you think this act is permissible (all right). Being impartial, you won't think this act is permissible unless you think it would be permissible for your bike to be stolen in the same situation. Being conscientiousness, you won't think this unless you're willing that your bike be stolen in the same situation. So if you're conscientious and impartial, then you won't steal Detra's bicycle unless you're willing that your bike be stolen in the same situation. Here's a diagram:

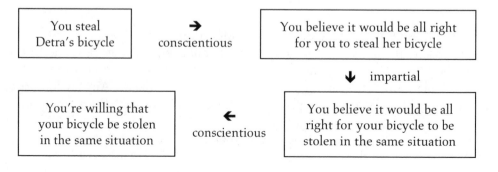

So if we're conscientious and impartial, then we'll follow GR: we won't do something to another unless we're willing that it be done to us in the same situation. So if we violate GR, then we violate either conscientiousness or impartiality or both. So if we assume that we ought to be conscientious and impartial, then we can *deduce* that we ought to follow the golden rule.

So GR follows from the requirements to be conscientious and impartial. But why be conscientious and impartial? Why care about consistency at all?

Different views could answer differently. Maybe we ought to be consistent because this is inherently right; our minds grasp the duty to be consistent as the first duty of a rational being. Or maybe we accept consistency norms because they are commanded by God, are useful to social life, accord with how we want to live, or promote our self-interest (since inconsistency brings painful "cognitive dissonance" and social sanctions). Or perhaps demands to be conscientious and impartial are consistency conditions built into our moral language. I'll abstract from these issues here and assume only that there's *some* reason to be consistent, in a broad sense that includes being conscientious and impartial. I won't worry about the details. I'm trying to develop consistency norms that appeal to a wide range of approaches – even though these approaches may explain and justify the norms differently.

To incorporate GR into our logical framework, we need to add requirements to be *conscientious* and *impartial*. Our belief logic already has part of the conscientiousness requirement. We already can prove the imperative analogue of the first step of our GR argument:

<table>
<tr><td rowspan="9">Don't *act* to do A to X without *believing* that it's all right for you to do A to X.[1]</td><td></td><td></td><td colspan="2">[∴ ~(u:Aux • ~u:RAux)</td></tr>
<tr><td>*</td><td>1</td><td>asm: (u:Aux • ~u:RAux)</td></tr>
<tr><td></td><td>2</td><td>∴ u:Aux {from 1}</td></tr>
<tr><td>*</td><td>3</td><td>∴ ~u:RAux {from 1}</td></tr>
<tr><td>*</td><td>4</td><td>u ∴ ~RAux {from 3}</td></tr>
<tr><td></td><td>5</td><td>u ∴ O~Aux {from 4}</td></tr>
<tr><td></td><td>6</td><td>u ∴ Aux {from 2}</td></tr>
<tr><td></td><td>7</td><td>u ∴ ~Aux {from 5}</td></tr>
<tr><td></td><td>8</td><td>∴ ~(u:Aux • ~u:RAux)
{from 1; 6 contradicts 7}</td></tr>
</table>

However, we can't yet prove the imperative analogue of our GR argument's third step – which also deals with conscientiousness:

> Don't *believe* that it would be all right for X to do A to you in the same situation without *being willing* that X do A to you in the same situation.

The hard part here is to symbolize "in the same situation." If we ignore this for

---

[1] For discussion on this principle, see my "Acting commits one to ethical beliefs," *Analysis* 42 (1983), pages 40–3.

the moment, then what we need is this:

> Don't *believe* that it would be all right for X to do A
> to you without *being willing* that X do A to you.

We'll interpret "being willing that A be done" as "accepting 'A *may* be done.'" Here the permissive "A may be done" isn't another way to say "A is all right." Instead, it's a member of the imperative family, but weaker than "Do A," expressing only one's consent to the action. We'll symbolize "A *may* be done" as "M$\underline{A}$." Then we can symbolize the imperative mentioned above as follows:

$$\sim(\underline{u}{:}RA\underline{u}x \cdot \sim\underline{u}{:}MA\underline{u}x) \quad = \quad \begin{array}{l}\text{Don't combine (1) } \textit{believing} \text{ "It would} \\ \text{be all right for X to do A to me" with} \\ \text{(2) } \textit{not accepting} \text{ "X may do A to me."}\end{array}$$

To prove this, we need a principle like "$\square(R\underline{A} \supset M\underline{A})$" – which says that a permissibility judgment entails the corresponding permissive. This is like the prescriptivity principle ("Hare's Law") discussed in Section 12.4, which says that an ought judgment entails the corresponding imperative: "$\square(O\underline{A} \supset \underline{A})$."[1]

Our biggest task is how to symbolize and prove the impartiality requirement and the imperative analogue of our GR argument's second step:

<table>
<tr>
<td>Don't combine (1) believing that it's all right for you to do A to X with (2) not believing that it would be all right for X to do A to you in the same situation.</td>
<td>$\sim(\underline{u}{:}RA\underline{u}x \cdot \sim\underline{u}{:}...)$</td>
</tr>
</table>

To symbolize this, we need to replace "..." with a formula that means "it would be all right for X to do A to you in *the same situation*." And to prove this, we need an inference rule to reflect universalizability – which is one of the few principles on whose truth almost all moral philosophers agree.

The *universalizability principle* (U) says that whatever is right (wrong, good, bad, etc.) in one case would also be right (wrong, good, bad, etc.) in any exactly or relevantly similar case, regardless of the individuals involved. Here are three equivalent formulations for "all right" (similar forms work for "ought"):

---

[1] For discussion on this "$\square(R\underline{A} \supset M\underline{A})$" principle, see my "How incomplete is prescriptivism?" *Mind* 93 (1984), pages 103–7. My "$\square(R\underline{A} \supset M\underline{A})$" and "$\square(O\underline{A} \supset \underline{A})$" assume that violations of conscientiousness involve a strict logical inconsistency. One who didn't accept this, but who still thought that violations of conscientiousness were in some way objectionable, could endorse the weaker principles "$(R\underline{A} \supset M\underline{A})$" and "$(O\underline{A} \supset \underline{A})$" – and weaker versions of the corresponding inference rules; the golden rule proof at the end of this chapter would still work.

Universalizability (U)

If it's all right for X to do A, then it would be all right for anyone else to do A in the same situation.

If act A is permissible, then there is some universal property (or conjunction of such properties) F, such that: (1) act A is F, and (2) in any actual or hypothetical case every act that is F is permissible.

$$(R\underline{A} \supset (\exists F)(F\underline{A} \cdot \blacksquare(X)(FX \supset RX)))$$

The second phrasing, which is more technically precise, uses the notion of a "universal property." A *universal property* is any non-evaluative property describable without proper names (like "Gensler" or "Cleveland") or pointer terms (like "I" or "this"). Let me give examples. Suppose I am tempted to steal my neighbor Patrick's new computer. This possible act has several properties or characteristics; for example, it is:

- *wrong* (evaluative term),
- an act of stealing *Pat's* computer (proper name), and
- something *I* would be doing (pointer word).

These aren't universal, since they use evaluative terms, proper names, or pointer words. But the act also has universal properties; for example, it is:

- an act of stealing a new computer from one's neighbor,
- an act whose agent has blue eyes, and
- an act that would greatly distress the computer's owner.

U says that the morality of an act depends on its universal properties (like those of the second group), properties expressible without evaluative terms, proper names, or pointer words. Two acts with the same universal properties must have the same moral status, regardless of the individuals involved.

Here's an important corollary of universalizability:

U*   If it's all right for you to do A to X, then it would be all right for X to do A to you in the exact same situation.

=   If it's all right for you to do A to X, then, for some universal property F, F is the complete description of your-doing-A-to-X in universal terms, and, in any actual or hypothetical case, if X's-doing-A-to-you is F, then it would be all right for X to do A to you.

$$(RA\underline{u}x \supset (\exists F)(F^*A\underline{u}x \cdot \blacksquare(FA\underline{x}u \supset RA\underline{x}u)))$$

U* relates closely to the second step in our argument for GR.

14.5 GR logical machinery

Now we'll add logical machinery to formulate and prove our version of the golden rule. This involves adding:

- letters for universal properties and for actions,
- "M" ("may") for permissives,
- "■" ("in every actual or hypothetical case") for hypothetical cases, and
- "*" for the complete description of an act in universal terms.

We also need to add inference rules. This section will get complicated; you may need to read it a couple of times to follow what's happening.

First, we'll use letters of two new sorts (both can be used in quantifiers):

- "F," "G," "H," and these with primes stand for universal properties of actions (including conjunctions of such properties).
- "$\underline{X}$," "$\underline{Y}$," "$\underline{Z}$," and these with primes stand for actions.

These examples use letters for universal properties:

$$\text{F}\underline{A} \quad \begin{array}{l} = \quad \text{Act A has universal property F.} \\ = \quad \text{Act A is F (e.g., act A is an act of stealing).} \end{array}$$

$$(\text{F}\underline{A} \supset \sim \text{R}\underline{A}) \quad = \quad \text{If act A is an act of stealing, then act A is wrong.}$$

$$\text{G}\underline{A} \quad \begin{array}{l} = \quad \text{Act A is an act of a blue-eyed philosophy teacher} \\ \quad \quad \text{stealing a bicycle from an impoverished student.} \end{array}$$

We translate "F$\underline{A}$" as "Act A is F" (not as "Imperative 'Do A' is F"). This next example uses a universal-property quantifier:

$$(\text{F})(\text{F}\underline{A} \equiv \text{F}\underline{B}) \quad \begin{array}{l} = \quad \text{Acts A and B have all the same universal properties.} \\ = \quad \text{For every universal property F, act A has property F} \\ \quad \quad \text{if and only if act B has property F.} \end{array}$$

These examples use action quantifiers:

$$(\exists \underline{X})\text{F}\underline{X} \quad \begin{array}{l} = \quad \text{Some act has universal property F.} \\ = \quad \text{For some act X, X has universal property F.} \end{array}$$

$$(\underline{X})(\text{F}\underline{X} \supset \text{O}\underline{X}) \quad \begin{array}{l} = \quad \text{Every act that is F ought to be done.} \\ = \quad \text{For every act X, if act X is F, then act X ought to be done.} \end{array}$$

$$(\underline{X})(\exists \text{F})\text{F}\underline{X} \quad \begin{array}{l} = \quad \text{Every act has some universal property.} \\ = \quad \text{For every act X there's some universal property F, such} \\ \quad \quad \text{that act X is F.} \end{array}$$

Our two new kinds of letter require two new formation rules:

> 1. The result of writing "F," "G," "H," or one of these with primes, and then an imperative wff is itself a descriptive wff.
> 2. The result of writing "(" or "(∃," and then "F," "G," "H," "$\underline{X}$," "$\underline{Y}$," "$\underline{Z}$," or one of these with primes, and then ")" is a quantifier.

Assume expanded versions of our quantifier rules for the new quantifiers. We have to substitute the right sort of thing for the quantified letter:

> For *individual variables*: x, y, z, x', ..., substitute individual constants: a, b, c, d, ...
>
> For *universal-property variables*: F, G, H, F', ..., substitute universal-property letters not bound to quantifiers: F, G, H, F', ...
>
> For *action variables*: $\underline{X}$, $\underline{Y}$, $\underline{Z}$, $\underline{X}'$, ..., substitute imperative wffs: A$\underline{a}$, $\underline{B}$, A$\underline{xy}$, ...[1]

When "M" is prefixed to an imperative wff, we'll translate it as "may":[2]

> 3. The result of prefixing an imperative wff with "M" is a wff.

$$MA \quad = \quad \text{Act A may be done.}$$

$$MA\underline{xu} \quad = \quad \text{X may do A to you.}$$

$$
\begin{array}{rcl}
 & = & \text{You accept "X may do A to me."} \\
u{:}MA\underline{xu} & = & \text{You consent to X's doing A to you.} \\
 & = & \text{You're willing that X do A to you.}
\end{array}
$$

Permissives like "MA" are weaker members of the imperative family. They express our consent to the act, but not necessarily our positive desire that the act take place. We can consistently consent both to the act and to its omission – saying "You may do A and you may omit A." Here are further wffs:

$$\sim M{\sim}\underline{A} \quad = \quad \text{Act A may not be omitted.}$$

$$
\begin{array}{rcl}
 & = & \text{You accept "X may not omit doing A to me."} \\
u{:}{\sim}M{\sim}A\underline{xu} & = & \text{You demand that X do A to you.}
\end{array}
$$

---

[1] The last case requires two technical provisos. Suppose that we drop a quantifier containing an action variable and substitute an imperative wff for the variable. Then we must be sure that (1) this imperative wff contains no variable that also occurs in a quantifier in the derived wff, and (2) if we dropped an existential quantifier, this substituted imperative wff must be an underlined capital letter that isn't an action variable and that hasn't occurred before in the proof.

[2] Capital letters have various uses, depending on context. In "((M · Ma) ⊃ (Mbc · M$\underline{A}$))," for example, "M" is used first for a statement, then for a property of an individual, then for a relation between individuals, and finally for "may." It's usually clearer to use different letters.

"M<u>A</u>" is weaker and "~M~<u>A</u>" is stronger than "<u>A</u>."[1]

Inference rule G1 is the principle that "A is all right" entails "A may be done." G1 holds regardless of what imperative wff replaces "<u>A</u>":[2]

$$\text{G1} \quad \boxed{\text{R}\underline{\text{A}} \quad \rightarrow \quad \text{M}\underline{\text{A}}}$$

Given this and the rules for "M," "O," and "R," we also can prove the reverse entailment from "M<u>A</u>" to "R<u>A</u>." Then either of the two logically entails the other; so accepting one commits a person to accepting the other. But the distinction between the two doesn't vanish. "R<u>A</u>" is true or false; to accept "R<u>A</u>" is to believe that something is true. But "M<u>A</u>" isn't true or false; to accept "M<u>A</u>" isn't to believe something but to will something, to consent to the idea of something being done.

Some of our inference rules for "M" and "■" involve new kinds of world. A *world prefix* is now any string of zero-or-more instances of letters from the set <W, D, H, P, a, b, c, ...> – where <a, b, c, ...> is the set of small letters. Here "P," "PP," "PPP," and so on are "permission worlds," much like deontic worlds. A permission world that depends on a given world W1 is a possible world that contains the indicative judgments of W1 and some set of imperatives prescribing actions jointly permitted by the permissives of W1.

Inference rules G2 to G4 (which won't be used in our GR proof) govern permissions and are much like the deontic rules. G2 and G3 hold regardless of what pair of contradictory imperative wffs replaces "<u>A</u>" / "~<u>A</u>":

$$\text{G2} \quad \boxed{\begin{array}{c} \text{~M}\underline{\text{A}} \quad \rightarrow \quad \text{P}\therefore \text{~}\underline{\text{A}}, \\ \text{use a blank or any string of P's} \end{array}}$$

In G2, the world prefix of the derived line must be either the same as that of the earlier line or else the same except that it adds one or more P's at the end.

$$\text{G3} \quad \boxed{\begin{array}{c} \text{M}\underline{\text{A}} \quad \rightarrow \quad \text{P}\therefore \underline{\text{A}}, \\ \text{use a } new \text{ string of P's} \end{array}}$$

---

[1] The relationship between permissives and standard imperatives is tricky. See my *Formal Ethics* (London: Routledge, 1996), pages 185–6, and my "How incomplete is prescriptivism?" *Mind* 93 (1984), pages 103–7.

[2] Thinking that an act is *all right* commits one to *consenting* to the idea of it being done (or, equivalently, *being willing* that it be done). We also could use words like "approve," "accept," "condone," or "tolerate" – in one sense of these terms. The sense of "consent" that I have in mind refers to an inner attitude incompatible with inwardly objecting to (condemning, disapproving, forbidding, protesting, objecting to) the act. Consenting here is a minimal attitude and needn't involve favoring or advocating or welcoming the act. It's consistent to both consent to the idea of A being done and also consent to the idea of A not being done.

In G3, the world prefix of the derived line must be the same as that of the earlier line except that it adds a *new* string (a string not occurring in earlier lines) of one or more P's at the end. G4 mirrors the deontic indicative transfer rule; it holds regardless of what descriptive or deontic wff replaces "A":

$$\text{G4} \qquad \boxed{\quad \text{P}\therefore \text{A} \quad \rightarrow \quad \text{A} \quad}$$

In G4, the world prefixes in the derived and deriving lines must be identical except that one ends in one or more additional P's.

"■" is a modal operator somewhat like "□":

> 4.   The result of prefixing any wff with "■" is a wff.

"■" translates as "in every actual or hypothetical case" or "in every possible world having the same basic moral principles as those true in the actual world." Here's a wff using "■":

$$\blacksquare(\text{F}\underline{\text{A}} \supset \text{O}\underline{\text{A}})$$

= If act A is or were F, then act A ought to be done.
= In every actual or hypothetical case, if act A is F, then act A ought to be done.

Suppose that, while act A may or may not have property F (e.g., it may or may not maximize pleasure), still, if it did, then it would be what ought to be done. We'll use "■(F$\underline{\text{A}}$ ⊃ O$\underline{\text{A}}$)" for this idea. "(F$\underline{\text{A}}$ ⊃ O$\underline{\text{A}}$)" is too weak to express this (since this wff is trivially true if "F$\underline{\text{A}}$" is false); "□(F$\underline{\text{A}}$ ⊃ O$\underline{\text{A}}$)" is too strong (because there's no such entailment). So we'll use "■" to formulate claims about what would be right or wrong in hypothetical situations (such as imagined exactly reversed situations).

We can now symbolize the universalizability principle:

> U   If act A is permissible, then there is some universal property (or conjunction of such properties) F, such that: (1) act A is F, and (2) in any actual or hypothetical case every act that is F is permissible.
>
> $$(\text{R}\underline{\text{A}} \supset (\exists \text{F})(\text{F}\underline{\text{A}} \cdot \blacksquare(\underline{\text{X}})(\text{F}\underline{\text{X}} \supset \text{R}\underline{\text{X}})))$$

G5 and G6 are the "all right" and "ought" forms of the corresponding inference rules. These hold regardless of what imperative wff replaces "$\underline{\text{A}}$," what universal-property variable replaces "F," and what action variable replaces "$\underline{\text{X}}$":

$$\begin{array}{lll}
\text{G5} & \text{R}\underline{\text{A}} \rightarrow & (\exists \text{F})(\text{F}\underline{\text{A}} \cdot \blacksquare(\underline{\text{X}})(\text{F}\underline{\text{X}} \supset \text{R}\underline{\text{X}})) \\
\text{G6} & \text{O}\underline{\text{A}} \rightarrow & (\exists \text{F})(\text{F}\underline{\text{A}} \cdot \blacksquare(\underline{\text{X}})(\text{F}\underline{\text{X}} \supset \text{O}\underline{\text{X}}))
\end{array}$$

In G5 and G6, the world prefix of the derived and deriving lines must be identical and must contain no "W." The proviso prevents us from being able to prove that violations of universalizability are logically self-contradictory (as I don't think they are).

The rules for "■" resemble those for "□." Recall that our expanded world prefixes can use "H," "HH," and "HHH"; these represent *hypothetical situation worlds*, which are possible worlds having the same basic moral principles as those of the actual world (or whatever world the H-world depends on). G7 and G8 hold regardless of what pair of contradictory wffs replaces "A" / "~A":

$$\text{G7} \quad \boxed{\begin{array}{c} \blacksquare A \;\rightarrow\; H \therefore A, \\ \text{use a blank or any string of H's} \end{array}}$$

In G7, the world prefixes in the derived and deriving lines must either be the same or the same except that one adds one or more H's at the end.

$$\text{G8} \quad \boxed{\begin{array}{c} \sim\blacksquare A \;\rightarrow\; H \therefore \sim A, \\ \text{use a } new \text{ string of H's} \end{array}}$$

In G8, the derived line's world prefix must be the same as that of the earlier line except that it adds a *new* string (a string not occurring in earlier lines) of one or more H's at the end. Rule G9 (which won't be used in our proof of the golden rule) says that "□" and "■" are equivalent when prefixed to descriptive wffs; this holds regardless of what *descriptive* wff replaces "A":

$$\text{G9} \quad \boxed{\blacksquare A \;\leftrightarrow\; \square A}$$

Our final symbol is "*"; this is used with universal-property letters to represent the complete description of an action in universal terms. Here's the rule for constructing wffs with "*," with an example:

> 5. The result of writing "F," "G," "H," or these with primes, then "*," and then an imperative wff is itself a descriptive wff.

$$\text{F*}\underline{A} \quad \begin{array}{ll} = & \text{F is the complete description of act A in universal terms.} \\ = & \text{F is the description of act A in universal terms which includes} \\ & \text{all the universal properties of act A.} \end{array}$$

"F*$\underline{A}$" means the same as this longer wff:

$(F\underline{A} \cdot (G)(G\underline{A} \supset \Box(\underline{X})(F\underline{X} \supset G\underline{X})))$

=   Act A is F, and every universal property G that A has is
          included as part of F.

=   Act A is F, and, for every universal property G that A has,
          it's logically necessary that every act that's F also is G.

We adopt the corresponding inference rule G10, which lets us go back and forth
between "F*$\underline{A}$" and this longer wff. G10 holds regardless of what distinct
universal-property letters replace "F" and "G," what imperative wff replaces
"$\underline{A}$," and what action variable replaces "$\underline{X}$":

G10 $\boxed{F*\underline{A} \quad \leftrightarrow \quad (F\underline{A} \cdot (G)(G\underline{A} \supset \Box(\underline{X})(F\underline{X} \supset G\underline{X})))}$

Rule G11, our final inference rule, says that every act has a complete description in universal terms (even though it may be too long to write down). G11 is
an axiom; it lets us put wff "$(\underline{X})(\exists F)F*\underline{X}$" on any line of a proof:

G11 $\boxed{(\underline{X})(\exists F)F*\underline{X}}$

We'll use "*" in symbolizing "exactly similar situation." Let's take an
example. Let "A$\underline{m}$x" represent the act of my attacking X. Suppose this act has
complete description F:

F*A$\underline{m}$x   =   My-attacking-X has *complete universal description* F.

Let's flesh this out. Let "G," "G'," ... represent my universal properties; these
include properties like being a logician. Let "H," "H'," ... represent X's universal properties; these might include being an impoverished student. Let "R,"
"R'," ... represent the relationships between X and me; these might include X's
being my student. Now property F would look like this, which describes the
actual situation:

FA$\underline{m}$x   =   My-attacking-X is an act of someone who
          is G, G', ... attacking someone who is H,
          H', ... and related to me in ways R, R', ...

Now we imagine an *exactly similar situation* if we imagine the situation where
X's-attacking-me has this same description F:

FA$\underline{x}$m   =   X's-attacking-me is an act of someone who
          is G, G', ... attacking someone who is H,
          H', ... and related to X in ways R, R', ...

In this imagined exactly similar situation, X is in my exact place – and I am in

X's exact place. All our universal properties and relationships are switched.
We can now symbolize the reversed-situation corollary of universalizability:

U*   If it's all right for you to do A to X, then it would be all right for X
to do A to you in the exact same situation.

=   If it's all right for you to do A to X, then, for some universal
property F, F is the complete description of your-doing-A-to-X in
universal terms, and, in any actual or hypothetical case, if X's-
doing-A-to-you is F, then it would be all right for X to do A to you.

$$(RA\underline{u}x \supset (\exists F)(F^*A\underline{u}x \cdot \blacksquare(FA\underline{x}u \supset RA\underline{x}u)))$$

Also, and most importantly, we can symbolize the golden rule:

GR   Treat others only as you consent to being treated in the same situation.

=   Don't combine *acting* to do A to X with *being unwilling* that A be done
to you in the same situation.

=   Don't combine (1) accepting "Do A to X" with (2) not accepting "For
some universal property F, F is the complete description in universal
terms of my-doing-A-to-X, and, in any actual or hypothetical situation,
if X's-doing-A-to-me is F, then X may do A to me."

$$\sim(\underline{u}{:}A\underline{u}x \cdot \sim\underline{u}{:}(\exists F)(F^*A\underline{u}x \cdot \blacksquare(FA\underline{x}u \supset MA\underline{x}u)))$$

While we're at it, here are symbolizations of two other consistency principles
mentioned in Section 14.2:

Impartiality: Make similar evaluations about similar actions,
regardless of the individuals involved.

=   Don't accept "Act A is permissible" without accepting "Any
act exactly or relevantly similar to act A is permissible."

=   Don't accept "Act A is permissible" without accepting "For
some universal property F, act A is F and, in any actual or
hypothetical situation, any act that is F is permissible."

$$\sim(\underline{u}{:}R\underline{A} \cdot \sim\underline{u}{:}(\exists F)(F\underline{A} \cdot \blacksquare(\underline{X})(F\underline{X} \supset R\underline{X})))$$

> **Formula of universal law:** Act only as you're willing for anyone to act in the same situation – regardless of imagined variations of time or person.[1]
>
> = Don't combine *acting* to do A with *not being willing* that any similar action be done in the same situation.
>
> = Don't combine (1) accepting "Do A" with (2) not accepting "For some universal property F, F is the complete description in universal terms of my doing A, and, in any actual or hypothetical situation, any act that is F may be done."
>
> $$\sim(\underline{u}{:}A\underline{u} \cdot \sim\underline{u}{:}(\exists F)(F^*A\underline{u} \cdot \blacksquare(\underline{X})(F\underline{X} \supset M\underline{X})))$$

This "formula of universal law" covers imagined cases where I am in the place of *anyone* affected by my action; so it's a generalized GR that applies equally to situations involving more than two people. It also can apply to situations involving only one person (for example, cases where my present action can harm my future self).

14.6   The symbolic GR proof

Before we do our proof of the golden rule, let's review the larger picture.

We began this chapter by sketching various dimensions of ethical rationality. Then we narrowed our focus, first to rationality as consistency, and then to a single consistency principle – the golden rule. We had to formulate GR carefully to avoid absurd implications. We arrived at this wording:

Golden rule	GR forbids this combination:
Treat others only as you consent to being treated in the same situation.	• I do something to another. • I'm unwilling that this be done to me in the same situation.

Then we sketched an intuitive proof of the golden rule, using the example of stealing Detra's bicycle. Then we noted that incorporating GR and its proof into our logical framework requires adding impartiality and strengthening conscientiousness. So we added logical machinery to do this. And so now we are ready to give a formal proof of the golden rule.

---

[1] My "formula of universal law" resembles Immanuel Kant's principle. His wording went, "Act only on that maxim through which you can at the same time will that it should be a universal law." I'm not claiming that Kant explicitly intended his principle in exactly my sense.

Our proof goes as follows ("#" marks lines that use our new inference rules):

$[\therefore \sim(\underline{u}{:}A\underline{u}x \cdot \sim\underline{u}{:}(\exists F)(F^*A\underline{u}x \cdot \blacksquare(FA\underline{x}u \supset MA\underline{x}u)))$

1	asm: $(\underline{u}{:}A\underline{u}x \cdot \sim\underline{u}{:}(\exists F)(F^*A\underline{u}x \cdot \blacksquare(FA\underline{x}u \supset MA\underline{x}u)))$	
2	$\therefore \underline{u}{:}A\underline{u}x$ {from 1}	
3	$\therefore \sim\underline{u}{:}(\exists F)(F^*A\underline{u}x \cdot \blacksquare(FA\underline{x}u \supset MA\underline{x}u))$ {from 1}	
4	$u \therefore \sim(\exists F)(F^*A\underline{u}x \cdot \blacksquare(FA\underline{x}u \supset MA\underline{x}u))$ {from 3}	
5	$u \therefore A\underline{u}x$ {from 2}	
6	u asm: $\sim RA\underline{u}x$ {we need to derive "$RA\underline{u}x$"}	
7	$u \therefore O\sim A\underline{u}x$ {from 6}	
8	$u \therefore \sim A\underline{u}x$ {from 7}	
9	$u \therefore RA\underline{u}x$ {from 6; 5 contradicts 8}	
# 10	$u \therefore (\exists F)(FA\underline{u}x \cdot \blacksquare(\underline{X})(FX \supset RX))$ {from 9 by G5}	
11	$u \therefore (GA\underline{u}x \cdot \blacksquare(\underline{X})(GX \supset RX))$ {from 10}	
12	$u \therefore GA\underline{u}x$ {from 11}	
13	$u \therefore \blacksquare(\underline{X})(GX \supset RX)$ {from 11}	
# 14	$u \therefore (\underline{X})(\exists F)F^*X$ {by rule G11}	
15	$u \therefore (\exists F)F^*A\underline{u}x$ {from 14}	
16	$u \therefore H^*A\underline{u}x$ {from 15}	
# 17	$u \therefore (HA\underline{u}x \cdot (F)(FA\underline{u}x \supset \square(\underline{X})(HX \supset FX)))$ {from 16 by G10}	
18	$u \therefore HA\underline{u}x$ {from 17}	
19	$u \therefore (F)(FA\underline{u}x \supset \square(\underline{X})(HX \supset FX))$ {from 17}	
20	$u \therefore (GA\underline{u}x \supset \square(\underline{X})(HX \supset GX))$ {from 19}	
21	$u \therefore \square(\underline{X})(HX \supset GX)$ {from 12 and 20}	
22	$u \therefore (F)\sim(F^*A\underline{u}x \cdot \blacksquare(FA\underline{x}u \supset MA\underline{x}u))$ {from 4}	
23	$u \therefore \sim(H^*A\underline{u}x \cdot \blacksquare(HA\underline{x}u \supset MA\underline{x}u))$ {from 22}	
24	$u \therefore \sim\blacksquare(HA\underline{x}u \supset MA\underline{x}u)$ {from 16 and 23}	
# 25	$uH \therefore \sim(HA\underline{x}u \supset MA\underline{x}u)$ {from 24 by G8}	
26	$uH \therefore HA\underline{x}u$ {from 25}	
27	$uH \therefore \sim MA\underline{x}u$ {from 25} ◄┄┄┄┄┄	
28	$uH \therefore (\underline{X})(HX \supset GX)$ {from 21}	
29	$uH \therefore (HA\underline{x}u \supset GA\underline{x}u)$ {from 28}	
30	$uH \therefore GA\underline{x}u$ {from 26 and 29}	
# 31	$uH \therefore (\underline{X})(GX \supset RX)$ {from 13 by G7}	
32	$uH \therefore (GA\underline{x}u \supset RA\underline{x}u)$ {from 31}	
33	$uH \therefore RA\underline{x}u$ {from 30 and 32}	
# 34	$uH \therefore MA\underline{x}u$ {from 33 by G1} ◄┄┄┄┄	
35	$\therefore \sim(\underline{u}{:}A\underline{u}x \cdot \sim\underline{u}{:}(\exists F)(F^*A\underline{u}x \cdot \blacksquare(FA\underline{x}u \supset MA\underline{x}u)))$	

{from 1; 27 contradicts 34}

While this is a difficult proof, you should be able to follow the individual lines and see that everything follows correctly.

Our proof begins as usual; we assume the opposite of what we want to prove and then try to derive a contradiction. Soon we get lines 4 and 5 (where 5 is addressed to yourself):

Line 4 | X may not do A to me in an exactly similar situation. | Do A to X. | Line 5

Using line 4, we get these key lines:

16 Let H be the complete description of my doing A to X.
26 In an imagined situation, X's-doing-A-to-me is H.
27 In our imagined situation, X may not do A to me.

We use line 5 to get "It's all right for me to do A to X":

5 Do A to X.   (This is addressed to yourself.)
6 ⌐ Assume that it's *not* all right for me to do A to X.
7 │ ∴ I ought not to do A to X.
8 ∟ ∴ Don't do A to X.   (This is addressed to yourself.)
9 ∴ It's all right for me to do to X.   {8 contradicts 5}

Then we use universalizability on "It's all right for me to do A to X" to get "Any act relevantly or exactly similar to my-doing-A-to-X would be all right." We specify that G is the morally relevant complex of properties here; so:

12 My-doing-A-to-X has property G.
13 Any act that has property G would be all right.

We get a contradiction in a few more lines:

16 H is the complete description of my doing A to X.   {above}
12 My-doing-A to-X has property G.   {above}
21 ∴ G is part of H – and every act that is H is G.   {from 16 & 12}
26 In our imagined situation, X's-doing-A-to-me is H.   {above}
30 ∴ In our imagined situation, X's-doing-A-to-me is G.   {from 21 & 26}
13 Any act that has property G would be all right.   {above}
33 ∴ In our imagined situation, X's-doing-A-to-me is all right.   {from 30 & 13}
34 ∴ In our imagined situation, X may do A to me.   {from 33}

Since 34 contradicts 27, we derive our conclusion. This ends our proof of the golden rule:[1]

Always treat others as you want to be treated; that is
the summary of the Law and the Prophets. (Mt 7:12)

---

[1] If you want a challenging exercise, try to prove the impartiality and universal law formulas, as formulated at the end of the previous section. Answers are in the back of the book.

CHAPTER 15
Metalogic

Metalogic studies logical systems. It focuses not on using these systems to test concrete arguments but rather on the systems themselves. This chapter provides an introduction to metalogic.

15.1 Metalogical questions

Metalogic is the study of logical systems; when we do metalogic, we try to prove things about these systems. Here's an example. Recall our first two rules in Section 6.1 for forming propositional wffs:

> 1. Any capital letter is a wff.
> 2. The result of prefixing any wff with "~" is a wff.

It follows from these that there's no longest wff – since, if there were a longest wff, then we could make a longer one by adding another "~." This simple proof is about a logical system, so it's part of *metalogic*.

Consider our system of propositional logic. Metalogic asks questions like: Do we need all five symbols ("~," "•," "∨," "⊃," and "≡")? Could we define some symbols in terms of others? Did we set up our proof system right? Are any of the inference rules defective? Can we prove self-contradictions or invalid arguments? Do we have enough inference rules to prove all valid propositional arguments? Could other approaches systematize propositional logic?

These are typical metalogical questions. This book focuses on logic, not metalogic (which can get highly technical). But this chapter will do a little metalogic, to give you an idea of what this is like.

15.2 Symbols

We don't need all five propositional symbols ("~," "•," "∨," "⊃," and "≡"). We could symbolize and test the same arguments if we had just "~" and "•"; then, instead of writing "(P ∨ Q)," we could write "~(~P • ~Q)":

$$(P \lor Q) \quad = \quad \sim(\sim P \cdot \sim Q)$$
$$\text{At least one is true} \quad = \quad \text{Not both are false.}$$

The two forms are equivalent, in that both are true or false under the same conditions; we could show this using a truth table. Similarly, we could express "⊃" and "≡" using "~" and "·":

$$(P \supset Q) \quad = \quad \sim(P \cdot \sim Q)$$
$$\text{If P then Q} \quad = \quad \text{We don't have P true and Q false.}$$

$$(P \equiv Q) \quad = \quad (\sim(P \cdot \sim Q) \cdot \sim(Q \cdot \sim P))$$
$$\text{P if and only if Q} \quad = \quad \text{We don't have P true and Q false, and}$$
$$\text{we don't have Q true and P false.}$$

Or we might translate the other symbols into "~" and "∨":

$$(P \cdot Q) \quad = \quad \sim(\sim P \lor \sim Q)$$
$$(P \supset Q) \quad = \quad (\sim P \lor Q)$$
$$(P \equiv Q) \quad = \quad (\sim(P \lor Q) \lor \sim(\sim P \lor \sim Q))$$

Or we might use just "~" and "⊃" – in light of these equivalences:

$$(P \cdot Q) \quad = \quad \sim(P \supset \sim Q)$$
$$(P \lor Q) \quad = \quad (\sim P \supset Q)$$
$$(P \equiv Q) \quad = \quad \sim((P \supset Q) \supset \sim(Q \supset P))$$

It's even possible to get by using just the symbol "|" for NAND; "(P | Q)" means "not both P and Q." We can then define "~P" as "(P | P)" and "(P · Q)" as "((P | Q) | (P | Q))." It's not very intuitive, but it works.

Systems with only one or two symbols are more elegantly simple but harder to use. However, logicians are sometimes more interested in proving results about a system than in using it to test arguments; and it may be easier to prove these results if we use fewer symbols.

Another approach is to use all five symbols but divide them into undefined (primitive) symbols and defined ones. We could take "~" and either "·" or "∨" or "⊃" as undefined, and then define the others using these. We'd then view the defined symbols as abbreviations; whenever we liked, we could eliminate them and use only the undefined symbols.

How do we know that our five symbols suffice to formulate wffs for every possible truth table? Suppose we have a truth table for two letters that comes out as below and we want to replace "??" with a wff that gives this table:

A B	??
0 0	0
0 1	1
1 0	1
1 1	0

How do we know
that some wff gives
this truth table?

To construct the wff, we can put an OR between the true cases (rows 2 and 3):
A-is-false-and-B-is-true [row 2] OR A-is-true-and-B-is-false [row 3]:

$$((\sim A \cdot B) \lor (A \cdot \sim B))$$

So we can, using just NOT, AND, and OR, rather mechanically come up with a wff that expresses any specific truth table. (If the formula is always false, use a wff like "$(A \cdot \sim A)$," which is always false.)

There are further options about notation. While we use capital letters for statements, some logicians use small letters (often just "p," "q," "r," and "s") or Greek letters. Some use "-" or "¬" for negation, "&" or "∧" for conjunction, "→" for conditional, or "↔" for equivalence. Various conventions are used for dropping parentheses. It's easy to adapt to these differences.

Polish notation avoids parentheses and has shorter formulas. "K," "A," "C," and "E" go in place of the left-hand parentheses for "·," "∨," "⊃," and "≡"; and "N" is used for "∼." Here are four examples:

$\sim(P \cdot Q)$	=	NKpq	$((P \cdot Q) \supset R)$	=	CKpqr
$(\sim P \cdot Q)$	=	KNpq	$(P \cdot (Q \supset R))$	=	KpCqr

Advocates of Polish notation say they can actually understand the formulas.

15.3 Soundness

The most important questions of metalogic are about whether a system is **sound** (won't prove bad things – so every argument provable in the system is valid) and **complete** (can prove every good thing – so every valid argument expressible in the system is provable in the system).

Could the following case happen? A student named Logicus found a flaw in our proof system. Logicus produced a formal proof of a propositional argument; and he then showed by a truth table that this argument is invalid. So some arguments provable on our proof system are invalid.

People have found such flaws in logical systems. How do we know that our propositional system is free from such flaws? How can we prove soundness?

> *Soundness*: Any propositional argument for which we
> can give a formal proof is valid (on the truth-table test).

We first must show that all the propositional inference rules are *truth pre-serving* (which means that, when applied to true wffs, they yield only further true wffs). We have 13 inference rules: 6 S-rules, 6 I-rules, and RAA. It's easy (but tedious) to use the truth-table method of Section 6.6 to show that the S- and I-rules are truth preserving. All these rules pass the test (as you could check for yourself); when applied to true wffs, they yield only true wffs.

RAA is more difficult to check. First we show that the *first* use of RAA in a proof is truth preserving. Suppose all previous not-blocked-off lines in a proof are true, and we use RAA to derive a further line; we have to show that this further line is true:

$$
\begin{array}{lll}
1 & \dots = 1 & \Leftarrow \\
2 & \dots = 1 & \Leftarrow
\end{array}
\quad \text{Suppose all these are true.}
$$

$$
\begin{array}{l}
\ulcorner \text{ asm: } \sim A \\
\ \ \dots \\
\ \ \therefore B \\
\lfloor \therefore \sim B \\
\ \ \therefore A
\end{array}
$$

We derive a contradiction.

$\leftarrow$ Does A then have to be true?

From previous true lines plus assumption "~A," we derive contradictory wffs "B" and "~B" using S- and I-rules. We just saw that the S- and I-rules are truth preserving. So if the lines used to derive "B" and "~B" were all true, then both "B" and "~B" would have to be true, which is impossible. Hence the lines used to derive them can't all be true. So if the lines before the assumption are all true, then assumption "~A" has to be false. So its opposite ("A") has to be true. So the first use of RAA in a proof is truth preserving.

We can similarly show that if the first use of RAA in a proof is truth pre-serving, then the second must also be. And we can show that if the first n uses of RAA are truth preserving, then the n+1 use must also be. Then we can apply the principle of mathematical induction:

Mathematical Induction

Suppose that something holds in the first case, and if it holds in the first n cases, then it holds in the n+1 case. Then it holds in all cases.

Using this principle, it follows that *all* uses of RAA are truth preserving.

Now suppose an argument is provable in our propositional system. Then there's some proof that derives the conclusion from the premises using truth-preserving rules. So if the premises are true, then the conclusion also must be true – and so the argument is valid. So if an argument is provable in our propositional system, then it's valid. This establishes soundness.

Isn't this reasoning circular? Aren't we just assuming principles of proposi-tional inference (like *modus ponens*) as we defend our propositional system? Of course we are. Nothing can be proved without assuming logical rules. We aren't attempting the impossible task of proving things about a logical system without assuming any logical rules. Instead, we're doing something more modest. We're trying to show, relying on ordinary reasoning, that we didn't make certain errors in setting up our system.

The consistency of our system is an easy corollary of its soundness. Let's say that a wff is a **theorem** if it's provable from zero premises. "(P ∨ ~P)" is an example of a theorem; we can prove it rather simply by assuming its opposite and then deriving a contradiction:

$$
\begin{array}{lll}
 & [\ \therefore (P \lor \sim P) & \text{Valid} \\
* \quad 1 & \quad \ulcorner \text{asm: } \sim(P \lor \sim P) \\
2 & \quad \mid \therefore \sim P \quad \{\text{from 1}\} \\
3 & \quad \llcorner \therefore P \quad \{\text{from 1}\} \\
4 & \therefore (P \lor \sim P) \quad \{\text{from 1; 2 contradicts 3}\}
\end{array}
$$

By our soundness result, since "∴ (P ∨ ~P)" is provable it must be valid on the truth-table test. So then it must be impossible for "(P ∨ ~P)" to be false. So then "(P ∨ ~P)" must have an all-1 truth table. And the more general result follows, that all theorems of our system must have all-1 truth tables.

Now a system is **consistent** provided that no two contradictory formulas are both theorems. We just showed that all theorems of our system have all-1 truth tables. But no two contradictory formulas both have all-1 truth tables (since if a formula has all 1's then its contradictory has all 0's). So no two contradictory formulas are both theorems of our propositional system. So our propositional system is consistent.

15.4 Completeness

Our soundness proof shows that our propositional system won't prove invalid arguments. You probably didn't doubt this. But you may have had doubts about whether our system is strong enough to prove all valid propositional arguments. After all, the single-assumption method of doing proofs wasn't strong enough; Section 7.3 uncovered valid arguments that require multiple assumptions. How do we know that our expanded method is enough? Maybe Logicus will find a further propositional argument that's valid but not provable; then we'd have to strengthen our system still further. To calm these doubts, we'll show that our propositional system is complete:

Completeness: Every valid propositional argument is provable.

Our completeness proof will show that if we correctly apply the proof strategy of Section 7.3 to a valid propositional argument then we get a proof. Recall that this strategy has five steps (which you might want to review): 1-START, 2-S&I, 3-RAA, 4-ASSUME, and 5-REFUTE. Let's assume that we correctly apply this strategy to a propositional argument. Then:

We'll end in the RAA step with all assumptions blocked off, or end in the REFUTE step, or keep going endlessly.
If we end in the RAA step with all assumptions blocked off, then we'll get a proof.
If we end in the REFUTE step, then the argument is invalid.
We won't keep going endlessly.
∴ If the argument is valid, then we'll get a proof.

$((A \lor F) \lor E)$
$(A \supset P)$
$(F \supset \sim V)$
$\sim E$
$\therefore (V \supset P)$

Premise 1 is true because our proof strategy has only two stopping points; so we'll stop at one or the other or we won't stop. Premise 2 is true because our proof strategy (especially the S&I and RAA steps) mirrors the Section 7.1 definition of "proof." Now we have to argue for premises 3 and 4.

Premise 3 says "If we end in the REFUTE step, then the argument is invalid." This is true because, when we reach the REFUTE step, all the complex wffs are dissolved into smaller parts and eventually into simple wffs, the larger forms are true if the smaller parts are true, and the simple wffs we end up with are consistent and thus give truth conditions making all the other wffs true – thus making the premises of the original argument true while its conclusion is false – thus showing that the original argument is invalid.

Here's a chart (where α and β represent any wffs):

This form:	dissolves into these:
$\sim\sim\alpha$	α [S-rule]
$(\alpha \cdot \beta)$	α and β [S-rule]
$\sim(\alpha \cdot \beta)$	$\sim\alpha$ or $\sim\beta$ [I-rule or otherwise]
$(\alpha \lor \beta)$	α or β [I-rule or otherwise]
$\sim(\alpha \lor \beta)$	$\sim\alpha$ and $\sim\beta$ [S-rule]
$(\alpha \supset \beta)$	$\sim\alpha$ or β [I-rule or otherwise]
$\sim(\alpha \supset \beta)$	α and $\sim\beta$ [S-rule]
$(\alpha \equiv \beta)$	$(\alpha \supset \beta)$ and $(\beta \supset \alpha)$ [S-rule]
$\sim(\alpha \equiv \beta)$	$(\alpha \lor \beta)$ and $\sim(\alpha \cdot \beta)$ [S-rule]

The truth of the items in the right column would insure the truth of the corresponding items in the left column.

The left column gives the nine complex wff forms possible in our system. The right column shows the smaller parts that these complex wff forms will have dissolved into by the time we reach the REFUTE step. Forms that dissolve using an S-rule always dissolve into the same smaller parts. Other forms can dissolve in multiple ways. Consider "$\sim(A \cdot B)$." We might be able to use an I-rule on this to derive "$\sim A$" or "$\sim B$." If not, then we can break "$\sim(A \cdot B)$" by assuming one part or its negation, which will (immediately or after using an I-rule) give us "$\sim A$" or "$\sim B$." So when we reach the REFUTE step, all not-blocked-off complex wffs will be *starred* or *broken*, and thus dissolved into the parts given above.

Each complex wff is true if the parts it dissolves into are true. We can check that this is so by going through the nine cases in the box. For example, $\sim\sim\alpha$ dissolves into α, and is true if α is true. $(\alpha \cdot \beta)$ dissolves into α and β, and is true if both of these are true. Similarly, $\sim(\alpha \cdot \beta)$ goes into $\sim\alpha$ or $\sim\beta$, and is true if either of these is true.

Our *refutation* is the set of all the simple not-blocked-off wffs and is consistent (or else we'd have applied RAA). This refutation gives truth conditions making all the other not-blocked-off wffs true too (since these other wffs dissolved into the simple parts that make up the refutation). So our refutation gives truth conditions making *all* the not-blocked-off lines true. But these lines include the premises and the denial of the conclusion (of the original argument). So our refutation gives truth conditions making the premises and the denial of the conclusion all true. So the argument is *invalid*. So if we correctly apply our strategy to a propositional argument and end in the REFUTE step, then the argument is invalid. This establishes premise 3.

Now we have to argue for premise 4: "We won't keep going endlessly." This is a concern, since the proof strategy for some systems can go into an endless loop (Section 9.5). That won't happen for us in propositional logic, since here the complexity of the wffs that are neither starred nor blocked off nor broken keeps decreasing as we go on, and eventually, if we don't get a proof, goes to zero, at which point we get a refutation. If you want the tedious details, you'll have to suffer through the next paragraph.

Let the *complexity level of a wff* be the number of instances in it of "$\cdot$," "$\vee$," "$\supset$," and "$\sim\sim$" (double negation), plus three times the number of instances of "$\equiv$." So *simple wffs* "A" and "$\sim$A" have complexity 0, "$(P \cdot Q)$," "$\sim(P \vee Q)$," "$\sim(\sim P \supset \sim Q)$," and "$\sim\sim P$" have complexity 1, "$((P \cdot Q) \supset R)$" has complexity 2, and "$(P \equiv Q)$" has complexity 3. Let the *complexity level of a stage of a proof* be the sum of the complexity levels of the lines to that point that are not either starred or blocked off or broken. When we START by assuming the opposite of the conclusion, the argument has a certain complexity level; for example, the sample problem at the start of Chapter 7 has complexity 3. Each S&I step (for example, going from "$(P \supset Q)$" and "P" to "Q" – or from "$(P \equiv Q)$" to "$(P \supset Q)$" and "$(Q \supset P)$") decreases the complexity level by at least one.[1] Each ASSUME (multiple assumption) will immediately or in the next step (through an application of an I-rule) reduce the complexity level by at least one.[2] RAA is trickier. If we apply RAA on the initial assumption, then the

---

[1] One rare occasions, an S&I step can reduce the complexity level by more than one. Suppose that we have "$(A \cdot B)$" and "$(B \cdot A)$" and simplify one of them into "A" and "B." The conjunction we simplify is *starred* and the other one is *broken*, so the complexity level is reduced by two.

[2] Suppose that we need to break "$(A \supset B)$" and so we assume "A"; then we can conclude "B" and star "$(A \supset B)$," which will reduce the complexity by one. Suppose that instead we assume "$\sim$A"; then "$(A \supset B)$" is broken, which immediately reduces the complexity by one.

proof is done, there is no endless loop, and so let's ignore this case. If we apply RAA on a non-initial assumption, then the complexity level may temporarily increase (due to our having to erase multiple stars); but the overall effect is to decrease the complexity from what it was before we made the non-initial assumption in question.[1] So the complexity level of the proof keeps decreasing. Since the proof starts with a finite complexity level which keeps going down, then, if we don't get a proof, then we'll eventually end with a complexity level of 0 – which (if we can derive nothing further) will move us to the REFUTE step which ends the strategy. So we won't get an endless loop.

So if we correctly apply our strategy to a propositional argument and the argument is valid, then we'll get a proof. This establishes completeness. So we've proved both soundness and completeness for our system:

Soundness: Every provable propositional argument is valid.
Completeness: Every valid propositional argument is provable.

From both together, we conclude that a propositional argument is provable in our system if and only if it's valid.

15.5   An axiomatic system

Our propositional system is an *inferential system*, since it uses mostly **inference rules** (rules that let us derive formulas from earlier formulas). It's also possible to systematize propositional logic as an *axiomatic system*, which uses mostly **axioms** (formulas that can be put on any line, regardless of earlier lines). Both approaches can be set up to be equally powerful – so that anything provable with one is provable with the other. Axiomatic systems tend to have a simpler structure, while inferential systems tend to be easier to use. The pioneers of symbolic logic used axiomatic systems.

I'll now sketch a version of an axiomatic system from *Principia Mathematica*.[2] We'll use the definitions of "wff," "premise," and "derived line" from our propositional system – and this definition of "proof":

> A *proof* is a vertical sequence of zero or more premises followed by one or more derived lines, where each derived line is an axiom or follows from earlier lines by the inference rule or the substitution of definitional equivalents.

[1] Recall that we make an additional assumption in order to break a complex wff. For example, we need to break "(A ⊃ B)" and so we assume "A." If this assumption dies, we conclude "~A" and then "(A ⊃ B)" is broken (which reduces the complexity level). If instead we assumed "~A," then when this assumption dies then we derive "A"; we then can use this with "(A ⊃ B)" to get "B" – and then star "(A ⊃ B)" (which reduces the complexity level). So when an additional assumption dies, then the complexity level is decreased from what it was before we made the assumption.

[2] Bertrand Russell and Alfred North Whitehead (Cambridge: Cambridge University Press, 1910).

There are four axioms; these axioms, and the inference rule and definitions, hold regardless of which wffs uniformly replace "A," "B," and "C":

Axiom 1. $((A \lor A) \supset A)$
Axiom 2. $(A \supset (A \lor B))$
Axiom 3. $((A \lor B) \supset (B \lor A))$
Axiom 4. $((A \supset B) \supset ((C \lor A) \supset (C \lor B)))$

The system has one inference rule (*modus ponens*): "$(A \supset B)$, $A \rightarrow B$." It takes "$\lor$" and "$\sim$" as undefined; it defines "$\supset$," "$\cdot$," and "$\equiv$" as follows:

Definition 1. $(A \supset B) = (\sim A \lor B)$
Definition 2. $(A \cdot B) = \sim(\sim A \lor \sim B)$
Definition 3. $(A \equiv B) = ((A \supset B) \cdot (B \supset A))$

The proof of "$(P \lor \sim P)$" in our inferential system is trivially simple (Section 15.3). The axiomatic proof is rather difficult:

1   ∴ $(((P \lor P) \supset P) \supset ((\sim P \lor (P \lor P)) \supset (\sim P \lor P)))$ {from axiom 4, substituting "$(P \lor P)$" for "A," "P" for "B," and "$\sim P$" for "C"}
2   ∴ $((P \lor P) \supset P)$ {from axiom 1, substituting "P" for "A"}
3   ∴ $((\sim P \lor (P \lor P)) \supset (\sim P \lor P))$ {from 1 and 2}
4   ∴ $(P \supset (P \lor P))$ {from axiom 2, substituting "P" for "A" and "P" for "B"}
5   ∴ $(\sim P \lor (P \lor P))$ {from 4, substituting things equivalent by definition 1}
6   ∴ $(\sim P \lor P)$ {from 3 and 5}
7   ∴ $((\sim P \lor P) \supset (P \lor \sim P))$ {from axiom 3, substituting "$\sim P$" for "A" and "P" for "B"}
8   ∴ $(P \lor \sim P)$ {from 6 and 7}

Since there's no automatic strategy, creating such proofs requires guesswork and intuition. And we might work for hours trying to prove an argument that's actually invalid. Axiomatic systems tend to be painful to use.

15.6   Gödel's theorem

Now we'll consider metalogic's most surprising discovery: Gödel's theorem.

Let's define a **formal system** (or *calculus*) to be an artificial language with notational grammar rules and notational rules for determining validity. Formal systems typically are either inferential (our usual approach) or axiomatic.

It's fairly easy to put propositional logic into a sound and complete formal system. Our inferential system does the job – as does the axiomatic system of Russell and Whitehead. In either system, a propositional argument is valid if and only if it's provable.

You might think that arithmetic could similarly be put into a sound and complete system. If we succeeded, we'd have an inferential or axiomatic system that could prove any truth of arithmetic but no falsehood. Then a statement of arithmetic would be true if and only if it's provable in the system.

But this is impossible. **Gödel's theorem** shows that we can't systematize arithmetic in this way. For any attempted formalization, one of two bad things will happen: some true statements of arithmetic won't be provable (making the system incomplete), or some false statements of arithmetic will be provable (making the system unsound). Gödel's theorem shows that any formal system attempting to encompass arithmetic will be incomplete or unsound.

You may find Gödel's theorem hard to believe. Arithmetic seems to be an area where everything can be proved one way or the other. But Kurt Gödel in 1931 showed the world that this was wrong. The reasoning behind his theorem is difficult; here I'll just try to give a glimpse of what it's about.[1]

What exactly is this "arithmetic" that we can't systematize? "Arithmetic" here is roughly like high-school algebra, but limited to positive whole numbers. It includes truths like these three:

$$2+2=4$$
$$\text{If } x+y=z, \text{ then } y+x=z.$$
$$\text{If } xy=18 \text{ and } x=2y, \text{ then } x=6 \text{ and } y=3.$$

More precisely, *arithmetic* is the set of truths and falsehoods that can be expressed using symbols for the vocabulary items in these boxes:

Mathematical vocabulary	*Logical vocabulary*
positive numbers: 1, 2, 3, … plus, times to the power of parentheses, equals	not, and, or, if-then variables: x, y, z, … every, some parentheses, equals

Gödel's theorem claims that no formal system with symbols for all the items in these two boxes can be both sound and complete.

The notions in our mathematical box can be reduced to a sound and complete formal system: one that we'll call the "number calculus." And the notions in our logical box can be reduced to a sound and complete formal system: our quantificational system. But combining these two systems produces a monster that can't be put into a sound and complete formal system.

We'll now construct a *number calculus* (NC) that uses seven symbols:

---

[1] My little book, *Gödel's Theorem Simplified* (Langham, Md.: University Press of America, 1984), tried to explain the theorem. Refer to this book for further information.

$$/ \quad + \quad \cdot \quad \wedge \quad (\quad) \quad =$$

"/" means "one" ("1"). We'll write 2 as "//" ("one one"), 3 as "///" ("one one one" – think of three sticks in a row), and so on. "+" is for "plus," "·" for "times," and "^" for "to the power of." Our seven symbols cover all the notions in our mathematical box.

Meaningful sequences of NC symbols are *numerals, terms,* and *wffs*:

> 1. Any string consisting of one or more instances of "/" is a *numeral.*
> 2. Every numeral is a *term.*
> 3. The result of joining any two terms by "+," "·," or "^" and enclosing the result in parentheses is a *term.*
> 4. The result of joining any two terms by "=" is a *wff.*

Here are examples (with the more usual equivalents below):

Numerals:	//	///////	
	2	7	
Terms:	///////	(// · //)	((/ + /) ^ //)
	7	2 · 2	$(1+1)^2$
Wffs:	/// = ///	(// + //) = ////	
	3=3	2+2=4	

Our NC will be able to prove just the true wffs. NC uses one axiom and six inference rules; here's our axiom (in which any numeral can replace "a"):

$$\text{Axiom:} \quad a = a$$

Any instance of this (any self-identity using the same numeral on both sides) is an axiom: "/=/" ["1=1"], "//=//" ["2=2"], "///=///" ["3=3"], and so on.

Our inference rules let us substitute one string of symbols for another. We'll use "↔" to say that we can substitute the symbols on either side for those on the other side. We have two rules for "plus" (where "a" and "b" in our inference rules stand for any numerals):

$$\text{R1.} \quad (a+/) \leftrightarrow a/$$
$$\text{R2.} \quad (a+/b) \leftrightarrow (a/+b)$$

For example, R1 lets us interchange "(///+/)" ["3+1"] and "////" ["4"]. R2 lets us interchange "(//+//)" ["2+2"] and "(///+/)" ["3+1"] – moving the "+" one "/" to the right. We'll see R3 to R6 in a moment.

An *NC proof* is a vertical sequence of wffs, each of which is either an axiom or else follows from earlier members by one of the inference rules R1 to R6. A *theorem* is any wff of a proof.

Using our axiom and inference rules R1 and R2, we can prove any true wff of NC that doesn't use "•" or "^." Here's a proof of "(//+//)=////" ["2+2=4"]:

1. ////=////   {from the axiom}
2. (///+/)=////   {from 1 using R1}
3. (//+//)=////   {from 2 using R2}

We start with a self-identity. We get line 2 by substituting "(///+/)" for "/////" (as permitted by rule R1). We get line 3 by further substituting "(//+//)" for "(///+/)" (as permitted by rule R2). So "(//+//)=////" is a theorem.

Here are our rules for "times" and "to the power of":

R3. (a • /) ↔ a
R4. (a • /b) ↔ ((a • b) + a)
R5. (a ^ /) ↔ a
R6. (a ^ /b) ↔ ((a ^ b) • a)

Our NC is sound and complete; any wff of NC is true if and only if it's provable in NC. This is easy to show, but we won't do the proof here.

Suppose we take our number calculus, add the symbols and inference rules of our quantificational logic, add a few more axioms and inference rules, and call the result the "arithmetic calculus" (AC). We could then symbolize any statement of arithmetic in AC. So we could symbolize these:

If x+y=z, then y+x=z.
=   ((x+y)=z ⊃ (y+x)=z)

If xy=8 and x=2y, then x=4 and y=2.
=   (((x•y)=//////// • x=(//•y)) ⊃ (x=//// • y=//))

x is even.
=   For some number y, x = 2 times y.
=   (∃y)x=(// • y)

x is prime.
=   For every number y and z, if x = y times z, then y=1 or z=1.
=   (y)(z)(x=(y • z) ⊃ (y=/ ∨ z=/))

Here's Goldbach's conjecture (which is still neither proved nor disproved):

Every even number is the sum of two primes.
=   (x)((∃y)x=(2 • y) ⊃ (∃x')(∃x'')(x=(x'+x'') • ((y)(z)(x'=(y • z)
    ⊃ (y=/ ∨ z=/)) • (y)(z)(x''=(y • z) ⊃ (y=/ ∨ z=/))))))

Gödel's theorem shows that any such arithmetic calculus has a fatal flaw: either it *can't* prove some arithmetic truths, or it *can* prove some arithmetic falsehoods. This flaw comes not from an accidental defect in our choice of axioms and inference rules, but from the fact that any such system can encode messages about itself.

To show how this works, it's helpful to use a version of AC with minimal vocabulary. The version that we've sketched so far uses these symbols:

$$/ \quad + \quad \cdot \quad \wedge \quad (\quad) \quad = \quad \sim \quad \vee \quad \supset \quad \exists \quad x, y, z, x', \ldots$$

We'll now economize. Instead of writing "$\wedge$" ("to the power of"), we'll write "$\cdot\cdot$." We'll drop "$\vee$" and "$\supset$," and express the same ideas using "$\sim$" and "$\cdot$" (Section 15.2). We'll use "n," "nn," "nnn," "nnnn," ... for our variables (instead of "x," "y," "z," "x'," ...). We'll drop "$\exists$," and write "$\sim$(n)$\sim$" instead of "($\exists$n)." Our minimal-vocabulary version of AC uses only eight symbols:

$$/ \quad + \quad \cdot \quad (\quad) \quad = \quad \sim \quad n$$

Any statement of arithmetic can be symbolized by combining these symbols.

Our strategy for proving Gödel's theorem goes as follows. First we give ID numbers to AC formulas. Then we see how AC formulas can encode messages about other AC formulas. Then we construct a special formula, called the Gödel formula G, that encodes this message about itself: "G isn't provable." G asserts its own unprovability; this is the key to Gödel's theorem.

It's easy to give ID numbers to AC formulas. Let's assign to each of the eight symbols a digit from 1 to 8:

Symbol:	/	+	$\cdot$	(	)	=	$\sim$	n
ID Number:	1	2	3	4	5	6	7	8

Thus "/" has ID # 1 and "+" has ID # 2. To get the ID number for a formula, we replace each symbol by its one-digit ID number. So we replace "/" by "1," "+" by "2," and so on. Here are two examples:

The ID # for: "/=/"   The ID # for: "(//+//)"
    is: 161   is: 4112115

The ID numbers follow patterns. For example, each numeral has an ID number consisting of all 1's:

Numeral:	/	//	///	////
ID Number:	1	11	111	1111

So we can say:

Formula # n is a numeral	if and only if	n consists of all 1's.

We can express the right-hand box as the equation "(nine-times-n plus one) equals some power of ten," or "$(\exists x)9n+1=10^x$," which can be symbolized in an AC formula.[1] This AC formula is true of any number n if and only if formula # n is a numeral. This is how system AC encodes messages about itself.

An AC theorem is any formula provable in AC. The ID numbers for theorems follow definite but complex patterns. It's possible to find an equation that's true of any number n if and only if formula # n is a theorem. If we let "n is …" represent this equation, we can say:

The equation in the right-hand box would be very complicated.

To make things more intuitive, let's pretend that all and only theorems have *odd* ID numbers. Then "n is odd" encodes "Formula # n is a theorem":

Formula # n is a theorem	if and only if	n is odd.

For example, "161 is odd" encodes the message that formula # 161 (which is "$/=/$") is a theorem:

Formula # 161 is a theorem	if and only if	161 is odd.

Then "n is even" would encode the message that formula # n is a non-theorem:

Formula # n is a non-theorem	if and only if	n is even.

Imagine that "485…" is some specific very large number. Let the following box represent the AC formula that says that 485… is even:

This formula would encode the following message:

Formula # 485… is a non-theorem.

---

[1] The AC formula for this equation is "$\sim(nn)\sim(((///////// \cdot n) + /) = (////////// \cdot\cdot nn))$." This formula has ID # 748857444111111111385215641111111111338855. It's important that the statements in our right-hand boxes can be symbolized in AC formulas with definite ID numbers. It isn't important that we write out the formulas or their ID numbers.

So the AC formula is true if and only if formula # 485... is a non-theorem. Now suppose this formula itself happens to have ID number 485.... Then the formula would be talking about itself, declaring that it itself is a non-theorem. This is what the Gödel formula G does. G, which itself has a certain ID number, encodes the message that the formula with this ID number is a non-theorem. G in effect says this:

G	G is not a theorem.

So G encodes the message "G is not a theorem." But this means that G is true if and only if it isn't a theorem.

So G is true if and only if it isn't provable. Now G, as a formula of arithmetic, is either true or false. Is G true? Then it isn't provable – and our system contains unprovable truths. Or maybe G is false? Then it's provable – and our system contains provable falsehoods. In either case, system AC is flawed.

We can't remove the flaw by adding further axioms or inference rules. No matter what we add to the arithmetic calculus, we can use Gödel's technique to find a formula of the system that's true-but-unprovable or false-but-provable. Hence arithmetic can't be reduced to any sound and complete formal system.

This completes our sketch of the reasoning behind Gödel's proof. To fill in the details would require answering two further questions:

- Consider the equation that's true of any number n if and only if formula # n is a theorem. This equation would have to be much more complicated than "n is odd." How can we produce this equation?
- If we have this equation, how do we then produce a formula with a given number that says that the formula with that number is a non-theorem?

The answers to these questions are too complicated to go into here. The important thing is that the details can be worked out; we won't here worry about how to work them out.[1]

Most people find the last two chapters surprising. We tend to think that *everything* can be proved in math, and that *nothing* can be proved in ethics. But Gödel's theorem shows that not everything can be proved in math. And our golden-rule formalization shows that some important ideas (like the golden rule) can be proved in ethics. Logic can surprise us.

---

[1] For the technical details, see my *Gödel's Theorem Simplified* (Langham, Md.: University Press of America, 1984).

CHAPTER 16
History of Logic

Logic was born in ancient Greece, and then reborn about a hundred years ago. Since then, logic has grown and expanded even more, and has contributed to the emergence of the computer age. We can better understand and appreciate logic by studying its history.

16.1 Ancient logic

The formal study of valid reasoning began with **Aristotle** (384–322 BC) in ancient Greece. An unprecedented emphasis on reasoning prepared for Aristotle's logic. Greeks used complex reasoning in geometry, to prove results like the Pythagorean theorem. Sophists taught rich young men how to gain power by arguing effectively (and often by verbal trickery). The early philosophers Parmenides and Heraclitus reasoned about being and non-being, anticipating later disputes about the law of non-contradiction, and Zeno reasoned about paradoxes. Socrates and Plato gave models of careful philosophical reasoning, testing ideas by trying to derive absurdities from them and seeking beliefs that could be held consistently after a careful examination.

Of course, reasoning is an important ability of humans as such, and did not begin in ancient Greece. Our reasoning ability raises big questions. Is it biologically based, built into our brains by evolution because it aided survival? Or does our reasoning ability have a divine origin, since we are made in the "image and likeness" of an intelligent God? Or do both explanations have a place and fit together harmoniously? Logic raises fascinating issues for other disciplines.

As an area of study, logic started with Aristotle. As far as we know, he was the first to formulate a correct principle of inference, to use letters for terms, and to construct an axiomatic system. He focused on the logic of "all," "no," and "some." He created syllogistic logic (Chapter 2), which studies arguments like these (which use statements of the form "all A is B," "no A is B," "some A is B," or "some A is not B"):

Valid argument	→	All humans are mortal.	all H is M
		All Greeks are humans.	all G is H
		∴ All Greeks are mortal.	∴ all G is M

This argument is *valid* because of its formal structure, as given by the formulation on the right; any argument having this same structure will be valid. If we change the structure, we may get an invalid argument, like this one:

Invalid		All Romans are mortal.	all R is M
argument	➔	All Greeks are mortal.	all G is M
		∴ All Greeks are Romans.	∴ all G is R

This is *invalid* because its form is wrong. Aristotle defended valid forms by deriving them from forms he saw as self-evidently valid; he criticized invalid forms by showing that some substitution for the letters leads to true premises and a false conclusion.

Aristotle's logic of syllogisms is about *logic in a narrow sense*, since it deals with what follows from what. Aristotle also pursued other topics that connect with appraising arguments, such as definitions and fallacies; these are about *logic in a broader sense*.

Aristotle proposed two principles of thought. His **law of non-contradiction** states that the same property cannot at the same time both belong and not belong to the same object in the same respect. So "S is P" and "S is not P" cannot both be true at the same time – unless we take "S" or "P" differently in the two statements. Aristotle saw this law as so certain that it could not be proved by anything more certain; he thought that not all knowledge could be demonstrated, since otherwise we'd need an infinity of arguments, whereby every premise of every argument is proved by a further argument. Those who deny the law of non-contradiction assume it in their deliberations; to drive this point home, we might pretend to agree that contradictions are fine and then bombard them with contradictions until they plead for us to stop. Aristotle also supported the **law of excluded middle**, that either "S is P" or "S is not P" is true. Some deviant logicians today dispute both laws (Chapter 17).

Aristotle also investigated the logic of "necessary" and "possible," which is now called *modal logic* (Chapters 10 and 11). In an intriguing section, he discusses future contingents (future events that may or may not happen). Suppose that there may be a sea battle tomorrow. If "There will be a sea battle tomorrow" (abbreviated as "S" below) is *now* either true or false, this seems to imply that whether the battle occurs is a matter of necessity:

> Either it's true that S or it's false that S.
> If it's true that S, then it's necessary that S.
> If it's false that S, then it's necessary that not-S.
> ∴ Either it's necessary that S or it's necessary that not-S.

Aristotle rejected the conclusion, since he thought there was no necessity either way. He seemed to deny the first premise and thus the universal validity of the law of excluded middle (which he elsewhere defends); if we interpret him this way (which is controversial) then he anticipated many-valued logic in positing a third truth value besides true and false (Section 17.1). But an alternative solution is possible. Many think that premises 2 and 3 have a box-inside/box-outside ambiguity (Section 10.1): taking them as "$(A \supset \Box B)$" makes them doubtful while taking them as "$\Box(A \supset B)$" makes the argument invalid.

After Aristotle, **Stoics** and others developed a logic that focused on "if-then," "and," and "or," much like our propositional logic (Chapters 6 and 7). Stoic logicians defended, for example, an important form of inference that later came to be called *modus tollens* (denying mode):

Valid *argument*	➜	If your view is correct, then such and such is true. Such and such is false. ∴ Your view is not correct.	If C then S Not-S ∴ Not-C

Stoic logicians also investigated modal logic. Unlike logicians today, they often took "necessary" and "possible" in a temporal sense, as something like "true at all times" and "true at some times." They were concerned with whether there was a strong modal argument for *fatalism*, the view that every event happens of inherent necessity (see problem 10 of Section 10.3b).

There was much debate over how to understand the conditional "If A then B" (Section 17.4). Philo of Megara saw "If A then B" as true if and only if it's not *now* the case that A is true and B is false; this fits the modern truth table for "if-then" but led to controversy. Diodorus Chronos saw "If A then B" as true if and only if it's *never* at any time the case that A is true while B is false.

At first, the logics of Aristotle and the Stoics were seen as rivals. They differed in three main ways:

- Aristotle focused on "all," "no," and "some." Stoics focused on "if-then," "and," and "or."
- Aristotle used letter variables and expressed arguments as long conditionals, like "If all A is B, and all C is A, then all C is B." Stoics used number variables and expressed arguments as sets of statements, like "If 1 then 2. But not-2. Therefore, not-1."
- Aristotle saw logic not as part of philosophy but rather as a general tool for any kind of thinking. Stoics saw logic as one of the three branches of philosophy (the other two being physics and ethics). But both agreed that students should study logic early, before going into other areas.

Later thinkers combined the two approaches into what is now called **traditional logic**. For the next two thousand years or so, the logic of Aristotle, with additions from the Stoics, ruled in the Western world.

Roughly at the same time, another tradition of logic rose up independently in India, China, and Tibet. This is sometimes called **Buddhist logic**, even though it was pursued also by Hindus and others. It studied many of the areas that were important in the West, including inference, fallacies, and language.

A common pattern in Buddhist logic is the five-line syllogism:

> Here there is fire, {conclusion}
>   because there is smoke. {premise}
> Wherever there is smoke there is fire, as in a kitchen. {rule & example}
> Here there is smoke. {premise}
> ∴ Here there is fire. {conclusion}

The first two lines here repeat the last two; the last three lines express a valid deductive inference:

> All cases of smoke are cases of fire.
> This is a case of smoke.
> ∴ This is a case of fire.

This reconstruction omits "as in a kitchen," which suggests an inductive justification of the universal premise (Chapter 5); in our experience of smoke and fire (as in the kitchen), smoke always seems to involve fire.

The Eastern logic tradition is as yet poorly understood in the West; it covers many thinkers over many centuries, with few texts translated into Western languages and many texts being difficult to interpret. Some commentators emphasize similarities between East and West; they see human thinking as essentially the same everywhere. Others emphasize differences and caution against imposing a Western framework on Eastern thought. And some deviant logicians see the Eastern tradition as very congenial to their views.

Many see the East as more mystical than logical; for example, Zen Buddhism delights in using paradoxes (like the sound of one hand clapping) to move us beyond logical thinking toward a mystical enlightenment. But East and West both have logical and mystical elements. Sometimes these elements come together in the same individual, as in Ludwig Wittgenstein, who in the early 20th century invented truth tables but also had a strongly mystical side.

16.2 Medieval logic

Medieval logicians carried on the basic framework of Aristotle and the Stoics, as logic became increasingly more important in higher education.

The Christian thinker **Boethius** (480–524) was important in the transition to the Middle Ages. He wrote on logic, including commentaries; he clearly explained the modal box-inside/box-outside ambiguity as he defended the compatibility of divine foreknowledge with human freedom (examples 4 and 14 of Section 10.3b). He also translated Aristotle's logic into Latin. Most of these translated works were lost until the 12th century, except for *Categories* and *On Interpretation*, which became the main source of logic for several centuries; the tradition based on these was later called the *logica vetus* (old logic).

The Arab world dominated in logic from about 800–1200. Some Arab logicians were Christian, but most were Muslim; both groups saw logic as an important tool for theology and for areas like medicine. First they focused on translating Aristotle into Arabic; then they wrote commentaries, textbooks, and original works on logic and other areas. They worked on topics like modal logic, conditionals, universals, predication, existence, and syllogistic statements. Baghdad and Moorish Spain were centers of logic studies.

The 11th and 12th centuries brought a resurgence of logic in Christian Europe, first with Anselm and Peter Abelard, and later with the appearance in Latin of more of Aristotle's logical works (particularly the *Prior Analytics*, *Posterior Analytics*, *Topics*, and *Sophistical Refutations*); the *logica nova* (new logic) was based on these latter works. There was much interest in the problem of universals and in how terms signify. Peter of Spain and William of Sherwood wrote influential logic textbooks.

The clever Barbara-Celarent verse became a tool for instructing students about Aristotle's logic:

Barbara, Celarent, Darii, Ferioque, prioris;
Cesare, Camestres, Festino, Baroco, secundae;
tertia, Darapti, Disamis, Datisi, Felapton,
Bocardo, Ferison, habet; quarta insuper addit
Bramantip, Camenes, Dimaris, Fesapo, Fresison.

Each capitalized name here represents a valid syllogism. The vowels "A," "I," "E," and "O" in the names signify specific sentence forms ("negative" is misspelled below to make the mnemonic work in English):

A	all – is –	A ffirmative universal
I	some – is –	aff I rmative particular
E	no – is –	n E gotive universal
O	some – is not –	neg O tive particular

So "Barbara," with AAA vowels, has three "all" statements:

all M is P
all S is M
∴ all S is P

$\frac{MP}{SM}$ = figure 1

Aristotelian syllogisms have two premises. It's traditional to use "M," "S," and "P" for the terms. The *middle term* "M" is common to both premises; the *predicate* "P" of the conclusion also occurs in the first premise, while the *subject* "S" of the conclusion also occurs in the second premise. There are four possible figures, or arrangements of the premise letters:

1 (prioris)	2 (secundae)	3 (tertia)	4 (quarta)
MP	PM	MP	PM
SM	SM	MS	MS

The four axioms of Aristotle's system are the valid forms of the first figure –
Barbara, Celarent, Darii, and Ferio:

Barbara	Celarent	Darii	Ferio
all M is P	no M is P	all M is P	no M is P
all S is M	all S is M	some S is M	some S is M
∴ all S is P	∴ no S is P	∴ some S is P	∴ some S is not P

The other 15 forms can be derived as theorems. The consonants give clues on
how to do this; for example, "m" tells us to switch the order of the premises.

Thomas Aquinas (1224–74), the most influential medieval philosopher, had
little impact on the development of logic; but he made much use of logic in his
writings. In light of the sheer bulk of his writings and his heavy stress on
argumentation, he may have produced a greater number of philosophical arguments than anyone else who has ever lived.

Fourteenth-century logicians include William of Ockham and Jean Buridan.
Ockham is best known for "Ockham's Razor" (that we should accept the
simplest theory that adequately explains the data) and his attempt to avoid
metaphysics in the analysis of language; but he also developed principles of
modal logic. Buridan is best known for his claim that a dog placed exactly
between two bowls of food would choose one randomly; but he also formulated
the standard rules for valid syllogisms, one version of which says that a
syllogism is *valid* just if it satisfies all of these conditions:

- Every term distributed in the conclusion must be distributed in the premises. (A term is *distributed* in a statement just if the statement makes some
  claim about every entity that the term refers to; equivalently, a distributed
  term is one that occurs just after "all" or anywhere after "no" or "not.")
- The middle term must be distributed in at least one premise. (The *middle
  term* is the term common to both premises; if we violate this rule, we commit the fallacy of the *undistributed middle*.)
- If the conclusion is negative, exactly one premise must be negative. (A
  statement is *negative* if it contains "no" or "not"; otherwise it is positive.)
- If the conclusion is positive, both premises must be positive.

Logic was important in the Middle Ages – both in philosophical writings and
in higher education. The world's first universities were then springing up in
Europe, and these put a strong emphasis on logic. One sign of the influence of
medieval logic is the persistence of Latin terms (like *modus ponens, a priori/a
posteriori*, and *de re/de dicto*) even today.

16.3 Enlightenment logic

Aristotelian logic dominated until the end of the 19th century. Several logicians contributed to syllogistic logic; for example, Leonhard Euler diagrammed "all A is B" by putting an A-circle inside a larger B-circle, Lewis Carroll entertained us with silly syllogisms and points about logic in *Alice in Wonderland*, and John Venn gave us diagrams for testing syllogisms (Section 2.6). But most logicians would have agreed with the philosopher Immanuel Kant, who claimed that Aristotle had invented and perfected logic; nothing else of fundamental importance could be learned or added, although we might improve teaching techniques. Kant would have been shocked to learn about the revolution in logic that came about a hundred years after him.

The German thinkers Georg W. F. Hegel and Karl Marx provided a side current. Hegel proposed that logic should recognize contradictions in nature as the key to understanding how thought evolves historically; one view provokes its opposite, and then the two tend to come together in a higher synthesis. Marx also saw contradictions in the world as real; he applied this idea to political struggles and revolution. Critics objected that the *dialectical logic* of Hegel and Marx confuses conflicting properties in the world (like hot/cold or capitalist/proletariat) with logical self-contradictions (like the same object being both white and, in the same sense and time and respect, also non-white).

The philosopher Gottfried Leibniz, one of the inventors of calculus, had insight into future developments. He proposed the idea of a symbolic language that would reduce reasoning to something like arithmetic calculation. If controversies arose, the parties could take up their pencils and say, "Let us calculate." Leibniz created a logical notation much like that of Boole (and much earlier than Boole); but his work on this was published after Boole.

Many thinkers tried to invent an algebraic notation for logic. Augustus De Morgan proposed that we symbolize "all A is B" as "A))B" and "some A is B" as "A()B"; a letter on the concave side of the parenthesis is distributed. He became known for his *De Morgan laws* for propositional logic:

> Not both A and B   =   Either not-A or not-B
> Not either A or B   =   Both not-A and not-B

De Morgan complained that the logic of his day could not handle relational arguments like "All dogs are animals; therefore all heads of dogs are heads of animals" (problem 25 of Section 9.5b – which our logic can handle).

The **Boolean algebra** of **George Boole** (1815–64) was a breakthrough, since it allowed something like mathematical calculation to be used to check the correctness of inferences. Boole used letters for sets; so "M" might stand for the set of mortals and "H" for the set of humans. Putting two letters together represents the *intersection* of the sets; so "HM" represents the set of those who are *both human and mortal*. Then we can symbolize "All humans are mortal" as "H = HM," which says that the set of humans = the set of those who are both human and mortal. We can symbolize a syllogism as a series of equations:

	All humans are mortal.	H = HM
Valid →	All Greeks are humans.	G = GH
argument	∴ All Greeks are mortal.	∴ G = GM

In the algebraic version, we can derive the conclusion from the premises by substituting equals for equals. Start with the second premise: G = GH. Cross out "H" and write "HM" (the first premise says H = HM); this give us G = GHM. Then cross out "GH" and write "G" (the second premise says G = GH); this gives us G = GM.

Boolean formulas, like those on the left below (which use a later symbolism), can be interpreted to be about sets or about statements:

-A	The set of non-As	Not-A
A∩B	The intersection of sets A and B	A and B
A∪B	The union of sets A and B	A or B

So if "A" represents the set of animals, then "-A" is the set of non-animals; but if "A" represents the statement that Aristotle is a logician, then "-A" is the statement that Aristotle is not a logician. The same laws cover both interpretations; for example, "A∩B = B∩A" works regardless of whether we are talking about sets or statements. When we speak of *Boolean operators* today, we often have in mind the statement interpretation; such Boolean operators include "and," "or," "not," and other propositional connectives.

Boole, who is considered the father of *mathematical logic*, thought that logic belonged with mathematicians instead of philosophers. But the effect of his work was to make logic a subject shared by both groups, each getting the slice of the action that fits it better. While Boole's work was important, a far greater revolution in logic was soon to come.

16.4   Frege and Russell

Gottlob Frege (1848–1925) created modern logic with his 1879 *Begriffsschrift* ("Concept Writing"). This slim book of 88 pages introduced a symbolism that, for the first time, let us combine in every conceivable way the "all," "no," and "some" of Aristotle with the "if-then," "and," and "or" of the Stoics. So we can now symbolize forms like "If everything that is A or B is then C and D, then everything that is non-D is non-A." Thus the gap between Aristotle and the Stoics was overcome in a higher synthesis. Frege also showed how to analyze arguments with relations (like "x loves y") and multiple quantifiers. So we can now show that "There is someone that everyone loves" entails "Everyone loves someone" – but not conversely. Frege presented his logic as a genuine *formal system*, with purely notational rules for determining the grammaticality of formulas and the correctness of proofs.

Frege's work, despite its importance, was largely ignored until **Bertrand Russell** (1872–1970) came to praise it in the early years of the 20th century. Part of the problem was that Frege used a strange and unintuitive symbolism; few people took the time to master his many pages of complex, tree-like diagrams. Frege used lines for "not," "if-then," and "all":

Not-A   If A then B   For all x

———┬—A   ┬—B   —x—
                    └—A

These combine to symbolize forms like "Not all A is non-B," which in our quantificational symbolism is "$\sim(x)(Ax \supset \sim Bx)$":

Not all A is non-B   =   ———┬—x—┬—┬—Bx
                                   └—Ax

This was also his way to write "Some A is B" (which is "$(\exists x)(Ax \cdot Bx)$" in our symbolism); he had no simpler notation for "some" or "and."

Logic was part of Frege's project of showing that arithmetic is reducible to logic; he wanted to show that all the basic concepts of arithmetic (like numbers and addition) are definable in purely logical terms and that all the truths of arithmetic are provable using just axioms and inference rules of logic. Frege used set theory. In particular, he used a seemingly harmless axiom that every condition on x (like "x is a cat") picks out a set containing just those elements that satisfy that condition. For example, the condition "x is a cat" picks out the set of cats. But consider that some sets are members of themselves (the set of abstract objects is itself an abstract object) while other sets are not (the set of cats is not itself a cat). By Frege's axiom, "x is not a member of itself" picks out the set containing just those things that are not members of themselves. Call this "set R." So any x is a member of R, if and only if x is not a member of x (here "$\in$" means "is a member of" and "$\notin$" means "is not a member of"):

For all x, $x \in R$ if and only if $x \notin x$.

Bertrand Russell asked in a 1902 letter to Frege: What about set R itself? By the above principle, R is a member of R, if and only if R is not a member of R:

$R \in R$ if and only if $R \notin R$.

So is R a member of itself? If it is, then it isn't – and if it isn't, then it is; either way we get a contradiction. Since this contradiction, called **Russell's paradox**, was provable in Frege's system, that system was flawed. Frege was crushed, since his life work collapsed. His attempts to fix the problem weren't successful. He never fully recovered.

Russell greatly admired Frege and his groundbreaking work in logic; the two minds worked along similar lines. But the paradox showed that Frege's approach needed fixing. So Russell, with his former teacher Alfred North Whitehead, worked to develop logic and set theory in a way that avoided the contradiction. They also developed a more intuitive symbolism (much like what we use in this book), based on the work of Giuseppe Peano. The result was the massive *Principia Mathematica*, which was published in 1910–1913. *Principia* had a huge influence and became the standard formulation of the new logic.

16.5   After *Principia*

Classical symbolic logic includes propositional and quantificational logic (Chapters 6 to 9). An approach to these is "classical" if it accords with the systems of Frege and Russell about which arguments are valid, regardless of differences in symbolization and proof techniques. Classical symbolic logic gradually became the new orthodoxy in the 20th century, replacing the Aristotelian logic that had dominated for over 20 centuries.

Much of the work in logic that followed *Principia Mathematica* revolved around classical symbolic logic. Different proof techniques were developed; while Frege and Russell used an axiomatic approach, later logicians invented inferential and truth-tree methods that were easier to use. Different ways of symbolizing arguments were developed, including the "Polish notation" of a remarkable school of logic that was strong in Poland between the world wars. Ludwig Wittgenstein and Emil Post independently invented truth tables, which clarified our understanding of logical connectives (like "if-then," "and," and "or") and led to a criterion of validity based on semantics – on the meaning of the connectives and how they contribute to truth or falsity; Alfred Tarski and others expanded the semantic approach to quantificational logic.

Much work was done in **metalogic**, which is the study of logical systems (Chapter 15). **Kurt Gödel** showed that Russell's axiomatization of classical logic was, given certain semantic assumptions, correct: just the right things were provable. But he also showed, against Frege and Russell, that arithmetic cannot be reduced to any formal system: no consistent set of axioms and inference rules would suffice to prove all arithmetic truths; this result, called **Gödel's theorem**, is perhaps the most striking and surprising result of 20th-century logic. Alonzo Church showed that the problem of determining validity in quantificational logic cannot be reduced to an mechanical algorithm. There was also much activity in the neighboring area of *set theory*, which after Russell's paradox became increasingly complex and controversial.

There was also much work in **philosophy of logic** (Chapter 18), which deals with philosophical questions about logic, such as: Are logical truths dependent on human conventions (so different conventions might produce different logical truths) or on the objective nature of reality (perhaps giving us the framework of any possible language that would be adequate to describe reality)? Can logic help us to clarify metaphysical issues, such as what kinds of entity ultimately exist? Should we assume abstract entities (like properties and propositions) when we do logic? How can we resolve logical paradoxes (such as Russell's paradox and the liar paradox)? Are logical truths empirical or *a priori*? Does logic distort ordinary beliefs and ordinary language, or does it correct them? What is the definition and scope of logic?

Logic was important in the development of computers. The basic insight behind computers is that logical functions like "and" and "or" can be simulated electrically by *logic gates*; this idea goes back to the American logician Charles Sanders Peirce in the 1880s and was rediscovered by Claude Shannon in 1938. If we connect a large number of logic gates in the right way and add memory and input-output devices, we get a computer. Logicians like John von Neumann, Alan Turing, and Arthur Burks helped design the first large-scale electronic computers. Since logic is important for computers, in both hardware and software, it's studied today in computer science departments. So now three main departments study logic – philosophy, mathematics, and computer science – each from a different perspective.

Logic today is also an important part of *cognitive science*, which is an interdisciplinary approach to thought that includes areas like linguistics, psychology, biology (especially areas dealing with brain and sensory systems), computers (especially artificial intelligence), and other branches of philosophy (especially epistemology and philosophy of mind).

As classical symbolic logic became the new orthodoxy, it started to be questioned. Two types of non-classical logic came into being. **Supplementary logics** accepted that classical logic was fine as far as it went but needed to be supplemented by other logics in order to deal, for example, with "necessary" and "possible." **Deviant logics** thought that classical logic was wrong on some points and needed to be changed.

The most important *supplementary logic* is modal logic, which deals with "necessary" and "possible" (Chapters 10 and 11). Ancient and medieval logicians pursued modal logic; but 20th-century logicians mostly ignored it until C. I. Lewis started publishing on it in 1932. Modal logic then became controversial. Willard Van Orman Quine argued that it was based on a confusion; he contended that logical necessity was unclear and that quantified modal logic led to an objectionable metaphysics of necessary properties. There was lively debate on modal logic for many years. Then, in 1959, Saul Kripke presented a possible-worlds way to explain modal logic; this made more sense of it and gave it new respect among logicians. Possible worlds have proved useful in other areas and are now a common tool in logic; and several philoso-phers (including Alvin Plantinga) have defended a metaphysics of necessary properties. Today, modal logic is a well-established extension of classical logic.

Other extensions apply to ethics ("A ought to be done" or "A is good"), theory of knowledge ("X believes that A" or "X knows that A"), the part-whole relationship ("X is a part of Y"), temporal relationships (about "It will be true at some future time that A" and "It was true at some past time that A"), and other areas (Chapters 12 to 14). Most logicians would agree that classical logic needs to be supplemented in order to apply to certain kinds of argument.

Deviant logics say that classical symbolic logic is wrong on some points and needs to be changed (Chapter 17). Some propose using more than two truth values. Maybe we need a third truth value for "half-true": so "1" = "true," "0" = "false," and "½" = "half-true"; truth tables and alternative propositional logics have been set up on this many-valued basis. Or maybe we need a fuzzy-logic range of truth values, from completely true (1.00) to completely false (0.00); then statements would be more or less true. Or perhaps "A" and "not-A" can both be false (intuitionist logic) or can both be true (paraconsistent logic). Or perhaps the classical approach to "if-then" is flawed; some suggested logics even reject *modus ponens* ("If A then B, A ∴ B") and *modus tollens* ("If A then B, not-B ∴ not-A"). These and other deviant logics have been proposed. Today there is much questioning of basic logical principles.

This brief history of logic has focused on deductive logic and related areas. There has also been much interest in informal logic (Chapters 3 and 4), induct-ive logic (Chapter 5), and history of logic (this chapter).

So logic has a complex history – from Aristotle and the Stoics in ancient Greece, through the Middle Ages and the Enlightenment, to the turmoil of the 19th century and the transformation of logic with Frege and Russell, and into the 20th- and 21ˢᵗ-century development of classical and non-classical logics and the birth of the computer age.[1]

---

[1] For further study on the history of logic, I suggest P. H. Nidditch's *The Development of Mathe-matical Logic* (London: Routledge & Kegan Paul, 1962) and, for primary sources, Irving M. Copi and James A. Gould's *Readings on Logic* (New York: Macmillan, 1964). Also useful are William C. Kneale and Martha Kneale's *The Development of Logic* (Oxford: Clarendon, 1962) and Joseph M. Bocheński's *A History of Formal Logic*, ed. and trans. Ivo Thomas (Notre Dame, Ind.: University of Notre Dame Press, 1961).

CHAPTER 17

Deviant Logics

Deviant logics reject standard assumptions. Most logicians since Aristotle have assumed, for example, that statements are either true or false, but not both, and that *true* and *false* are the only truth values. Deviant logics question such ideas. Maybe we need more than two truth values (many-valued logic). Or maybe "A" and "not-A" can both be true (paraconsistent logic) or can both be false (intuitionist logic). Or maybe the standard IF-THEN inferences are mistaken (relevance logic).

Deviant logics are controversial. Some are happy that logic is becoming, in some circles, as controversial as other areas of philosophy. Others defend orthodox logic and see deviant logics as the road to intellectual chaos; they fear what would happen if thinkers could not take it for granted that *modus ponens* and *modus tollens* are valid and that contradictions are to be avoided.

17.1 Many-valued logic

Most logicians assume that there are only two truth values: *true* and *false*. Our propositional logic in Chapter 6 accepts this "bivalence principle," symbolizing true as "1" and false as "0." This is consistent with there being truth-value gaps for sentences that are meaningless (like "Glurklies glurkle") or vague (like "Her shirt is white," when it's between white and gray). Logic needn't worry about such sentences, since arguments using them are already defective; so we can just stipulate that capital letters stand for statements that *are* true or false.

Many-valued logics accept more than two truth values. Three-valued logic might use "1" for true, "0" for false, and "½" for *half-true*. This last category might apply to statements that are unknowable, or too vague to be true-or-false, or plausible but unproved, or meaningless, or about future events not yet decided either way. A three-valued truth table for NOT looks like this:

P	~P	
0	1	If P is false, then ~P is true.
½	½	If P is half-true, then ~P is half-true.
1	0	If P is true, then ~P is false.

This table shows how the other connectives work:

P	Q	$(P \cdot Q)$	$(P \vee Q)$	$(P \supset Q)$	$(P \equiv Q)$
0	0	0	0	1	1
0	½	0	½	1	½
0	1	0	1	1	0
½	0	0	½	½	½
½	½	½	½	1	1
½	1	½	1	1	½
1	0	0	1	0	0
1	½	½	1	½	½
1	1	1	1	1	1

An AND takes the value of the lower conjunct, and an OR takes the value of the higher disjunct. An IF-THEN is true if the consequent is at least as true as the antecedent and is half-true if the consequent is a little less true than the antecedent. An IF-AND-ONLY-IF is true if both parts have the same truth value and is half-true if they differ a little.

Given these truth tables, some standard laws of logic fail. "$(P \vee {\sim}P)$" (the law of excluded middle) and "${\sim}(P \cdot {\sim}P)$" (the law of non-contradiction) would sometimes be only half true. And "$(P \supset Q)$" would not be equivalent to "${\sim}(P \cdot {\sim}Q)$," since they differ in truth value if P and Q are both ½. We could avoid all these results by making "$(\frac{1}{2} \vee \frac{1}{2})$" true and "$(\frac{1}{2} \cdot \frac{1}{2})$" false; but then "P" would strangely not be logically equivalent to "$(P \vee P)$" or to "$(P \cdot P)$."

Fuzzy logic proposes that we accept an infinity of truth values; these can be represented by real numbers between 0.00 (fully false) and 1.00 (fully true). Then we might define a "valid argument" as one in which, if the premises have at least a certain truth value (perhaps .9), then so does the conclusion; *modus ponens* then fails (since if "A" and "$(A \supset B)$" are both .9, then "B" might be less than .9) as do other logical principles. Some propose an even fuzzier logic whose truth values are vague values like "very true" or "slightly true."

Fuzzy logic is used in devices like clothes dryers to permit precise control. A crisp-logic dryer might have a rule that if the shirts are dry then the heat is turned off; a fuzzy-logic dryer might say that if the shirts are dry to degree n then the heat is turned down to degree n. We could get the same result using standard logic and a relation "Dxn" that means "shirt x is dry to degree n" – thus moving from "degrees of truth" to qualifications on the predicate "dry" (which applies in a more-or-less fashion).

Opponents say many-valued logic is weird and arbitrary and has little application to real-life arguments. Even if this is so, the many-valued approach has other applications. It can be used, for example, in computer memory systems with more than two states. And it can be used to show the independence of axioms for propositional logic (Section 15.5); an axiom can be shown to be independent of the other axioms of a certain system if, for example, the other axioms (and theorems derived from these) always have a value of "7" on a given truth-table scheme, while this axiom sometimes has a value of "6."

17.2 Paraconsistent logic

Aristotle's **law of non-contradiction** states that the same property cannot at the same time both belong and not belong to the same object in the same respect. So "S is P" and "S is not P" cannot both be true at the same time – unless we take "S" or "P" differently in the two statements. Aristotle saw this law as certain but unprovable. He claimed that those who deny the law of non-contradiction assume it in their deliberations; wouldn't these same people complain if we bombarded them with contradictions?

Aristotle mentions Heraclitus as denying the law of non-contradiction. The 19th-century German thinker Georg W. F. Hegel proposed that logic should recognize contradictions in nature as the key to understanding how thought evolves historically; one view provokes its opposite, and then the two tend to come together in a higher synthesis. Karl Marx also saw contradictions in the world as real; he applied this idea to political struggles and revolution. Critics object that the *dialectical logic* of Hegel and Marx often confuses conflicting properties in the world (like hot/cold or capitalist/proletariat) with logical self-contradictions (like the same object being both white and, in the same sense and time and respect, also non-white).

In standard propositional logic, the law of non-contradiction is symbolized as "$\sim$(P $\cdot$ $\sim$P)" and is accepted as a *truth-table tautology* – a formula that is true in all possible cases:

P	$\sim$(P $\cdot$ $\sim$P)
0	1
1	1

"This is false: I went to Paris and I did not go to Paris."

"P and not-P" is always false in standard logic, which presupposes that "P" stands for the same statement throughout. English is looser and lets us shift the meaning of a phrase in the middle of a sentence. "I went to Paris and I did not go to Paris" may express a truth if it means "I went to Paris (in that I landed once at the Paris airport) – but I did not really go there (in that I saw almost nothing of the city)." Because of the shift in meaning, this would better translate as "(P $\cdot$ $\sim$Q)," which wouldn't violate the law of non-contradiction.

Some recent logicians, like Graham Priest, claim that *sometimes* a statement and its contradictory are both true. Such **dialethist** logicians do not say that *all* statements and their denials are true – but just that *some* are. Here are examples where "A and not-A" might be claimed to be true:

- "We do and do not step into the same river." (Heraclitus)
- "God is spirit and is not spirit." (the mystic Pseudo-Dionysius)
- "The moving ball is here and not here." (Hegel and Marx)
- "The round square is both round and not-round." (Meinong)
- "The one hand claps and does not clap." (Eastern paradox)
- "Sara is a child and not a child." (paradoxical speech)
- "What I am telling you now is false." (liar paradox)
- "The electron did and did not go in the hole." (quantum physics)

Most logicians contend that these are not genuine cases of "A and not-A," at least if they are taken in a sensible way, since we must take the two instances of "A" to represent different ideas. For example, "Sara is a child and not a child" can be sensible only if it really means something like "Sara is a *child-in-age* but not a *child-in-sophistication*." Paradoxical speech, although sometimes nicely provocative, does not make sense if taken literally. Dialethists try to show that some of their allegedly true self-contradictions resist such analyses.

In standard propositional logic we can, from a single self-contradiction, deduce the truth of every statement and its denial. But then, if we believed a self-contradiction and also believed all the logical consequences of our beliefs, we'd contract the dreaded disease of *contradictitis* – whereby we'd believe every statement and also its contradictory – bringing chaos to human speech and thought. Here's an intuitive derivation showing how, given the contradictory premises "A is true" and "A is not true," we can deduce any arbitrary statement "B" (this "A, ~A ∴ B" inference is called the **explosion principle**):

1   A is true. {premise}
2   A is not true. {premise}
3 ∴ At least one of these two is true: A or B. {from 1: if A is true then at least one of the two, A or B, is true}
4 ∴ B is true. {from 2 and 3: if at least one of the two, A or B, is true and it isn't A, then it's B}

Dialethists respond by rejecting standard logic. Instead, they defend a **paraconsistent logic** – a logic that rejects the explosion principle; this lets them contain an occasional self-contradiction without leading to an "anything goes" logical nihilism. In the above argument, they reject line 4 and thus the "(A ∨ B), ~A ∴ B" form (*disjunctive syllogism*). Suppose, they say, B is false and A is both-true-and-false (!); then, they say, "(A ∨ B)" is true (since "A" is true), "~A" is true (since "A" is also false), but "B" is false – and so disjunctive syllogism is invalid.

Paraconsistent logicians have developed their own truth tables to explain their view. One option uses "1" for true and "0" for false, but permits "A" and "not-A" have these independently of each other; so we have four possibilities:

P	~P	
0	0	P and not-P are both false.
0	1	P is false and not-P is true.
1	0	P is true and not-P is false.
1	1	P and not-P are both true.

This approach rejects the usual understanding of "not," whereby "not-A" has the opposite truth value as "A." In paraconsistent logic, disjunctive syllogism is invalid, since it can have true premises and a false conclusion (here "(A ∨ B)" is true because the first part is true):

A ~A B	(A ∨ B),	~A	∴	B	
1 1 0	1	1		0	← Invalid

Similarly, the explosion principle, which permits us to deduce any arbitrary statement from a self-contradiction, is invalid:

A ~A B	A,	~A	∴	B	
1 1 0	1	1		0	← Invalid

Paraconsistent logic lets logic go on normally for the most part – so most of the arguments in this book that came out as valid or invalid on standard logic would come out the same way as before; but it also permits an occasional self-contradiction to be true. Thus it denies that a strict adherence to the law of non-contradiction is necessary for coherent thought.

Critics object that it makes no sense to permit "A" and "not-A" to both be true, at least if we take "not" in anything close to its normal sense. If we reject the usual truth table for "not," which makes "not-A" always have the opposite truth value of "A," then what is left of the meaning of "not"?

Critics also object that permitting "A" and "not-A" to both be true lets irrational people off too easily. Consider politicians or students who regularly contradict themselves, asserting "A" and then a few breaths later asserting "not-A," and yet defend themselves by appealing to the "new logic" which permits both to be true at once. Surely this is lame and sophistical.

Some who accept the law of non-contradiction (and thus reject dialethism) see some value in paraconsistent logic. They point out that people or computers sometimes have to derive conclusions from inconsistent premises. Suppose our best set of data about a crime or some area of science is flawed and inconsistent; we still might want to derive the best conclusions we can from this data. The "anything and its opposite follows from inconsistent data" approach of classical logic is unhelpful. Paraconsistent logic is claimed to be able to do better.

Critics question whether paraconsistent logic can do better. Suppose our data is inconsistent. Then our data has errors and so can't be relied upon to provide reliable conclusions. So we need to clear up the inconsistency first, perhaps by rejecting the least solidly based statements that led to the inconsistency. Put differently, we need to look for what follows (using standard logic) from the most probable consistent subset of the data.

Critics also claim that the rejection of disjunctive syllogism lessens the usefulness of paraconsistent logic for real-life cases. Suppose we know that either A or B committed the murder – and then later we find out that A didn't commit the murder. We need to be able to conclude that B then committed the murder. But with paraconsistent logic we cannot conclude this.

While most logicians accept the law of non-contradiction, they defend it in different ways. Some philosophers see it as a useful language convention. We could imagine a tribe where vague statements (like "This shirt is white") in borderline circumstances are said to be *both true and false* (instead of *neither true nor false*). We could choose to speak this way; and we could easily translate between this and normal speech. If so, then perhaps a strict adherence to the law of non-contradiction is at least partly conventional. Some who look at the matter this way see the law of non-contradiction as a convention that is less confusing and pragmatically better than what paraconsistent logicians offer us.

Others reject this conventionalist view and see the law of non-contradiction as expressing a deep metaphysical truth about reality. They see paraconsistent logicians as offering, not an alternative way of speaking, but rather a clever but incoherent metaphysics. Regardless of our verdict here, dialethism and paraconsistent logic do offer interesting challenges that make us think more deeply about logic.

17.3   Intuitionist logic

Aristotle supported the **law of excluded middle**, that either "S is P" or "S is not P" is true. Standard propositional logic accepts this law as "(A ∨ ~A)" ("A or not-A"), which has an all-1 truth table and thus is true in all possible cases. **Intuitionist logicians**, like the Dutch mathematicians Luitzen Brouwer and Arend Heyting, reject this law when applied to some areas of mathematics. They similarly reject the law of *double negation* "(~~A ⊃ A)" ("If not-not-A, then A"). They believe that "A" and "~A" are sometimes both false in cases that involve infinite sets. To emphasize these differences, intuitionists tend to use "¬" for negation instead of "~."

Intuitionist mathematicians see the natural numbers (0, 1, 2, . . .) as grounded in our experience of counting. Mathematical truths are constructions of the human mind; mathematical formulas should not be considered *true* unless the mind can prove their truth. Consider Goldbach's conjecture: "Every even number is the sum of two primes." This seems to hold for every even number we pick: 2 (1+1), 4 (3+1), 6 (5+1), 8 (7+1), 10 (7+3), and so on. But no one has proved or disproved that it holds for *all* even numbers. Some think Goldbach's conjecture must be true or false objectively, even though we may never prove which it is. Intuitionists disagree. They say truth in mathematics is provability; if we assume that neither Goldbach's conjecture nor its negation is provable, we must conclude that neither it nor its negation is true. This is why intuitionists think that, in some cases involving infinite sets (like the set of even numbers), neither "A" nor "~A" is true, and so both are false. The law of excluded middle does apply, however, if we use *finite* sets; so "Every even number under 1,000,000,000 is the sum of two primes" is true or false, and we could write a computer program that could in principle eventually tell us which it is.

Some philosophers of a non-realist slant reject the law of excluded middle in other areas. Suppose you think the only basic objective truths are ones about your individual experience, like "I feel warmth" or "I sense redness." You might be willing to say that there are objective truths about material objects (like "I am holding a red pen"), but only if these truths can be verified by your experience. You might even hold that what is *true* is what is *verified by your experience*. But often your experience verifies neither "A" nor "not-A"; in these cases, neither "A" nor "not-A" would be true, and so both would be false. On this basis, you might hold, for example, that "There is a God" and "There is no God" are both false – since neither is verified by your experience. On this basis, you might reject the law of excluded middle.

Critics of a realist sort think these approaches are bad metaphysics. Goldbach's conjecture about mathematics is either objectively true or objectively false; and our experience offers some support (but not conclusive proof) that it is true. Similarly, "There is a God" is objectively true or false, even though we may not have conclusive proof either way. It's an error to identity "true" with "verified," since we may imagine unverified truths; in fact, there is a whole world of truths and falsehoods that may not be accessible to our finite minds.

17.4   Relevance logic

Classical propositional logic analyzes "If P then Q" in a simple way, as just denying that we have P-true-and-Q-false:

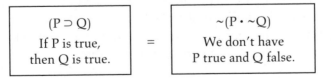

An IF-THEN understood this way is called a **material implication**. A material implication is automatically true if the antecedent is false or the consequent is true; this leads to the so-called *paradoxes of material implication*:

> From "not-A" we can infer "If A then B." So from "Pigs don't fly" we can infer "If pigs fly, then I'm rich."

> From "B" we can infer "If A then B." So from "Pigs don't fly" we can infer "If I'm rich, then pigs don't fly."

While many logicians see such results as odd but harmless, relevance logicians see them as wrong and want to reconstruct logic to avoid them.

Relevance logicians oppose evaluating the truth of "If A then B" just by the truth values of the parts; they say an IF-THEN can be true only if the parts are *relevant* to each other. While they do not spell out this "relevance" requirement in any complete way, they insist that logic should not be able to prove theorems like "If P-and-not-P, then Q," in which the antecedent and consequent do not share any letters. Since paraconsistent logic (Section 17.2) also rejects the idea that a self-contradiction entails every statement, there is a natural affinity between the two approaches; many relevance logics are also paraconsistent. Relevance logics often symbolize their *relevant implication* as "→," to contrast with the "⊃" of *material implication*.

Defenders of material implication say much in response. They often appeal to *conversational implication* to diffuse objections based on the paradoxes of material implication. Paul Grice claimed that what is true may not be sensible to assert in ordinary speech. He suggested, as a rule of communication, that we should not make a weaker claim rather than a stronger one unless we have a special reason. Suppose you tell your five children, "At least three of you will get Christmas presents" – while in fact you know that all five will get presents. Saying this suggests or insinuates that it is false or doubtful that all five will get presents. This is due to speech conventions, not logical entailments. "At least three will get presents" does not logically entail the falsity of "All five will get presents." But saying the first in most circumstances suggests that the second is false or doubtful. Similarly, there's not much point in telling people "If P then Q" on the basis of knowing not-P or knowing Q – since it's better to tell them straight off that not-P or that Q. There's generally a point to telling people "If P then Q" only if there is some special connection between the two, some way of going from one to the other. But, again, this has to do with speech conventions, not with truth conditions for "If P then Q."

Some defenders of material implication claim that the so-called paradoxes of material implication are perfectly correct and can be defended by intuitive arguments. For example, we can derive "If not-A then B" from "A":

> 1   A is true. (Premise)
> 2   ∴ Either A is true or B is true.   {from 1}
> 3   ∴ If A is not true, then B is true.   {from 2}

Relevance logic must reject this plausible derivation; it must deny that 2 follows from 1, that 3 follows from 2, or that deducibility is *transitive* (if 3 follows from 2, and 2 from 1, then 3 follows from 1). Doing any of these violates our logical intuitions at least as much as do the material-implication paradoxes. So relevance logics, although they try to avoid unintuitive results about conditionals, cannot achieve this goal; they all result in oddities at least as bad as the ones they are trying to avoid. Another problem is that a wide range of conflicting relevance logics have been proposed; these disagree much among themselves on which arguments involving conditionals are valid.

Relevance logicians have found other conditional arguments that, while valid on the traditional view, seem to them to be invalid. Some examples even question the validity of *modus ponens* ("If A then B, A ∴ B"). One allegedly questionable *modus ponens* inference involves measles:

If you have red spots, then $(R \supset M)$
   you have measles.
You have red spots.   R
∴ You have measles.   ∴ M

This is claimed to be invalid because you might have red spots for some other reason. Another objection, from Vann McGee, is more complex. Back in 1980, three main candidates ran for US president: two Republicans (Ronald Reagan, who won with over 50 percent of the vote, and John Anderson, who got about 7 percent of the vote and was thought to have no chance to win) and a Democrat (Jimmy Carter, who got just over 40 percent of the vote). Consider this argument, given just before the actual election:

If a Republican will win, then if Reagan does not $(W \supset (\sim R \supset A))$
   win then Anderson will win.
A Republican will win.   W
∴ If Reagan does not win, then Anderson will win.   ∴ $(\sim R \supset A)$

Here it seems right to believe the premises but not the conclusion (since clearly if Reagan does not win, then Carter will win, not Anderson). So again, this instance of *modus ponens* is claimed to be invalid.

Defenders of *modus ponens* claim that these two examples confuse a genuine IF-THEN with a statement of conditional probability. Compare these three ways of taking "If you have red spots, then you have measles":

1. *Unqualified IF-THEN*: "If you have red spots, then you have measles."

2. *Conditional Probability*: "The probability is high that you have measles, given that you have red spots."

3. *Qualified IF-THEN*: "If you have red spots and other causes can be excluded, then you have measles."

The premise about measles, if a genuine IF-THEN, has to mean 1, and not 2 or 3; but then its truth excludes the red spots having other causes in such a way that you do not have measles. The truth of this IF-THEN doesn't entail that we are *certain* that there are no other causes; but if *in fact* there are other causes (so you have red spots but not measles), then the IF-THEN is false. A similar analysis will take care of the Reagan argument.

Even if we reject relevance logic in favor of orthodox propositional logic, still there are relatives of the standard IF-THEN that cannot plausibly be interpreted as material implications. We already mentioned *conversational implication* (where saying A suggests or insinuates a further statement B) and *conditional probability* (where fact A would make fact B probable to a given degree). There are also, for example, *logical entailments* ("B logically follows from A" – which Chapter 10 symbolizes as "□(A ⊃ B)") and *counterfactuals* ("If A had happened then B would have happened" – which is sometimes symbolized as "(A □→ Q)"). So conditionals and their near relatives form a diverse family, going from very strong logical entailments, through standard flavors of IF-THEN, and down to mere suggestion or insinuation. Even apart from relevance logic, conditionals raise many logical issues.

It should not surprise us that there are deep controversies about basic principles of logic. Every area, including claims about material objects like "I see a chair," raises controversies if we push things far enough. But not all alternative views are equally reasonable. I would contend that, despite the controversies, I really do see a chair. And I would contend that most assumptions about logic that have been held since the time of Aristotle are equally solid.[1]

---

[1] I do think, however, that in the context of quantified modal logic (Section 11.4) there is much to be said for *free logic*, which is deviant. For further information on deviant logics, see Graham Priest's *An Introduction to Non-Classical Logic*, 2nd ed. (Cambridge: Cambridge University Press, 2008) and J. C. Beall and Bas C. van Fraassen's *Possibilities and Paradox* (Oxford: Oxford University Press, 2003).

CHAPTER 18
Philosophy of Logic

Philosophy of logic deals with issues about logic that are broadly philosophical, especially ones about the nature of reality (metaphysics) or the foundations of knowledge (epistemology). Of the many possible issues, we will here deal with these: Are there abstract entities, and does logic presuppose them? Does logic give us the key to understand the structure of reality? What is the basis for logical laws – are they empirical or true by convention? What is truth, and how do different views on truth affect logic? What is the scope of logic?

18.1 Abstract entities

Metaphysics studies the nature of reality from a broad perspective. It considers views like *materialism* (only the physical is ultimately real), *idealism* (only the mental is ultimately real), and *dualism* (both the physical and the mental are ultimately real). Another issue is whether there are **abstract entities** – entities, roughly, that are neither physical (like apples) nor mental (like feelings); alleged examples include numbers, sets, and properties.

Logic can lead quickly us to abstract entities. Consider this argument:

> This is green.
> This is an apple.
> ∴ Some apple is green.

When we discuss this argument, we may seem to talk about abstract entities:

- the *set* of green things; this set seems to be not a physical or mental entity, but rather an abstract entity.
- the *property* of greenness, which can apply either to the color as experienced or to its underlying physical basis; in either case, greenness seems to be not a concrete mental or physical entity, but rather something more abstract that has physical or mental instances.
- the *concept* of greenness, which is what terms for "green" in various languages mean.
- the *word* "green" and the *sentence* "This is green," which are abstract patterns that have written and auditory instances.

- the *proposition* that this is green, which is what we claim to be true when we assert "This is green" in English or similar things in other languages.

Platonists, as logicians use the term, are those who straightforwardly accept the existence of abstract objects, regardless of whether they accept other parts of Plato's philosophy. *Nominalists*, in contrast, are unhappy about this proliferation of entities and want to limit what exists to concrete physical or mental entities; nominalism's challenge is to make sense of logic while rejecting abstract entities. Intermediate views are possible; maybe we should accept abstract entities, not as independently real entities that we discover, but rather as creations or fictions of the mind.

Disputes about abstract entities go back to ancient and medieval debates about forms and universals, and continue to rage today.

18.2   Metaphysical structures

Does logic give us the key to understand the metaphysical structure of reality? **Ludwig Wittgenstein**, in his *Tractatus Logico-Philosophicus* (1922), argued that it does. He claimed that the world is the totality of facts. If we state all the facts, we completely describe reality. Facts are about simple objects. An atomic statement pictures a fact in such a way that the elements of the statement mirror the simple objects of the world. Language, when completely analyzed, breaks down into such atomic statements. Complex statements are built from atomic ones using logical connectives like "and," "or," and "not." Wittgenstein invented truth tables to show how this works. Some complex statements, like "It's raining or not raining," are true in all cases, regardless of which atomic statements are true; these complex statements are certain but lack content.

While Wittgenstein thought that atomic statements were the simplest, most basic truths, he was vague on whether they dealt with physical facts or with experiences. In any case, genuine complex statements have to be constructible out of atomic statements using the logical connectives of propositional logic (Chapter 6). Statements not so constructible are nonsensical. Wittgenstein thought that most philosophical issues (for example, about values or God) were nonsensical. Paradoxically, he thought that his own theory (starting with his claim that the world is the totality of facts) is nonsensical too; it goes beyond language. He ended on a mystical note: the most important things in life (his own theory, values, God, the meaning of life) cannot be put into words.

Bertrand Russell was impressed by Wittgenstein's views but tried to make them more sensible and less paradoxical. Russell's *logical atomism* held that an ideal language – one adequate to describe reality completely – must be based on quantificational logic (Chapters 8 and 9) and thus must include quantifiers like "all" and "some." It must also include terms that refer to the ultimately simple elements of reality – which include objects, properties, and relations. He debated whether the basic entities of the world were physical, or mental, or perhaps something neutral between the two.

Russell thought that, while logical analysis can reveal metaphysical structures, yet ordinary language can lead us into bad metaphysics (Section 9.6). Suppose you say "There is nothing in the box." Some might be led to think that "nothing" is the name of a mysterious object in the box. This is wrong. Instead, "There is nothing in the box" just means "It is false that there is something in the box." Or suppose you say "The average American has 2.4 children." While "the average American" doesn't refer to an actual entity, the sentence as a whole is meaningful; the sentence means that the average number of children that Americans have is 2.4. "Nothing" and "the average American" are **logical constructs**; they are merely ways of speaking and do not directly refer to actual objects. Russell went on to ask whether things like sets, numbers, material objects, persons, electrons, and experiences were real entities or logical constructs. Logical analysis is the key to answering such questions. We must see, for example, whether statements about material objects can be reduced to sensations, or whether statements about minds can be analyzed as being about behavior.

In much the same spirit, **Willard V. O. Quine** pursued **ontology**, which is about what kinds of entity ultimately exist. His slogan, "To be is to be the value of a bound variable," was intended to clarify ontological disputes. The slogan means that the entities that our theory commits us to are the entities that our quantified variables (like "for all x" and "for some x") must range over for the statements of our theory to be true. So if we say, "There is some feature that Shakira and Britney have in common," then we must accept *features* (*properties*) as part of our ontology – unless we can show that our reference to them is just an avoidable way of speaking (a "logical construct" in Russell's sense). Quine accepted *sets* in his ontology, because he thought these abstract entities were needed for mathematics and science; in picking an ontology, he appealed to pragmatic considerations. He rejected properties, concepts, and propositions because he thought they were less clear.

In his later years, Ludwig Wittgenstein supported an *ordinary language* approach and rejected his earlier idea of basing metaphysics on logic. His *Philosophical Investigations* (1953) argued that his earlier work was a mistake, since it imposed a framework on reality instead of fairly investigating what it is like. His new slogan became "Don't think, but look!" Don't say that reality *has* to be such and such, because that is what your preconceptions say it must be; instead, look and see how it is. He now contended that few concepts had strict analytic definitions. His favorite example was "game," which he claimed had no strict definition. Games typically involve a competition between sides, winning and losing, a combination of skill and luck, and so forth. But none of these is essential to a game; solitaire involves no competition, ring-around-the-rosie involves no winning or losing, cutting cards involves no skill, and checkers involves no luck. While games tend to share some family resemblances, any attempted strict analysis of "game" is easily refuted by giving examples of games that violate the analysis. We distort language if we think that all statements must be analyzable into simple concepts that reflect metaphysically simple elements of reality. There is no one "ideal language" that perfectly mirrors reality; instead, there are various *language games* that humans construct for various purposes. Logic is a language game, invented to help us appraise the correctness of reasoning; we distort logic if we see it as giving us a special key to understand the metaphysical structure of reality.

So we see a range of views here about the connection of logic with metaphysics, with Wittgenstein holding different views at different times.[1]

18.3 The basis for logical laws

Let's consider **logical laws** like *modus ponens* and the law of non-contradiction:

- *Modus ponens*: If A then B, A, therefore B.
- Non-contradiction: A and not-A cannot both be true, unless A is taken differently in both instances.

Why are such logical laws correct, and how do we know that they are correct? Thinkers have proposed a bewildering range of answers. Here we'll consider five influential answers: supernaturalism, psychologism, pragmatism, conventionalism, and realism.[2]

1. **Supernaturalism** holds that all laws of every sort – whether about physics, morality, mathematics, or logic – depend on God. Radical supernaturalists say that God creates the logical laws or at least makes them true. God could make a world where *modus ponens* and the law of non-contradiction fail; and he could violate the law of non-contradiction – for example, by making "You're reading this sentence" and "You're not reading this sentence" both true. So logical laws are contingent: they could have been false. Moderate supernaturalists, on the other hand, say that logical laws express God's perfect nature. God's perfection require that he be consistent, that his created world follow the laws of logic, and that he desire that we be consistent and logical. Since God's nature is necessary, the laws of logic are also necessary. Supernaturalists of both sorts hold that God builds the laws of logic into our minds, so these laws appear to us to be "self-evident" when adequately reflected upon.

Critics raise objections to supernaturalism. Some contend that the laws of

---

[1] For further metaphysical issues raised by logic, see Section 3.4 (about the logical positivist critique of metaphysics), Section 9.2 (about the substitution of identicals and the nature of mind), and Sections 11.2 to 11.4 (about Aristotelian essentialism).

[2] Sections 17.2 and 17.4 presented deviant logics that reject non-contradiction and *modus ponens*. Here we'll assume the correctness of these laws.

logic hold for every possible world, including ones where there is no God; so God cannot provide the basis for these logical laws. Others say that, since beliefs about logic are more certain than beliefs about God, it's wrong to base logic on God. Still others say that God accepts logical laws because they're inherently valid; logical laws aren't valid just because God chooses to accept them (radical supernaturalism) or just because they accord with his nature (moderate supernatualism).

2. **Psychologism** holds that logical laws are somehow based on how we think. Logic is part of our natural history and is built into our biological structure. Humans evolved to walk on two feet, to have hand–eye coordination, to communicate with each other by speech, and to think logically; these promote our survival and are part of our genetic and biological makeup. Radical psychologism says that logic *describes* how we think; logical laws are psychological laws about thinking. Moderate psychologism, on the other hand, sees logic as built into us in a more subtle way; we are so built that at reflective moments we see inconsistency and illogicality as defects – even though at weaker moments our thinking may suffer from such defects. When we reflect on our inconsistencies, we tend to develop an uncomfortable anxiety that psychologists call "cognitive dissonance"; this is as much a part of our natural history and biological structure as is thirst. So the laws of logic are built into our instincts.

Critics raise objections to psychologism. Radical psychologism, which claims that logical laws describe our thinking, would make it impossible for us to be illogical or inconsistent. But people often reason invalidly or express inconsistent ideas; so logical laws don't necessarily reflect how we think. Moderate psychologism recognizes this problem and is more subtle; it sees logical laws as reflecting, instead, instinctive norms about thinking that are built into us and that we recognize at more reflective moments. This approach gives a plausible evolutionary and biological explanation of how logic can be instinctive in us. But the approach fails if it's taken to explain what makes logical laws true or solidly based. Suppose evolution gave us an instinctive belief in the flatness of the earth; it wouldn't follow that the earth actually *was* flat – or that this belief was so solidly based that we couldn't criticize it. Similarly, the instinctiveness of the laws of logic wouldn't make these logical laws correct or solidly based; maybe our instincts on these matters are right or maybe they're wrong – we'd have to investigate further.

There's also a problem with basing our knowledge of logical laws on evolution theory. We need logic to appraise the correctness of scientific theories like evolution; so our knowledge of logic cannot without circularity rest on our knowledge of scientific theories. In addition, our knowledge of logic is more solidly based than our knowledge of scientific theories.

3. **Pragmatism** holds that logical laws are based on experience. The broad consensus of humanity is that logic works; when we think things out in a logical and consistent way, we are more apt to find the truth and satisfy our

needs. This empirical and pragmatic test provides the only firm basis for logic or for any other way of thinking.

Critics raise objections to pragmatism. They agree that, yes, logical thinking does work. But logic works because its laws hold of inherent necessity; but then logical laws cannot be based on experience. Our experience can show us that something *is* true (for example, that this flower is red); but it cannot show us that something *must* be true (that its opposite is *impossible*). Let's compare logic with mouse traps. We can test various mouse traps to see how well they work; a given trap might catch a mouse or might not – both are possible. But it isn't possible for a logical law to fail – for example, for "If A then B" and "A" to both be true while "B" was false. The inherent necessity of logical laws shows that they cannot be based on experience.

Besides, we cannot know that logic works unless we appeal to much observation and reasoning – where the reasoning presupposes logical laws. So the pragmatist defense of logical laws is ultimately circular.

4. **Conventionalism** holds that logical laws are based on verbal conventions. We use logical words like "and," "or," "if-then," and "not" according to rules that can be expressed in basic truth tables. Given these basic truth tables (Sections 6.2 to 6.6), we can show *modus ponens* to be valid (since its truth table never gives true premises and a false conclusion); we can similarly show the law of non-contradiction to be true (since its truth table comes out as true in all cases). Thus we can justify logical laws using conventions about what the logical words mean. Conventionalism easily explains why logical laws are inherently necessary; if we deny logical laws, we contradict ourselves – since we violate the meaning of logical words like "and," "or," "if-then," and "not." It also explains how we can know logical laws in an *a priori* manner, independent of sense experience; as is the case with "All bachelors are unmarried," logical laws are true by virtue of the meaning of words (Sections 3.6 and 3.7) – and so we can grasp their truth by becoming clear on what they mean. A final advantage of conventionalism is that it explains the status of logical laws without appealing to beliefs that are controversial or difficult to defend, like God, evolution, a Platonism about abstract entities, or a mysterious ability of the human mind to grasp abstract truths. The conventionality of logic opens the door to the idea that there could be alternative logics that are equally correct but follow different conventions.

Critics raise objections to conventionalism. First, the attempt to prove *modus ponens* by appealing to truth tables is circular:

If the truth table for *modus ponens* never gives true premises
  and a false conclusion, then *modus ponens* is valid.   If A then B
The truth table for *modus ponens* never gives true premises   A
  and a false conclusion.   ∴ B
∴ *Modus ponens* is valid.

This argument itself uses *modus ponens*; so it's circular, since it assumes from the start that *modus ponens* is valid. Second, conventionalism confuses the logical laws themselves (which are necessary truths) with how we express them (which depends on language conventions). If we changed our language, the logical laws would still be true, but we'd have to express them using different words. Third, conventionalism makes logical laws too arbitrary, since they could fail if we changed our conventions. For example, both *modus ponens* and the law of non-contradiction fail on some many-valued conventions (Section 17.1). But logical laws seem to have an inherent correctness that doesn't depend on which language conventions we adopt.

5. **Realism** holds that logical laws are objective, independent, abstract truths. We *discover* logical laws; we don't construct or create them. Logical laws are not reducible to the mental (to how we think or even to how God thinks), nor to the physical, nor are they merely useful tools, nor are they based on conventions. Logical laws govern our world, and every possible world, because violations of the logical laws are impossible; it cannot be, for example, that A and not-A are both true. The logical laws become "self-evident" to us when adequately reflected upon. This doesn't mean that logical intuitions are infallible; beginning logic students tend to have poor intuitions about whether an argument is valid or invalid. But logical intuitions can be trained; we develop our logical intuitions by, for example, testing proposed inference forms by examining concrete cases in which a form's validity or invalidity is more obvious. The best evidence for a principle of logic is that it appears evident to a mind that is well-trained in logic and that serious attempts to find good objections to the principle continually fail.

Critics raise objections to realism. Many object that realism makes logical laws too mysterious. Suppose you're a materialist; you hold that all facts about the universe are ultimately expressible in the language of physics and chemistry. How do objective, irreducible logical facts fit into such a universe? Are logical facts composed of chemicals, or what sort of weird thing are they? And how could we ever know such mysterious logical facts? In addition, objective, abstract logical laws seem to presuppose abstract entities (Section 18.1); but abstract entities have no place in a materialistic world. A dualist view that accepts only mind and matter would have similar doubts about realism.

Logicians for the most part (except for deviant logicians – see Chapter 17) agree on what the logical laws are. But logicians differ widely on what these laws are based on and how we can know them to be correct.

18.4 Truth and paradoxes

The concept of **truth** is important to logic. A *valid argument* is often defined as one in which it's impossible to have the premises all true and the conclusion false. And truth comes up further in propositional logic (with truth tables and the truth-assignment test) and in refutations of invalid arguments (which are possible situations making the premises all true and the conclusion false).

There are many philosophical issues about truth. For example, is classical logic right in assuming that statements are either true or false, but not both, and that *true* and *false* are the only truth values? Some deviant logics deny these assumptions (Chapter 17).

What sort of thing do "true" and "false" apply to? Suppose you point to a green apple and say "This is green." Should we say that what is true is the *sentence* "This is green," or perhaps the sentence as used on this occasion (where you point to a certain object)? If so, then is this sentence concrete physical marks or sounds, or is it a more abstract pattern that has written or auditory instances? Or perhaps what is true-or-false is not sentences, but rather *propositions*, which are the *assertions* that we use language to make. But then are are propositions something mental, or are they abstract entities, like the meaning of "This is green"?

What does it mean to call something *true*? To be "true," according to various theories, is:

- to correspond to the facts (correspondence theory),
- to cohere with our other beliefs (coherence theory),
- to be useful to believe (pragmatist theory),
- to be verified (verification theory), or
- to be what we would agree to under cognitively ideal conditions (ideal consensus theory); or perhaps
- "It's true that A" is just a verbose way to assert A (redundancy theory).

The pragmatist and verification analyses require that we give up the law of excluded middle, since it can happen that neither a statement nor its negation is useful to belief, or that neither is verified. These two analyses could also support many-valued logic (Section 17.1), since a statement can be useful to believe (or can be verified) to various degrees. Thus different answers to the "What is truth?" question can support different approaches to logic.

Alfred Tarski once proposed an adequacy condition, called "convention T," that any definition of truth must satisfy; here's an example of convention T:

> The sentence "Snow is white" is *true*,
>   if and only if snow *is* white.

This equivalence raises problems for many definitions of "true" that water down the notion's objectivity. For example, the view that "true" just means "accepted in our culture" leads to an absurdity. Imagine that we lived on a tropical island where snow *is* white (in high-mountain cracks that are never visited or seen) but yet we don't believe that it's white; then on the proposed view *snow could be white while "Snow is white" was not be true* – which is absurd. A similar objection works against the pragmatist and verification views. This time imagine that we lived on that same tropical island and that "Snow is white" was neither useful to believe nor verified. Again, on the pragmatist and verification views, *snow could be white while "Snow is white" was not true* – which is absurd.

The **liar paradox** raises questions about the nature of truth. The liar paradox is a statement that asserts its own falsity and thus, paradoxically, appears to be both true and false. Consider claim P:

(P)   P is false.

Is P true? Then things must be as P says they are, and thus P has to be false. Is P false? Then things are as P says they are, and thus P has to be true. So if P is either true or false, then it has to be both true and false.

Graham Priest and others claim that P is *both true and false*, which requires rejecting Aristotle's law of non-contradiction (Section 17.2). The more common view is that P is *neither true nor false*, which requires rejecting or qualifying Aristotle's law of excluded middle. But why is P neither true nor false?

Bertrand Russell, to deal with such paradoxes, proposed a *theory of types* that outlaws certain forms of self-reference. Very roughly, there are ordinary objects (type 0), properties of these (type 1), properties of these properties (type 2), and so on. Any meaningful statement can talk only about objects of a lower type; so no speech can talk meaningfully about itself. P violates this condition, and so is meaningless – and thus neither true nor false.

However, Russell's theory seems to refute itself. "Any meaningful statement can talk only about objects of a lower type," to be useful, has to restrict *all statements, of every type*; but then it violates its own rule and declares itself meaningless. So the paradox reappears.

Tarski, to deal with the paradox, proposed that no language can contain its own truth predicate; to ascribe truth or falsity to a statement in a given language, we must ascend to a higher-level language, called the *metalanguage*. P violates this condition and so is meaningless – and thus neither true nor false.

Opponents say Tarski's view is too restrictive. English and other languages *do* contain their own truth predicates, and they need to do this for many purposes. So it would be better to have a less sweeping restriction to take care of the liar paradox. But there is little agreement about what this restriction should be.

Epimenides of Crete in the sixth century BC proposed the liar paradox, and St Paul mentioned it in his letter to Titus (1:12). It has been widely discussed ever since. While most logicians think that a theory of truth must deal with the paradox, how best to do this is still unclear.

18.5   The scope of logic

"Logic" is often defined in ways like "the analysis and appraisal of arguments," "the study of valid reasoning," "the science of the principles governing the validity of inference," or "the art and science of right reasoning." These definitions work out much the same in practice.

The meaning of "logic" is more complicated than this, since the term can be used in a narrow and a broad sense. *Logic in the narrow sense* is the study of deductive reasoning, which is about what logically follows from what. *Logic in the broad sense* includes also various other studies that relate to the analysis and appraisal of arguments, studies like informal logic, inductive logic, meta-logic, and philosophy of logic (Chapters 3–5, 15, and 18).

Even if we take "logic" in this narrow deductive sense, there still is some unclarity on what it includes. Suppose you say, "I have $30; therefore I have more than $20." Is this part of logic, part of mathematics, or both?

Willard V. O. Quine suggested that we limit "logic" to classical propositional and quantificational logic (Chapters 6 to 9), which he saw as fairly uncontroversial and as focusing on topic-neutral terms like "and" and "not" that arise in every area of study. Philosophical extensions to this, like modal and deontic logic (Chapters 10 to 12), focus on terms like "necessary" and "ought" that are too colorful and topic-specific to be part of logic; these areas, if legitimate at all (and he had his doubts) are part of philosophy in general, not part of logic. Mathematical extensions, like set theory and axiomatizations of arithmetic, belong to mathematics. And deviant logics (Chapter 17) are illegitimate.

Most logicians today tend to use "(deductive) logic" in a broader way that is hard to pin down. Deductive logic is commonly taken to include, besides classical symbolic logic and traditional syllogistic logic, philosophical extensions (like modal and deontic logic), deviant logics, and sometimes even mathematical extensions (like set theory). Logic is seen as part of at least three disciplines – philosophy, mathematics, and computer science – which approach it from different angles. Any attempt to give sharp and final boundaries to the term "logic" would be artificial.[1]

---

[1] Philosophy of logic, as traditionally practiced, tends to ignore issues that logic raises for ethics; I think these issues are important, especially the demand for consistency in thought-and-action that leads to the golden rule (Chapters 12 to 14). For further study about philosophy of logic, I suggest Willard V. O. Quine's *Philosophy of Logic*, 2nd ed. (Cambridge, Mass.: Harvard University Press, 1986), which is a good introduction to this area from an influential logician and philosopher, and Colin McGinn's *Logical Properties: Identity, Existence, Predication, Necessity, Truth* (Oxford: Clarendon, 2000), which gives an opposing view; reading both together should give an idea of alternative perspectives in this area.

Appendix
For Further Reading

If you've mastered much of this book and want to read more, you might consult my *Historical Dictionary of Logic* (Lanham, Md.: Scarecrow Press [Rowman & Littlefield], 2006). This is an encyclopedia of logic; it contains a series of short, nontechnical articles arranged alphabetically, on a broad range of topics – including figures and historical periods, branches of logic, specialized vocabulary, controversies, and relationships to other disciplines – and a 13-page chronology listing major events in the history of logic. It also has an extensive 52-page bibliography of readings in logic, a recommended list of 63 works in various categories, and a smaller list of works for beginners. The beginner list includes these books:

- P. H. Nidditch's *The Development of Mathematical Logic* (London: Routledge & Kegan Paul, 1962): a sketch of the history of logic and its most important results, from Aristotle through the 20th century.
- Willard Van Orman Quine's *Philosophy of Logic*, 2nd ed. (Cambridge, Mass.: Harvard University Press, 1986): a good but contentious introduction to this area from an influential logician and philosopher.
- Colin McGinn's *Logical Properties: Identity, Existence, Predication, Necessity, Truth* (Oxford: Clarendon, 2000): an opposing view on philosophy of logic from that of Quine's book.
- Graham Priest's *An Introduction to Non-Classical Logic*, 2nd ed. (Cambridge: Cambridge University Press, 2008) a defense of deviant logic by its most eloquent defender, who argues that the standard systems of logic are flawed and need to be revamped (technical parts may be skipped).
- Ian Hacking's *An Introduction to Probability and Inductive Logic* (Cambridge: Cambridge University Press, 2001): a lively introduction to inductive logic and its applications.
- George S. Boolos and Richard C. Jeffrey's *Computability and Logic*, 3rd ed. (Cambridge: Cambridge University Press, 1989): a technical treatment of topics such as Turing machines, uncomputable functions, the Skolem-Löwenheim theorem, and Gödel's theorem (a slow read, but clear and interesting and doesn't presume much mathematics).

If you're just starting, you might pick one or two of these that interest you. If you're so advanced that you need further suggestions, consult my *Historical Dictionary of Logic*.

Answers to Selected Problems

For each exercise set in the book, answers are given for problems 1, 3, 5, 10, 15, 20, 25, and so on.

2.1a

1. t is S
3. no L is B
5. all D is H
10. a is s
15. m is A

2.2a

1. This isn't a syllogism, because "D" and "E" occur only once.
3. This isn't a syllogism, because "Y" occurs three times and "G" occurs only once.
5. This isn't a syllogism, because "Z is N" isn't a wff.

2.2b

1. w is not s̲
3. no R̲ is S̲
5. all P̲ is B

2.2c

1. no P* is B*   Invalid
   some C is not B*
   ∴ some C* is P*
3. no H* is B*   Invalid
   no H* is D*
   ∴ some B* is not D
5. ∴ g is g*   Valid
10. all D* is A   Invalid
    ∴ all A is D*

2.3a

1. all S* is D   Valid
   all D* is U
   ∴ all S is U*

3. all T* is C   Valid
   no C* is R*
   ∴ no T is R
5. all M* is R   Valid
   some P is M
   ∴ some P* is R*
10. all S* is Y   Invalid
    m is Y
    ∴ m* is S*
15. all N* is L   Valid
    m is N
    ∴ m* is L*
20. b is W   Invalid
    u is W
    ∴ u* is b*
25. some S is W   Valid
    all S* is L
    all L* is H
    ∴ some W* is H*

2.3b

1. We can't prove either "Bob stole money" or "Bob didn't steal money." 2 & 6 yield no valid argument with either conclusion.
3. 4 & 8 & 9 prove David stole money: "d is W, all W is H, all H is S ∴ d is S."
5. This would show that our data was inconsistent and hence contains false information.

2.4a

1. all J is F
3. all S is R
5. some H is L
10. no S is H
15. all M is B
20. some H is not G

2.5a

1. "No human acts are free" or "No free acts are human acts."
3. "Some free acts are determined" or "Some determined acts are free."
5. No conclusion validly follows.
10. "No culturally taught racial feelings are rational" or "No rational thing is a culturally taught racial feelings."
15. "Some who like raw steaks like champagne" or "Some who like champagne like raw steaks."
20. "No basic moral norms are principles based on human nature" or "No principles based on human nature are basic moral norms."
25. "No moral judgments are objective truths" or "No objective truths are moral judgments."

2.6a

1. Valid

   no B is C
   all D is C
   ∴ no D is B

3. Valid

   all E is F
   some G is not F
   ∴ some G is not E

5. Valid

   all A is B
   all B is C
   ∴ all A is C

10. Invalid

    some V is W
    some W is Z
    ∴ some V is Z

2.7a

1. all R* is G   Valid
   all G* is T
   all T* is V
   all V* is U
   ∴ all R is U*

3. g is A   Valid
   all A* is R
   no R* is C*
   ∴ g* is not C

5. no S* is A*   Valid
   all W* is A
   ∴ no S is W

Premise 2 (implicit but false) is "All garments that should be worn next to the skin while skiing are garments that absorb moisture."

10. all P* is O   Valid
    all O* is E
    no M* is E*
    ∴ no M is P

15. e is C   Invalid
    all S* is C
    ∴ e* is S*

20. all N* is C   Valid
    no E* is C*
    g is E
    ∴ g* is not N

Premise 3 (implicit) is "God exists" is an existence claim.

25. all D* is F   Valid
    some P is not F*
    ∴ some P* is not D

3.1a

1. "Cop" is negative. "Police" is more neutral.
3. "Heroic" is positive. These are negative: "reckless," "foolhardy," "brash," "rash," "careless," "imprudent," and "daredevil."
5. "Elderly gentleman" is positive. "Old man" is negative.
10. "Do-gooder" is negative. "Person concerned for others" and "caring human being" are positive.
15. "Booze" is negative or neutral. "Cocktail" is positive, while "alcohol," "liquor," and "intoxicant" are neutral.
20. "Babbling" is negative. "Talking," "speaking," and "discussing" are neutral.
25. "Bribe" is negative. "Payment" and "gift" are neutral or positive.

30. "Whore" is negative. "Prostitute" is more neutral.

3.2a

1. If you make a false statement that you think is true, that isn't a lie.

3. (1) One who believes in God may not make God his or her ultimate concern. (2) One may have an ultimate concern (such as making money) without believing in God. (3) "Object of ultimate concern" is relative in a way that "God" isn't: "Is there an object of ultimate concern?" invites the question "For whom?" – while "Is there a God?" doesn't.

5. Since "of positive value" is no more clearly understood than "good," this definition does little to clarify what "good" means. And there's the danger of circularity if we go on to define "of positive value" in terms of "good."

10. (1) If I believe that Michigan will beat Ohio State next year, it still might not be true. (2) If "true" means "believed," then both these statements are true (since both are believed by someone): "Michigan will beat Ohio State next year" and "Michigan won't beat Ohio State next year." (3) "Believed" is relative in a way that "true" isn't: "Is this believed?" invites the question "By whom?" – while "Is this true?" doesn't.

15. This set of definitions is circular.

3.2b

1. This is true according to cultural relativism. Sociological data can verify what is "socially approved," and this is the same as what is "good."

3. This is true. The norms set up by my society determine what is good in my society, so these norms couldn't be mistaken.

5. This is undecided. If our society approves of respecting the values of other societies, then this respect is good. But if our society disapproves of respecting the values of other societies, then this respect is bad.

10. This is true according to CR.

15. This is false (and self-contradictory) according to cultural relativism.

20. This is undecided, since cultural relativism leaves unspecified which of these various groups is "the society in question."

3.4a

1. This is meaningful on LP (it could be verified) and PR (it could make a practical difference in terms of sensations or choices).

3. This is meaningful on both views.

5. This is probably meaningless on both views (unless the statement is given some special sense).

10. This is meaningless on LP (at least on the version that requires public verifiability). It's meaningful on PR (since its truth could make a practical difference to Manuel's experience).

15. Since this (LP) isn't able to be tested empirically, it's meaningless on LP. [To avoid this result, a positivist could claim that LP is true by definition and hence analytic (Section 3.6). Recall that LP is qualified so that it applies only to synthetic statements. But then the positivist has to use "meaningless" in the unusual sense of "synthetic but not empirical" instead of in the intended sense of "true or false." This shift takes the bite out of the claim that a statement is "meaningless." A believer can readily agree that "There is a God" is "meaningless" if all this means is that "There is a God" isn't synthetic-but-not-empirical.] It's meaningful on PR (its truth could make a difference to our choices about what we ought to believe).

3.5a

(These answers were adapted from those given by my students)

1. "Is ethics a <u>science</u>?" could mean any of the following:
- Are ethical judgments true or false independently of human feelings and opinions? Can the truth of some ethical judgments be known?
- Can ethics be systematized into a set of rules that will tell us unambiguously what we ought to do in all (or most) cases?
- Can ethical principles be proved using the methods of empirical science?
- Is there some rational method for arriving at ethical judgments that would lead people to agree on their ethical judgments?
- Can a system of ethical principles be drawn up in an axiomatic form, so that ethical theorems can be deduced from axioms accessible to human reason?

3. "Is this belief part of <u>common sense</u>?" could mean any of the following:

- Is this belief accepted instinctively or intuitively, as opposed to being the product of reasoning or education?
- Is this belief so entrenched that subtle reasoning to the contrary, even if it seems flawless, has no power to convince us?
- Is this belief something that people of good "horse sense" will accept regardless of their education?
- Is this belief obviously true?
- Is this belief universally accepted?

[In each case we could further specify the group we are talking about – for example, "Is this belief obviously true to anyone who has ever lived (to all those of our own country, or to practically all those of our own country who haven't been exposed to subtle reasoning on this topic)?"]

5. "Are values <u>relative</u> (or <u>absolute</u>)?" could mean any of the following:

- Do different individuals and societies disagree (and to what extent) on values?
- Do people disagree on basic moral principles (and not just on applications)?
- Are all (or some) values incapable of being proved or rationally argued?
- Is it wrong to claim that a moral judgment is correct or incorrect rather than claiming that it's correct or incorrect relative to such and such a group? Do moral judgments express social conventions rather than truths that hold independently of such conventions?
- Do right and wrong always depend on circumstances (so that no sort of action could be always right or always wrong)?
- In making concrete moral judgments, do different values have to be weighed against each other?
- Are all things that are valued only valued as a means to something else (so that nothing is valued for its own sake)?

10. "Is that judgment based on <u>reason</u>?" could be asking whether the judgment is based on the following:

- Self-evident truths, the analysis of concepts, and logical deductions from these (reason versus experience).
- The foregoing plus sense experience, introspection, and inductive arguments (reason versus faith).
- Some sort of thinking or experience or faith (as opposed to being based on mere emotion).
- The thinking and experience and feelings

of a sane person (as opposed to those of an insane person).

- An adequate and impartial examination of the available data.
- A process for arriving at truth in which everyone correctly following it would arrive at the same conclusions.
- What is reasonable to believe, or what one ought to believe (or what is permissible to believe) from the standpoint of the seeking of truth.

[We could be asking whether a given person bases his or her judgment on one of the foregoing, or whether the judgment in question could be based on one of the foregoing.]

15. "Do you have a <u>soul</u>?" could mean any of the following:

- Do you have a personal identity that could in principle survive death and the disintegration of your body?
- Are you capable of conscious thinking and doing?
- Would an exhaustive description of your material constituents and observable behavior patterns fail to capture important elements of what you are?
- Are you composed of two quite distinct beings – a thinking being without spatial dimensions and a material being incapable of thought?
- Are you capable of caring deeply about anything?
- Are you still alive?

3.6a

1. Analytic.
3. Synthetic.
5. Analytic.
10. Analytic.
15. Analytic.
20. Most philosophers think this is synthetic. St Anselm, Descartes, and Charles Hartshorne argued that it was analytic. See examples 3 and 4 of Section 6.7b, and examples 9 and 26 of Section 10.3b.
25. Most say synthetic, but some say analytic.

3.7a

1. *A priori.*
3. *A posteriori.*
5. *A priori.*
10. *A priori.*
15. *A priori.*

20. Most philosophers think this could only be known *a posteriori*. Some philosophers think it can be known *a priori* (see comments on problem 20 of the last section).

25. Most philosophers think this could only be known *a priori*, but a few think it could be known *a posteriori*.

4.2a

1. Complex question (like "Are you still beating your wife?").

3. Pro-con. The candidate might be a crook. Or an opposing candidate might be even more intelligent and experienced.

5. Appeal to the crowd.

10. Genetic.

15. Appeal to authority.

20. None of the labels fit exactly. This vague claim (what is a "discriminating backpacker"?) is probably false (discriminating backpackers tend to vary in their preferences). The closest labels are "appeal to authority," "appeal to the crowd," "false stereotype," or perhaps "appeal to emotion." There's some "snob appeal" here too, but this isn't one of our categories.

25. *Post hoc ergo propter hoc.*

30. Appeal to opposition.

35. Appeal to emotion.

40. *Post hoc ergo propter hoc.*

45. *Ad hominem* or false stereotype.

50. *Post hoc ergo propter hoc.* The conclusion might still be true, but we'd need a longer argument to show this; many argue, for example, that Bush's deregulation of banking caused the financial crisis.

55. Ambiguous.

60. Black and white, or complex question.

4.2b

1. Complex question.

3. Ambiguity.

5. False stereotype.

10. Appeal to authority.

15. Pro-con.

20. Genetic.

25. Black and white.

30. *Ad hominem.*

35. Appeal to the crowd.

40. Part-whole.

45. Appeal to authority, *ad hominem,* or appeal to emotion.

50. Circular.

55. Complex question.

60. Circular (but it still might be true).

4.3a

(The answers for 3 and 5 are representative correct answers; other answers may be correct.)

1. There are no universal duties.
   If everyone ought to respect the dignity of others, then there are universal duties.
   ∴ Not everyone ought to respect the dignity of others.

3. If we have ethical knowledge, then either ethical truths are provable or there are self-evident ethical truths.
   We have ethical knowledge.
   Ethical truths aren't provable.
   ∴ There are self-evident ethical truths.

5. All human concepts derive from sense experience.
   The concept of logical validity is a human concept.
   ∴ The concept of logical validity derives from sense experience.

10. If every rule has an exception, then there's an exception to this idea too; but then some rule doesn't have an exception. Statement 10 implies its own falsity and hence is self-refuting.

15. If it's impossible to express truth in human concepts, then statement 15 is false. Statement 15 implies its own falsity and hence is self-refuting.

4.4a

(These are examples of answers and aren't the only "right answers.")

1. If the agent will probably get caught, then offering the bribe probably isn't in the agent's self-interest.
   The agent will probably get caught. (One might give inductive reasoning for this.)
   ∴ Offering the bribe probably isn't in the agent's self-interest.

3. Some acts that grossly violate the rights of some maximize good consequences (in the sense of maximizing the total of everyone's interests).
   No acts that grossly violate the rights of some are right.
   ∴ Some acts that maximize good consequences aren't right.

5. Any act that involves lying is a dishonest act (from the definition of "dishonest"). Offering the bribe involves lying (falsifying records, and the like).
∴ Offering the bribe is a dishonest act.

10. Science adequately explains our experience.
If science adequately explains our experience, then the belief that there is a God is unnecessary to explain our experience.
∴ The belief that there is a God is unnecessary to explain our experience.

Or: Science doesn't adequately explain certain items of our experience (why these scientific laws govern our universe and not others, why our universe exhibits order, why there exists a world of contingent beings at all, moral obligations, and so on).
If science doesn't adequately explain certain items of our experience, then the belief that there is a God is necessary to explain our experience.
∴ The belief that there is a God is necessary to explain our experience.

15. The idea of logical validity is an idea gained in our earthly existence.
The idea of logical validity isn't derived from sense experience.
∴ Some ideas gained in our earthly existence don't derive from sense experience.

5.2a

1. There are 32 such cards out of the 103 remaining cards. So your probability is 32/103 (about 31.1 percent).

3. Coins have no memory. The probability of heads is 50 percent.

5. The probability that Michigan will win the Rose Bowl is 80 percent times 60 percent times 30 percent, or 14.4 percent.

10. You get a number divisible by three 12 out of 36 times. You don't get it 24 out of 36 times. Thus, mathematically fair betting odds are 2 to 1 (24 to 12) against getting a number divisible by three.

15. In 100 such cases, Ohio State would pass 60 times and run 40 times. If we set up to stop the pass, we'd stop them 58 times out of 100 [(60 · 70 percent) + (40 · 40 percent)]. If we set up to stop the run, we'd stop them 62 times out of 100 [(60 · 50 percent) + (40 · 80 percent)]. So we should set up to stop the run.

5.3a

1. You shouldn't believe it. It's only 12.5 percent (50 · 50 · 50 percent) probable.

3. You shouldn't believe it. It's 37.5 percent probable, since it happens in 3 of the 8 possible combinations.

5. You shouldn't believe it. It isn't more probable than not; it's only 50 percent probable.

10. You should buy the Enormity Incorporated model. If you buy the Cut-Rate model, there's an expected replacement cost of $360 ($600 times 60 percent) in addition to the $600 purchase price. This makes the total expected cost $960. The expected cost on the Enormity Incorporated model is $900.

5.4a

1. This is a poor argument, since the sample has little variety.

3. This is a poor argument, since the sample is very small and lacks variety.

5. This is a good inductive argument (if you aren't in the polar regions where the sun doesn't come up at all for several weeks in the winter). In standard form, the argument goes: "All examined days are days when the sun comes up; a large and varied group of days has been examined; tomorrow is a day; so probably tomorrow is a day when the sun comes up."

10. This weakens the argument. Some students cram logic mainly for the Law School Admissions Test (since this test contains many logic problems). You might not have known this, however.

5.5a

1. This doesn't affect the strength of the argument, since the color of the book has little to do with the contents.

3. This weakens the argument. It's less likely that a course taught by a member of the mathematics department would include a discussion of analogical reasoning.

5. This weakens the argument. An abstract approach that stresses theory is less likely to discuss analogical reasoning.

10. This weakens the argument. A book with only 10 pages on inductive reasoning is less likely to include analogical reasoning.

15. This weakens the argument, since it's a significant point of difference between the two cases.

5.7a

1. Using the method of agreement, we conclude that either having a few drinks causes a longer reaction time, or having a longer reaction time causes a person to have a few drinks. The second alternative is less likely in terms of our background information. So we conclude that having a few drinks probably causes a longer reaction time.

3. The method of agreement seems to lead to the conclusion that the soda caused the hangover. However, we know that scotch, gin, and rum all contain alcohol. So soda isn't the only factor common to all four cases; there's also the alcohol. So the method of agreement doesn't apply here. To decide whether the soda or the alcohol caused the hangover, Michelle would have to experiment with drinking soda but no alcohol, and drinking alcohol but no soda.

5. Using the method of agreement, we'd conclude that either factor K caused cancer or cancer caused factor K. If we found some drug to eliminate factor K, then we could try it and see whether it eliminates cancer. If eliminating factor K eliminated cancer, then it's likely that factor K caused cancer. But if factor K came back after we eliminated it, then it's likely that cancer caused factor K.

10. Using the method of disagreement, we'd conclude that eating raw garlic doesn't by itself necessarily cause mosquitoes to stop biting you.

15. Using the method of agreement, we'd conclude that either the combination of factors (heating or striking dry matches in the presence of oxygen) causes the match to light, or else the lighting of the match causes the combination of factors. The latter is implausible (it involves a present fire causing a past heating or striking). So probably the combination of factors causes the match to light.

20. By the method of variation, it's likely that an increase in the electrical voltage is the cause of the increase in the electrical current, or the electrical current is the cause of the electrical voltage, or something else caused them both. We know (but perhaps little Will doesn't) that we can have a voltage without a current (such as when nothing is plugged in to our electrical socket) but we can't have a current without a voltage. So we'd think that voltage causes current (and not vice versa) and reject the "electrical current is the cause of the electrical voltage" alternative. So we'd conclude that probably an increase in the electrical voltage is the cause of the increase in the electrical current, or else some other factor (Will's curiosity, for example) caused both increases.

25. By the method of difference, wearing a single pair of socks probably is (or is part of) the cause of the blisters, or the blisters are (or are part of) the cause of wearing a single pair of socks. The latter is impossible, since a present event can't cause a past event. So probably wearing a single pair of socks is (or is part of) the cause of the blisters. Since we know that we don't get blisters from wearing a single pair of socks without walking, we'd conclude that wearing a single pair of socks is only part of the cause of the blisters.

5.8a

1. The problem is how to do the experiment so that differences in air resistance won't get in the way. We could build a 100-foot tower on the moon (or some planet without air), drop a feather and a rock from the top, and see if both strike the ground at the same time. Or we might go to the top of a high building and drop two boxes that are identical except that one is empty while the other is filled with rocks. In this second case, the two boxes have the same air resistance but different weights.

3. We could study land patterns (hills, rock piles, eccentric boulders, and so on) left by present-day glaciers in places like Alaska, compare land patterns of areas that we are fairly sure weren't covered by glaciers, and compare both with those of Wisconsin. Mill's method of agreement might lead us to conclude that glaciers probably caused the land patterns in Wisconsin. To date the glacier, we'd have to find some "natural calendar" (such as the yearly rings in tree trunks, yearly sediment layers on the bottoms of lakes, corresponding layers in sedimentary rocks, or carbon breakdown) and connect it with Wisconsin climatic changes or land patterns.

5. We could give both groups an intelligence test. The problem is that the first child might test higher, not because of greater innate intelligence, but because of differences in how the first and the last child are brought up. (The last child, but not the first, is normally brought up with other children around and by older parents.) To eliminate this factor, we might test adopted children. If we find that a child born first and one born last tend to test equally (or unequally) in the same sort of adoptive environment, then we could conclude that the two groups tend (or don't tend) to have the same innate intelligence.

10. See the answer to problem 3. Any data making statement 3 probable would make 10 improbable. In addition, if we found any "natural calendar" that gives a strong inductive argument concerning any events occurring over 5,000 years ago, this also would make 10 unlikely. [Of course, these are only inductive arguments; it's possible for the premises to be all true and the conclusion false.]

6.1a

1. $\sim(A \cdot B)$
3. $((A \cdot B) \vee C)$
5. $((A \supset B) \vee C)$
10. $(A \supset \sim(\sim B \cdot \sim C))$
15. $(\sim(E \vee P) \supset \sim R)$
20. E   ["$(M \vee F)$" is wrong, since the English sentence doesn't mean "Everyone is male or everyone is female."]

6.2a

1. 1
3. 1
5. 0
10. 1
15. 0

6.3a

1. $\sim(1 \cdot 0) = \sim 0 = 1$
3. $\sim(\sim 1 \cdot \sim 0) = \sim(0 \cdot 1) = \sim 0 = 1$
5. $(\sim 0 \equiv 0) = (1 \equiv 0) = 0$
10. $(\sim 1 \vee \sim(0 \supset 0)) = (0 \vee \sim 1) = (0 \vee 0) = 0$
15. $\sim((1 \supset 1) \supset (1 \supset 0)) = \sim(1 \supset 0) = \sim 0 = 1$

6.4a

1. $(? \cdot 0) = 0$
3. $(? \vee \sim 0) = (? \vee 1) = 1$
5. $(0 \supset ?) = 1$

10. $(? \supset \sim 0) = (? \supset 1) = 1$

6.5a

1.
P Q	$(P \equiv \sim Q)$
0 0	0
0 1	1
1 0	1
1 1	0

3.
P Q R	$(P \vee (Q \cdot \sim R))$
0 0 0	0
0 0 1	0
0 1 0	1
0 1 1	0
1 0 0	1
1 0 1	1
1 1 0	1
1 1 1	1

5.
P Q	$((P \equiv Q) \supset Q)$
0 0	0
0 1	1
1 0	1
1 1	1

6.6a

1. Invalid: second row has 110.

C D	$(C \supset D)$,	D	$\therefore$	C
0 0	1	0		0
0 1	1	1		0
1 0	0	0		1
1 1	1	1		1

3. Valid: no row has 110.

T B	$(T \supset B)$,	$(T \supset \sim B)$	$\therefore$	$\sim T$
0 0	1	1		1
0 1	1	1		1
1 0	0	1		0
1 1	1	0		0

5. Invalid: row 4 has 1110. (I once got a group together but couldn't get Grand Canyon backcountry reservations. So we instead explored canyons near Escalante, Utah. This made R=0, T=1, and E=1.)

R T E	$((R \cdot T) \supset E)$,	T	$\sim R$	$\therefore$	$\sim E$
0 0 0	1	0	1		1
0 0 1	1	0	1		0
0 1 0	1	1	1		1
0 1 1	1	1	1		0
1 0 0	1	0	0		1
1 0 1	1	0	0		0
1 1 0	0	1	0		1
1 1 1	1	1	0		0

10. Invalid: row 1 has 110.

S E R	$(S \supset (E \cdot \sim R))$,	$\sim E$	$\therefore$	R
0 0 0	1	1		0
0 0 1	1	1		1
0 1 0	1	0		0
0 1 1	1	0		1
1 0 0	0	1		0
1 0 1	0	1		1
1 1 0	1	0		0
1 1 1	0	0		1

6.7a

1. $\sim(N^1 \equiv H^1) \neq 1$ Valid
   $N^1 = 1$
   $\therefore \sim H^1 = 0$

3. $((T \vee M^1) \supset Q^0) \neq 1$ Valid
   $M^1 = 1$
   $\therefore Q^0 = 0$

5. $((L^0 \cdot F^1) \supset S^1) = 1$ Invalid
   $S^1 = 1$
   $F^1 = 1$
   $\therefore L^0 = 0$

10. $(\sim T^0 \supset (P^1 \supset J^0)) \neq 1$ Valid
    $P^1 = 1$
    $\sim J^0 = 1$
    $\therefore T^0 = 0$

15. $A^1 = 1$ Valid
    $\sim A^1 \neq 1$
    $\therefore B^0 = 0$

(An argument with inconsistent premises is always valid: if the premises can't all be true, we can't have premises all true and conclusion false. But such an argument can't be sound, since the premises can't all be true. This argument is controversial – see Section 17.2.)

6.7b

1. C   Valid
   A
   $((C \cdot A) \supset (F \vee I))$
   $\sim I$
   $\therefore F$

3. $((U \cdot \sim R) \supset C)$ Valid
   $\sim C$
   U
   $\therefore R$

5. $((S \cdot \sim M) \supset D)$ Valid
   $\sim D$
   S
   $\therefore M$

10. $(I \supset (U \vee \sim P))$ Invalid
    $\sim U$
    $\sim P$
    $\therefore I$

15. $((M \cdot S) \supset G)$ Valid
    S
    $\sim G$
    $\therefore \sim M$

20. $((I \cdot \sim D) \supset R)$ Valid
    $\sim D$
    I
    $\therefore R$

6.8a

1. $(S \supset (Y \cdot I))$
3. $(Q \vee R)$
5. $(\sim T \supset \sim P)$
10. $(A \supset E)$ *or, equivalently,* $(\sim E \supset \sim A)$
15. $(S \supset W)$

6.9a

1. $(S \supset \sim K)$ Valid
   K
   $\therefore \sim S$

The implicit premise 2 is "We can know something that we aren't presently sensing."

3. $((B \cdot \sim Q) \supset O)$ Invalid
   $\sim B$
   $\therefore \sim O$

5. $(S \supset A)$ Valid
   $\sim A$
   $\therefore \sim S$

The implicit premise 2 is "The basic principles of ethics aren't largely agreed upon by intelligent people who have studied ethics."

10. $(K \supset (P \vee S))$ Valid
    $\sim P$
    $\sim S$
    $\therefore \sim K$

15. $(O \supset (H \vee C))$ Valid
    $\sim C$
    O
    $\therefore H$

20. G   Valid
    $\sim S$
    $((M \cdot G) \supset S)$
    $\therefore \sim M$

6.10a

1.	P, U	10.	H, I	
3.	no conclusion	15.	no conclusion	
5.	~R, ~S	20.	no conclusion	

6.11a

1.	~T	10.	no conclusion	
3.	~B	15.	F	
5.	no conclusion	20.	Y	

6.12a

1.	~U	10.	~A	
3.	no conclusion	15.	no conclusion	
5.	P, ~Q			

6.13a

1.	(A · B), C	5.	no conclusion	
3.	no conclusion			

7.1a

1.　Valid
```
*  1    (A ⊃ B)
     [ ∴ (~B ⊃ ~A)
*  2   ┌ asm: ~(~B ⊃ ~A)
   3   │ ∴ ~B   {from 2}
   4   │ ∴ A    {from 2}
   5   └ ∴ ~A   {from 1 and 3}
   6  ∴ (~B ⊃ ~A)   {from 2; 4 contradicts 5}
```

3.　Valid
```
*  1    (A ⊃ B)
*  2    (~A ⊃ B)
     [ ∴ B
   3   ┌ asm: ~B
   4   │ ∴ ~A   {from 1 and 3}
   5   └ ∴ A    {from 2 and 3}
   6  ∴ B   {from 3; 4 contradicts 5}
```

5.　Valid
```
*  1    (A ∨ B)
*  2    (A ⊃ C)
*  3    (B ⊃ D)
     [ ∴ (C ∨ D)
*  4   ┌ asm: ~(C ∨ D)
   5   │ ∴ ~C   {from 4}
   6   │ ∴ ~D   {from 4}
   7   │ ∴ ~A   {from 2 and 5}
   8   │ ∴ B    {from 1 and 7}
   9   └ ∴ ~B   {from 3 and 6}
  10  ∴ (C ∨ D)   {from 4; 8 contradicts 9}
```

10.　Valid
```
*  1    (A ⊃ (B ⊃ C))
     [ ∴ ((A · B) ⊃ C)
*  2   ┌ asm: ~((A · B) ⊃ C)
*  3   │ ∴ (A · B)   {from 2}
   4   │ ∴ ~C        {from 2}
   5   │ ∴ A         {from 3}
   6   │ ∴ B         {from 3}
*  7   │ ∴ (B ⊃ C)   {from 1 and 5}
   8   └ ∴ ~B        {from 4 and 7}
   9  ∴ ((A · B) ⊃ C)   {from 2; 6 contradicts 8}
```

7.1b

1.　Valid
```
*  1    ((H · T) ⊃ B)
   2    H
     [ ∴ (T ⊃ B)
*  3   ┌ asm: ~(T ⊃ B)
   4   │ ∴ T         {from 3}
   5   │ ∴ ~B        {from 3}
*  6   │ ∴ ~(H · T)  {from 1 and 5}
   7   └ ∴ ~T        {from 2 and 6}
   8  ∴ (T ⊃ B)   {from 3; 4 contradicts 7}
```

3.　Valid
```
*  1    (W ⊃ (F ∨ M))
   2    ~F
*  3    (M ⊃ A)
     [ ∴ (W ⊃ A)
*  4   ┌ asm: ~(W ⊃ A)
   5   │ ∴ W         {from 4}
   6   │ ∴ ~A        {from 4}
*  7   │ ∴ (F ∨ M)   {from 1 and 5}
   8   │ ∴ ~M        {from 3 and 6}
   9   └ ∴ M         {from 2 and 7}
  10  ∴ (W ⊃ A)   {from 4; 8 contradicts 9}
```

5.　Valid
```
*  1    (~W ⊃ ~G)
*  2    (~A ⊃ ~P)
*  3    (~W ∨ ~A)
     [ ∴ (~P ∨ ~G)
*  4   ┌ asm: ~(~P ∨ ~G)
   5   │ ∴ P   {from 4}
   6   │ ∴ G   {from 4}
   7   │ ∴ W   {from 1 and 6}
   8   │ ∴ A   {from 2 and 5}
   9   └ ∴ ~A  {from 3 and 7}
  10  ∴ (~P ∨ ~G)   {from 4; 8 contradicts 9}
```
(This could also be translated without the NOTs – by letting "W," for example, stand for "God doesn't want to prevent evil.")

10.　Valid
```
*  1    (I ⊃ ~R)
```

```
*    2     (~R ⊃ ~T)
     3     T
*    4     (~I ⊃ F)
          [ ∴ F
     5   ┌ asm: ~F
     6   │ ∴ R   {from 2 and 3}
     7   │ ∴ ~I  {from 1 and 6}
     8   └ ∴ I   {from 4 and 5}
     9    ∴ F   {from 5; 7 contradicts 8}
```

7.2a

```
1.    Invalid                          ┌─────────┐
*    1    (A ∨ B)                       │ ~A, B   │
         [ ∴ A                          └─────────┘
     2    asm: ~A
     3    ∴ B   {from 1 and 2}

3.    Invalid                          ┌─────────┐
     1    ~(A • ~B)                     │ B, ~A   │
         [ ∴ ~(B • ~A)                  └─────────┘
*    2    asm: (B • ~A)
     3    ∴ B   {from 2}
     4    ∴ ~A  {from 2}

5.    Invalid                          ┌─────────┐
     1    ((A ⊃ B) ⊃ (C ⊃ D))          │ A, ~D,  │
*    2    (B ⊃ D)                       │ ~B, C   │
*    3    (A ⊃ C)                       └─────────┘
         [ ∴ (A ⊃ D)
*    4    asm: ~(A ⊃ D)
     5    ∴ A   {from 4}
     6    ∴ ~D  {from 4}
     7    ∴ ~B  {from 2 and 6}
     8    ∴ C   {from 3 and 5}

10.   Invalid                          ┌─────────┐
*    1    ~(~A • ~B)                    │ ~C, ~D, │
     2    ~C                            │ E, ~A, B│
*    3    (D ∨ ~A)                      └─────────┘
*    4    ((C • ~E) ⊃ ~B)
     5    ~D
         [ ∴ ~E
     6    asm: E
     7    ∴ ~A   {from 3 and 5}
     8    ∴ B    {from 1 and 7}
     9    ∴ ~(C • ~E)   {from 4 and 8}
```

7.2b

```
1.    Invalid                          ┌─────────┐
     1    (S ⊃ K)                       │ M, ~S, K│
*    2    (M ⊃ K)                       └─────────┘
     3    M
         [ ∴ S
     4    asm: ~S
```

```
     5    ∴ K   {from 2 and 3}

3.    Valid
     1    E
*    2    (E ⊃ ~R)
*    3    ((I • ~A) ⊃ R)
     4    I
         [ ∴ A
     5   ┌ asm: ~A
     6   │ ∴ ~R   {from 1 and 2}
*    7   │ ∴ ~(I • ~A)  {from 3 and 6}
     8   └ ∴ A   {from 4 and 7}
     9    ∴ A   {from 5; 5 contradicts 8}

5.    Valid
*    1    (E ⊃ W)
*    2    (W ⊃ (~R • I))
         [ ∴ (R ⊃ ~E)
*    3   ┌ asm: ~(R ⊃ ~E)
     4   │ ∴ R   {from 3}
     5   │ ∴ E   {from 3}
     6   │ ∴ W   {from 1 and 5}
     7   │ ∴ (~R • I)   {from 2 and 6}
     8   └ ∴ ~R   {from 7}
     9    ∴ (R ⊃ ~E)   {from 3; 4 contradicts 8}

10.   Valid
*    1    (G ∨ H)
*    2    ((G • K) ⊃ F)
*    3    (H ⊃ C)
*    4    ((C • K) ⊃ U)
         [ ∴ (K ⊃ (U ∨ F))
*    5   ┌ asm: ~(K ⊃ (U ∨ F))
     6   │ ∴ K   {from 5}
*    7   │ ∴ ~(U ∨ F)   {from 5}
     8   │ ∴ ~U   {from 7}
     9   │ ∴ ~F   {from 7}
*   10   │ ∴ ~(G • K)   {from 2 and 9}
*   11   │ ∴ ~(C • K)   {from 4 and 8}
    12   │ ∴ ~G   {from 6 and 10}
    13   │ ∴ H    {from 1 and 12}
    14   │ ∴ C    {from 3 and 13}
    15   └ ∴ ~C   {from 6 and 11}
    16    ∴ (K ⊃ (U ∨ F))   {from 5; 14 contra 15}
```

```
15.   Invalid                          ┌─────────┐
*    1    (A ⊃ B)                       │ H, A, B,│
*    2    (B ⊃ (F ⊃ M))                 │ ~M, ~F  │
*    3    (M ⊃ ~H)                      └─────────┘
     4    H
         [ ∴ ~A
     5    asm: A
     6    ∴ B   {from 1 and 5}
*    7    ∴ (F ⊃ M)   {from 2 and 6}
     8    ∴ ~M   {from 3 and 4}
     9    ∴ ~F   {from 7 and 8}
An "F" premise would make it valid.
```

20.　Valid

* 1　　(~A ⊃ (F · C))
* 2　　(~G ⊃ ~F)
　　[∴ (~A ⊃ G)
* 3　┌ asm: ~(~A ⊃ G)
　4　│ ∴ ~A　{from 3}
　5　│ ∴ ~G　{from 3}
* 6　│ ∴ (F · C)　{from 1 and 4}
　7　│ ∴ F　{from 6}
　8　│ ∴ C　{from 6}
　9　└ ∴ ~F　{from 2 and 5}
　10　∴ (~A ⊃ G)　{from 3; 7 contradicts 9}

25.　Valid

* 1　　(F ⊃ (E · S))
* 2　　(E ⊃ T)
* 3　　(T ⊃ T´)
* 4　　(T´ ⊃ X)
* 5　　((X · T´) ⊃ Y)
* 6　　((X · Y) ⊃ ~S)
　　[∴ ~F
　7　┌ asm: F
* 8　│ ∴ (E · S)　{from 1 and 7}
　9　│ ∴ E　{from 8}
　10　│ ∴ S　{from 8}
　11　│ ∴ T　{from 2 and 9}
　12　│ ∴ T´　{from 3 and 11}
　13　│ ∴ X　{from 4 and 12}
* 14　│ ∴ ~(X · Y)　{from 6 and 10}
　15　│ ∴ ~Y　{from 13 and 14}
* 16　│ ∴ ~(X · T´)　{from 5 and 15}
　17　└ ∴ ~X　{from 12 and 16}
　18　∴ ~F　{from 7; 13 contradicts 17}

7.3a

1.　Valid

* 1　　(A ⊃ B)
　2　　(A ∨ (A · C))
　　[∴ (A · B)
* 3　┌ asm: ~(A · B)
　4　│┌ asm: ~A　{break 1}
　5　││ ∴ (A · C)　{from 2 and 4}
　6　│└ ∴ A　{from 5}
　7　│ ∴ A　{from 4; 4 contradicts 6}
　8　│ ∴ B　{from 1 and 7}
　9　└ ∴ ~B　{from 3 and 7}
　10　∴ (A · B)　{from 3; 8 contradicts 9}

3.　Valid

* 1　　(B ⊃ A)
* 2　　~(A · C)
　3　　(B ∨ C)
　　[∴ (A ≡ B)
* 4　┌ asm: ~(A ≡ B)
　5　│ ∴ (A ∨ B)　{from 4}

* 6　│ ∴ ~(A · B)　{from 4}
　7　│┌ asm: ~B　{break 1}
　8　││ ∴ C　{from 3 and 7}
　9　││ ∴ ~A　{from 2 and 8}
　10　│└ ∴ A　{from 5 and 7}
　11　│ ∴ B　{from 7; 9 contradicts 10}
　12　│ ∴ A　{from 1 and 11}
　13　│ ∴ ~C　{from 2 and 12}
　14　└ ∴ ~A　{from 6 and 11}
　15　∴ (A ≡ B)　{from 4; 12 contradicts 14}

5.　Valid

* 1　　((A ⊃ B) ⊃ C)
* 2　　(C ⊃ (D · E))
　　[∴ (B ⊃ D)
* 3　┌ asm: ~(B ⊃ D)
　4　│ ∴ B　{from 3}
　5　│ ∴ ~D　{from 3}
　6　│┌ asm: ~(A ⊃ B)　{break 1}
　7　││ ∴ A　{from 6}
　8　│└ ∴ ~B　{from 6}
　9　│ ∴ (A ⊃ B)　{from 6; 4 contradicts 8}
　10　│ ∴ C　{from 1 and 9}
　11　│ ∴ (D · E)　{from 2 and 10}
　12　└ ∴ D　{from 11}
　13　∴ (B ⊃ D)　{from 3; 5 contradicts 12}

7.3b

1.　Valid

* 1　　((F · P) ∨ (A · P))
* 2　　(P ⊃ G)
　　[∴ (P · G)
* 3　┌ asm: ~(P · G)
* 4　│┌ asm: (F · P)　{break 1}
　5　││ ∴ F　{from 4}
　6　││ ∴ P　{from 4}
　7　││ ∴ G　{from 2 and 6}
　8　│└ ∴ ~G　{from 3 and 6}
　9　│ ∴ ~(F · P)　{from 4; 7 contradicts 8}
* 10　│ ∴ (A · P)　{from 1 and 9}
　11　│ ∴ A　{from 10}
　12　│ ∴ P　{from 10}
　13　│ ∴ G　{from 2 and 12}
　14　└ ∴ ~G　{from 3 and 12}
　15　∴ (P · G)　{from 3; 13 contradicts 14}

3.　Valid

* 1　　(A ≡ (H ∨ B))
　2　　~H
　　[∴ (A ≡ B)
* 3　┌ asm: ~(A ≡ B)
* 4　│ ∴ (A ⊃ (H ∨ B))　{from 1}
　5　│ ∴ ((H ∨ B) ⊃ A)　{from 1}
　6　│ ∴ (A ∨ B)　{from 3}
* 7　│ ∴ ~(A · B)　{from 3}

```
  8   ┌ asm: ~A   {break 4}
  9   │ ∴ ~(H ∨ B)  {from 5 and 8}
 10   │ ∴ ~B   {from 9}
 11   └ ∴ B   {from 6 and 8}
 12     ∴ A   {from 8; 10 contradicts 11}
*13     ∴ (H ∨ B)  {from 4 and 12}
 14     ∴ ~B   {from 7 and 12}
 15   └ ∴ B   {from 2 and 13}
 16   ∴ (A ≡ B)  {from 3; 14 contradicts 15}
```

5. Valid

```
* 1      (~C ⊃ ~M)
* 2      (~M ⊃ ~E)
  3      (C ⊃ A)
* 4      (A ⊃ E)
   [  ∴ (E ≡ C)
* 5   ┌ asm: ~(E ≡ C)
* 6   │ ∴ (E ∨ C)  {from 5}
  7   │ ∴ ~(E • C)  {from 5}
  8   │ ┌ asm: C   {break 1}
 .9   │ │ ∴ A   {from 3 and 8}
 10   │ │ ∴ E   {from 4 and 9}
 11   │ │ ∴ M   {from 2 and 10}
 12   │ └ ∴ ~E   {from 7 and 8}
 13   │ ∴ ~C   {from 8; 10 contradicts 12}
 14   │ ∴ ~M   {from 1 and 13}
 15   │ ∴ ~E   {from 2 and 14}
 16   │ ∴ ~A   {from 4 and 15}
 17   └ ∴ E   {from 6 and 13}
 18   ∴ (E ≡ C)  {from 5; 15 contradicts 17}
```

10. Valid

```
* 1      ((D • L) ⊃ (F • A))
  2      ((D • ~L) ⊃ (G • A))
   [  ∴ (D ⊃ A)
* 3   ┌ asm: ~(D ⊃ A)
  4   │ ∴ D   {from 3}
  5   │ ∴ ~A   {from 3}
  6   │ ┌ asm: ~(D • L)  {break 1}
  7   │ │ ∴ ~L   {from 4 and 6}
  8   │ │ ┌ asm: ~(D • ~L)  {break 2}
  9   │ │ └ ∴ L   {from 4 and 8}
 10   │ │ ∴ (D • ~L)  {from 8; 7 contradicts 9}
 11   │ │ ∴ (G • A)  {from 2 and 10}
 12   │ │ ∴ G   {from 11}
 13   │ └ ∴ A   {from 11}
*14   │ ∴ (D • L)  {from 6; 5 contradicts 13}
 15   │ ∴ L   {from 14}
*16   │ ∴ (F • A)  {from 1 and 14}
 17   │ ∴ F   {from 16}
 18   └ ∴ A   {from 16}
 19   ∴ (D ⊃ A)  {from 3; 5 contradicts 18}
```

7.4a

1. Invalid

```
 1      ~(A • B)
    [ ∴ (~A • ~B)
**2    asm: ~(~A • ~B)
  3     asm: ~A   {break 1}
  4     ∴ B   {from 2 and 3}
```

~A, B

3. Invalid

```
 1      (A ⊃ B)
 2      (C ⊃ (~D • E))
    [ ∴ (D ∨ F)
* 3    asm: ~(D ∨ F)
  4    ∴ ~D   {from 3}
  5    ∴ ~F   {from 3}
  6     asm: ~A   {break 1}
  7      asm: ~C   {break 2}
```

~D, ~F, ~A, ~C

5. Invalid

```
 1      (A ⊃ (B • C))
**2      ((D ⊃ E) ⊃ A)
    [ ∴ (E ∨ C)
* 3    asm: ~(E ∨ C)
  4    ∴ ~E   {from 3}
  5    ∴ ~C   {from 3}
  6     asm: ~A   {break 1}
**7      ∴ ~(D ⊃ E)  {from 2 and 6}
  8      ∴ D   {from 7}
```

~E, ~C, ~A, D

7.4b

1. Invalid

```
 1      (M ⊃ ~B)
 2      ~M
 3      (B ⊃ (P • G))
    [ ∴ G
  4    asm: ~G
  5     asm: ~B   {break 3}
```

3. Invalid

```
 1      (~R ⊃ (O • ~S))
    [ ∴ (R ⊃ (C • S))
* 2    asm: ~(R ⊃ (C • S))
  3    ∴ R   {from 2}
  4    ∴ ~(C • S)  {from 2}
  5     asm: ~C   {break 4}
```

R, ~C

5. Invalid

```
 1      ((A • L) ⊃ (D • M))
 2      (M ⊃ ~C)
 3      (S ⊃ L)
    [ ∴ ((A • ~S) ⊃ C)
* 4    asm: ~((A • ~S) ⊃ C)
* 5    ∴ (A • ~S)  {from 4}
  6    ∴ ~C   {from 4}
```

```
   7      ∴ A   {from 5}
   8      ∴ ~S   {from 5}
** 9        asm: ~(A · L)   {break 1}
  10        ∴ ~L   {from 7 and 9}
```

10.   Valid

```
   1      H
   2      P
   3      ~H′
*  4      (M ⊃ ((H · P) ⊃ H′))
   5      (~M ⊃ S)
      [ ∴ (~M · S)
   6    ┌ asm: ~(~M · S)
   7    │ ┌ asm: ~M   {break 4}
   8    │ │ ∴ S   {from 5 and 7}
   9    │ └ ∴ ~S   {from 6 and 7}
  10    │ ∴ M   {from 7; 8 contradicts 9}
* 11    │ ∴ ((H · P) ⊃ H′)   {from 4 and 10}
* 12    │ ∴ ~(H · P)   {from 3 and 11}
  13    └ ∴ ~P   {from 1 and 12}
  14    ∴ (~M · S)   {from 6; 2 contradicts 13}
```

15.   Invalid   ┌─────────────────┐
                        │ N, F, ~E, ~W   │
                        └─────────────────┘
```
   1      ((E · F) ⊃ W)
   2      ((W · M) ⊃ (B · ~N))
      [ ∴ (N ⊃ ~F)
*  3      asm: ~(N ⊃ ~F)
   4      ∴ N   {from 3}
   5      ∴ F   {from 3}
** 6        asm: ~(E · F)   {break 1}
   7        ∴ ~E   {from 5 and 6}
   8          asm: ~(W · M)   {break 2}
   9          asm: ~W   {break 8}
```

8.1a

```
 1.    ~Cx
 3.    (∃x)~Cx
 5.    (x)Cx
10.    ~(∃x)(Lx · Ex)
15.    (∃x)(Ax · (Dx · ~Bx))
20.    ~(x)(Cx ⊃ Px)
25.    (x)(Cx · Lx)
```

8.2a

1.   Valid

```
   1      (x)Fx
      [ ∴ (x)(Gx ∨ Fx)
*  2    ┌ asm: ~(x)(Gx ∨ Fx)
*  3    │ ∴ (∃x)~(Gx ∨ Fx)   {from 2}
*  4    │ ∴ ~(Ga ∨ Fa)   {from 3}
   5    │ ∴ ~Ga   {from 4}
   6    │ ∴ ~Fa   {from 4}
   7    └ ∴ Fa   {from 1}
   8    ∴ (x)(Gx ∨ Fx)   {from 2; 6 contradicts 7}
```

3.   Valid

```
*  1      ~(∃x)(Fx · Gx)
*  2      (∃x)Fx
      [ ∴ (∃x)~Gx
*  3    ┌ asm: ~(∃x)~Gx
   4    │ ∴ (x)~(Fx · Gx)   {from 1}
   5    │ ∴ Fa   {from 2}
   6    │ ∴ (x)Gx   {from 3}
*  7    │ ∴ ~(Fa · Ga)   {from 4}
   8    │ ∴ ~Ga   {from 5 and 7}
   9    └ ∴ Ga   {from 6}
  10    ∴ (∃x)~Gx   {from 3; 8 contradicts 9}
```

5.   Valid

```
   1      (x)(Fx ⊃ Gx)
*  2      (∃x)Fx
      [ ∴ (∃x)(Fx · Gx)
*  3    ┌ asm: ~(∃x)(Fx · Gx)
   4    │ ∴ Fa   {from 2}
   5    │ ∴ (x)~(Fx · Gx)   {from 3}
*  6    │ ∴ (Fa ⊃ Ga)   {from 1}
   7    │ ∴ Ga   {from 4 and 6}
*  8    │ ∴ ~(Fa · Ga)   {from 5}
   9    └ ∴ ~Ga   {from 4 and 8}
  10    ∴ (∃x)(Fx · Gx)   {from 3; 7 contradicts 9}
```

10.   Valid

```
   1      (x)(Fx ≡ Gx)
*  2      (∃x)~Gx
      [ ∴ (∃x)~Fx
*  3    ┌ asm: ~(∃x)~Fx
   4    │ ∴ ~Ga   {from 2}
   5    │ ∴ (x)Fx   {from 3}
*  6    │ ∴ (Fa ≡ Ga)   {from 1}
*  7    │ ∴ (Fa ⊃ Ga)   {from 6}
   8    │ ∴ (Ga ⊃ Fa)   {from 6}
   9    │ ∴ ~Fa   {from 4 and 7}
  10    └ ∴ Fa   {from 5}
  11    ∴ (∃x)~Fx   {from 3; 9 contradicts 10}
```

8.2b

1.   Valid

```
   1      (x)(Dx ⊃ Bx)
   2      (x)Dx
      [ ∴ (x)Bx
*  3    ┌ asm: ~(x)Bx
*  4    │ ∴ (∃x)~Bx   {from 3}
   5    │ ∴ ~Ba   {from 4}
*  6    │ ∴ (Da ⊃ Ba)   {from 1}
   7    │ ∴ ~Da   {from 5 and 6}
   8    └ ∴ Da   {from 2}
   9    ∴ (x)Bx   {from 3; 7 contradicts 8}
```

3.   Valid

```
*  1      ~(∃x)(Fx · Ox)
```

2   (x)(Cx ⊃ Ox)
    [∴ ~(∃x)(Fx • Cx)
* 3 ┌ asm: (∃x)(Fx • Cx)
   4 │ ∴ (x)~(Fx • Ox) {from 1}
* 5 │ ∴ (Fa • Ca) {from 3}
   6 │ ∴ Fa {from 5}
   7 │ ∴ Ca {from 5}
* 8 │ ∴ (Ca ⊃ Oa) {from 2}
   9 │ ∴ Oa {from 7 and 8}
* 10 │ ∴ ~(Fa • Oa) {from 4}
  11 └ ∴ ~Oa {from 6 and 10}
  12 ∴ ~(∃x)(Fx • Cx) {from 3; 9 contra 11}

5.   Valid

   1   (x)(Kx ⊃ Ex)
* 2   ~(∃x)(Ex • Kx)
    [∴ ~(∃x)Kx
* 3 ┌ asm: (∃x)Kx
   4 │ ∴ (x)~(Ex • Kx) {from 2}
   5 │ ∴ Ka {from 3}
* 6 │ ∴ (Ka ⊃ Ea) {from 1}
   7 │ ∴ Ea {from 5 and 6}
* 8 │ ∴ ~(Ea • Ka) {from 4}
   9 └ ∴ ~Ea {from 5 and 8}
  10 ∴ ~(∃x)Kx {from 3; 7 contradicts 9}

10.   Valid

* 1   ~(∃x)(Bx • Cx)
* 2   (∃x)(Lx • Cx)
   3   (x)(Cx ⊃ Rx)
    [∴ (∃x)(Rx • (Cx • ~Bx))
* 4 ┌ asm: ~(∃x)(Rx • (Cx • ~Bx))
   5 │ ∴ (x)~(Bx • Cx) {from 1}
* 6 │ ∴ (La • Ca) {from 2}
   7 │ ∴ (x)~(Rx • (Cx • ~Bx)) {from 4}
   8 │ ∴ La {from 6}
   9 │ ∴ Ca {from 6}
* 10 │ ∴ (Ca ⊃ Ra) {from 3}
  11 │ ∴ Ra {from 9 and 10}
* 12 │ ∴ ~(Ba • Ca) {from 5}
  13 │ ∴ ~Ba {from 9 and 12}
* 14 │ ∴ ~(Ra • (Ca • ~Ba)) {from 7}
* 15 │ ∴ ~(Ca • ~Ba) {from 11 and 14}
  16 └ ∴ Ba {from 9 and 15}
  17 ∴ (∃x)(Rx • (Cx • ~Bx)) {from 4; 13 contradicts 16}

8.3a

1.   Invalid   a, b

* 1   (∃x)Fx   ┌──────┐
    [∴ (x)Fx   │ Fa, ~Fb │
* 2 asm: ~(x)Fx └──────┘
   3 ∴ Fa {from 1}
* 4 ∴ (∃x)~Fx {from 2}
   5 ∴ ~Fb {from 4}

3.   Invalid   a, b

* 1   (∃x)(Fx ∨ Gx)   ┌────────┐
* 2   ~(x)Fx   │ Fa, ~Ga │
    [∴ (∃x)Gx   │ ~Fb, ~Gb │
* 3 asm: ~(∃x)Gx   └────────┘
* 4 ∴ (Fa ∨ Ga) {from 1}
* 5 ∴ (∃x)~Fx {from 2}
   6 ∴ (x)~Gx {from 3}
   7 ∴ ~Fb {from 5}
   8 ∴ ~Ga {from 6}
   9 ∴ Fa {from 4 and 8}
  10 ∴ ~Gb {from 6}

5.   Invalid   a

* 1   ~(∃x)(Fx • Gx) ┌─────────┐
   2   (x)~Fx   │ ~Ga, ~Fa │
    [∴ (x)Gx   └─────────┘
* 3 asm: ~(x)Gx
   4 ∴ (x)~(Fx • Gx) {from 1}
* 5 ∴ (∃x)~Gx {from 3}
   6 ∴ ~Ga {from 5}
   7 ∴ ~Fa {from 2}
   8 ∴ ~(Fa • Ga) {from 4}

10.   Invalid   a,b

* 1   (∃x)~Fx   ┌────────┐
* 2   (∃x)~Gx   │ Ga, ~Fa │
    [∴ (∃x)(Fx ≡ Gx) │ Fb, ~Gb │
* 3 asm: ~(∃x)(Fx ≡ Gx) └────────┘
   4 ∴ ~Fa {from 1}
   5 ∴ ~Gb {from 2}
   6 ∴ (x)~(Fx ≡ Gx) {from 3}
* 7 ∴ ~(Fa ≡ Ga) {from 6}
* 8 ∴ (Fa ∨ Ga) {from 7}
   9 ∴ ~(Fa • Ga) {from 7}
  10 ∴ Ga {from 4 and 8}
* 11 ∴ ~(Fb ≡ Gb) {from 6}
* 12 ∴ (Fb ∨ Gb) {from 11}
  13 ∴ ~(Fb • Gb) {from 11}
  14 ∴ Fb {from 5 and 12}

8.3b

1.   Invalid   a, b

* 1   (∃x)(Bx • Gx)   ┌────────┐
    [∴ (x)(Bx ⊃ Gx) │ Ba, Ga │
* 2 asm: ~(x)(Bx ⊃ Gx) │ Bb, ~Gb │
* 3 ∴ (∃x)~(Bx ⊃ Gx) {from 2} └────────┘
* 4 ∴ (Ba • Ga) {from 1}
   5 ∴ Ba {from 4}
   6 ∴ Ga {from 4}
* 7 ∴ ~(Bb ⊃ Gb) {from 3}
   8 ∴ Bb {from 7}
   9 ∴ ~Gb {from 7}

3. Invalid

```
*   1      (∃x)Sx
*   2      ~(x)Cx
    [ ∴ (∃x)(Sx • ~Cx)
*   3      asm: ~(∃x)(Sx • ~Cx)
    4    ∴ Sa   {from 1}
*   5    ∴ (∃x)~Cx   {from 2}
    6    ∴ (x)~(Sx • ~Cx)   {from 3}
    7    ∴ ~Cb   {from 5}
*   8    ∴ ~(Sa • ~Ca)   {from 6}
    9    ∴ Ca   {from 4 and 8}
*  10    ∴ ~(Sb • ~Cb)   {from 6}
   11    ∴ ~Sb   {from 7 and 10}
```

a, b

```
Sa, Ca
~Sb, ~Cb
```

5. Valid

```
    1      (x)((Vx • Cx) ⊃ Px)
    2      (x)(Dx ⊃ (Cx • ~Px))
    [ ∴ ~(∃x)(Dx • Vx)
*   3    ┌ asm: (∃x)(Dx • Vx)
*   4    │ ∴ (Da • Va)   {from 3}
    5    │ ∴ Da   {from 4}
    6    │ ∴ Va   {from 4}
*   7    │ ∴ ((Va • Ca) ⊃ Pa)   {from 1}
*   8    │ ∴ (Da ⊃ (Ca • ~Pa))   {from 2}
*   9    │ ∴ (Ca • ~Pa)   {from 5 and 8}
   10    │ ∴ Ca   {from 9}
   11    │ ∴ ~Pa   {from 9}
*  12    │ ∴ ~(Va • Ca)   {from 7 and 11}
   13    └ ∴ ~Ca   {from 6 and 12}
   14    ∴ ~(∃x)(Dx • Vx)   {from 3; 10 contra 13}
```

10. Valid

```
    1      (x)(Sx ⊃ Vx)
    [ ∴ (x)(~Vx ⊃ ~Sx)
*   2    ┌ asm: ~(x)(~Vx ⊃ ~Sx)
*   3    │ ∴ (∃x)~(~Vx ⊃ ~Sx)   {from 2}
*   4    │ ∴ ~(~Va ⊃ ~Sa)   {from 3}
    5    │ ∴ ~Va   {from 4}
    6    │ ∴ Sa   {from 4}
*   7    │ ∴ (Sa ⊃ Va)   {from 1}
    8    └ ∴ ~Sa   {from 5 and 7}
    9    ∴ (x)(~Vx ⊃ ~Sx)   {from 2; 6 contra 8}
```

15. Invalid

```
*   1      ~(∃x)(Px • Bx)
*   2      (∃x)(Cx • ~Bx)
    [ ∴ (∃x)(Cx • Px)
*   3      asm: ~(∃x)(Cx • Px)
    4    ∴ (x)~(Px • Bx)   {from 1}
*   5    ∴ (Ca • ~Ba)   {from 2}
    6    ∴ (x)~(Cx • Px)   {from 3}
    7    ∴ Ca   {from 5}
    8    ∴ ~Ba   {from 5}
    9    ∴ ~(Pa • Ba)   {from 4}
*  10    ∴ ~(Ca • Pa)   {from 6}
   11    ∴ ~Pa   {from 7 and 10}
```

a

```
Ca, ~Ba, ~Pa
```

8.4a

```
 1.   (Cg ∨ Eg)
 3.   ((x)Lx ⊃ (x)Ex)
 5.   ((∃x)Ex ⊃ R)
10.   ((x)Ex ⊃ (x)(Lx ⊃ Ex))
15.   ~(∃x)Ex or, equivalently, (x)~Ex
20.   ~(∃x)(Lx • Ex) or, equiv, (x)~(Lx • Ex)
```

8.5a

1. Valid

```
    1      (x)(Fx ∨ Gx)
    2      ~Fa
    [ ∴ (∃x)Gx
*   3    ┌ asm: ~(∃x)Gx
    4    │ ∴ (x)~Gx   {from 3}
*   5    │ ∴ (Fa ∨ Ga)   {from 1}
    6    │ ∴ Ga   {from 2 and 5}
    7    └ ∴ ~Ga   {from 4}
    8    ∴ (∃x)Gx   {from 3; 6 contradicts 7}
```

3. Invalid

```
*   1      ((x)Ex ⊃ R)
    [ ∴ (x)(Ex ⊃ R)
*   2      asm: ~(x)(Ex ⊃ R)
*   3    ∴ (∃x)~(Ex ⊃ R)   {from 2}
*   4    ∴ ~(Ea ⊃ R)   {from 3}
    5    ∴ Ea   {from 4}
    6    ∴ ~R   {from 4}
*   7    ∴ ~(x)Ex   {from 1 and 6}
*   8    ∴ (∃x)~Ex   {from 7}
    9    ∴ ~Eb   {from 8}
```

a, b

```
Ea
~Eb
~R
```

5. Invalid

```
*   1      ((∃x)Fx ⊃ (∃x)Gx)
    [ ∴ (x)(Fx ⊃ Gx)
*   2      asm: ~(x)(Fx ⊃ Gx)
*   3    ∴ (∃x)~(Fx ⊃ Gx)   {from 2}
*   4    ∴ ~(Fa ⊃ Ga)   {from 3}
    5    ∴ Fa   {from 4}
    6    ∴ ~Ga   {from 4}
    7    ┌ asm: ~(∃x)Fx   {break 1}
    8    │ ∴ (x)~Fx   {from 7}
    9    └ ∴ ~Fa   {from 8}
   10    ∴ (∃x)Fx   {from 7; 5 contradicts 9}
*  11    ∴ (∃x)Gx   {from 1 and 10}
   12    ∴ Gb   {from 11}
```

a, b

```
Fa
~Ga
Gb
```

10. Invalid

```
*   1      ~(∃x)(Fx • Gx)
    2      ~Fd
    [ ∴ Gd
    3      asm: ~Gd
    4    ∴ (x)~(Fx • Gx)   {from 1}
    5    ∴ ~(Fd • Gd)   {from 4}
```

d

```
~Fd, ~Gd
```

15.   Valid
* 1   ((∃x)Ex ⊃ R)
       [∴ (x)(Ex ⊃ R)
* 2   ┌ asm: ~(x)(Ex ⊃ R)
* 3   │ ∴ (∃x)~(Ex ⊃ R)   {from 2}
* 4   │ ∴ ~(Ea ⊃ R)   {from 3}
  5   │ ∴ Ea   {from 4}
  6   │ ∴ ~R   {from 4}
* 7   │ ∴ ~(∃x)Ex   {from 1 and 6}
  8   │ ∴ (x)~Ex   {from 7}
  9   └ ∴ ~Ea   {from 8}
 10   ∴ (x)(Ex ⊃ R)   {from 2; 5 contradicts 9}

8.5b

1.   Valid
  1   (x)Cx
* 2   (Cw ⊃ G)
       [∴ G
  3   ┌ asm: ~G
  4   │ ∴ ~Cw   {from 2 and 3}
  5   └ ∴ Cw   {from 1}
  6   ∴ G   {from 3; 4 contradicts 5}

3.   Valid
  1   (x)(Bx ⊃ Cx)
  2   Bw
* 3   (Cw ⊃ G)
       [∴ G
  4   ┌ asm: ~G
  5   │ ∴ ~Cw   {from 3 and 4}
* 6   │ ∴ (Bw ⊃ Cw)   {from 1}
  7   └ ∴ Cw   {from 2 and 6}
  8   ∴ G   {from 4; 5 contradicts 7}

5.   Valid
  1   (x)(Ex ⊃ (Ix ∨ Fx))
       [∴ (~(∃x)Ix ⊃ (x)(~Fx ⊃ ~Ex))
* 2   ┌ asm: ~(~(∃x)Ix ⊃ (x)(~Fx ⊃ ~Ex))
* 3   │ ∴ ~(∃x)Ix   {from 2}
* 4   │ ∴ ~(x)(~Fx ⊃ ~Ex)   {from 2}
  5   │ ∴ (x)~Ix   {from 3}
* 6   │ ∴ (∃x)~(~Fx ⊃ ~Ex)   {from 4}
* 7   │ ∴ ~(~Fa ⊃ ~Ea)   {from 6}
  8   │ ∴ ~Fa   {from 7}
  9   │ ∴ Ea   {from 7}
* 10 │ ∴ (Ea ⊃ (Ia ∨ Fa))   {from 1}
* 11 │ ∴ (Ia ∨ Fa)   {from 9 and 10}
  12 │ ∴ Ia   {from 8 and 11}
  13 └ ∴ ~Ia   {from 5}
  14   ∴ (~(∃x)Ix ⊃ (x)(~Fx ⊃ ~Ex))   {from 2;
         12 contradicts 13}

10.   Valid
  1   (x)(Ax ⊃ Px)
* 2   (Ae • Ad)

       [∴ (Pe • Pd)
* 3   ┌ asm: ~(Pe • Pd)
  4   │ ∴ Ae   {from 2}
  5   │ ∴ Ad   {from 2}
* 6   │ ∴ (Ad ⊃ Pd)   {from 1}
  7   │ ∴ Pd   {from 5 and 6}
  8   │ ∴ ~Pe   {from 3 and 7}
* 9   │ ∴ (Ae ⊃ Pe)   {from 1}
 10   └ ∴ Pe   {from 4 and 9}
 11   ∴ (Pe • Pd)   {from 3; 8 contradicts 10}

15.   Valid
* 1   (T ⊃ (H • (x)(Mx ⊃ Ex)))
  2   (x)(Ex ⊃ Ix)
  3   Mt
  4   ~It
       [∴ ~T
  5   ┌ asm: T
* 6   │ ∴ (H • (x)(Mx ⊃ Ex))   {from 1 and 5}
  7   │ ∴ H   {from 6}
  8   │ ∴ (x)(Mx ⊃ Ex)   {from 6}
* 9   │ ∴ (Et ⊃ It)   {from 2}
 10   │ ∴ ~Et   {from 4 and 9}
* 11 │ ∴ (Mt ⊃ Et)   {from 8}
 12   └ ∴ Et   {from 3 and 11}
 13   ∴ ~T   {from 5; 10 contradicts 12}

20.   Valid
* 1   ~(∃x)(~Cx • Ix)
  2   (x)(Ex ⊃ Ix)
       [∴ (x)(Ex ⊃ Cx)
* 3   ┌ asm: ~(x)(Ex ⊃ Cx)
  4   │ ∴ (x)~(~Cx • Ix)   {from 1}
* 5   │ ∴ (∃x)~(Ex ⊃ Cx)   {from 3}
* 6   │ ∴ ~(Ea ⊃ Ca)   {from 5}
  7   │ ∴ Ea   {from 6}
  8   │ ∴ ~Ca   {from 6}
* 9   │ ∴ (Ea ⊃ Ia)   {from 2}
 10   │ ∴ Ia   {from 7 and 9}
* 11 │ ∴ ~(~Ca • Ia)   {from 4}
 12   └ ∴ ~Ia   {from 8 and 11}
 13   ∴ (x)(Ex ⊃ Cx)   {from 3; 10 contra 12}

9.1a

1.   La
3.   ~a=p
5.   (∃x)(∃y)(~x=y • (Lx • Ly))
10.   (∃x)(Lx • ~(∃y)(~y=x • Ly))
15.   (Ra • ~a=f)

9.2a

1.   Invalid
  1   Fa
      [∴ ~(∃x)(Fx • ~x=a)

       a, b
┌─────────────┐
│ Fa, ~Fb   │
│ ~b=a   │
└─────────────┘

* 2   asm: (∃x)(Fx • ~x=a)
* 3   ∴ (Fb • ~b=a) {from 2}
  4   ∴ Fb {from 3}
  5   ∴ ~b=a {from 3}

3.   Valid

  1   a=b
  2   b=c
   [∴ a=c
  3   ┌ asm: ~a=c
  4   └ ∴ ~b=c {from 1 and 3}
  5   ∴ a=c {from 3; 2 contradicts 4}

5.   Invalid

  1   ~a=b
  2   ~c=b
   [∴ a=c
  3   asm: ~a=c

a, b, c

~a=b, ~a=c
~c=b

10.   Invalid

   [∴ (∃x)(∃y)~y=x
* 1   asm: ~(∃x)(∃y)~y=x
  2   ∴ (x)~(∃y)~y=x {from 1}
* 3   ∴ ~(∃y)~y=a {from 2}
  4   ∴ (y)y=a {from 3}
  5   ∴ a=a {from 4}

a

a=a

9.2b

1.   Valid

  1   k=n
  2   Bn
  3   Tk
   [∴ (∃x)(Tx • Bx)
* 4   ┌ asm: ~(∃x)(Tx • Bx)
  5   │ ∴ Bk {from 1 and 2}
  6   │ ∴ (x)~(Tx • Bx) {from 4}
* 7   │ ∴ ~(Tk • Bk) {from 6}
  8   └ ∴ ~Bk {from 3 and 7}
  9   ∴ (∃x)(Tx • Bx) {from 4; 5 contradicts 8}

3.   Valid

  1   Oc
  2   ~Op
   [∴ ~p=c
  3   ┌ asm: p=c
  4   └ ∴ ~Oc {from 2 and 3}
  5   ∴ ~p=c {from 3; 1 contradicts 4}

5.   Invalid

  1   ~Bm
  2   ~Bu
   [∴ u=m
  3   asm: ~u=m

m, u

~Bm, ~Bu
~u=m

10.   Valid

* 1   (Ku ∨ Kt)

  2   ~Ku
   [∴ ~u=t
  3   ┌ asm: u=t
  4   │ ∴ Kt {from 1 and 2}
  5   └ ∴ ~Kt {from 2 and 3}
  6   ∴ ~u=t {from 3; 4 contradicts 5}

15.   Valid

* 1   (∃x)(Lx • ~(∃y)(~y=x • Ly))
  2   Lp
  3   Fp
   [∴ (x)(Lx ⊃ Fx)
* 4   ┌ asm: ~(x)(Lx ⊃ Fx)
* 5   │ ∴ (∃x)~(Lx ⊃ Fx) {from 4}
* 6   │ ∴ ~(La ⊃ Fa) {from 5}
  7   │ ∴ La {from 6}
  8   │ ∴ ~Fa {from 6}
* 9   │ ∴ (Lb • ~(∃y)(~y=b • Ly)) {from 1}
  10 │ ∴ Lb {from 9}
* 11 │ ∴ ~(∃y)(~y=b • Ly) {from 9}
  12 │ ∴ (y)~(~y=b • Ly) {from 11}
* 13 │ ∴ ~(~a=b • La) {from 12}
  14 │ ∴ a=b {from 7 and 13}
* 15 │ ∴ ~(~p=b • Lp) {from 12}
  16 │ ∴ p=b {from 2 and 15}
  17 │ ∴ ~Fb {from 8 and 14}
  18 └ ∴ ~Fp {from 16 and 17}
  19   ∴ (x)(Lx ⊃ Fx) {from 4; 3 contradicts 18}

9.3a

1.   (Lto • Lot)
3.   (x)(Rx ⊃ Ltx)
5.   ((x)Lxo • ~(x)Lox)
10.   (x)(Lxx ⊃ Lox)
15.   (x)(Cgx ⊃ Lgx)
20.   (x)(Cgx ⊃ Ggx)

9.4a

1.   (x)(Rx ⊃ (y)Lyx) or, *equivalently,*
      (x)(y)(Ry ⊃ Lxy)
3.   (∃x)(Rx • (∃y)Lyx) or, *equivalently,*
      (∃x)(∃y)(Ry • Lxy)
5.   (x)(Rx ⊃ (∃y)(Iy • Lxy))
10.   ~(∃x)(Ix • (y)Lxy)
15.   ((x)Ltx ⊃ (∃x)(Ix • (y)Lxy))
20.   (x)(∃y)Cyx
25.   (x)(y)(Cxy ⊃ Lxy)

9.5a

1.   Invalid

  1   (x)Lxa
   [∴ (x)Lax
* 2   asm: ~(x)Lax

a, b

Lab, Laa
~Lab

* 3 ∴ (∃x)~Lax {from 2}
4 ∴ ~Lab {from 3}
5 ∴ Laa {from 1}
6 ∴ Lba {from 1}

3. Invalid

1 (x)(y)(Lxy ⊃ x=y)
 [∴ (x)Lxx
* 2 asm: ~(x)Lxx
* 3 ∴ (∃x)~Lxx {from 2}
4 ∴ ~Laa {from 3}
5 ∴ (y)(Lay ⊃ a=y) {from 1}
6 ∴ (Laa ⊃ a=a) {from 5}

a

~Laa

5. Valid

1 (x)(y)Lxy
 [∴ (x)(y)((Fx · Gy) ⊃ Lxy)
* 2 ┌ asm: ~(x)(y)((Fx · Gy) ⊃ Lxy)
* 3 │ ∴ (∃x)~(y)((Fx · Gy) ⊃ Lxy) {from 2}
* 4 │ ∴ ~(y)((Fa · Gy) ⊃ Lay) {from 3}
* 5 │ ∴ (∃y)~((Fa · Gy) ⊃ Lay) {from 4}
* 6 │ ∴ ~((Fa · Gb) ⊃ Lab) {from 5}
* 7 │ ∴ (Fa · Gb) {from 6}
8 │ ∴ ~Lab {from 6}
9 │ ∴ Fa {from 7}
10 │ ∴ Gb {from 7}
11 │ ∴ (y)Lay {from 1}
12 │ ∴ (y)Lby {from 1}
13 │ ∴ Laa {from 11}
14 └ ∴ Lab {from 11}
15 ∴ (x)(y)((Fx · Gy) ⊃ Lxy) {from 2; 8 contradicts 14}

10. Valid

1 Lab
2 Lbc
 [∴ (∃x)(Lax · Lxc)
* 3 ┌ asm: ~(∃x)(Lax · Lxc)
4 │ ∴ (x)~(Lax · Lxc) {from 3}
5 │ ∴ ~(Laa · Lac) {from 4}
* 6 │ ∴ ~(Lab · Lbc) {from 4}
7 └ ∴ ~Lbc {from 1 and 6}
8 ∴ (∃x)(Lax · Lxc) {from 3; 2 contra 7}

15. Valid

1 (x)(y)(Lxy ⊃ (Fx · ~Fy))
 [∴ (x)(y)(Lxy ⊃ ~Lyx)
* 2 ┌ asm: ~(x)(y)(Lxy ⊃ ~Lyx)
* 3 │ ∴ (∃x)~(y)(Lxy ⊃ ~Lyx) {from 2}
* 4 │ ∴ ~(y)(Lay ⊃ ~Lya) {from 3}
* 5 │ ∴ (∃y)~(Lay ⊃ ~Lya) {from 4}
* 6 │ ∴ ~(Lab ⊃ ~Lba) {from 5}
7 │ ∴ Lab {from 6}
8 │ ∴ Lba {from 6}
9 │ ∴ (y)(Lay ⊃ (Fa · ~Fy)) {from 1}
10 │ ∴ (y)(Lby ⊃ (Fb · ~Fy)) {from 1}
* 11 │ ∴ (Lab ⊃ (Fa · ~Fb)) {from 9}

* 12 │ ∴ (Fa · ~Fb) {from 7 and 11}
13 │ ∴ Fa {from 12}
14 │ ∴ ~Fb {from 12}
* 15 │ ∴ (Lba ⊃ (Fb · ~Fa)) {from 10}
16 │ ∴ (Fb · ~Fa) {from 8 and 15}
17 └ ∴ Fb {from 16}
18 ∴ (x)(y)(Lxy ⊃ ~Lyx) {from 2; 14 contradicts 17}

9.5b

1. Valid

1 (x)Ljx
 [∴ (∃x)Lxu
* 2 ┌ asm: ~(∃x)Lxu
3 │ ∴ (x)~Lxu {from 2}
4 │ ∴ Ljj {from 1}
5 │ ∴ Lju {from 1}
6 └ ∴ ~Lju {from 3}
7 ∴ (∃x)Lxu {from 2; 5 contradicts 6}

3. Invalid

1 Oab
 [∴ Oba
2 asm: ~Oba

a,b

Oab, ~Oba

To make it valid, we need the premise that "older than" is asymmetrical: "(x)(y)(Oxy ⊃ ~Oyx)" – "In every case, if a first person is older than the second, then the second isn't older than the first."

5. Invalid

1 (x)(∃y)Dxy
 [∴ (∃y)(x)Dxy
* 2 asm: ~(∃y)(x) Dxy
3 ∴ (y)~(x)Dxy {from 2}
* 4 ∴ (∃y)Day {from 1}
5 ∴ Dab {from 4}
6 ∴ ~(x)Dxb {from 3}
7 ∴ (∃x)~Dxb {from 6}

a,b

Dab, Dba
~Daa, ~Dbb

Endless loop: we add further wffs to make the premise true and conclusion false. "~Dab, ~Dba, Daa, Dbb" also refutes the argument.

10. Valid

* 1 (∃x)(y)Lyx
 [∴ (∃x)Lxx
* 2 ┌ asm: ~(∃x)Lxx
3 │ ∴ (y)Lya {from 1}
4 │ ∴ (x)~Lxx {from 2}
5 │ ∴ Laa {from 3}
6 └ ∴ ~Laa {from 4}
7 ∴ (∃x)Lxx {from 2; 5 contradicts 6}

15. Valid

1 (x)((∃y)Lxy ⊃ (y)Lyx)
2 Lrj

[∴ Liu

```
   3  ┌ asm: ~Liu
*  4  │ ∴ ((∃y)Lry ⊃ (y)Lyr)  {from 1}
   5  │ ┌ asm: ~(∃y)Lry  {break 4}
   6  │ │ ∴ (y)~Lry  {from 5}
   7  │ └ ∴ ~Lrj  {from 6}
   8  │ ∴ (∃y)Lry  {from 5; 2 contradicts 7}
   9  │ ∴ (y)Lyr  {from 4 and 8}
  10  │ ∴ Lur  {from 9}
* 11  │ ∴ ((∃y)Luy ⊃ (y)Lyu)  {from 1}
  12  │ ┌ asm: ~(∃y)Luy  {break 11}
  13  │ │ ∴ (y)~Luy  {from 12}
  14  │ └ ∴ ~Lur  {from 13}
  15  │ ∴ (∃y)Luy  {from 12; 10 contradicts 14}
  16  │ ∴ (y)Lyu  {from 11 and 15}
  17  └ ∴ Liu  {from 16}
  18  ∴ Liu  {from 3; 3 contradicts 17}
```

20. Valid

```
   1  (x)(Gx ⊃ (y)((Ey • Cxy) ⊃ Pxy))
   2  (x)(Ox ⊃ (y)(Ey ⊃ Cxy))
   3  ((∃x)(y)(Ey ⊃ Pxy) ⊃ ~(∃x)Ex)
*  4  (∃x)Ex
      [ ∴ (~Og ∨ ~Gg)
*  5  ┌ asm: ~(~Og ∨ ~Gg)
   6  │ ∴ Og  {from 5}
   7  │ ∴ Gg  {from 5}
*  8  │ ∴ (Gg ⊃ (y)((Ey • Cgy) ⊃ Pgy))  {fm 1}
   9  │ ∴ (y)((Ey • Cgy) ⊃ Pgy)  {fm 7 and 8}
* 10  │ ∴ (Og ⊃ (y)(Ey ⊃ Cgy))  {from 2}
  11  │ ∴ (y)(Ey ⊃ Cgy)  {from 7 and 8}
  12  │ ∴ Ea  {from 4}
* 13  │ ∴ ~(∃x)(y)(Ey ⊃ Pxy)  {from 3 and 4}
  14  │ ∴ (x)~(y)(Ey ⊃ Pxy)  {from 13}
* 15  │ ∴ ~(y)(Ey ⊃ Pgy)  {from 14}
* 16  │ ∴ (∃y)~(Ey ⊃ Pgy)  {from 15}
* 17  │ ∴ ~(Eb ⊃ Pgb)  {from 16}
  18  │ ∴ Eb  {from 17}
  19  │ ∴ ~Pgb  {from 17}
* 20  │ ∴ ((Eb • Cgb) ⊃ Pgb)  {from 9}
* 21  │ ∴ (Eb ⊃ Cgb)  {from 11}
  22  │ ∴ Cgb  {from 18 and 21}
* 23  │ ∴ ~(Eb • Cgb)  {from 19 and 20}
  24  └ ∴ ~Eb  {from 22 and 23}
  25  ∴ (~Og ∨ ~Gg)  {from 5; 18 contra 24}
```

25. Valid

```
   1  (x)(Dx ⊃ Ax)
      [ ∴ (x)((∃y)(Dy • Hxy) ⊃ (∃y)(Ay • Hxy))
*  2  ┌ asm: ~(x)((∃y)(Dy • Hxy) ⊃
      │        (∃y)(Ay • Hxy))
*  3  │ ∴ (∃x)~((∃y)(Dy • Hxy) ⊃
      │        (∃y)(Ay • Hxy))  {from 2}
*  4  │ ∴ ~((∃y)(Dy • Hay) ⊃
      │        (∃y)(Ay • Hay))  {from 3}
*  5  │ ∴ (∃y)(Dy • Hay)  {from 4}
*  6  │ ∴ ~(∃y)(Ay • Hay)  {from 4}
```

```
*  7  │ ∴ (Db • Hab)  {from 5}
   8  │ ∴ Db  {from 7}
   9  │ ∴ Hab  {from 7}
  10  │ ∴ (y)~(Ay • Hay)  {from 6}
* 11  │ ∴ ~(Ab • Hab)  {from 10}
  12  │ ∴ ~Ab  {from 9 and 11}
* 13  │ ∴ (Db ⊃ Ab)  {from 1}
  14  └ ∴ Ab  {from 8 and 13}
  15  ∴ (x)((∃y)(Dy • Hxy) ⊃ (∃y)(Ay • Hxy))
         {from 2; 12 contradicts 14}
```

10.1a

1. □G
3. ~□M
5. □(R ⊃ P)
10. Ambiguous: (R ⊃ □R) or □(R ⊃ R)
15. (A ⊃ □B)
20. □(H ∨ T)
25. (R ⊃ □E)
30. □(G ⊃ □G)

10.2a

1. Valid

```
*  1  ◇(A • B)
      [ ∴ ◇A
*  2  ┌ asm: ~◇A
*  3  │ W ∴ (A • B)  {from 1}
   4  │ ∴ □~A  {from 2}
   5  │ W ∴ A  {from 3}
   6  │ W ∴ B  {from 3}
   7  └ W ∴ ~A  {from 4}
   8  ∴ ◇A  {from 2; 5 contradicts 7}
```

3. Valid

```
*  1  ~◇(A • ~B)
      [ ∴ □(A ⊃ B)
*  2  ┌ asm: ~□(A ⊃ B)
   3  │ ∴ □~(A • ~B)  {from 1}
*  4  │ ∴ ◇~(A ⊃ B)  {from 2}
*  5  │ W ∴ ~(A ⊃ B)  {from 4}
   6  │ W ∴ A  {from 5}
   7  │ W ∴ ~B  {from 5}
*  8  │ W ∴ ~(A • ~B)  {from 3}
   9  └ W ∴ B  {from 6 and 8}
  10  ∴ □(A ⊃ B)  {from 2; 7 contradicts 9}
```

5. Valid

```
*  1  (◇A ∨ ◇B)
      [ ∴ ◇(A ∨ B)
*  2  ┌ asm: ~◇(A ∨ B)
   3  │ ∴ □~(A ∨ B)  {from 2}
   4  │ ┌ asm: ◇A  {break 1}
   5  │ │ W ∴ A  {from 4}
   6  │ │ W ∴ ~(A ∨ B)  {from 3}
```

```
    7  | └ W ∴ ~A   {from 6}
*   8  | ∴ ~◇A   {from 4; 5 contradicts 7}
    9  | ∴ □~A   {from 8}
*  10  | ∴ ◇B   {from 1 and 8}
   11  | WW ∴ B   {from 10}
*  12  | WW ∴ ~(A ∨ B)   {from 3}
   13  | WW ∴ ~A   {from 12}
   14  └ WW ∴ ~B   {from 12}
   15  ∴ ◇(A ∨ B)   {from 2; 11 contradicts 14}
```

10.   Valid

```
    1     □(A ⊃ B)
       [ ∴ (□A ⊃ □B)
*   2   ┌ asm: ~(□A ⊃ □B)
    3   │ ∴ □A   {from 2}
*   4   │ ∴ ~□B   {from 2}
*   5   │ ∴ ◇~B   {from 4}
    6   │ W ∴ ~B   {from 5}
*   7   │ W ∴ (A ⊃ B)   {from 1}
    8   │ W ∴ ~A   {from 6 and 7}
    9   └ W ∴ A   {from 3}
   10   ∴ (□A ⊃ □B)   {from 2; 8 contradicts 9}
```

10.2b

1.   Valid

```
    1     □(T ⊃ L)
*   2     ◇(T • ~I)
       [ ∴ ◇(L • ~I)
*   3   ┌ asm: ~◇(L • ~I)
*   4   │ W ∴ (T • ~I)   {from 2}
    5   │ ∴ □~(L • ~I)   {from 3}
    6   │ W ∴ T   {from 4}
    7   │ W ∴ ~I   {from 4}
*   8   │ W ∴ (T ⊃ L)   {from 1}
    9   │ W ∴ L   {from 6 and 8}
*  10   │ W ∴ ~(L • ~I)   {from 5}
   11   └ W ∴ ~L   {from 7 and 10}
   12   ∴ ◇(L • ~I)   {from 3; 9 contradicts 11}
```

3.   Valid

```
*   1     (C ⊃ □(T ⊃ M))
*   2     ~□M
    3     □(~T ⊃ ~~T)
       [ ∴ ~C
    4   ┌ asm: C
    5   │ ∴ □(T ⊃ M)   {from 1 and 4}
*   6   │ ∴ ◇~M   {from 2}
    7   │ W ∴ ~M   {from 6}
*   8   │ W ∴ (~T ⊃ ~~T)   {from 3}
*   9   │ W ∴ (T ⊃ M)   {from 5}
   10   │ W ∴ ~T   {from 7 and 9}
   11   └ W ∴ ~~T   {from 8 and 10}
   12   ∴ ~C   {from 4; 10 contradicts 11}
```

5.   Valid

```
*   1     ◇(G • T)
```

```
    2     □(T ⊃ E)
       [ ∴ ◇(G • E)
*   3   ┌ asm: ~◇(G • E)
*   4   │ W ∴ (G • T)   {from 1}
    5   │ ∴ □~(G • E)   {from 3}
    6   │ W ∴ G   {from 4}
    7   │ W ∴ T   {from 4}
*   8   │ W ∴ (T ⊃ E)   {from 2}
    9   │ W ∴ E   {from 7 and 8}
*  10   │ W ∴ ~(G • E)   {from 5}
   11   └ W ∴ ~E   {from 6 and 10}
   12   ∴ ◇(G • E)   {from 3; 9 contradicts 11}
```

10.   Valid

```
    1     □((R • B) ⊃ ~N)
*   2     ◇(R • B)
       [ ∴ ~□(R ⊃ N)
    3   ┌ asm: □(R ⊃ N)
*   4   │ W ∴ (R • B)   {from 2}
    5   │ W ∴ R   {from 4}
    6   │ W ∴ B   {from 4}
*   7   │ W ∴ ((R • B) ⊃ ~N)   {from 1}
    8   │ W ∴ ~N   {from 4 and 7}
*   9   │ W ∴ (R ⊃ N)   {from 3}
   10   └ W ∴ N   {from 5 and 9}
   11   ∴ ~□(R ⊃ N)   {from 3; 8 contradicts 10}
```

15.   Valid

```
    1     □(~T ⊃ T)
       [ ∴ □T
*   2   ┌ asm: ~□T
*   3   │ ∴ ◇~T   {from 2}
    4   │ W ∴ ~T   {from 3}
*   5   │ W ∴ (~T ⊃ T)   {from 1}
    6   └ W ∴ T   {from 4 and 5}
    7   ∴ □T   {from 2; 4 contradicts 6}
```

10.3a

1.   Invalid

```
*   1     ◇A
       [ ∴ □A
*   2     asm: ~□A
    3     W ∴ A   {from 1}
*   4     ∴ ◇~A   {from 2}
    5     WW ∴ ~A   {from 4}
```

W	A
WW	~A

3.   Invalid

```
*   1     ◇A
*   2     ◇B
       [ ∴ ◇(A • B)
*   3     asm: ~◇(A • B)
    4     W ∴ A   {from 1}
    5     WW ∴ B   {from 2}
    6     ∴ □~(A • B)   {from 3}
*   7     W ∴ ~(A • B)   {from 6}
    8     W ∴ ~B   {from 4 and 7}
```

W	A, ~B
WW	B, ~A

* 9   WW ∴ ~(A · B)   {from 6}
  10   WW ∴ ~A   {from 5 and 9}

5.   Invalid
  1   (□A ⊃ □B)
       [∴ □(A ⊃ B)
* 2   asm: ~□(A ⊃ B)
* 3   ∴ ◊~(A ⊃ B)   {from 2}
* 4   W ∴ ~(A ⊃ B)   {from 3}
  5   W ∴ A   {from 4}
  6   W ∴ ~B   {from 4}
** 7   asm: ~□A   {break 1}
** 8   ∴ ◊~A   {from 7}
  9   WW ∴ ~A   {from 8}

W	A, ~B
WW	~A

10.   Invalid
* 1   ~□A
  2   □(B ≡ A)
       [∴ ~◊B
* 3   asm: ◊B
* 4   ∴ ◊~A   {from 1}
  5   W ∴ B   {from 3}
  6   WW ∴ ~A   {from 4}
* 7   W ∴ (B ≡ A)   {from 2}
* 8   W ∴ (B ⊃ A)   {from 7}
  9   W ∴ (A ⊃ B)   {from 7}
  10   W ∴ A   {from 5 and 8}
* 11   WW ∴ (B ≡ A)   {from 2}
* 12   WW ∴ (B ⊃ A)   {from 11}
  13   WW ∴ (A ⊃ B)   {from 11}
  14   WW ∴ ~B   {from 6 and 12}

W	A, B
WW	~A, ~B

10.3b

1.   Valid
* 1   (P ⊃ □(T ⊃ B))
* 2   ◊(T · ~B)
       [∴ ~P
  3   ┌ asm: P
  4   │ ∴ □(T ⊃ B)   {from 1 and 3}
* 5   │ W ∴ (T · ~B)   {from 2}
  6   │ W ∴ T   {from 5}
  7   │ W ∴ ~B   {from 5}
* 8   │ W ∴ (T ⊃ B)   {from 4}
  9   └ W ∴ B   {from 6 and 8}
  10   ∴ ~P   {from 3; 7 contradicts 9}

3.   Invalid
  1   □(B ⊃ B)
       [∴ (B ⊃ □B)
* 2   asm: ~(B ⊃ □B)
  3   ∴ B   {from 2}
* 4   ∴ ~□B   {from 2}
* 5   ∴ ◊~B   {from 4}
  6   W ∴ ~B   {from 5}
  7   ∴ (B ⊃ B)   {from 1}
  8   W ∴ (B ⊃ B)   {from 1}

	B
W	~B

5.   Invalid
  1   □(R ⊃ F)
  2   □(U ⊃ ~R)
       [∴ ~□(F ⊃ U)
  3   asm: □(F ⊃ U)
  4   ∴ (R ⊃ F)   {from 1}
  5   ∴ (U ⊃ ~R)   {from 2}
  6   ∴ (F ⊃ U)   {from 3}
  7   asm: ~R   {break 4}
  8   asm: ~F   {break 6}

~R, ~F

10.   Invalid
  1   □(D ∨ ~D)
* 2   (□D ⊃ ~F)
* 3   (□~D ⊃ ~F)
       [∴ ~F
  4   asm: F
* 5   ∴ ~□D   {from 2 and 4}
* 6   ∴ ~□~D   {from 2 and 4}
* 7   ∴ ◊~D   {from 3}
* 8   ∴ ◊D   {from 4}
  9   W ∴ ~D   {from 5}
  10   WW ∴ D   {from 6}
  11   W ∴ (D ∨ ~D)   {from 1}
  12   WW ∴ (D ∨ ~D)   {from 1}
  13   ∴ (D ∨ ~D)   {from 1}
  14   asm: D   {break 13}

	F, D
W	~D
WW	D

15.   Valid
* 1   (M ⊃ □(S ⊃ G))
* 2   ◊(S · ~G)
       [∴ ~M
  3   ┌ asm: M
  4   │ ∴ □(S ⊃ G)   {from 1 and 3}
* 5   │ W ∴ (S · ~G)   {from 2}
  6   │ W ∴ S   {from 5}
  7   │ W ∴ ~G   {from 5}
* 8   │ W ∴ (S ⊃ G)   {from 4}
  9   └ W ∴ G   {from 6 and 8}
  10   ∴ ~M   {from 3; 7 contradicts 9}

20.   Valid
* 1   (M ⊃ □(A ⊃ B))
* 2   ◊(~B · A)
       [∴ ~M
  3   ┌ asm: M
  4   │ ∴ □(A ⊃ B)   {from 1 and 3}
* 5   │ W ∴ (~B · A)   {from 2}
  6   │ W ∴ ~B   {from 5}
  7   │ W ∴ A   {from 5}
* 8   │ W ∴ (A ⊃ B)   {from 4}
  9   └ W ∴ ~A   {from 6 and 8}
  10   ∴ ~M   {from 3; 7 contradicts 9}

25.   Valid
* 1   ◊(W · D)
  2   □(W ⊃ F)

```
        [ ∴ ◇(F · D)
*   3   ┌ asm: ~◇(F · D)
*   4   │ W ∴ (W · D)   {from 1}
    5   │ ∴ □~(F · D)   {from 3}
    6   │ W ∴ W   {from 4}
    7   │ W ∴ D   {from 4}
*   8   │ W ∴ (W ⊃ F)   {from 2}
    9   │ W ∴ F   {from 6 and 8}
*  10   │ W ∴ ~(F · D)   {from 5}
   11   └ W ∴ ~F   {from 7 and 10}
   12   ∴ ◇(F · D)   {from 3; 9 contradicts 11}
```

11.1a

1.   Valid in B or S5.

```
*   1   ◇□A
        [ ∴ A
    2   ┌ asm: ~A
    3   │ W ∴ □A   {from 1}  # ⇒ W
    4   └ ∴ A   {from 3}  need B or S5
    5   ∴ A   {from 2; 2 contradicts 4}
```

3.   Valid in S4 or S5.

```
*   1   ◇◇A
        [ ∴ ◇A
*   2   ┌ asm: ~◇A
*   3   │ W ∴ ◇A   {from 1}  # ⇒ W
    4   │ ∴ □~A   {from 2}
    5   │ WW ∴ A   {from 3}  W ⇒ WW
    6   └ WW ∴ ~A   {from 4}  need S4 or S5
    7   ∴ ◇A   {from 2; 5 contradicts 6}
```

5.   Valid in S5.

```
*   1   (□A ⊃ □B)
        [ ∴ □(□A ⊃ □B)
*   2   ┌ asm: ~□(□A ⊃ □B)
*   3   │ ∴ ◇~(□A ⊃ □B)   {from 2}
*   4   │ W ∴ ~(□A ⊃ □B)   {from 3}  # ⇒ W
    5   │ W ∴ □A   {from 4}
*   6   │ W ∴ ~□B   {from 4}
*   7   │ W ∴ ◇~B   {from 6}
    8   │ WW ∴ ~B   {from 7}  W ⇒ WW
    9   │ ┌ asm: ~□A   {break 1}
   10   │ │ ∴ ◇~A   {from 9}
   11   │ │ WWW ∴ ~A   {from 10}  # ⇒ WWW
   12   │ └ WWW ∴ A   {from 5}  need S5
   13   │ ∴ □A   {from 9; 11 contradicts 12}
   14   │ ∴ □B   {from 1 and 13}
   15   └ WW ∴ B   {from 14}  need S4 or S5
   16   ∴ □(□A ⊃ □B)   {from 2; 8 contra 15}
```

10.   Valid in B or S5.

```
*   1   ◇A
        [ ∴ ◇□◇A
*   2   ┌ asm: ~◇□◇A
    3   │ W ∴ A   {from 1}  # ⇒ W
    4   │ ∴ □~□◇A   {from 2}
```

```
*   5   │ W ∴ ~□◇A   {from 4}  any system
*   6   │ W ∴ ◇~◇A   {from 5}
*   7   │ WW ∴ ~◇A   {from 6}  W ⇒ WW
    8   │ WW ∴ □~A   {from 7}
    9   └ W ∴ ~A   {from 8}  need B or S5
   10   ∴ ◇□◇A   {from 2; 3 contradicts 9}
```

15.   Valid in S4 or S5.

```
    1   □A
        [ ∴ □□□A
*   2   ┌ asm: ~□□□A
*   3   │ ∴ ◇~□□A   {from 2}
*   4   │ W ∴ ~□□A   {from 3}  # ⇒ W
*   5   │ W ∴ ◇~□A   {from 4}
*   6   │ WW ∴ ~□A   {from 5}  W ⇒ WW
*   7   │ WW ∴ ◇~A   {from 6}
    8   │ WWW ∴ ~A   {from 7}
        │       WW ⇒ WWW
    9   └ WWW ∴ A   {from 1}  need S4 or S5
   10   ∴ □□□A   {from 2; 8 contradicts 9}
```

11.1b

1.   Valid in S5.

```
    1   □(N ⊃ □N)
*   2   ◇N
        [ ∴ □N
*   3   ┌ asm: ~□N
    4   │ W ∴ N   {from 2}  # ⇒ W
*   5   │ ∴ ◇~N   {from 3}
    6   │ WW ∴ ~N   {from 5}  # ⇒ WW
*   7   │ W ∴ (N ⊃ □N)   {from 1}  any system
    8   │ W ∴ □N   {from 4 and 7}
    9   └ WW ∴ N   {from 8}  need S5
   10   ∴ □N   {from 3; 6 contradicts 9}
```

3.   This side is valid in S5.

```
    1   □(N ⊃ □N)
        [ ∴ ~(◇N · ◇~N)
*   2   ┌ asm: (◇N · ◇~N)
*   3   │ ∴ ◇N   {from 2}
*   4   │ ∴ ◇~N   {from 2}
    5   │ W ∴ N   {from 3}  # ⇒ W
    6   │ WW ∴ ~N   {from 4}  # ⇒ WW
*   7   │ W ∴ (N ⊃ □N)   {from 1}  any system
    8   │ W ∴ □N   {from 5 and 7}
    9   └ WW ∴ N   {from 8}  need S5
   10   ∴ ~(◇N · ◇~N)   {from 2; 6 contradicts 9}
```

The other side is valid in S4 or S5.

```
*   1   ~(◇N · ◇~N)
        [ ∴ □(N ⊃ □N)
*   2   ┌ asm: ~□(N ⊃ □N)
*   3   │ ∴ ◇~(N ⊃ □N)   {from 2}
*   4   │ W ∴ ~(N ⊃ □N)   {from 3}  # ⇒ W
    5   │ W ∴ N   {from 4}
*   6   │ W ∴ ~□N   {from 4}
```

*	7	W ∴ ◇~N {from 6}
	8	WW ∴ ~N {from 7} W ⇒ WW
	9	⌐ asm: ~◇N {break 1}
	10	│ ∴ □~N {from 9}
	11	└ W ∴ ~N {from 10} any system
	12	∴ ◇N {from 9; 5 contradicts 11}
*	13	∴ ~◇~N {from 1 and 12}
	14	∴ □N {from 13}
	15	└ WW ∴ N {from 14} need S4 or S5
	16	∴ □(N ⊃ □N) {from 2; 8 contradicts 15}

5.   Valid in S4 or S5.

	1	□T
*	2	◇~L
*	3	(N ⊃ □(□T ⊃ L))
		[∴ ~N
	4	⌐ asm: N
	5	│ W ∴ ~L {from 2} # ⇒ W
	6	│ ∴ □(□T ⊃ L) {from 3 and 4}
*	7	│ W ∴ (□T ⊃ L) {from 6} any system
*	8	│ W ∴ ~□T {from 5 and 7}
*	9	│ W ∴ ◇~T {from 8}
	10	│ WW ∴ ~T {from 9} W ⇒ WW
	11	└ WW ∴ T {from 1} need S4 or S5
	12	∴ ~N {from 4; 10 contradicts 11}

11.2a

1.   (x)◇Ux

3.   □Uj

5.   (Ns • ◇~Ns)

10.   (x)(Nx ⊃ □Ax)

15.   ◇(x)(Cx ⊃ Tx)

20.   (∃x)□Ux

11.3a

1.   Valid

*	1	(∃x)□Fx
		[∴ □(∃x)Fx
*	2	⌐ asm: ~□(∃x)Fx
	3	│ ∴ □Fa {from 1}
*	4	│ ∴ ◇~(∃x)Fx {from 2}
*	5	│ W ∴ ~(∃x)Fx {from 4}
	6	│ W ∴ (x)~Fx {from 5}
	7	│ W ∴ Fa {from 3}
	8	└ W ∴ ~Fa {from 6}
	9	∴ □(∃x)Fx {from 2; 7 contradicts 8}

3.   Valid

		[∴ □(∃x)x=a
*	1	⌐ asm: ~□(∃x)x=a
*	2	│ ∴ ◇~(∃x)x=a {from 1}
*	3	│ W ∴ ~(∃x)x=a {from 2}
	4	│ W ∴ (x)~x=a {from 3}
	5	│ W ∴ ~a=a {from 4}

	6	└ W ∴ a=a {to contradict 5}
	7	∴ □(∃x)x=a {from 1; 5 contradicts 6}

5.   Valid

*	1	◇(x)Fx
		[∴ (x)◇Fx
*	2	⌐ asm: ~(x)◇Fx
	3	│ W ∴ (x)Fx {from 1}
*	4	│ ∴ (∃x)~◇Fx {from 2}
*	5	│ ∴ ~◇Fa {from 4}
	6	│ ∴ □~Fa {from 5}
	7	│ W ∴ Fa {from 3}
	8	└ W ∴ ~Fa {from 6}
	9	∴ (x)◇Fx {from 2; 7 contradicts 8}

10.   Valid

*	1	(∃x)◇Fx
		[∴ ◇(∃x)Fx
*	2	⌐ asm: ~◇(∃x)Fx
*	3	│ ∴ ◇Fa {from 1}
	4	│ ∴ □~(∃x)Fx {from 2}
	5	│ W ∴ Fa {from 3}
*	6	│ W ∴ ~(∃x)Fx {from 4}
	7	│ W ∴ (x)~Fx {from 6}
	8	└ W ∴ ~Fa {from 7}
	9	∴ ◇(∃x)Fx {from 2; 5 contradicts 8}

11.3b

1.   Invalid

	1	Bi
		[∴ □(x)(~Bx ⊃ ~x=i)
*	2	asm: ~□(x)(~Bx ⊃ ~x=i)
*	3	∴ ◇~(x)(~Bx ⊃ ~x=i) {from 2}
*	4	W ∴ ~(x)(~Bx ⊃ ~x=i) {from 3}
*	5	W ∴ (∃x)~(~Bx ⊃ ~x=i) {from 4}
*	6	W ∴ ~(~Ba ⊃ ~a=i) {from 5}
	7	W ∴ ~Ba {from 6}
	8	W ∴ a=i {from 6}
	9	W ∴ ~(~Bi ⊃ ~i=i) {from 6 and 8}
	10	W ∴ ~Bi {from 7 and 8}

a, i
Bi
~Bi, ~Ba
a=i

W

3.   Valid

	1	~a=p
*	2	(((∃x)□x=p • ~(x)□x=p) ⊃ S)
		[∴ S
	3	⌐ asm: ~S
*	4	│ ∴ ~((∃x)□x=p • ~(x)□x=p)
		│ {from 2 and 3}
	5	│ ⌐ asm: ~(∃x)□x=p {break 4}
	6	│ │ ∴ (x)~□x=p {from 5}
	7	│ │ ∴ ~□p=p {from 6}
	8	│ │ ∴ ◇~p=p {from 7}
	9	│ │ W ∴ ~p=p {from 8}
	10	│ └ W ∴ p=p {to contradict 9}
*	11	│ ∴ (∃x)□x=p {from 5; 9 contradicts 10}
	12	│ ∴ (x)□x=p {from 4 and 11}

13 | ∴ □a=p {from 12}
14 └ ∴ a=p {from 13}
15 ∴ S {from 3; 1 contradicts 14}

5.   Invalid

                                    a, b

  1   □(∃x)Ux
    [∴ (∃x)□Ux | Ua, ~Ub |
* 2   asm: ~(∃x)□Ux   W | Ub, ~Ua |
  3   ∴ (x)~□Ux {from 3}
* 4   ∴ (∃x)Ux {from 1}
  5   ∴ Ua {from 4}
* 6   ∴ ~□Ua {from 3}
* 7   ∴ ◇~Ua {from 6}
  8   W ∴ ~Ua {from 7}
* 9   W ∴ (∃x)Ux {from 1}
 10   W ∴ Ub {from 1}

Endless loop: add "~Ub" to the actual world to make the conclusion false.

10.   Valid

* 1   ◇(Ts • ~Bs)
  2   □(x)(Tx ⊃ Px)
    [∴ ~□(x)(Px ⊃ Bx)
  3   ┌ asm: □(x)(Px ⊃ Bx)
* 4 | W ∴ (Ts • ~Bs) {from 1}
  5 | W ∴ Ts {from 4}
  6 | W ∴ ~Bs {from 4}
  7 | W ∴ (x)(Tx ⊃ Px) {from 2}
  8 | W ∴ (x)(Px ⊃ Bx) {from 3}
* 9 | W ∴ (Ts ⊃ Ps) {from 7}
 10 | W ∴ Ps {from 5 and 9}
* 11 | W ∴ (Ps ⊃ Bs) {from 8}
 12   └ W ∴ ~Ps {from 6 and 11}
 13   ∴ ~□(x)(Px ⊃ Bx) {from 3; 10
              contradicts 12}

15.   Valid (but line 11 requires S5 or B).

* 1   ◇(∃x)Ux
  2   □(x)(Ux ⊃ □Ox)
    [∴ (∃x)Ox
* 3   ┌ asm: ~(∃x)Ox
* 4 | W ∴ (∃x)Ux {from 1}
  5 | ∴ (x)~Ox {from 3}
  6 | W ∴ Ua {from 4}
  7 | W ∴ (x)(Ux ⊃ □Ox) {from 2}
  8 | ∴ ~Oa {from 5}
* 9 | W ∴ (Ua ⊃ □Oa) {from 7}
 10 | W ∴ □Oa {from 6 and 9}
 11   └ ∴ Oa {from 10}
 12   ∴ (∃x)Ox {from 3; 8 contradicts 11}

12.1a

1.   (L̲ ∨ S̲)
3.   (A̲ ⊃ W) *or, equivalently,* (~W ⊃ ~A̲)
5.   ~(A̲ • B̲)
10. ((x)Ax ⊃ Au̲)

15.   (B ⊃ ~A̲)
20.   (∃x)(Sx̲ • Wx)

12.2a

1.   Valid

  1   ~A̲
    [∴ ~(A̲ • B̲)
  2   ┌ asm: (A̲ • B̲)
  3   └ ∴ A̲ {from 2}
  4   ∴ ~(A̲ • B̲) {from 2; 1 contradicts 3}

3.   Invalid

                          | ~B, A̲, ~A |

  1   (A ⊃ B̲)
    [∴ (~B ⊃ ~A̲)
* 2   asm: ~(~B ⊃ ~A̲)
  3   ∴ ~B {from 2}
  4   ∴ A̲ {from 2}
  5   asm: ~A {break 1}

5.   Valid

* 1   ~◇(A̲ • B̲)
* 2   ~(C̲ • ~A̲)
    [∴ ~(C̲ • B̲)
* 3   ┌ asm: (C̲ • B̲)
  4 | ∴ □~(A̲ • B̲) {from 1}
  5 | ∴ C̲ {from 3}
  6 | ∴ B̲ {from 3}
  7 | ∴ A̲ {from 2 and 5}
* 8 | ∴ ~(A̲ • B̲) {from 4}
  9   └ ∴ ~A̲ {from 6 and 8}
 10   ∴ ~(C̲ • B̲) {from 3; 7 contradicts 9}

10.   Valid

* 1   ~(A̲ • ~B̲)
    [∴ (~A̲ ∨ B̲)
* 2   ┌ asm: ~(~A̲ ∨ B̲)
  3 | ∴ A̲ {from 2}
  4 | ∴ ~B̲ {from 2}
  5   └ ∴ B̲ {from 1 and 3}
  6   ∴ (~A̲ ∨ B̲) {from 2; 4 contradicts 5}

12.2b

1.   Valid

* 1   (C̲ ∨ E̲)
  2   V
* 3   (V ⊃ ~C̲)
    [∴ E̲
  4   ┌ asm: ~E̲
  5 | ∴ C̲ {from 1 and 4}
  6   └ ∴ ~C̲ {from 2 and 3}
  7   ∴ E̲ {from 4; 5 contradicts 6}

3.   Valid

* 1   (G ⊃ ~E̲)

  2   G
  [∴ ~<u>E</u>
  3 ┌ asm: <u>E</u>
  4 └ ∴ ~<u>E</u> {from 1 and 2}
  5 ∴ ~<u>E</u> {from 3; 3 contradicts 4}

5. Valid

* 1   (B ⊃ <u>C</u>)
  2   B
  [∴ <u>C</u>
  3 ┌ asm: ~<u>C</u>
  4 └ ∴ <u>C</u> {from 1 and 2}
  5 ∴ <u>C</u> {from 3; 3 contradicts 4}

10. Valid

  1   w=l
  [∴ (G<u>u</u>w ∨ ~G<u>u</u>l)
* 2 ┌ asm: ~(G<u>u</u>w ∨ ~G<u>u</u>l)
  3 │ ∴ ~G<u>u</u>w {from 2}
  4 │ ∴ ~G<u>u</u>l {from 1 and 3}
  5 └ ∴ G<u>u</u>l {from 2}
  6 ∴ (G<u>u</u>w ∨ ~G<u>u</u>l) {from 2; 4 contra 5}

15. Invalid

  1   (T ⊃ M)   ┌─────────────┐
  2   T   │ <u>T</u>, ~<u>M</u>, ~T │
  [∴ <u>M</u>   └─────────────┘
  3   asm: ~<u>M</u>
  4   asm: ~T {break 1}

20. Invalid
                                    a
  1   (x)(Hx ⊃ E<u>x</u>)   ┌──────────────┐
  [∴ (x)(~Ex ⊃ ~H<u>x</u>)   │ ~Ea, H<u>a</u>, ~Ha │
* 2   asm: ~(x)(~Ex ⊃ ~H<u>x</u>) └──────────────┘
* 3   ∴ (∃x)~(~Ex ⊃ ~H<u>x</u>) {from 2}
* 4   ∴ ~(~Ea ⊃ ~H<u>a</u>) {from 3}
  5   ∴ ~Ea {from 4}
  6   ∴ H<u>a</u> {from 4}
  7   ∴ (Ha ⊃ E<u>a</u>) {from 1}
  8   asm: ~Ha {break 7}

12.3a

1. (A ⊃ O~<u>B</u>)
3. (O~<u>A</u> ⊃ ~<u>A</u>)
5. □(<u>A</u> ⊃ R<u>A</u>)
10. O~(<u>B</u> • ~<u>A</u>)
15. (~◇(x)Ax ⊃ O~A<u>u</u>)
20. R(x)(~Tx ⊃ S<u>x</u>)

12.4a

1. Valid

  1   O~<u>A</u>
  [∴ O~(<u>A</u> • <u>B</u>)
* 2 ┌ asm: ~O~(<u>A</u> • <u>B</u>)

* 3 │ ∴ R(<u>A</u> • <u>B</u>) {from 2}
* 4 │ D ∴ (<u>A</u> • <u>B</u>) {from 3}
  5 │ D ∴ <u>A</u> {from 4}
  6 │ D ∴ <u>B</u> {from 4}
  7 └ D ∴ ~<u>A</u> {from 1}
  8 ∴ O~(<u>A</u> • <u>B</u>) {from 2; 5 contradicts 7}

3. Valid

  1   b=c
  [∴ (OF<u>a</u>b ⊃ OF<u>a</u>c)
* 2 ┌ asm: ~(OF<u>a</u>b ⊃ OF<u>a</u>c)
  3 │ ∴ OF<u>a</u>b {from 2}
  4 │ ∴ ~OF<u>a</u>c {from 2}
  5 └ ∴ OF<u>a</u>c {from 1 and 3}
  6 ∴ (OF<u>a</u>b ⊃ OF<u>a</u>c) {from 2; 4 contra 5}

5. Invalid

  [∴ O(<u>A</u> ⊃ O<u>A</u>)
* 1   asm: ~O(<u>A</u> ⊃ O<u>A</u>)
* 2   ∴ R~(<u>A</u> ⊃ O<u>A</u>) {from 1}
* 3   D ∴ ~(<u>A</u> ⊃ O<u>A</u>) {from 2}
  4   D ∴ <u>A</u> {from 3}
* 5   D ∴ ~O<u>A</u> {from 3}
* 6   D ∴ R~<u>A</u> {from 5}
  7   DD ∴ ~<u>A</u> {from 6}

10. Valid

* 1   (A ⊃ O<u>B</u>)
  [∴ O(A ⊃ <u>B</u>)
* 2 ┌ asm: ~O(A ⊃ <u>B</u>)
* 3 │ ∴ R~(A ⊃ <u>B</u>) {from 2}
* 4 │ D ∴ ~(A ⊃ <u>B</u>) {from 3}
  5 │ D ∴ A {from 4}
  6 │ D ∴ ~<u>B</u> {from 4}
  7 │ ∴ A {from 5 by indicative transfer}
  8 │ ∴ O<u>B</u> {from 1 and 7}
  9 └ D ∴ <u>B</u> {from 8}
  10 ∴ O(A ⊃ <u>B</u>) {from 2; 6 contradicts 9}

15. Valid

  1   O<u>A</u>
  2   O<u>B</u>
  [∴ ◇(A • B)
  3 ┌ asm: ~◇(A • B)
  4 │ ┌ asm: O(<u>A</u> • <u>B</u>) {assume to get
     │ │   opposite using 3 and Kant's Law}
  5 │ └ ◇(A • B) {from 4 using Kant's Law}
* 6 │ ∴ ~O(<u>A</u> • <u>B</u>) {from 4; 3 contradicts 5}
* 7 │ ∴ R~(<u>A</u> • <u>B</u>) {from 6}
* 8 │ D ∴ ~(<u>A</u> • <u>B</u>) {from 7}
  9 │ D ∴ <u>A</u> {from 1}
  10 │ D ∴ <u>B</u> {from 2}
  11 └ D ∴ ~<u>B</u> {from 8 and 9}
  12 ∴ ◇(A • B) {from 3; 10 contradicts 11}

20. Invalid

  1   O(x)(Fx ⊃ G<u>x</u>)

2   OF<u>a</u>
   [∴ OG<u>a</u>
* 3   asm: ~OG<u>a</u>
* 4   ∴ R~G<u>a</u> {from 3}
   5   D∴ ~G<u>a</u> {from 4}
   6   D∴ (x)(Fx ⊃ G<u>x</u>) {from 1}
   7   D∴ F<u>a</u> {from 2}
* 8   D∴ (Fa ⊃ G<u>a</u>) {from 6}
   9   D∴ ~Fa {from 5 and 8}
  10   ∴ ~Fa {from 9 by indicative transfer}

25.   Valid
* 1   (A ∨ O<u>B</u>)
   2   ~A
   [∴ O<u>B</u>
* 3 ⌐ asm: ~O<u>B</u>
   4 └ ∴ O<u>B</u> {from 1 and 2}
   5   ∴ O<u>B</u> {from 3; 3 contradicts 4}

12.4b

1.   Valid
* 1   ~R(<u>B</u> · <u>D</u>)
   2   O<u>D</u>
   [∴ ~<u>B</u>
   3 ⌐ asm: <u>B</u>
   4 │ ∴ O~(<u>B</u> · <u>D</u>) {from 1}
   5 │ ∴ <u>D</u> {from 2}
* 6 │ ∴ ~(<u>B</u> · <u>D</u>) {from 4}
   7 └ ∴ ~<u>D</u> {from 3 and 6}
   8   ∴ ~<u>B</u> {from 3; 5 contradicts 7}

3.   Valid
   1   A
   2   O~<u>A</u>
* 3   ((A · ◇~A) ⊃ F)
   [∴ F
   4 ⌐ asm: ~F
* 5 │ ∴ ~(A · ◇~A) {from 3 and 4}
* 6 │ ∴ ~◇~A {from 1 and 5}
   7 └ ∴ ◇~A {from 2 by Kant's Law}
   8   ∴ F {from 4; 6 contradicts 7}

5.   Invalid
   [∴ (O<u>A</u> ⊃ A)
* 1   asm: ~(O<u>A</u> ⊃ A)
   2   ∴ O<u>A</u> {from 1}
   3   ∴ ~A {from 1}
   4   ∴ <u>A</u> {from 2}

10.   Invalid
* 1   R(∃x)A<u>x</u>
   [∴ (x)RA<u>x</u>
* 2   asm: ~(x)RA<u>x</u>
* 3   D∴ (∃x)A<u>x</u> {from 1}
* 4   ∴ (∃x)~RA<u>x</u> {from 2}
   5   D∴ A<u>a</u> {from 3}

* 6   ∴ ~RA<u>b</u> {from 4}
   7   ∴ O~A<u>b</u> {from 6}
   8   D∴ ~A<u>b</u> {from 7}

15.   Valid
* 1   (O~<u>K</u> ⊃ O~<u>I</u>)
* 2   (R<u>N</u> ⊃ R<u>I</u>)
   [∴ (O~<u>K</u> ⊃ O~<u>N</u>)
* 3 ⌐ asm: ~(O~<u>K</u> ⊃ O~<u>N</u>)
   4 │ ∴ O~<u>K</u> {from 3}
* 5 │ ∴ ~O~<u>N</u> {from 3}
* 6 │ ∴ R<u>N</u> {from 5}
   7 │ ∴ O~<u>I</u> {from 1 and 4}
* 8 │ ∴ R<u>I</u> {from 2 and 6}
   9 │ DD∴ <u>I</u> {from 8}
  10 └ DD∴ ~<u>I</u> {from 7}
  11   ∴ (O~<u>K</u> ⊃ O~<u>N</u>) {from 3; 9 contra 10}

20.   Valid
   1   N
   2   □(<u>B</u> ⊃ <u>D</u>)
   3   □(<u>D</u> ⊃ (N ⊃ <u>S</u>))
   [∴ O(<u>S</u> ∨ ~<u>B</u>)
* 4 ⌐ asm: ~O(<u>S</u> ∨ ~<u>B</u>)
* 5 │ ∴ R~(<u>S</u> ∨ ~<u>B</u>) {from 4}
* 6 │ D∴ ~(<u>S</u> ∨ ~<u>B</u>) {from 5}
   7 │ D∴ ~<u>S</u> {from 6}
   8 │ D∴ <u>B</u> {from 6}
* 9 │ D∴ (<u>B</u> ⊃ <u>D</u>) {from 2}
  10 │ D∴ <u>D</u> {from 8 and 9}
* 11 │ D∴ (<u>D</u> ⊃ (N ⊃ <u>S</u>)) {from 3}
* 12 │ D∴ (N ⊃ <u>S</u>) {from 10 and 11}
  13 │ D∴ ~N {from 7 and 12}
  14 └ ∴ ~N {from 13 by indicative transfer}
  15   ∴ O(<u>S</u> ∨ ~<u>B</u>) {from 4; 1 contradicts 14}

25.   Valid
* 1   (R<u>P</u> ⊃ O<u>S</u>)
* 2   ~◇S
   [∴ O~<u>P</u>
* 3 ⌐ asm: ~O~<u>P</u>
   4 │ ∴ □~S {from 2}
* 5 │ ∴ R<u>P</u> {from 3}
   6 │ ∴ O<u>S</u> {from 1 and 5}
* 7 │ ∴ ◇S {from 6 by Kant's Law}
   8 │ W∴ S {from 7}
   9 └ W∴ ~S {from 4}
  10   ∴ O~<u>P</u> {from 3; 8 contradicts 9}

13.1a

1.   u:~G
3.   ~u:G
5.   □(u:G ⊃ ~u:~G)
10.   ~(<u>u</u>:A · <u>u</u>:~A)

13.2a

1. Valid
*   1   ~◇(A · B)
     [∴ ~(u:A · u:B)
*   2   ┌ asm: (u:A · u:B)
   3   │ ∴ □~(A · B)   {from 1}
   4   │ ∴ u:A   {from 2}
   5   │ ∴ u:B   {from 2}
   6   │ u ∴ A   {from 4}
*   7   │ u ∴ ~(A · B)   {from 3}
   8   │ u ∴ ~B   {from 6 and 7}
   9   └ u ∴ B   {from 5}
  10   ∴ ~(u:A · u:B)   {from 2; 8 contradicts 9}

3. Invalid
*   1   ~◇(A · B)
     [∴ (u:A ⊃ ~u:B)
*   2   asm: ~(u:A ⊃ ~u:B)
   3   ∴ □~(A · B)   {from 1}
   4   ∴ u:A   {from 2}
   5   ∴ u:B   {from 2}
   6   u ∴ B   {from 5}
*   7   u ∴ ~(A · B)   {from 3}
   8   u ∴ ~A   {from 6 and 7}

5. Invalid
*   1   ~◇(A · B)
     [∴ (u:~A ∨ u:~B)
*   2   asm: ~(u:~A ∨ u:~B)
   3   ∴ □~(A · B)   {from 1}
*   4   ∴ ~u:~A   {from 2}
*   5   ∴ ~u:~B   {from 2}
   6   u ∴ A   {from 4}
   7   uu ∴ B   {from 5}
*   8   u ∴ ~(A · B)   {from 3}
   9   u ∴ ~B   {from 6 and 8}
*   10   uu ∴ ~(A · B)   {from 3}
   11   uu ∴ ~A   {from 7 and 10}

10. Valid
*   1   ~◇(A · B)
     [∴ ~(u:A · ~u:~B)
*   2   ┌ asm: (u:A · ~u:~B)
   3   │ ∴ □~(A · B)   {from 1}
   4   │ ∴ u:A   {from 2}
*   5   │ ∴ ~u:~B   {from 2}
   6   │ u ∴ B   {from 5}
*   7   │ u ∴ ~(A · B)   {from 3}
   8   │ u ∴ ~A   {from 6 and 7}
   9   └ u ∴ A   {from 4}
  10   ∴ ~(u:A · ~u:~B)   {from 2; 8 contra 9}

13.2b

1. Valid
   1   □(A ⊃ B)
*   2   ~u:B
     [∴ ~u:A
   3   ┌ asm: u:A
   4   │ u ∴ ~B   {from 2}
*   5   │ u ∴ (A ⊃ B)   {from 1}
   6   │ u ∴ ~A   {from 4 and 5}
   7   └ u ∴ A   {from 3}
   8   ∴ ~u:A   {from 3; 6 contradicts 7}

3. Invalid
   1   u:A
     [∴ ~u:~A
   2   asm: u:~A
   3   u ∴ ~A   {from 2}

5. Invalid
     [∴ (u:A ∨ u:~A)
*   1   asm: ~(u:A ∨ u:~A)
*   2   ∴ ~u:A   {from 1}
*   3   ∴ ~u:~A   {from 1}
   4   u ∴ ~A   {from 2}
   5   uu ∴ A   {from 3}

10. Invalid
     [∴ (A ⊃ u:A)
*   1   asm: ~(A ⊃ u:A)
   2   ∴ A   {from 1}
*   3   ∴ ~u:A   {from 1}
   4   u ∴ ~A   {from 3}

13.3a

1. u:Sa
3. u:OSa
5. u:Sa
10. (u:OAu ⊃ Au)
15. (u:Axu ⊃ Aux)

13.4a

1. Valid
     [∴ ~(u:A · u:~A)
*   1   ┌ asm: (u:A · u:~A)
   2   │ ∴ u:A   {from 1}
   3   │ ∴ u:~A   {from 1}
   4   │ u ∴ A   {from 2}
   5   └ u ∴ ~A   {from 3}
   6   ∴ ~(u:A · u:~A)   {from 1; 4 contra 5}

3.　Invalid

[∴ (u:B<u>a</u> ∨ u:~B<u>a</u>)
* 1　　asm: ~(<u>u</u>:B<u>a</u> ∨ <u>u</u>:~B<u>a</u>)
* 2　　∴ ~<u>u</u>:B<u>a</u>　{from 1}
* 3　　∴ ~<u>u</u>:~B<u>a</u>　{from 1}
　 4　　u ∴ ~B<u>a</u>　{from 2}
　 5　　uu ∴ B<u>a</u>　{from 3}

5.　Invalid

　 1　　u:(x)OA<u>x</u>
[∴ <u>u</u>:A<u>u</u>
* 2　　asm: ~<u>u</u>:A<u>u</u>
　 3　　u ∴ ~A<u>u</u>　{from 2}

10.　Valid

　 1　　□(<u>A</u> ⊃ <u>B</u>)
[∴ ~(<u>u</u>:O<u>A</u> · ~<u>u</u>:<u>B</u>)
* 2　┌ asm: (<u>u</u>:O<u>A</u> · ~<u>u</u>:<u>B</u>)
　 3　│ ∴ <u>u</u>:O<u>A</u>　{from 2}
* 4　│ ∴ ~<u>u</u>:<u>B</u>　{from 2}
　 5　│ u ∴ ~<u>B</u>　{from 4}
* 6　│ u ∴ (<u>A</u> ⊃ <u>B</u>)　{from 1}
　 7　│ u ∴ ~<u>A</u>　{from 5 and 6}
　 8　│ u ∴ O<u>A</u>　{from 3}
　 9　└ u ∴ <u>A</u>　{from 8}
　 10　∴ ~(<u>u</u>:O<u>A</u> · ~<u>u</u>:<u>B</u>)　{from 2; 7 contra 9}

13.4b

1.　Valid

[∴ ~(<u>u</u>:(x)OA<u>x</u> · ~<u>u</u>:A<u>u</u>)
* 1　┌ asm: (<u>u</u>:(x)OA<u>x</u> · ~<u>u</u>:A<u>u</u>)
　 2　│ ∴ <u>u</u>:(x)OA<u>x</u>　{from 1}
* 3　│ ∴ ~<u>u</u>:A<u>u</u>　{from 1}
　 4　│ u ∴ ~A<u>u</u>　{from 3}
　 5　│ u ∴ (x)OA<u>x</u>　{from 2}
　 6　│ u ∴ OA<u>u</u>　{from 5}
　 7　└ u ∴ A<u>u</u>　{from 6}
　 8　∴ ~(<u>u</u>:(x)OA<u>x</u> · ~<u>u</u>:A<u>u</u>)　{from 1; 4 contradicts 7}

3.　Valid

　 1　　□(<u>E</u> ⊃ (N ⊃ <u>M</u>))
[∴ ~((<u>u</u>:<u>E</u> · <u>u</u>:N) · ~<u>u</u>:<u>M</u>)
* 2　┌ asm: ((<u>u</u>:<u>E</u> · <u>u</u>:N) · ~<u>u</u>:<u>M</u>)
* 3　│ ∴ (<u>u</u>:<u>E</u> · <u>u</u>:N)　{from 2}
* 4　│ ∴ ~<u>u</u>:<u>M</u>　{from 2}
　 5　│ ∴ <u>u</u>:<u>E</u>　{from 3}
　 6　│ ∴ <u>u</u>:N　{from 3}
　 7　│ u ∴ ~<u>M</u>　{from 4}
* 8　│ u ∴ (<u>E</u> ⊃ (N ⊃ <u>M</u>))　{from 1}
　 9　│ u ∴ <u>E</u>　{from 5}
* 10　│ u ∴ (N ⊃ <u>M</u>)　{from 8 and 9}
　 11　│ u ∴ ~N　{from 7 and 10}
　 12　└ u ∴ N　{from 6}
　 13　∴ ~((<u>u</u>:<u>E</u> · <u>u</u>:N) · ~<u>u</u>:<u>M</u>)　{from 2; 11

contradicts 12}

5.　Valid

[∴ ~(<u>u</u>:(x)O~K<u>x</u> · ~<u>u</u>:(N ⊃ ~K<u>u</u>))
* 1　┌ asm: (<u>u</u>:(x)O~K<u>x</u> · ~<u>u</u>:(N ⊃ ~K<u>u</u>))
　 2　│ ∴ <u>u</u>:(x)O~K<u>x</u>　{from 1}
* 3　│ ∴ ~<u>u</u>:(N ⊃ ~K<u>u</u>)　{from 1}
* 4　│ u ∴ ~(N ⊃ ~K<u>u</u>)　{from 3}
　 5　│ u ∴ N　{from 4}
　 6　│ u ∴ K<u>u</u>　{from 4}
　 7　│ u ∴ (x)O~K<u>x</u>　{from 2}
　 8　│ u ∴ O~K<u>u</u>　{from 7}
　 9　└ u ∴ ~K<u>u</u>　{from 8}
　 10　∴ ~(<u>u</u>:(x)O~K<u>x</u> · ~<u>u</u>:(N ⊃ ~K<u>u</u>))　{from 1; 6 contradicts 9}

10.　Invalid

[∴ (u:A<u>u</u> ⊃ u:RA<u>u</u>)
* 1　　asm: ~(u:A<u>u</u> ⊃ <u>u</u>:RA<u>u</u>)
　 2　　∴ u:A<u>u</u>　{from 1}
* 3　　∴ ~<u>u</u>:RA<u>u</u>　{from 1}
* 4　　u ∴ ~RA<u>u</u>　{from 3}
　 5　　u ∴ O~A<u>u</u>　{from 4}

13.5a

1.　O<u>u</u>:S<u>a</u>
3.　R<u>u</u>:OS<u>a</u>
5.　(x)~R<u>x</u>:G
10.　(O<u>u</u>:x=x · (x=x · u:x=x))
15.　(O<u>u</u>:A ≡ ~◇(u:A · ~A))
20.　(u:A<u>x</u>u ⊃ OA<u>u</u>x)
25.　((~Du · O<u>u</u>:Bj) ⊃ O<u>u</u>:Fj)

13.6a

1.　Valid

　 1　　□(A ⊃ B)
* 2　　~R<u>u</u>:B
[∴ ~R<u>u</u>:A
* 3　┌ asm: R<u>u</u>:A
　 4　│ ∴ O~<u>u</u>:B　{from 2}
　 5　│ D ∴ <u>u</u>:A　{from 3}
* 6　│ D ∴ ~<u>u</u>:B　{from 4}
　 7　│ Du ∴ ~B　{from 6}
* 8　│ Du ∴ (A ⊃ B)　{from 1}
　 9　│ Du ∴ ~A　{from 7 and 8}
　 10　└ Du ∴ A　{from 5}
　 11　∴ ~R<u>u</u>:A　{from 3; 9 contradicts 10}

3.　Valid

* 1　　R(~<u>u</u>:A · ~<u>u</u>:~A)
[∴ ~O<u>u</u>:A
　 2　┌ asm: O<u>u</u>:A
　 3　│ D ∴ (~<u>u</u>:A · ~<u>u</u>:~A)　{from 1}
　 4　│ D ∴ <u>u</u>:A　{from 2}

5   └ D ∴ ~u:A {from 3}
6   ∴ ~Ou:A {from 2; 4 contradicts 5}

5. Invalid

   1   Oa:(C · D)
     [∴ Ob:C
* 2   asm: ~Ob:C
* 3   ∴ R~b:C {from 2}
* 4   D ∴ ~b:C {from 3}
   5   Db ∴ ~C {from 4}
   6   D ∴ a:(C · D) {from 1}
* 7   Da ∴ (C · D) {from 6}
   8   Da ∴ C {from 7}
   9   Da ∴ D {from 7}

10. Valid

   1   Ou:(A ⊃ OBu)
     [∴ ~(u:A · ~u:Bu)
* 2 ┌ asm: (u:A · ~u:Bu)
   3 │ ∴ u:A {from 2}
* 4 │ ∴ ~u:Bu {from 2}
   5 │ u ∴ ~Bu {from 4}
   6 │ ∴ u:(A ⊃ OBu) {from 1}
   7 │ u ∴ A {from 3}
* 8 │ u ∴ (A ⊃ OBu) {from 6}
   9 │ u ∴ OBu {from 7 and 8}
 10 └ u ∴ Bu {from 9}
 11 ∴ ~(u:A · ~u:Bu) {from 2; 5 contra 10}

13.6b

1. Valid

   1   Ou:G
     [∴ ~Ru:~G
* 2 ┌ asm: Ru:~G
   3 │ D ∴ u:~G {from 2}
   4 │ D ∴ u:G {from 1}
   5 │ Du ∴ ~G {from 3}
   6 └ Du ∴ G {from 4}
   7 ∴ ~Ru:~G {from 2; 5 contradicts 6}

3. Valid

     [∴ O~(u:OAu · ~u:Au)
* 1 ┌ asm: ~O~(u:OAu · ~u:Au)
* 2 │ ∴ R(u:OAu · ~u:Au) {from 1}
* 3 │ D ∴ (u:OAu · ~u:Au) {from 2}
   4 │ D ∴ u:OAu {from 3}
* 5 │ D ∴ ~u:Au {from 3}
   6 │ Du ∴ ~Au {from 5}
   7 │ Du ∴ OAu {from 4}
   8 └ Du ∴ Au {from 7}
   9 ∴ O~(u:OAu · ~u:Au) {from 1; 6
       contradicts 8}

5. Valid

   1   □(E ⊃ C)
* 2   Ou:E

     [∴ Ou:C
* 3 ┌ asm: ~Ou:C
* 4 │ ∴ R~u:C {from 3}
* 5 │ D ∴ ~u:C {from 4}
   6 │ Du ∴ ~C {from 5}
* 7 │ Du ∴ (E ⊃ C) {from 1}
   8 │ Du ∴ ~E {from 6 and 7}
   9 │ D ∴ u:E {from 2}
 10 └ Du ∴ E {from 9}
 11 ∴ ~Ou:E {from 3; 8 contradicts 10}

10. Valid

   1   a:F
   2   Oa:F
   3   ~F
   4   C
   5   a:(F ∨ C)
   6   ~K
     [∴ (((Oa:(F ∨ C) · (F ∨ C))
       · a:(F ∨ C)) · ~K)
* 7 ┌ asm: ~(((Oa:(F ∨ C) · (F ∨ C)) ·
      │ a:(F ∨ C)) · ~K)
* 8 │ ∴ ~((Oa:(F ∨ C) · (F ∨ C)) · a:(F ∨ C))
      │ {from 6 and 7}
* 9 │ ∴ ~(Oa:(F ∨ C) · (F ∨ C)) {from 5
      │ and 8}
 10 │ ┌ asm: ~(F ∨ C) {break 9}
 11 │ └ ∴ ~C {from 10}
 12 │ ∴ (F ∨ C) {from 10; 4 contradicts 11}
* 13 │ ∴ ~Oa:(F ∨ C) {from 9 and 12}
* 14 │ ∴ R~a:(F ∨ C) {from 13}
* 15 │ D ∴ ~a:(F ∨ C) {from 14}
 16 │ D ∴ a:F {from 2}
 17 │ Du ∴ ~(F ∨ C) {from 15}
 18 │ Du ∴ F {from 16}
 19 └ Du ∴ ~F {from 17}
 20 ∴ (((Oa:(F ∨ C) · (F ∨ C)) · a:(F ∨ C))
      · ~K) {from 7; 18 contradicts 19}

15. Valid

   1   Ou:(M ⊃ F)
     [∴ ~(u:M · ~u:F)
* 2 ┌ asm: (u:M · ~u:F)
   3 │ ∴ u:M {from 2}
* 4 │ ∴ ~u:F {from 2}
   5 │ u ∴ ~F {from 4}
   6 │ ∴ u:(M ⊃ F) {from 1}
   7 │ u ∴ M {from 3}
* 8 │ u ∴ (M ⊃ F) {from 6}
   9 └ u ∴ ~M {from 5 and 8}
 10 ∴ ~(u:M · ~u:F) {from 2; 7 contra 9}

20.   Invalid

1   O~(u:A · ~u:B)
    [∴ (u:A ⊃ u:B)
* 2   asm: ~(u:A ⊃ u:B)
3   ∴ u:A   {from 2}
4   ∴ ~u:B   {from 2}
5   ∴ ~(u:A · ~u:B)   {from 1}
** 6   asm: ~u:A   {break 5}
7   u ∴ ~A   {from 6}

25.   Valid

1   Ou:(P ⊃ OAu)
2   Ou:P
    [∴ u:Au
* 3   ┌ asm: ~u:Au
4   │ u ∴ ~Au   {from 3}
5   │ ∴ u:(P ⊃ OAu)   {from 1}
6   │ ∴ u:P   {from 2}
* 7   │ u ∴ (P ⊃ OAu)   {from 5}
8   │ u ∴ P   {from 6}
9   │ u ∴ OAu   {from 7 and 8}
10 └ u ∴ Au   {from 9}
11   ∴ u:Au   {from 3; 4 contradicts 10}

30.   Invalid

1   (x)Rx:A   a, b
    [∴ R(x)x:A   D ┌─────────────┐
* 2   asm: ~R(x)x:A   DD │ a:A, ~b:A   │
3   ∴ O~(x)x:A   {from 2}   ├─────────────┤
* 4   ∴ Ra:A   {from 1}   │ b:A, ~a:A   │
5   D ∴ a:A   {from 4}   └─────────────┘
* 6   D ∴ ~(x)x:A   {from 3}
* 7   D ∴ (∃x)~x:A   {from 6}
* 8   D ∴ ~b:A   {from 7}
9   Db ∴ ~A   {from 8}
* 10   ∴ Rb:A   {from 1}
11   DD ∴ b:A   {from 10}

Endless loop: add "~a:A" to world DD to make the conclusion false. (You weren't required to give a refutation.)

14.6 (See footnote at end of Chapter 14)

1.   [∴ ~(u:RA · ~u:(∃F)(FA · ■(X)(FX ⊃ RX)))
* 1 ┌ asm: (u:RA · ~u:(∃F)(FA · ■(X)(FX ⊃
     │   RX)))
2 │ ∴ u:RA   {from 1}
* 3 │ ∴ ~u:(∃F)(FA · ■(X)(FX ⊃ RX))   {fm 1}
* 4 │ u ∴ ~(∃F)(FA · ■(X)(FX ⊃ RX))   {fm 3}
5 │ u ∴ RA   {from 2}
6 │ u ∴ (∃F)(FA · ■(X)(FX ⊃ RX))
     └   {from 5 by G5}
7   ∴ ~(u:RA · ~u:(∃F)(FA · ■(X)(FX ⊃ RX)))
         {from 1; 4 contradicts 6}

2.   [∴ ~(u:Au · ~u:(∃F)(F*Au · ■(X)(FX ⊃
         MX)))

* 1 ┌ asm: (u:Au · ~u:(∃F)(F*Au · ■(X)(FX ⊃
     │   MX)))
2 │ ∴ u:Au   {from 1}
* 3 │ ∴ ~u:(∃F)(F*Au · ■(X)(FX ⊃ MX))
     │   {from 1}
* 4 │ u ∴ ~(∃F)(F*Au · ■(X)(FX ⊃ MX))
     │   {from 3}
5 │ u ∴ Au   {from 2}
6 │ ┌ u asm: ~RAu
7 │ │ u ∴ O~Au   {from 6}
8 │ └ u ∴ ~Au   {from 7}
9 │ u ∴ RAu   {from 6; 5 contradicts 8}
* 10 │ u ∴ (∃F)(FAu · ■(X)(FX ⊃ RX))
     │   {from 9 by G5}
* 11 │ u ∴ (GAu · ■(X)(GX ⊃ RX))
     │   {from 10}
12 │ u ∴ GAu   {from 11}
13 │ u ∴ ■(X)(GX ⊃ RX)   {from 11}
14 │ u ∴ (X)(∃F)F*X   {by rule G11}
* 15 │ u ∴ (∃F)F*Au   {from 14}
16 │ u ∴ H*Au   {from 15}
* 17 │ u ∴ (HAu · (F)(FAu ⊃ □(X)(HX ⊃ FX)))
     │   {from 16 by G10}
18 │ u ∴ HAu   {from 17}
19 │ u ∴ (F)(FAu ⊃ □(X)(HX ⊃ FX))   {fm 17}
* 20 │ u ∴ (GAu ⊃ □(X)(HX ⊃ GX))   {fm 19}
21 │ u ∴ □(X)(HX ⊃ GX)   {from 12 and 20}
22 │ u ∴ (F)~(F*Au · ■(X)(FX ⊃ MX))   {fm 4}
* 23 │ u ∴ ~(H*Au · ■(X)(HX ⊃ MX))   {fm 22}
24 │ u ∴ ~■(X)(HX ⊃ MX)   {fm 16 & 23}
* 25 │ uH ∴ ~(X)(HX ⊃ MX)   {fm 24 by G8}
* 26 │ uH ∴ (∃X)~(HX ⊃ MX)   {from 25}
* 27 │ uH ∴ ~(HB ⊃ MB)   {from 26}
28 │ uH ∴ HB   {from 27}
29 │ uH ∴ ~MB   {from 27}
30 │ uH ∴ (X)(HX ⊃ GX)   {from 21}
* 31 │ uH ∴ (HB ⊃ GB)   {from 30}
32 │ uH ∴ GB   {from 28 and 31}
33 │ uH ∴ (X)(GX ⊃ RX)   {from 13 by G7}
* 34 │ uH ∴ (GB ⊃ RB)   {from 33}
35 │ uH ∴ RB   {from 32 and 34}
36 └ uH ∴ MB   {from 35 by G1}
37   ∴ ~(u:Au · ~u:(∃F)(F*Au · ■(X)(FX ⊃
         MX)))   {from 1; 29 contradicts 36}

Index

Abelard, P., 355
Abstract entities, 359, 361, 373–5, 378–80
Actual world, 228, 232, 236f, 243, 249f, 263, 265, 281–3, 285, 429f
Actualism, 262, 264
Ad hominem / ad rem, 62f
Affirming the consequent, 116
Agreement method, 100
Algorithm, 219, 360
Ambiguity, 18, 45, 48, 55–7, 77–9, 102, 119, 230f, 242f, 254–7, 261, 352–4
Analytic statement, 49–53, 375
Ancient logic, 351–4
Anderson, J., 371
And-gate, 152
Anselm, St, 136, 239, 245, 247, 252f, 260, 355, 387
Antecedent, 122, 139, 364, 369f
Anthropic principle, 112, 122, 132
A posteriori / a priori, 49, 51–4, 88, 356, 361, 378f
Appalachian Trail, 56, 80, 92, 96, 143, 177, 196
Appeal to … ; see entries without these initial words
Aquinas, St Thomas, 15, 136, 220, 225, 246, 356
Arab logic, 355
Argument, 2–5, 55–9, 71, 74–9, 80–2, 269f
Aristotelian essentialism, 254f, 259, 265f
Aristotelian view, 32f, 196, 239
Aristotle, 7, 24, 32f, 65, 116, 138, 220, 245, 254f, 259, 265f, 274, 351–8, 360, 362f, 365, 368, 372, 381, 383
Arithmetic, 160, 167, 344–50, 357, 359f, 368f, 382
Association, 120
Assumption, 153–6, 168–171, 175, 232f, 339–43
Authority, appeal to, 61–3
Axiom, 208, 331, 343–51, 356, 359f, 364f,
Ayer, A. J., 31, 44, 202, 244; see also logical positivism

B- and B+ rules, 293–6, 310–12
Barbara-Celarent, 355f
Barcan, R., 258

Barcan inference, 258, 263
Beall, J., 372
Begging the question, 56, 99, 109
Belief logic, 290–312
Belief world, 292–6
Berkeley, G., 196
Beside the point, 57f
Best-explanation inference, 111f, 132
Bible, 1, 22, 65, 68, 72, 158, 165, 192, 318, 335, 381
Biconditional, 123, 155f
Biting the bullet, 75
Black-and-white thinking, 63
Bocheński, J., 362
Boethius, 244, 246, 354f
Boole, G., 357f
Boolean algebra, 357f
Boolos, G., 383
Box inside / box outside, 230f, 242–4, 246, 254–7, 352–4
Brandt, R., 24
Brouwer, L., 268f
Buddhist logic, 353f
Buridan, J., 356
Burks, A., 152, 317, 361
Bush, G. W., 66, 69, 388

Calculus, 344f, 347, 350, 357; see also formal system
Carroll, L., 357
Carson, T., 238
Carter, J., 371
Castañeda, H–N, 138, 267, 275
Cause, 60, 99–102, 317
Cellini, 121
Charity, principle of, 29, 77, 141
Chisholm, R., 239, 289, 306
Chrysippus, 245; see also Stoics
Church, A., 219, 360
Church's theorem, 219, 360
Circular, 39, 42f, 55f, 109f, 115–17, 339f, 377–9
Clarifying definition, 41
Classical symbolic logic, 360–3
Cognitive science, 361
Coherence criterion, 109, 111, 314, 380
Collins, F., 112

Deontic Logic

A = Do A.

O<u>A</u> = It's obligatory that A.

R<u>A</u> = It's permissible that A.

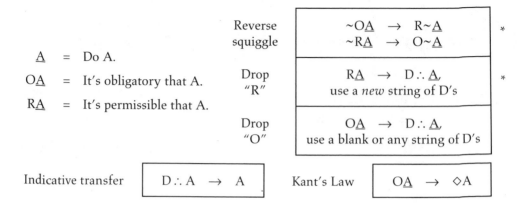

Reverse squiggle	~O<u>A</u> → R~<u>A</u> ~R<u>A</u> → O~<u>A</u>
Drop "R"	R<u>A</u> → D ∴ <u>A</u>, use a *new* string of D's
Drop "O"	O<u>A</u> → D ∴ <u>A</u>, use a blank or any string of D's

Indicative transfer | D ∴ A → A | Kant's Law | O<u>A</u> → ◇A |

Belief Logic

u:A = You believe A.

u:<u>A</u> = You will A.

<u>u</u>:A = Believe A.

<u>u</u>:<u>A</u> = Will A.

B-	~<u>u</u>:A → u ∴ ~A, use a *new* string of u's
B+	<u>u</u>:A → u ∴ A, use any string of u's

Inductive Logic

Statistical syllogism	N percent of A's are B's. X is an A. This is all we know about the matter. ∴ It's N percent probable that X is a B.
Sample-projection syllogism	N percent of examined A's are B's. A large and varied group of A's has been examined. ∴ Probably roughly N percent of all A's are B's.
Analogy syllogism	Most things true of X also are true of Y. X is A. This is all we know about the matter. ∴ Probably Y is A.